The Frank J. Fabozzi Series

Handbook of
Alternative Assets

Handbook of
Alternative Assets

Mark J. P. Anson

JOHN WILEY & SONS

I would like to dedicate this book to my wife, Mary Hayes,
for her incredible support and indulgence;
to my children Madeleine and Marcus
for playing quietly while Daddy was working on his book;
and to my editor, Frank Fabozzi, for keeping me on track and on point.

Published by John Wiley & Sons, Inc.
Published simultaneously in Canada.

No part of this publication may be reproduced, stored in a retrieval system or
transmitted in any form or by any means, electronic, mechanical, photocopying,
recording, scanning or otherwise, except as permitted under Sections 107 or 108
of the 1976 United States Copyright Act, without either the prior written permission of the Publisher, or authorization through payment of the appropriate per-copy
fee to the Copyright Clearance Center, 222 Rosewood Drive, Danvers, MA 01923,
(978) 750-8400, fax (978) 750-4744. Requests to the Publisher for permission
should be addressed to the Permissions Department, John Wiley & Sons, Inc., 605
Third Avenue, New York, NY 10158-0012, (212) 850-6011, fax (212) 850-6008,
E-Mail: PERMREQ@WILEY.COM.

This publication is designed to provide accurate and authoritative information in
regard to the subject matter covered. It is sold with the understanding that the
publisher is not engaged in rendering professional services. If professional advice
or other expert assistance is required, the services of a competent professional
person should be sought.

Wiley also publishes its books in a variety of electronic formats. Some content
that appears in print may not be available in electronic books.

ISBN: 0-471-21826-X

Printed in the United States of America.

10 9 8 7 6 5 4 3 2 1

About the Author

Mark Anson is the Chief Investment Officer for the California Public Employees' Retirement System (CalPERS). CalPERS has over $151 billion in assets under management. Mark earned his law degree from the Northwestern University School of Law in Chicago where he was the Production Editor of the Law Review, and his Ph.D. and Masters in Finance from the Columbia University Graduate School of Business in New York where he graduated *Beta Gamma Sigma*. Mark is a member of the New York and Illinois State Bar Associations. He has also earned the Chartered Financial Analyst, Certified Public Accountant, Certified Management Accountant, and Certified Internal Auditor degrees. In addition, Mark has received the Series 3, 4, 7, 8, 24, and 63 NASD securities industry licenses. Mark is an author of two other books on the financial markets and has published over 40 articles on the topics of hedge funds, private equity, risk management, derivatives, and portfolio management.

as much as possible and provide the intuition behind my argument constr-

Preface

Over the past several years, I have conducted quite a bit of independent research with respect to the alternative asset classes discussed in this book. Yet, I had never stopped to consider alternative assets within a comprehensive framework. This book provides that framework.

Early on, I make that statement that alternative assets are really alternative investment strategies within an existing class rather than a new asset class. This is an important point to remember because alternative assets are used more often to expand the investment opportunities within an existing asset class rather than as a hedge of that asset class.

This book has two broad objectives. The first is to introduce the reader to the various types of alternative assets that exist in the financial markets. In this respect, parts of this book are more descriptive in nature.

In the descriptive chapters, I attempt to do away with technical financial jargon, and instead, provide examples of alternative assets that are easy to understand. When I run up against technical terms used in describing alternative assets, I provide simple examples to lay a foundation of intuition behind the jargon. My goal is to educate and to inform, not to dazzle the reader with my grasp of technical financial nomenclature.

Second, this book provides chapters with original research with respect to alternative assets. In this respect, certain chapters are more quantitative as is necessary to develop empirical results. Again, I try to stay away from financial jargon as much as possible and provide the intuition behind my empirical conclusions. Yet, I believe that these chapters can serve as reference material for mathematical conclusions regarding alternative assets.

Overall, my goal is to provide information that has practical value to an investor. Therefore, this book focuses less on the theoretical development of alternative assets and more on the practical concepts needed to invest successfully. I have used many of the concepts discussed in this book when investing in alternative assets.

Finally, this book provides my ideas, research, experience, and opinions with respect to the alternative asset industry. Undoubtedly, some readers may disagree with my thoughts, ideas, and opinions, but this is good. It means that I have stimulated the thought process of those readers to critically evaluate alternative assets as well as my own conclusions. The greater the critical eye brought to the alternative asset investment universe, the greater the probability of success in that universe.

In sum, I hope that this book stimulates the reader with respect to alternative assets. If so, I will have considered this book to be a worthwhile effort.

As a final note, this book reflects my individual opinions and insights, and not those of my employer, the California Public Employees' Retirement System.

Mark Anson
December 17, 2001

Table of Contents

Chapter 1

What is an Alternative Asset Class?

P art of the difficulty of working with alternative asset classes is defining them. Are they a separate asset class or a subset of an existing asset class? Do they hedge the investment opportunity set or expand it? Are they listed on an exchange or do they trade in the over-the-counter market?

In most cases, alternative assets are a subset of an existing asset class. This may run contrary to the popular view that alternative assets are separate asset classes.[1] However, we take the view that what many consider separate "classes" are really just different investment strategies within an existing asset class.

Additionally, in most cases, they expand the investment opportunity set, rather than hedge it. Last, alternative assets are generally purchased in the private markets, outside of any exchange. While hedge funds, private equity, and credit derivatives meet these criteria, we will see that commodity futures prove to be the exception to these general rules.

Alternative assets, then, are just alternative investments within an existing asset class. Specifically, most alternative assets derive their value from either the debt or equity markets. For instance, most hedge fund strategies involve the purchase and sale of either equity or debt securities. Additionally, hedge fund managers may invest in derivative instruments whose value is derived from the equity or debt markets.

In this book, we classify five types of alternative assets: hedge funds, commodity and managed futures, private equity, credit derivatives, and corporate governance. Hedge funds and private equity are the best known of the alternative asset world. Typically these investments are accomplished through the purchase of limited partner units in a private limited partnership. Commodity futures can be either passive investing tied to a commodity futures index, or active investing through a commodity pool or advisory account. Private equity is the investment strategy of investing in companies before they issue their securities publicly, or taking a public company private. Credit derivatives can be purchased through limited partnership units, as a tranche of a special purpose vehicle, or directly through the purchase of distressed debt securities. Last, corporate governance is a form of shareholder activism designed to improve the internal controls of a public company.

---

[1] See, for example, Chapter 8 in David Swensen, *Pioneering Portfolio Management* (New York: The Free Press, 2000).

We will explore each one of these alternative asset classes in detail, providing practical advice along with useful research. We begin this chapter with a review of *super* asset classes.

SUPER ASSET CLASSES

There are three *super* asset classes: capital assets, assets that are used as inputs to creating economic value, and assets that are a store of value.[2]

Capital Assets

Capital assets are defined by their claim on the future cash flows of an enterprise. They provide a source of ongoing value. As a result, capital assets may be valued based on the net present value of their expected future cash flows.

Under the classic theory formulated by Franco Modigliani and Merton Miller, a corporation cannot change its value (in the absence of tax benefits) by changing the method of its financing.[3] Modigliani and Miller demonstrated that the value of the firm is dependent upon its cash flows. How those cash flows are divided between their shareholders and bondholders is irrelevant to firm value.

Consequently, capital assets are distinguished not by their possession of physical assets, but rather, by their claim on the cash flows of an underlying enterprise. Hedge funds, private equity funds, and credit derivatives investments all fall within the super asset class of capital assets because their values are determined by the present value of expected future cash flows.

As a result, we can conclude that it is not the types of securities in which they invest that distinguishes hedge funds, private equity funds, or credit derivatives from traditional asset classes. Rather, it is the alternative investment strategies that they pursue that distinguishes them from traditional stock and bond investments.

Assets that Can be Used as Economic Inputs

Certain assets can be consumed as part of the production cycle. Consumable or transformable assets can be converted into another asset. Generally, this class of asset consists of the physical commodities: grains, metals, energy products, and livestock. These assets are used as economic inputs into the production cycle to produce other assets, such as automobiles, skyscrapers, new homes, and appliances.

These assets generally cannot be valued using a net present value analysis. For example, a pound of copper, by itself, does not yield an economic stream of revenues. However, the copper can be transformed into copper piping that is used in an office building, or as part of the circuitry of an appliance.

[2] See Robert Greer, "What is an Asset Class Anyway?" *The Journal of Portfolio Management* (Winter 1997).
[3] Franco Modigliani and Merton Miller, "The Cost of Capital, Corporation Finance, and the Theory of Investment," *American Economic Review* (June 1958).

While consumable assets cannot produce a stream of cash flows, we will demonstrate in Chapter 11, which deals with commodities, that this asset class has excellent diversification properties for an investment portfolio. In fact, the lack of dependence on future cash flows to generate value is one of the reasons why commodities have important diversification potential vis à vis capital assets.

Assets that are a Store of Value

Art is considered the classic asset that stores value. It is not a capital asset because there are no cash flows associated with owning a painting or a sculpture. Consequently, art cannot be valued using a discounted cash flow analysis. It is also not an asset that is used as an economic input because it is a finished product.

Art requires ownership and possession. Its value can only be realized through its sale and transfer of possession. In the meantime, the owner retains the artwork with the expectation that it will at least yield a price equal to that which the owner paid for it.

There is no rational way to gauge whether the price of art will increase or decrease because its value is derived purely from the subjective (and private) visual enjoyment that the right of ownership conveys. Therefore, to an owner, art is a store of value. It conveys neither economic benefits nor is used as an economic input, but retains the value paid for it.

Gold and precious metals are another example of a store of value asset. In some parts of the world (India, for example), gold and silver are the primary means of maintaining wealth. In these countries, residents do not have access to the same range of financial products that are available to residents of more developed nations. Consequently, they accumulate their wealth through a tangible asset as opposed to a capital asset.

However, the lines between the three super classes of assets can become blurred. For example, gold can be leased to jewelry and other metal manufacturers. Jewelry makers lease gold during periods of seasonal demand, expecting to purchase the gold on the open market and return it to the lessor before the lease term ends. The gold lease provides a stream of cash flows that can be valued using a discounted cash flow analysis. However, the lease rate of gold is usually small in relation to the market price of gold.[4]

Precious metals can also be used as a transformable/consumable asset because they have the highest level of thermal and electrical conductivity amongst the metals. Silver, for example, is used in the circuitry for most telephones and light switches. Gold is used in the circuitry for TVs, cars, airplanes, computers, and rocket ships.

Real Estate

We provide a brief digression to consider where real estate belongs in our classification scheme. Real estate is a distinct asset class, but is it an alternative one? For

---

[4] For instance, the 12-month lease rate for gold in January 2001 was 1.3375% compared to a spot price of gold of $265 per ounce.

the purposes of this book we do not consider real estate to be an alternative asset class. The reasons are several.

First, real estate was an asset class long before stocks and bonds became the investment of choice. In fact, in times past, land was the single most important asset class. Kings, queens, lords, and nobles measured their wealth by the amount of property that they owned. "Land barons" were aptly named. Ownership of land was reserved only for the most wealthy members of society.

However, over the past 200 years, our economic society changed from one based on the ownership of property to the ownership of legal entities. This transformation occurred as society moved from the agricultural age to the industrial age. Production of goods and services became the new source of wealth and power.

Stocks and bonds were born to support the financing needs of new enterprises that manufactured material goods and services. In fact, stocks and bonds became the "alternatives" to real estate instead of vice versa. With the advent of stock and bond exchanges, and the general acceptance of owning equity or debt stakes in companies, it is sometimes forgotten that real estate was the original and primary asset class of society.

In fact, it was only 20 years ago in the United States that real estate was the major asset class of most individual investors. It was not until the long bull market started in 1983 that investors began to diversify their wealth into the "alternative" assets of stocks and bonds.

Second, given the long-term presence of real estate as an asset class, several treatises have been written concerning its valuation.[5] These treatises provide a much more extensive examination of the real estate market than can be covered within the scope of this book.

Finally, we do not consider real estate to be an alternative asset class as much as we consider it to be an additional asset class. Real estate is not an alternative asset to stocks and bonds. Instead, it is a fundamental asset class that should be included within every diversified portfolio. The alternative assets that we consider in this book are meant to diversify the stock and bond holdings within a portfolio context.

ASSET ALLOCATION

Asset allocation is generally defined as the allocation of an investor's portfolio across a number of asset classes.[6] Asset allocation by its very nature shifts the

---

[5] See, for example, Howard Gelbtuch, David MacKmin, and Michael Milgrim, eds., *Real Estate Valuation in Global Markets* (New York: Appraisal Institute, 1997); James Boykin and Alfred Ring, *The Valuation of Real Estate* (Englewood Cliffs, NJ: Prentice Hall, 1993); Austin Jaffe and C.F. Sirmans, *Fundamentals of Real Estate Investment*, 3d ed. (Englewood Cliffs, NJ: Prentice Hall, 1994); and Jack Cummings, *Real Estate Finance & Investment Manual* (Englewood Cliffs, NJ: Prentice Hall, 1997).

[6] See William Sharpe, "Asset Allocation: Management Style and Performance Measurement," *The Journal of Portfolio Management* (Winter 1992).

emphasis from the security level to the portfolio level. It is an investment profile that provides a framework for constructing a portfolio based on measures of risk and return. In this sense, asset allocation can trace its roots to Modern Portfolio Theory and the work of Harry Markowitz.[7]

Asset Classes and Asset Allocation

Initially, asset allocation involved four asset classes: equity, fixed income, cash, and real estate. Within each class, the assets could be further divided into sub-classes. For example, stocks can be divided into large capitalized stocks, small capitalized stocks, and foreign stocks. Similarly, fixed income can be broken down into U.S. Treasury notes and bonds, investment-grade bonds, high-yield bonds, and sovereign bonds.

The expansion of newly defined "alternative assets" may cause investors to become confused about their diversification properties and how they fit into an overall diversified portfolio. Investors need to understand the background of asset allocation as a concept for improving return while reducing risk.

For example, in the 1980s the biggest private equity game was taking public companies private. Does the fact that a corporation that once had publicly traded stock but now has privately traded stock mean that it has jumped into a new asset class? We maintain that it does not. Furthermore, public offerings are the primary exit strategy for private equity; public ownership begins where private equity ends.[8]

Considered within this context, a separate asset class does not need to be created for private equity. Rather this type of investment can be considered as just another point along the equity investment universe. Rather than hedging the equity class as another separate class all together, private equity expands the equity asset class.

Similarly, credit derivatives expand the fixed income asset class, rather than hedge it. We will also demonstrate that hedge funds can be characterized by their market (equity) or their fixed income (credit) exposures. Commodities fall into a different class of assets than equity, fixed income, or cash, and will be treated separately in this book.

Last, corporate governance is a strategy for investing in public companies. It seems the least likely to be an alternative investment strategy. However, we will demonstrate that a corporate governance program bears many of the same characteristics as other alternative investment strategies.

Strategic versus Tactical Allocations

Alternative assets should be used in a tactical rather than strategic allocation. Strategic allocation of resources is applied to fundamental asset classes such as

---

[7] See Harry Markowitz, *Portfolio Selection* (New Haven, CT: Cowles Foundation, Yale University Press, 1959).

[8] See Jeffery Horvitz, "Asset Classes and Asset Allocation: Problems of Classification," *The Journal of Private Portfolio Management* (Spring 2000).

equity, fixed income, cash, and real estate. These are the basic asset classes that must be held within a diversified portfolio.

Strategic asset allocation is concerned with the long-term asset mix. The strategic mix of assets is designed to accomplish a long-term goal such as funding pension benefits or matching long-term liabilities. Risk aversion is considered when deciding the strategic asset allocation, but current market conditions are not. In general, policy targets are set for strategic asset classes with allowable ranges around those targets. Allowable ranges are established to facilitate flexibility in the management of the investment portfolio.

Tactical asset allocation is short-term in nature. This strategy is used to take advantage of current market conditions that may be more favorable to one asset class over another. The goal of funding long-term liabilities has been satisfied by the target ranges established by the strategic asset allocation. The goal of tactical asset allocation is to maximize return.

Tactical allocation of resources depends on the ability to diversify within an asset class. This is where alternative assets have the greatest ability to add value. Their purpose is not to hedge the fundamental asset classes, but rather to expand them. Consequently, alternative assets should be considered as part of a broader asset class.

As already noted, private equity is simply one part of the spectrum of equity investments. Granted, a different set of skills is required to manage a private equity portfolio compared to public equity securities. However, private equity investments simply expand the equity investment universe. Consequently, private equity is an alternative investment strategy within the equity universe as opposed to a new fundamental asset class.

Another example is credit derivatives. These are investments that expand the frontier of credit risk investing. The fixed income world can be classified simply as a choice between U.S. Treasury securities that are considered to be default free, and spread products that contain an element of credit risk. Spread products include any fixed income investment that does not have a credit rating on par with the U.S. government. Consequently, spread products trade at a credit spread relative to U.S. Treasury securities that reflects their risk of default.

Credit derivatives are a way to diversify and expand the universe for investing in spread products. Traditionally, fixed income managers attempted to establish their ideal credit risk and return profile by buying and selling traditional bonds. However, the bond market can be inefficient and it may be difficult to pinpoint the exact credit profile to match the risk profile of the investor. Credit derivatives can help to plug the gaps in a fixed income portfolio, and expand the fixed income universe by accessing credit exposure in more efficient formats.

Efficient versus Inefficient Asset Classes

Another way to distinguish alternative investment strategies is based on the efficiency of the marketplace. The U.S. public stock and bond markets are generally considered to be the most efficient marketplaces in the world. Often, these markets are referred to as "semi-strong efficient." This means that all publicly available information regarding a publicly traded corporation, both past information and present, is fully priced in that company's traded securities.

Yet, inefficiencies exist in all markets, both public and private. If there were no informational inefficiencies in the public equity market, there would be no case for active management. Nonetheless, inefficiencies that do exist in the public markets eventually dissipate. The reason is that information is easy to acquire and disseminate in the publicly traded securities markets. Top quartile active managers in the public equity market earn excess returns (over their benchmarks) of only 1% to 2% a year.

In contrast, with respect to alternative assets, information is very difficult to acquire. Most alternative assets (with the exception of commodities) are privately traded. This includes private equity, hedge funds, and credit derivatives.

Consider venture capital, one subset of the private equity market. Investments in start-up companies require intense research into the product niche the company intends to fulfill, the background of the management of the company, projections about future cash flows, exit strategies, potential competition, beta testing schedules, and so forth. This information is not readily available to the investing public. It is time-consuming and expensive to accumulate. Further, most investors do not have the time or the talent to acquire and filter through the rough data regarding a private company. One reason why alternative asset managers charge large management and incentive fees is to recoup the cost of information collection.

This leads to another distinguishing factor between alternative investments and the traditional asset classes: the investment intermediary. Continuing with our venture capital example, most investments in venture capital are made through limited partnerships, limited liability companies, or special purpose vehicles. It is estimated that 80% of all private equity investments in the United States are funneled through a financial intermediary.

Last, investments in alternative assets are less liquid than their public markets counterparts. Investments are closely held and liquidity is minimal. Further, without a publicly traded security, the value of private securities cannot be determined by market trading. The value of the private securities must be estimated by book value, appraisal, or determined by a cash flow model.

OVERVIEW OF THIS BOOK

This book is organized into five sections. Section I reviews hedge funds. Chapter 2 begins with a brief history on the birth of hedge funds and an introduction to the types of hedge fund investment strategies. Chapter 3 provides some practical guidance as to how to build a hedge fund investment program. In Chapter 4 we discuss the selection of hedge funds. Chapter 5 is devoted to conducting due diligence, including both a qualitative and quantitative review. In Chapter 6 we introduce a classification scheme for hedge funds and analyze their return distributions. In Chapter 7, we consider some of the risks associated with hedge fund investing. In Chapter 8 we review the regulatory framework in which hedge funds operate. Last, in Chapter 9 we consider whether hedge funds should be "institutionalized."

Section II is devoted to commodity and managed futures. We begin with a brief review in Chapter 10 of the economic value inherent in commodity futures contracts. Chapter 11 describes how an individual or institution may invest in commodity futures, including an introduction to commodity futures benchmarks. Chapter 12 considers commodity futures within a portfolio framework, while Chapter 13 examines the managed futures industry.

Section III covers the spectrum of private equity. In Chapter 14 we provide an introduction to venture capital, while Chapter 15 is devoted to leveraged buyouts. In Chapter 16 we show how debt may be a component of the private equity marketplace. In Chapter 17 we review the economics associated with private equity investments, and in Chapter 18 we introduce alternative investment strategies within the private equity marketplace. Last, we consider some issues with respect to private equity benchmarks in Chapter 19.

Section IV is devoted to credit derivatives. In Chapter 20 we review the importance of credit risk, and provide examples of how credit derivatives are used in portfolio management. In Chapter 21 we review the collateralized debt obligation market. Specifically, we review the design, structure, and economics of collateralized bond obligations and collateralized loan obligations.

Finally, we devote Chapter 22 to corporate governance as an alternative investment strategy.

Throughout this book we attempt to provide descriptive material as well as empirical examples. Our goal is both to educate the reader with respect to these alternative investment strategies as well as to provide a reference book.

Section I

Hedge Funds

Chapter 2

Introduction to Hedge Funds

The term "hedge fund" is a term of art. It is not defined in the Securities Act of 1933 or the Securities Exchange Act of 1934. Additionally, "hedge fund" is not defined by the Investment Company Act of 1940, the Investment Advisers Act of 1940, the Commodity Exchange Act, or, finally, the Bank Holding Company Act. So what is this investment vehicle that every investor seems to know about but for which there is scant regulatory guidance?

As a starting point, we turn to the *American Heritage Dictionary* (third edition) which defines a hedge fund as:

> An investment company that uses high-risk techniques, such as borrowing money and selling short, in an effort to make extraordinary capital gains.

Not a bad start, but we note that hedge funds are not investment companies, for they would be regulated by the Securities and Exchange Commission under the Investment Company Act of 1940.[1] Additionally, some hedge funds, such as market neutral and market timing have conservative risk profiles and do not "swing for the fences" to earn extraordinary gains.

We define hedge funds as:

> A privately organized investment vehicle that manages a concentrated portfolio of public securities and derivative instruments on public securities, that can invest both long and short, and can apply leverage.

Within this definition there are five key elements of hedge funds that distinguish them from their more traditional counterpart, the mutual fund.

First, hedge funds are private investment vehicles that pool the resources of sophisticated investors. One of the ways that hedge funds avoid the regulatory scrutiny of the SEC or the CFTC is that they are available only for high net worth investors. Under SEC rules, hedge funds cannot have more than 100 investors in the fund. Alternatively, hedge funds may accept an unlimited number of "qualified purchasers" in the fund. These are individuals or institutions that have a net worth in excess of $5,000,000.

---

[1] In fact, hedge funds take great pains to avoid being regulated by the SEC as an investment company. The National Securities Markets Improvement Act of 1996 greatly relieved hedge funds of certain regulatory burdens by allowing an unlimited number of "qualified purchasers" in a hedge fund.

There is a penalty, however, for the privacy of hedge funds. Although they may escape the regulatory burden of U.S. agencies, they cannot raise funds from investors via a public offering. Additionally, hedge funds may not advertise broadly or engage in a general solicitation for new funds. Instead, their marketing and fundraising efforts must be targeted to a narrow niche of very wealthy individuals and institutions. As a result, the predominant investors in hedge funds are family offices, endowments, and, to a lesser extent, pension funds.

Second, hedge funds tend to have portfolios that are much more concentrated than their mutual fund brethren. Most hedge funds do not have broad securities benchmarks. The reason is that most hedge fund managers claim that their style of investing is "skill-based" and cannot be measured by a market return. Consequently, hedge fund managers are not forced to maintain security holdings relative to a benchmark; they do not need to worry about "benchmark" risk. This allows them to concentrate their portfolio only on those securities that they believe will add value to the portfolio.

Another reason for the concentrated portfolio is that hedge fund managers tend to have narrow investment strategies. These strategies tend to focus on only one sector of the economy or one segment of the market. They can tailor their portfolio to extract the most value from their smaller investment sector or segment.

Third, hedge funds tend to use derivative strategies much more predominately than mutual funds. Indeed, in some strategies, such as convertible arbitrage, the ability to sell or buy options is a key component of executing the arbitrage. The use of derivative strategies may result in non-linear cash flows that may require more sophisticated risk management techniques to control these risks.

Fourth, hedge funds may go both long and short securities. The ability to short public securities and derivative instruments is one of the key distinctions between hedge funds and traditional money managers. Hedge fund managers incorporate their ability to short securities explicitly into their investment strategies. For example, equity long/short hedge funds tend to buy and sell securities within the same industry to maximize their return but also to control their risk. This is very different from traditional money managers that are tied to a long-only securities benchmark.

Finally, hedge funds use leverage, sometimes, large amounts. Mutual funds, for example, are limited in the amount of leverage they can employ; they may borrow up to 33% of their net asset base. Hedge funds do not have this restriction. Consequently, it is not unusual to see some hedge fund strategies that employ leverage up to 10 times their net asset base.

We can see that hedge funds are different than traditional long-only investment managers. We next discuss the history of the hedge fund development.

A BRIEF HISTORY OF HEDGE FUNDS

The first hedge fund was established in 1949, the Jones Hedge Fund. Alfred Winslow Jones established a fund that invested in U.S. stocks, both long and short.

The intent was to limit market risk while focusing on stock selection. Consequently, this fund was not tied to a securities benchmark and may be properly classified as an equity long/short fund.

Jones operated in relative obscurity until an article was published in *Fortune* magazine that spotlighted the Jones Hedge Fund.[2] The interest in Jones' product was large, and within two years a survey conducted by the SEC established that the number of hedge funds had grown from one to 140.

Unfortunately, many hedge funds were liquidated during the bear market of the early 1970s, and the industry did not regain any interest until the end of the 1980s. The appeal of hedge funds increased tremendously in the 1990s. By 1998, the President's Working Group on Financial Markets estimated that there were up to 3,500 hedge funds with $300 billion in capital and up to $1 trillion in total assets.[3] Compare this size to mutual funds, where the amount of total assets was $5 trillion in 1998.

Therefore, the hedge fund industry is about 20% of the size of the mutual fund industry. Still the interest in hedge funds is growing. And despite the start of the Jones Hedge Fund five decades ago, the industry is still relatively new. Another estimate of the hedge fund industry is that it has grown from $50 billion in capital in 1990 to $362 billion in 1999. However, the hedge fund market is highly fragmented, with less than 20 funds managing $3 billion or more.[4] The fragmented nature of the hedge fund industry is indicative of its nascent beginning.

Long Term Capital Management

The hedge fund market hit another speedbump in 1998 when Long Term Capital Management (LTCM) of Greenwich, Connecticut had to be rescued by a consortium of banks and brokerage firms. At the time LTCM was considered to be one of the largest and best of the hedge fund managers.

LTCM was founded in 1994 by several executives from Salomon Brothers Inc. as well as well-known academics in the field of finance. The reputation of the founding principals of LTCM were such that the fund enjoyed instant prestige within the hedge fund community.

LTCM implemented a variety of strategies best known as "relative value" trades. It earned returns, net of fees of approximately 40% in 1995 and 1996, and about 20% in 1997.[5] At the end of 1997, LTCM returned $2.7 billion to its investors, but did not noticeably reduce its investment positions. In 1998, its capital base was $4.8 billion.

---

[2] See Carol Loomis, "The Jones Nobody Keeps Up With," *Fortune*, April 1966, pp. 237–247.
[3] See The President's Working Group on Financial Markets, "Hedge Funds, Leverage, and the Lessons of Long-Term Capital Management," April 1999.
[4] See Chip Cummins, "Hedge Funds Not Worried About Pending U.S. Regulations," *Dow Jones International News* (March 28, 2000); and *The New York Times*, "Hedge Fund Industry Creates a Dinosaur: The Macro Manager," May 6, 2000, Section B.
[5] The President's Working Group on Financial Markets, p. 16.

On August 31, 1998, LTCM's balance sheet showed $125 billion in assets with a capital base of $4.8 billion. This was a greater than 25 to 1 leverage ratio. In addition, the fund had over 60,000 trades on its books. The gross notional amount of the fund's futures contracts totaled $500 billion, the notional amount of its swap positions totaled $750 billion, and its options and other over-the-counter derivative positions totaled $150 billion.[6] The leverage ratio implied by these derivative positions was a whopping 291.67 to 1.

Unfortunately, all parties come to an end, and LTCM's positions began to unravel as a result of the Russian bond crisis. In August 1998, the Russian government defaulted on the payment of its outstanding bonds. This caused a worldwide liquidity crisis with credit spreads expanding rapidly around the globe. The Federal Reserve Bank stepped in and acted quickly with three rate reductions within six months, but this was not enough to salvage LTCM.

With spreads widening, instead of contracting as LTCM's pricing models had predicted, LTCM quickly accumulated paper losses. The lost value of their paper positions led to margin calls from several of LTCM's prime brokers. LTCM was forced to liquidate some of its positions in illiquid markets that were temporarily out of balance. This caused more losses, which led to more margin calls, and LTCM's financial positions began to spiral downward.

The situation for LTCM was bleak, and large financial institutions feared that if LTCM were forced to liquidate the majority of its portfolio there would be a negative impact in the financial markets. Finally, on September 23, at the neutral site of the Federal Reserve Bank of New York, 14 banks and brokerage firms met and agreed to provide a capital infusion of $3.6 billion to LTCM. In return the consortium of banks and brokerage firms received 90% ownership of LTCM.

While the cause of LTCM's demise was clear, the real question is how did LTCM achieve such a huge amount of credit such that it could leverage its cash positions at a 25 to 1 ratio, and its derivative positions at almost a 300 to 1 ratio? It was simple: LTCM did not reveal its full trading positions to any of its counterparties. Each counterparty was kept in the dark about the size of LTCM's total credit exposure with all other counterparties. As a result, LTCM was able to amass a huge amount of credit and nearly send a shock wave of epic proportions through the financial markets.

In the next section we review the relative value strategy of LTCM as well as other primary hedge fund strategies.

HEDGE FUND STRATEGIES

In Chapter 1 we indicated that hedge funds invest in the same equity and fixed income securities as traditional long-only managers. Therefore, it is not the alternative "assets" in which hedge funds invest that differentiates them from long-only managers, but rather, it is the alternative investment strategies that they pursue.

---

[6] *Id.* at p. 17.

In this section we review several alternative strategies that hedge funds apply. In general, some hedge funds have considerable exposure to the financial markets. This would be the *long/short, global macro hedge fund or short selling players*. Other hedge funds take little market exposure, but use leverage to magnify the size of their bets. These are the *arbitrage hedge funds*. Last there are hedge fund strategies that take little credit or market risk. These are the *market neutral* and *market timing strategies*.

Equity Long/Short

Equity long/short managers build their portfolios by combining a core group of long stock positions with short sales of stock or stock index options/futures. Their net market exposure of long positions minus short positions tends to have a positive bias. That is, equity long/short managers tend to be long market exposure. The length of their exposure depends on current market conditions. For instance, during the great stock market surge of 1996–1999, these managers tended to be mostly long their equity exposure. However, as the stock market turned into a bear market in 2000, these managers decreased their market exposure as they sold more stock short or sold stock index options and futures.

For example, consider a hedge fund manager in 2000 who had a 100% long exposure to tobacco industry stocks and had a 20% short exposure to semiconductor stocks. The beta of the S&P Tobacco index is 0.5, and for the Semi-Conductor index it is 1.5. The weighted average beta of the portfolio is:

$$[1.0 \times 0.5] + [-0.20 \times 1.5] = 0.20$$

Beta is a well-known measure of market exposure (or systematic risk). A portfolio with a beta of 1.0 is considered to have the same stock market exposure or risk as a broad-based stock index such as the S&P 500.

According to the Capital Asset Pricing Model, the hedge fund manager has a conservative portfolio. The expected return of this portfolio according the model is:[7]

$$6\% + 0.20 \times (-9.5\% - 6\%) = 2.9\%$$

However, in 2000, the total return on the S&P Tobacco Index was 98% while for the Semi-conductor Index it was –31%. This "conservative" hedge fund portfolio would have earned the following return in 2000:

$$[1.0 \times 98\%] + [-0.20 \times -31\%] = 104.20\%$$

This is a much higher return than that predicted by the Capital Asset Pricing Model.

[7] The Capital Asset Pricing Model is expressed as:

E(Return on Portfolio) = Risk-free rate + Beta × (Return on the Market – Risk-free rate)

In 2000, the return on the market, represented by the S&P 500 was –9.5%, while the risk-free rate was about 6%.

This example serves to highlight two points. First, the ability to go both long and short in the market is a powerful tool for earning excess returns. The ability to fully implement a strategy not only about stocks and sectors that are expected to increase in value but also stocks and sectors that are expected to decrease in value allows the hedge fund manager to maximize the value of his market insights.

Second, the long/short nature of the portfolio can be misleading with respect to the risk exposure. This manager is 80% net long. Additionally, the beta of the combined portfolio is only 0.20. From this an investor might conclude that the hedge fund manager is pursuing a low risk strategy. However, this is not true. What the hedge fund manager has done is to make two explicit bets: that tobacco stocks will appreciate in value and that semi-conductor stocks will decline in value.

The Capital Asset Pricing Model assumes that investors hold a well-diversified portfolio. That is not the case with this hedge fund manager. Most hedge fund managers build concentrated rather than highly diversified portfolios. Consequently, traditional models (such as the Capital Asset Pricing Model) and associated risk measures (such as beta) may not apply to hedge fund managers.

Equity long/short hedge funds essentially come in two flavors: fundamental or quantitative. *Fundamental long/short hedge funds* conduct traditional economic analysis on a company's business prospects compared to its competitors and the current economic environment. These managers will visit with corporate management, talk with Wall Street analysts, contact customers and competitors, and essentially conduct bottom-up analysis. The difference between these hedge funds and long-only managers is that they will short the stocks that they consider to be poor performers and buy those stocks that are expected to outperform the market. In addition, they may leverage their long and short positions.

Fundamental long/short equity hedge funds tend to invest in one economic sector or market segment. For instance, they may specialize in buying and selling internet companies (sector focus) or buying and selling small market capitalization companies (segment focus).

In contrast, *quantitative equity long/short hedge fund managers* tend not to be sector or segment specialists. In fact, it is quite the reverse. Quantitative hedge fund managers like to cast as broad a net as possible in their analysis.

These managers use mathematical analysis to review past company performance in light of several quantitative factors. For instance, these managers may build regression models to determine the impact of market price to book value (price/book ratio) on companies across the universe of stocks as well as different market segments or economic sectors. Or, they may analyze changes in dividend yields on stock price performance.

Typically, these managers build multifactor models, both linear and quadratic, and then test these models on historical stock price performance. Backtesting involves applying the quantitative model on prior stock price performance to see if there is any predictive power in determining whether the stock of a particular company will rise or fall. If the model proves successful using historical data, the hedge fund manager will then conduct an "out of sample" test of the model.

This involves testing the model on a subset of historical data that was not included in the model building phase.

If a hedge fund manager identifies a successful quantitative strategy, it will apply its model mechanically. Buy and sell orders will be generated by the model and submitted to the order desk. In practice, the hedge fund manager will put limits on its model such as the maximum short exposure allowed or the maximum amount of capital that may be committed to any one stock position. In addition, quantitative hedge fund managers usually build in some qualitative oversight to ensure that the model is operating consistently.

In Exhibit 1, a graph of a hypothetical investment of $1,000 in an Equity Long/Short fund of funds compared to the S&P 500 is provided. In this chapter, we use data from Hedge Fund Research, Inc. (HFRI), a database of about 1,100 hedge funds.[8] The time period is 1990 through 2000. As can be seen, the returns to this strategy were quite favorable compared to the stock market.

Global Macro

As their name implies, global macro hedge funds take a macroeconomic approach on a global basis in their investment strategy. These are top-down managers who invest opportunistically across financial markets, currencies, national borders, and commodities. They take large positions depending upon the hedge fund manager's forecast of changes in interest rates, currency movements, monetary policies, and macroeconomic indicators.

Global macro managers have the broadest investment universe. They are not limited by market segment or industry sector, nor by geographic region, financial market, or currency. Additionally, global macro may invest in commodities. In fact, a fund of global macro hedge funds offers the greatest diversification of investment strategies.

Exhibit 1: HFRI Equity Long/Short Index

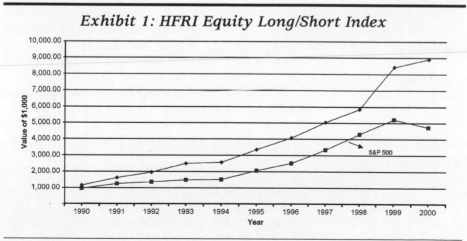

[8] More information on the HFRI database may be found at www.hfr.com.

Exhibit 2: HFRI Global Macro Index

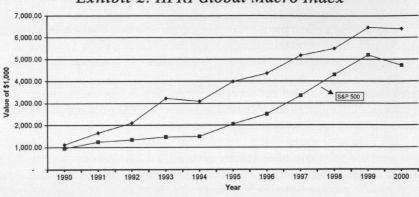

Global macro funds tend to have large amounts of investor capital. This is necessary to execute their macroeconomic strategies. In addition, they may apply leverage to increase the size of their macro bets. As a result, global macro hedge funds tend to receive the greatest attention and publicity in the financial markets.

The best known of these hedge funds was the Quantum Hedge Fund managed by George Soros. It is well documented that this fund made significant gains in 1992 by betting that the British pound would devalue (which it did). This fund was also accused of contributing to the "Asian Contagion" in the fall of 1997 when the government of Thailand devalued its currency, the baht, triggering a domino effect in currency movements throughout southeast Asia.

In recent times, however, global macro funds have fallen on hard times.[9] One reason is that many global macro funds were hurt by the Russian bond default in August 1998 and the bursting of the technology bubble in March 2000. These two events caused large losses for the global macro funds.

A second reason, as indicated above, is that global macro hedge funds had the broadest investment mandate of any hedge fund strategy. The ability to invest widely across currencies, financial markets, geographic borders, and commodities is a two-edged sword. On the one hand, it allows global macro funds the widest universe in which to implement their strategies. On the other hand, it lacks focus. As more institutional investors have moved into the hedge fund marketplace, they have demanded greater investment focus as opposed to free investment reign.

Exhibit 2 provides a comparison of global macro hedge funds to the S&P 500 over the period 1990–2000. During this time period global macro hedge funds earned favorable returns.

Short Selling

Short selling hedge funds have the opposite exposure of traditional long-only managers. In that sense, their return distribution should be the mirror image of

[9] See The *New York Times* (May 6, 2000).

long-only managers: they make money when the stock market is declining and lose money when the stock market is gaining.

These hedge fund managers may be distinguished from equity long/short managers in that they generally maintain a net short exposure to the stock market. However, short selling hedge funds tend to use some form of market timing. That is, they trim their short positions when the stock market is increasing and go fully short when the stock market is declining. When the stock market is gaining, short sellers maintain that portion of their investment capital not committed to short selling in short-term interest rate bearing accounts.

The past 10 years have seen predominantly a strong bull market in the United States. There have been some speed bumps: the short recession of 1990–1991 and the soft landing of 1994. But for the most part, the U.S. equity market has enjoyed strong returns in the 1990s. As a result, short sellers have had to seek other markets such as Japan, or result to more market timing to earn positive results. Later, when we review the distributions of hedge funds, we will see if short sellers have been successful in pursuing other markets or in market timing.

Exhibit 3 presents the returns to short selling hedge funds over the period 1990–2000. As might be expected, these hedge funds underperformed the S&P 500.

Convertible Bond Arbitrage

Hedge fund managers tend to use the term "arbitrage" somewhat loosely. Arbitrage is defined simply as riskless profits. It is the purchase of a security for cash at one price and the immediate resale for cash of the same security at a higher price. Alternatively, it may be defined as the simultaneous purchase of security A for cash at one price and the selling of identical security B for cash at a higher price. In both cases, the arbitrageur has no risk. There is no market risk because the holding of the securities is instantaneous. There is no basis risk because the securities are identical, and there is no credit risk because the transaction is conducted in cash.

Exhibit 3: HFRI Short Selling Index

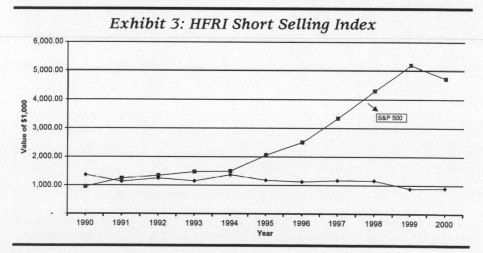

Instead of riskless profits, in the hedge fund world, arbitrage is generally used to mean low-risk investments. Instead of the purchase and sale of identical instruments, there is the purchase and sale of similar instruments. Additionally, the securities may not be sold for cash, so there may be credit risk during the collection period. Last, the purchase and sale may not be instantaneous. The arbitrageur may need to hold onto his positions for a period of time, exposing him to market risk.

Convertible arbitrage funds build long positions of convertible bonds and then hedge the equity component of the bond by selling the underlying stock or options on that stock. Equity risk can be hedged by selling the appropriate ratio of stock underlying the convertible option. This hedge ratio is known as the "delta" and is designed to measure the sensitivity of the convertible bond value to movements in the underlying stock.

Convertible bonds that trade at a low premium to their conversion value tend to be more correlated with the movement of the underlying stock. These convertibles then trade more like stock than they do a bond. Consequently a high hedge ratio, or delta, is required to hedge the equity risk contained in the convertible bond. Convertible bonds that trade at a premium to their conversion value are highly valued for their bond-like protection. Therefore, a lower delta hedge ratio is necessary.

However, convertible bonds that trade at a high conversion value act more like fixed income securities and therefore have more interest rate exposure than those with more equity exposure. This risk must be managed by selling interest rate futures, interest rate swaps, or other bonds. Furthermore, it should be noted that the hedging ratios for equity and interest rate risk are not static, they change as the value of the underlying equity changes and as interest rates change. Therefore, the hedge fund manager must continually adjust his hedge ratios to ensure that the arbitrage remains intact.

If this all sounds complicated, it is, but that is how hedge fund managers make money. They use sophisticated option pricing models and interest rate models to keep track of the all of moving parts associated with convertible bonds. Hedge fund managers make arbitrage profits by identifying pricing discrepancies between the convertible bond and its component parts, and then continually monitoring these component parts for any change in their relationship.

Consider the following example. A hedge fund manager purchases 10 convertible bonds with a par value of $1,000, a coupon of 7.5%, and a market price of $900. The conversion ratio for the bonds is 20. The conversion ratio is based on the current price of the underlying stock, $45, and the current price of the convertible bond. The delta, or hedge ratio, for the bonds is 0.5. Therefore, to hedge the equity exposure in the convertible bond, the hedge fund manager must short the following shares of underlying stock:

10 bonds × 20 conversion ratio × 0.5 hedge ratio = 100 shares of stock.

To establish the arbitrage, the hedge fund manager purchases 10 convertible bonds and sells 100 shares of stock. With the equity exposure hedged, the convertible bond is transformed into a traditional fixed income instrument with a 7.5% coupon.

Additionally, the hedge fund manager earns interest on the cash proceeds received from the short sale of stock. This is known as the "short rebate." The cash proceeds remain with the hedge fund manager's prime broker, but the hedge fund manager is entitled to the interest earned on the cash balance from the short sale (a rebate).[10] We assume that the hedge fund manager receives a short rebate of 4.5%. Therefore, if the hedge fund manager holds the convertible arbitrage position for one year, he expects to earn interest not only from his long bond position, but also from his short stock position.

The catch to this arbitrage is that the price of the underlying stock may change as well as the price of the bond. Assume the price of the stock increases to $47 and the price of the convertible bond increases to $920. If the hedge fund manager does not adjust the hedge ratio during the holding period, the total return for this arbitrage will be:

Appreciation of bond price:	$10 \times (\$920 - \$900)$	=	$200
Appreciation of stock price:	$100 \times (\$45 - \$47)$	=	-$200
Interest on bonds:	$10 \times \$1,000 \times 7.5\%$	=	$750
Short rebate:	$100 \times \$45 \times 4.5\%$	=	$202.50
Total:			$952.50

If the hedge fund manager paid for the 10 bonds without using any leverage, the holding period return is:

$$\$952.50 \div \$9000 = 10.58\%$$

However, suppose that the hedge fund manager purchased the convertible bonds with $4,500 of initial capital and $4,500 of borrowed money. We suppose that the hedge fund manager borrows the additional investment capital from his prime broker at a prime rate of 6%.

Our analysis of the total return is then:

Appreciation of bond price:	$10 \times (\$920 - \$900)$	=	$200
Appreciation of stock price:	$100 \times (\$47 - \$45)$	=	-$200
Interest on bonds:	$10 \times \$1,000 \times 7.5\%$	=	$750
Short rebate:	$100 \times \$45 \times 4.5\%$	=	$202.5
Interest on borrowing:	$6\% \times \$4,500$	=	-$270
Total:			$682.5

And the total return on capital is:

$$\$682.5 \div \$4,500 = 15.17\%$$

---

[10] The short rebate is negotiated between the hedge fund manager and the prime broker. Typically, large, well-established hedge fund managers receive a larger short rebate.

Exhibit 4: HFRI Convertible Arbitrage Index

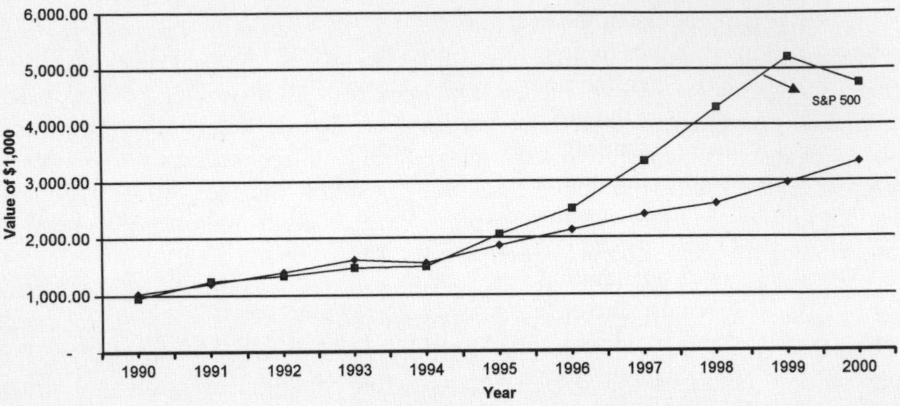

The amount of leverage used in convertible arbitrage will vary with the size of the long positions and the objectives of the portfolio. Yet, in the above example, we can see how using a conservative leverage ratio of 2:1 in the purchase of the convertible bonds added almost 500 basis points of return to the strategy. It is easy to see why hedge fund managers are tempted to use leverage. Hedge fund managers earn incentive fees on every additional basis point of return they earn. Further, even though leverage is a two-edged sword — it can magnify losses as well as gains — hedge fund managers bear no loss if the use of leverage turns against them. In other words, hedge fund manages have everything to gain by applying leverage, but nothing to lose.

Additionally, leverage is inherent in the shorting strategy because the underlying equity stock must be borrowed to be shorted. Convertible arbitrage leverage can range from two to six times the amount of invested capital. This may seem significant, but it is lower than other forms of arbitrage.

Convertible bonds are subject to credit risk. This is the risk that the bonds will default, be downgraded, or that credit spreads will widen. There is also call risk. Last, there is the risk that the underlying company will be acquired or will acquire another company (i.e., event risk), both of which can have a significant impact on the company's stock price and credit rating. These events are only magnified when leverage is applied.

Exhibit 4 plots the value of convertible arbitrage strategies versus the S&P 500. Convertible arbitrage earns a consistent return but does not outperform stocks in strong bull equity markets.

Fixed Income Arbitrage

Fixed income arbitrage involves purchasing one fixed income security and simultaneously selling a similar fixed income security. The sale of the second security is done to hedge the underlying market risk contained in the first security. Typically, the two securities are related either mathematically or economically such that they move similarly with respect to market developments. Generally, the difference in pricing between the two securities is small, and this is what the fixed income arbitrageur hopes to gain. By buying and selling two fixed income securities that are tied together, the hedge fund manager hopes to capture a pricing discrepancy that will cause the prices of the two securities to converge over time.

Fixed income arbitrage does not need to use exotic securities. It can be nothing more than buying and selling U.S. Treasury bonds. In the bond market, the most liquid securities are the *on-the-run* Treasury bonds. These are the most currently issued bonds by the U.S. Treasury Department. However, there are other U.S. Treasury bonds outstanding that have very similar characteristics to the on-the-run Treasury bonds. The difference is that *off-the-run* bonds were issued at an earlier date, and are now less liquid than the on-the-run bonds. As a result, price discrepancies occur. The difference in price may be no more than one-half or one quarter of a point ($25) but can increase in times of uncertainty when investor money shifts to the most liquid U.S. Treasury bond.

Nonetheless, when held to maturity, the prices of these two bonds should converge to their par value. Any difference will be eliminated by the time they mature, and any price discrepancy may be captured by the hedge fund manager. Fixed income arbitrage is not limited to the U.S. Treasury market. It can be used with corporate bonds, municipal bonds, sovereign debt, or mortgage backed securities.

Fixed income arbitrage may also include trading among fixed income securities that are close in maturity. This is a form of yield curve arbitrage. These types of trades are usually driven by temporary imbalances in the term structure.

Consider Exhibit 5. This was the term structure for U.S. Treasury securities in July 2000. Notice that there are "kinks" in the term structure between the 3-month and the 5-year time horizon. Kinks in the yield curve can happen at any maturity and usually reflect an increase (or decrease) in liquidity demand around the focal point. These kinks provide an opportunity to profit by purchasing and selling Treasury securities that are similar in maturity.

Consider the kink that peaks at the 2-year maturity. The holder of the 2-year Treasury security profits by rolling down the yield curve. In other words, if interest rates remain static, the 2-year Treasury note will age into a lower yielding part of the yield curve. Moving down the yield curve will mean positive price appreciation. Conversely, Treasury notes in the 3- to 5-year range will roll up the yield curve to higher yields. This means that their prices are expected to depreciate.

An arbitrage trade would be to purchase a 2-year Treasury note and short a 3-year note. As the 3-year note rolls up the yield curve, it should decrease in value while the 2-year note should increase in value as it rolls down the yield curve.

This arbitrage trade will work as long as the kink remains in place. However, this trade does have its risks. First, shifts in the yield curve up or down can affect the profitability of the trade because the two securities have different maturities. To counter this problem, the hedge fund manager would need to purchase and sell the securities in the proper proportion to neutralize the differences in duration. Also, liquidity preferences of investors could change. The kink could reverse itself, or flatten out. In either case, the hedge fund manager will lose money. Conversely, the liquidity preference of investors could increase, and the trade will become even more profitable.

A subset of fixed income arbitrage uses mortgage-backed securities (MBS). MBS represent an ownership interest in an underlying pool of individual mortgage loans. Therefore, an MBS is a fixed income security with underlying prepayment options. MBS hedge funds seek to capture pricing inefficiencies in the U.S. MBS market.

MBS arbitrage can be between fixed income markets such as buying MBS and selling U.S. Treasuries. This investment strategy is designed to capture credit spread inefficiencies between U.S. Treasuries and MBS. MBS trade at a credit spread over U.S. Treasuries to reflect the uncertainty of cash flows associated with MBS compared to the certainty of cash flows associated with U.S. Treasury bonds.

As noted above, during a flight to quality, investors tend to seek out the most liquid markets such as the on-the-run U.S. Treasury market. This may cause credit spreads to temporarily increase beyond what is historically or economically justified. In this case the MBS market will be priced "cheap" to U.S. Treasuries. The arbitrage strategy would be to buy MBS and sell U.S. Treasury, where the interest rate exposure of both instruments is sufficiently similar so as to eliminate most (if not all) of the market risk between the two securities. The expectation is that the credit spread between MBS and U.S. Treasuries will decline and the MBS position will increase in value relative to U.S. Treasuries.

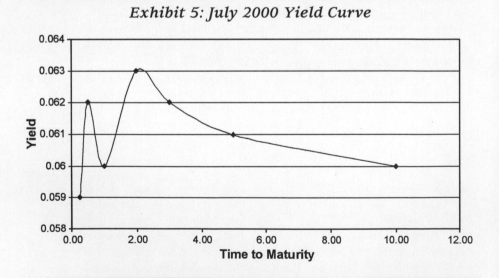

Exhibit 5: July 2000 Yield Curve

Exhibit 6: HFRI Fixed Income Arbitrage Index

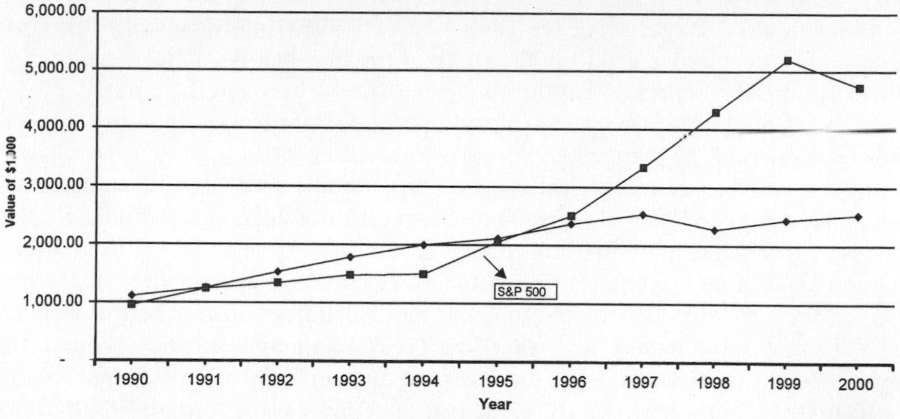

MBS arbitrage can be quite sophisticated. MBS hedge fund managers use proprietary models to rank the value of MBS by their option-adjusted spread (OAS). The hedge fund manager evaluates the present value of an MBS by explicitly incorporating assumptions about the probability of prepayment options being exercised. In effect, the hedge fund manager calculates the option-adjusted price of the MBS and compares it to its current market price. The OAS reflects the MBS' average spread over U.S. Treasury bonds of a similar maturity, taking into account the fact that the MBS may be liquidated early from the exercise of the prepayment option by the underlying mortgagors.

The MBS that have the best OAS compared to U.S. Treasuries are purchased, and then their interest rate exposure is hedged to zero. Interest rate exposure is neutralized using Treasury bonds, options, swaps, futures, and caps. MBS hedge fund managers seek to maintain a duration of zero. This allows them to concentrate on selecting the MBS that yield the highest OAS.

There are many risks associated with MBS arbitrage. Chief among them are duration, convexity, yield curve rotation, prepayment risk, credit risk (for private label MBS), and liquidity risk. Hedging these risks may require the purchase or sale of other MBS products such as interest-only strips and principal-only strips, inverse floaters, U.S. Treasuries, interest rate futures, swaps, and options.

What should be noted about fixed income arbitrage strategies is that they do not depend on the direction of the general financial markets. Arbitrageurs seek out pricing inefficiencies between two securities instead of making bets on the market. Consequently, we do not expect fixed income arbitrage strategies to have a high correlation with either stock market returns or bond market returns. Exhibit 6 demonstrates that fixed income arbitrage earns a steady return year after year regardless of the movement of the stock market.

Merger Arbitrage

Merger arbitrage is perhaps the best-known arbitrage among investors and hedge fund managers. Merger arbitrage generally entails buying the stock of the firm that is to be acquired and selling the stock of the firm that is the acquirer. Merger arbitrage managers seek to capture the price spread between the current market prices of the merger partners and the value of those companies upon the successful completion of the merger.

The stock of the target company will usually trade at a discount to the announced merger price. The discount reflects the risk inherent in the deal; other market participants are unwilling to take on the full exposure of the transaction-based risk. Merger arbitrage is then subject to event risk. There is the risk that the two companies will fail to come to terms and call off the deal. There is also the risk that another company will enter into the bidding contest, ruining the initial dynamics of the arbitrage. Last, there is regulatory risk. Various U.S. and foreign regulatory agencies may not allow the merger to take place for antitrust reasons. Merger arbitrageurs specialize in assessing event risk and building a diversified portfolio to spread out this risk.

Merger arbitrageurs conduct significant research on the companies involved in the merger. They will review current and prior financial statements, EDGAR filings, proxy statements, management structures, cost savings from redundant operations, strategic reasons for the merger, regulatory issues, press releases, and competitive position of the combined company within the industries it competes. Merger arbitrageurs will calculate the rate of return that is implicit in the current spread and compare it to the event risk associated with the deal. If the spread is sufficient to compensate for the expected event risk, they will execute the arbitrage.

Once again, the term "arbitrage" is used loosely. As discussed above, there is plenty of event risk associated with a merger announcement. The profits earned from merger arbitrage are not riskless. As an example, consider the announced deal between Tellabs and Ciena in 1998.

Ciena owned technology that allowed fiber optic telephone lines to carry more information. The technology allowed telephone carriers to get more bandwidth out of existing fiber optic lines. Tellabs made digital connecting systems. These systems allowed carriers to connect incoming and outgoing telephonic lines as well as allow many signals to travel over one phone circuit.

Tellabs and Ciena announced their intent to merge on June 3, 1998 in a one for one stock swap. One share of Tellabs would be issued for each share of Ciena. The purpose of the merger was to position the two companies to compete with larger entities such as Lucent Technologies. Additionally, each company expected to leverage their business off of the other's customer base. Tellabs price at the time was about $66 while that of Ciena's was at $57.

Shortly after the announcement, the share price of Tellabs declined to about $64 while that of Ciena's increased to about $60. Still, there was $4 of merger premium to extract from the market if the deal were completed. A merger arbitrage hedge fund manager would employ the following strategy:

      Short 1000 shares of Tellabs at $64
      Purchase 1000 shares of Ciena at $60

Unfortunately, the deal did not go according to plan. During the summer, Ciena lost two large customers, and it issued a warning that its third quarter profits would decline. Ciena's stock price plummeted to $15 by September. In mid-September the deal fell apart. The shares of Ciena were trading at such a discount to Tellabs' share price that it did not make economic sense to complete the merger, when Ciena's shares could be purchased cheaply on the open market. In addition, Tellabs share price declined to about $42 on earnings concerns.

      By the time the merger deal fell through, the hedge fund manager would have to close out his positions:

      Buy 1000 shares of Tellabs stock at $42
      Sell 1000 shares of Ciena at $15

The total return for the hedge fund manager would be:

Gain on Tellabs shares:	$1000 \times (\$64 - \$42)$	=	$22,000
Loss of Ciena shares:	$1000 \times (\$15 - \$60)$	=	–$45,000
Short rebate on Tellabs:	$4.5\% \times 1000 \times \$64 \times (110/360)$	=	$880
Total:		=	–$22,120

For a total return on invested capital of:

      $-\$22,120 \div \$60,000 = -36.87\%$

      Further, suppose the hedge fund manager had used leverage to initiate this strategy, borrowing one half of the invested capital from his prime broker for the initial purchase of the Ciena shares. The total return would then be:

Gain on Tellabs shares:	$1000 \times (\$64 - \$42)$	=	$22,000
Loss of Ciena shares:	$1000 \times (\$15 - \$60)$	=	–$45,000
Short rebate on Tellabs:	$4.5\% \times 1000 \times \$64 \times (110/360)$	=	$880
Financing cost:	$6\% \times 500 \times \$60 \times (110/360)$	=	–$550
Total:		=	–$22,670

The return on invested capital is now:

      $-\$22,670 \div \$30,000 = -75.57\%$

      On an annualized basis, this is a return of –247%. This example of a failed merger demonstrates the event risk associated with merger arbitrage. When deals fall through, it gets ugly. Furthermore, the event risk is exacerbated by the amount of leverage applied in the strategy. It is estimated that Long Term Capital Management of Greenwich, Connecticut had a 4 million share position in the Tellabs-Ciena merger deal, much of it supported by leverage.

Exhibit 7: HFRI Merger Arbitrage Index

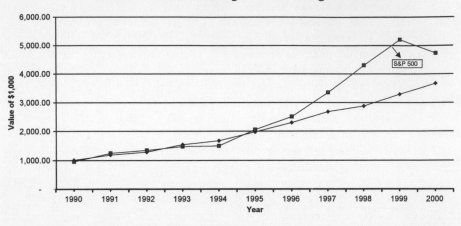

Some merger arbitrage managers only invest in announced deals. However, other hedge fund managers will invest on the basis of rumor or speculation. The deal risk is much greater with this type of strategy, but so too is the merger spread (the premium that can be captured).

To control for risk, most merger arbitrage hedge fund managers have some risk of loss limit at which they will exit positions. Some hedge fund managers concentrate only in one or two industries, applying their specialized knowledge regarding an economic sector to their advantage. Other merger arbitrage managers maintain a diversified portfolio across several industries to spread out the event risk.

Like fixed income arbitrage, merger arbitrage is deal driven rather than market driven. Merger arbitrage derives its return from the relative value of the stock prices between two companies as opposed to the status of the current market conditions. Consequently, merger arbitrage returns should not be highly correlated with the general stock market. Exhibit 7 highlights this point. Similar to fixed income arbitrage, merger arbitrage earns steady returns year after year.

Relative Value Arbitrage

Relative value arbitrage might be better named the smorgasbord of arbitrage. This is because relative value hedge fund managers are catholic in their investment strategies; they invest across the universe of arbitrage strategies. The best known of these managers was Long Term Capital Management (LTCM). Once the story of LTCM unfolded, it was clear that their trading strategies involved merger arbitrage, fixed income arbitrage, volatility arbitrage, stub trading, and convertible arbitrage.

In general, the strategy of relative value managers is to invest in spread trades: the simultaneous purchase of one security and the sale of another when the economic relationship between the two securities (the "spread") has become mis-priced. The mispricing may be based on historical averages or mathematical equa-tions. In either case, the relative value arbitrage manager purchases the security that is "cheap" and sells the security that is "rich." It is called relative value arbi-trage because the cheapness or richness of a security is determined relative to a second security. Consequently, relative value managers do not take directional bets on the financial markets. Instead, they take focussed bets on the pricing rela-tionship between two securities regardless of the current market conditions.

Relative value managers attempt to remove the influence of the financial markets from their investment strategies. This is made easy by the fact that they simultaneously buy and sell similar securities. Therefore, the market risk embed-ded in each security should cancel out. Any residual risk can be neutralized through the use of options or futures. What is left is pure security selection: the purchase of those securities that are cheap and the sale of those securities that are rich. Relative value managers earn a profit when the spread between the two secu-rities returns to normal. They then unwind their positions and collect their profit.

We have already discussed merger arbitrage, convertible arbitrage, and fixed income arbitrage. Two other popular forms of relative value arbitrage are stub trading and volatility arbitrage.

Stub trading is an equity-based strategy. Frequently, companies acquire a majority stake in another company, but their stock price does not fully reflect their interest in the acquired company. As an example, consider Company A whose stock is trading at $50. Company A owns a majority stake in Company B, whose remain-ing outstanding stock, or stub, is trading at $40. The value of Company A should be the combination of its own operations, estimated at $45 a share, plus its majority stake in Company B's operations, estimated at $8 a share. Therefore, Company A's share price is undervalued relative to the value that Company B should contribute to Company A's share price. The share price of Company A should be about $53, but instead, it is trading at $50. The investment strategy would be to purchase Company A's stock and sell the appropriate ratio of Company B's stock.

Let's assume that Company A's ownership in Company B contributes to 20% of Company A's overall revenues. Therefore, the operations of Company B should contribute one fifth to Company A's share price. Therefore, a proper hedg-ing ratio would be four shares of Company A's stock to Company B's stock.

The arbitrage strategy is:

Buy four shares of Company A stock at $4 \times \$50 = \$200$
Sell one share of Company B stock at $1 \times \$40 = \$40$

The relative value manager is now long Company A stock and hedged against the fluctuation of Company B's stock. Let's assume that over three months the share price of Company B increases to $42 a share, the value of Company A's opera-tions remains constant at $45, but now the shares of Company A correctly reflect the contribution of Company B's operations. The value of the position will be:

Value of Company A's operations:	$4 \times \$45$	=	$180
Value of Company B's operations:	$4 \times \$42 \times 20\%$	=	$33.6
Loss on short of Company B stock:	$1 \times (\$40 - \$42)$	=	−$2
Short rebate on Company B stock:	$1 \times \$40 \times 4.5\% \times 3/12$ =		$0.45
Total:		=	$212.05

The initial invested capital was $200 for a gain of $12.05, or 6.02% over three months. Suppose the stock of Company B had declined to $30, but Company B's operations were properly valued in Company A's share price. The position value would be:

Value of Company A's operations:	$4 \times \$45$	=	$180
Value of Company B's operations:	$4 \times \$30 \times 20\%$	=	$24
Gain on short of Company B's stock:	$1 \times (\$40 - \$30)$	=	$10
Short rebate on Company B's stock:	$1 \times \$40 \times 4.5\% \times 3/12$ =		$0.045
Total:		=	$214.45

The initial invested capital was $200 for a gain of $14.45, or 7.22% over three months. For stub trading to work there must be some market catalyst such that the contribution of Company B is properly reflected in Company A's share price.

Volatility arbitrage involves options and warrant trading. Option prices contain an *implied* number for volatility. That is, it is possible to observe the market price of an option and back out the value of volatility implied in the current price using various option pricing models. The arbitrageur can then compare options on the same underlying stock to determine if the volatility implied by their prices are the same.

The implied volatility derived from option pricing models should represent the expected volatility of the underlying stock that will be realized over the life of the option. Therefore, two options on the same underlying stock should have the same implied volatility. If they do not, an arbitrage opportunity may be available. Additionally, if the implied volatility is significantly different from the historical volatility of the underlying stock, then relative value arbitrageurs expect the implied volatility will revert back to its historical average. This allows hedge fund managers to determine which options are priced "cheap" versus "rich." Once again, relative value managers sell those options that are rich based on the implied volatility *relative* to the historical volatility and buy those options with cheap volatility relative to historical volatility.

Exhibit 8 presents the value of relative value arbitrage compared to the S&P 500. This strategy demonstrates steady returns without much influence from the direction of the stock market.

Event Driven

Event driven hedge funds attempt to capture mispricing associated with capital market transactions. These transactions include mergers and acquisitions, spin-offs, tracking stocks, reorganizations, bankruptcies, share buy-backs, special dividends, and any other significant market event.

Exhibit 8: HFRI Relative Value Arbitrage Index

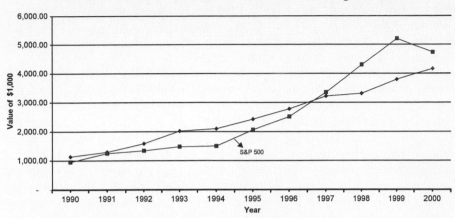

Exhibit 9: HFRI Event Driven Index

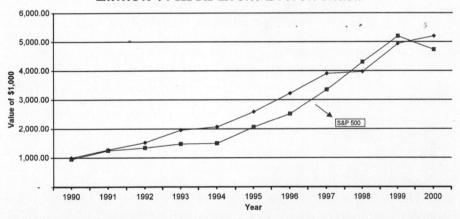

By their nature, these special events are non-recurring. Consequently, the market may take time to digest the information associated with these transactions, providing an opportunity for event driven managers to act quickly and capture a premium in the market. Additionally, some of these events may be subject to certain conditions such as shareholder or regulatory approval. Therefore, there is event risk associated with this strategy. The profitability of this type of strategy is dependent upon the successful completion of the transaction within the expected time frame.

We should not expect event driven strategies to be influenced by the general stock market, since these are company specific events, not market driven events. However, in Exhibit 9 we do see that the value of event driven strategies does closely parallel that value of the S&P 500. This could be because the strong stock market of 1990s encouraged more capital market transactions.

Market Neutral

Our last two categories are different from the previous hedge fund strategies in that they employ little or no leverage and maintain little or no market exposure. In fact, the very nature of their programs is to limit or eliminate market exposure altogether. We start with market neutral hedge funds.

Market neutral hedge funds also go long and short the market. The difference is that they maintain integrated portfolios which are designed to neutralize market risk. This means being neutral to the general stock market as well as having neutral risk exposures across industries. Security selection is all that matters.

Market neutral hedge fund managers generally apply the rule of one alpha.[11] This means that they build an integrated portfolio designed to produce only one source of alpha. This is distinct from equity long/short managers that build two separate portfolios: one long and one short, with two sources of alpha. The idea of integrated portfolio construction is to neutralize market and industry risk and concentrate purely on stock selection. In other words, there is no "beta" risk in the portfolio either with respect to the broad stock market or with respect to any industry. Only stock selection, or alpha, should remain.

Market neutral hedge fund managers generally hold equal positions of long and short stock positions. Therefore, the manager is dollar neutral; there is no net exposure to the market either on the long side or on the short side.

Market neutral investors generally apply no leverage because there is no market exposure to leverage. However, some leverage is always inherent when stocks are borrowed and shorted. Nonetheless, the nature of this strategy is that it has minimal credit risk.

Generally, market neutral managers follow a three-step procedure in their strategy. The first step is to build an initial screen of "investable" stocks. These are stocks traded on the manager's local exchange, with sufficient liquidity so as to be able to enter and exit positions quickly, and with sufficient float so that the stock may be borrowed from the hedge fund manager's prime broker for short positions. Additionally, the hedge fund manager may limit his universe to a capitalization segment of the equity universe such as the mid-cap range.

Second, the hedge fund manager typically builds factor models. These are linear and quadratic regression equations designed to identify those economic factors that consistently have an impact on share prices. This process is very similar to that discussed with respect to equity long/short hedge fund manages. Indeed, the two strategies are very similar in their portfolio construction methods. The difference is that equity long/short managers tend to have a net long exposure to the market while market neutral managers have no exposure.

Factor models are used for stock selection. These models are often known as "alpha engines." Their purpose is to find those financial variables that influence stock prices. These are bottom-up models that concentrate solely on

---

[11] See Bruce Jacobs and Kenneth Levy, "The Law of One Alpha," *The Journal of Portfolio Management* (Summer 1995).

corporate financial information as opposed to macroeconomic data. This is the source of the manager's skill — his stock selection ability.

The last step is portfolio construction. The hedge fund manager will use a computer program to construct his portfolio in such a way that it is neutral to the market as well as across industries. The hedge fund manager may use a commercial "optimizer" — computer software designed to measure exposure to the market and produce a trade list for execution based on a manager's desired exposure to the market — or he may use his own computer algorithms to measure and neutralize risk.

Most market neutral managers use optimizers to neutralize market and industry exposure. However, more sophisticated optimizers attempt to keep the portfolio neutral to several risk factors. These include, size, book to value, price/earnings ratios, and market price to book value ratios. The idea is to have no intended or unintended risk exposures that might compromise the portfolio's neutrality.

Market neutral programs tend to be labeled "black boxes." This is a term for sophisticated computer algorithms that lack transparency. The lack of transparency associated with these investment strategies comes in two forms. First, hedge fund managers, by nature, are secretive. They are reluctant to reveal their proprietary trading programs. Second, even if a hedge fund manager were to reveal his proprietary computer algorithms, these algorithms are often so sophisticated and complicated that they are difficult to comprehend.

We will have more to say about transparency in Chapter 4 regarding the selection of hedge fund managers and whether the hedge fund industry should be institutionalized. For now it is sufficient to point out that black boxes tend to be problematic for investors.

We would expect market neutral hedge fund managers to produce returns independent of the stock market (they are neutral to the stock market). Exhibit 10 confirms this expectation.

Exhibit 10: HFRI Equity Market Neutral Index

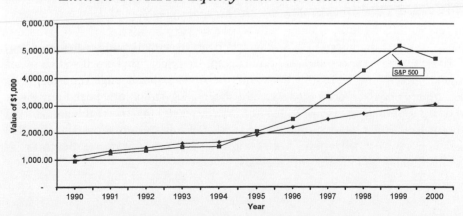

Market Timers

Market timers, as their name suggests, attempt to time the most propitious moments to be in the market, and invest in cash otherwise. More specifically, they attempt to time the market so that they are fully invested during bull markets, and strictly in cash during bear markets.

Unlike equity long/short strategies or market neutral strategies, market times use a top-down approach as opposed to a bottom-up approach. Market timing hedge fund managers are not stock pickers. They analyze fiscal and monetary policy as well as key macroeconomic indicators to determine whether the economy is gathering or running out of steam.

Macroeconomic variables they may analyze are labor productivity, business investment, purchasing managers' surveys, commodity prices, consumer confidence, housing starts, retail sales, industrial production, balance of payments, current account deficits/surpluses, and durable goods orders.

They use this macroeconomic data to forecast the expected gross domestic product (GDP) for the next quarter. Forecasting models typically are based on multifactor linear regressions, taking into account whether a variable is a leading or lagging indicator and whether the variable experiences any seasonal effects.

Once market timers have their forecast for the next quarter(s) they position their investment portfolio in the market according to their forecast. Construction of their portfolio is quite simple. They do not need to purchase individual stocks. Instead, they buy or sell stock index futures and options to increase or decrease their exposure to the market as necessary. At all times, contributed capital from investors is kept in short-term, risk-free, interest bearing accounts. Treasury bills are often purchased which not only yield a current risk-free interest rate, but also can be used as margin for the purchase of stock index futures.

When a market timer's forecast is bullish, he may purchase stock index futures with an economic exposure equivalent to the contributed capital. He may apply leverage by purchasing futures contracts that provide an economic exposure to the stock market greater than that of the underlying capital. However, market timers tend to use limited amounts of leverage.

When the hedge fund manager is bearish, he will trim his market exposure by selling futures contracts. If he is completely bearish, he will sell all of his stock index futures and call options and just sit on his cash portfolio. Some market timers may be more aggressive and short stock index futures and buy stock index put options to take advantage of bear markets. In general though, market timers have either long exposure to the market or no exposure. Consequently, this is a conservative hedge fund strategy in the same mode as market neutral programs. Exhibit 11 confirms this analysis.

Exhibit 11: HFRI Market Timing Index

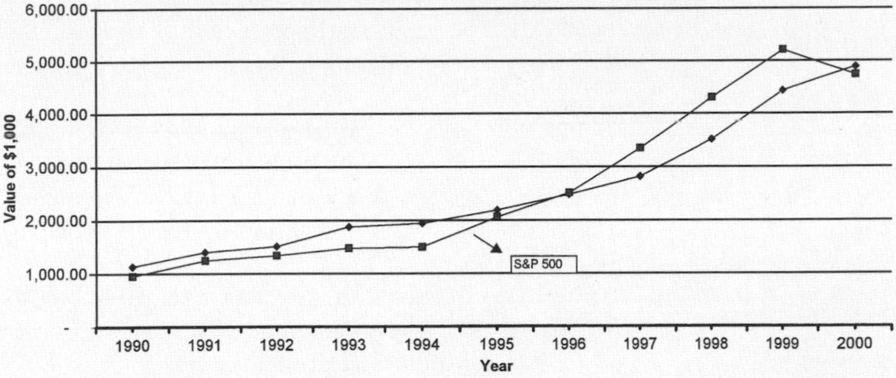

CONCLUSION

This chapter was intended to provide an overview of the hedge fund market; it was not intended to draw any conclusions about the value of hedge funds as an investment vehicle. The issues associated with hedge fund investing will be addressed in the following chapters. In the meantime, there are three key points that the reader should take from this chapter.

First, the hedge fund industry has grown dramatically over the past decade. Although it is only about one-fifth the size of the mutual fund industry, its growth potential is much higher. New managers enter the hedge fund industry on a daily basis and new capital, particularly from pension funds, is being drawn to the industry.

Second, the hedge fund strategies discussed above invest in the same securities as traditional long-only managers. This is a key point that we made in Chapter 1, but it bears repeating. Hedge fund managers use the same securities as long-only managers. However, the distinguishing feature of hedge fund managers is the strategies in which they employ those securities. Therefore, hedge fund managers do not employ alternative assets, but rather, alternative strategies.

Last, there are many different hedge fund strategies. Which is best for the investor? That will really depend upon the strategic approach that the investor wishes to take. Some investors may be more focussed on equity-based strategies. For them, equity long/short funds or merger arbitrage might be appropriate. For an investor with a fixed income bias, convertible arbitrage, fixed income arbitrage, or relative value arbitrage may be appropriate. Suffice it to say that there is suffi-cient variety in the hedge fund marketplace to suit most investors.

Chapter 3

Establishing a Hedge Fund Investment Program

T he hedge fund market has demonstrated tremendous growth over the past decade. The amount invested in this market has grown from an estimated $50 billion in 1990 to $362 billion in 1999. However, the hedge fund market is highly fragmented. Conservative estimates put the number of hedge funds at over 2500 funds, with less than 20 funds managing $3 billion or more.[1] The fragmented nature of the hedge fund market creates both opportunities and hazards for new investors in this arena.

This chapter addresses the opportunities associated with hedge funds. We will discuss the hazards in later chapters. We begin with a review of the research on hedge funds where we address questions regarding the benefits of hedge funds within an investment portfolio, whether their performance is persistent, and whether hedge funds undermine the financial markets. We then consider the investment strategies that may be applicable to hedge funds.

SHOULD HEDGE FUNDS BE PART OF AN INVESTMENT PROGRAM?

Before considering hedged funds as part of a strategic investment program, we must first ask the question: Are they worth it? Initially, we must consider the return potential of hedge funds. Second, we must determine whether hedge funds have a place within a diversified portfolio that includes stocks and bonds.

Goldman, Sachs & Co. and Financial Risk Management Ltd. in two reports study the returns to hedge funds over two time periods, 1993–1997 and 1994–1998.[2] Over the first time period, they find the return to four categories of hedge funds, Market Neutral, Event Driven, Equity Long/Short, and Tactical Trading, to earn average annual returns of 13.37%, 17.25%, 19.29%, and 19.48%, respectively. This compared to an average annual return for the S&P 500 of 20.25% over the same time period. However, the volatility for each class of hedge funds was significantly lower than that for the S&P 500.

---

[1] See Chip Cummins, "Hedge Funds Not Worried about Pending U.S. Regulations," *Dow Jones International News* (March 28, 2000); and *The New York Times*, "Hedge Fund Industry Creates a Dinosaur: The Macro Manager" (May 6, 2000), Section B.

[2] See Goldman, Sachs & Co. and Financial Risk Management Ltd., "The Hedge Fund 'Industry' and Absolute Return Funds," *The Journal of Alternative Investments* (Spring 1999), pp. 11–27; and "Hedge Funds Revisited," *Pension and Endowment Forum* (January 2000).

Further, the correlation with the S&P 500 ranged from 0.06 (Market Neutral) to 0.6 (Equity L/S). A portfolio of 60% S&P 500, 30% Lehman Aggregate Bond Index, and 10% absolute return hedge fund index outperformed the Pension Plan Index of 60/40 stocks/bonds by 78 basis points per year with a reduction in portfolio standard deviation of 31 basis points.

Over the second time period, which included the bailout of the Long Term Capital Management hedge fund group, the four hedge fund groups earned an average annual return of 11.9% for Market Neutral, 12.7% for Event Driven, 15.15% for Equity Long/Short, and 16.98% for Tactical Trading. The average annual return for the S&P 500 was 24.06% during this time period. Correlation of returns with the S&P 500 increased during this period ranged from 0.38 (Market Neutral) to 0.77 (Equity Long/Short). A portfolio of 60% S&P 500, 30% Lehman Aggregate Bond Index, and 10% hedge funds increased the total return by 48 basis points per year over the 60/40 Pension Plan Index, but portfolio volatility also increased by 14 basis points.

For the time period 1991–1995, Schneeweis and Spurgin document a range of hedge fund average annual returns of 7.8% for short selling funds to 27.9% for global macro funds.[3] Average annual standard deviation calculations ranged from 3.1% for market neutral funds to 18.4% for emerging market hedge funds. Correlation coefficients of the Hedge Fund Research hedge fund indices with the S&P 500 ranged from −0.60 for short selling hedge funds to 0.74 to hedge funds focussing on growth sectors.

Separately, Schneeweis finds that a portfolio consisting of 80% that is equally weighted with U.S. stocks and U.S. bonds and 20% hedge funds outperforms the stand alone stock and bond portfolio in terms or expected return, standard deviation, Sharpe ratio, and *drawdown*.[4] (Drawdown is a measure of the decline in net asset value of an investment portfolio.) A similar test using international stocks yields the same results.

Liang finds for the time period 1990–1996 that an equally weighted portfolio of 921 hedge funds earned a total return of 208% compared to 156% for the S&P 500.[5] Monthly standard deviation for the hedge fund group was 4.04% compared to 3.37% for the S&P 500. Liang regressed the returns from 16 different hedge fund styles on the returns to stocks, bonds, currencies, and commodities. He found R-squares that ranged from 0.20 for currency based hedge funds to 0.77 for emerging market hedge funds, with the composite R-square for all hedge funds to be 0.23. Liang also compared his sample of hedge funds to a sample of mutual funds. He found that the average Sharpe ratio for hedge funds to be 0.44, while for mutual funds it was 0.26.

---

[3] See Thomas Schneeweis and Richard Spurgin, "Multifactor Analysis of Hedge Fund, Managed Futures, and Mutual Fund Return and Risk Characteristics," *The Journal of Alternative Investments* (Fall 1998), pp. 1–24.

[4] See Thomas Schneeweis, "The Benefits of Hedge Funds: Asset Allocation for the Institutional Investor," Center for International Securities and Derivatives Markets (September 2000).

[5] See Bing Liang, "On the Performance of Hedge Funds," *Financial Analysts Journal* (July/August 1999), pp. 72–83.

Peskin, Urias, Anjilvel, and Boudreau find that over the time period of January 1990 through June 2000, the average annual return for all hedge funds in their sample was 18.9%, with a volatility of 5.5% and a Sharpe ratio of 2.5.[6] This compares quite favorably to the return for the S&P 500 of 17.2%, volatility of 13.7%, and a Sharpe ratio of 0.9.

Edwards and Liew find that over the time period 1989–1996, an equally weighted fund of hedge funds earned an average annual return of 11.2% with a correlation coefficient with the S&P 500 of 0.37.[7] An unconstrained optimization including stocks, bonds, and fund of funds, selected an allocation of 84% to an equally-weighted fund of hedge funds, 7% to the S&P 500, and 10% to long-term corporate bonds.

Brown, Goetzmann, and Ibbotson study the period 1989–1995.[8] They find that an equally weighted portfolio of offshore hedge funds earned an average return of 13.26%. Average annual standard deviations ranged from 6.16% for commodity pools to 22.15% for event driven hedge funds. Correlation coefficients with the S&P 500 ranged from –0.70 for short selling funds to 0.83 for opportunistic funds investing in the U.S. markets.

Ackermann, McEnally, and Ravenscraft review hedge funds within a portfolio context.[9] They find that over the period 1988–1995 the addition of hedge funds to either a stock, bond, or balanced portfolio results in an improved Sharpe ratio.

Fung and Hsieh[10] conduct a hedge fund performance attribution analysis similar to that performed by Sharpe for mutual funds.[11] They find low R-squares between the returns to hedge funds and those of traditional asset classes. Almost half (48%) of the hedge fund regression equations had an R-square below 25%. Further, they found that 25% of the hedge funds were negatively correlated with the standard asset classes.

The body of research on hedge funds demonstrates two key qualifications for hedge funds. First, that over the time period of 1989–2000, the returns to hedge funds were positive. The highest returns were achieved by global macro hedge funds, and the lowest returns were achieved by short selling hedge funds. Not all categories of hedge funds beat the S&P 500. However, in many cases, the volatility associated with hedge fund returns was lower than that of the S&P 500.[12]

---

[6] See Michael Peskin, Michael Urias, Satish Anjilvel, and Bryan Boudreau, "Why Hedge Funds Make Sense," Morgan Stanley Dean Witter Quantitative Strategies (November 2000).

[7] See Franklin Edwards and Jimmy Liew, "Hedge Funds versus Managed Futures as an Asset Class," *The Journal of Derivatives* (Summer 1999), pp. 45–62.

[8] See Stephen J. Brown, William N. Goetzmann and Roger G. Ibbotson, "Offshore Hedge Funds: Survival and Performance, 1989–1995," *The Journal of Business* (vol. 72), pp. 91–117.

[9] See Carl Ackermann, Richard McEnally, and David Ravenscraft, "The Performance of Hedge Funds: Risk, Return, and Incentives," *The Journal of Finance* (June 1999), pp. 833–873.

[10] See William Fung and David Hsieh, "Empirical Characteristics of Dynamic Trading Strategies: The Case of Hedge Funds," *The Review of Financial Studies* (Summer 1997), pp. 275–302.

[11] William Sharpe, "Asset Allocation: Management Style and Performance Measurement," *The Journal of Portfolio Management* (1992), pp. 7–19.

[12] See Goldman, Sachs & Co. and Financial Risk Management Ltd., "The Hedge Fund 'Industry' and Absolute Return Funds" and "Hedge Funds Revisited."

Second, the empirical research demonstrates that hedge funds provide good diversification benefits. In other words, hedge funds do, in fact, hedge other financial assets. Correlation coefficients with the S&P 500 range from –0.7 for short selling hedge funds to 0.83 for opportunistic hedge funds investing in the U.S. markets.[13] The less than perfect positive correlation with financial assets indicates that hedge funds can expand the efficient frontier for asset managers.

In summary, the recent research on hedge funds indicates consistent, positive performance with low correlation with traditional asset classes. The conclusion is that hedge funds can expand the investment opportunity set for institutions, offering both return enhancement as well as diversification benefits.

Nonetheless, there are several caveats to keep in mind with respect to the documented results for hedge funds. First, most of the empirical research on hedge funds was conducted over the same and, relatively short, time period of the early to mid-1990s. This was a time of stable economic growth. As a result, it is not surprising that the existing research has produced consistent, favorable results.

Second, most of the research on hedge funds was done before 1998 when Long Term Capital Management of Greenwich, Connecticut had to be rescued by a consortium of large banks and brokerage firms. The fallout from this near disaster was felt throughout the hedge fund industry with less competent firms folding their operations. Recent research provides clear evidence that shocks to one segment of the hedge fund industry can be felt across many different hedge fund strategies.[14] We will analyze this issue in more detail in a later chapter. Additionally, the recent roller-coaster ride in the U.S. stock markets has forced at least one large hedge fund shop to close its doors and has severely humbled another hedge fund giant.[15]

Third, some form of bias (survivorship bias, self-selection bias, and catastrophe bias) exist in the empirical studies. All of the cited studies make use of a hedge fund database. The building of these databases results in certain biases becoming embedded in the data. These biases, if not corrected, can unintentionally inflate the documented returns to hedge funds. It has been estimated that these three biases can add from 100 to 400 basis points to the estimated total return of hedge funds. We will address this issue in greater detail in Chapters 6 and 7 that cover risk management.

IS HEDGE FUND PERFORMANCE PERSISTENT?

This is the age-old question with respect to all asset managers, not just hedge funds: Can the manager repeat her good performance? This issue, though, is par-

---

[13] See Brown, Goetzmann, and Ibbotson, "Offshore Hedge Funds: Survival and Performance, 1989–1995," and Schneeweis and Spurgin, "Multifactor Analysis of Hedge Fund, Managed Futures, and Mutual Fund Return and Risk Characteristics."

[14] See Goldman, Sachs & Co. and Financial Risk Management Ltd., "The Hedge Fund "Industry" and Absolute Return Funds" and "Hedge Funds Revisited;" and Mark Anson, "Financial Market Dislocations and Hedge Fund Returns," working paper, 2001.

[15] See *The New York Times*, "Hedge Fund Industry Creates a Dinosaur: The Macro Manager," May 6, 2000, Section B.

ticularly acute for the hedge fund marketplace because hedge fund managers often claim that the source of their returns is "skill-based" rather than dependent upon general financial market conditions. Unfortunately, the existing evidence is mixed, and there is no clear conclusion.

Brown, Goetzmann, and Ibbotson present a year-by-year cross-sectional regression (parametric analysis) of past hedge fund returns on current hedge fund returns.[16] Over the six years studied, they find that three of the years have positive slopes (indicating persistent positive performance) and three years have negative slopes (indicating no persistence). In other words, it is only a 50–50 chance that good performance in one year will be followed by good performance in the following year. They conclude that there is no evidence of performance persistence in their hedge fund sample.

Park and Staum measure skill by the ratio of excess return as measured by the Capital Asset Pricing model divided by the standard deviation of the hedge fund manager's returns.[17] They use this skill statistic to rank hedge fund managers on a year-by year basis and then compare this ranking to the following year's skill ranking. Using a non-parametric test, they find strong evidence that hedge fund manager skill persists from year to year.

Agarwal and Naik use both a parametric (regression) test and a non-parametric (ranking) test to measure the persistence of hedge fund performance.[18] They find that under both tests a considerable amount of performance persistence exists at the quarterly horizon. However the persistence is reduced as one moves to yearly returns, indicating that performance persistence among hedge fund managers is primarily short term in nature.

Peskin, Urias, Anjilvel, and Boudreau find results similar to Agarwal and Naik.[19] They find that performance among hedge fund managers persists on a monthly basis, but it is much less so on an annual basis.

A different approach to performance persistence looks at the persistence of volatility in hedge fund returns. Specifically, other researchers have noted that the volatility of returns is more persistent over time than the size or direction of the return itself. Schneeweis[20] and Park and Staum[21] demonstrate that the best forecast of future returns is one that is consistent with prior volatility, instead of a forecast that is based upon prior returns.

---

[16] See Brown, Goetzmann, and Ibbotson, "Offshore Hedge Funds: Survival and Performance, 1989–1995."
[17] See James Park and Jeremy Staum, "Performance Persistence in the Alternative Investment Industry," working paper (1999).
[18] See Vikas Agarwal and Narayan Naik, "Multi-Period Performance Persistence Analysis of Hedge Funds," *The Journal of Financial and Quantitative Analysis* (September 2000), pp. 327–342.
[19] See Peskin, Urias, Anjilvel, and Boudreau, "Why Hedge Funds Make Sense."
[20] See Thomas Schneeweis, "Evidence of Superior Performance Persistence in Hedge Funds: An Empirical Comment," *The Journal of Alternative Investments* (Fall 1998), pp. 76–80.
[21] See Park and Staum, "Performance Persistence in the Alternative Investment Industry."

DO HEDGE FUNDS UNDERMINE THE FINANCIAL MARKETS?

Hedge funds have often been made scapegoats for whatever ails the financial markets. This can be traced back to George Soros' currency attack on the British Pound Sterling. In 1992, George Soros bet heavily and correctly that the British government would not be able to support the pound and that the pound would devalue.

In 1997, Soros was once again blamed for a currency crisis by the Malaysian Prime Minister Mahathir bin Mohammad. The Prime Minister attributed the crash in the Malaysian ringgit to speculation in the currency markets by hedge fund managers, including George Soros.

Brown, Goetzmann, and Park test specifically whether hedge funds caused the crash of the Malaysian ringgit.[22] They regress the monthly percentage change in the exchange rate on the currency exposure maintained by hedge funds. Reviewing the currency exposures of 11 large global macro hedge funds, they conclude that there is no evidence that the Malaysian ringgit was affected by hedge fund manager currency exposures. Additionally, they test the hypothesis that global hedge funds precipitated the slide of a basket of Asian currencies (the "Asian Contagion") in 1997. They find no evidence that hedge funds contributed to the decline of the several Asian currencies in the fall of 1997.

Fung and Hsieh measure the market impact of hedge fund positions on several financial market events from the October 1987 stock market crash to the Asian Contagion of 1997.[23] They found that there were certain instances where hedge funds did have an impact on the market, most notably with the devaluation of the pound sterling in 1992. However, in no case was there evidence that hedge funds were able to manipulate the financial markets away from their natural paths driven by economic fundamentals. For instance, the Sterling came under pressure in 1992 due to large capital outflows from the UK. The conclusion is that, for instance, George Soros bet correctly against the Sterling and exacerbated its decline, but he did not trigger the devaluation.

A HEDGE FUND INVESTMENT STRATEGY

The above discussion demonstrates that hedge funds can expand the investment opportunity set for investors. The question now becomes: What is to be accomplished by the hedge fund investment program? The strategy may be simply a search for an additional source of return. Conversely, it may be for risk management purposes. Whatever its purpose, an investment plan for hedge funds may consider one of four strategies. Hedge funds may be selected on an opportunistic basis, as a hedge fund of funds, as part of a joint venture, or as an absolute return strategy.

[22] See Stephen Brown, William Goetzmann, and James Park, "Hedge Funds and the Asian Currency Crisis," *The Journal of Portfolio Management* (Summer 2000), pp. 95–101.
[23] See William Fung and David Hsieh, "Measuring the Market Impact of Hedge Funds," *The Journal of Empirical Finance* (2001).

Opportunistic Hedge Fund Investing

The term "hedge fund" can be misleading. Hedge funds do not necessarily have to hedge an investment portfolio. Rather, they can be used to expand the investment opportunity set. This is the opportunistic nature of hedge funds — they can provide an investor with new investment opportunities that she cannot otherwise obtain through traditional long only investments.

There are several ways hedge funds can be opportunistic. First, many hedge fund managers can add value to an existing investment portfolio through specialization in a sector or in a market strategy. These managers do not contribute portable alpha. Instead, they contribute above market returns through the application of superior skill or knowledge to a narrow market or strategy.

Consider a portfolio manager whose particular expertise is the biotechnology industry. She has followed this industry for years and has developed a superior information set to identify winners and losers. On the long only side the manager purchases those stocks that she believes will increase in value, and avoids those biotech stocks she believes will decline in value. However, this strategy does not utilize her superior information set to its fullest advantage. The ability to go both long and short biotech stocks in a hedge fund is the only way to maximize the value of the manager's information set. Therefore, a biotech hedge fund provides a new opportunity: the ability to extract value on both the long side and the short side of the biotech market.

The goal of this strategy is to identify the best managers in a specific economic sector or specific market segment that complements the existing investment portfolio. These managers are used to enhance the risk and return profile of an existing portfolio, rather than hedge it.

Opportunistic hedge funds tend to have a benchmark. Take the example of the biotech long/short hedge fund. An appropriate benchmark would be the AMEX Biotech Index that contains 17 biotechnology companies. Alternatively, if the investor believed that the biotech sector will outperform the general stock market, she could use a broad based stock index such as the S&P 500 for the benchmark. The point is that opportunistic hedge funds are not absolute return vehicles (discussed below). Their performance can be measured relative to a benchmark.

As another example, most institutional investors have a broad equity portfolio. This portfolio may include an index fund, external value and growth managers, and possibly, private equity investments. However, along the spectrum of this equity portfolio, there may be gaps in its investment line-up. For instance, many hedge funds combine late stage private investments with public securities. These hybrid funds are a natural extension of an institution's investment portfolio because they bridge the gap between private equity and index funds. Therefore a new opportunity is identified: the ability to blend private equity and public securities within one investment strategy. We will discuss this strategy further in our section on private equity.

Exhibit 1: Implementing an Opportunistic Hedge Fund Strategy

Diversified Hedge Fund Portfolio	Equity-Based Hedge Fund Portfolio
Equity Long/Short	Equity Long/Short
Short Selling	Short Selling
Market Neutral	Market Neutral
Merger Arbitrage	Merger Arbitrage
Event Driven	Event Driven
Convertible Arbitrage	Convertible Arbitrage
Global Macro	
Fixed Income Arbitrage	
Relative Value Arbitrage	
Market Timers	

Again, we come back to one of our main themes: that alternative "assets" are really alternative investment strategies, and these alternative strategies are used to expand the investment opportunity set rather than hedge it. In summary, hedge funds may be selected not necessarily to reduce the risk of an existing investment portfolio, but instead, to complement its risk and return profile. Opportunistic investing is designed to select hedge fund managers that can enhance certain portions of a broader portfolio.

Another way to consider opportunistic hedge fund investments is that they are finished products because their investment strategy or market segment complements an institutional investor's existing asset allocation. In other words, these hybrid funds can plug the gaps of an existing portfolio. No further work is necessary on the part of the institution because the investment opportunity set has been expanded by the addition of the hybrid product. These "gaps" may be in domestic equity, fixed income, or international investments. Additionally, because opportunistic hedge funds are finished products, it makes it easier to establish performance benchmarks.

Constructing an opportunistic portfolio of hedge funds will depend upon the constraints under which such a program operates. For example, if an investor's hedge fund program is not limited in scope or style, then diversification across a broad range of hedge fund styles would be appropriate. If, however, the hedge fund program is limited in scope to, for instance, expanding the equity investment opportunity set, the choices will be less diversified across strategies. Exhibit 1 demonstrates these two choices.

Hedge Fund of Funds

A *hedge fund of funds* is an investment in a group of hedge funds, from five to more than 20. The purpose of a hedge fund of funds is to reduce the idiosyncratic risk of any one hedge fund manager. In other words, there is safety in numbers.

This is simply modern portfolio theory (MPT) applied to the hedge fund marketplace. Diversification is one of the founding principles of MPT, and it is as applicable to hedge funds as it is to stocks and bonds.

Henker reviews the diversification benefits for three styles of hedge funds: equity long/short, event driven, and relative value.[24] Using random sampling within each hedge fund style, he finds that a portfolio of about five funds captures most of the diversification benefits that can be achieved within each style. The reduction of risk is achieved because of the heterogeneous return characteristics of hedge funds comprising the fund of funds portfolio. The fact that hedge funds within the same style have different return patterns is consistent with the findings of Fung and Hsieh.[25] They found no evidence of "herding" among hedge funds that pursued currency investment strategies.

Park and Staum consider the optimal diversification for a random pool of hedge funds selected from a database of 1,230 hedge funds of all different styles.[26] Consistent with Henker, they demonstrate that a fund of funds portfolio of five hedge funds can eliminate approximately 80% of the idiosyncratic risk of the individual hedge fund managers. After five hedge funds, the diversification benefits decline significantly. They find that a fund of funds portfolio of 20 hedge funds can diversify away about 95% of the idiosyncratic risk.

What, then, is left in terms of return with a hedge fund of funds? Along with the diversification of risk, fund of funds also provide diversification of return. That is, the return on a fund of funds product is generally below that of individual hedge fund styles. Generally, the return is cash-plus with cash defined as LIBOR and the plus equal to 100 to 200 basis points.

This low volatility, cash-plus product may be applied in one of three ways: risk budgeting, portable alpha, or cash substitute.

Risk Budgeting

It seems odd to think of hedge funds as a risk budgeting tool. However, the empirical studies cited above demonstrate that fund of funds have a low standard deviation and a low correlation with traditional asset classes. Therefore, they are excellent candidates for risk budgeting.

We digress for a moment to discuss risk budgeting. Risk budgeting is a subset of the risk management process. It is the process of measuring the risk that an investor is actually taking, assessing the investor's appetite for risk, quantifying how much risk the investor is willing to take, and then deciding how to allocate that risk across a diversified portfolio. The process of allocating risk across a portfolio is what is known as risk budgeting. Risk budgeting allows a manager to set risk target levels throughout her portfolio.

Consider Exhibit 2. In this exhibit, we present the monthly expected return, standard deviation, and Sharpe ratios for the S&P 500, the Salomon Smith

[24] See Thomas Henker, "Naive Diversification for Hedge Funds," *The Journal of Alternative Assets* (Winter 1998), pp. 33–38.

[25] See Fung and Hsieh, "Measuring the Market Impact of Hedge Funds."

[26] See James Park and Jeremy Staum, "Fund of Funds Diversification: How Much is Enough?" *The Journal of Alternative Investments* (Winter 1998), pp. 39–42.

Barney Broad Investment Grade (BIG) bond index, the NASDAQ index, Morgan Stanley Capital's Europe, Australia and Far East (EAFE) index, and three hedge fund indices. The period covered is January 1990 through June 2000. The three hedge fund indices are two composite hedge fund indices of all hedge funds in the MAR and HFR databases and an HFR hedge fund of funds index.

From Exhibit 2, we can see that hedge fund indices, including that for hedge fund of funds, have higher Sharpe ratios compared to that for stocks and bonds. But hedge funds should not be considered in isolation. To asses their true value to a diversified portfolio, we need to see how hedge fund returns are correlated with the returns to stocks and bonds.

Suppose an investor has a monthly risk budget of 5% for her overall portfolio and she wishes to invest in small-capitalized stocks. From Exhibit 2 we can see that small-cap stocks have the highest expected return. Unfortunately, the monthly expected volatility for the NASDAQ stocks is 6.5%, which exceeds her risk budget.

The investor can solve her problem by combining a hedge fund of funds investment with small-cap stocks to meet her risk budget of 5%. Consider Exhibit 3. This exhibit is a correlation matrix that demonstrates that the returns received from hedge funds are less than perfectly correlated with stocks and bonds. For example, we can see that the correlation of the returns to the HFR FOF index with the returns to small-cap stocks is 0.54. Using the information in Exhibits 2 and 3 we can determine the optimal allocation to hedge fund of funds and small-cap stocks such that the investor can stay within her risk budget. The calculation is:

$$0.05 = \text{square root of } \{[w(\text{FOF})]^2 \times 0.0182^2 + [1 - w(\text{FOF})]^2 \times 0.065^2 + 2 \times [w(\text{FOF})] \times [1 - w(\text{FOF})] \times 0.0182 \times 0.065 \times 0.54\}$$

where

> $w(\text{FOF})$ is the weight in the portfolio allocated to a hedge fund of funds
> $1 - w(\text{FOF})$ is the weight in the portfolio allocated to small-cap stocks

Exhibit 2: Expected Return, Standard Deviation, and Sharpe Ratios

Asset Class	Expected Return	Standard Deviation	Sharpe Ratio
S&P 500	1.21%	3.94%	17.94%
BIG	0.63%	1.11%	11.80%
NASDAQ	1.94%	6.50%	22.19%
EAFE	0.49%	4.91%	0.91%
MAR	0.90%	1.37%	29.21%
HFR	1.41%	2.07%	44.06%
HFR FOF	1.00%	1.82%	27.28%

Exhibit 3: Correlation Matrix

	S&P500	BIG	NASDAQ	EAFE	MAR	HFR Comp	HFR FOF
S&P 500	1.00	0.41	0.73	0.55	0.50	0.65	0.38
BIG	0.41	1.00	0.25	0.21	0.20	0.18	0.13
NASDAQ	0.73	0.25	1.00	0.46	0.55	0.83	0.54
EAFE	0.55	0.21	0.46	1.00	0.37	0.50	0.31
MAR	0.50	0.20	0.55	0.37	1.00	0.82	0.87
HFR Comp	0.65	0.18	0.83	0.50	0.82	1.00	0.80
HFR FOF	0.38	0.13	0.54	0.31	0.87	0.80	1.00

Solving the equation for w(FOF) yields a value of 0.715. That is, the investor needs to invest 71.5% of her portfolio in a hedge fund of funds and 28.5% in small-cap stocks to remain within her risk budget of 5% monthly standard deviation.

Consider the power of a hedge fund of funds in this example. Without hedge funds, the investor could not allocate any of her portfolio to small-cap stocks because the monthly standard deviation of small-cap stocks of 6.5% exceeded her risk budget of 5%. However, when combined with a fund of funds product, the investor can allocate up to 28.5% of her portfolio to small-cap stocks.

Simply put, the investor uses hedge funds to "buy" units of risk that can then be allocated to other portions of her portfolio. This may run counter to intuition because hedge funds are perceived to be risky investments; yet, in Exhibit 2 we can see that the risk associated with a portfolio of hedge funds, as measured by the monthly standard deviation, is lower than large-cap stocks, small-cap stocks, and foreign stocks. Additionally, hedge fund returns have less than perfect correlation with stock returns. Therefore, they can be useful risk budgeting tools.

Risk budgeting can change portfolio asset allocations by highlighting the less than perfect correlation between two investment strategies. In the risk budgeting world, different asset classes or investment strategies are assigned different hurdle rates. These hurdle rates quantify an asset's correlation with the overall portfolio.

For example, most portfolios have a large exposure to large-cap stocks. But from Exhibit 3, we can see that hedge fund of funds have the lowest correlation with large-cap stocks. As a result, the hurdle rate for hedge fund of funds would be lower than other asset classes or strategies.

Elton, Gruber, and Retnzler provide the calculation for determining the hurdle rate for hedge fund of funds vis-à-vis large-cap stocks.[27] In a study of commodity pools within a portfolio context, they show that a commodity pool should be added to an existing portfolio if the following equation is satisfied:

$$(R_c - R_f)/\sigma_c > (R_p - R_f) \times \rho_{c,p}/\sigma_p \tag{1}$$

[27] See Edwin Elton, Martin Gruber, and Joel Rentzler, "Professionally Managed, Publicly Traded Commodity Funds," *The Journal of Business* (1987), pp. 175–199.

where

R_c is the expected return to the commodity pool
R_p is the expected return to the portfolio
R_f is the risk-free rate
$\rho_{c,p}$ is the correlation between the returns to the commodity pool and the portfolio
σ_c is the volatility of returns to the commodity pool
σ_p is the volatility of returns to the portfolio

We can take Equation (1) and transform it into a hurdle rate calculation for hedge fund of funds:

$$R_h = (R_p - R_f) \times \rho_{h,p} \times \sigma_h / \sigma_p + R_f \tag{2}$$

Defining the S&P 500 as the portfolio, the hurdle rate for hedge fund of funds is:

Hurdle Rate = $(0.0121 - 0.005) \times 0.38 \times 0.0182/0.0394 + 0.005 = 0.0062$

In other words, hedge fund of funds must earn a rate of at least 62 basis points per month to be a valuable addition for risk budgeting purposes. Given that the expected return for hedge fund of funds is 1% per month, the hurdle rate is met, and a hedge fund of funds is a valuable risk budgeting tool.

Compare this result to that obtained for international stocks. Using the EAFE stock index, we perform the same risk budgeting calculation for international stocks vis-à-vis large cap stocks. The question is whether international stocks are appropriate risk budgeting tools versus large cap stocks. Plugging in the values from Exhibits 2 and 3 into Equation (2) we get:

Hurdle Rate = $(0.0121 - 0.005) \times 0.55 \times 0.0491/0.0394 + 0.005 = 0.0098$

The hurdle rate for international stocks is 98 basis points per month. From Exhibit 2, we can see that the expected return is only 49 basis points per month. Therefore, international stocks are not suitable risk budgeting tools with respect to large-cap stocks.

Portable Alpha

Portable alpha can be obtained from a diversified pool of hybrid managers with low correlation to traditional asset classes. This is a combination strategy of investing with multiple managers to achieve a portable alpha.

The idea is to invest with several hedge fund managers to achieve a distribution of returns that are uncorrelated with either stocks or bonds. Generally, this product yields a return equal to a cash rate of return plus a premium. The premium is the portable alpha. It represents the extra return that can be achieved with a hedge fund of funds above that which can be earned from investing in short term cash instruments such as Treasury bills or high-grade commercial paper. The portable alpha is then applied to the equity or fixed income portion of the portfolio with futures contracts.

For example, Exhibit 3 demonstrates that the HFR fund of funds index has the lowest correlation with the returns to the S&P 500, even lower than that of investment grade bonds. Furthermore, Exhibit 2 shows that hedge fund of funds earn a monthly return of 1%, 37 basis points greater than that for investment grade bonds. This extra return may be considered the "alpha." It is the return earned above that of a fixed income rate of return while providing an alternative investment that is less correlated with equity returns than that of traditional fixed income investments.

Consider an investor who has $1 billion to invest in large-cap U.S. stocks. The expected return for large cap stocks is 1.21% per month. Instead of investing the full $1 billion in the S&P 500, she invests $500 million in the S&P 500, and $500 million in hedge fund of funds. In addition, the investor purchases S&P 500 equity futures contracts such that the combination of hedge fund of funds plus equity futures contracts will be equivalent to an economic exposure of $500 million invested in the S&P 500. This process is known as "equitization," and the investor does it to equitize her hedge fund of funds investment.

We digress for a moment to discuss the embedded financing cost associated with a portable alpha strategy. To prevent arbitrage in the financial markets, the S&P 500 futures contract reflects a short-term risk-free rate of financing. That is, the difference in the futures price and the current spot price of the S&P 500 reflects the relevant risk-free rate. This is because speculators who buy or sell the S&P 500 futures contracts must hedge their position by selling or buying the underlying stocks. To purchase or borrow the underlying stocks, the speculator must borrow, and this cost of short-term financing is reflected in the pricing of the S&P 500 futures contract.[28] Therefore, any portable alpha strategy must earn at least the cost of the cost of short term financing embedded within the futures contract. Otherwise, the alpha will be negative, not positive.

For our example, we use the return of the 3-month U.S. Treasury bill as the short-term financing rate reflected in the S&P 500 futures contracts. Over the period January 1990 through June 2000, this rate was about 0.5% per month. Therefore, the hedge fund of funds strategy must earn at least 0.5% per month to provide an excess return, or alpha.

In building the portable alpha strategy, we note that the systematic, or market, risk of hedge fund of funds is not zero. Therefore, we will need to take

---

[28] For instance, suppose this were not the case. Suppose that the futures contract was priced "rich" compared to the underlying S&P 500 stocks. Then the arbitrage would be to borrow cash to finance the purchase of the S&P 500 stocks and sell the futures contract to lock in an arbitrage profit. To prevent a risk-free arbitrage, therefore, futures contracts must reflect the cost of financing.

into account that our portable alpha strategy already contains a small component of systematic or market risk. From Exhibits 2 and 3 we can calculate the beta of the hedge fund of funds, using the S&P 500 as the proxy for the market:[29]

$$\text{beta} = [0.38 \times 0.0182 \times 0.0394]/0.0394^2 = 0.175$$

The low beta value of the hedge fund of funds strategy demonstrates that it has minimal market risk. Our goal is to add equity futures contracts to our $500 million investment in the hedge fund of funds until the combination of futures contracts and our hedge fund of funds investment matches the systematic risk of $500 million invested in the S&P 500. We then determine how much extra return we receive from this portable alpha strategy compared to what we could earn by purchasing large-cap stocks.

By definition, we establish the S&P 500 as the market portfolio. Therefore, its beta, or measure of systematic risk is 1.0. We know that the beta of the hedge fund of funds strategy is 0.175. We need to add sufficient S&P 500 futures contracts so that combination of hedge fund of funds and equity futures contracts matches the systematic risk of $500 million invested in the S&P 500. This means that the equity futures contracts must contribute $1 - 0.175 = 0.825$, or 82.5%, of the systematic risk of the portable alpha strategy.

Since our goal is to match the systematic, or beta, risk of an investment of $500 million in the S&P 500, we must purchase equity futures contracts such that they contribute 82.5% of the beta risk of the portable alpha strategy. This amount is:

$$82.5\% \times \$500 \text{ million} = \$412.50 \text{ million of equity futures contracts.}$$

Given an S&P 500 market value of about 1250 at the end of February 2001, this would translate into $412,500,000 ÷ [$250 × 1250] = 1,320 S&P 500 futures contracts.[30]

Finally, we now come to the amount of portable alpha we achieve with this strategy. The $500 million invested in the hedge fund of funds earns an expected monthly return of 1%. Plus we have an investment in S&P 500 futures contracts that provides a return that is equivalent to 82.5% of that earned by an investment of $500 million in the S&P 500. In total, this portable alpha strategy is expected to earn a monthly return of:

$$1\% + 0.825 \times 1.21\% = 2\%$$

---

[29] The beta of an asset relative to the market portfolio is defined as:

$$\text{beta} = \rho(a,m) \times \sigma(a) \times \sigma(m)/\sigma(m)^2$$

where

    $\rho(a, m)$ is the correlation coefficient between the asset return and the market return

    $\sigma(a)$ is the standard deviation of the asset's returns

    $\sigma(m)$ is the standard deviation of the market's returns

[30] Every point of the S&P 500 index is worth $250 dollars under the S&P 500 futures contract. Therefore, one S&P 500 contract represents $250 × 1250 = $312,500 of economic exposure to the S&P 500.

To summarize, the portable alpha strategy requires a cash investment in the hedge fund of funds of $500 million. Equity futures contracts are added so that the combination of hedge fund of funds and equity futures contracts matches the systematic, or beta, risk of an investment of $500 million in the S&P 500. The portable alpha strategy earns the combination return from the hedge fund of funds and equity futures contracts.

The last piece that we must account for is the embedded financing cost in the S&P 500 futures contracts. We assumed that this was 0.50% per month. Therefore, our portable alpha strategy earns a net return of 2% − 0.5% = 1.5% per month. Compare this to the expected return of 1.21% of investing only in the S&P 500. The portable alpha strategy outperforms the S&P 500 by 29 basis points per month. On a $500 million dollar investment, this is an additional $1.45 million earned each month ($17,400,000 per year) above that earned by investing in large cap stocks.

This portable alpha strategy demonstrates part of the allure of hedge funds. The ability to use low market risk strategies to build portable alpha strategies that can outperform traditional investment strategies can add significant value to an investment portfolio.

If this example seemed like a lot of work, it is. For this reason, we classify hedge fund of funds that produce a portable alpha as an unfinished product. It is unfinished because the investor must finish the product by deciding where, when, and how to add the alpha to its portfolio. Futures, such as equity futures, must be used to match the systematic risk of a passive equity portfolio while maintaining the excess return or alpha generated by the fund of funds portfolio.

Portable alpha strategies are "beta driven" because the purpose is to add an excess return component while maintaining a similar systematic risk as the overall asset class. Equity futures or fixed income futures are added to "equitize" or "fixed incometize" the generated alpha, matching the beta or market risk of the asset class, but at the same time, adding the portable alpha. The investor receives the market return plus the alpha.

It is important to note that few institutions have the internal staff necessary to build a hedge fund of funds product. Typically, an outside manager must be hired to build this type of product for the institution. Furthermore, this process is not cheap; hedge fund of funds managers may charge management fees of 1 to 3% on top of the hedge fund managers' fees. Also, Brown, Goetzmann, and Ibbotson suggest that a fund of funds selector does not produce superior returns.[31]

Cash Substitute

Exhibit 2 demonstrates that the three hedge fund indices have significantly lower risk than large-cap, small-cap, or foreign stocks. In fact, the MAR index of hedge funds generates a risk profile that is just slightly greater than investment grade bonds while generating greater return. The same is true for the HFR composite hedge fund index and the hedge fund of funds index.

---

[31] See Brown, Goetzman, and Ibbotson, "Offshore Hedge Funds: Survival and Performance, 1989–1995."

This has led some researchers to consider whether hedge funds can replace cash or bonds in an efficient portfolio. Lamm studies the issue of hedge funds as a cash substitute.[32] He combines hedge funds with stocks and bonds in an efficient frontier analysis. He finds that hedge funds enter efficient frontiers across all risk levels because of their superior risk-adjusted returns. More importantly, Lamm finds that hedge funds enter efficient portfolios largely at the expense of bonds. That is, hedge funds primarily displace cash and bonds in efficient portfolios. This suggests that hedge funds may be used as a cash substitute.

We note that in Exhibit 2 the three hedge fund indices have superior Sharpe ratios compared to investment grade bonds. While the volatility associated with hedge funds is greater than investment grade bonds, it is marginally so. Conversely, the volatility of hedge fund returns is considerably less than that for the three categories of stock investments. Additionally, hedge funds earn higher returns than bonds.

Exhibit 3 demonstrates that hedge fund returns have a low correlation with the returns to large-cap, small-cap, and foreign stocks. Therefore, hedge funds have a risk profile similar to bonds in terms of risk and correlation with stock returns. Yet, hedge funds earn a better return than investment grade bonds. This makes hedge funds a potential substitute for bonds in an efficient portfolio.

Joint Venture

As noted in the introduction, the hedge fund market is fragmented with most hedge fund managers controlling a relatively small amount of assets. This provides a good opportunity to enter into a joint venture with an emerging hedge fund manager.

The greatest challenge for any new hedge fund manager is attracting sufficient capital to achieve a critical mass. Park, Brown, and Goetzmanm find the attrition rate for hedge funds is about 15% per year, while Brown, Goetzmann, and Ibbotson find that few hedge funds survive more than three years.[33] A large institutional investor can provide the necessary capital along with the stability and the credibility necessary to achieve this critical mass. In such a situation, a hedge fund manager receives a much greater benefit than just the fees collected.

In return for these start-up benefits, the institution can ask for reduced fees and a potential equity stake in the manager's revenues. As the hedge fund manager increases its assets under management, the institution will share in this growth. Additionally, the institution can earn excellent returns from its hedge fund investment with a lower fee structure. This form of collaboration can produce good long-term returns for both the institutional investor and the hedge fund manager.

---

[32] See R. McFall Lamm, Jr., "Portfolios of Alternative Assets: Why Not 100% Hedge Funds?" *The Journal of Investing* (Winter 1999).

[33] See James Park, Stephen Brown, and William Goetzmann, "Performance Benchmarks and Survivorship Bias for Hedge Funds and Commodity Trading Advisors," *Hedge Fund News* (August 1999); and Brown, Goetzmann, and Ibbotson, "Offshore Hedge Funds: Survival and Performance, 1989–1995."

Another new development in the hedge fund marketplace is the hedge fund management company. These are asset management companies that build a stable of hedge fund managers by acquiring equity ownership in the hedge fund manager. This business model is similar to that for mutual funds established by traditional money managers.

In the mutual fund industry, a corporation is established that advises each individual mutual fund. The investment adviser registers the mutual fund company with the Securities and Exchange Commission, sells shares of the mutual fund to investors, and performs all of the necessary accounting and operational duties. The fees earned from providing investment advice to the mutual fund flow upward to the advisory company.

Similarly, hedge fund management companies take care of all of the regulatory, operational, and marketing issues for the hedge fund manager, and in return, receive an equity stake in the management and profit sharing fees earned by the hedge fund manager. These hedge fund management companies need investment capital for two reasons.

First, they need working capital to acquire hedge fund managers for their management company. Second, they need investment capital to place with their hedge fund managers. In return, an investor can receive an equity stake in the hedge fund management company, or the individual hedge fund manager and receive the benefit of a hedge fund investment.

This strategy is a combination of private equity and hedge fund investing, and it offers several advantages. First many institutional investors maintain a private equity staff. Using this staff to enter into another arena in the alternative asset world allows an institution to apply its investment experience in a new venue. This "portable expertise" is analogous to portable alpha in that it can be added to other avenues of the alternative asset market.

Second, private equity investments tend to be structured as funds or pools. This legal structure is similar (but not identical) to that for hedge funds.[34] Consequently, private equity investors tend to have considerable experience sorting through the issues of pooled investors in an alternative asset vehicle.

Lastly, the linking of private equity and hedge fund investing is a natural evolution in alternative asset investing. The expansion of the investment opportunity set need not be done through the selection of discrete pockets of alternative assets; combinations of alternative assets will work just as well.

Absolute Return

Hedge funds are often described as "absolute return" products. This term comes from the skill-based nature of the industry. Hedge fund managers generally claim that their investment returns are derived from their skill at security selection

---

[34] For example, private equity funds often offer an incentive fee recapture provision known as a "clawback." Conversely, hedge funds typically offer an incentive fee hurdle rate known as a "high water mark." We will discuss more of these differences in Section III where private equity is covered.

rather than that of broad asset classes. This is due to the fact that most hedge fund managers build concentrated portfolios of relatively few investment positions and do not attempt to track a stock or bond index. The work of Fung and Hsieh, discussed earlier, shows that hedge funds generate a return distribution that is very different from mutual funds.[35]

Further, given the generally unregulated waters in which hedge fund managers operate, they have greater flexibility in their trading style and execution than traditional long-only managers. This flexibility provides a greater probability that a hedge fund manager will reach his return targets. As a result, hedge funds have often been described as absolute return vehicles that target a specific annual return regardless of what performance might be found among market indices. In other words, hedge fund managers target an absolute return rather than determine their performance relative to an index.

All traditional long-only managers are benchmarked to some passive index. The nature of benchmarking is such that it forces the manager to focus on his benchmark and his tracking error associated with that benchmark. This focus on benchmarking leads traditional active managers to commit a large portion their portfolios to tracking their benchmark. The necessity to consider the impact of every trade on the portfolio's tracking error relative to its assigned benchmark reduces the flexibility of the investment manager.

In addition, long-only active managers are constrained in their ability to short securities. They may only "go short" a security up to its weight in the benchmark index. If the security is only a small part of the index, the manager's efforts to short the stock will be further constrained. The inability to short a security beyond its benchmark weight deprives an active manager of a significant amount of the mispricing in the marketplace. Furthermore, not only are long-only managers unable to take advantage of overpriced securities, but they also cannot fully take advantage of underpriced securities because they cannot generate the necessary short positions to balance the overweights with respect to underpriced securities.

The flexibility of hedge fund managers allows them to go both long and short without benchmark constraints. This allows them to set a target rate of return or an "absolute return."

Specific parameters must be set for an absolute return program. These parameters will direct how the hedge fund program is constructed and operated and should include risk and return targets as well as the type of hedge fund strategies that may be selected. Absolute return parameters should operate at two levels: that of the individual hedge fund manager and for the overall hedge fund program. The investor sets target return ranges for each hedge fund manager but sets a specific target return level for the absolute return program. The parameters for the individual managers may be different than that for the program. For example, acceptable levels of volatility for individual hedge fund managers may be greater than that for the program.

---

[35] See Fung and Hsieh, "Empirical Characteristics of Dynamic Trading Strategies: The Case of Hedge Funds."

Exhibit 4: An Absolute Return Strategy

Absolute Return Portfolio	Individual Hedge Fund Managers
Target Return: 15%	Expected Return: 10% to 25%
Target Risk: 7%	Target Risk: 5% to 15%
Largest Acceptable Drawdown: 10%	Largest Drawdown: 10% to 20%
Liquidity: Semi-annual	Liquidity: Semi-annual
Hedge Fund Style: Equity-based	Hedge Fund Style: Equity L/S, Market Neutral, Merger Arbitrage, Short Selling, Event Driven, Convertible Arbitrage
Length of Track Record: 3 years	Minimum Track Record: 3 years

The program parameters for the hedge fund managers may be based on such factors as volatility, expected return, types of instruments traded, leverage, and historical drawdown. Other qualitative factors may be included such as length of track record, periodic liquidity, minimum investment, and assets under management. Liquidity is particularly important because an investor needs to know with certainty her time frame for cashing out of an absolute return program if hedge fund returns turn sour.

Exhibit 4 demonstrates an absolute return program strategy. Notice that the return for the portfolio has a specific target rate of 15%, while for the individual hedge funds, the return range is 10% to 25%. Also, the absolute return portfolio has a target level for risk and drawdowns, while for the individual hedge funds, a range is acceptable.

However, certain parameters are synchronized. Liquidity, for instance, must be the same for both the absolute return portfolio and that of the individual hedge fund managers. The reason is that a range of liquidity is not acceptable if the investor wishes to liquidate her portfolio. She must be able to cash out of each hedge fund within the same time frame as that established for the portfolio.

CONCLUSION

Recent research indicates that hedge fund investments can expand the investment opportunity set for investors. The returns to hedge funds are generally positive, have lower volatility than the S&P 500, and have less than perfect correlation with traditional asset classes. Consequently, hedged funds provide a good opportunity to diversify a portfolio.

An investor must decide what is the best strategy for investing in hedge funds. Hedge funds may be invested in as part of an opportunistic strategy, as part of a fund of funds strategy, as part of a private equity investment strategy, or as an absolute return strategy. In each case, hedge funds can add value to an existing portfolio.

Opportunistic hedge fund investing runs counter to the name "hedge funds." This strategy uses hedge funds to expand the investment opportunity set, not hedge it. Typically, opportunistic hedge funds will have a benchmark associated with their performance.

Hedge fund of funds strategies may have one of three purposes. Fund of funds products may be used for risk budgeting, portable alpha, or as a fixed income substitute. In each case, the fixed income-like volatility associated with a fund of funds product makes it an excellent portfolio diversifier.

A private equity hedge fund strategy provides two sources of potential alpha. The investor receives the benefits of a hedge fund investment strategy and that of a private equity strategy. If the hedge fund manager is successful, the investor will receive good returns from the hedge fund investment strategy as well as an equity kicker.

Finally, absolute return strategies target a specific risk and return profile. The goal is to produce a consistent return no matter in which part of the economic cycle the investor may find herself.

This chapter provided both the rationale and the strategy for investing in hedge funds. The next two chapters will address the tactical issues of hedge fund manager selection and due diligence, respectively.

Chapter 4

Selecting a
Hedge Fund Manager

A considerable amount of research has been dedicated to determining the economic value added of hedge funds (see our discussion in Chapter 3). Yet, despite the mounting evidence regarding the value of hedge funds, very little has been written regarding the selection of hedge fund managers. In this chapter we address some practical issues to consider in establishing a hedge fund investment program.

We begin this chapter with a graphical description of the hedge fund industry compared to the traditional world of long-only investments. We use this description throughout the chapter to describe the types of hedge fund programs encountered. Next, we present three essential questions that must be answered when selecting a hedge fund manager. Lastly, we summarize a few conclusions regarding a hedge fund investment program.

A GRAPHICAL PRESENTATION OF THE HEDGE FUND INDUSTRY

It should be no surprise to most investors that hedge funds operate differently from traditional long-only investment managers. Long-only managers typically invest in either the equity or bond market, but do not leverage their investment bets. Therefore, their investment programs have considerable market risk exposure, but very little leverage or credit risk exposure.[1]

Consider Exhibit 1. This exhibit plots market risk versus credit risk for several styles of long-only managers. We use a relative scale of 0 to 5 where 0 represents no exposure to financial market risk and 5 represents the maximum exposure. The same relative scale is applied with respect to credit risk.

---

[1] For an excellent and more detailed discussion on this type of classification, see CrossBorder Capital, "TSS(II)-Tactical Style Selection: Integrating Hedge Funds into the Asset Allocation Framework," *Hedge Fund Research* (August 2000).

A prior version of this paper appeared as Mark Anson, "Selecting a Hedge Fund Manager," *The Journal of Wealth Management* (Winter 2000).

Exhibit 1: Long Only Investments

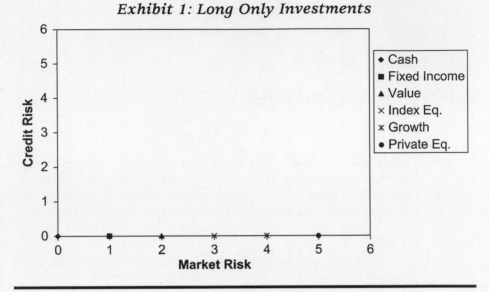

As Exhibit 1 demonstrates, traditional long-only managers have considerable exposure to market risk but minimal exposure to credit risk. At one end of the scale are money market cash managers. To avoid "breaking the buck" these managers do not take any credit risk or market risk. They invest in the most liquid and creditworthy of short-term financial paper. Typically, this includes high-grade 90-day commercial paper and 90-day U.S. Treasury obligations.

At the other end of the scale are private equity managers. They take no credit risk, but have the greatest exposure to market risk. Most private equity funds, for instance, have lock-up periods between 7 and 10 years. Investments made by private equity funds are in non-public securities for which no readily available market exists. Liquidity is low, and investors are exposed to the long-term prospects of the equity market.

In between the cash managers and the private equity managers, and along the increasing scale of market risk, we find fixed income managers, value managers, equity index managers, and growth managers.

The graphical analysis changes considerably for hedge fund managers. Exhibit 2 demonstrates the market versus credit risk exposures for several major styles of hedge funds. Near the zero axis we find market neutral funds — those hedge funds with no market exposure (market neutral) and low leverage. Market neutral funds use limited amounts of leverage because there is no market exposure to leverage or magnify.

Along the credit risk axis, we see that the exposure to credit risk increases for merger arbitrage, convertible arbitrage, and fixed income arbitrage. The use of leverage, or credit risk, is a major factor that distinguishes hedge fund managers from traditional long-only managers.

Exhibit 2: Hedge Funds

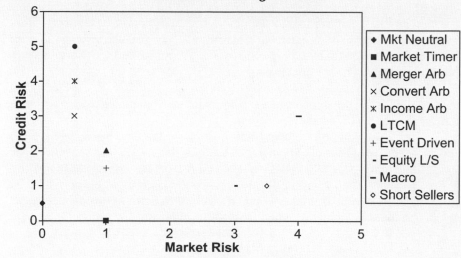

Merger arbitrage, for example, usually applies low leverage, in the range of two to one. Recall that merger arbitrage involves buying the equity securities of the target company and selling the equity securities of the acquiring company. Although the terms of the merger are announced for all to see, the companies may sell at a discount to the announced price to reflect the uncertainty associated with the completion of the merger. Despite the offsetting positions, there may still be some residual market risk because the two merger partners are corporations whose fortunes depend somewhat on the general market conditions.

Other arbitrage hedge funds, such as convertible arbitrage, have a small market exposure but a large credit exposure. This is because arbitrage funds take small market bets but use leverage (sometimes, considerable amounts) to magnify the size of the market bets.

As we discussed in Chapter 2, these types of hedge funds extract their profits from relative value trades. They trade based on relatively small price discrepancies in the market, but use large amounts of leverage to extract the most value from these small discrepancies.

Long Term Capital Management (LTCM) of Greenwich, Connecticut was the best-known example of these relative value/arbitrage players. It has been well documented that LTCM used massive amounts of leverage to extract value from its relatively small market bets.[2] Consequently, we use it to define the upper boundary for credit exposure.

Equity long/short and global macro hedge funds have exposure to both credit risk and market risk. Global macro funds tend to make large bets on the

---

[2] See The President's Working Group on Financial Markets, "Hedge Funds, Leverage, and the Lessons of Long Term Capital Management," (April 28, 1999).

direction of certain currencies, commodities, stock markets, or bond markets. Generally, global macro funds have the ability to invest across the investment spectrum and national borders in the placing of their bets. Consequently, they have a large market exposure. Global macro funds may also use leverage to magnify the size of their bets. George Soros and Julian Robertson were the best known of the macro hedge fund managers.

Long/short equity hedge funds, by their very nature, are exposed to the stock market. Also, this type of hedge fund manager sometimes uses leverage to increase the value of long/short positions.

The main point of Exhibits 1 and 2 is that hedge fund managers have risk profiles that differ considerably from that of traditional long-only investments. In particular, hedge funds often take considerable credit risk in their investment strategies.

Exhibits 1 and 2 form a focal point for the analysis of hedge funds. We will come back to these diagrams several times in the course of this book, expanding them at times to highlight certain parts of the alternative investment industry.

THREE FUNDAMENTAL QUESTIONS

Although the first hedge fund was introduced more than 40 years ago,[3] the hedge fund industry is still relatively new because it has attracted attention only within the past decade. In fact, most of the academic research on hedge funds was conducted during the 1990s. As a result, for most hedge fund managers, a two- to three-year track record is considered long term. In fact, Park, Brown and Goetzmann find that the attrition rate in the hedge fund industry is about 15% per year and that the half-life for hedge funds is about 2.5 years. Liang documents an attrition rate of 8.54% per year for hedge funds. Weisman indicates that relying on a hedge fund manager's past performance history can lead to disappointing investment results.[4] Consequently, performance history, while useful, cannot be relied upon solely in selecting a hedge fund manager.

Beyond performance numbers, there are three fundamental questions that every hedge fund manager should answer during the initial screening process. The answers to these three questions are critical to understanding the nature of the hedge fund manager's investment program. The three questions are:

1. What is the investment objective of the hedge fund?
2. What is the investment process of the hedge fund manager?
3. What makes the hedge fund manager so smart?

[3] Alfred W. Jones introduced the first hedge fund in 1949. See David Purcell and Paul Crowley, "The Reality of Hedge Funds," *The Journal of Investing* (Fall 1999), pp. 26–44.
[4] See James Park, Stephen J. Brown, and William N. Goetzmann, "The Performance Benchmarks and Survivorship Bias of Hedge Funds and Commodity Trading Advisors," *Hedge Fund News* (August 1999); Bing Liang "Hedge Fund Performance: 1990–1999," *Financial Analysts Journal* (January/February 2001), pp. 11–18; and Andrew Weisman, "The Dangers of Historical Hedge Fund Data," working paper (2000).

A hedge fund manager should have a clear and concise statement of its investment objective. Second, the hedge fund manager should identify its investment process. For instance, is it quantitatively or qualitatively based? Last, the hedge fund manager must demonstrate that he or she is smarter than other money managers.

The questions presented in this chapter are threshold issues. These questions are screening tools designed to reduce an initial universe of hedge fund managers down to a select pool of potential investments. They are not, however, a substitute for a thorough due diligence review. We address that subject in the next chapter. Instead, these questions can identify potential hedge fund candidates for which due diligence is appropriate.

Investment Objective

The question of a hedge fund manager's investment objective can be broken down into three questions:

1. In which markets does the hedge fund manager invest?
2. What is the hedge fund manager's general investment strategy?
3. What is the hedge fund manager's benchmark, if any?

Although these questions may seem straightforward, they are often surprisingly difficult to answer. Consider the following language from a hedge fund disclosure document:

> The principal objective of the Fund is capital appreciation, primarily through the purchase and sale of securities, commodities, and other financial instruments including without limitation, stocks, bonds, notes, debentures, and bills issued by corporations, municipalities, sovereign nations or other entities; options, rights, warrants, convertible securities, exchangeable securities, synthetic and/or structured convertible or exchangeable products, participation interests, investment contracts, mortgages, mortgage and asset-backed securities, real estate and interests therein; currencies, other futures, commodity options, forward contracts, money market instruments, bank notes, bank guarantees, letters of credit, other forms of bank obligations; other swaps and other derivative instruments; limited partnership interests and other limited partnership securities or instruments; and contracts relating to the foregoing; in each case whether now existing or created in the future.

Let's analyze the above statement in light of our three investment objective questions.

Question 1: In which markets does the hedge fund manager invest? Answer: In every market known to exist.

By listing every possible financial, commodity, or investment contract currently in existence (or to exist in the future), the hedge fund manager has covered all options, but has left the investor uninformed. Unfortunately, the unlimited nature of the hedge fund manager's potential investment universe does not help to narrow the scope of the manager's investment objective.

Question 2: What is the hedge fund manager's general strategy? Answer: Capital appreciation.

This answer too, is uninformative. Rarely does any investor invest in a hedge fund for capital *depreciation*. Generally, hedge funds are not used as tax shelters. Furthermore, many institutional investors are tax-exempt so that taxes are not a consideration. Capital appreciation is assumed for most investments, including hedge funds. The above language is far too general to be informative.

Question 3: What is the manager's benchmark, if any? Answer: There is no effective benchmark. The manager's investment universe is so widespread as to make any benchmark useless.

Unfortunately, the above disclosure language, while very detailed, discloses very little. It does cover all of the manager's legal bases, but it does not inform the investor.

Where does this manager fall within the hedge fund spectrum in Exhibit 2? The very broad nature of this hedge fund's investment objective places it in the global macro category. Its investment universe is far too broad to be an arbitrage fund. By the same token, its strategy is too expansive to be considered an equity long/short program. Its only appropriate category is global macro.

By contrast, consider the following language from a second hedge fund disclosure document.

> The Fund's investment objective is to make investments in public
> securities that generate a long-term return in excess of that gener-
> ated by the overall U.S. public equity market while reducing the
> market risk of the portfolio through selective short positions.

This one sentence answers all three investment objective questions. First, the manager identifies that it invests in the U.S. public equity market. Second, the manager discloses that it uses a long/short investment strategy. Lastly, the manager states that its objective is to outperform the overall U.S. equity market. Therefore, a suitable benchmark might be the S&P500, the Russell 1000, or a sector index.

From Exhibit 2, this hedge fund is clearly identified as an equity long/short strategy. Its primary purpose is to take on market risk, not credit risk.

In summary, long-winded disclosure statements are not necessary. A well-thought out investment strategy can be summarized in one sentence.

Investment Process

Most investors prefer a well-defined investment process that describes how an investment manager makes its investments. The articulation and documentation of the process can be just as important as the investment results generated by the process. Consider the following language from another hedge fund disclosure document:

> The manager makes extensive use of computer technology in both the formulation and execution of many investment decisions. Buy and sell decisions will, in many cases, be made and executed algorithmically according to quantitative trading strategies embodied in analytical computer software running the manager's computer facilities or on other computers used to support the Fund's trading activities.

This is a "black box." A black box is the algorithmic extension of the hedge fund manager's brain power. Computer algorithms are developed to quantify the manager's skill or investment insight.

For black box managers, the black box itself is the investment process. It is not that the black boxes are bad investments. In fact, the hedge fund research indicates that proprietary quantitative trading strategies can be quite successful.[5] Rather, the issue is whether good performance results justify the lack of a clear investment process.

Black box programs tend to be used in arbitrage or relative value hedge fund programs. From Exhibit 2 we can see that these types of programs fall along the credit risk axis. Hedge fund managers use quantitative computer algorithms to seek out pricing discrepancies between similar securities or investment contracts. They then sell the investment that appears to be "expensive" and buy the investment that appears to be "cheap." The very nature of arbitrage programs is to minimize market risk. Leverage is then applied to extract the most value from their small net exposure to market risk.

A black box is just one example of process versus investment results. The hedge fund industry considers itself to be "skill-based." However, it is very difficult to translate manager skill into a process. This is particularly true when the performance of the hedge fund is dependent upon the skill of a specific individual.

Let's consider another, well publicized skill-based investment process. In the spring of 2000, the hedge funds headed by George Soros stumbled, leading to the departure of Stanley Druckenmiller, the chief investment strategist for Soros

---

[5] See CrossBorder Capital. "Choosing Investment Styles to Reduce Risk," *Hedge Fund Research*, (October 1999); Goldman, Sachs & Co. and Financial Risk Management Ltd., "The Hedge Fund "Industry" and Absolute Return Funds," *The Journal of Alternative Investments* (Spring 1999); and "Hedge Funds Revisited," *Pension and Endowment Forum* (January 2000).

Fund Management. The *Wall Street Journal* documented the concentrated skill-based investment style of this hedge fund group:

> For years, [Soros Fund Management] fostered an entrepreneurial culture, with a cadre of employees battling wits to persuade Mr. Druckenmiller to invest.
>
> "[Mr. Druckenmiller] didn't scream, but he could be very tough. It could be three days or three weeks of battling it out until he's convinced, or you're defeated."[6]

The above statement does not describe an investment process. It is a description of an individual. The hedge fund manager's investment analysis and decision-making is concentrated in one person. This is a pure example of "skill-based" investing. There is no discernible process. Instead, all information is filtered through the brain of one individual. In essence, the institutional investor must trust the judgment of one person.

Mr. Druckenmiller compiled an exceptional track record as the manager of the Soros Quantum Fund. However, the concentration of decision-making authority is not an economic risk, it is a process risk.

Investors should accept economic risk but not process risk. Soros Fund Management is a well-known global macro hedge fund manager. From Exhibit 2 we can see that fundamental risks of an investment in a global macro fund are credit risk and market risk.

Investors are generally unwilling to bear risks that are not fundamental to their tactical and strategic asset allocations. Process risk is not a fundamental risk. It is an idiosyncratic risk of the hedge fund manager's structure and operations.

Generally, process risk is not a risk that investors wish to bear. Nor is it a risk for which they expect to be compensated. Furthermore, how would an investor go about pricing the process risk of a hedge fund manager? It can't be quantified, and it can't be calibrated. Therefore, there is no way to tell whether an institutional investor is being properly compensated for this risk.[7]

Process risk also raises the ancillary issue of lack of transparency. Skill-based investing usually is opaque. Are the decisions of the key individual quantitatively based? Qualitatively based? There is no way to really tell. This is similar to the problems discussed earlier with respect to black boxes.

To summarize, process risk cannot be quantified and it is not a risk that investors are willing to bear. Process risk also raises issues of transparency. Investors want clarity and definition, not opaqueness and amorphousness.

---

[6] *The Wall Street Journal*, "Shake-Up Continues at Soros's Hedge-Fund Empire," May 1, 2000, page C1.

[7] See James Park and Jeremy Staum, "Fund of Funds Diversification: How Much is Enough?" *The Journal of Alternative Investments* (Winter 1998). They demonstrate that idiosyncratic process risks can largely be eliminated through a diversified fund of funds program. They indicate that a portfolio of 15 to 20 hedge funds can eliminate much of the idiosyncratic risk associated with hedge fund investments.

What Makes the Hedge Fund Manager so Smart?

Before investing money with a hedge fund manager, an investor must determine one of the following. The hedge fund manager must be able to demonstrate that he or she is smarter than the next manager. One way to be smarter than another hedge fund manager is to have superior skill in filtering information. That is, the hedge fund manager must be able to look at the same information set as another manager but be able to glean more investment insight from that data set.

Alternatively, if the hedge fund manager is not smarter than the next manager, he must demonstrate that he has a better information set; his competitive advantage is not filtering information, but gathering it. To be successful, a hedge fund manager must demonstrate one or both of these competitive advantages.

Generally speaking, quantitative, computer-driven managers satisfy the first criteria. That is, hedge fund managers that run computer models access the same information set as everyone else, but have better (smarter) algorithms to extract more value per information unit than the next manager. These managers tend to be relative value managers.

Relative value managers extract value by simultaneously comparing the prices of two securities and buying and selling accordingly. This information is available to all investors in the marketplace. However, it is the relative value managers that are able to process the information quickly enough to capture mispricings in the market. These arbitrage strategies fall along the credit risk axis in Exhibit 2.

Alternatively, hedge fund managers that confine themselves to a particular market segment or sector generally satisfy the second criteria. They have a larger information set that allows them to gain a competitive edge in their chosen market. Their advantage is a proprietary information set accumulated over time rather than a proprietary data filtering system.

Consider the following statement from a hedge fund disclosure document:

> The Adviser hopes to achieve consistently high returns by focusing
> on small- and mid-cap companies in the biotechnology market.

The competitive advantage of this type of manager is his or her knowledge not only about a particular economic sector (biotechnology), but also about a particular market segment of that sector (small- and mid-cap). This type of manger tends to take more market risk exposure than credit risk exposure and generally applies equity long/short programs (see Exhibit 2).

Identifying the competitive advantage of the hedge fund manager is the key to determining whether the hedge fund manager can sustain performance results. We indicated in Chapter 3 that the issue of performance persistence is undecided.

Therefore, an investor cannot rely on historical hedge fund performance data as a means of selecting good managers from bad managers. Furthermore, every hedge fund disclosure document contains some variation of the following language:

> Past performance is no indication of future results.

Essentially, this statement directs the investor to ignore the hedge fund manager's performance history.

To asses the likelihood of performance persistence, the investor must then determine whether the hedge fund manager is an information gatherer or an information filterer. Consider the following language from a hedge fund disclosure document.

> The General Partner will utilize its industry expertise, contacts, and databases developed over the past 11 years to identify _____ company investment ideas outside traditional sources and will analyze these investment opportunities using, among other techniques, many aspects of its proven methodology in determining value.

This hedge fund manager has a superior information set that has been developed over 11 years. It is an information gatherer. Consistent with Exhibit 2, this manager applies an equity long/short program within a specific market sector.

Finally, consider the following disclosure language from a merger arbitrage hedge fund manager:

> [The] research group [is] staffed by experienced M&A lawyers with detailed knowledge of deal lifecycle, with extensive experience with corporate law of multiple US states, US and foreign securities laws regarding proxy contests, and antitrust laws (both of the US and EU), and who have made relevant filings before regulators and have closed a wide variety of M&A transactions.

This hedge fund manager is an information filterer. Its expertise is sifting through the outstanding legal and regulatory issues associated with a merger and determining the likelihood that the deal will be completed.

To summarize, a good lesson is that successful hedge fund managers know the exact nature of their competitive advantage, and how to exploit it.

CONCLUSION

The preponderance of the academic evidence indicates that hedge funds are a valuable addition to a diversified portfolio. However, the empirical research does not provide much guidance on how to select a hedge fund manager. In this chapter, we have presented three basic questions that should be answered by each hedge fund manager.

These questions address the tactical issue of selecting a hedge fund manager. In Chapter 3 we presented the strategic framework for constructing a hedge fund investment program. Once the hedge fund strategy is selected, manager selection becomes critical.

Selecting a hedge fund manager is made all the more difficult given the ambivalent evidence regarding the persistence of hedge fund manager performance. In Chapter 3 we indicated that the evidence on performance persistence among hedge fund managers is inconclusive. Therefore, investors cannot rely solely on past performance history in selecting the hedge fund manager.

This makes the tactical questions presented in this chapter all the more important. In particular, an investor must evaluate whether the hedge fund manager can sustain performance. With respect to this issue, the answer lies with determining what makes the hedge fund manager so smart.

Chapter 5

Due Diligence for Hedge Fund Managers

I n our prior chapters we addressed the questions of what (What are hedge funds?), why (Why should hedge funds be included in an investment portfolio?), and how (How should a hedge fund manager be selected?). We now turn to the question of who. Who should be selected as your hedge fund manager will depend on due diligence.

Due diligence starts the initial process of building a relationship with a hedge fund manager. It is an unavoidable task that investors must follow in order to choose a manager. Due diligence is the process of identifying the best and the brightest of the hedge fund managers. This is where the investor must roll up her sleeves and get into the devilish details that can prove to be so elusive with hedge fund managers.

Due diligence consists of seven parts: structure, strategy, performance, risk, administrative, legal, and references. This chapter reviews each part of the due diligence procedure. In the appendix to the chapter, we provide a due diligence checklist.

STRUCTURAL REVIEW

The structural review defines the organization of the hedge fund manager. We start with the basics: How is the fund organized? It is important to remember that the hedge fund manager and the hedge fund are separate legal entities with different legal structures and identities. We then consider the structure of the hedge fund manager, any regulatory registrations, and key personnel.

Fund Organization

The hedge fund manager may invest the hedge fund's assets through an off-shore master trust account or fund. An off-shore master trust account is often used to take into account the various tax domiciles of the hedge fund's investors. Often, a hedge fund manager will set up two hedge funds, one on-shore (U.S.-based) and one off-shore. Master trusts are typically established in tax neutral sites such as Bermuda or the Cayman Islands.

The purpose of the master trust is to invest the assets of the both the on-shore hedge fund and the off-shore hedge fund in a consistent (if not, identical) manner so that both hedge funds share the benefit of the hedge fund manager's insights.

Investors in either fund are not disadvantaged by this structure. Instead, it allows the tax consequences to flow down to the tax code of each investor's domicile country.

Master trusts/funds are often viewed suspiciously as tax evasion vehicles. This is not their purpose. Their purpose is tax neutrality, not evasion. In Bermuda, for example, master trust funds do not pay any corporate income tax. They only pay a corporate licensing fee. Therefore, there are no adverse tax consequences to the hedge fund investors at the master trust level.

Instead, the tax consequences for the investors will depend upon their domicile. Investors in the on-shore U.S.-based hedge fund are subject to the U.S. Internal Revenue Code. Investors in the off-shore fund are subject to the tax code of their respective domicile. Therefore, master trust vehicles are used to accommodate the different tax domiciles of foreign and domestic investors.

Consider a hedge fund manager who has two investors: one based in the United States and one in France. Where should she locate her hedge fund? If she locates the hedge fund in the United States, the U.S. investor will be happy, but the French investor may have to pay double the income taxes: both in the United States and in France. The best way to resolve this problem is to set up two hedge funds, one on-shore and one off-shore. In addition, a master trust account is established in a tax neutral site. The hedge fund manager can then invest the assets of both hedge funds through the master trust account and each investor will be liable only for the taxes imposed by the revenue code of their respective countries.[1] Exhibit 1 demonstrates the master trust structure.

Exhibit 1: Master Trust Account

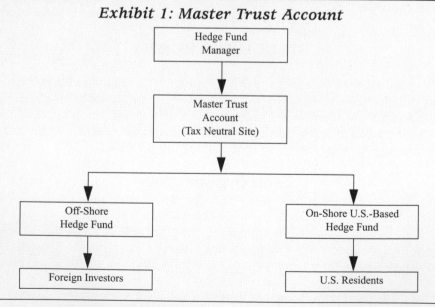

[1] In reality, the United States and France have a tax treaty so the threat of double taxation is minimal. However there are many countries that do not have tax treaties, and the potential for double taxation is a reality.

Hedge fund structures do not have to be as complicated as that presented in Exhibit 1. The majority of hedge fund managers in the United States operate only within the United States, have only an on-shore hedge fund, and accept only U.S. investors. Nonetheless, the popularity of hedge fund investing has resulted in operating structures that are sometimes as creative as the hedge fund strategies themselves.

Hedge Fund Manager Organization

First, the basics: Where is the hedge fund manager located, are there any satellite offices, and where is the nearest office to the investor? These questions can be very important if the hedge fund manager operates overseas and there are significant time differences between the manager's business hours and that of the investor.

Second, an organization chart is mandatory. Who is the Chief Executive Officer, the Chief Investment Officer, and Chief Operating Officer? A warning: It is not a good business plan if they are all the same person. Hedge fund managers should do what they do best: invest money and leave the operating details to someone else.

Of special importance is the Chief Financial Officer. The CFO will be the investor's most important link with the hedge fund manager after an investment is made because the CFO will be responsible for reporting the hedge fund manager's performance numbers. Consequently, the investor should make certain that the CFO has strong background in accounting, preferably a Certified Public Accountant, a Chartered Accountant, or another professional accounting designation. Last, the investor must determine who are the senior managers in charge of trading, information systems, marketing, and research and development.

The educational and professional background of all principals should be documented. It should be determined whether they have graduate degrees, whether there are any Chartered Financial Analysts, and what was their prior investment experience before starting a hedge fund.

Another warning: Many equity long/short hedge fund managers were former long-only managers. Yet, shorting stocks is very different than going long stocks. The ability to locate and borrow stock, limit losses in a bull market, and short on the uptick rule are special talents that cannot be developed overnight.

Before investing money with a long/short hedge fund manager, an investor should find out where the hedge fund manager learned to short stocks. If it is a hedge fund manager that previously managed a long-only portfolio, chances are that she might not have much experience with respect to shorting stocks, and therefore, will be learning to short stocks with your money.

Ownership

Ownership of the hedge fund manager must be documented. It is important to know who owns the company that advises the hedge fund. This is important for "key person" provisions of the contractual documentation.

Additionally, ownership is important for ensuring that there is a proper alignment of interests with the hedge fund manager's employees as well as retention of employment. By sharing the ownership of the hedge fund management company with key employees, the hedge fund manager can ensure proper alignment of interests as well as retention of key personnel.

Registrations

The investor should document the regulatory registrations of the hedge fund manager. The hedge fund manager might be registered with the Securities and Exchange Commission as an Investment Adviser under the Investment Adviser's Act of 1940. If so, the hedge fund manager must file annually Form ADV with the SEC that contains important financial and structural information regarding the hedge fund manager.

Alternatively, the hedge fund manager might be registered with the National Futures Association (NFA) and the Commodity Futures Trading Commission (CFTC) as either a Commodity Trading Advisor (CTA) or a Commodity Pool Operator (CPO). The NFA is the self-regulatory organization for the managed futures industry. It is approved by the CFTC to handle all registrations for CTAs and CPOs. Also, the hedge fund manager might be registered with the NFA as an introducing broker or futures commission merchant. If the hedge fund manager is registered as either a CTA, CPO, introducing broker, or futures commission merchant, it must obey the rules and regulations of the NFA and the CFTC.

If the hedge fund manager is registered with either the SEC or the CFTC, the investor should ascertain the date of the original registration and whether there are any civil, criminal, or administrative actions outstanding against the hedge fund manager. This information must be filed with either the NFA (for the managed futures industry) or the SEC (for investment advisers).

Outside Service Providers

The investor must document who is the hedge fund manager's outside auditors, prime broker, and legal counsel. Each of these service providers must be contacted.

First, the investor should receive the hedge fund manager's last annual audited financial statement as well as the most current statement. Any questions regarding the financial statements should be directed to the CFO and the outside auditors. Any opinion from the auditors other than an unqualified opinion must be explained by the outside auditors. Additionally, outside auditors are a good source of information regarding the hedge fund manager's accounting system and operations.

The hedge fund manager's prime broker is responsible for executing the hedge fund manager's trades, lending securities to short, and providing short-term financing for leverage. It is essential that the investor contact the prime broker because the prime broker is in the best position to observe the hedge fund manager's trading positions.

There was an incident on President's Day in 1997 where a prime broker contacted one of its hedge fund manager clients and demanded a margin call. In a margin call the prime broker demands that the hedge fund manager post more cash or collateral to cover either her short positions or her borrowing from the manager.

Margin calls can happen for several reasons. First and foremost, a short position can move against a hedge fund manager creating a large negative balance with the hedge fund manager's prime broker. To protect itself from the credit exposure to the hedge fund manager, the prime broker will make a margin call, in effect, demanding that the hedge fund manager either put up cash or more securities as collateral to cover the prime broker's credit exposure to the hedge fund manager.

On this particular President's Day, a prime broker made a margin call on a hedge fund manager that invested in the mortgage-backed securities market. The essence of the margin call is that the prime broker was skeptical of the market value of positions that the hedge fund manager claimed. The prime broker demanded that the hedge fund manager either confirm the market value of her positions by soliciting bids in the mortgage-backed securities market to buy some of the hedge fund manager's portfolio, or post more collateral.

Unfortunately, President's Day is a national holiday when banks and insurance companies, two key investors in the mortgage-backed securities market, are closed. As a result the market for mortgage-backed securities was very thin that day and the hedge fund manager had no choice but to be a price taker. Additionally, the hedge fund manager's marking to market values proved to be optimistic. The resulting fire sale had a significant impact on the hedge fund manager's performance.

This unfortunate example demonstrates the important relationship between the prime broker community and the hedge fund community. Every hedge fund manager has at least one prime broker, and these prime brokers monitor the hedge fund manager's portfolio.

Finally, the investor should speak with the hedge fund manager's outside counsel. This is important for two reasons. First, outside counsel is typically responsible for keeping current all regulatory registrations of the hedge fund manager. Second, outside counsel can inform the investor of any criminal, civil, or administrative actions that might be pending against the hedge fund manager. Outside counsel is also responsible for preparing the hedge fund manager's offering document. This is with whom the investor will negotiate should an investment be made with the hedge fund manager.

STRATEGIC REVIEW

The second phase of due diligence is a review of the hedge fund manager's investment strategy. This should include a clear statement of the hedge fund manager's style, the markets in which she invests, what competitive advantage the hedge fund manager brings to the table, the source of her investment ideas, and what benchmark, if any, is appropriate for the hedge fund.

Investment Style

In Chapter 2, we listed several styles of hedge fund managers. While these are the major hedge fund styles, they are by no means exhaustive. The creativity of hedge fund managers is such that there are as many styles as there are colors of the rainbow.

For instance, relative value arbitrage is a hedge fund style frequently seen. Recall that relative value arbitrage compares two similar securities and buys the security that is "cheap" relative to the other security while selling the security that is relatively "rich." Relative value arbitrage can be subdivided into economic arbitrage and statistical arbitrage. Economic arbitrage compares the pricing fundamentals of two similar securities to determine if the prices set by the market are inconsistent with the fundamentals. If an inconsistency is identified, the "cheap" security is purchased and the "rich" security is sold. The hedge fund manager will hold on to these positions until the market corrects itself and the two security prices are in proper balance. This holding period may be a day, week, or several months. In some cases, it may be necessary to hold the two securities to maturity (in the case of bonds).

Conversely, "stat arb" is another form of relative value arbitrage where the trading is based not on economic fundamentals, but rather, on statistical anomalies that temporarily occur in the market. Typically, these anomalies occur only for a moment or for a day at most. Consequently, statistical arbitrage is a very short-term relative value trading program with positions entered and exited within the same trading day.

Additionally, economic relative value or statistical arbitrage can occur in the fixed income, equity, or convertible bond markets. Exhibit 2 diagrams how an investment strategy should be documented.

Investment Markets

Next, the investor should document in which markets the hedge fund manager invests. Recall that this was one of our basic questions presented in Chapter 4. For an equity long/short manager, the answer is obvious. Recall the following language from Chapter 4:

> The Fund's investment objective is to make investments in public securities that generate a long-term return in excess of that generated by the overall U.S. public equity market while reducing the market risk of the portfolio through selective short positions.

From this statement, it is clear that this manager is an equity long/short manager investing in the U.S. equity market.

For other hedge fund managers, however, the answer is not so obvious. For instance, global macro managers typically have the broadest investment mandate possible. They can invest across the world equity, bond, commodity, and currency markets. Pinning down a global macro manager may be akin to picking up mercury. Nonetheless, the investor should document as best she can in what markets the hedge fund manager invests. If the hedge fund manager is a global macro manager, the investor may have to accept that the manager can and will invest in whatever market it deems fit.

The investor should also determine the extent to which the hedge fund manager invests in derivative securities. Derivatives are a two-edged sword. On the one hand, they can hedge an investment portfolio and reduce risk. On the other hand, they can increase the leverage of the hedge fund and magnify the risks taken by the hedge fund manager.

Investment Securities

Closely related to the investment markets are the types of securities in which the hedge fund manager invests. For some strategies, it will be straightforward. For instance, the sample language provided above indicates that the hedge fund manager will invest in the stock of U.S. companies.

However, other strategies will not be so clear. Recall the language in Chapter 4 where one hedge fund manager listed every security, futures contract, option, and derivative contract "in each case whether now existing or created in the future." This manager needs to be pinned down, and the due diligence checklist is the place to do it.

Exhibit 2: Documenting a Hedge Fund Investment Strategy

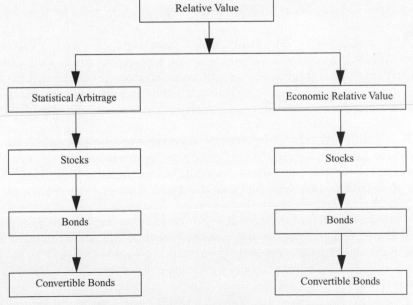

Oftentimes, hedge fund disclosure documents are drafted in very broad and expansive terms. The reason is that the hedge fund manager does not want to be legally bound into an investment corner. The purpose of due diligence is not to legally bind the hedge fund manager but to document the types of securities necessary to effect her investment strategy.

It is very important that the investor determine the hedge fund manager's strategy for using derivatives, the type of derivatives used, and in which markets will derivatives be purchased. Of particular concern is the extent to which hedge fund manager may "short volatility."

Shorting volatility is a strategy where hedge fund managers sell out of the money call or put options against their investment portfolio. If the options expire unexercised, the hedge fund manager receives the option premiums and this increases the return for the hedge fund. However, if the options are exercised against the hedge fund manager, significant negative results may occur. In Chapter 7 on risk management, we demonstrate the dangers of shorting volatility.

Benchmark

Establishing a benchmark for hedge fund managers is one of the thorniest issues facing the industry. We will have quite a bit to say about this in Chapter 9. For now, suffice it to say that hedge fund managers eschew benchmarks.

One reason is the skill-based nature of their investment styles. Manager skill cannot be captured by a passive securities benchmark. Skill, in fact, is orthogonal to passive investing.

Second, most hedge fund managers apply investment strategies that cannot be captured by a passive securities index. For instance, it can be argued that a long-only passive equity index is not an appropriate benchmark for an equity long/short hedge fund. Additionally, hedge fund managers also use derivative instruments, such as options, that have non-linear payout functions. Passive securities indices do not reflect non-linear payout strategies.

Last, hedge fund managers tend to maintain concentrated portfolios. The nature of this concentration makes the investment strategy of the hedge fund manager distinct from a broad-based securities index.

Nonetheless, some performance measure must be established for the hedge fund manager. For instance, if the hedge fund manager runs a long/short equity fund concentrating on the semi-conductor sector of the technology industry, a good benchmark would be the SOX/semi-conductor index maintained by the Philadelphia Stock Exchange.

If the hedge fund manager does not believe that any index is appropriate for his strategy, then a *hurdle rate* must be established. Hurdle rates are most appropriate for absolute return hedge fund managers whose rate of return is not dependent upon the general economic prospects of a sector or a broad-based market index.

Competitive Advantage

Recall our question from Chapter 4: What makes the hedge fund manager so smart? We made the point that the best hedge fund managers know the exact nature of their competitive advantage, and how to exploit it. This advantage must be documented as part of the due diligence process.

Another way to ask this question is: What makes the hedge fund manager different from the other managers? For instance, there are many merger arbitrage managers. However, some invest only in announced deals while some speculate on potential deals. Some merger arbitrage funds invest in cross-border deals while others stay strictly within the boundaries of their domicile. Some participate in deals only of a certain market capitalization range while others are across the board. And finally, some merger arbitrage funds use options and convertible securities to capture the merger premium while others invest only in the underlying equity.

As another competitive advantage, some merger arbitrage experts develop large in-house legal staffs to review the regulatory (anti-trust) implications of the announced deals. These managers rely on their expert legal analysis to determine whether the existing merger premium is rich or cheap. They exploit the legal issues associated with the merger instead of the economic issues.

Current Portfolio Position

This part of the due diligence is meant to provide a current snapshot of the hedge fund. First, the investor should ascertain the fund's current long versus short exposure. Additionally, the investor should determine the amount of cash that the hedge fund manager is keeping and why. Too much cash indicates an investment strategy that may be stuck in neutral.

The investor should also ascertain how many investments the hedge fund manager currently maintains in the fund. As we have previously discussed, hedge fund managers typically run concentrated exposure. Therefore, the investor is exposed to more stock specific risk than market risk. Again, this is the essence of hedge fund management: Hedge fund managers do not take market risk, they take security specific risk. This stock or security specific risk is the source of the hedge fund manager's returns.

Last, the investor should ask the hedge fund manager how she has positioned the hedge fund portfolio in light of current market conditions. This should provide insight not only as to how the hedge fund manager views the current financial markets, but also her investment strategy going forward.

Source of Investment Ideas

What is the source of the hedge fund manager's investment ideas? Does she wait until "it just hits her?" Conversely, is there a rigorous process for sourcing investment ideas? Idea generation is what hedge fund investing is all about. This is the source of the manager's skill.

The source of investment ideas is closely tied in with the nature of competitive advantage. The hedge fund manager's competitive advantage could be her research department that generates investment ideas better or faster than other hedge fund managers. Conversely, some hedge fund managers, such as merger arbitrage managers, wait for deals to be announced in the market.

In addition, the investor should determine in which type of market the hedge fund manager's ideas work best. Do they work best in bear markets, bull markets, flat markets, or none at all? For instance, an absolute return hedge fund manager (a manager with a hurdle rate for a benchmark) should be agnostic with respect to the direction of the market. Otherwise, an argument could be made that the hedge fund manager's performance should be compared to a market index.

Capacity

A frequent issue with hedge fund managers is the capacity of their investment strategy. Hedge fund manager's have investment strategies that are more narrowly focused than traditional long-only managers. As a consequence, their investment strategies frequently have limited capacity. This is more the case for hedge fund managers that target small sectors of the economy or segments of the financial markets.

For instance, the convertible bond market is much smaller than the U.S. equity market. Consequently, a convertible bond hedge fund manager may have more limited capacity than an equity long/short manager. Global macro hedge fund managers, with their global investment mandate, have the largest capacity. This large capacity is derived from their unlimited ability to invest across financial instruments, currencies, borders, and commodities.

Capacity is an important issue for the investor because the hedge fund manager might dilute her skill by allowing a greater number of investors into the hedge fund than is optimal from an investment standpoint. This may result in too much money chasing too few deals.

PERFORMANCE REVIEW

List of Funds and Assets Under Management

First, the investor should document how many hedge funds the hedge fund manager advises and the assets under management for each fund. The investor should know the size of the hedge fund manager's empire. This is important not only for the collection of performance data, but also it may give the investor some sense of the hedge fund manager's investment capacity.

There are three important questions to ask. How long has the hedge fund manager been actively managing a hedge fund? Have her performance results been consistent over time? Are the investment strategies the same or different for each hedge fund?

In Chapter 4, we noted that the attrition rate in the hedge fund is very high, up to 15% a year according to one study. Successful hedge fund managers have a long-term track record with consistent results. However, "long-term" in the hedge fund industry is a relative term. For hedge funds, five years is generally sufficient to qualify as long-term.

Additionally, if a hedge fund manager manages more than one hedge fund, the investment strategy and style should be documented for both. If the hedge funds follow the same style, then the issue of trade allocation must be resolved. The investor should determine how the hedge fund manager decides which trades go into which hedge fund.

Drawdowns

Drawdowns are a common phenomenon in the hedge fund industry. Simply defined, a drawdown is a decline in the net asset value of the hedge fund. Drawdowns are not unique to the hedge fund industry; they also occur in the mutual fund industry. However, in the long-only world of mutual funds, drawdowns are often motivated by declines in market indices. This reflects the market risk associated with mutual funds.

The difference with hedge funds is that they eschew market risk in favor of stock specific risk. The amount of stock specific risk in the hedge fund is reflective of the hedge fund manager's skill level of finding overpriced and underpriced securities regardless of the condition of the general financial markets. Therefore, drawdowns in the hedge fund world indicate a lapse of hedge fund manager skill.

Hedge fund managers often claim that their industry is skill-based. This claim is a two-edged sword. On the one hand, it protects hedge fund managers from being compared to a passive long-only index as a benchmark. On the other hand, it also means that when the hedge fund declines in value, the blame rests solely with the hedge fund manager and not with the condition of the financial markets.

Therefore, it is important to measure how much a lapse of hedge fund manager skill cost the fund, and how long it took for the hedge fund manager to regain her skill and recoup the losses. Last, the hedge fund manager should explain her temporary loss of skill.

Statistical Data

This section covers the basic summary information that is expected of all active managers: the average return over the life of the fund as well as the standard deviation (volatility) or returns and the Sharpe ratio.

As an aside, Sharpe ratios can be misleading statistics when measuring hedge fund performance because of the non-linear strategies that hedge fund managers can pursue. We provide an example of this danger in Chapter 7 on risk management.

Additionally, if a benchmark can be identified for the hedge fund, then the systematic risk of the hedge fund with that benchmark should be measured. This statistic is known as the beta of the hedge fund and it measures the extent by which the hedge fund returns move in tandem with the benchmark.

Also, if a benchmark is identified, then an Information Ratio (IR) statistic can be calculated. This is the excess return of the hedge fund (the returns to the hedge fund minus the returns to the benchmark) divided by the standard deviation of the excess returns. The IR measures the amount of active return that is earned for each unit of active risk exposure. As a rule of thumb, successful long-only managers generally earn an IR between 0.25 to 0.50. With respect to hedge funds, an investor should expect to receive an IR between 1 and 1.5.

Withdrawals

Withdrawals can be detrimental to fund performance. If a hedge fund manager is fully invested at the time of a redemption request, fund performance will suffer. First, the hedge fund manager must sell securities to fund the withdrawal. This means transaction costs that would not otherwise be incurred will be charged to the fund and will be borne by all investors. Additionally, to the extent that a hedge fund manager cannot liquidate a portion of her investment strategy on a pro rata basis to fund the withdrawal, there may be a loss to the hedge fund from foregone investment opportunities.

Finally, the less liquid the securities in which the hedge fund manager invests, the greater will be these costs. Equity long/short hedge funds usually have the lowest cost associated with a withdrawal because the equity markets are typically the most liquid markets in which to transact. However, more arcane investment strategies and securities such as mortgage-backed arbitrage can have significant costs associated with a withdrawal.

Recall the incident discussed above with respect to a prime broker executing a margin call on President's Day to a mortgage-backed hedge fund manager. The timing of the margin call had severe implications for fund performance. A withdrawal request is similar to a margin call in that a hedge fund investor demands that the hedge fund manager liquidate some of her positions to fund the redemption request. The results, if unexpected, can have a negative impact of fund performance.

RISK REVIEW

Risk Management

Three important questions must be answered: What risks are managed? How is risk measured? How is risk managed?

First, it is important to determine what risks the hedge fund manager monitors. Does she have limits on the percentage of the portfolio that may be invested in any one company or security? Additionally, does the manager monitor her gross long exposure, gross short exposure, and net market exposure? To what extent can the manager be long and to what extent can she be short the market?

Risk can be measured through measures of standard deviation, semi-variance, Sortino measures, by value-at-risk, and by style analysis. The investor must document what type of risk measurement system the hedge fund manager applies.

Last, the investor must determine how the hedge fund manager manages the risk of her positions. As indicated above, one way to control risk is by setting limits on the size of any investment position. This is particularly important because of the concentrated nature of most hedge fund portfolios.

Another way to manage risk is to set an upper boundary on the standard deviation of the hedge fund's returns. Alternatively, the hedge fund manager could set a limit on the amount of *active risk* (the standard deviation of excess returns) in the hedge fund.

Two additional risks that must be discussed are *short volatility risk* and *counterparty risk*. As already mentioned, hedge fund managers can sell options as part of their investment strategy. When a hedge fund manager sells an option, she collects the option premium at the time of the sale. If the option expires unexercised, the hedge fund manager keeps the option premium and the hedge fund's returns will be increased by the amount of the option premium. However, if the option is exercised against the manager, this may have a negative impact on the hedge fund performance.

Additionally, hedge fund managers frequently trade in over-the-counter derivative instruments. These are essentially private contracts between two parties: the hedge fund manager and her counterparty. The counterparty to such trades is often a large Wall Street investment house or large money center bank. Nonetheless, when a hedge fund manager negotiates these custom derivative contracts with a counterparty, the hedge fund manager takes on the credit risk that her counterparty will fulfill its obligations under the derivative contract.

Exchange-traded derivative contracts such as listed futures and options contracts do not have this counterparty risk because the clearinghouse for the exchange will make good on any defaulted contract. However, in the over-the-counter world of derivatives, the hedge fund manager must rely on its counterparty's good faith and credit to perform its obligations under the derivative contract.

In sum, the investor must determine how the hedge fund manager looks at risk, what are the most important risk exposures in the portfolio, and how the hedge fund manager reacts to excess risk.

Leverage

Some hedge fund managers specifically limit the leverage they will employ. This limit is typically set in the limited partnership agreement so that the hedge fund manager is legally bound to stay within a leverage limit. Nonetheless, within the leverage limit, the hedge fund manager has considerable flexibility.

Also, many hedge fund managers never set a limit on the amount of leverage that they may apply.

If leverage is applied, the investor should document the highest amount of leverage used by the hedge fund manager as well as the average leverage of the fund since inception. As we indicated in Chapter 2, one of the reasons for the demise of Long Term Capital Management was the massive amount of leverage employed in its strategy. While leverage can be a successful tool if employed correctly, it will have a significantly detrimental impact on hedge fund performance during periods of minimal liquidity.

Risk Officer

Last, and most important, who monitors risk? The chief investment officer and the chief risk officer should not be the same person. If so, there is a conflict in risk control because risk management should function separately from investment management. Without this independence, there can be no assurance that risk will be properly identified and managed.

Often the chief financial officer serves as the risk officer. This is a good solution as long as the CFO is not also the chief investment officer (rarely is this the case). In the smaller hedge fund shops, this is the usual procedure. However, larger hedge funds have established a chief risk officer who monitors the hedge fund manager's positions across all hedge funds and separate accounts.

If the amount of leverage is not contractually specified in the limited partnership agreement, then the risk manager must set the limit. Even if there is a limit on leverage, the risk manager must monitor the leverage in each hedge fund to ensure that it is consistent with that fund's investment strategy. Finally, the risk manager should establish the position limits for any one investment within a hedge fund portfolio.

ADMINISTRATIVE REVIEW

Civil, Criminal, and Regulatory Actions

The hedge fund manager should fully disclose all civil, criminal, and regulatory actions against the hedge fund manager or any of its principals over the past five years. Normally a three-year history is asked for, but five years is also common.

The hedge fund manager may balk at listing civil or criminal actions previously or currently pending against its principals. However, in addition to the expected red flags that legal actions raise, this is necessary information for two more reasons.

First, a history of civil or criminal actions filed against one of the hedge fund manager's principals is a valuable insight into that principal's character. Given the litigious nature of current society, it would not be unusual for a principal to be involved in a civil lawsuit outside the operating business of the hedge fund. However, a pattern of such lawsuits might indicate trouble.

Second, lawsuits are distracting. They take a toll in terms of time, money, and emotions. Such a distraction could impede a principal's performance with respect to the hedge fund.

Employee Turnover

Given the skill-based nature (or claim, thereof) of the hedge fund industry, a hedge fund manager's personnel is its most valuable resource. This is where the skill resides.

A complete list of hired and departing employees is important for three reasons. First, as previously discussed, a good hedge fund manager knows her competitive advantage and how to exploit it. One type of competitive advantage is the people employed by the hedge fund manager. Preserving this workforce may be one of the keys to maintaining her advantage.

Second, similar to lawsuits, turnover is distracting. It takes time, money, and sometimes emotions to recruit new talent. Additionally, new employees take time to come up the learning curve and comprehend all of the nuances of a hedge fund manager's investment strategy.

Last, high employee turnover may be indicative of a volatile Chief Executive Officer. If the employees do not have faith enough in the CEO to remain with the hedge fund manager, why should the investor?

Account Representative

This is very simple. A primary contact person should be designated. This representative will handle issues regarding performance, withdrawals, increased investment, distributions, and meetings. Ideally it should be someone other than the Chief Executive Officer, whose job it is to keep the hedge fund manager on course rather than take client phone calls.

Disaster Planning

Disaster planning was particularly important with the Y2K concerns. However, its import has not been diminished with the passing of the new millennium. Hedge fund managers employ sophisticated trading models that require considerable computing power. This is especially true for those hedge fund managers that employ quantitative arbitrage models.

The hedge fund manager should have a recovery plan if a natural or other disaster shuts down its trading and investment operations. This plan could be leasing space at a disaster recovery site owned by a computer service provider, a back-up trading desk at another remote location, or the sharing of facilities with other trading desks.

Consider the simple case of a power "brown-out." How would the hedge fund manager monitor its investment positions? How would it monitor its risks? How would it trade without the use of its analytical computer programs? The hedge fund manager must have a back-up plan to address these questions.

LEGAL REVIEW

Type of Investment

Most hedge fund investments are structured as limited partnerships. Limited partnership units are purchased by the investor where the number of units that the investor owns entitles her to a pro rata share of the returns earned by the hedge fund.

Some hedge fund managers offer separate accounts for their investors. These are individual investment accounts that are dedicated solely to one investor. There are pros and cons of both types of investments.

In a limited partnership structure, the hedge fund manager acts as the general partner, and invests a portion of her own capital in the hedge fund side by side with that of the limited partners. This ensures an alignment of interests between the hedge fund manager and her investors.

Also, a limited partnership provides a "financial firewall" for the investor. Limited partnership laws protect the limited partners so that they are at risk only to the extent of their capital committed. Therefore, the limited partner's maximum downside is known with certainty. Any excess risk is borne by the hedge fund manager as the general partner.

Separate accounts do not have the advantages of alignment of interests or financial firewalls. There is more risk associated with this type of investment. However, there are two advantages of a separate account.

First, the investor need only worry about her own motivations. In our section on Performance Review, we discussed how withdrawals of capital from a hedge fund can be detrimental to the fund's performance. Therefore, the withdrawal of capital by one limited partner could disadvantage the remaining investors in the hedge fund. With a separate account, this issue does not exist because there is only one investor per account.

Second, separate accounts facilitate reporting and risk management. In a limited partnership, the investor receives her pro rata share of the fund's return and owns a pro rata share of each individual investment. Reporting these pro rata shares, or aggregating them for risk management purposes, can be cumbersome. However, with a separate account, all gains, losses, and investments are owned 100% by the investor. This simplifies any reporting or risk management requirements.

Fees

The standard in the hedge fund industry is "1 and 20." This means a 1% management fee and a 20% profit sharing or incentive fee. However, this structure is by no means uniform. Some of the larger hedge funds charge up to a 3% management fee and a 30% incentive fee, while some newer hedge funds may charge less than the standard "1 and 20."

In addition to the fee structure, the investor should determine how frequently fees are collected. Typically, management fees are collected on a quarterly basis, but they may also be structured semi-annually or annually. Incentive fees are usually collected on an annual basis.

The investor should also determine if there is a "high watermark" or a "clawback" with respect to the incentive fees. A high watermark means that a hedge fund manager cannot collect any incentive fee until she exceeds the highest previous net asset value.

This is particularly important because of the nature of drawdowns. If a hedge fund manager suffers a drawdown, she should not collect any incentive fees while she recoups this lost value. Incentive fees should begin only after the manager has regained the lost fund value and produced new value for her investors. Most hedge funds have high watermarks.

Clawbacks are rare in the hedge fund world. They are much more common in the private equity marketplace. As its name implies, a clawback provision allows the investors in the fund to "claw back" incentive fees previously received by the hedge fund manager. Clawback arrangements generally apply if, over the life of the fund, the hedge fund manager has failed to produce an agreed upon hurdle rate.

Lock-Ups and Redemptions

While lock-up periods are the standard in the private equity world, they are much less common in hedge funds. However, more and more hedge funds are requiring lock-up periods for their investors. A lock-up period is just that: The investor's capital is "locked-up" for a designated period. During this time, the investor cannot redeem any part of her investment.

Lock-up periods provide two benefits. First, they give the hedge fund manager time to implement her investment strategy. Imagine how difficult it might be to implement a sophisticated investment strategy while at the same time worrying about how to fund redemption requests.

Second, we have already pointed out that ill-timed withdrawals of capital by one limited partner in a hedge fund can disadvantage the remaining investors. During the lock-up period, this is not an issue. Nervous investors have no choice but to have their capital committed for a specified period of time. Confident investors can be assured that their investment will not be undermined by a fickle limited partner.

Withdrawals and redemptions are specified in the limited partnership agreement. Some hedge funds provide monthly liquidity, but the norm is quarterly or semi-annual redemption rights. Also, limited partners typically must give notice to the hedge fund manager that they intend to redeem. This notice period can be from 30 to 90 days in advance of the redemption. The purpose of the notice is to give the hedge fund manager the ability to position the hedge fund's portfolio to finance the redemption request.

Subscription Amount

All hedge funds have a minimum subscription amount. Generally, this amount is quite high for two reasons. First, the hedge fund manager needs sufficient investment capital to implement his investment strategy. Second, higher capital commitments ensure that only sophisticated investors with a large net worth will subscribe in the hedge fund. Hedge fund investing is not for the average investor. Rather, they are designed for sophisticated investors who can appreciate and accept the risks associated with hedge funds.

Some hedge funds may also have a maximum subscription amount. This is done so that no single investor becomes too large relative to other investors in the fund. Also, the hedge fund manager may have capacity issues that require limits on an investor's capital contribution.

Advisory Committee

Advisory committees serve as a source of objective input for the hedge fund manager. They are comprised of representatives from the hedge fund manager and investors in the hedge fund.

Advisory committees may provide advice on the valuation of certain investments, particularly illiquid investments. The committee may advise the hedge fund manager when it is time to mark down or mark up an illiquid security where objective market prices are not available.

The advisory committee may also advise the hedge fund manager as to whether she should open up the hedge fund for new investors, and how much more capacity the hedge fund manager should take. Before, allowing new investors into the fund, the hedge fund manager may wish to seek the counsel of the advisory committee to see if the existing investors have concerns about capacity or the types of additional investors that may be allowed to invest.

While advisory committees are a useful device for control by the hedge fund limited partners, they are more common in the private equity world than with hedge funds. We will discuss this point further in Chapter 18 where crossover funds are covered.

REFERENCE CHECKS

Service Providers

We indicated previously, in the Structural Review section, the importance of speaking with a hedge fund manager's primary service providers. For instance, with respect to the outside auditors, the investor should ask when the last audit was conducted and whether the auditors issued an unqualified opinion. Additionally, the investor should inquire about any issues that outside auditors have raised with the hedge fund manager over the course of their engagement.

With respect to the prime broker, the investor should inquire how frequently margin calls have been made, the size of the calls, and whether any calls have not been met. Remember that the prime broker is in the best position to evaluate the market value of the hedge fund manager's investments. A discussion with the prime broker should give the investor a reality check whether or not the hedge fund manager is recognizing the proper value of the hedge fund's portfolio.

Legal counsel is important to check on the veracity of any civil, criminal, or regulatory actions against the hedge fund manager or its principals. This conversation should confirm those actions listed by the hedge fund manager under the Administrative Review. Last, the legal counsel can confirm the status of any regulatory registrations under which the hedge fund manager operates.

Existing Clients

Talking to existing clients is a necessary step to check the veracity of the hedge fund manager's statements and to measure his "client responsiveness."

Typical questions to ask are: Have the financial reports been timely? Have the reports been easy to understand? Has the hedge fund manager responded positively to questions about financial performance? Has the hedge fund manager done what she said she would do (maintain her investment strategy)? What concerns does the current investor have regarding the hedge fund manager of the hedge fund's performance? Would the existing client invest more money with the hedge fund manager?

In sum, this is a chance for a prospective investor to ask current investors for their candid opinion of the hedge fund manager. If the prospective investor has any doubts regarding the hedge fund manager, these doubts should be either confirmed or dispelled.

CONCLUSION

Is this chapter we addressed the question of who. We provided a comprehensive discussion on due diligence with respect to selecting a hedge fund manager. This process is not a simple exercise. A thorough investor should expect to spend 50 to 75 hours of their time reviewing a hedge fund manager.[2]

In the Appendix, we provide an easy to follow due diligence checklist. In developing this checklist, we attempted to err on the side of being overly inclusive. An investor may choose to use all of this checklist, expand it, or edit it to suit his or her purposes. We believe, however, that the attached checklist is a good starting point for the best practices with respect to hedge fund due diligence.

---

[2] We know of at least one hedge fund of funds manager that spends between 75 and 100 hours of due diligence with each hedge fund manager.

APPENDIX TO CHAPTER 5

DUE DILIGENCE EXECUTIVE SUMMARY

Name of Hedge Fund _____

Hedge Fund Manager_____

Address_____

Phone Number_____

Facsimile Number_____

Chief Executive Officer_____

Key Contact Person_____

Hedge Fund Style_____

Assets under Management_____

Years of Operation_____

DUE DILIGENCE CHECKLIST

1. STRUCTURAL REVIEW

Type of Investment

    Hedge Fund (name)_____

    Separate Account_____

    Other (specify)_____

    On-Shore Account or Fund?   ____Yes ____No

    Master Trust Account?   ____Yes ____No

Hedge Fund Manager

    Main Business Office_____

                   _____

    Nearest Satellite Office_____

    Telephone Number_____

    Facsimile Number_____

    Type of Legal Entity_____

    Ownership Structure_____

                   _____

Key Personnel

    Chief Executive Officer_____

    Chief Operating Officer_____

    Chief Investment Officer_____

    Chief Financial Officer_____

    Head of Trading_____

Attach biographies of key principals: include education, work experience, and professional degrees (this may be taken from the offering memorandum).

Regulatory Registrations (please check)

Commodity Pool Operator_____

Commodity Trading Advisor_____

Investment Adviser_____

Investment Company_____

Broker-Dealer_____

Futures Commission Merchant_____

Introducing Broker_____

Other_____

If any of the above were checked, please indicate the regulatory authority with whom the hedge fund manager is registered, and the date of the registration.

Outside Service Providers

Independent Auditor_____

Legal Counsel_____

Prime Broker_____

II. STRATEGIC REVIEW

Hedge Fund Style (e.g., Market Neutral, Global Macro, etc.)

_____

Description of investment strategy

_____
_____
_____

Description of instruments used to implement strategy

_____
_____
_____

What is your benchmark or hurdle rate?

_____

What is your competitive advantage?/What makes your strategy different from other hedge fund managers?

_____
_____
_____

How many investments are in your current portfolio?

_____
_____
_____

What is your current long/short/cash position?

_____
_____

What is your current strategy given the current market conditions?

_____

_____

_____

What is the source of your investment ideas?

_____

_____

_____

In which markets do your strategies perform best?

_____

_____

_____

What is the maximum capacity of your strategy?

_____

_____

_____

III. PERFORMANCE DATA

List all funds managed, assets under management for each fund, and date of performance inception.

_____

_____

_____

List the maximum drawdown for each fund, including: % of drawdown, recovery period, and reason for drawdown.

_____

_____

_____

Provide the average return, standard deviation, Sharpe Ratio, and number of positive versus negative months of performance for each fund since inception. Also please attach a track record for each fund.

_____

_____

_____

List the largest withdrawal from each fund including: the date, percentage of equity, and reason for the withdrawal.

_____

_____

_____

If there is a benchmark for each fund, provide each fund's beta relative to the benchmark and information ratio.

_____

_____

IV. RISK

Risk Management

What risks are measured?_____

How is risk measured?_____

How is risk managed?_____

Are position limits used?_____

What is your gross long exposure, your gross short exposure, and your net market exposure?

_____

What types of derivatives do you use in your investment strategy, and how do you monitor the risks associated with these instruments?_____

_____

_____

_____

How do you monitor counterparty credit risk?_____

_____

_____

_____

Leverage

What is the current level of leverage?_____

What is the maximum amount of leverage that may be employed in your strategy?

_____

Historically, what is the maximum amount of leverage that you have employed?

_____

Historically, what is the average leverage amount employed?_____

Risk Officer

Who is responsible for monitoring risk?_____

If the person responsible for risk is also the Chief Investment Officer or another investment person, please explain how the risk function can remain independent.

_____

_____

_____

V. ADMINISTRATION

Have there been any civil, criminal, or regulatory actions against the hedge fund manager or any of its principals within the last three years?

_____

_____

_____

Has there been any significant turnover or personnel within the last three years?

_____

_____

_____

Who will be the primary account representative for our investment?

_____

_____

_____

What is your disaster recovery plan?

_____

_____

_____

VI. LEGAL REVIEW

What type of investment product is being offered?

_____

_____

What is the management fee?

_____

What is the incentive fee?

_____

Is there any fee recapture or "high watermark"?

_____

Is there a lock-up period?

_____

How frequently can an investor redeem its investment?

_____

What is the minimum and maximum subscription?

_____

Is there an advisory committee?

_____

VII. REFERENCES

Accounting firm contact

_____

Prime broker contact

_____

Legal counsel contact

_____

Existing investors (please provide at least two)

_____

_____

Chapter 6

Risk Management Part 1: Hedge Fund Return Distributions

Most of the prior studies of hedge funds have generally examined hedge funds within a mean-variance efficient frontier. Generally, Sharpe ratios are used to compare hedge fund returns to those of stock and bond indices. However, hedge funds may pursue investment strategies that have non-linear payoffs or are exposed to significant event risk, both of which may not be apparent from a Sharpe ratio analysis. Consequently, the distributions associated with hedge funds may demonstrate properties that cannot be fully captured by the mean and variance.

The purpose of this chapter is to take some of the "mystery" out of hedge funds by examining their return distributions. Analyzing these return distributions will provide us with necessary insight to understand and manage the risks associated with hedge fund investing. Additionally, we should be able to determine whether there is, in fact, skill at work.

We start with a brief review of the hedge fund literature on mapping the distribution of returns to hedge funds. We then expand on our prior description of hedge funds versus traditional long-only investors. We use this graphical description to classify and examine the type of return distributions we might expect from hedge funds. Last, we discuss the risk management implications for hedge funds.

A REVIEW OF HEDGE FUND STUDIES

In Chapter 3, we provided an extensive review of the research literature regarding hedge fund returns. A growing body of empirical research demonstrates that hedge funds can be a valuable addition to a diversified portfolio of stocks and bonds. We briefly summarize those articles that consider hedge funds within a portfolio context.

These portfolio optimization studies demonstrate that the low correlation between the returns to hedge funds and those of traditional asset classes make hedge funds a valuable portfolio addition. Goldman Sachs & Co. and Financial Risk Management Ltd. find that a portfolio of 60% S&P 500, 30% Lehman

Aggregate Bond Index, and 10% hedge funds outperformed a 60/40 allocation of stocks/bonds by 78 basis points while reducing portfolio volatility by 31 basis points.[1] Edwards and Liew find that an unconstrained optimization including stocks, bonds, and fund of hedge funds, selects an 84% allocation to an equally-weighted fund of hedge funds, 7% to the S&P500, and 10% to corporate bonds.[2] Purcell and Crowley find that the inclusion of hedge funds in a diversified portfolio can increase expected returns by as much as 200 basis points.[3] Ackermann, McEnally, and Ravenscraft find, using mean-variance analysis, that hedge funds augment the diversification potential of portfolios comprised of domestic stocks, foreign stocks, and bonds.[4]

In summary, the prior research indicates that hedge funds are a valuable addition to a diversified portfolio within a mean-variance efficient frontier. Yet, hedge fund returns may exhibit properties that cannot be described by the first two moments of a distribution.

The moments of a distribution are statistics that describe the shape of the distribution. When an investor invests capital in a security, a hedge fund, or some other asset, she receives a distribution of returns from that investment. This distribution of returns can be described by certain statistics called "moments." Everyone is familiar with the first moment of a distribution, this is the mean, or average return, and it is denoted by $E(R)$. The second moment of the distribution is denoted by $E(R^2)$, and it is used to determine the variance and the standard deviation of the distribution.

The normal, or bell-shaped, distribution can be completely described by its first two moments. Often in finance, the returns to most securities are assumed to follow a normal distribution. However, several studies have demonstrated that hedge funds generate returns that differ significantly from those generated by traditional financial asset classes.

Fung and Hsieh attempt to analyze the returns to hedge funds by applying the factor or style analysis conducted by William Sharpe with respect to mutual funds.[5] In his 1992 study, Sharpe compared the returns of mutual funds to the returns from financial asset class indices to determine the amount of variation in mutual fund returns explained by asset class returns. His results indicated that up to 90% of mutual fund returns are explained by asset class returns.

---

[1] Goldman, Sachs & Co. and Financial Risk Management Ltd. "The Hedge Fund "Industry" and Absolute Return Funds," *The Journal of Alternative Investments* (Spring 1999).

[2] Edwards, Franklin and Jimmy Liew. "Hedge Funds versus Managed Futures as Asset Classes," *The Journal of Derivatives* (Summer 1999).

[3] Purcell, David and Paul Crowley. "The Reality of Hedge Funds," *The Journal of Investing* (Fall 1999), pp. 26–44.

[4] Carl Ackermann, Richard McEnally, and David Ravenscraft, "The Performance of Hedge Funds: Risk, Return, and Incentives," *The Journal of Finance* (June 1999).

[5] See William Fung and David Hsieh, "Empirical Characteristics of Dynamic Trading Strategies: The Case of Hedge Funds," *Review of Financial Studies*, Vol. 10 (1997); and William Sharpe, "Asset Allocation: Management Style and Performance Measure," *Journal of Portfolio Management* (1992).

Fung and Hsieh find that the amount of variation of hedge fund returns that is explained by financial asset class returns is low; R-square measures were less than 25% for almost half of the hedge funds studied. They then apply a principal components analysis based on a hedge fund's trading style. They find that five different trading styles (systems/opportunistic, global/macro, value, systems/ trend following, and distressed) explain about 45% of the cross sectional variation in hedge fund returns.

Liang conducts a style analysis similar to Sharpe and finds R-squares in the range of 20% for hedge funds that invest in foreign exchange to 77% for hedge funds that invest in emerging markets.[6] Schneeweis and Spurgin conduct a regression analysis of the returns to various hedge fund categories to the returns of stocks, bonds, commodities, and currency returns.[7] They find R-square measures that range from near zero for relative value hedge funds to 0.67 for hedge funds that pursue primarily a long equity investment strategy.

These studies indicate that hedge fund return patterns do not map as well on to financial assets as do mutual fund returns. It is possible that hedge funds generate return distributions that are very different from traditional financial assets. In this chapter, we consider some common characteristics shared between hedge fund returns and those of financial asset classes and their impact on the shape of hedge fund return distributions.

A GENERAL CLASSIFICATION FOR HEDGE FUNDS

Recall that in Chapter 4 we provided a graphical comparison between hedge funds and traditional long-only managers. Long-only managers typically invest in either the equity or bond market, but do not leverage their investment bets. Therefore, their investment programs have considerable market risk exposure, but very little leverage or credit risk exposure.

We present again Exhibit 1 where we plot market risk versus credit risk for several styles of long-only managers. Again, we use a relative scale of 0 to 5 where 0 represents no exposure to market risk and 5 represents the maximum exposure. The same relative scale is applied along the horizontal axis with respect to credit risk. As Exhibit 1 demonstrates, traditional long-only managers have considerable exposure to market risk but minimal exposure to credit risk.

In Exhibit 2, we graph the ten different hedge fund styles that we discussed in Chapter 2. We can separate these hedge funds into three broad groups: (1) those hedge funds that have market risk, (2) those hedge funds that have credit risk, and (3) those hedge funds that minimize credit and market risk.

---

[6] Bing Liang, "On the Performance of Hedge Funds," *Financial Analysts Journal* (July/August 1999).
[7] Thomas Schneeweis and Richard Spurgin, "Multifactor Analysis of Hedge Fund, Managed Futures, and Mutual Fund Return and Risk Characteristics," *The Journal of Alternative Investments* (Fall 1998), pp. 1–24.

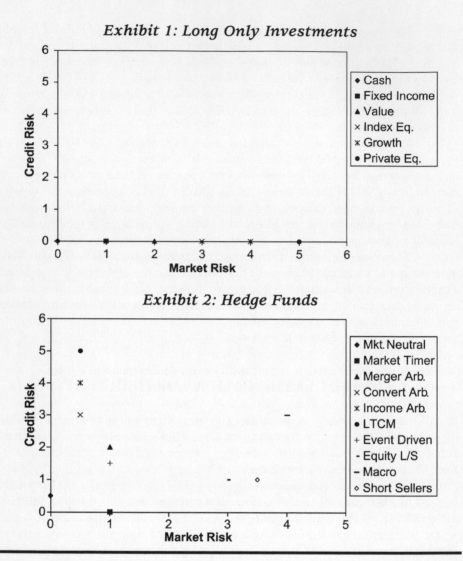

Exhibit 1: Long Only Investments

Exhibit 2: Hedge Funds

Equity long/short, short selling, and macro/directional hedge funds have exposure to market risk. Long/short equity hedge funds are exposed to the stock market, but this exposure varies depending on the ratio of long positions to short positions. Short sellers also have market exposure. They take the opposite position of long-only mangers. Global macro funds tend to make large bets on the direction of certain currencies, stock markets, or bond markets. Consequently, they have a large market exposure. Global macro funds may also use leverage to magnify the size of their bets.

Hedge fund managers that apply arbitrage strategies have significant exposure to credit risk. Arbitrage funds take small market bets but use leverage (sometimes, considerable amounts) to magnify the size of the market bets. In Exhibit 2, the arbitrage strategies line up along the credit risk axis.

Last, market neutral or market timing funds have small exposures to credit risk and market risk. These funds attempt to avoid or limit their exposure to risk in an attempt to limit the volatility of their returns. The tradeoff is that they earn lower returns than other hedge fund strategies.

We expect that those hedge funds that have credit risk exposure should have a distribution of returns that resembles that for fixed income investments that are also exposed to credit risk. Credit risk distributions are generally exposed to significant downside risk. This risk is embodied in the form of credit events such as downgrades, defaults, and bankruptcies.

This downside return distribution can be described in terms of *kurtosis* and *skewness*. Kurtosis is a term used to describe the general condition that the probability mass associated with the tails of a distribution, or outlier events, is different from that of a normal distribution. The condition of large tails in the distribution is known as *leptokurtosis*. This term describes a distribution of returns that has significant mass concentrated in outlier events. Therefore, to say a distribution of returns is leptokurtic is to mean that the distribution of returns has a greater exposure to outlier events.

The converse of leptokurtosis is *platykurtosis* — the condition where the tails of a distribution are thinner than that expected by a normal distribution.[8] A platykurtic distribution has less probability mass concentrated in outlier events. Generally, platykurtic distributions are less risky than leptokurtic distributions because they have less exposure to extreme events.

The skew of a distribution is again measured relative to a normal (i.e., bell-shaped) distribution. A normal distribution has no skew, it is perfectly symmetrical. Distributions with a negative skew indicate downside exposure, while a positive skew indicates an upward bias.

Credit risky investments experience leptokurtosis because they are exposed to event risk: the risk of downgrades, defaults, and bankruptcies. In fact, credit risk is a general way to describe the several types of event risk affecting the return distribution of credit risky investments. In addition, credit risky investments also tend to have a negative skew. The combination of leptokurtosis and negative skew results in large downside tails associated with the return distribution. This translates into considerable downside risk.

We expect that arbitrage funds that line up along the credit risk axis should also demonstrate similar distributions, that is, fat downside tails with a distribution skewed to the left. The fat downside tails and the skewed distribution reflect the event risk inherent in arbitrage investment strategies.

Conversely, those hedge funds that have more market exposure should exhibit symmetrical distributions. This should be consistent with the findings of

---

[8] My wife Mary calls this "scrunching the bell curve."

Fama[9] and Blume[10] who found that the returns to stocks to have no skew. However, they also observed that equity market returns exhibit the condition of leptokurtosis, or fat tails in the distribution. Consequently, we expect hedge funds with market exposure to also exhibit leptokurtosis.

Finally, there are the hedge funds that minimize credit risk and market risk. This would be the market neutral and market timing hedge funds. We would expect these hedge funds to have a small skew or none at all and exhibit low values of leptokurtosis, or even, *platykurtosis* — where the tails of the distribution are thinner than a normal distribution.

HEDGE FUND RETURN DISTRIBUTIONS

We use data from Hedge Fund Research Inc., a database containing information on more than 1,000 hedge funds representing over $100 billion of assets under management. We examine the returns to hedge fund strategies over the time period of January 1990 through June 2000.[11] We review the same ten strategies that were discussed in Chapter 2.

The time period of 1990–2000 is chosen because January 1990 is the starting date for data in the HFR hedge fund indices. Additionally, the time period of 1990–2000 was witness to numerous financial cycles beginning with the U.S. recession of 1990–1991. Further, there was the Latin America crisis (the "Tequilla Crisis") brought about by the devaluation of the Mexican Peso in December 1994, two periods of Federal Reserve Bank tightening (1994–1995 and 1999–2000), and two periods of Federal Reserve Bank easing (1991 and 1997–1998). Finally, there was the Asian Contagion in 1997 followed by a major liquidity crisis brought about by the Russian bond default in August 1998. In sum, this time period was sufficiently diverse in economic cycles and crises that it should provide a robust return distribution for each hedge fund style.

Exhibit 3 presents the monthly expected returns, standard deviations, and Sharpe ratios for the asset classes and the different hedge fund styles over the time period January 1990 through June 2000. Except for short selling hedge funds, the Sharpe ratios of the hedge fund indices are higher than those for stocks and bonds. However, as alluded to earlier, Sharpe ratios may not fully capture the risks associated with hedge fund return distributions. For this reason we also include two additional distribution statistics, the skew and kurtosis.

---

[9] See Eugene Fama, *Foundations of Finance* (New York: Basic Books, 1976).
[10] Marshall Blume, "Portfolio Theory: a Step Toward its Practical Application," *The Journal of Business* (April 1970).
[11] One significant caveat must be mentioned with respect to using hedge fund indices for economic analysis. Hedge funds are not as accessible to all investors as are stocks and bonds. Normally, the hedge fund managers impose minimum net worth or earning power requirements on an investment in their fund. Additionally, there are issues of capacity when pursuing alternative investment as well as regulatory restrictions as to the number of investors in a hedge fund. Consequently, an index of hedge funds is not investable compared to a stock or bond index.

Exhibit 3: Expected Returns and Sharpe Ratios
January 1990 through June 2000

Hedge Fund Strategy	Expected Return	Standard Deviation	Sharpe Ratio	Skew	Kurtosis
Equity Long/Short	1.83%	2.62%	0.525	0.113	1.802
Short Selling	0.20%	6.38%	−0.039	0.088	1.761
Global Macro	1.51%	2.67%	0.396	0.153	0.102
Convertible Arbitrage	0.96%	1.01%	0.501	−1.496	3.487
Event Driven	1.32%	1.93%	0.45	−1.629	6.728
Merger Arbitrage	1.04%	1.31%	0.446	−3.294	14.938
Fixed Income Arbitrage	0.74%	1.42%	0.2	−1.733	8.444
Relative Value Arbitrage	1.14%	1.16%	0.589	−1.251	10.545
Equity Market Neutral	0.89%	0.93%	0.47	−0.087	0.323
Market Timing	1.27%	1.96%	0.421	0.109	−0.457
S&P 500	1.20%	3.92%	0.19	−0.499	1.443
SSMB High Yield Index	0.78%	2.13%	0.157	−0.434	4.233

For comparison, we include two financial asset classes that demonstrate market risk and credit risk. For market risk, we use large-capitalization stocks represented by the S&P 500 Index. For credit risk, we use high-yield bonds represented by the Salomon Smith Barney High Yield Composite Index. These two asset classes provide us with distribution benchmarks for analyzing hedge fund returns. We analyze the returns to these two financial asset classes over the same time period as for hedge funds.

We take the raw data contained in the HFRI database, and recalibrate it to plot a frequency distribution of the returns associated with each hedge fund investment style. Such a distribution provides a graphical depiction of the range and likelihood of returns associated with a hedge fund return. We calculate the mean, standard deviation, skew, and kurtosis associated with the returns to each hedge fund strategy.

Skewness and kurtosis are defined by the third and fourth moments of the distribution, respectively. Normal distributions can be defined by the first two moments of the distribution — the mean and the variance. Therefore, for a normal distribution, a Sharpe ratio is an appropriate measure for risk and return. However, if higher moments of the distribution are present, a Sharpe ratio may not capture the complete risk and return profile. As we examine each hedge fund return distribution, we will refer back to the values of skew and kurtosis in Exhibit 3.

We begin by graphing the frequency distribution for large-cap stocks and high-yield grade bonds. We use these two asset classes to capture market risk and credit risk, respectively. In Exhibit 4 we can see that the S&P 500 has a distribution with a negative skew of −0.499 and a low but positive value of kurtosis of 1.44.

The positive value of kurtosis indicates that the return distribution of the S&P 500 has greater probability mass in the tail of the distribution than would be expected compared to a normal distribution. This means that there are more outlier events associated with the distribution of returns to the S&P 500 than would be predicted by a normal distribution. A negative value for kurtosis would indicate the reverse — that there is less probability mass in the tails (fewer outlier events) than a normal distribution.

The negative skew found in the returns to stocks is contrary to the findings of both Fama and Blume discussed earlier. This could be due to the different time period examined in this study compared to earlier research rather than indicating a fundamental change in the distribution of equity returns.

A negative skew indicates that the mean of the distribution is to the left of (less than) the median of the distribution. This means that there are more frequent large return observations to the left of the distribution (negative returns) and there are more small and mid-range positive return observations to the right of the distribution. In other words, large negative outlying returns occur more frequently than large positive outlying returns, indicating a bias to the downside.

A positive skew indicates the reverse of a negative skew. It indicates that the mean of the distribution is to the right of the median and that there are more frequent large positive returns than there are large negative returns. A positive skew demonstrates a bias to the upside.

For high-yield bonds, the return distribution is distinctly non-normal. In Exhibit 5 we see a negative skew value of -0.434 as well as a large positive value of kurtosis of 4.233. This distribution demonstrates significant leptokurtosis. Specifically, the distribution of returns to high-yield bonds demonstrates a significant downside tail. This "fat" tail reflects the event risk of downgrades, defaults, and bankruptcies. We note again that credit risk is simply another way to describe event risk. Credit spreads can also increase as a result of event risk; the Russian bond default is a perfect example.

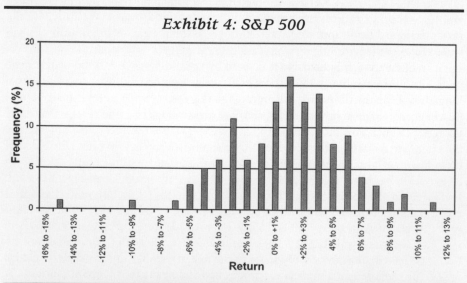

Exhibit 4: S&P 500

Exhibit 5: Salomon Smith Barney High Yield Index

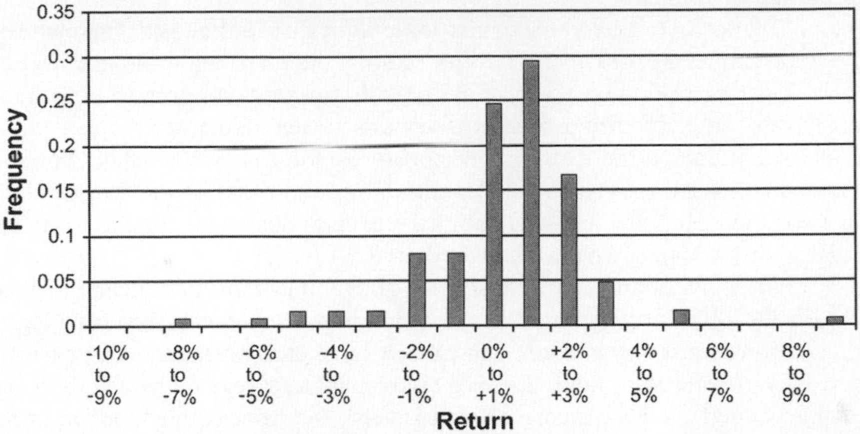

Hedge Funds that Exhibit Market Risk

We use Exhibits 4 and 5 for comparison as we examine the distributions associated with hedge fund returns. We begin with those hedge funds that take more market risk than credit risk. These include global macro hedge funds, short selling hedge funds, and equity long/short hedge funds.

Equity Long/Short Hedge Funds

This type of investing focuses on stock selection. This is the source of what many hedge fund mangers claim is "skill-based" investing. Rather than mimic an equity benchmark, these managers focus their skill on a particular market segment or industry sector to generate their returns.

Equity long/short strategies tend to have a long bias. That is, equity long/short managers tend to be more on the long side of the market than they are on the short side. Partly this is because it is more difficult to borrow stocks to short, and partly it is because many long/short equity managers came from the traditional long-only investment world and thereby have a long bias. Therefore, we would expect equity long/short hedge fund return distributions to also demonstrate the leptokurtic properties of the S&P 500.

Yet, the ability to short stocks at appropriate times should reduce some of the outlier events associated with the stock market. Therefore, while we still expect a positive value of kurtosis, we also expect it to be less than the broad stock market. Furthermore, the ability to go both long and short in the stock market should give equity long/short hedge fund managers an advantage over long-only passive investing. This added dimension to their strategy should reduce the negative skew associated with long-only investing.

Exhibit 6 presents the distribution for the HFRI Equity Long/Short Hedge Index. We see that this distribution has a positive skew of 0.113. This is particularly noteworthy given the negative skew observed with respect to the S&P 500 returns over the same time period.

The positive skew to the equity long/short distribution is a demonstration of hedge fund manager skill. The ability to shift the distribution of stock returns from a negative skew to a positive skew is a concrete example of skill-based investing for which the hedge fund industry is so often associated.

Additionally, the distribution of returns for equity long/short investing has a positive kurtosis value (1.802), consistent with that of the stock market. However, the value of kurtosis is slightly greater than that for the S&P 500, instead of less which is what we had predicted.

One explanation might be that these hedge fund managers attempt to generate a "double alpha" strategy. That is, they attempt to add value by investing long in those companies that they expect to increase in value and short those companies that they expect to decrease in value. This is a double alpha strategy in that the short sales are not generated to reduce exposure to market risk, but instead, to provide additional value through stock selection. The double alpha strategy would also be consistent with a positive skew if manager skill can indeed select both winners and losers. However, it is possible that the pursuit of a double alpha strategy increases the hedge fund's exposure to outlier events, resulting in a larger value of kurtosis for the distribution than would be predicted by observing the returns to the broad stock market.

Short Selling Hedge Funds

Short selling hedge funds perform well in down markets and poorly in up markets. Short selling hedge funds should be the mirror image of long-only investments. However, they may attempt to limit their short positions in up markets, thus timing their positions to limit their losses when the financial markets are improving. Consequently, we might expect a slight positive skew to their return distribution.

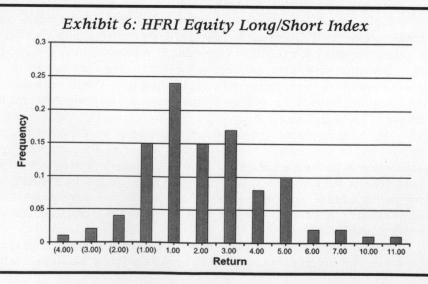

Exhibit 6: HFRI Equity Long/Short Index

Exhibit 7: HFRI Short Selling Index

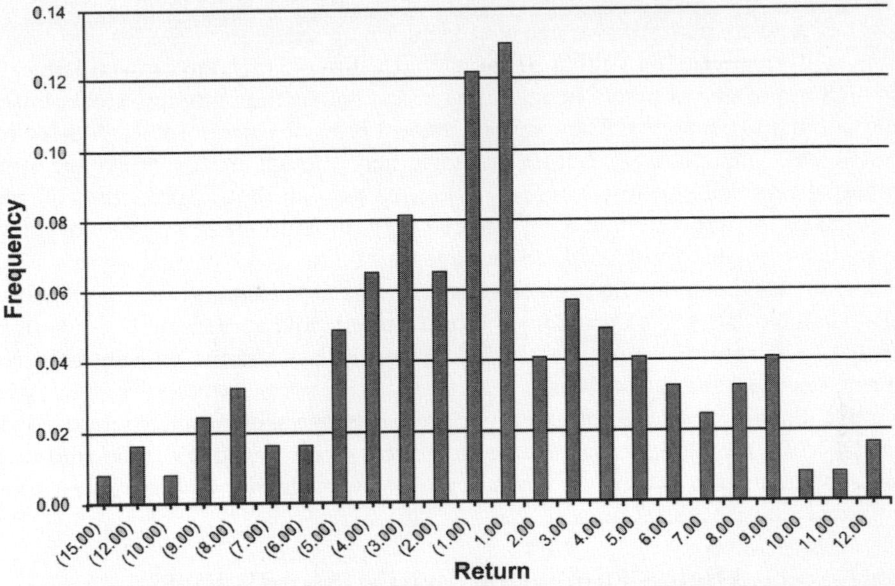

With respect to fat tails, we would expect to see a value of kurtosis similar to that for long-only stocks. This is because they have the reverse position from a traditional long-only manager. Short selling hedge funds are down when long-only managers are up and vice versa. Consequently, their returns should reflect the same type of kurtosis as that for a long-only equity benchmark.

Exhibit 7 presents the frequency distribution for the HFRI Short Selling Index. We can see that this distribution has a slight positive skew (0.088) and with a kurtosis (1.761) similar to that of the general stock market. We note that this distribution is centered slightly above zero. Short selling hedge funds, on average, earn a positive return of about 0.2% per month.

Given the positive returns associated with the stock market over the time period 1990–2000, the positive return to short selling hedge funds indicates a bias to market timing. This bias allowed them to produce a positive skew to their return distribution. The ability to generate a positive skew while maintaining a level of kurtosis similar to the general stock market is an indication of manager skill.

Global Macro Hedge Funds

Exhibit 8 presents the distribution for the HFRI Macro Hedge Fund Index. Surprisingly, this distribution more closely resembles a normal distribution than that demonstrated by large-cap stocks or high-yield bonds. Global macro funds exhibit a slightly positive skew (0.153) with a low value of leptokurtosis (0.102).

This is contrary to what we expected. Given the large exposure to market risk for global macro funds, we expected to see significant leptokurtosis. Furthermore, to the extent that macro funds apply leverage, we expected to see a negative skew, consistent with that observed for high-yield bonds. Instead, we find the reverse: a positive skew value and almost no leptokurtosis.

One explanation could be the global nature of their investment strategy. By definition, global macro hedge funds invest across the currency, stock, bond, and commodity markets. They are not limited either by geographic scope or by asset class. Their broad investment mandate may allow them to achieve the most widely diversified portfolio where the idiosyncratic distribution properties of specific markets are diversified away. Indeed the Global Macro Hedge Fund Index includes 46 hedge funds with an average asset size of $252 million investing across financial, commodity, and currency markets around the world. This breadth of investment strategies provides the best opportunity to achieve a diversified portfolio of returns, minimize the impact of outlier events, and, perhaps, to approximate a normal distribution.

In any event, the ability to produce a positive skew to their return distribution while providing less exposure to outliers (a lower value of kurtosis) than the general stock market indicates that global macro hedge fund managers have provided a positive level of skill.

Hedge Funds that Exhibit Credit Risk

The second general category of hedge funds lines up along the credit risk axis in Exhibit 2. We have merger arbitrage at the bottom of the credit risk axis and relative value arbitrage at the top end of the credit risk axis.

Exhibit 8: HFRI Global Macro Index

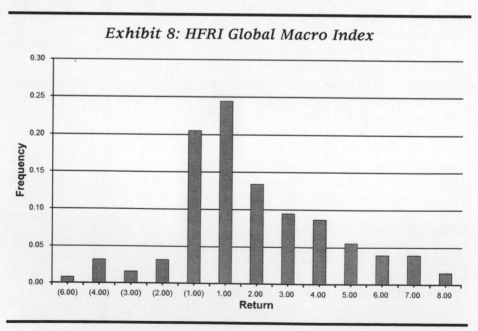

The investment strategies of these funds involve taking only a little market exposure — hence their label as arbitrage funds. However, these hedge funds magnify that exposure through credit risk. Additionally, these funds are exposed to event risk: the risk that one part of their arbitrage strategy will not perform as expected. Their exposure to event risk should be demonstrated with a large, downside tail in their return distributions. In other words, they should exhibit distributions with a large value of kurtosis and a negative skew. Moreover, as we move up the credit risk axis, we should expect the distribution of returns to the hedge fund strategy to exhibit larger downside tails.

Convertible Arbitrage

Convertible arbitrage funds seek to buy undervalued convertible bonds and then hedge out the systematic risk associated with them. For convertible bonds that trade more like equity, the hedge fund manager shorts an appropriate ratio of stock (the delta) to neutralize the equity position. For convertible bonds that trade more like fixed income instruments, the hedge fund manager may short interest rate futures to hedge the interest rate risk. In either case the investor is betting that the option to exchange the bond for stock is mispriced by the market.

The upside potential of the trade is typically known with precision — it is usually based on an option pricing model. However, the downside cannot be determined with the same certainty. Convertible arbitrage can fail because of redemption risk — the risk that the company may redeem the convertible bonds and the option value will be lost. In addition there is the credit risk associated with distressed security investing. If the company goes bankrupt, the bonds and any equity option attached to them may be worthless. In sum, convertible arbitrage is exposed to event risk.

In addition, convertible arbitrage funds employ leverage. This leverage is implicit in the margin account used to borrow stock or bonds for the short position. In addition, these funds may borrow additional capital to boost their returns. For these reasons, we expect a large downside tail and a negative skew to the distribution.

Exhibit 9 confirms these expectations. We observe a negative skew of −1.496 and large kurtosis value of 3.487. These observations are consistent with the redemption risk and event risk faced by convertible bond arbitrageurs. The large positive value of kurtosis and negative value for skew translates into significant downside risk. We conclude that convertible arbitrage has significant event risk similar to credit risky investments.

Our last issue is to determine whether there is any skill at work. From Exhibit 9, we can see that 75% of the time an investor should expect to receive a return of about 1% a month from convertible arbitrage. This consistency of return is an indication of skill.

To provide a perspective of this skill, compare Exhibit 9 to that of Exhibit 4 for stocks and Exhibit 5 for high-yield bonds. We can see that the frequency of returns for stocks and bonds is much more dispersed than it is for convertible arbitrage. Therefore, although convertible arbitrage does expose an investor to significant downside risk, there is a trade-off: monthly performance that is far more consistent than what an investor can expect from either the stock market or high-yield market.

Event Driven Hedge Funds

Event driven hedge funds have exposure to both market risk and credit risk. The market risk comes from their investment in significant transactional events such as mergers and acquisitions, spin-offs, liquidations, reorganizations, recapitalizations, share buy-backs, and other events. The very nature of the investing exposes this type of hedge fund to event risk: the risk that the anticipated event will not come to fruition. Additionally, these hedge funds may apply leverage to amplify their investment bets. Consequently, we would expect to see large/fat tails in the distribution and a negative skew to the distribution to reflect the event risk associated with this strategy.

Exhibit 10 confirms this analysis. Event driven hedge funds have a large negative skew value of −1.629 and a large positive kurtosis value of 6.728. This is consistent with the exposure to event risk.

Also, event driven hedge funds produce performance results that are only slightly more consistent than that for high-yield bonds. Unfortunately, it is hard to argue that there is much skill at work with respect to this strategy.

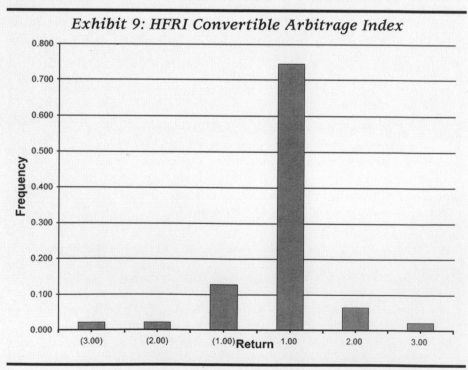

Exhibit 9: HFRI Convertible Arbitrage Index

Exhibit 10: HFRI Event Driven Index

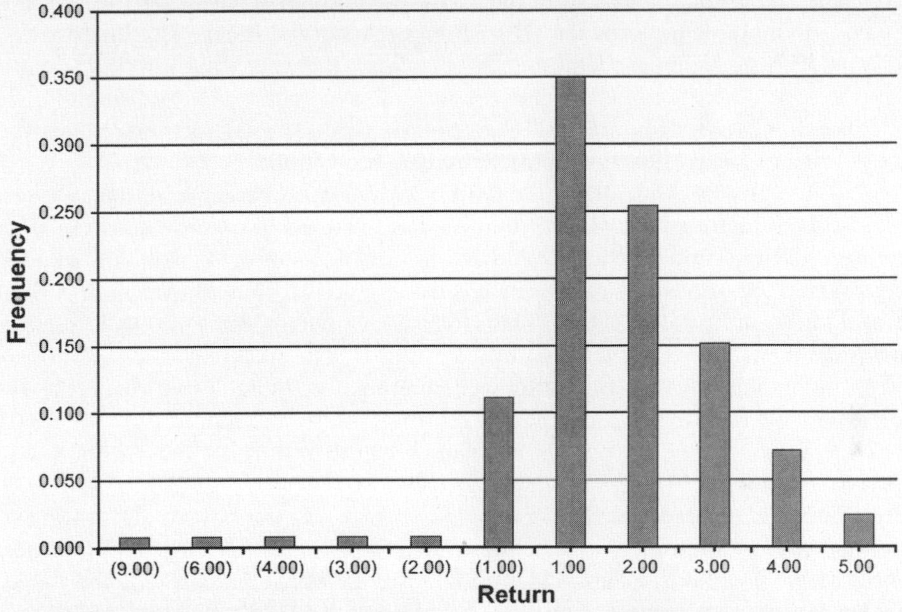

Merger Arbitrage Hedge Funds

Merger arbitrage hedge funds seek to capture the spread between the market prices of two companies engaged in a merger and the value of those securities upon successful completion of the merger or takeover. The spread in the market reflects the unwillingness of other market participants to take on the risk that the transaction will not be completed. Mergers collapse because the two firms may fail to come to complete agreement on terms, government agencies may intervene (e.g. review of possible monopolies), or because a third party may bid on the target firm.

Some hedge fund managers transact only in announced deals, while others will take on more transaction risk based on speculation or rumors of mergers. In either case, the transaction risk is large. If a deal craters, merger arbitrage funds stand to lose a considerable portion of their investment. Consequently, we expect the distribution of returns to demonstrate a large downside tail. This is similar to what we find with credit risk — the risk of bankruptcy has the ability to wipe out an investment in that company.

In addition to the event risk of a collapsed deal, merger arbitrage funds also apply leverage. Leverage exposes merger arbitrage funds to additional event risk that should magnify the tails of the distribution.

The upside potential for merger arbitrage is limited. Once the terms of a merger deal are announced, the amount of value to be gained is known with precision. There is no upside beyond what is offered in the current spread. The greater the transaction risk, the larger the spread, but the spread represents all the merger arbitrage manager can expect to earn. Because the upside to a merger deal is limited, and the downside can be considerable, we expect to see a distribution with a negative skew.

Exhibit 11 presents the HFRI Merger Arbitrage Index. This distribution is consistent with our expectations. A very large kurtosis value of 14.938 indicates a large downside tail associated with failed merger deals. Additionally, we observe a negative skew of −3.294 to the distribution that further reflects the transaction or "deal" risk associated with merger arbitrage.

Despite the large downside tail associated with merger arbitrage, Exhibit 11 also demonstrates very consistent positive returns. About 88% of the time merger arbitrage funds deliver 1% to 2% returns per month. This is similar with the consistency of positive returns discovered for convertible arbitrage above, and is an indication of positive skill. Therefore, when merger deals go "bad," merger arbitrage managers experience significant losses. The trade off is that the overwhelming majority of the time, they generate positive monthly returns in the 1% to 2% range with a long-term expected return of 1.04% per month.

Fixed Income Arbitrage Hedge Funds

Fixed income arbitrage, as its name suggests, involves the buying and selling of similar types of fixed income securities to capitalize on mispricing opportunities. For example, fixed income arbitrage funds may combine an interest only mortgage-backed strip and a principal only mortgage-backed strip to form a traditional mortgage pass-through certificate and then sell a similar pass-through certificate to take advantage of any differences in price. Leverage is applied to extract the most value from any difference in price.

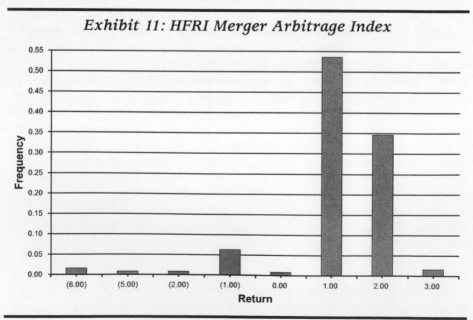

Exhibit 11: HFRI Merger Arbitrage Index

Exhibit 12: HFRI Fixed Income: Arbitrage Index

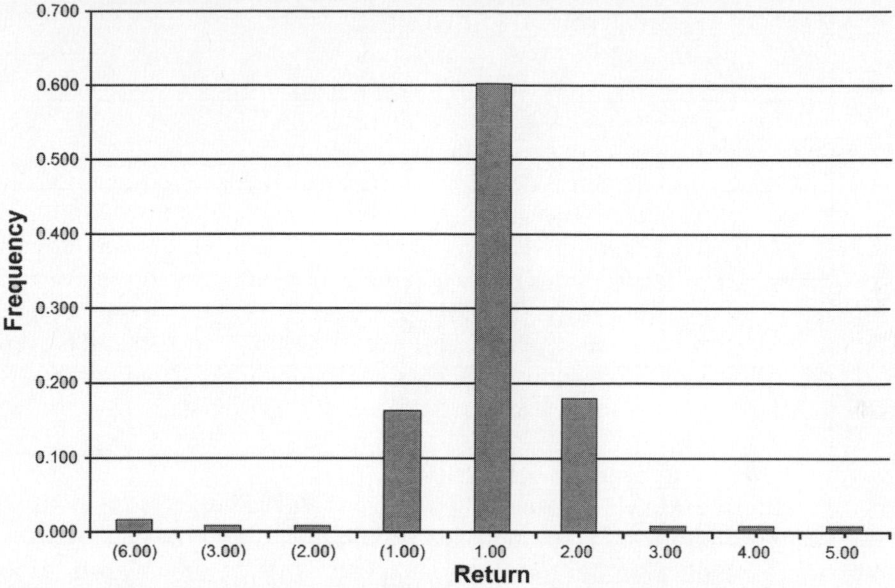

Fixed income arbitrage is dependent upon the prices of the two similar securities converging. However, there are many events that might prevent this conversion. For instance, the Federal Reserve Bank may decide to cut interest rates, encouraging mortgage refinancing, and thereby speeding up the rate by which mortgage holders prepay their mortgage debt. The change in prepayment rates is a considerable risk for a mortgage-backed fixed income hedge fund manger. This type of event risk should manifest itself in a large downside tail to the return distribution.

Exhibit 12 presents a distribution consistent with this conclusion: a large positive value of kurtosis of 8.44 and a negative skew of −1.733. In sum, a large downside tail indicates significant exposure to event risk. However, like convertible arbitrage and merger arbitrage, fixed income arbitrage produces consistent monthly returns. Sixty percent of the time, fixed income arbitrage produces a return of about 1% per month. This is much more consistent than either the stock market or the high-yield market.

Relative Value Arbitrage

In Exhibit 2 we expect relative value hedge funds to have the greatest exposure to credit risk. These funds seek out arbitrage or relative value opportunities wherever they exist: merger arbitrage, convertible arbitrage, fixed income arbitrage, mortgage-backed securities arbitrage, and options arbitrage. Often, they apply considerable leverage in their investment strategies. Long Term Capital Management is the best example of a relative value hedge fund.

Exhibit 13: HFRI Relative Value Arbitrage Index

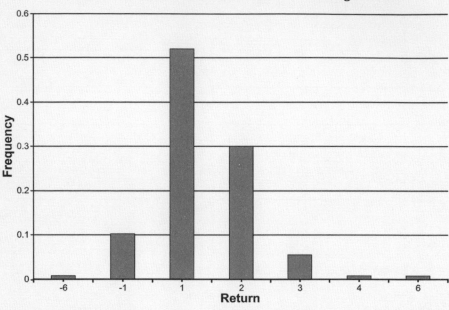

Exhibit 13 presents the results for the HFRI Relative Value Arbitrage Index. Similar to the other arbitrage funds, we find a large ("fat") downside tail and a large, negative skew to the distribution. Relative value funds have a large positive value of kurtosis equal to 10.54, indicating large fat tails. Additionally, relative value hedge funds also have a large negative skew value of −1.25. This is consistent with event risk expected of this investment strategy.

Relative arbitrage managers also produce consistent results. For over 80% of the months observed, returns were in the 1% to 2% range, with a long-term average just over 1% per month. As previously noted, consistency of performance results is an indication of manager skill.

Hedge Funds that Have Low Market and Credit Risk

Our last broad category of hedge funds is different from the previous hedge fund strategies in that hedge funds in this category employ little or no leverage and maintain little or no market exposure. In fact, the very nature of these programs is to minimize market and credit exposure altogether. Two strategies fit this profile: market neutral funds and market timing hedge funds.

Market Neutral

Market neutral hedge funds go long and short the market. These funds seek to maintain neutral exposure to the general stock market as well as having neutral risk exposures across industries. The hedge fund manager builds an integrated portfolio so that market and industry exposures cancel out. Security selection is all that matters. There is no "beta," or market risk in the portfolio either with respect to the broad stock market or with respect to any industry. Only the alpha associated with stock selection should remain.

Furthermore, these funds apply only a small amount of credit risk. There is no market or industry risk to leverage, but the fund will incur leverage from the stocks it borrows to establish the short positions.

With minimal market and credit risk exposure, we would expect a distribution that does not have a negative skew (either from market or credit risk) or large tails. In fact, if a market neutral hedge fund manager is successful in removing credit risk and market risk from his portfolio, we would expect to see the statistical biases of skewness and leptokurtosis disappear.

Exhibit 14 confirms our expectations. First, we can see that the distribution of returns for market neutral hedge funds is centered around 0.89%. That is, the average monthly return to market neutral hedge funds is 89 basis points. This is a good demonstration of manager skill: the ability to remove market and credit risk and earn a positive return.

Moreover, the values for skewness and kurtosis are quite low. Skew is −0.087, indicating a very mild, almost negligible skew to the left. This is a considerable improvement from the skew associated with the returns to high-yield bonds and stock returns.

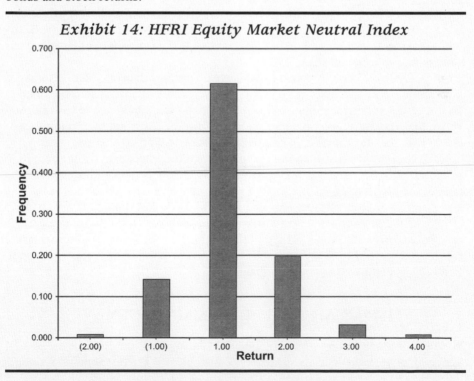

Exhibit 14: HFRI Equity Market Neutral Index

Finally, the value of kurtosis is 0.323. Again, this number is quite favorable compared to a normal distribution, and it is considerably smaller than stocks or high-yield bonds. It indicates that the market neutral distribution of returns exhibit only mild leptokurtosis — the tails of the distribution are only slightly larger than that for a normal distribution.

In summary, market neutral hedge funds exhibit the properties of minimal credit and market risk, consistent with their intended strategy.

Market Timers

Recall from Chapter 2 that market timers attempt to time the most economically beneficial moments to be in the stock market, and invest in cash otherwise. More specifically, they attempt to time the market so that they are fully invested during bull markets, and strictly in cash during bear markets. This is a top down approach to investing; market timers analyze fiscal and monetary policy as well as key macroeconomic indicators to determine whether the economy is gathering or running out of steam.

The ability to move in and out of the stock market, and conversely, out of and into cash, should provide market timers with two advantages. First, they have the opportunity to avoid the downturns associated with the stock market. If they are successful, they should be able to shift the negative skew associated with the stock market to a positive, or at least, a neutral skew. Second, since they are not fully invested in the stock market at all times, they should avoid some of the outlier events associated with the stock market. This means that the tails of the distribution for market timers should be close to normal. The condition of leptokurtosis should be low or nonexistent.

Exhibit 15 confirms these advantages. First, the distribution of returns for market timing hedge funds has a small positive skew of 0.109. Therefore, market timers have demonstrated that shifting between the stock market and cash can add value. Specifically, market timers are able to shift the distribution of returns associated with the stock market from a negative skew to a positive skew.

Second, the distribution of returns to market timers exhibits the condition of *platykurtosis*. The value of kurtosis is −0.457. This is the condition where the tails of the distribution have a smaller probability density than the tails of a normal distribution; the tails are *thinner* than normal. Market timing is the only style of hedge fund investing that demonstrates this condition. Not only are market timers successfully able to avoid the outlier events associated with stock market returns, they are able to provide a distribution of returns that is less exposed to large events compared to a normal distribution.

IMPLICATIONS FOR RISK MANAGEMENT

Before risk management of hedge funds can be applied, the risks of the several hedge fund strategies must be understood. Specifically, the distribution of returns

of each hedge fund strategy must be analyzed to determine its shape and properties. In this chapter we found that many hedge fund return distributions exhibit
properties that are distinctly non-normal. The issue before us is how to apply this
information when constructing a hedge fund program. We offer some practical
observations and suggestions.

One observation is: Do not construct a hedge fund program based on
only one type of hedge fund strategy. As indicated in Exhibits 6 through15, the
different hedge fund styles exhibit different return distributions. Therefore, benefits can be obtained by diversifying across hedge fund strategies. This is plain old
portfolio theory: Do not put all of your eggs into one hedge fund basket.

Hedge Funds that Exhibit Market Risk

The good news here is that three types of market risk hedge funds — equity long/
short, global macro, and short selling — exhibit risk profiles that are no worse
than the overall stock market, and in some cases, better.

Consider equity long/short hedge funds. These hedge funds demonstrate
a value of leptokurtosis of 1.8 and a skew factor of 0.113. First, the value of kurtosis is similar to that of the S&P 500. Therefore, this type of hedge fund strategy
exposes the investor to outlier events at about the same rate as investing in the
S&P 500. This is comforting for those investors that already invest in the stock
market. If an investor can understand and accept the risk of the U.S. stock market,
the risk profile for equity long/short hedge funds is not much different.

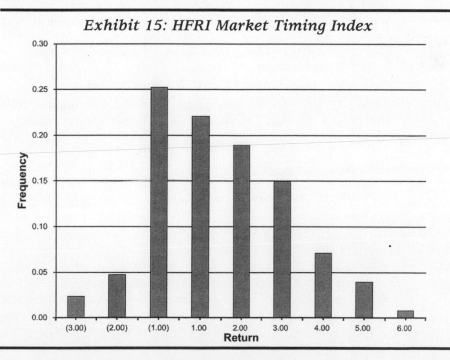

Exhibit 15: HFRI Market Timing Index

There is, however, one distinct advantage of equity long/short strategies, and that is the positive skew factor for this strategy compared to the negative skew for the S&P 500. This means that equity long/short hedge fund managers have been able to shift the distribution of returns from the left, or downside, of the distribution, to the right, or upside, of the distribution. In other words, there are more positive observations to the right of the median of the distribution for long/short managers than there are negative observations to the left of the median. Therefore, equity long/short managers demonstrate a positive upward bias to their returns, compared to the S&P 500 with about the same exposure to outlier events.

In summary, there is a shift in the skew of the stock return distribution from negative to positive with only a slight increase in leptokurtosis. This seems a good trade off although we know of no statistic that measures a skew/kurtosis ratio similar to a mean/standard deviation Sharpe ratio.

The simplest way to reduce the impact of outlier events is to diversify. Therefore, equity long/short programs should be diversified across industry sector and market capitalization. Additionally, equity long/short strategies should be combined with other hedge fund strategies to diversify the sources of return and risk.

Last, we note that short selling and global macro hedge funds also have positive skews and positive values of kurtosis. Yet, the leptokurtosis for short sellers is not that much greater than the general stock market, and for global macro funds, the value of kurtosis is smaller than that for U.S. stocks. Consequently, short selling hedge funds are exposed to about the same amount of outlier events as the stock market while global macro funds actually reduce the exposure to outlier events. Therefore, short selling hedge funds pose a risk that is only slightly greater than that for stocks but in return, a positive skew is observed. While global macro hedge funds not only have a positive skew, they have less outlier risk.

Hedge Funds that Exhibit Credit Risk

Exhibits 9 through 13 indicated that the arbitrage group of hedge funds exhibit properties similar to a credit risk distribution: large (fat) downside risk exposures. These large downside tail exposures reflect the event risk inherent in arbitrage strategies.

Consider merger arbitrage. As Exhibit 11 demonstrates, about 53% of the time you should expect to earn about 1% per month, and about 35% of the time, you should earn 2% per month. Therefore, about 88% of the time you should receive a return of 1% to 2% per month with merger arbitrage. These results are very favorable compared to the S&P 500 where the frequency of returns are much more dispersed. Therefore, the consistency with which merger arbitrage funds deliver performance is less risky than that for the S&P 500. Further, the standard deviation of merger arbitrage returns is one third that for the S&P 500.

However, merger arbitrage is exposed to event risk. Exhibit 11 shows that merger arbitrage has the largest negative skew and the largest value of leptokurtosis. This means that when deals break down, significant losses will be incurred.

The reason is that merger arbitrage is similar to selling a put option or selling insurance.

With a short put option, the hedge fund manager sells the put and collects a cash premium from the sale. If the put expires unexercised, the hedge fund manager keeps the premium and adds it to the total return. However, if the underlying asset price is less than the strike price of the put option at maturity, the option will be exercised against the hedge fund manager. The manager must either purchase the underlying asset at the strike price (which is above the market price), or settle the option in cash. In both cases, the hedge fund manager incurs a loss.

The payoff for a short put option is presented in Exhibit 16. Notice that the short put option earns a consistent payout until the strike price is reached, and then declines in value. This is similar to the payout expected from merger arbitrage: a consistent payout, but a loss of value if the merger is not completed. Therefore, the distribution of returns associated with a short put option strategy will also be skewed to the left, because a short put option holder is exposed to downside risk.

Another way to consider this risk is that it is similar to the sale of an insurance contract. Insurers sell insurance policies and collect premiums. In return for collecting the insurance premium, they take on the risk that there will be no unfortunate economic events.

Therefore, an insurance contract is like the sale of a put option. If nothing happens, the insurance company gets to keep the insurance/option premium. However, if there is an event, the insurance policy holder can "put" its policy back to the insurance company for a payout. The insurance company must then pay the face value (the strike price) of the insurance contract and accept a loss. Insurers make money by spreading these insurance contracts across many different types of policyholders and thereby diversifying the risk of loss on any one economic event.

Exhibit 16: Payoff to a Short Put Option

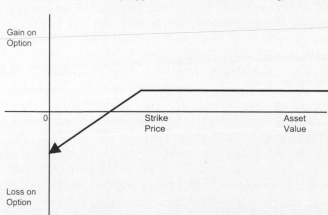

Merger arbitrage hedge funds can then be viewed as insurance agents. What they are insuring is the risk of loss should the deal collapse. By purchasing the stock of the target company and selling the stock of the acquiring company stock from investors who do not have as much confidence in the merger deal, merger arbitrage hedge funds accept/insure against the risk of the deal collapsing. If the merger fails, they are on the hook for the loss instead of the shareholders from whom they purchased or sold shares.

When viewed as insurance agents, three risk management suggestions can be made for merger arbitrage funds. First, apply the same principles as insurance companies: Diversify the risks. It is better to invest with two or three merger arbitrage funds than with one, because this will spread the insurance risk among three different funds. Second, do not invest in merger arbitrage funds that concentrate in the same industry, or market capitalization range. This will concentrate and compound the insurance risk. Last, limit the amount of leverage that the merger arbitrage manager may apply. The more the leverage, the larger the size of the short put option risk.

While we used merger arbitrage to highlight the downside risk exposure, this risk is similar for every arbitrage strategy. Each of these strategies have a similar short put option exposure. They are at risk to outlier events.

For instance, recall our discussion of the demise of Long Term Capital Management in Chapter 2. LTCM was a relative value arbitrage hedge fund manager. LTCM made a number of bets on the relative value of similar securities. This strategy worked well as long as a severe economic event did not occur. Year in and year out LTCM was able to collect option-like premiums in the financial markets for insuring that the prices of similar securities would converge.

However, a disastrous economic event eventually occurred: the default by the Russian government on its bonds. Instead of converging as LTCM had bet they would, prices of similar securities diverged. LTCM's short put option profile worked against it, and it lost massive amounts of capital.[12] Those investors that had sold their positions to LTCM benefited, and just like an insurance company, LTCM was forced to accept the losses. Additionally, the huge leverage LTCM employed only exacerbated its short put option exposure.

In summary, arbitrage funds act like insurance companies: If there is a disastrous financial event, they bear the loss. This is consistent with the ideas of Fung and Hsieh.[13] This exposure is exacerbated to the extent arbitrage funds apply leverage. Therefore, a simple risk management tool is to invest with arbitrage hedge funds that employ limited leverage. A two-to-one ratio should be sufficient for these funds to effect their strategies.

---

[12] See Philippe Jorion, "Risk Management Lessons Learned from Long Term Capital Management," working paper (2000).

[13] William Fung and David Hsieh, "A Primer on Hedge Funds," *Journal of Empirical Finance*, forthcoming.

Hedge Funds that Have Low Market and Credit Risk

Our initial reaction to market neutral funds is that risk management should be easy. Indeed, our discussion of Exhibit 14 indicates limited exposure to market, industry, or credit risk. What the investor is exposed to is residual stock risk.

Market neutral portfolios are not without risk. Exhibit 14 indicates that the monthly standard deviation is 0.93%. This is about one fourth of the monthly risk observed for the S&P 500. Therefore, market neutral funds are less risky than the general stock market, but they are not riskless. Investors sometimes associate "market neutral" with "risk free."

Nonetheless, the risk associated with this type of hedge fund strategy is less than that for the stock market. If the investor is already comfortable with investments in the stock market, market neutral programs will fit within their existing risk profile. The only risk management comment is the one that applies throughout this chapter: diversify. Broaden the investment base with more than one risk neutral manager, so that stock specific risk does not become concentrated in the same company names.

Finally, we consider the market timing hedge funds. These hedge funds have greater risk than market neutral funds; the standard deviation of their returns is 1.96%, about twice that of market neutral hedge funds. However, market timers demonstrate about one half the risk of the S&P 500. Therefore, this strategy is also lower in risk compared to the general stock market. Add to this conclusion a distribution of returns that has a positive skew and a lower than normal exposure to outlier events, and you have a reasonably low risk investment strategy. Yet, diversification applies to market timers as it does to every other hedge fund strategy.

CONCLUSION

This chapter explored the different nature of hedge fund strategies by providing a frequency distribution of their returns. We observe that those hedge funds that tend to take on more market risk than credit risk have similar return distributions to large cap stocks. Conversely, those hedge funds that have more credit risk than market risk have return distributions that resemble credit risk securities. Last, those hedge funds that take minimal credit risk and market risk did demonstrate return distributions that were consistent with lower risk profiles.

Finally, we find considerable evidence of hedge fund manager skill throughout the hedge fund manager strategies examined. This skill manifested itself in one of three ways: the ability to shift the distribution of returns from a negative skew to a positive skew; the ability to shrink the tails of the return distribution (reduce exposure to outlier events); and last, the ability to produce consistent returns with greater frequency than observed in the stock and bond markets.

Chapter 7

Risk Management Part II: Additional Hedge Fund Risks

R isk management extends beyond the economic risks undertaken by a hedge fund manager. Chapter 6 documented the credit and market risk exposure of several hedge fund strategies. However, there are several other risks that an institution should consider when investing in hedge funds.

Beyond the economic risks of a hedge fund investment, there are seven additional risk factors that are a concern to an investor: process risk, mapping risk, transparency risk, risk measurement risk, data risk, performance measurement risk, and event risk. *Process risk* relates to the "skill-based" style of hedge fund investing. *Mapping risk* considers the lack of additivity of individual hedge fund risk profiles. *Transparency risk* is the risk of non-disclosure. *Risk measurement risk* highlights the problems associated with risk management statistics. *Data risk* considers the biases inherent in hedge fund performance data. *Performance measurement risk* exposes the dangers of relying on historical hedge fund performance data. Last, *event risk* measures the extent to which hedge fund returns are affected by financial market returns.

PROCESS RISK

Most investors prefer a well-defined investment process that describes how an investment manager makes its investments. In Chapter 4 we highlighted the investment process as one of the three basic questions that must be answered when selecting a hedge fund manager. In Chapter 5 we indicated that the hedge fund manager's investment process must be documented as part of the due diligence process. Yet, documenting a hedge fund manager's investment process is not always a straightforward task. Consider the following language from a hedge fund disclosure document that we initially presented in Chapter 4:

> The General Partner makes extensive use of computer technology in both the formulation and execution of many investment decisions. Buy and sell decisions will, in many cases, be made and executed algorithmically according to quantitative trading strategies embodied in analytical computer software running the General Partner's computer facilities or on other computers used to support the Fund's trading activities.

Hedge fund processes that depend primarily on computer algorithms generally lack transparency. This is what is meant by a "black box." Hedge fund managers that can be classified as information filterers rely on sophisticated computer programs to sift through current market data to find securities that appear to be mispriced. Yet, to describe a hedge fund manager's investment process as "computer programs" is insufficient documentation. The problem is that for black box managers, the black box itself is the investment process.

The lack of transparency in the investment process is what we describe as "process risk." There are two ways to manage this risk. The first is quite direct: Don't invest in what you cannot document. This is a blunt risk management policy, but if an investor cannot understand the investment process, chances are, he may not be able to comprehend the risks associated with the process. This is especially true for a hedge fund manager that will not let an investor examine its investment algorithms.

The second way to manage this risk is to "pop the hood" of the hedge fund manager's black box. It is not necessary to read the underlying computer code behind every computer algorithm. Instead, the investor must understand the structure of the algorithms.

First, the investor should determine that different computer algorithms are used to evaluate different financial instruments. As an example, mortgage-backed securities and convertible bonds are affected by different economic variables and pricing dynamics. One computer algorithm size does not fit all of the financial markets.

Second, the investor should determine that the computer algorithm includes all relevant variables. For instance, with respect to convertible bond arbitrage, appropriate economic inputs might be the underlying stock price, the historical volatility, the implied volatility, the current term structure of interest rates, the credit rating of the instrument, the duration of the bond, the convertible strike price, and any call provisions in the bond indenture.

Third, the investor should determine what the computer algorithms attempt to accomplish. Convertible arbitrage funds, for example, build long positions of convertible bonds and then hedge the equity component of the bond by selling the underlying stock or options on that stock. Equity risk can be hedged by selling the appropriate ratio, or "delta," of stock underlying the convertible option. The delta is a measure of the sensitivity of the convertible bond value to movements in the underlying stock, and it changes as the price of the underlying stock changes. Therefore, convertible bond arbitrage algorithms must be designed to measure and track the delta hedge ratio and to provide a signal as to when an existing hedge ratio must be adjusted.

Black boxes are an example of a sophisticated process risk. However, process risk need not be embedded in a computer program, it can also exist with an individual.

In Chapter 4 we also made reference to the recent poor performance of the hedge funds run by George Soros. Mr. Soros had long ago ceded day-to-day investment management of his hedge funds to Stanley Druckenmiller. In the spring of 2000, the *Wall Street Journal* documented the concentrated skill-based investment style of this hedge fund group:

> For years, [Soros Fund Management] fostered an entrepreneurial culture, with a cadre of employees battling wits to persuade Mr. Druckenmiller to invest.
>
> "[Mr. Druckenmiller] didn't scream, but he could be very tough. It could be three days or three weeks of battling it out until he's convinced, or you're defeated."[1]

This is another example of process risk. There is no documented investment process. Instead, there is one person. An investor may be able to document the existence of a person, but not the thought process of that individual. Filtering all information through the brain of one individual raises two issues.

First, the investment process is dependent upon a single person. Should that person leave the hedge fund, the investment process will leave with him. Hedge fund documents often contain a "key person" provision for this reason. If a key investment person leaves or dies, then the investors have the right to withdraw from the hedge fund.

Second, hedge fund investment strategies that are dependent upon one person also lack of transparency. Skill-based investing usually is opaque. There is no way to really tell whether the decisions of the key investment person are quantitatively or qualitatively based.

Investors should accept the fundamental economic risks of the asset classes in which they invest. However, investors are generally unwilling to bear risks that are not fundamental to their tactical and strategic asset allocations.

Process risk is not a fundamental risk. It is an idiosyncratic risk of the hedge fund manager's structure and operations. Generally, it is not a risk that investors wish to bear. Unfortunately, process risk is peculiar to the hedge fund industry because of the industry's "skill-based" nature.

The solution to this problem is diversification. Modern portfolio theory (MPT) teaches us that a diversified basket of stocks will eliminate most, if not all, of the idiosyncratic risk of the individual companies, leaving only market risk to be compensated. Similarly, MPT can be applied to hedge fund investing. Park and Staum[2] and Henker[3] indicate that a portfolio of 15 to 20 hedge fund managers can eliminate up to 95% of the idiosyncratic/process risk associated with hedge fund managers.

---

[1] The *Wall Street Journal*, "Shake-Up Continues at Soros's Hedge-Fund Empire," May 1, 2000, page C1.

[2] James Park and Jeremy Staum, "Fund of Funds Diversification: How Much is Enough?" *The Journal of Alternative Investments* (Winter 1998).

[3] Thomas Henker, "Naive Diversification for Hedge Funds," *The Journal of Alternative Investments* (Winter 1998).

MAPPING RISK

Another issue with hedge fund risk management is that there is no standard platform for measuring risk and no standard format for reporting risk. Different hedge funds map risk differently. For example, hedge fund managers may use different time periods and different confidence levels to measure the value at risk of their portfolios. Consequently, it is difficult to combine the risks of several hedge funds.

A good example of the mapping problem is the work done by Fung and Hsieh[4] and Liang.[5] Both studies attempt to analyze the returns to hedge funds by applying the factor or style analysis conducted by William Sharpe with respect to mutual funds.[6] In his 1992 study, Sharpe compared the returns of mutual funds to the returns from financial asset class indices to determine the amount of variation in mutual fund returns explained by asset class returns. His results indicated that up to 90% of mutual fund returns are explained by asset class returns.

Fung and Hsieh apply Sharpe's style analysis to hedge funds. They find that the amount of variation of hedge fund returns that is explained by financial asset class returns is low; R-square measures were less than 25% for almost half of the hedge funds studied. Fung and Hsieh then apply a principal components analysis based on a hedge fund's trading style. They find that five different trading styles (systems/opportunistic, global/macro, value, systems/trend following, and distressed) explain about 45% of the cross sectional variation in hedge fund returns.

Liang conducts a style analysis similar to Sharpe and finds R-squares in the range of 20% for hedge funds that invest in foreign exchange to 77% for hedge funds that invest in emerging markets.

The point of these studies is that hedge fund returns do not map as well onto standard asset classes as do mutual funds. One reason is the skill-based nature of the hedge fund industry; hedge fund managers tend to hold concentrated portfolios that do not resemble passive indices. Another reason is that hedge funds often invest in derivative instruments that have non-linear payoffs, and non-linear derivative instruments map poorly onto linear (financial) asset classes.

Recall Exhibits 1 and 2 in Chapter 6. In Chapter 6 we compared long-only and hedge fund investment strategies over two dimensions: market risk and credit risk. We demonstrated that hedge fund managers have risk profiles that are different than traditional long-only investments. In particular, many hedge fund strategies take considerable credit risk in their investment strategies, while traditional long-only managers take on market risk. Consequently, the risk analysis applied to long-only managers is not sufficient for hedge fund managers.

---

[4] William Fung and David Hsieh, "Empirical Characteristics of Dynamic Trading Strategies: The Case of Hedge Funds," *Review of Financial Studies*, vol. 10, 1997.

[5] Bing Liang, "On the Performance of Hedge Funds," *Financial Analysts Journal* (July/August 1999).

[6] William Sharpe, "Asset Allocation: Management Style and Performance Measure, *Journal of Portfolio Management*, vol. 18, 1992.

Second, different hedge fund managers have different types of concentrated risk exposure that cannot simply be added to give a total exposure. For instance, equity long/short hedge funds have considerable market risk, but have little credit exposure. Conversely, arbitrage hedge funds, such as convertible arbitrage, have a small market exposure but a large credit exposure. This is because arbitrage funds take small market bets but use leverage (sometimes considerable amounts) to magnify the size of the market bets. Even if they all measured risk in a consistent manner, their risk exposures are sufficiently different such that combining them into one risk statistic would be misleading.

Two solutions to the mapping problem are possible. First, institutions can act as global risk managers. It is the hedge fund manager's responsibility to generate the excess returns, and the investor's job to manage the risks that arise from that investment. This is a macro approach to risk management.

Under this solution, the investor loads each hedge fund manager's risk exposures into her risk management system and determines the risk of her overall portfolio. This solution has the advantage that the investor controls the mapping of the risk exposures rather than the individual hedge fund managers. The difficulty is getting sufficient performance data from the hedge fund manager to be able to measure the manager's exposures accurately.

This may be less difficult than it seems. As a starting point, from Exhibit 2 in Chapter 6, hedge fund managers can be generally classified as those having market exposure and those having credit exposure. Once the primary risk exposure has been identified, this risk can be more finely parsed.

For example, if it is a long/short equity hedge fund, whose primary exposure is market risk, the investor needs to determine in which market sector or segment the manager invests. Then the investor can determine the manager's average net exposure to that market sector or segment. Consider an equity hedge fund manager who is long/short the technology sector. An appropriate measure of the risk for this manager would be her net exposure to a technology index such as the Standard & Poor's Technology Index. Using this benchmark, the investor can determine the beta (market risk) exposure of the hedge fund manager to the technology sector. In addition, the investor can determine whether the hedge fund manager's ability to invest both long and short has provided a return in excess of that provided by the sector benchmark.

As a second solution, the investor could ask for each hedge fund manager's investment positions. This is a micro approach.

Unfortunately, this is problematic for two reasons. First, hedge fund managers are reluctant to reveal their individual investment positions. Hedge fund managers, in general, do not like to disclose their investment positions because these tend to be the manager's proprietary data. The concern is that the distribution of such detailed information might erode the hedge fund manager's competitive edge should this information be inadvertently disclosed.

Another difficulty is that the investor must aggregate all of the individual positions across the several hedge fund programs within its risk management system. This requires a very sophisticated internal risk management system to collect individual hedge fund positions and combine them into reportable risk exposures, not to mention the pragmatic difficulties of having the hedge fund managers transmit their daily positions to the investor.

One possibility is that the hedge fund managers could report this information to a central agent such as a prime broker who could use its risk platform to prepare the risk analysis. However, this would require hedge funds to voluntarily report their positions to a central prime broker who may not be the prime broker for the hedge fund. Unfortunately, this "hearsay reporting," while a theoretical solution, is far from a practical solution. Most hedge funds do not wish to report their daily positions to several prime brokers: their own and those of their clients. Consequently, until hearsay reporting becomes a reality, it is likely that most investors will have to be global risk managers.

TRANSPARENCY RISK

We alluded to transparency risk as an ancillary issue associated with process risk. Transparency is a consistent issue with hedge fund managers because of their unregulated nature. Mutual fund managers, for example, are required under the Investment Company Act of 1940 to present annually a full financial disclosure including a list of their securities holdings. Commodity pool operators and Commodity trading advisors are required under the Commodity Exchange Act to make similar disclosures. Hedge fund managers that operate outside the regulatory jurisdiction of the SEC or the CFTC typically do not provide as complete disclosure as their regulated counterparts.

Hedge funds generally provide an annual financial statement and performance review. However, hedge funds rarely disclose their existing portfolio positions. Without an accounting of their trading and portfolio positions, three issues arise for the investor.

The first is the authenticity of the hedge fund manager's performance. For instance, did an equity long/short manager really earn 10% in the current quarter from stock selection, or did she make market timing bets on the S&P 500 using SPX futures contracts? Without a position report, there is no way to establish the provenance of the hedge fund manager's performance results.

Second, without disclosure of trading and portfolio positions, an investor cannot appropriately monitor and measure the risks of the hedge fund manager. Again, using the example of an equity long/short manager, did the manager earn 10% in the quarter from long/short stock selections in the media sector of the economy as described in the manager's offering memorandum, or did she stray into other sectors?

Third, without transparency, investors cannot aggregate risks across their entire investment program to understand the implications at the portfolio level. It will be difficult for an investor to verify whether the hedge fund managers in her program are making stock selections in the same economic sector, and therefore, compounding their collective risk positions instead of diversifying them.

Hedge fund managers are reluctant to disclose their trading and portfolio positions for several reasons. First, hedge fund managers contend that if they were to disclose their investment positions, other managers might be able to reverse engineer the hedge fund manager's investment strategy. In effect, a snapshot of the hedge fund manager's portfolio might reveal useful investment information to other market participants.

A second concern for hedge fund managers is that if they disclose to the financial markets their investment intentions, they will not be able to execute their trades as advantageously as possible. Essentially, this contention is that other market participants might line up in an attempt to "pick off" the hedge fund manager as she attempts to either establish or unwind her investment portfolio.

In an effort to resolve the competing needs and concerns of investors and hedge fund managers, the International Association of Financial Engineers and the Global Association of Risk Professionals jointly sponsored a Steering Committee on "Hedge Fund Risk Disclosure." This industry committee consists of hedge fund managers, investors, risk management professionals, and prime brokers. The purpose of the Steering Committee is to establish transparency guidelines that will satisfy hedge fund managers and investors alike.

The Steering Committee reached the conclusion that full, daily position reporting by hedge fund managers is not the solution. First, daily position reporting may compromise the hedge fund manager's investment strategy. Second, the vast quantity of position data generated by a hedge fund manager may overwhelm an investor's risk monitoring system.

The Steering Committee concluded that exposure reporting combined with delayed position reporting was sufficient for risk monitoring and management purposes. Exposure reporting is the practice of reporting the risk exposures of the hedge fund manager instead of her individual trading positions. These exposures are known as "risk buckets." It is much more practical to manage risk buckets than it is to manage individual trading positions. In fact, the practice of risk management is to measure and manage the aggregate risk exposures across a diversified portfolio. Risk buckets accomplish this task by identifying the factors that most impact the value of an investment portfolio.

For instance, exposure reporting might indicate the total dollar exposure to each industry or sector in which the hedge fund manager invests. It might also report the top ten investment positions, as well as net market exposure, total long exposure and total short exposure. Exposure reporting might also indicate the amount of leverage in the portfolio as well as the duration and convexity (for a bond portfolio), or beta exposure (for a stock portfolio). Last, exposure reporting might indicate the extent to which the hedge fund manager is exposed to market events (short volatility).

Second, the Steering Committee concluded that position reporting could be reported with a sufficient lag to protect the hedge fund manager's investment strategy. Ninety days, for example, might be a sufficient delay between when a hedge fund manager executes a trade and when the manager reports its positions to an investor. The investor can satisfy itself that the hedge fund manager has not incurred any style drift, while the hedge fund manager is secure in the secrecy of her positions.

RISK MANAGEMENT RISK

Value at risk (VAR) is a statistical method of quantifying a potential risk of loss. VAR can be defined as the maximum loss that can be expected under normal market conditions over a specified time horizon and at a specified level of confidence. For instance, a VAR calculation might determine that, with a 95% level of confidence, the worst loss that a hedge fund manager might incur over one month's trading horizon is $10 million.

VAR calculations are based on several statistical inputs: the level of confidence, the time horizon, the volatility of the underlying asset, and the expected return of the underlying asset. The level of confidence is chosen by the hedge fund manager. For example, a 95% confidence level translates into a 1 in 20 chance of the loss exceeding $10 million. The manager also chooses the time horizon. This might be daily if the risk being monitored is a trading desk, monthly if the risk is a hedge fund performance, or annually for long-only managers.

The volatility and expected return of the underlying asset are determined by historical data. Hedge fund managers might wish to look only at the most recent data, possibly the last 90 trading days, to ensure the most current information regarding the hedge fund manager's return distribution. Alternatively, a hedge fund manager might wish to look at a longer period of time such as a year or more to capture the long-term volatility and expected return associated with her performance.

This short discussion highlights the first risk in VAR. The hedge fund manager has control over three critical variables that underlie the VAR calculation: confidence level, time horizon, and time period over which to measure volatility and expected return. Hedge fund managers will have different time horizons, confidence levels, and measuring period. VAR is not applied consistently across hedge fund managers, and therefore, cannot be properly compared from hedge fund manager to manager.

A second risk is that VAR measures are not additive. VAR is a statistic that measures the likelihood of a loss exceeding a certain threshold dollar amount over a specified period of time. It is a measure of probability that is dependent upon a manager's time horizon, specified confidence level, and asset mix. Given that hedge fund managers may have different time horizons, confidence levels, and asset mixes, VAR measures will vary widely across hedge fund managers. Additionally, different types of hedge fund strategies will have different types of risk exposures.

Exhibit 1: VAR Calculation for Monthly S&P 500 Returns

Time Period: Jan 90 through Dec 99

Expected Monthly Return	1.27%
Standard Deviation of Monthly Returns	3.87%
Expected Return + 1.96 standard deviations	8.85%
Expected Return − 1.96 standard deviations	−6.31%

Exhibit 2: Monthly Returns to the S&P 500: 1990

Month	Return
January	−6.88%
February	0.85%
March	2.43%
April	−2.69%
May	9.25%
June	−0.89%
July	−0.52%
August	−9.43%
September	−5.12%
October	−0.67%
November	5.99%
December	2.48%

Third, VAR is often based on the assumption that the returns to an underlying asset, such as a hedge fund investment, are normally distributed. Under this assumption, VAR considers only the mean and standard deviation of a distribution of returns. However, as we indicated in Chapter 6, the return distributions to hedge fund managers are distinctly non-normal. In particular, most of the hedge fund strategies examined in Chapter 6 demonstrated either considerable kurtosis or skewness, or both. VAR analysis based on the assumption of normality will not capture these additional risk factors.

Fourth, VAR is based on "normal" market conditions (i.e., that market outliers occur infrequently). In fact, outlier events occur more frequently than predicted by a normal distribution of returns. Consequently, VAR calculations based on the assumption may lead to unfortunate surprises.

Consider the S&P 500 over the time period 1990–1999. Exhibit 1 demonstrates the summary statistics and VAR analysis for the monthly return to the S&P 500 over this time period. The expected monthly return was 1.27% and the standard deviation of S&P 500 returns was 3.87%. Under the assumption of normally distributed returns, VAR analysis would say that, with a 97.5% level of confidence, the monthly returns on the S&P 500 should not exceed 1.96 standard deviations from the expected return. Therefore, a VAR of 97.5% confidence interval would predict that the return to the S&P 500 in any given month should not exceed 8.85% or be less than −6.31%. In other words, there is a 1 in 40 chance that the monthly return to the S&P 500 will exceed 8.85% or be less than −6.31%.

Despite the 97.5% confidence level from the VAR analysis, consider the monthly returns to the S&P 500 in the year 1990. Exhibit 2 demonstrates that in 1990, there were three months that exceeded the VAR confidence interval. The months of January, May, and August exceeded the 97.5% confidence interval predicted by VAR. Therefore the "1 in 40" event that should occur only once in every 40 months occurred three times within a space of 12 months. This example simply highlights that the financial markets are uncertain and descriptive statistics such as VAR can only describe, they cannot predict.

Therefore, if VAR is to be used in hedge fund risk management, it must be used with care. First, the VAR calculations of hedge fund managers must be synchronized. An investor should ask its hedge fund managers to use consistent time horizons, confidence levels, and measuring periods.

Second, the VAR calculations of the hedge fund managers cannot be added together to achieve a total VAR for a hedge fund program. However, this is good news because the total VAR for a hedge fund program will be less than the sum of the individual VAR calculations for each hedge fund manager. The reason is that the returns to each hedge fund manager will be less than perfectly correlated with the returns to other hedge fund managers.[7]

The hedge fund managers should be selected so that their investment programs are different from one another. This means that there will be offsetting risks among the hedge fund managers. As a result, the VAR for a hedge fund program will be less than the sum of the VAR calculations for the individual hedge fund managers.

Third, VAR cannot be used to capture the complete risk profile of a hedge fund manager. Additional information will be necessary. In particular, the extent to which a hedge fund manager is short volatility must be determined. In Chapter 6 we demonstrated how arbitrage hedge fund managers mimic a strategy of selling put options. This is a short volatility strategy, and the expected loss from this strategy should be calculated.

Last, the financial markets are anything but normal. Financial events have a way of occurring with greater frequency than expected. One way to compensate for this in a VAR calculation is to increase the confidence level. By specifying a 1 in 100 probability (99% level of confidence) in the VAR calculation, an investor can project a more realistic expectation of the worst loss that might occur. For instance, using our example of the S&P 500, if we had used a 99% confidence level for assessing VAR, only one month in 1990 (August) would have exceeded the confidence range.

DATA RISK

Much of the desire to invest in hedge funds stems from the academic research regarding the performance of this asset class. The empirical studies with respect

---

[7] In fact, the individual VAR calculations would be additive only if the returns to each hedge fund were perfectly correlated.

to hedge funds demonstrate convincingly that hedge funds are a valuable addition to a diversified portfolio. In summary, these studies demonstrate that an allocation to hedge funds can increase the overall return to the portfolio while reducing its risk.[8] However, there are several caveats with respect to these studies.

First, almost all of these studies were conducted during the same, and relatively brief, period of the early to mid 1990s. Given that these studies examined the return behavior of hedge funds during the same time period, it is not surprising that they find consistent performance. Additionally, the fact that they also find consistently positive performance is a tribute to the lack of financial market turmoil during most of the 1990s.

However, the dual punch of the Russian bond crisis and the Long Term Capital Management disaster in 1998 were sufficient to send ripple effects throughout the hedge fund industry. Therefore, prior empirical studies must be taken with a grain of salt. In the last section of this chapter we examine instances of market turmoil to determine how hedge funds operate during troubled times.

A second reason to be skeptical of hedge fund performance data is the inherent biases found in hedge fund databases used in most of the research regarding hedge funds.[9] As a reminder, hedge funds are generally organized as private investment vehicles and do not generally disclose their investment activities to the public. Therefore, many hedge funds do not disclose their performance record to a reporting service in the same way that mutual funds do. A complete performance record of every hedge fund is simply unobtainable.

For example, Liang found that across 16 different hedge fund styles, the highest Sharpe ratio achieved was 1.11 (for merger arbitrage) and the average Sharpe ratio across all hedge funds was 0.36.[10] However, another recent study across 21 hedge funds styles found Sharpe ratios as high as 3.63 (for relative value) with an average Sharpe ratio across all hedge funds of 2.23.[11]

These are large differences. Part of the difference might be explained by time periods that overlapped but were not synchronized (but this would then indicate the time sensitivity of hedge fund returns). However, the more likely explanation is that the two studies used different databases. Therefore, the different results indicate that some portion of performance depends on the database used in the study. Most of the databases that track hedge fund performance did not come into existence until the early 1990s, the starting period for most of the hedge fund research to date. Consequently, the performance of hedge funds prior to 1990 may be lost forever.

There is no complete database of hedge funds. Liang documents that two large hedge fund databases, Hedge Fund Research, Inc. and Tass Management

---

[8] For a more detailed summary of these studies, see our discussion in Chapter 3.

[9] For a thorough discussion on the subject of data biases, see William Fung and David Hsieh, "Hedge Fund Performance Benchmarks: Information Content and Measurement Biases," working paper, Fuqua School of Business, Duke University, May 2000.

[10] See Liang, "On the Performance of Hedge Funds."

[11] See Andrew Lo, "Risk Management for Hedge Funds: An Introduction and Overview," working paper, MIT Sloan School of Management, April 2000.

Ltd., have only 465 hedge funds in common in their respective databases.[12] This overlap represents 40% of the HFR database and only 28.5% of the Tass database. Consequently, it is not possible to observe the full universe of hedge funds.

Within this imperfect framework there are three data biases that can affect the reported performance of hedge funds. The first is survivorship bias. Survivorship bias arises when a database of hedge funds includes only surviving hedge funds. Those hedge funds that have ceased operations may be excluded from the database. This leads to an upward bias in performance reporting because presumably, those hedge funds that ceased operations performed poorly. In other words, only the good hedge funds survive, and their positive performance adds an upward bias to the reported financial returns.

In addition, the database may be biased downwards in risk relative to the universe of all hedge funds because those hedge funds that ceased operations may have had more volatile returns (the cause for their demise). Survivorship bias is a natural result of the way the hedge fund industry (or any new financial industry) evolved. Databases were not developed until sufficient interest by the academic and institutional community rendered such a service necessary. By that time, many hedge funds that had started and failed were never recorded.

Survivorship bias has been documented in the mutual fund industry. One way to measure this bias is to obtain the population of all funds that operated during a certain period. The average return of all funds operating during that period is compared to the average return generated by the funds in existence at the end of the period. The difference is the amount of survivorship bias.[13]

The amount of survivorship bias in the hedge fund industry has been estimated at 2% to 3% per year.[14] This is the amount of upward bias reflected in the returns reported to a hedge fund database if not corrected for hedge funds that ceased operations. Clearly, this is a very large bias that, if not corrected, can provide misleading conclusions about the investment benefits of hedge funds.

Survivorship bias is all the more important in the hedge fund industry compared to the mutual fund industry because of the high turnover rate. It has been estimated that the average life of a hedge fund is about three years and that the yearly attrition rate is greater than 15%.[15] Consequently, hedge funds cease

---

[12] Bing Liang, "Hedge Funds: The Living and the Dead," *Journal of Financial and Quantitative Analysis*, (September 2000), pp. 309–326.

[13] See Burton Malkiel, "Returns from Investing in Equity Mutual Funds 1971 to 1991," *Journal of Finance*, 1995.

[14] See Fung and Hsieh, "Performance Characteristics of Hedge Funds and Commodity Funds: Natural versus Spurious Biases;" and Stephen Brown, William Goetzmann, and Roger Ibbotson, "Offshore Hedge Funds: Survival and Performance, 1989–1995," *Journal of Business*, 1999; and Liang, "Hedge Funds: The Living and the Dead."

[15] See Franklin Edwards and Jimmy Liew, "Hedge Funds versus Managed Futures as Asset Classes," *The Journal of Derivatives* (Summer 1999); and James Park, Stephen Brown, and William Goetzmann, "Performance Benchmarks and Survivorship Bias for Hedge Funds and Commodity Trading Advisors," *Hedge Fund News* (August 1999).

operations with great frequency, and this should be expected to exacerbate the survivorship problem.

Ackermann, McEnally, and Ravenscraft, however, find no systematic bias in their study of hedge funds.[16] Specifically, they find that there are competing forces in survivorship bias: termination bias and self-selection bias. Some funds stop reporting their information because they terminate their operations while other funds stop reporting their performance because they have become so successful that it is no longer in their best interests to publicly report their performance.

A second bias affecting hedge fund performance results is selection bias. Generally, those hedge funds that are performing well have an incentive to report their results to a database in order to attract new investors into the fund. This would result in hedge funds included in the database having better performance than those that are excluded because of their (presumably) poor performance.

A process known as "backfilling" further magnifies this selection bias. When a database adds a hedge fund's historical performance to its pool of funds, it "backfills" the hedge fund's performance to the date it began operations. This creates an instant history of hedge fund returns. Because a hedge fund manager holds the option of when to reveal her historical performance, it is reasonable to expect that she will disclose the performance when her results look most favorable. This leads to an upward bias in performance results within the hedge fund database. To eliminate a backfill bias, it has been estimated that the first 12 to 24 months of reported data should be eliminated from a hedge fund manager's performance history.

There is a converse to the selection bias. It is also possible that those hedge funds that are very successful have no incentive to report their performance to a database because they have already attracted a sufficient number of investors to their fund. This would lead to a downward bias of hedge fund performance reported by the databases. Ackermann, McEnally, and Ravenscraft find that selection bias is offset with no impact on hedge fund reported performance, while Fung and Hsieh find that selection bias adds approximately 1.4% to reported hedge fund returns.[17]

Finally, a third bias is called "catastrophe" or "liquidation" bias. This bias arises from the fact that hedge funds that are performing poorly and likely to cease operations stop reporting their performance before they actually close shop. A hedge fund that is performing poorly and likely to go out of business has no incentive to continue to report its performance. Indeed, the hedge fund probably has greater issues to deal with such as liquidating positions to fund customer redemptions than reporting its performance.

---

[16] See Carl Ackermann, Richard McEnally, and David Ravenscraft, "The Performance of Hedge Funds: Risk, Return, and Incentives," *The Journal of Finance* (June 1999), pp. 833–874.

[17] See William Fung and David Hsieh, "Performance Characteristics of Hedge Funds and Commodity Funds: Natural versus Spurious Biases," *The Journal of Financial and Quantitative Analysis*, 2000; and Ackermann, McEnally, and Ravenscraft, "The Performance of Hedge Funds: Risk, Return, and Incentives."

Exhibit 3: Biases Associated with Hedge Fund Data

Bias	Park, Brown, and Goetzmann	Brown, Goetzmann, and Ibbotson	Fung and Hsieh	Ackermann, McEnally, and Ravenscraft
Survivorship	2.6%	3%	3%	No impact
Selection	1.9%	Not estimated	1.4%	No impact
Catastrophe	Not estimated	Not estimated	Not estimated	0.7%
Total	4.5%	3%	4.4%	0.7%

Sources: James Park, Stephen Brown, and William Goetzmann, "Performance Benchmarks and Survivorship Bias for Hedge Funds and Commodity Trading Advisors," *Hedge Fund News* (August 1999); Stephen Brown, William Goetzmann, and Roger Ibbotson, "Offshore Hedge Funds: Survival and Performance, 1989–1995," *Journal of Business*, 1999; William Fung and David Hsieh, "Performance Characteristics of Hedge Funds and Commodity Funds: Natural versus Spurious Biases," *The Journal of Financial and Quantitative Analysis*, 2000; and, Carl Ackermann, Richard McEnally, and David Ravenscraft, "The Performance of Hedge Funds: Risk, Return, and Incentives," *The Journal of Finance* (June 1999), pp. 833–874.

Catastrophe bias results in an upward bias in returns and a downward bias in risk because poor performance history is excluded from the data bias. Ackermann, McEnally, and Ravenscraft attempted to measure this bias by contacting hedge fund managers directly to determine their return performance subsequent to the termination of reporting. Their study measures the impact of liquidation bias to be approximately 70 basis points.

As Exhibit 3 demonstrates, the combination of survivorship and selection bias can add up to 450 basis points in hedge fund returns before the impact of catastrophe bias is considered. As a consequence, it is safe to say that studies of hedge funds, if not properly discounted for inherent data biases, will inflate the returns to hedge funds.

In summary, there are several biases that are embedded in the historical returns to hedge funds. These biases tend to increase the returns to hedge fund performance. This creates the risk of inflated expectations with regard to the performance of hedge funds.

Every hedge fund disclosure document contains the language: "Past Performance is no indication of future results." This is all the more apparent when considering the data biases associated with historical hedge fund performance.

PERFORMANCE MEASUREMENT RISK

The Sharpe ratio is the statistic most often used to compare the performance of two investment managers. It is a measure of risk-adjusted returns. It divides the performance of an investment manager in excess of the risk-free rate by the standard deviation of that manager's performance results. Its purpose is to provide a basis to compare the performance of different managers that may invest in different financial assets.

However, there are some practical difficulties with using a Sharpe ratio analysis to compare hedge fund returns. As previously indicated, many hedge funds use derivatives with non-linear payoff structures as part of their investment plan. These non-linear instruments can lead to misleading Sharpe ratio conclusions.

In Chapter 6, we demonstrated that many hedge fund managers have investment styles that contain a short option exposure. When a hedge fund manager shorts/sells an option, she collects the option premium. If the option expires worthless, the hedge fund manager pockets the option premium at no cost and can thereby increase her total return.

Selling options results in an asymmetric payoff profile. The upside potential is limited to the option premium collected, while the downside can be quite large depending on the size of the market event. As we indicated in Chapter 6, this type of strategy is similar to selling insurance contracts against a decline in the financial markets.

Short options exposure also helps to boost a manager's Sharpe ratio because the hedge fund manager collects the option premium and deposits it in a cash account with low volatility. The result is high total return with low (apparent) risk. Portfolio optimization techniques will tend to over-allocate to these hedge fund managers because of their high total return and Sharpe ratio and the fact that the risk inherent in short option positions did not manifest itself during the hedge fund manager's short operating history.

This over-allocation process is sometimes referred to as a "short volatility bias," and it is a dangerous trap for unaware investors.[18] Hedge fund managers using a short volatility strategy can pump up their returns with low risk in the short run by collecting option premiums. Selling options is just like selling insurance: Premiums continue to be collected and invested in short-term cash instruments until some catastrophe hits the financial markets and the options are exercised just like an insurance policy. This strategy will work until a hedge fund manager experiences a "volatility event."

To the extent that risk-adjusted returns are inflated through the short selling of options, portfolio optimizers will tend to over-allocate to those strategies. Yet, allocating to these hedge fund managers will increase portfolio risk rather than reduce it because the portfolio has now increased its exposure to a financial market catastrophe event.

The trap is that hedge fund managers can boost their short-term risk-adjusted performance through a short volatility strategy only to increase their exposure to a volatility event. Portfolio optimizers base their selections only on patent risk, the volatility of the hedge fund manager's returns to date. However, optimizers do not incorporate latent risk (i.e., the risk of a volatility event).

To highlight this problem, consider the following example. A hedge fund manager accepts a $1,000,000 investment from a pension fund and invests this

---

[18] See Andrew Weisman and Jerome Abernathy, "The Danger of Historical Hedge Fund Data," working paper, 1999.

money in 6-month U.S. Treasury bills. In addition, at the beginning of every month, the hedge fund manager sells fairly priced out-of-the-money call options and out-of-the-money put options on the S&P 500 that will expire at the end of the month. (This type of option strategy is known as a "strangle.") The strike prices are chosen to be 2.5 standard deviations away from the current market price. The hedge fund manager invests the option premiums received in U.S. Treasury bills. The hedge fund manager writes enough of these options to generate a return equal to 1.5 times that of the risk-free rate.

Since a 2.5 standard deviation event occurs only about 1% of the time, the manager has a 99% chance of outperforming the risk-free rate in any one month. In other words, it would take a "one in one hundred" type market event to trigger the exercise of the options in any given month. This means that a volatility event is expected once about every eight years (100 months divided by 12). A volatility event occurs when the S&P 500 trades outside the 2.5 standard deviation range of the put/call option strangle.

In the meantime, the manager collects the option premiums and produces impressive Sharpe ratios. In addition, a sufficient track record is established that can be fed into an optimizer resulting in the selection of the hedge fund manager. This hedge fund house of cards will come tumbling down, however, when the market turns against this short volatility investment strategy. The large short option exposure will result in a large negative cumulative return for the hedge fund manager that will wipe out most of the hedge fund manager's prior gains.

Let's put some actual numbers on this. For simplicity, we will assume that the U.S. Treasury bill rate stays constant at 6% a year. Using monthly data from 1995 through 1999, we find that the monthly standard deviation of the S&P 500 Index is about 4%. Therefore, a 2.5 standard deviation move up or down means that the S&P 500 would have to increase or decrease by more than 10% for the put/call option strangle to be exercised against the hedge fund manager.

Option pricing simulation shows that a 10% out-of-the-money option strangle on the S&P 500 would cost about $7.50 per strangle. The goal of the hedge fund manager is to collect enough option premiums each month to generate a rate of return that is 150% greater than the Treasury-bill rate. Therefore, each month, the hedge fund manager must leverage her invested capital by selling enough strangles so that her return on invested capital is 9% or 1.5 times the Treasury bill rate of 6%.

As an example, assume that in the first month the hedge fund manager receives $1,000,000 from her client which she invests for 1 month at 9%. This would generate an end of period total of ($1,000,000) × (1.0075) = $1,007,500. The catch is that the manager invests the money in U.S. Treasury bills earning 6%. Therefore, the hedge fund manager must sell enough put/call strangles and take in enough option premium so as to generate a total return equal to $1,007,500. The calculation is:

$$(\$1,000,000 + \text{option premiums}) \times (1 + 0.06/12) = \$1,007,500$$

The amount of option premiums is $2,487. At an expected cost of $7.50, the hedge fund manager must sell 331 put/call strangles to generate a return of 9%.

This strategy will work until a volatility event occurs and the expected loss of capital results. At that point, the S&P 500 will move by more than the 10% limit (2.5 standard deviations) so that the strangle will be exercised. Also, as the size of the investment increases, the hedge fund manager must sell more and more options to maintain the 9% return.

We performed a Monte Carlo Simulation to determine how long it would take for a volatility event to occur. We estimate our parameters over a 60-month period of January 1995 through December 1999. Running 5,000 simulations, our model estimated that it would take 80 months (almost seven years) for the options to be exercised against the hedge fund manager. This is a little less than we predicted initially for our "1 in 100" event. Our simulation indicated that a volatility event could occur as early as the first month and take as long as 237 months. Additionally, we used a conservative estimate that the option is in the money by 10 S&P 500 points when exercised.

Exhibit 4 demonstrates what happens when the manager employs this strategy. It works fine for the first almost seven years. Then a volatility event occurs and the options are exercised against the portfolio manager. The exercise of the options does not wipe out all of the manager's gains, but it does eliminate a good portion. In the end, the manager is left with an effective annual return of 2.85%, well below that of U.S. Treasury bills.

Exhibit 4: Short Volatility Investment Strategy

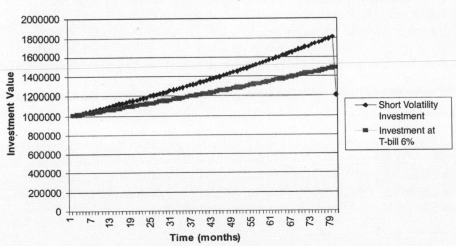

Exhibit 5: Performance Statistics for Short Volatility Investment Strategy

	Pre-Volatility Event	Post-Volatility Event
Average Annual Return	9%	2.85%
Excess Return	3%	−3.15%
Standard Deviation	0.42%	3.71%
Sharpe Ratio	7.14	−0.85

Exhibit 5 shows the returns and Sharpe ratios generated by the hedge fund manager before the volatility event and after the volatility event. As can be seen, the hedge fund manager looks like a star before the volatility event, but is unmasked once the event occurs. Unfortunately, before the volatility event is reached, the hedge fund manager can achieve a stellar track record. The low volatility associated with Treasury bill returns allows the hedge fund manager to achieve a large, positive Sharpe ratio before the volatility event occurs.

The volatility event, however, not only decreases the total return of the investment strategy, it also increases the volatility of the hedge fund manager's returns. In the month that the options are exercised against the hedge fund manager, the hedge fund earns a −33% return. This severe decline in one month causes the volatility of the hedge fund manager's returns to jump from 0.42% to 3.71%. Therefore, the volatility event reveals the latent risk associated with the hedge fund manager's strategy.

The above example may seem extreme, but at least one well-known hedge fund manager employed this strategy (and lost). Victor Niederhoffer was a well-known trader and author of a successful book: *The Education of a Speculator*. Dr. Niederhoffer, generally considered to be an excellent investor and savvy trader, earned a doctorate from the University of Chicago Graduate School of Business. He built trading programs based on statistical analysis. After analyzing stock market returns over many prior years, Dr. Niederhoffer believed that the stock market would never fall by more than 5% on any given day. He put this idea to work by selling out-of-the-money put options on stock index futures. His strategy worked successfully for several years. In fact, he was able to generate a 20% compound annual return.[19] However, his investment strategy eventually hit a "volatility event."

On October 27, 1997, the S&P 500 declined by 7%. The put options that Victor Niederhoffer had sold increased in value dramatically, and he was faced with a margin call of $50 million from his prime brokers. Unable to meet the margin call, his brokers liquidated his trading positions and wiped out his hedge fund portfolio. He was forced to close his hedge fund door.

---

[19] See David Segal, "Market's Crash Destroys Trader: A Risky Bet Brings Down a Millionaire Money Manager," The *Washington Post* (November 17, 1997), p. A1.

Curiously, Mr. Niederhoffer's analysis did not include (or, even more curious, chose to ignore) the history of the market crash on October 19, 1987. On that day, the S&P 500 declined by 20%.[20]

The above simulation and the history of Dr. Niederhoffer highlight the problems associated with the short selling of options. Short volatility positions can increase performance of the hedge fund manager, but they expose the hedge fund to large downside risk should a volatility event occur.

Unfortunately, there is no simple solution for this problem but there are some practical suggestions. First, hedge fund managers with short track records and high Sharpe ratios should be scrutinized carefully. They may not have experienced a volatility event sufficient to damage their performance history. It is possible that selecting managers based on their history of risk-adjusted returns may in fact be a negative selection process if their trading history is too short.

Second, this gets to the age-old issue with respect to the hedge fund industry: transparency. Just what is the hedge fund manager doing? How is she generating her excess performance? To what extent does she use options (particularly, short options) in her trading strategies? In Chapter 5 we included these questions as part of our due diligence process.

Last, new analytical tools are needed. Risk-adjusted ratios were developed for the linear investment world of traditional long-only investment managers and mutual funds. Additional analysis is needed to account for the non-linear investment strategies employed by many hedge funds.

EVENT RISK

Hedge funds, by their very name are supposed to hedge the risk and return profile of a diversified portfolio. Indeed many, if not most, hedge fund managers claim that their return distributions are "skill-based;" that is, returns are not readily identifiable with the returns to financial asset classes. This argument is the source for the additional claim that hedge funds are "total return" or "absolute return" investments, for which no benchmark is appropriate. The lack of an identifiable benchmark for a hedge fund would indicate that hedge fund returns are independent of financial market returns.

In addition, we would also expect the returns to hedge funds to be independent of each other. Again, this stems from the skill-based, absolute return claim of hedge fund managers. If hedge fund returns are truly skill-based, not only should they be independent of the returns in the financial markets, but also their returns should be uncorrelated with each other. Benchmarks would be inappropriate.

We put these claims to the test by conducting an event analysis. The third quarter of 1998 saw two serious financial events that added considerable turmoil to

---

[20] The history of Victor Niederhoffer's trading strategy is documented in Philippe Jorion, "Risk Management Lessons Learned from Long Term Capital Management," working paper (2000).

the financial markets. First, in August 1998, The Russian government defaulted on its outstanding treasury bonds. Credit spreads on all types of debt widened significantly relative to U.S. Treasury bonds, and liquidity in many debt markets was reduced. It is this type of financial turmoil that hedge funds are expected to hedge. If hedge fund managers truly generate returns through pure skill, such economic events should have very little impact on the distribution of returns from hedge funds.

Second, in September of 1998, Long Term Capital Management (LTCM) of Greenwich, Connecticut, one of the best known and largest of the hedge fund managers, almost collapsed. A consortium of commercial and investment banks, acting in consultation with the Federal Reserve Bank of New York, fearing the possible reverberations in the financial markets, injected $3.6 billion of fresh capital into LTCM. Again, if hedge fund managers derive their returns from pure skill, their returns should be independent of each other, and events such as LTCM, should have very little impact on their return distribution.

First, we examine the returns to hedge funds in the month of August 1998. Again, if hedge funds returns are generated independent of the financial markets, we would expect to see their returns unaffected by the Russian bond crisis during this time. Second, we examine the returns to hedge funds in the month of September 1998. If hedge funds offer skill-based returns independent of each other, we should expect to see no impact on their performance from the near demise of LTCM.

We use the data from the Hedge Fund Research Inc. hedge fund indices. We examine the same hedge fund styles that were examined in Chapter 6. Using data from 1990 through 1998 we conducted an event analysis.

Economists and other financial researchers often ask the question, What is the impact of an economic event on the value of a financial asset? Under the principle of efficient capital markets, the effect of the event should be reflected immediately in the asset value. Therefore, the economic impact of the event can be measured using asset prices over a short interval of time.

The objective of an event study is to measure the difference between the actual returns observed with respect to an investment and the returns that are expected to occur in the absence of the observed event. The difference between the actual returns observed and those expected is called the "abnormal" or "excess" return. The excess returns are observed around the event date, and conclusions are drawn as to whether the event had a significant impact on an asset class.[21]

We focus on two event months, August and September 1998. These two months should capture much of the turmoil caused by the Russian bond default and the LTCM near-collapse. We acknowledge that these two events are intertwined. For instance, the Russian bond debacle resulted in widening credit spreads that caused spillover effects on LTCM's positions even though this hedge fund did not own any Russian Bonds. To capture the interconnected nature of these two events, we also measure the combined excess return of August and September 1998.

---

[21] For a review of event studies and their application to hedge funds, see Mark Anson, "Financial Market Dislocations and Hedge Fund Returns," working paper (2001).

Exhibit 6: Hedge Fund Excess Returns

Strategy	Aug-98	T Stat	Sep-98	T Stat	Aug-Sept	T Stat
Equity L/S	−9.37%	−4.37	1.44%	0.67	−7.93%	−2.62
Global Macro	−5.46%	−2.00	−2.26%	−0.83	−7.73%	−2.00
Short Selling	18.98%	3.54	−4.60%	−0.86	14.38%	1.90
Convertible Arb	−4.11%	−4.37	−1.99%	−2.11	−6.10%	−4.58
Merger Arbitrage	−6.73%	−5.33	0.70%	0.56	−6.03%	−3.38
Fixed Income Arb	−2.16%	−1.93	−7.43%	−6.63	−9.59%	−6.05
Relative Value	−7.03%	−6.82	−1.04%	−1.01	−8.06%	−5.53
Event Driven	−10.34%	−6.08	−2.06%	−1.21	−12.40%	−5.16
Market Neutral	−2.63%	−3.30	−0.15%	−0.19	−2.78%	−2.47
Market Timing	−0.44%	−0.25	−1.49%	−0.87	−1.92%	−0.79
S&P 500	−15.70%	−4.46	5.12%	1.45	−10.58%	−2.13
High Yield	−8.31%	−4.22	0.53%	0.27	−7.78%	−2.79
U.S. Treasury	2.00%	1.60	2.10%	1.68	4.11%	2.32

Exhibit 6 presents the results of our analysis.[22] For each hedge fund style, we present the excess returns for August and September 1998. We also present the t-statistics associated with these two event months. Student t-statistics greater than or equal to, in absolute value, 1.68, 1.97, and 2.3 are significant at the 10%, 5%, and 1% level of confidence, respectively. Last, we present the cumulative excess return for the two-month event period of August and September 1998 combined.

For comparison, in Exhibit 6 we also present the excess returns associated with large-cap stocks, high-yield bonds, and U.S. Treasury bonds. We include these traditional asset classes to determine how they reacted to the Russian bond default and the LTCM crisis.

As might be expected, both large-cap stocks and high-yield bonds were significantly negatively impacted by the Russian bond default. Also, there was a flight to quality as indicated by the positive excess returns earned by U.S. Treasury bonds during this time period. In addition, large-cap stocks quickly recovered in September while high-yield bonds suffered only a one-month decline in August. Last, the two-month event period is significantly negative for large-cap stocks and high-yield bonds, but significantly positive for U.S. Treasury bonds.

In Exhibit 6 the t-statistic for all hedge fund styles is statistically negative at the 1% level for August 1998 except for short sellers and market timers. Short sellers earned significantly positive excess returns during this time period, while market timers show no demonstrable impact. Our first conclusion is that, except for short sellers and market timers, hedge funds did not offer significant diversification benefits during this market event, and were, in fact, affected by the same turmoil that impacted the traditional financial markets. Even market neutral hedge funds demonstrated significantly negative excess returns.

---

[22] For each hedge fund style we use the 102 months of data prior to August 1998 to calculate the mean and standard deviation of the index.

With respect to the near disaster of LTCM, the results are mixed. Some hedge fund strategies demonstrate significant negative excess returns in September 1998, while others are insignificant. However, when we examine the two-month event period, we find the cumulative excess returns to be significantly negative for all hedge fund strategies except for short sellers and market timers.

Several lessons can be gleaned from this analysis. First, many of the mispricing (arbitrage) opportunities that hedge funds attempt to capture can require an investment horizon of several months or greater. Additionally, arbitrage strategies generally make the assumption of normal liquidity. However, when that liquidity dried up as a result of the Russian bond default, many of mispricing relationships increased instead of decreasing, thus creating large, temporary paper losses. This situation was further exacerbated by margin calls from prime brokers which forced some hedge fund managers to liquidate their positions and turned paper losses into realized losses.

Second, many lending institutions that provided liquidity to hedge funds were themselves invested in the same markets and under pressure to manage their own risk exposures. These institutions were unable to provide liquidity to the market at the time hedge fund managers needed it the most.

Finally, hedge fund manager received redemption calls from their investors during this period. This forced hedge fund managers to liquidate positions to fund their customer's redemption requests. Hedge fund managers were faced with a liquidity mismatch between the investment horizon of their arbitrage strategies and the investment horizon of their investors. This is similar to a mismatch between the duration of an institution's liabilities and assets. Pension funds and banks long ago learned the lessons of immunization, but hedge fund managers were forced to learn this lesson the hard way in 1998.

In conclusion, what this event analysis demonstrates is that hedge fund returns are influenced by the same financial market dislocations as traditional asset classes. An absence of liquidity in the financial markets can have the same impact on hedge fund managers as it does for long-only managers. A hedge fund manager may have all of its economic risks appropriately balanced or hedged only to be caught in a liquidity crisis. This is all the more exacerbated to the extent that a hedge fund manager invests in less liquid financial markets or custom-tailored derivative transactions.

SUMMARY

The hedge fund industry has received tremendous attention over the past decade as an alternative investment strategy to hedge traditional portfolio returns. However, as a new investment strategy, there are new risks that bear consideration. In this chapter we presented seven risk factors associated with hedge fund investments that must be considered in addition to the market exposures received. These seven factors do not diminish the value of hedge fund investments, but they are useful for developing realistic expectations with respect to the value added of hedge funds in a diversified portfolio.

Chapter 8

Regulation of Hedge Funds

In prior chapters we have mentioned briefly the unregulated waters in which hedge funds operate. In this chapter we review the relevant regulatory authorities and consider what jurisdiction they have over hedge fund managers. While we will try to keep this chapter as brief as possible, brevity is not the hallmark of the laws that regulate the financial industry. The securities and commodities laws can be both arcane and tedious.[1]

Further, the debate continues as to whether hedge funds should be regulated. There is no convenient answer to this question, but its pertinence has increased in the wake of Long Term Capital Management. We will attempt to address this issue at the end of the chapter.

We begin the chapter with a review of the federal securities laws and their application to hedge funds. Specifically, we examine how these laws apply to the sale of hedge fund limited partnership units as well as how hedge funds are classified within the securities law framework. We then consider the regulations of the Commodity Exchange Act and their application to hedge fund managers. Last, we review several initiatives that were born in the wake of the Long Term Capital Management bailout.

THE SECURITIES ACT OF 1933

The Securities Act of 1933 (the "1933 Act") was born out of the Great Depression. With the collapse of the stock market in 1929 and the economic depression that followed, Congress sought to make the financial markets a safer place for investors. The 1933 Act was enacted to regulate the initial sale of securities to investors.

Prior to the 1933 Act, the initial sale of securities to investors was unregulated. Legitimate corporations and partnerships as well as scam artists could produce an offering document with misleading and material misstatements contained therein. Furthermore, there was no central authority to review offering documents before they were distributed to investors. As a consequence, investor sentiment in the stock market hit bottom.

Enacted almost 70 years ago, the Securities Act of 1933 continues to this day essentially in its original form. We highlight two key provisions of the 1933 Act that apply to hedge funds. First, the general law of the 1933 Act is that there

---

[1] This is one reason why hedge fund attorneys are well paid: They are trained to master the arcane and the tedious.

can be no sale of any security without a registration statement filed with the Securities and Exchange Commission (SEC). Second, there are exceptions to the general rule, of which hedge fund managers may take advantage.

The Initial Sale of Securities

Section 5(a) of the 1933 Act states:

> Unless a registration statement is in effect as to a security, it shall be unlawful for any person, directly or indirectly:
>
> (1) To make use of any means or instruments of transportation or communication in interstate commerce or of the mails to sell such security through the use or medium of any prospectus or otherwise; or
> (2) To carry or cause to be carried through the mails or in interstate commerce, by any means or instruments of transportation, any security for the purposes of sale or delivery after sale.

First, notice that the 1933 Act applies to the sale of a security. Hedge fund managers might argue that the offering of limited partnership units in a hedge fund is not a sale of a security. However, under Section 2(a)(1), the 1933 Act defined the term broadly:

> The term "security" means any note, stock, treasury stock, bond, debenture, evidence of indebtedness, certificate of interest or participation in any profit-sharing agreement, collateral-trust certificate, preorganization certificate or subscription, transferable share, investment contract, voting-trust certificate, certificate of deposit for a security, fractional undivided interest in oil, gas or other mineral rights...

Clearly, the purchase of limited partnership units in a hedge fund may be classified as a "certificate of interest or participation in any profit-sharing agreement." Consequently, hedge fund managers fall within the jurisdiction of Section 5(a).

As an aside, notice how broad the regulatory language is. We provided only a portion of the language of Section 2(a)(1). The lengths to which Congress went to define a security indicates that they intended the term to be construed as broadly as possible, and the courts have implemented this intent. Additionally, in Section 5(a), the phrase "to make use of any means or instruments of transportation or communication in interstate commerce or of the mails" is just as applicable today to the internet and Federal Express as it was to the telegraph and the U.S. postal service in 1933.

Section 5(a) sets out that before a public sale of securities can be made, a registration statement must be effective. This registration statement must be filed with the SEC for its review. The form and content of the registration statement is further spelled out in the 1933 Act.[2] The SEC will review the registration statement and return it with comments. The comments must be addressed in amendments ("pre-effective" amendments) that are filed to the original registration statement. Depending upon the comments and questions raised by the SEC, several pre-effective amendments might be required.

Finally, when all of the SEC's comments and questions are satisfied and all material information is properly disclosed, the SEC will declare a registration statement "effective." This is a key point. It is a violation of the 1933 Act to say that the SEC has "approved" the registration statement. This might mislead investors to believe that the SEC has approved the merits of the investment securities being offered. Consequently, the SEC never "approves" a registration statement; it merely informs the registrant that it has no further issues and that the registration statement is now "effective."

Once effective, a registration statement is called a prospectus, and it is good for one year. If a registrant wishes to sell securities after one year, it must file a post-effective amendment to update the current prospectus. The post-effective amendment will go through the same review process as the original registration statement.[3]

As the above discussion indicates, the registration process can be long and legally intensive. Yet most hedge funds manage to avoid it. There are two ways.

The first is simple: Avoid the jurisdiction of the SEC. This is accomplished by operating an "off-shore" hedge fund. Off-shore hedge funds are organized in a jurisdiction outside of the United States in places such as Bermuda or the Cayman Islands. In addition, these off-shore funds sell their limited partnership interests to non-U.S. investors. By operating outside of the borders of the United States, and by selling their limited partnership interests to non-U.S. investors, hedge funds can avoid the registration requirements of the SEC.

The second way to avoid the lengthy registration process is to find an exemption from registration within the 1933 Act. These "safe harbors" are listed in Section 4 of the 1933 Act. Specifically, Section 4(2) of the 1933 Act states that:

> The provisions of Section 5 shall not apply to: Transactions by an issuer not involving a public offering.

In summary, if a hedge fund manager can avoid a "public offering" of its limited partnership units, it may forego the lengthy registration process. This is what is meant by a "private offering." It is any sale of a security that is not done as part of a public offering where a registration statement must be filed.

---

[2] The 1933 Act spells out several types of registration statements that may be submitted. For example, an S-1 registration statement must be filed with the SEC for an initial public offering of a security. Given the first time offering of the security, an S-1 registration statement requires the greatest disclosure. However, for secondary offerings, less disclosure is required, and short form registration statements may be filed.

[3] Mutual funds, for example, continually sell units in their fund year after year. Consequently, each year, every mutual fund must file a post-effective amendment to its original prospectus to keep the sale of its mutual fund units current.

Congress enacted Section 4(2) to provide relief from the lengthy registration process when the likelihood that the public would benefit from this process was remote. Issuers, like hedge funds, can rely on the Section 4(2) exemption if they make private offerings to investors who are either sophisticated investors or institutional investors. Generally these type of non-public offerings fall within Regulation D.

Regulation D

Under the 1933 Act, Congress has provided issuers with ready-made safe harbors from the registration requirements. The most often-used are "The Rules Governing the Limited Offer and Sale of Securities Without Registration under the Securities Act of 1933." These rules are universally known as "Regulation D."

Under Regulation D, a hedge fund must file a Notice of Sale with the SEC within 15 days of the first sale made of hedge fund units. Additionally, there are two important rules that must be followed: Rule 506 and Rule 501.

Rule 506 is titled "Exemption for Limited Offers and Sales Without Regard to Dollar Amount of the Offering." It states:

(a) *Exemption*. Offers and sales of securities by an issuer that satisfy the conditions in paragraph (b) of this rule shall be deemed to be transactions not involving any public offering within the meaning of Section 4(2) of the [1933] Act.

(b) *Conditions to be Met*. (1) *General Conditions*. To qualify for an exemption under this rule, offers and sales must satisfy all terms and conditions of Rules 501 and 502. (2) *Specific Conditions*. (i) *Limitation on the Number of Purchasers*. There are no more than, or the issuer reasonably believes that there are no more than 35 purchasers of securities from the issuer in any offering under this rule. (ii) *Nature of Purchasers*. Each purchaser who is not an accredited investor either alone or with his purchaser representative has such knowledge and experience in financial and business matters that he is reasonably capable of evaluating the merits and risks of the prospective investment, or the issuer reasonably believes immediately prior to making any sale that such purchaser comes within this description.

Rule 501 provides terms and definitions for the other rules contained in Regulation D (including Rule 506). Two key provisions apply. First, under Rule 501(e):

Calculation of Number of Investors. For purposes of calculating the number of purchasers under Rule 506(b), the following shall apply: (1) The following purchasers shall be excluded: (iv) any accredited investor.

Therefore, under Rule 506 (b) and Rule 501(e), a hedge fund manager can sell her limited partnership units to an unlimited number of accredited investors, and to no more than 35 non-accredited investors.

The second important provision is Rule 501(a) that defines the term "accredited investor." This rule provides a laundry list of what constitutes an accredited investor. Essentially, the definition includes any large institutional investor or organization, provided that it was not formed for the specific purpose of acquiring the securities offered and that it has total assets in excess of $5,000,000. With respect to individuals, an accredited investor is defined as:

> Any natural person whose individual net worth, or joint net worth with that person's spouse, at the time of his purchase exceeds $1,000,000; or

> Any natural person who had an individual income in excess of $200,000 in each of the two most recent years or joint income with that person's spouse in excess of $300,000 in each of those years and has a reasonable expectation of reaching the same income level in the current year.

In summary, "high net worth" individuals under Rule 501 must have a net worth in excess of $1,000,000 or make $200,000 a year ($300,000 if they include their spouse). The high net worth test is particularly important for the hedge fund industry, because family offices and wealthy investors have been the mainstay investor of the hedge fund industry for years.

In Exhibit 1 we provide a flowchart for how hedge fund managers navigate the waters of the 1933 Act. A hedge fund manager has three choices. She can file a registration statement with the SEC to sell limited partnership interests in her hedge fund, she can take advantage of the ready-made safe harbors under Regulation D, or she can take her hedge fund off-shore. Most hedge fund managers follow the second choice; they take advantage of the provisions of Regulation D and sell only to accredited investors. Other hedge fund managers simply move off-shore and find non-U.S. clients. Very few hedge fund managers take the time to go through a full SEC registration process.

One last important point needs to be made with respect to the 1933 Act. Regulation D is explicit that it serves only as a safe harbor from the registration requirements of the 1933 Act, but it is not a safe harbor from the anti-fraud provisions of the 1933 Act. In fact, there is no safe harbor from the anti-fraud provisions of the 1933 Act. Section 17 of the 1933 Act states that:

> (a) It shall be unlawful for any person in the offer or sale of any securities by the use of any means or instruments of transportation or communication in interstate commerce or by the use of the mails, directly or indirectly:

> (1) To employ any device, scheme, or artifice to defraud, or

(2) To obtain money or property by means of any untrue statement of a material fact or omission to state a material fact necessary in order to make the statements made, in light of the circumstances under which they were made, not misleading, or

(3) To engage in any transaction, practice, or course of business which operates or would operate as a fraud or deceit upon the purchaser.

Exhibit 1: The Securities Act of 1933

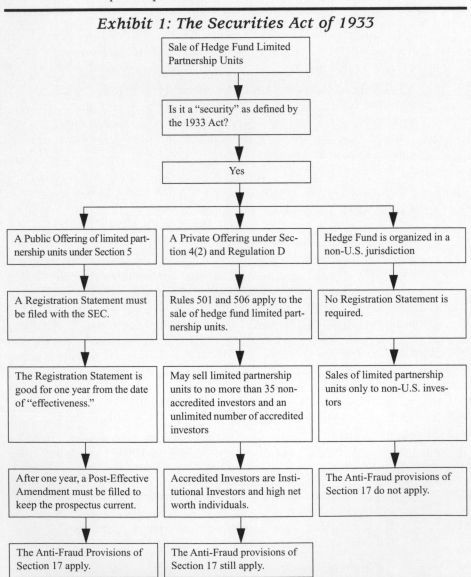

Section 17 of the 1933 Act is applicable to a hedge fund manager whether she offers her limited partnership units for sale in a public or private offering. Even if the hedge fund manager avails herself of Regulation D, the SEC will have jurisdiction over the hedge fund manager, and may prosecute the hedge fund manager for any material misstatement or failure to disclose a material fact in the sale of limited partnership units.

The anti-fraud provisions of Section 17 do not apply, however, to an off-shore fund selling to non-U.S. investors. The reason is that Section 17 was designed to protect investors domiciled in the United States. Also, the hedge fund manager has no base of operations in the United States over which the SEC could assert jurisdiction.

THE SECURITIES EXCHANGE ACT OF 1934

The Securities Exchange Act of 1934 (the "1934 Act") addressed several important issues. First, it created the Securities and Exchange Commission. Recall under Section 5 of the 1933 Act, a public sale of securities requires a registration statement to be filed. Unfortunately, the 1933 Act did not address to whom or where registration statements should be sent. The 1934 Act clarified this process by establishing the SEC.

Second, the 1934 Act imposed rules and regulations on the behavior and conduct of broker-dealers. Many brokers failed during the Great Depression from lack of capital, while others closed their doors because they were "fly by night" operations. The 1934 Act ensures that all broker-dealers are properly registered with the SEC, that they maintain adequate capital for times of market stress, that they file periodic financial reports with the SEC, and that they conduct their business within the rules and regulations of a central authority.[4]

Third, the 1934 Act established rules and regulations regarding the secondary trading of issued securities. It is the secondary trading of securities that has implications for the hedge fund industry.

Limited partnership units in a hedge fund may be transferred from an existing limited partner to a new limited partner. While the hedge fund partnership agreement may have conditions on this transfer, this is still a secondary sale of securities.

When the hedge fund manager sells the limited partnership units to the initial investors, this is considered a *primary offering* or *initial public offering* of securities. Primary offerings and IPOs are governed by the 1933 Act. However, the offer or sale of securities that were previously distributed in an IPO is covered by the 1934 Act.

---

[4] The SEC has delegated a portion of its authority to the National Association of Securities Dealers, Inc. to define the industry standard of conduct for broker-dealers.

Rule 10b-5

The 1934 Act applies to resales of limited partnership interests by the investors in the hedge fund, rather than the hedge fund manager. In particular, all secondary sales of limited partnership interests in a hedge fund are subject to Rule 10b-5: *Employment of Manipulative and Deceptive Devices.*

Rule 10b-5 states:

> It shall be unlawful for any person, directly or indirectly, by the use of any means or instrumentality of interstate commerce, or of the mails, or of any facility of any national securities exchange:
>
> (1) To employ any device, scheme, or artifice to defraud,
> (2) To make any untrue statement of a material fact or to omit to state a material fact necessary in order to make the statements made, in light of the circumstances under which they were made, not misleading, or
> (3) To engage in any act, practice, or course of business which operates or would operate as a fraud or deceit upon any persons,
>
> in connection with the purchase or sale of any security.

Notice that the language of Rule 10b-5 parallels the anti-fraud language in Section 17 of the 1933 Act. Congress ensured that the same anti-fraud standard applies for the secondary sale of securities as well as for initial public offerings.

Rule 10b-5 is sometimes known as the "Insider Trading Rule." One of its purposes is to prevent corporate insiders, people who know more about a corporation's prospects and business, from taking advantage of outsiders by way of their superior knowledge about the company in question. However, this rule is general enough to capture any secondary sale of securities where one party is in possession of material non-public information and uses this non-public information to its advantage.

For instance, a limited partner in a hedge fund might be aware that the hedge fund manager is about to be indicted on criminal charges, but this information has not been publicly announced. This is material non-public information, and the limited partner must disclose it to prospective buyers if he intends to sell his limited partnership interests. Conversely, the hedge fund manager would need to disclose this information only if she intends to sell new limited partnership interests to either existing or new limited partners.

THE INVESTMENT COMPANY ACT OF 1940

The Investment Company Act of 1940 (the "Company Act") was designed to regulate investment pools. Today, this act primarily regulates the mutual fund industry. Mutual funds are investment companies for purposes of the Company Act and the SEC.

Under Section 3(a) of the Company Act, an investment company:

Means any issuer which is or holds itself out as being engaged primarily, or proposes to engage primarily, in the business of investing, reinvesting, or trading in securities.

While this definition clearly incorporates mutual funds, it is also broad enough to encompass hedge funds. Hedge funds are investment companies for purposes of the Company Act. Falling within the jurisdiction of the Company Act means that hedge funds must adhere to the same registration requirements under Section 8 of the Company Act as do mutual funds.[5] Fortunately, the Company Act also provides two ready-made safe harbors of which hedge fund managers may take advantage.

First, Section 3(c)(1) of the Company Act states, in part:

Notwithstanding subsection 3(a), none of the following persons is an investment company within the meaning of this title:

(1) Any issuer whose outstanding securities (other than short-term paper) are beneficially owned by not more than one hundred persons and which is not making and does not presently propose to make a public offering of its securities.

"3(c)(1) funds," as they are known, can be offered to any type of investor, sophisticated and unsophisticated, accredited and non-accredited, provided that the hedge fund manager does not allow more than 100 investors into the fund. For smaller hedge fund managers, the 100 person limit should not be an issue. For larger hedge funds, however, that wish to attract additional capital, the 100 person limit may prove binding.

In 1996, Congress added a new paragraph 7 to Section 3(c) of the Company Act. This paragraph recognizes that an investment pool might contain many investors that are sophisticated, and consequently, might not need the oversight of the SEC. Section 3(c)(7) states, in part, that the following entity will not fall within the meaning of an investment company:

Any issuer, the outstanding securities of which are owned exclusively by persons who, at the time of acquisition of such securities, are qualified purchasers, and which is not making and does not at that time propose to make a public offering of such securities.

This new type of fund is often referred to as a "3(c)(7) fund," and it is designed for sophisticated investors. Prior to the introduction of Section 3(c)(7), hedge funds

---

[5] Even if a hedge fund failed to register with the SEC as an investment company, it would still be subject to the SEC jurisdiction under Section 7, *Transactions by Unregistered Investment Companies*. This section of the Company Act allows the SEC to assert jurisdiction over an investment company even if it has not registered with the SEC.

were limited to accepting no more than 100 investors in their fund. Any more than that, and they would have to register with the SEC as an investment company.[6] Section 3(c)(7) removes this limit and provides more flexibility for hedge fund managers.

The term "qualified purchaser" was introduced in the 1996 amendment to the Company Act. This term means:

(1) any natural person (including any person who holds a joint account, community property or other similar shared ownership interest in an issuer with that person's qualified spouse) who owns not less than $5,000,000 in investments;

(2) any company that owns not less than $5,000,000 in investments and that is owned directly or indirectly by or for 2 or more natural persons who are not related as siblings or spouse (including former spouse), or direct lineal descendants by birth or adoption, spouses of such persons, the estates of such persons, or foundations, charitable organizations, or trusts established by or for the benefit of such persons;

(3) any trust that is not covered by clause (2) and that was not formed for the specific purpose of acquiring the securities offered, as to which the trustee or other person authorized to make decisions with respect to the trust, and each settlor or other person who has contributed assets to the trust, is a person described in clause (1), (2), or (4); or

(4) any person, acting for its own account or the accounts of other qualified purchasers, who in the aggregate owns and invests on a discretionary basis, not less than $25,000,000 in investments.

Therefore, 3(c)(7) funds cater only to the very wealthy (with investments — not net worth — of at least $5,000,000) as well as endowments, pension plans, trust companies, and other investment organizations.

It is often stated that Section 3(c)(7) limits hedge funds to no more than 499 investors. This is not true; Section 3(c)(7) imposes no such limit. However, there is another practical limit established by Section 12 of the 1934 Act (Registration Requirements for Securities). Specifically, under Section 12(g)(1)(A)&(B) any issuer who is engaged in interstate commerce must register its securities with the SEC in a registration statement within a certain period of time after the issuer achieves $1,000,000 in total assets and has a class of equity security held of record by 500 or more persons.[7] Therefore, hedge fund managers that apply the Section 3(c)(7) safe harbor limit the number of investors in their fund to 499.

---

[6] An existing 3(c)(1) fund can become a 3(c)(7) fund providing it notifies its existing investors that future investors will be limited to qualified purchasers, and that it provides existing investors in the fund with an opportunity to redeem their interests in the hedge fund. See Section 3(c)(7)(B)(ii)(I)&(II).

[7] This is another way attorneys earn their keep. There is no cross reference between Sections 3(c)(7) of the Company Act and Section 12(g) of the 1934 Act.

Exhibit 2: The Investment Company Act of 1940

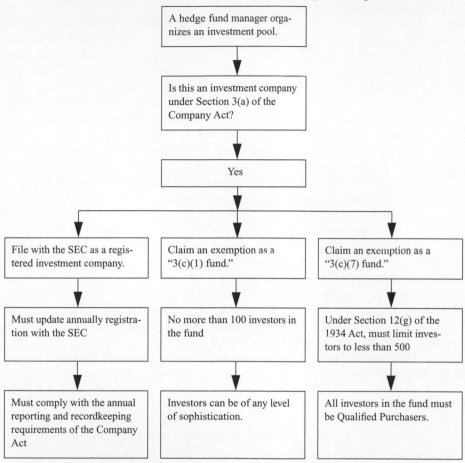

In Exhibit 2, we provide a review of the Company Act. We can see that a hedge fund manager has three choices. She can register the hedge fund as an investment company under Section 3(a) of the Company Act, however, this will expose the hedge fund to the same reporting, disclosure, and record keeping requirements of a typical mutual fund.

Alternatively, the hedge fund manager can take advantage of the exemptions under Sections 3(c)(1) or 3(c)(7). Under 3(c)(1), the hedge fund manager cannot accept more than 100 investors in the hedge fund. The trade-off is that investors can be of any level of sophistication. Under Section 3(c)(7), the hedge fund manager can have an unlimited number of investors in the hedge fund (practically limited to 499 persons by Section 12(g) of the 1934 Act). But, in return, 3(c)(7) investors must have large investment portfolios or be large institutional investors.

THE INVESTMENT ADVISERS ACT OF 1940

In the same breath that created the Company Act, Congress also established the Investment Advisers Act of 1940 (the "Advisers Act"). The purpose of the Advisers Act is to regulate those individuals that provide investment advice to investment companies, pension plans, endowments, and other individuals. Under the Advisers Act, an investment adviser is defined, in part, as:

> Investment adviser means any person who, for compensation, engages in the business of advising others, either directly or indirectly or through publications and writings, as to the value of securities or as to the advisability of investing in, purchasing, or selling securities, or who, for compensation as part of a regular business, issues or promulgates analyses or reports concerning securities...

This definition is broad enough to include hedge fund managers. For example, the Advisers Act does not address the issue of long or short investing. Instead, it addresses the business of giving advice on the value of securities, good or bad. Long or short investing is the investment adviser's strategy. Once again, this broad language is sufficient to include hedge fund managers within the federal securities laws. Section 203(a) of the Advisers Act requires investment advisers as defined above to register with the SEC.

Fortunately, Congress once again provided exceptions to the general rule. First, there is the small adviser exception. Section 203A (1) states:

> No investment adviser that is regulated or required to be regulated as an investment adviser in the state in which it maintains its principal office and place of business shall register under Section 203, unless the investment adviser (A) has assets under management of not less than $25,000,000; or (B) is an adviser to an investment company registered under Title I of this Act.

In other words, if the investment adviser does not manage assets greater than $24,999,999 and is not an investment adviser to a mutual fund, then it does not need to register with the SEC.

Second, there is the limited client exception. Under Section 203(b)(3) of the Advisers Act, the registration requirements of Section 203(a) do not apply to:

> Any investment adviser who during the course of the preceding 12 months has had fewer than 15 clients and who neither holds himself out generally to the public as an investment adviser nor acts as an investment adviser to any investment company registered under Title 1 of this Act.

For purposes of counting the number of people that an investment adviser advises, Section 203(b) provides that each hedge fund counts as one client no matter how many investors there may be in the hedge fund.[8] Therefore, for a hedge fund manager that only advises one or a small group of hedge funds, it is easy to stay within this exception. However, a growing phenomenon in the hedge fund industry is the management of separate accounts.

A separate account is an investment account for a single investor. More and more investors are asking for separate accounts because of the transparency that it provides. While a hedge fund manager may be reluctant to provide all of her positions contained within a hedge fund for many investors, she may be more willing to provide full transparency for an individual account. The reason is that the damage to a separate account from a breach of confidentiality will lay solely at the investor's feet. Should an investor in a separate account reveal the hedge fund manager's positions to the market, the investor will be harming only himself.

The growth of separate accounts may force a hedge fund manager to register as an investment adviser. Each separate account counts as one full "person," equivalent in counting status to one hedge fund for purposes of the Advisers Act. Therefore, most hedge fund managers that accept separate accounts have registered as an investment adviser. Registration as an investment adviser requires the hedge fund manager to file an annual disclosure form (Form ADV) with the SEC.

Finally, the anti-fraud provisions of Section 206 of the Advisers Act apply to all investment advisers whether registered or exempt. Essentially, it is illegal for any investment adviser to employ any scheme, to engage in any transaction, or to engage in any course of action which is fraudulent, deceptive, or manipulative.

Exhibit 3 demonstrates the choices for a hedge fund manager under the Advisers Act.

THE COMMODITY EXCHANGE ACT

The Commodity Exchange Act (the "CEA") was promulgated by Congress in 1974. The CEA accomplished two major goals. First, it established the Commodity Futures Trading Commission as the regulatory authority for the futures industry including the futures exchanges. Second, it established disclosure, record keeping, and reporting rules for commodity pool operators (CPOs), commodity trading advisors (CTAs), futures commission merchants (FCMs), and introducing brokers. It is the rules that regulate CPOs that are most pertinent to hedge fund managers.

---

[8] The key to counting the hedge fund as only one client is to manage the hedge fund in accordance with the terms of the limited partnership agreement or other organization document. In this way, the hedge fund manager is advising only the hedge fund and not its individual investors.

Exhibit 3: The Investment Advisers Act of 1940

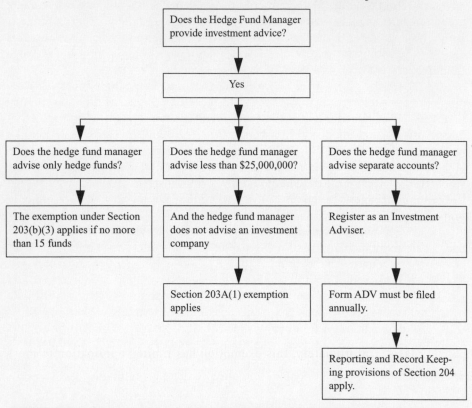

CPOs are a subset of the hedge fund universe. These are hedge fund managers who invest primarily in commodity futures contracts. We will discuss their strategies in the section on commodities investing. For now, we are concerned with their regulation.

Section 1.3(cc) of the CEA defines a CPO as:

Any person engaged in a business which is of the nature of an investment trust, syndicate, or similar form of enterprise, and who, in connection therewith, solicits, accepts, or receives from others, funds, securities, or property, either directly or indirectly or through capital contributions, the sale of stock or other forms of securities, or otherwise, for the purpose of trading in any commodity for future delivery or commodity option on or subject to the rules of any contract market, but does not include such persons not within the intent of this definition as the Commission may specify by rule or regulation or order.

In summary, any person who collects money from other individuals for the purpose of investing the money collectively in the commodity futures markets is a commodity pool operator.

If a hedge fund manager is a CPO under the definition of Section 1.3(cc), she must register with the CFTC[9] and the National Futures Association under Sections 4(m) and 4(n) and Rule 3.10.

Once registered, a CPO must obey the disclosure document requirements of Sections 4.21 and 4.24, the reporting requirements of Section 4.22, the record keeping requirements of section 4.23, and the performance disclosures of Section 4.25 of the CEA. These sections collectively detail the type of information the CPO must disclose to prospective investors in its offering documents, the financial information that it must present to existing investors in their Account Statements, and the format for presenting performance results in disclosure documents and annual reports. Last, the CPO must keep detailed books and records for the CFTC to audit.

However, as we have seen with respect to the regulation of the financial markets, Congress provided several exemptions from registering as a CPO. The CEA provides three safe harbors for CPOs.

First, under Section 4.5 certain entities are excluded from the definition of the term CPO. These include investment companies registered under the Investment Company Act of 1940, insurance companies, banks, trust companies, ERISA plans, other pension plans, and employee welfare plans. Section 4.5 is meant to exclude any entity that is regulated under another federal law such as the federal securities laws, the Employee Retirement Income Security Act, or federal banking laws. Unfortunately, this exemption has limited application to most hedge funds because they are not otherwise regulated by another federal agency.

To claim an exemption under Section 4.5, an entity must file a notice of eligibility with the CFTC. As part of the notice, the entity must represent that it will use commodity futures or commodity options contracts solely for bona fide hedging purposes.

Second, under Section 4.13, there are two safe harbors. First, Section 4.13(a) exempts a commodity pool operator from registration if: (1) she receives no compensation from operating the pool, (2) she operates only one pool, (3) she does not advertise the pool, and (4) she is not otherwise required to register with the CFTC. Second, section 4.13(b) exempts a CPO from registration if: (1) the total capital contributions received for all pools does not exceed $200,000 and (2) there are no more than 15 participants in any pool. Section 4.13 is meant to apply to the small CPO, most likely someone whose primary business is not managing a commodity pool. It is unlikely to apply to a hedge fund manager whose livelihood depends on receiving income from the pool.

Last, there is Section 4.7. This is the section most applicable to CPO/ hedge fund managers. This section is directed at entities whose primary business

---

[9] All registrations for Commodity Pool Operators as well as other business associated with the futures industry are filed with the National Futures Association. The NFA is the designated self-regulatory authority for the futures industry, and the CFTC has delegated the registration requirements to the NFA.

is managing a commodity pool. Section 4.7 does not exempt a CPO from register-ing with the CFTC and the NFA and filing annual reports thereto. However, it does exempt the CPO from the disclosure, reporting, and record keeping require-ments of Sections 4.21–4.25. The catch is that the CPO must sell its pool interests only to "Qualified Eligible Participants" (QEPs). Additionally the CPO must file a Claim for Exemption with the CFTC.

Section 4.7 provides a long laundry list of the standard types of institu-tional investors that qualify as a QEPs. These include banks, FCMs, broker-dealers, trusts, other CPOs and commodity trading advisors, insurance companies, invest-ment companies, and pension plans. In addition there is a test for individuals.

For individual investors, the CFTC chose to the use the same require-ments for an accredited investor (See Regulation D, above) but with an extra kicker. The accredited investor must also own securities with an aggregate market value of $2,000,000, or the investor must have had on deposit with a futures com-mission merchant within the last six months $200,000 in initial margin and option premiums for futures contracts and options thereon. Therefore, it is not enough for an accredited investor to have a high net worth or high earning potential, he must also have an existing investment portfolio worth at least $2 million or be actively involved in the futures markets (as demonstrated by his futures account activity).

Despite these three registration exemptions, the anti-fraud provisions of the CEA still apply. Section 6 of the CEA states, in part:

> It shall be unlawful for a commodity trading advisor, associated
> person of a commodity trading advisor, commodity pool operator,
> or associated person of a commodity pool operator, by use of the
> mails or any means or instrumentality of interstate commerce,
> directly or indirectly (A) to employ any device, scheme, or arti-
> fice to defraud any client or participant or prospective client or
> participant; or (B) to engage in any transaction, practice, or course
> of business which operates as a fraud or deceit upon any client or
> participant or prospective client or participant.

In conclusion, there are several ways for hedge funds to avoid either reg-istration as a CPO, or the disclosure, record keeping, and reporting requirements for CPOs. These paths are diagrammed in Exhibit 4. However, no matter which path a hedge fund manager might choose, she cannot avoid the anti-fraud section of the CEA.

THE PRESIDENT'S WORKING GROUP
ON FINANCIAL MARKETS

In the wake of the Long Term Capital Management (LTCM) bailout, a working group (the Working Group) was appointed by President Clinton to review the cir-cumstances that led up to the rescue of LTCM. The Working Group was spearheaded by Robert Rubin, Secretary of the Treasury; Arthur Levitt, Chairman of the SEC; Alan Greenspan, Chairman of the Federal Reserve System; and, Brooksley Born, Chairperson of the CFTC. This group produced a report titled "Hedge Funds, Leverage, and the Lessons of Long-Term Capital Management."[10]

Exhibit 4: The Commodity Exchange Act and Rules

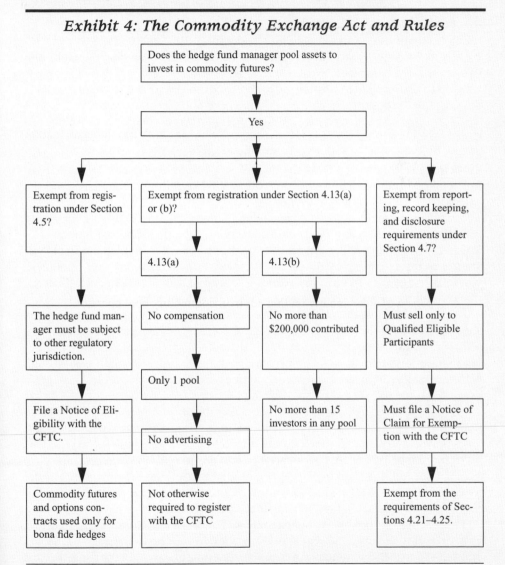

---

[10] See the President's Working Group on Financial Markets, "Hedge Funds, Leverage, and the Lessons of Long-Term Capital Management," April 28, 1999. Other participants in the working group included the Council of Economic Advisers, the Federal Deposit Insurance Corporation, the National Economic Council, the Federal Reserve Bank of New York, the Office of the Comptroller of the Currency, and the Office of Thrift Supervision.

The principal policy arising out of the events surrounding the LTCM episode regards how to constrain excessive leverage. As we previously discussed in Chapter 2, LTCM used massive amounts of leverage and had a leverage ratio in excess of 100 to 1. The concern was that extreme amounts of leverage concentrated with one investor can increase the likelihood of a general breakdown in the functioning of the financial markets.

To put LTCM's leverage into perspective, at the end of 1998, it had $1.5 trillion in derivative positions. In contrast, the six largest commercial banks and two investment banks combined had over $1 trillion of notional derivative positions.[11] LTCM had approximately 50% greater exposure to derivative instruments than the total exposure of eight large commercial and investment banks.

Yet, LTCM, and any hedge fund for that matter, cannot achieve significant leverage without the extension of credit by commercial and investment banks. Therefore, these financial institutions must take some of the blame/credit for helping to create the LTCM situation. The Working Group concluded that the financial institutions that extended credit to LTCM did not fully understand the extent to which LTCM was leveraged.

Consequently, one set of recommendations made by the Working Group was directed not at hedge funds but squarely at large financial institutions. The Working Group stated that financial institutions needed to implement improved standards for extending credit so that their own financial safety and soundness would be enhanced. In turn, the Working Group expected that financial institutions would then impose greater discipline on their borrowers.

Specifically, the Working Group concluded that financial institutions should establish procedures to measure and monitor counterparty risk exposure, set limits on credit exposure to any one institution, establish procedures for ongoing monitoring of credit quality, develop programs to mitigate credit risk through collateral calls, implement valuation practices for derivatives, and last, integrate credit risks and market risks.

In summary, the Working Group asked banks and other financial institutions to strengthen the risk management practices with respect to credit-based services provided to major counterparties in the derivatives and securities markets. This set of recommendations can be summarized into one rule: Know your customer.

Second, the Working Group concluded that the existing authority of the SEC, CFTC, and the Treasury Department should be expanded to monitor the risks posed by these market participants and the highly leveraged hedge fund counterparties that are their counterparties. The Working Group suggested that one method to enhance the regulatory overview would be to increase the SEC's and CFTC's risk assessment authority to include expanded reporting, record keeping, and examination of unregulated affiliates of broker dealers and future commission brokers. Many broker-dealers and FCMs form holding companies that are not registered either with the SEC or the CFTC, and these holding compa-

---

[11] Id.

nies transact in swaps and other OTC derivatives with hedge funds. Because they are not registered with any regulatory authority, these holding companies can transact outside the radar screen of the SEC, CFTC, and the Treasury Department. In addition, the Working Group recommended that these three regulators be granted the authority to require broker-dealers, FCMs, and their unregulated affiliates to report credit risk information by counterparty.

Last, the Working Group made two recommendations with respect to hedge funds. First, the Working Group recommended more frequent and meaningful disclosures by hedge funds. Specifically, the Working Group indicated that there should be improved transparency for hedge fund reporting, and pointed to the reporting requirements for CPOs as a possible standard for hedge funds.[12]

Second, the Working Group recommended that a group of hedge funds should draft and publish a set of sound risk management practices. It suggested that such practices should address the measurement of market risk, liquidity risk, stress testing, collateral management, internal controls, identification of position concentration, and frequent marking to market of trading positions and collateral. Last, the Working Group suggested that hedge funds should assess their performance against the sound practices for investors and counterparties.

THE GROUP OF FIVE HEDGE FUNDS

In February 2000, a group of five large hedge funds responded to the President's Working Group on Financial Markets.[13] Not surprisingly, this group of five of the largest hedge funds stopped short of endorsing any regulatory change to the hedge fund industry. However, it did conclude that hedge fund managers should work with regulators and counterparties to develop a broad consensus approach to public disclosure. Further, the Group of Five made several recommendations regarding the management of market risk, credit risk, and liquidity risk.

With respect to market risk, the Group of Five recommended that hedge fund managers should measure their aggregate market risk for each hedge fund portfolio as well as the relevant sub-components of the portfolio. These sub-components could be monitored by geographic region, industry sector, investment strategy, asset class, or by type of instrument used.

Additionally, the Group of Five recommended that hedge fund managers should perform stress tests to determine how potential changes in market conditions could impact the market risk of the hedge fund portfolio. Last, the Group of Five recommended that hedge fund managers should validate their market risk models via regular back testing on historical data.

---

[12] See Mark Anson, "Performance Presentation Standards: Which Rules Apply When?" *Financial Analysts Journal* (March/April 2001).

[13] The Group of Five consisted of Caxton Corporation, Kingdon Capital Management, LLC, Moore Capital Management, Inc., Soros Fund Management LLC, and Tudor Investment Corporation.

With respect to credit risk, the Group of Five recommended that hedge fund managers should establish policies and procedures to manage the Fund's exposure to potential defaults by trading counterparties. Specifically, hedge fund managers should identify acceptable counterparties based on a reasonable analysis of their credit worthiness and then set appropriate exposure limits. In addition the Group of Five recommended that hedge fund managers should seek to establish appropriate collateral provisions and other forms of credit support in their counterparty agreements.

These recommendations on credit risk mirror those made by the President's Working Group. Perhaps the clearest lesson learned from LTCM is the need for monitoring, measuring, and managing counterparty credit exposure.

Finally, liquidity risk is critical to a hedge fund manager's ability to continue trading in times of stress. During periods of financial market dislocations, a hedge fund manager may be faced with both margin calls from its brokers as well as redemption requests from its investors. As LTCM demonstrated, liquidity risk can have a devastating impact on performance.

The Group of Five recommended that hedge fund managers perform a liquidity analysis of their hedge fund portfolios. This analysis should take into account the investment strategies employed, the terms governing the rights of investors to redeem their partnership interests, and the liquidity of the assets in the portfolio. The Group of Five also suggested that hedge fund managers assess their cash and borrowing capacity under the worst historical drawdown for the fund as well as for stressed market conditions (when margin calls are frequent). Last, the Group of Five recommended that hedge fund managers should forecast their liquidity requirements and potential changes to liquidity measures.

While this report provided a clear set of risk management guidelines for the hedge fund industry, it may not become an industry standard for two reasons. First, the recommendations made by the Group of Five were at "the high end of what a risk management program should be."[14] The Group of Five consisted of five of the largest hedge fund managers in existence. Their recommendations may not be adopted by smaller hedge funds in the industry.

Second, none of the five hedge funds that sponsored the report pledged to adopt the recommendations. Although many of the practices recommended had been adopted by at least one member of the Group of Five, not all of the recommendations have been adopted by all of the members. Therefore, consistency of risk disclosure and risk management, even among the largest in the hedge fund industry, remains an issue.

CURRENT LEGISLATIVE INITIATIVES

In November 1999 Congressmen Edward Markey (House Democrat, Massachusetts) and Byron Dorgan (Senate Democrat, North Dakota) introduced the Deriva-

---

[14] See Mitchell Pacelle, "Five Hedge Funds' Report on Industry Stops Short of Call for New Regulation," The *Wall Street Journal* (February 8, 2000), p. c21.

tives Market Reform Act. The bill seeks to force public reporting by hedge funds and a group of family of funds with more than $1 billion in assets.

The act would require unregistered hedge funds with more than $1 billion under management to file reports quarterly with the SEC. These reports would include a statement of financial condition, income, cash flow, changes in equity, and a description of the models and methodologies the fund uses to assess and evaluate market risk. The bill would also give the SEC the power to regulate the disclosure of derivative positions, sudden changes in net asset value, and hedge fund leverage ratios.

The two Congressmen have pressed for hearings before the House Commerce Committee and the Senate Banking Committee. However, the bill has not yet found its way to the House or Senate floor for a vote.

A competing bill was introduced by Richard Baker, the chair of the House Banking subcommittee on Capital Markets. Dubbed the "Baker Bill," it targets hedge fund managers with $3 billion or more in assets under management or a group of family of funds with more than $20 billion in assets. The Baker Bill would require hedge fund managers that meet this criteria to file quarterly reports with the Federal Reserve System.

One criticism of the Baker Bill is that it might have a limited influence because only about 25 hedge fund managers, out of the approximately 3,000 plus universe, meet the threshold requirement of $3 billion of assets under management.[15] Nonetheless, the Baker Bill has passed through the House subcommittee. However, the bill has not been accepted for review by the Senate Banking Committee, and consequently, it remains bogged down at the committee level. Unfortunately, this leaves regulators and hedge funds alike speculating about what will be the next step in the regulatory road. At the time of this chapter, all that can be said is that the hedge fund industry is taking a "wait and see" approach.

CONCLUSION

This brief overview on the regulation of the hedge fund industry is meant to demonstrate the regulatory quagmire through which a hedge fund manager must navigate. For example, under the 1933 Act, we have a class of investors called "Accredited Investors," while under the Company Act we have "Qualified Purchasers," and under the CEA we have "Qualified Eligible Participants." Did we mention at the beginning of the chapter that the laws regulating the financial markets were arcane?

Nonetheless, there are several points to highlight. First, the laws of the financial markets can be confusing. Smart hedge fund legal counsel is an important component of a hedge fund's success.

---

[15] See Jamey Coddling, "Regulation Afoot?" *Futures* (May 1, 2000).

Second, within every piece of federal legislation are safe harbors that hedge fund managers have been quick to turn to their advantage. However, it is the use of these safe harbors that have led many pundits to claim that hedge funds are "unregulated." Yet these safe harbors generally provide that the hedge fund manager must contract only with sophisticated investors. The general public remains protected under the federal laws of the financial markets.

Third, even though hedge fund managers may take advantage of many of these safe harbors, the anti-fraud provisions of the federal laws still apply to hedge fund managers. Therefore, although they may avoid the registration, disclosure, record keeping, and reporting requirements of the securities and commodities laws, hedge fund managers are still on the hook for the most serious offenses: fraud, deceit, material misstatements, and failure to disclose material information.

Finally, the regulatory landscape for hedge funds remains uncertain. The President's Working Group on Financial Markets called for greater oversight of hedge funds. However, the Group of Five hedge funds countered that they could effectively police their own risk management practices. Nonetheless, legislation has been introduced into Congress calling for regulatory control of hedge funds. As of this writing, this regulation has yet to find its way out of committee status and to the floor of Congress for a vote.

Chapter 9

Should Hedge Funds Be Institutionalized?*

We conclude this section on hedge funds with a topic currently under debate in the investment world. Over the past decade, hedge funds have attracted increasing interest from institutional investors. The advent of institutions into the hedge fund world inevitably begs the question of whether hedge funds should be "institutionalized." However, while many people talk about institutionalization, few truly understand what it means.

Additionally, there may be pitfalls to this way of thinking. For example, in a penal sense, the term "institutionalize" refers to punishment that has been meted out through incarceration in a penitentiary. If hedge fund managers are to be institutionalized, we must consider what crimes they may have committed.

We begin this chapter by defining exactly what is meant by "institutionalization." We then consider whether the punishment fits the crime. Last we consider some consequences regarding the potential impact of institutionalization.

WHAT DOES "INSTITUTIONALIZATION" MEAN?

"Institutionalization" means three things. First, it means transparency. Second, it means a process. Third, it means relative returns.

Transparency

As a general rule, investors like transparency. This is particularly important for pension funds and endowment funds that are governed by a board of directors. The format and structure of these institutions is such that they must be able to "pop the hood" on any transaction to reveal in a clear and understandable manner the inner workings of the investment.

Unfortunately, transparency is another term that everyone talks about, but few really understand. For instance, some investors claim that they require complete "position" transparency. In other words, they demand to know every position that the hedge fund manager currently has outstanding. This is often done in the belief that more information is better than less.

Yet, this level of detailed information can overwhelm an investor. For instance, the President's Working Group on Financial Markets reported that Long

---

* This chapter was previously published in a substantially similar form in the *Journal of Investing*.

Term Capital Management had over 60,000 trading positions on its books.[1] Few investors, institutional or otherwise, have the capacity to digest this amount of information in a coherent manner. To be able to comprehend the information embedded in 60,000 trading position, the investor would need a trading and risk management system as sophisticated as LTCM's.

Furthermore, in the world of relative value arbitrage (LTCM's investment strategy) these positions can change dramatically in the course of a day's trading. Turnover is high, and the demand for position transparency would place a large reporting burden on the hedge fund manager as well as a risk management burden on the investor. Most investors simply do not have risk management systems sufficiently sophisticated to digest this dynamic pool of information.

Still, it is important to know the risks of a hedge fund manager. A solution to the information issue is "exposure" transparency. In this format, the hedge fund manager does not reveal her individual positions, but instead discloses her major risk components by sector, asset class, type of security, geographic location, etc.

Another issue is the format in which to present the information. In Chapter 8 we discussed how the Group of Five large hedge fund managers presented their best efforts at monitoring and controlling risk. However, these five hedge fund managers were not uniform in their acceptance of the risk management policies presented or how to disclose this information to their investors. Therefore, even among influential leaders in the hedge fund industry, transparency can have very different meanings.

In addition, there is the problem that many hedge fund managers have total discretion to invest in any market that they choose. In this instance, the issue of transparency is more subtle. Transparency should apply not only to a hedge fund manager's investment portfolio, but also to her investment strategy. Consider the following language from a hedge fund disclosure document:

> Consistent with the General Partner's opportunistic approach, there are no fixed limitations as to specific asset classes invested in by the Partnership. The Partnership is not limited with respect to the types of investment strategies it may employ or the markets or instruments in which it may invest.

In a nutshell, the hedge fund manager can invest in anything she wants. While her investment portfolio might be transparent at any point in time, her investment process is not. The manager's unlimited discretion means that investors simply do not know from day to day in which markets or securities the hedge fund manager will invest. The above investment strategy statement lacks focus, and consequently it is not transparent.

---

[1] See the President's Working Group on Financial Markets, "Hedge Funds, Leverage, and the Lessons of Long-Term Capital Management" (April 1999).

Finally, there is the "black box" nature of many hedge fund trading programs. Black boxes are a set of sophisticated computer algorithms that are developed to quantify a manager's skill or insight into an investment plan. By definition, black boxes are opaque. Black box managers tend to be secretive with respect to their technology to protect the proprietary nature of their trading scheme. This violates the principle of transparency that is fundamental to most investors.

Institutions, particularly public pension funds, tend to be open about their investment process and types of investments. Before an institution invests money with a black box manager, it must ascertain to its own satisfaction the accuracy and reliability of the fund manager's algorithms.

Yet, the proprietary nature of a black box strategy may make a hedge fund manager reluctant to reveal his quantitative insights. It is a delicate balance between protecting the manager's proprietary trading algorithms and providing sufficient disclosure to an institutional investor. Typically, this balance is struck in private one-on-one meetings between the institution's investment staff and the hedge fund manager.

Investment Process

Institutions prefer a well-defined investment process. The articulation and documentation of the process is just as important as the investment results generated by the process.

Return for a moment to our prior example of a black box. For black box managers, the black box itself is the investment process. Not only does it lack transparency, it is generally not well defined. The lack of definition makes investment committees or boards of directors suspicious of their value.

A black box is just one example of process versus investment results. The hedge fund industry considers itself to be "skill-based." However, it is very difficult to translate manager skill into a process. This is particularly true when the performance of the hedge fund is dependent upon the skill of specific individual.

Consider the following language from a hedge fund document regarding the hedge fund manager's arbitrage program:

> Mr. _____'s experience in the risk arbitrage department of
> _____ provides the General Partner with the specific
> expertise required for investing in special situations.

This is a clear statement that the hedge fund manager's investment analysis and decision-making is concentrated in one person. All information regarding arbitrage strategies is filtered by one individual.

Hedge fund managers can best be described as information processors. Some managers are better at gathering information and some hedge fund managers are better at filtering information. The statement above describes an information filterer.

Information filterers are the least transparent. The reason is that the filtering process is difficult to document. How does one document the individual described in the above statement other than to say he exists? The knowledge he carries in his brain is undoubtedly valuable, but it does not rise to the standard of an investment process.

Information filterers are the best example of "skill-based" investing. The investment process is either the human brain or a computer brain. Both, however, are difficult to describe.

Institutionalization then means that hedge fund managers will have to change their behavior. They will have to shift away from the dependence on the skill of any one individual or a computer black box, and they will have to translate their thought process to demonstrate a rigorous investment process.

Relative Returns

Institutions have been trained for years to expect relative returns. Manager returns are not reviewed in a vacuum. Instead, they are compared to a benchmark. This is true for both active and passive managers and internally versus externally managed funds. It is a fact of life that institutions use benchmarks and review a manager's performance based on relative as opposed to total returns.

Yet, hedge fund managers tend to claim (almost uniformly) that relative returns are not appropriate for their industry. After all, hedge funds are often referred to as absolute or total return products — investment vehicles for which no appropriate benchmark exists.

This also gets to the skill-based claim of most hedge fund managers: that their management styles and insight is based on their unique skill, and therefore it is inappropriate to establish any format for relative returns.

Skill-based claims fall short for two reasons. First, every active manager must have some base of skill. This is true not only for hedge fund managers but also for traditional long-only equity and fixed income managers. If these managers did not have skill, there would be no need for active management and all institutions would turn to passive investing.

Skill, therefore, is an essential element of all active management. Information ratios, used to measure the skill of a manager, are equally applicable to hedge fund managers as they are for traditional long-only managers.[2] The claim of many hedge fund managers that they should not be compared to a benchmark because their special "skill" differentiates them from traditional long-only investment managers does not ring true. In fact, it is all the more important to compare a hedge fund manager to a benchmark to identify and quantify the level of her skill.

Second, there are many efforts underway to develop reliable benchmarks for the hedge fund industry. For example, Evaluation Associates Capital Management provides competitive universe data across 14 different categories of hedge

---

[2] Information ratio is the excess return earned by a manager over a benchmark rate divided by the standard deviation of the excess return.

fund strategies. Additionally, there are current efforts by Morgan Stanley Capital International and Financial Risk Management Ltd. to develop a hedge fund index. Finally, in Chapters 2 and 7, we use data from Hedge Fund Research, Inc. to document the return patterns of ten different hedge fund trading strategies.

One criticism of hedge fund indices is that they are not investable. However, Credit Suisse First Boston and Tremont Advisors, Inc. have recently created an investable hedge fund index based on 291 hedge funds and 9 hedge fund investment strategies. Investors purchase units of an investment company that in turn invests the capital in limited partnership units in the hedge funds underlying the hedge fund index. Since the index is equally weighted among the 291 hedge funds, each dollar invested in the hedge fund investment company receives approximately $1/291 exposure to each hedge fund.

Furthermore, if a hedge fund manager's return is completely uncorrelated with financial assets, then an appropriate benchmark is a cash rate such as Treasury bills or LIBOR. This is also true for fund of funds managers. These managers are expected to provide a distribution of returns that is uncorrelated with financial assets and, therefore, any excess return should be measured against a short-term money market rate.

In summary, benchmarks are used not only to identify a manager's skill but also to quantify it. This is as useful for hedge fund managers as it is for traditional long-only managers. Also, there are existing benchmarks for the hedge fund industry with more on the way. Consequently, it is expected that relative performance will become a moving force in the hedge fund industry.

DOES THE PUNISHMENT FIT THE CRIME?

Having defined what "institutionalization" means, we now come to the crux of the issue: What offenses have hedge fund managers committed such that the investment community would wish to punish them?

The offenses that hedge fund managers have committed are twofold. First, hedge fund managers do not offer the transparency demanded by investors. This is all the more important in the highly fragmented world of the hedge fund industry.[3]

Consider the following report on Long Term Capital Management (LTCM) by The President's Working Group on Financial Markets (1999):

> An issue here is whether the LTCM Fund's investors and counterparties were aware of the nature of the exposures and risks the hedge fund had accumulated, such as the Fund's exposure to market liquidity and funding liquidity risks. They almost cer-

---

[3] See Chip Cummins, "Hedge Funds not Worried about Pending US Regulations," *Dow Jones International News* (March 28, 2000) estimates that there is at least $350 billion invested in over 2,500 hedge funds, but there are less than 20 funds managing $3 billion or more.

tainly were not adequately aware since, by most accounts, they exercised minimal scrutiny of the Fund's risk-management practices and risk profile.

The insufficient monitoring arose, in part, because of LTCM's practice of disclosing only minimal information to these parties, information such as balance sheet and income statements that did not reveal meaningful details about the Fund's risk profile and concentration of exposures in certain markets.

This opaqueness of LTCM's risk profile is an important part of the LTCM story and raises a number of concerns regarding credit-risk management and counterparty trading relationships.

The problem with LTCM is that while it was diversified across global markets, it was not diversified in its strategy. It had bet that volatility, credit, and liquidity spreads would narrow from historically high levels, when instead these spreads expanded after the Russian bond default in August 1998.[4] Furthermore, both LTCM's counterparties and its investors were not aware of the concentration of its risks.

LTCM may be the most extreme example of opaqueness, but it is undoubtedly not the only example. Investors do not need to see every trade ticket of a hedge fund manager but, at a minimum, they do need to see the risk positions of the hedge fund manager.

Investors can understand the risks of hedge fund investing and are willing to bear them, provided that they are disclosed. In addition, LTCM teaches the lesson that not only is it important to understand the economic risks of a hedge fund's position, it is also important to understand the credit and liquidity risks of those positions.

For instance, LTCM was faced with margin calls and investor redemption requests at a time when liquidity in the markets was virtually non-existent. In fact, the Group of Five hedge funds suggest that credit and liquidity risks were as important as market risk.[5]

Many hedge fund managers trade derivative instruments in the over-the-counter market. These instruments tend to be tailor-made and will not suit every party. Consequently, while a hedge fund manager may be hedged with respect to its economic risks, it may still be exposed to liquidity risk.

For example, with respect to LTCM, the liquidity of many markets in which it traded dried up at the time it needed liquidity the most.[6] Without a rescue package from Wall Street, the result would have been a disorderly "fire sale" which could have had an adverse impact on LTCM's capital as well as that of

---

[4] See The President's Working Group on Financial Markets (1999).

[5] The Group of Five hedge funds are: Caxton Corporation, Kingdon Capital Management, Moore Capital Management, Inc., Soros Fund Management, LLC, and Tudor Investment Corporation. See our discussion in Chapter 8.

[6] In fact many proprietary trading desks ("prop desks") at the investment banks had positions similar to LTCM. Therefore, they also suffered from the Russian Bond default and could not provide liquidity.

other market participants. As it was, the near collapse of LTCM had a profound effect across the hedge fund industry, depressing hedge fund returns in the third quarter of 1998 across a wide variety of investment styles.[7]

Lastly, hedge fund managers need to disclose their counterparty credit risks. For LTCM, the shoe was on the other foot in that its counterparties were exposed to LTCM's credit risk. Nonetheless, a hedge fund manager with significant counterparty risk may be faced with the unappealing prospect of liquidating collateral during a declining market.

In summary, a hedge fund manager must be willing to disclose not only its economic risk profile but also the link between market risk, liquidity risk, and credit risk.[8] The near collapse of LTCM demonstrates that value-at-risk models only capture economic or market risk. They do not capture liquidity and credit risks.

A second transgression of hedge fund managers is that they tend to concentrate their skill in one or two key individuals. Recall our discussion in Chapter 4 with respect to selecting a hedge fund manager. In that chapter we cited a *Wall Street Journal* article regarding Stanley Druckenmiller at Soros Fund Management. That article demonstrated how all of the investment decisions of the Soros Quantum Fund were funneled through Mr. Druckenmiller. This type of concentrated investment process is all too common in the hedge fund world.

In Chapter 4 we discussed that investors are unwilling to bear risks that are not fundamental to their tactical and strategic asset allocations. Process risk is not a fundamental risk. It is an idiosyncratic risk of the hedge fund manager's structure and operations.

Process risk also raises the ancillary crime of lack of transparency because skill-based investing usually is opaque. Whether the information is funneled through one key individual or through a set of computer programs, it is difficult to document the investment process.

This raises a further concern of how investors can ensure that a hedge fund manager maintains the same investment process. Without a well-documented investment process it is difficult to determine whether a hedge fund manager has strayed from her process. Possibly, an investor may determine if a hedge fund manager has strayed by reviewing performance numbers. But, this is detective work. An investor in a hedge fund should not have to become a private investigator. Changes in an investment process should be obvious. Yet, change cannot be measured unless an initial investment process is documented.

Finally, although hedge fund managers may be guilty of failing to provide transparency and an investment process, they are not guilty of failing to provide relative returns. The benchmarks discussed previously are relatively new, developed mostly over the last decade, and subject to certain biases and measurement errors.

---

[7] See Goldman Sachs & Co. and Financial Risk Management Ltd., "Hedge Funds Revisited," *Pension and Endowment Forum* (January 2000) and Mark Anson, "Financial Market Dislocations and Hedge Fund Returns," working paper, 2001.

[8] See The President's Working Group on Financial Markets (1999).

As a result, relative returns in the hedge fund industry are imperfect, and may not offer an accurate measure of a hedge fund manager's skill level.

In Chapter 7 we documented that current published hedge fund indices are subject to both survivorship bias and selection bias. These biases tend to inflate the returns to the index. Further, certain hedge fund indices are equal-weighted while others are value-weighted. Equal-weighted indices present a contrarian view because the index continually rebalances by selling winners and buying losers. Value-weighted indices represent a momentum investment strategy because those hedge funds that do well represent an increasing portion of the index.

Fung and Hsieh also find that broad-based hedge fund indices are prone to "style convergence" risk.[9] Broad-based hedged fund indices are helpful for institutional investors who wish to gain exposure to the current growth trend within the hedge fund industry. However, performance characteristics of broad hedge fund indices do not reflect the variety of hedge fund styles. In other words, mixing the wide range of hedge fund styles into a broader index does not work. Style convergence takes place and the index will be a poor benchmark from which to measure relative returns.

The result of style convergence is a higher correlation with traditional asset classes. Fund and Hsieh find that the hedge fund sub-indices based on different hedge fund styles have a much lower correlation with traditional asset classes. They conclude that for investors seeking diversification from traditional asset classes, broad-based hedge fund indices offer limited information content. In contrast, hedge fund sub-indices based on different strategies are better suited to the diversification goals of investors.

In summary, relative returns in the hedge fund arena are a new phenomenon. Many of the details are still being worked out, and it may be some time before a robust benchmark is developed. However, this is not the fault of the hedge fund managers. It merely reflects a continuing effort to bring the hedge fund industry into the institutional fold.

CONSEQUENCES OF INSTITUTIONALIZATION

Institutionalization denotes a certain form of punishment for behavior contrary to behavioral norms. We have defined what institutionalization means for the hedge fund industry. However, a few questions remain.

First, we must ask who is really being punished. Is it the hedge funds or the institutional investors? Investors want a product that offers certain characteristics of return, volatility, and correlation that can improve the risk and return profile of an existing diversified portfolio.[10] However, in developing a rigorous, well-

---

[9] William Fung and David Hsieh, "Hedge Fund Performance Benchmarks: Information Content and Measurement Biases," working paper, Fuqua School of Business, Duke University (May 2000).

[10] See Antoine Bernheim, "The Hedge Fund Landscape One Year after LTCM," *Hedge Fund News 1999*.

defined process, maximizing performance becomes secondary to risk control, predictability, and documentation.

Who then suffers the most? Is it the hedge fund manager who is forced to turn her skill into a documented investment process? Or is it the investor who has accepted the investment process in return for curbing the hedge fund manager's investment creativity?

There is no clear answer to this dilemma. However, investors must remain aware that by institutionalizing hedge fund managers, they will sacrifice some of the creative skill that makes the hedge fund industry so interesting and attractive in the first place.

A second issue is the "brain drain" of talent where a number of bright portfolio managers have left traditional long-only investment shops to start hedge funds. The long-only world is dominated by institutions. These managers fled to hedge funds where they could enjoy greater freedom and the ability to invest without institutional constraints.

This raises the issue of where these managers will next flee if the hedge fund industry becomes institutionalized. Possibly offshore. Possibly to some new financial management industry that has not yet been invented, but will provide limited access to institutional investors. As a result, it might be argued that instead of attempting to incarcerate the creativity of a successful manager, investors should leave the manager unfettered. Otherwise, the talented portfolio managers might be driven away forever.[11]

---

[11] At least one talented and successful hedge fund manager has closed his shop. Jeffery Vinik, former portfolio manager of Fidelity's Magellan Fund and manager of his own hedge fund, returned all of his client's money (with excellent returns) and shut down his very successful hedge fund in 2000.

Section II

Commodity and Managed Futures

Chapter 10
Introduction to Commodities

I n Chapter 1 we discussed how most alternative "asset classes" are really
alternative investment strategies within an existing asset class. This statement
applies to hedge funds, and private equity, for example. However, it does not
apply to commodities. Commodities are a separate asset class.

Capital assets such as stocks and bonds can be valued on the basis of the
net present value of expected future cash flows. Expected cash flows and discount
rates are a prime ingredient to determine the value of capital assets. Conversely,
commodities do not provide a claim on an ongoing stream of revenue in the same
fashion as stocks and bonds.[1] Consequently, they cannot be valued on the basis of
net present value, and interest rates have only a small impact on their value.

Commodities generally fall into the category of consumable or transformable assets. You can consume a commodity such as corn as either feedstock
or as food stock. Alternatively you can transform commodities like crude oil into
gasoline and other petroleum products. Consequently, they have economic value,
but they do not yield an ongoing stream of revenue.

Another distinction between capital assets and commodities is the global
nature of commodity markets. Worldwide, commodities markets are all dollar-
denominated. Further, the value of a particular commodity is dependent upon global supply and demand imbalances rather than regional imbalances. Consequently, commodity prices are determined globally rather than regionally.

This is very different from the equity markets where, for instance, you
have the U.S. stock market, foreign developed stock markets, and emerging markets. Foreign stock markets will reflect economic developments within their own
regions compared to the United States.

Consider Exhibit 1. In this exhibit we provide the correlation coefficients
between the S&P 500 and the FTSE 100 stock indices for the past decade. We can
see that the stock prices in the two countries are less than perfectly correlated
with a correlation coefficient of 0.63.

Exhibit 1: Correlation Coefficients

	S&P 500	FTSE	NY Crude	London Crude
S&P 500	1.00	0.63	−0.16	−0.17
FTSE	0.63	1.00	−0.19	−0.17
NY Crude	−0.16	−0.19	1.00	0.98
London Crude	−0.17	−0.17	0.98	1.00

[1] An exception to this rule are the precious metals such as gold, silver, and platinum which can be lent out
at a market lease rate.

Compare this to the correlation coefficient associated with the change in prices of crude oil listed on the New York Mercantile Exchange and the International Petroleum Exchange in London.[2] The correlation is 0.98. The change in crude oil prices in London and New York move in much closer lock step than stock prices in London and New York. This is because crude oil prices are determined by global economic factors instead of regional factors.

Note also, that the U.S. and UK stock markets are negatively correlated with the price of crude oil. This is not surprising given that energy products are the single most important input to any economy. We will come back to this point in the following chapters.

Finally, commodities do not conform to traditional asset pricing models such as the Capital Asset Pricing Model (CAPM). Under the CAPM, there are two components of risk: market or systematic risk and company specific or unsystematic risk. CAPM teaches us that investors should only be compensated for systematic risk or market risk because unsystematic risk (company specific risk) can be diversified away. CAPM uses a linear regression model to determine beta, a measure of an asset's exposure to systematic or market risk. The financial markets compensate for market risk by assigning a market risk premium above the risk-free rate.

Bodie and Rosansky[3] and Dusak[4] find that commodity beta values are not consistent with the CAPM. The reason is twofold. First, under CAPM, the market portfolio is typically defined as a portfolio of financial assets such as stocks and bonds, and commodity returns map poorly onto financial market returns. Consequently, distinctions between market/systematic risk and unsystematic risk cannot be made. Second, commodity prices are dependent upon global supply and demand factors, not what the market perceives to be an adequate risk premium for this asset class.

This brief introduction is meant to establish commodities as a separate asset class from stocks, bonds, and real estate. However, like stocks and bonds, there are different investment strategies within this asset class. In this chapter we describe the physical commodities markets in more detail and provide an overview of their pricing and underlying economics.

---

[2] In order to make a fair comparison of the correlation coefficients associated with the stock market returns of the U.S. and the UK and the crude oil markets in the U.S. and the UK, I converted FTSE prices into dollars. This removes any currency effects that might confound our analysis. Therefore, the correlation coefficients presented in Exhibit 1 are based on changes in dollar denominated prices. I am indebted to Peter Nguyen for pointing this out to me.

[3] See Zvi Bodie and Victor Rosansky, "Risk and Return in Commodity Futures," *Financial Analysts Journal* (May/June 1980).

[4] K. Dusak, "Futures Trading and Investor Returns: An Investigation of Commodity Market Risk Premiums," *Journal of Political Economy* (November–December 1973).

EXPOSURE TO COMMODITIES

Most investors do not include commodities in their investment portfolio. Part of the reason is lack of familiarity with this asset class. Another issue is how to gain exposure to commodity assets. There are four ways to obtain economic exposure to commodity assets.

Purchase the Underlying Commodity

An investor can simply purchase the underlying commodity to gain economic exposure. Actual ownership of physical commodities can be problematic, however. For instance, on the New York Mercantile Exchange, crude oil contracts are denominated in 1,000 barrel lots. Therefore, if an investor wished to own crude oil, she would have to find a storage tank with a minimum storage capacity of 1,000 barrels of oil.

Similarly, wheat, traded on the Chicago Board of Trade, is denominated in units of 5,000 bushels. These bushels must be stored in a silo. Most investors are not familiar with the storage issues of physical commodities, let alone willing to bear the storage costs of ownership associated with physical commodities.

However, there are parts of the world where physical ownership of commodities is still the major form of economic wealth. India, for example, is the second largest consumer of precious metals in the world, after the United States. The reason is that many parts of India are geographically remote, far removed from the financial services and products that are commonplace in the United States. Stocks, bonds, mutual funds, and even bank savings accounts are the exception not the rule. Consequently, people in these remote regions denominate their wealth in gold, silver, and platinum.

Natural Resource Companies

Another way to gain exposure to commodities is to own the securities of a firm that derives a significant part of its revenues from the purchase and sale of physical commodities. For instance, purchasing shares of Texaco might be considered a "pure play" on the price of oil since two-thirds of Texaco's revenues are derived from the exploration, refining, and marketing of petroleum products.

However, there are several reasons why this "pure play" might not work. First, part of the value of the stock in Texaco is dependent upon the movement of the general stock market. This is the CAPM, discussed above, and, as a result, an investment in the stock of any company will result in exposure to systematic, or market risk, as well as firm specific risk.

Systematic risk is measured by the beta of a stock. Beta measures the amount of market risk associated with a given security. A beta equal to one indicates the same level of systematic risk as the overall market, while a beta less than one indicates less risk than the market, and a beta greater than one indicates more risk than the market.

Exhibit 2: Beta Measures and Correlation Coefficients

	Stock Market Beta	Stock Market Correlation Coefficient	Crude Oil Beta	Crude Oil Correlation Coefficient
ExxonMobil	0.839	0.99	0.089	0.045
Texaco	0.531	0.94	0.025	0.001
Chevron	0.698	0.97	−0.010	0.001
Royal Dutch Shell	0.819	0.97	0.080	0.045

Consider Exhibit 2. In this exhibit, we list the correlation coefficients and the betas associated with the stock returns four large petroleum companies compared to the S&P 500 (the "market").[5] We also include correlation coefficients and betas for the stock returns of the four oil companies compared to the price of crude oil.

First, we can see that the oil companies all have large betas with respect to the S&P 500. This indicates that oil companies have significant stock market risk. Furthermore, the correlation coefficients between the stock returns of these four companies and the S&P 500 are very large. We can conclude that oil companies have considerable exposure to the general stock market.

The analysis changes when we examine the returns of these four companies to the prices of crude oil. Exhibit 2 indicates that the betas associated with crude oil prices are very low, less than 0.1 in all cases. In this case we define the market as the current price of crude oil traded in New York City. Further, one company, Chevron, has a negative beta (although small in absolute value terms) compared to oil prices indicating that its stock price reacts in the opposite direction from crude oil prices. In addition, the correlation coefficients between the oil company stock prices and crude oil stock prices are all close to zero. We can conclude the stock prices of oil companies are virtually independent of crude oil prices. Therefore, investing in an oil company as a "pure play" on crude oil prices provides an investor with significant stock market exposure and virtually no crude oil exposure.

Second, when an investor invests with an oil company (or any company for that matter) the investor assumes all of the idiosyncratic risks associated with that company. Continuing with our example of Texaco, in the 1980s it attempted an ill-fated merger with the Getty Oil Company even though the Getty Oil Company had an outstanding bid from Pennzoil. The result was massive litigation resulting in a several billion dollar verdict against Texaco, forcing the company to seek Chapter 11 bankruptcy protection. Further, in the 1990s, Texaco was the subject of a race discrimination lawsuit by many of its workers. This litigation cost Texaco several hundred million dollars.

Neither of these lawsuits, however, had anything to do with the price of oil. They were part of the idiosyncratic risk associated with the management prac-

---

[5] We use monthly data over the time period January 1990 through December 2000. We also note that on October 15, 2000 Texaco and Chevron announced an agreement to merge their respective companies. However, as of this writing the merger had not been completed and both companies continued to trade independently of each other.

tices of Texaco. Most investors seeking a pure play on oil would be disappointed to receive instead lengthy and expensive lawsuit exposure.

Additionally, there are other operating risks associated with an investment in any company. A company's financing policies, for example, affect the price of its stock. Texaco has a debt/equity ratio of about 1.20. This is a little above average for the oil industry. There is also operating leverage (i.e., the ratio of fixed to variable expenses). Oil companies tend to have high variable costs associated with their exploration, refining, and marketing programs. While financial and operating leverage affect the price of a stock, they have nothing to do with the price of oil.

Finally, even if all of the other risks associated with an investment in an oil company are accepted, the investor might find that the oil company has hedged away its oil exposure. Most large oil and energy companies maintain their own trading desks. One main goal of these trading desks is to hedge the risk associated with the purchase and sale of petroleum products. The reason is that oil companies, like most companies, prefer to smooth their annual earnings rather than be subject to large swings due to the price of oil.

The proof is demonstrated in Exhibit 2, where oil companies have low betas with respect to the price of crude oil. This is consistent with the fact that oil companies hedge away a considerable amount of their exposure to fluctuating oil prices.

Commodity Futures Contracts

The easiest way to gain exposure to commodity prices is through commodity futures contracts. Futures contracts offer several advantages. First, these contracts are traded on an exchange. Therefore, they share the same advantages as stock exchanges: a central marketplace, transparent pricing, clearinghouse security, uniform contract size and terms, and daily liquidity.

Second, the purchase of a futures contract does not require automatic delivery of the underlying commodity. An offsetting futures position can be initiated that will close out the position of the initial futures contract. In this way an investor can gain exposure to commodity prices without worrying about physical delivery. In fact only about 1% of all commodity futures contracts result in the actual delivery of the underlying commodity.

Third, futures contracts can be purchased without paying the full price for the commodity. When a futures contract is purchased, a down payment on the total futures price is required. This is called the *initial margin*. This margin requirement is a small percentage of the full purchase price of the underlying commodity, usually less than 10%. The initial margin is a good faith deposit to ensure full payment upon delivery of the underlying commodity. In the futures markets, the investor does not need to put up the total price for the underlying commodity unless she takes physical delivery of the commodity.

Futures accounts also have two other margin requirements. On a day by day basis, the value of the futures contract will fluctuate. Fluctuation of prices in the futures markets will cause the value of the investor's margin account to increase or decrease. This is called the *variation margin*. If the price of the futures contract increases, the holder of a long futures position will accrue positive variation margin. This adds to the equity in the futures margin account and may be withdrawn by the investor. Conversely, for an investor that has a short futures position, the increase in the price of the futures contract will result in a negative variation margin.

The *maintenance margin* is the minimum amount of equity that a futures margin account may have and is usually set at 75% to 80% of the initial margin. If subsequent variation margins reduce the equity in an investor's account down to the maintenance margin level, the investor will receive a *margin call* from the futures commission merchant. A margin call is a demand for additional cash to be contributed to the account to bring the equity in the account back over the maintenance margin level. If the investor cannot meet the margin call, the futures commission merchant has the right to liquidate the investor's positions in the account.

There can be some disadvantages to taking positions in futures contracts. First, if an investor wishes to maintain her exposure to commodity prices without taking physical delivery of the underlying contract, she will have to continually close out her existing futures position and re-establish a new position by entering into a new futures contract. This "rolling" of futures contracts can be costly depending on the term structure of the futures market. (We will discuss this more in detail below.)

Second, as we noted above, once a long futures position is established, there may be ongoing margin calls if the futures contract declines in value. Conversely, if an investor's futures contracts increase in value, she may withdraw the additional equity from her account. Nonetheless, managing the contributions and withdrawals from a futures account may require more activity than a traditional long-only security account. Futures accounts may only be opened with licensed futures commission merchants who are registered with the National Futures Association and the Commodity Futures Trading Commission.

Commodity-Linked Notes

The last way an investor can gain exposure to the commodity markets is through a commodity-linked note. This is where financial engineering and the commodities markets intersect. In its simplest form, a commodity-linked note is an intermediate term debt instrument whose value at maturity will be a function of the value of an underlying commodity futures contract or basket of commodity futures contracts.

Commodity-linked notes are not a new invention. In 1863, the Confederacy of the South issued a 20-year bond denominated in both Pounds Sterling and French Francs. Also, at the option of the bondholder, the bond could be converted into bales of cotton. This was a dual currency, commodity-linked bond.[6]

Commodity-linked notes have several advantages. First, the investor does not have to worry about the rolling of the underlying futures contracts. This becomes the problem of the issuer of the note who must roll the futures contracts to hedge the commodity exposure embedded in the note.

---

[6] See S. Warte Rawls III and Charles Smithson, "The Evolution of Risk Management Products," *The New Corporate Finance*, 2nd Ed., Donald H. Chew, Jr. (ed.) (New York: Irwin/McGraw-Hill, 1999).

Second, the note is, in fact, a debt instrument. Many investors may have restrictions on investing in the commodities markets. However, they can have access to commodity exposure through a debt instrument. The note is recorded as a liability on the balance sheet of the issuer, and as a bond investment on the balance sheet of the investor. In addition, the note can have a stated coupon rate and maturity just like any other debt instrument. The twist is that the investor accepts a lower coupon payment than it otherwise could receive in return for sharing in the upside of the commodity prices.

Last, the holder of the note does not have to worry about any tracking error issues with respect to the price of a single commodity or basket of commodities. Once again, this problem remains with the issuer.

In practice, commodity-linked notes are tied to the prices of commodity futures contracts or commodity options. Consider the following example. A pension fund is not allowed to trade commodity futures directly, but wants to invest in the commodity markets as a hedge against inflation. To diversify its portfolio, it purchases at par value from an investment bank a $1,000,000 structured note tied to the value of the Goldman Sachs Commodity Index (GSCI). The GSCI is a diversified basket of physical commodity futures contracts.

The note has a maturity of one year and is principal guaranteed, at maturity, the pension fund will receive at least the face value of the note. However, if the GSCI exceeds a certain level at maturity of the note the pension fund will share in this appreciation. Principal repayment therefore depends upon the settlement price of the GSCI index at the note's maturity. The pension fund has, in fact, a call option embedded in the note. If the GSCI exceeds a predetermined level (the strike price) at the maturity date, the pension fund will participate in the price appreciation.

The embedded call option on the GSCI is costly. The pension fund will pay for this option by receiving a reduced coupon payment (or no coupon) on the note. The closer to the money the call option is set, the lower will be the coupon payment. Assume that the strike price for a GSCI call option is set at 10% out of the money and that the coupon on the note is 2%.

Under normal circumstances, a plain vanilla note from the issuer would carry a coupon of 6%. Therefore, the pension fund is sacrificing 4% of coupon income for the price of the call option on the GSCI. Assume that at the time the note is issued, the GSCI is at the level of 1000. Therefore, the strike price on the call option (set 10% out of the money) is 1100. If, at maturity of the note, the value of the GSCI is above 1100, the investor will receive her 2% coupon plus the appreciation of the GSCI:

$$[1 + (GSCI_T - GSCI_x)/GSCI_x] \times \$1,000,000 + \$20,000$$

where

GSCI$_T$ is the value of the GSCI index at maturity of the note
GSCI$_x$ is the strike price for the call option embedded in the note

20,000 = 2% coupon × $1,000,000 face value note

If the option expires out of the money (the GSCI is less than or equal to 1100 at maturity), then the investor receives the return of her principal plus a 2% coupon. Exhibit 3 presents the possible payoffs to the structured note.

From Exhibit 3 we can see that the pension fund shares in the upside but is protected on the downside. The trade off for principal protection is a lower coupon payment and only a partial sharing in the upside (above the call strike price).

With respect to the issuer of the note, it will go out and purchase a one-year call option on the GSCI index with a strike price equal to 1100. If the option matures in the money, the issuer will pass on the price appreciation to the pension fund. In this way, the issuer maintains the commodity call option on its balance sheet, not the pension fund, but the pension fund gets the benefit of the option's payout.

Structured notes do not have to be principal protected. The pension fund can share fully in the upside as well as the downside. Consider a second note also with a $1,000,000 face value. However, this note shares fully in the change in value of the GSCI from the date the note is purchased. The trick here is that the change in value can be positive or negative. This is a commodity note linked to a futures contract instead of an option contract.

The note will pay a 5% coupon at maturity. Recall that the pension could otherwise purchase a regular one-year note from the same issuer (without commodity exposure) with a 6% coupon. The difference in coupon payments of 1% reflects the issuer's transaction and administration costs associated with the commodity-linked note. Compared to the prior example, a commodity-linked note with an embedded futures contract is less costly to issue than a note with an embedded commodity option.

Exhibit 3: Structured Note with a GSCI Call Option

GSCI	900	1000	1100	1200	1300
Principal	$1,000,000	$1,000,000	$1,000,000	$1,000,000	$1,000,000
Option Value	$0	$0	$0	$90,909	$181,818
Coupon	$20,000	$20,000	$20,000	$20,000	$20,000
Total Payment	$1,020,000	$1,020,000	$1,020,000	$1,110,909	$1,201,818
Total Return	2%	2%	2%	11.09%	20.18%

Exhibit 4: Structured note with a GSCI Futures Contract

GSCI	900	1000	1100	1200	1300
Principal	$1,000,000	$1,000,000	$1,000,000	$1,000,000	$1,000,000
Futures Value	−$100,000	$0	$100,000	$200,000	$300,000
Coupon	$50,000	$50,000	$50,000	$50,000	$50,000
Total Payment	$950,000	$1,050,000	$1,150,000	$1,250,000	$1,350,000
Total Return	−5%	5%	15%	25%	35%

The terms of the note state that at maturity the issuer will pay to the investor:

$$[1 + (GSCI_T - GSCI_0)/GSCI_0] \times \$1,000,000 + \$50,000$$

where

GSCI$_T$ is the value of the GSCI index at maturity of the note
GSCI$_0$ is the value of the GSCI index at the purchase date of the note

The payout for this second note is presented in Exhibit 4.

Notice the difference between Exhibits 3 and 4. In Exhibit 4 we can see that the pension fund shares in a linear payout stream: if the GSCI increases in value, the pension gains; if the GSCI declines in value, the pension fund loses. However, in Exhibit 3, the pension fund shares only in the gains, it does not share in the losses. This is a demonstration of the non-linear payout function associated with a commodity option. In contrast, a commodity note linked to a futures contract will provide an investor with a linear payout function.

Last, note that the pension fund has the opportunity for a much greater gain with the commodity note linked to a futures contract. However, in return for this upside potential, the pension fund must bear the risk of loss of capital should the GSCI decline below its initial level of 1000.[7] Another way of stating this is that with a commodity note linked to an option, the pension fund sacrifices some upside potential for the preservation of capital.

The financial engineering demonstrated in Exhibits 3 and 4 would not be necessary if the pension fund could invest directly in commodity futures and options. Engineering becomes necessary because of the pension fund's prohibition against purchasing commodities directly.

Commodity-linked notes are completely transparent because these notes utilize exchange-traded commodity futures and options contracts with daily pricing and liquidity. Furthermore, the equation to calculate their value is specified as part of the note agreement. As a result, pension funds, insurance companies, endowments, and other institutional investors may participate in viable securities that offer transparent exposure to a new asset class without a direct investment in that asset class.

In the above examples, it was assumed that the issuer was a large commercial bank that purchased the commodity futures or options and passed through either the gains or losses to the investor. However, commodity producers are also likely issuers of such notes.

---

[7] With respect to the issuer of the note, it will go out and purchase one-year futures contracts on the GSCI sufficient to cover the face value of the note. If the futures contracts increase in value, the issuer passes on this value to the pension fund. If the futures contracts decline in value, the issuer will close out its position at a loss. However, the issuer will be reimbursed for these losses because it does not have to return the full principal value of the note to the pension fund.

Consider an oil producer who would like to reduce its cost of debt financing. One way to lower the coupon rate on its debt would be to issue calls on crude oil attached to its bonds. As we demonstrated in Exhibit 3, if a commodity-linked note is tied to a call option, the coupon payment will be lower than what the issuer would otherwise offer. From the oil producer's perspective, any cash outflows as a result of the call option being exercised should be offset by the lower cost of financing it receives. From the investor's perspective, it trades a lower coupon payment on the note for the potential to share in the price appreciation of crude oil.

THE RELATIONSHIP BETWEEN
FUTURES PRICES AND SPOT PRICES

As we noted above, the easiest way to gain exposure to commodities is through commodity futures contracts. These contracts are transparent, are denominated in standard units, are exchange traded, have daily liquidity, and depend upon the spot prices of the underlying commodity. The last point, the relationship between spot and futures prices, must be developed to understand the dynamics of the commodity futures markets.

A futures contract obligates the seller of the futures contract to deliver the underlying asset at a set price at a specified time. Conversely, the buyer of a futures contract agrees to purchase the underlying asset at the set price and at a specified time. If the seller of the futures contract does not wish to deliver the underlying asset, she must close out her short futures position by purchasing an offsetting futures contract. Similarly, if the buyer of the futures contract does not wish to take delivery of the underlying asset, he must close out his long futures position by selling an offsetting futures contract. Only a very small percentage of futures contracts (usually less than 1%) result in delivery of the underlying asset.

There are three general types of futures contracts regulated by the Commodity Futures Trading Commission: financial futures, currency futures, and commodity futures. Commodity trading advisors and commodity pool operators invest in all three types of futures contracts. Additionally, many hedge fund managers apply arbitrage strategies with respect to financial and currency futures. The following examples demonstrate these arbitrage opportunities. We begin with financial futures.

Financial Futures

Financial futures include U.S. Treasury bond futures, agency futures, eurodollar CD futures, and stock index futures. In the United States, these contracts are traded on the Chicago Board of Trade, the Chicago Mercantile Exchange, and the FINEX division of the New York Cotton Exchange. Consider the example of a financial asset that pays no income.

Exhibit 5: Financial Asset Arbitrage when $F > Se^{r(T-t)}$

Time	Cash Inflow	Cash Outflow	Net Cash
t (initiate the arbitrage)	S (cash borrowed)	S (to purchase the asset)	$S - S = 0$
T (maturity of the futures contract)	F (price for future delivery of the asset)	$Se^{r(T-t)}$ (pay back principal and interest)	$F - Se^{r(T-t)}$

In the simplest case, if the underlying asset pays no income, then the relationship between the futures contract and the spot price is:

$$F = Se^{r(T-t)} \tag{1}$$

where

F = the price of the futures contract
S = the spot price of the underlying asset
e = the exponential operator, used to calculate continuous compounding
r = the risk-free rate
$T - t$ = the time until maturity of the futures contract

In words, the price of the futures contract depends upon the current price of the underlying financial asset, the risk-free rate and the time until maturity of the futures contract. Notice that the price of the futures contract depends upon the risk free rate and not the required rate of return for the financial asset. The reason that this is the case is because of arbitrage opportunities that exist for speculators such as hedge funds.

Consider the situation where $F > Se^{r(T-t)}$. A hedge fund manager could make a profit by applying the following strategy:

1. Borrow cash at the risk-free rate, r, and purchase the underlying asset at current price S.
2. Sell the underlying asset for delivery at time T and at the futures price F.
3. At maturity, deliver the underlying asset, pay the interest and principal on the cash borrowed, and collect the futures price F.

Exhibit 5 demonstrates this arbitrage strategy.

Two points about Exhibit 5 must be noted. First, to initiate the arbitrage strategy, no net cash is required. The cash outflow matches the cash inflow. This is one reason why arbitrage strategies are so popular.

Second, at maturity (time T), the hedge fund manager receives a positive net cash payout of $F - Se^{r(T-t)}$. How do we know that the net payout is positive? Simple, we know that at the initiation of the arbitrage strategy that $F > Se^{r(T-t)}$. Therefore, $F - Se^{r(T-t)}$ must be positive.

If the reverse situation were true at time t, $F < Se^{r(T-t)}$, then a reverse arbitrage strategy would make the same amount of profit: Buy the futures contract and sell short the underlying asset. This is demonstrated in Exhibit 6.

Exhibit 6: Financial Asset Arbitrage when $F < Se^{r(T\text{-}t)}$

Time	Cash Inflow	Cash Outflow	Net Cash
t (initiate the arbitrage)	S (the asset is sold short)	S (invested at interest rate r)	$S - S = 0$
T (maturity of the futures contract)	$Se^{r(T-t)}$ (receive principal and interest)	F (the price paid for the asset at maturity of the futures contract)	$Se^{r(T-t)} - F$

Exhibit 6 demonstrates the arbitrage profit $Se^{r(T-t)} - F$. How do we know this is a profit? Because we started with the condition that $Se^{r(T-t)} > F$. At maturity of the futures contract, the hedge fund manager will take delivery of the underlying asset at price F and use the delivery of the asset to cover her short position.

In general, futures contracts on financial assets are settled in cash, not by physical delivery of the underlying security.[8] However, this does not change the arbitrage dynamics demonstrated above. The hedge fund manager will simply close out her short asset position and long futures position at the same time and net the gains and losses. The profit will be the same as that demonstrated in Exhibit 6.

Most financial assets pay some form of income. Consider stock index futures contracts. A stock index tracks the changes in the value of a portfolio of stocks. The percentage change in the value of a stock index over time is usually defined so that it equals the percentage change in the total value of all stocks comprising the index portfolio. However, stock indices are usually not adjusted for dividends. In other words, any cash dividends received by an investor actually holding the stocks is not reflected in measuring the change in value of the stock index.

There are futures contracts on the S&P 500, the Nikkei 225 Stock Index, the NASDAQ 100 Index, the Russell 1000 Index, and the Dow Jones Industrials Stock Index. By far, the most popular contract is the S&P 500 futures contract (SPX) traded on the Chicago Mercantile Exchange.

Consider the S&P 500 futures contract. The pricing relationship as shown in equation (1) applies. However, equation (1) must be adjusted for the fact that the holder of the underlying stocks receives cash dividends, while the holder of the futures contract does not.

In Exhibit 5 we demonstrated how an arbitrage strategy may be accomplished by borrowing cash at the risk-free rate to purchase the underlying financial asset. With respect to stocks, the hedge fund manager receives the benefit of cash dividends from purchasing the stocks. The cash dividends received reduce the borrowing cost of the hedge fund manager. This must be factored into the futures pricing equation. We can express this relation as:

$$F = Se^{(r - q)(T - t)} \tag{2}$$

---

[8] However, certain futures exchanges allow for a procedure known as "exchange for physicals" where a holder of a financial asset can exchange the financial asset at maturity of the futures contract instead of settling in cash.

where the terms are the same as before, and q is equal to the dividend yield on the basket of stocks.

The dividend rate, q, is subtracted from the borrowing cost, r, to reflect the reduction in carrying costs from owning the basket of stocks. Consider the example of a 3-month futures contract on the S&P 500. Assume that the index is currently at 1200, that the risk-free rate is 6%, and that the current dividend yield on the S&P 500 is 2%. Using equation (2), the fair price for a 3-month futures contract on the S&P 500 is:

$$F = 1200e^{(0.06 - 0.02)(0.25)} = 1212$$

Notice again that the futures price on stock index futures does not depend upon the expected return on stocks. Instead, it depends on the risk-free rate and the dividend yield. Expected asset returns do not affect the pricing relationship between the current asset price and the future asset price because any expected return that the underlying asset should earn will also be reflected in the futures price. Therefore, the difference between the futures price and the spot price should reflect only the time value of money, adjusted for any income earned by the financial asset over the term of the futures contract.

Suppose that instead of a price of 1212, the three-month futures contract for the S&P 500 was priced at 1215. Then a hedge fund could establish the following arbitrage: borrow cash at an interest rate of 6% and purchase a basket of S&P 500 stocks worth $300,000 ($250 × 1200, where each point of the S&P 500 is worth $250 in the underlying futures contract), and sell the S&P 500 futures at a price of 1215. At the end of three months, the hedge fund would earn the following arbitrage profit:

Futures price received for the S&P 500 stocks
$$= 1215 \times \$250 = \qquad\qquad \$303,750$$
Plus dividend yield on stocks
$$= \$300,00 \times (e^{(0.02)\times(0.25)} - 1) = \qquad \$1,504$$
Less repayment of the loan plus interest
$$= \$300,000 \times e^{(0.06)\times(0.25)} = \qquad \$304,534$$
Equals Arbitrage Profits $\qquad\qquad\qquad\qquad\qquad\qquad$ $704

Exhibit 7 demonstrates the stock index arbitrage flow chart. A reverse arbitrage similar to Exhibit 6 can be implemented when $F < Se^{(r-q)(T-t)}$. That is, short the stocks, invest the cash at the risk-free rate, and buy the futures contract.

Exhibit 7: Stock Index Arbitrage when $F > Se^{(r-q)(T-t)}$

Time	Cash Inflow	Cash Outflow	Net Cash
t (initiate the arbitrage)	S (cash borrowed)	S (to purchase S&P 500 stocks)	$S - S = 0$
T (maturity of the futures contract)	F (price for future delivery of S&P 500 stocks)	$Se^{(r-q)(T-t)}$ (pay back principal and interest less dividends received)	$F - Se^{(r-q)(T-t)}$

Currencies

A foreign currency may be considered an income producing asset. The reason is that the holder of the foreign currency can earn interest at the risk-free rate prevailing in the foreign country. We define this foreign risk-free rate as f. Considered in this context, the relationship between a futures contract on a foreign currency and the current spot exchange rate can be expressed as:

$$F = Se^{(r-f)(T-t)} \tag{3}$$

where the terms are defined as before, and f is the risk free interest rate in the foreign country.

Equation (3) is similar to equation (2) because a foreign currency may be considered analogous to an income producing asset or a dividend paying stock. Equation (3) also expresses the well-known *interest rate parity theorem*. This theorem states that the exchange rate between two currencies will be dependent upon the differences in their interest rates.

Consider the exchange rate between the U.S. dollar and the Japanese yen. Assume that the current U.S. risk-free rate is 6% while that for the yen is approximately 1%. Also, assume that the current spot rate for yen to dollars is 120 yen per $US, or 0.00833 dollars per yen. A 3-month futures contract on the yen/dollar exchange rate would be:

$$F = 0.00833e^{(0.06 - 0.01)(0.25)} = 0.0084382$$

The futures price on Japanese yen for three months is 0.0084382 dollars per yen, or 118.51 yen per dollar.

To demonstrate a currency arbitrage when $F > Se^{(r-f)(T-t)}$ consider a hedge fund manager who can borrow 12,000 yen for three months at a rate of 1%. In three months time, the hedge fund manager will have to repay $12,000e^{(0.01 \times 0.25)} = 12,030$ yen. The manager converts the yen into dollars at the spot exchange rate of 120 yen/$1 = $100. This $100 can then be invested at the U.S. risk-free rate of interest for three months to earn $100e^{(0.060 \times 0.25)} = $101.50. If the three-month currency futures price on Japanese yen were the same as the spot exchange rate of 120 yen/$1, the hedge fund manager would need to sell 12,030/120 = $100.25 dollars to repay the yen loan. Since the manager receives $101.50 dollars back from her three-month investment in the United States, she will pocket the difference of $101.50 − $100.25 = $1.25 in arbitrage profits.

Exhibit 8 demonstrates that 150 yen of arbitrage profits may be earned if the futures contract price does not take into account the differences in the interest rates between the foreign and domestic currencies. The 150 yen of arbitrage profit may be converted back to dollars: 150 yen/120 = $1.25. Therefore, to prevent arbitrage, the currency futures price for Japanese yen must be 118.51 yen per $US. Then the amount of cash inflow received will be exactly equal to the cash outflow necessary to pay back the Japanese yen loan: $101.50 × 118.51 yen/$ = 12,030 yen.

Exhibit 8: Currency Arbitrage when $F > Se^{(r-f)(T-t)}$

Time	Cash Inflow	Cash Outflow	Net Cash
t (initiate the futures contract)	12,000 yen borrowed at 1%	12,000 yen/120 = $100 invested at 6%	0
T (maturity of the futures contract)	$101.50 from U.S. interest bearing account	12,030 yen to repay loan plus interest	($101.50 × 120) − 12,030 yen = 150 yen.

In practice, arbitrage opportunities do not occur as obviously as our example. Currency prices may be out of balance for only a short period of time. It is the nimble hedge fund manager that can take advantage of pricing discrepancies. Further, more famous hedge fund managers engage in currency speculation as opposed to currency arbitrage. In currency speculation, the hedge fund manager takes an unhedged position on one side of the market. Cash is committed to establish the position. The best example of this is George Soros' bet against the British pound sterling in 1992.

Commodity Futures

Commodities are not financial assets. Nonetheless, the pricing dynamics between spot prices and futures prices are similar to those for financial assets. However, there are important distinctions that will affect the pricing relationship.

First, as we discussed above, there are storage costs associated with physical commodities. These storage costs must be factored into the pricing equation. Storage costs can be considered as negative income. In other words, there is a cash outflow associated with holding the physical commodity. This is in contrast to financial assets discussed above. With financial assets, we demonstrated that income earned on the underlying asset will defray the cost of purchasing that asset. With physical commodities, however, there is both the cost of financing the purchase of the physical commodity and the storage cost associated with its ownership. This relationship may be expressed as:

$$F = Se^{(r+c)(T-t)} \qquad (4)$$

where the terms are as defined before, and c is the storage cost associated with ownership of the commodity.

In equation (4), the cost of storage, c, is added the cost of financing the purchase of the commodity. For example, consider a 1-year futures contract on crude oil. Assume that (1) it costs 2% of the price of crude oil to store a barrel of oil and the payment is made at the end of the year, (2) the current price of oil is $25, and (3) the risk-free rate of interest is 6%.[9] Then the future value of a 1-year crude oil futures contract is:

$$F = \$25e^{(0.06 + 0.02)(1)} = \$27.08$$

---

[9] If the storage costs are expressed as a dollar amount, then the appropriate equation is $F = (S + C)e^{r(T-t)}$ where C represents the present value of all storage costs incurred during the life of the futures contract.

Exhibit 9: Commodity Futures Arbitrage when $F > Se^{(r + c-y)(T-t)}$

Time	Cash Inflow	Cash Outflow	Net Cash
t (initiate the arbitrage)	S (cash borrowed)	S (to purchase the asset)	$S - S = 0$
T (maturity of the futures contract)	$F + S(e^{y(T-t)} - 1)$ (price for future delivery of the asset plus lease income)	$Se^{(r+c)(T-t)}$ (pay back principal and interest on loan plus storage costs)	$F + S(e^{y(T-t)} - 1)$ $- Se^{(r+c)(T-t)}$

A second difference between commodity futures and financial futures is the *convenience yield*. Consumers of physical commodities feel that there are benefits from the ownership of the commodity that are not obtained by owning a futures contract; that it is convenient to own the physical commodity. This benefit might be the ability to profit from temporary or local supply and demand imbalances, or the ability to keep a production line in process. Alternatively, the convenience yield for certain metals can be measured in terms of *lease rates*. Gold, silver, and platinum can be leased (loaned) to jewelry and electronic manufacturers with the obligation to repay the precious metal at a later date.

Taking both the cost of storage and the convenience yield into account, the price of a futures contract may be stated as:

$$F = Se^{(r + c - y)(T - t)} \tag{5}$$

where the terms are defined as before and y is the convenience yield.

Notice that the convenience yield is subtracted from the risk-free rate, r, and the storage cost, c. Similar to financial assets, the convenience yield, y, reduces the cost of ownership of the asset.

Consider the following example. The current price of an ounce of gold is $275, the risk-free rate is 6%, the cost of storage is 2% of the purchase price, and the lease rate to lend gold is 1%. A 6-month futures contract on gold will be:

$$F = \$275e^{(0.06 + 0.02 - 0.01)(0.5)} = \$284.80$$

Assume that $F > Se^{(r + c - y)(T - t)}$. Then an investor can earn an arbitrage profit by borrowing S to purchase the underlying commodity and selling the futures contract, F. This arbitrage is detailed in Exhibit 9.[10]

Exhibit 9 demonstrates the payment received from the arbitrage. At maturity of the futures contract, the investor receives a positive cash flow of $F + S(e^{y(T-t)} - 1) - Se^{(r+c)(T-t)}$. The amount $F + S(e^{y(T-t)} - 1)$ represents the futures

---

[10] In practice, storage costs are usually quoted in dollar terms rather than as a percentage of the commodity's value, while convenience yields are quoted as a percentage of the commodity's value. Consider the case where C is equal to the present value of the storage costs that must be paid over the life of the futures contract. Then equation (5) many be expressed as:

$$F = Se^{(r - y)(T - t)} + Ce^{r(T - t)}$$

price received at maturity of the contract plus any income from the lease of the commodity, and $Se^{(r + c)(T - t)}$ represents the cash that must be paid back for the loan, interest on the loan, and storage costs.

This arbitrage cannot work in reverse if the investor does not already own the commodity. Except for precious metals, commodities are difficult to borrow. Consequently, they cannot be shorted in the same fashion as financial assets. Furthermore, companies that own the underlying commodity do so for its consumption value rather than its investment value.

ECONOMICS OF THE COMMODITY MARKETS: NORMAL BACKWARDATION VERSUS CONTANGO

With this pricing framework in place, we turn to the economics of commodity consumption, production, and hedging. Commodity futures contracts exhibit a term structure similar to that of interest rates. This curve can be downward sloping or upward sloping. The reasons for the different curves will be determined by the actions of hedgers and speculators.

Consider a petroleum producer such as ExxonMobil. Through its exploration, developing, refining, and marketing operations, this company is naturally long crude oil exposure. This puts Exxon at risk to declining crude oil prices. To reduce this exposure, Exxon will sell crude oil futures contracts.[11]

From Exxon's perspective, by selling crude oil futures contracts it can separate its commodity price risk from its business risk (i.e., the ability to find crude oil, refine it and market it to consumers). By hedging, Exxon can better apply its capital to its business risks rather than holding a reserve of capital to protect against fluctuating crude oil prices. Simply stated, hedging allows for the more efficient use of Exxon's invested capital. However, there must be someone on the other side of the trade to bear the price risk associated with buying the futures contract. This is the speculator.

If Exxon transfers its risk to the speculator, the speculator must be compensated for this risk. The speculator is compensated by purchasing the futures contract from the petroleum producer at less than the expected future spot price of crude oil. That is, the price established in the commodity futures contract will be below the expected future spot price of crude oil. The speculator will be compensated by the difference between the futures price and the expected spot price. This may be expressed as:

$$E(S_T) > F_T \tag{6}$$

---

[11] As we discussed before, oil producers have energy trading desks to hedge their long crude oil exposure. Another way that Exxon hedges this risk is through long-term delivery contracts where the price of crude oil is fixed in the contract.

where

$E(S_T)$ = the expected spot price of the underlying commodity at time T (the maturity of the futures contract)

F_T = the agreed upon price in the futures contract to be paid at time T

If the inequality of equation (6) remains true at the maturity of the futures contract, the speculator will earn a profit of $S_T - F_T$. However, nothing is certain, commodity prices can fluctuate. It might turn out that the price agreed upon in the futures contract exceeds the spot price at time T. Then the speculator will lose an amount equal to $F_T - S_T$.

This is the risk that the petroleum producer transferred from its income statement to that of the speculator's. Therefore, to ensure the speculator is compensated more often than not for bearing the commodity price risk, it must be the case that agreed upon futures price F_T is sufficiently discounted compared to the expected future spot price S_T. This condition of the futures markets is referred to as *normal backwardation*, or simply, *backwardation*.

The term backwardation comes from John Maynard Keynes. Keynes was the first to theorize that commodity producers were the natural hedgers in the commodity markets and therefore would need to offer a risk premium to speculators in order to induce them to bear the risk of fluctuating commodity prices. This risk premium is represented by the difference of $E(S_T) - F_T$. Conversely, hedgers, because they are reducing their risks, are willing to enter into contracts where the expected payoff is slightly negative.

Backwardated commodity markets have downward sloping futures curves. The longer dated the futures contract the greater must be the discount compared to the expected future spot price to compensate the speculator for assuming the price risk of the underlying commodity for a longer period of time. Therefore, longer dated futures contracts are priced cheaper than shorter term futures contracts.

The reverse situation of a backwardated commodity market is a *contango market*. In a contango market, the inequality sign in equation (6) is reversed — the expected future spot price, S_T, is less than the current futures price, F_T.

A contango situation will occur when the hedger of the commodity is naturally short the underlying commodity. Consider the aircraft manufacturer, Boeing. The single largest raw material input in the construction of any jet aircraft is aluminum for the superstructure of the plane. Boeing is a major consumer of aluminum, but it does not own any aluminum mining interests. Therefore, it is naturally short aluminum and must cover this short exposure by purchasing aluminum to meet its manufacturing needs.

This puts Boeing at risk to rising aluminum prices. To hedge this risk, Boeing can purchase aluminum futures contracts.[12] However, a speculator must

---

[12] This is but one way that Boeing hedges its short exposure to aluminum. It can enter into long term contracts to purchase aluminum at fixed prices. These are essentially custom-tailored futures contracts, or forward contracts.

be lured to the market to sell the futures contract to Boeing and to take on commodity price risk. To entice the speculator, Boeing will be willing to purchase the futures contract at a price F_T that is greater than the expected future spot price:

$$F_T > E(S_T) \tag{7}$$

Boeing is willing to purchase the futures contract at an expected loss in return for eliminating the uncertainty over aluminum prices. The speculator will sell the futures contract and expect to earn a profit of $F_T - E(S_T)$. Of course, the speculator might earn more or less (or even lose money) depending upon the actual spot price of aluminum at maturity of the futures contract. If the inequality in equation (7) remains true at maturity of the aluminum futures contract, then the speculator will earn $F_T - S_T$.

The reader might ask why the speculator is necessary. Why doesn't Boeing negotiate directly with aluminum producers in fixed price contracts to lock in the price of aluminum and eliminate its commodity price exposure? To the extent it can, Boeing does. In fact, to the extent that commodity producers and commodity consumers can negotiate directly with one another, price risk can be eliminated without the need for speculators. However, the manufacture of aluminum does not always match Boeing's production cycle, and Boeing will have short-term demands for aluminum that will expose it to price risk. Speculators fill this gap.

Similarly, Exxon has a non-diversified exposure to crude oil. It can reduce the price risk associated with oil by selling its production forward. Yet, in many cases there may not be a willing consumer to purchase the forward production of crude oil. Therefore, Exxon must sell its future production at a discount to entice the speculator/investor into the market.

Contango futures markets have an upward sloping price curve. That is, the longer dated the futures contract, the greater must be the futures price that the speculator receives from selling the futures contract to the hedger. Higher prices reflect the additional risk that the speculator accepts over the longer period of time.

Backwardated versus contango markets also depend upon global supply and demand of the underlying commodity. Consider the case of crude oil. In early 1999, the market was awash in crude oil. Additional production from Iraq, a slowdown in Asian economies from the Asian Contagion in 1998, and lack of agreement (read cheating) by OPEC members led to a glut of crude oil. As a result, crude oil futures contracts reflected a contango market.

Exhibit 10 demonstrates this contango market. The futures prices presented in the graph are the crude oil futures prices that existed in January 1999. Notice that the further in time to maturity of the futures contract, the greater the price. This is in direct contrast to what we described in our example with Exxon. The reason is that in early 1999, with so much oil all about, petroleum producers began to shut in production. Oil wells were shut down because spot prices were so low. It was better for oil producers to wait for crude oil prices to rise and then resume production.

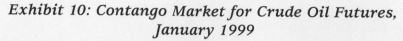

Exhibit 10: Contango Market for Crude Oil Futures, January 1999

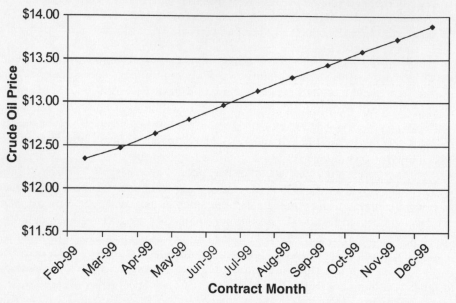

When this happened, it was the independent oil refiners and marketers (consumers of petroleum products) who became the hedgers in the market. These companies were naturally short crude oil and they bore the risk that crude oil prices would rise. To hedge this risk, they began to buy crude oil futures contracts to lock in the price of crude oil inputs. Speculators stepped in and provided the liquidity to the market by selling (instead of buying as in our prior example) crude oil futures contracts to the oil consumers. However, speculators sold the crude oil futures contracts at a premium to the expected future spot price to earn an appropriate return for bearing the crude oil price risk.

Eventually, OPEC got its act together, cut production, and policed its members. The reduction of crude oil to the marketplace brought the market back into backwardation. Exhibit 11 demonstrates the crude oil futures market as it existed one year later in January 2000. Longer dated futures contracts are priced at a discount to shorter dated futures contracts. This is a backwardated market.

Most commodity markets are backwardated most of the time. In fact the crude oil market is in backwardation approximately 70% of the time. The reason is that backwardated markets encourage commodity producers to produce. Consider Exhibit 11. In January 2000, Exxon had a choice: It could produce crude oil immediately and sell it at a price of $25.50 per barrel or it could sell it six months later at a price of $22.23. The choice is easy; Exxon would prefer to produce today and sell crude oil at a higher price rather than produce tomorrow and sell it a lower price. Therefore, backwardation is a necessary condition for current production of the underlying commodity.

However, sometimes supply and demand become unbalanced as was the case with crude oil in 1998 and early 1999. When this occurs, commodity futures markets can reverse their natural course and flip between backwardation and contango.

Exhibits 10 and 11 also highlight another useful point: the role of the speculator. The speculator does not care whether the commodity markets are in backwardation or contango; she is agnostic. All the speculator cares about is receiving an appropriate premium for the price risk she will bear. If the market is backwardated, the speculator is willing to purchase the futures contract from the hedger, but only at a discount. If the commodities market is in contango, the speculator will sell the futures contract, but only at a premium.

One last important point must be made regarding Exhibits 10 and 11. The speculator/investor in commodity futures can earn a profit no matter which way the commodity markets are acting. The conclusion is that the expected long-term returns to commodity investing are independent of the long-term commodity price trends. As we just demonstrated, the speculator is agnostic with respect to the current price trend of crude oil. Investment profits can be earned whether the market is in backwardation or contango. Therefore, profits in the commodity markets are determined by the supply and demand for risk capital, not the long-term pricing trends of the commodity markets.

Exhibit 11: Backwardated Market for Crude Oil Futures, January 2000

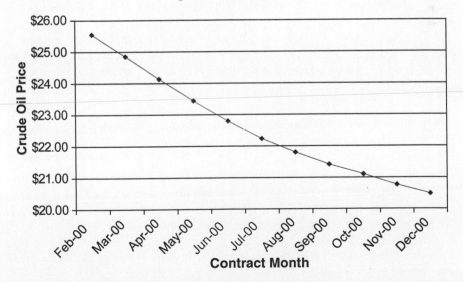

COMMODITY PRICES COMPARED TO FINANCIAL ASSET PRICES

We conclude this chapter by comparing commodity prices to financial asset prices. As we stated at the beginning of the chapter, financial asset prices reflect the long-term discounted value of a stream of expected future revenues. In the case of stock prices, this future revenue stream may be eternal. In the case of a bond, the time is finite but can be very long, 10 to 20 years of expected cash flows. Investors in financial assets are compensated for the risk of fluctuating cash flows, and this risk is reflected in the interest rate used to discount those cash flows.

Thus, long-term expectations and interest rates are critical for pricing financial assets. Conversely, speculators and investors in commodities earn returns for bearing short-term commodity price risk. By bearing the price risk for commodity producers and commodity consumers, commodity investors and speculators receive exposure to the hedger's short-term earnings instead of its long-term cash flows.

This short-term exposure to a hedger's earnings illustrates that commodities will be priced very differently from financial assets. Long-term expectations and interest rates have only a minimal impact on commodity prices. Therefore, commodity prices can react very differently from financial asset prices when short-term expectations and long-term expectations diverge. This divergence occurs naturally as part of the course of the business cycle.

For instance, at the bottom of a recession, the short-term expectation of the economy's growth is negative. Commodity prices will decline to reflect this lower demand for raw inputs. However, it is at the bottom of a recession when discount rates are low and when long-term earnings expectations are revised upwards that stocks and bonds begin to perform well. The converse is true at the peak of an expansion. Commodity prices are high, but long-term earnings expectations decline.

The different reactions to different parts of the business cycle indicate that commodities tend to move in the opposite direction of stocks and bonds. This has important portfolio implications that we will discuss in the following chapters. Suffice for now to understand that commodity prices follow different pricing dynamics than that of financial assets.

CONCLUSION

In this chapter we established commodity futures as a separate asset class distinct from financial assets. Futures contracts are important tools not only for hedgers but also for speculators. Many hedge funds make use of the futures markets either for arbitrage opportunities or to earn risk premiums.

We also laid the groundwork in terms of pricing dynamics and discussed the economics of commodity futures markets. In the next two chapters we will demonstrate how commodity futures can be added to a diversified portfolio to improve the overall risk and return profile of that portfolio.

Chapter 11

Investing in Commodity Futures

I n Chapter 10 we presented an introduction to the commodity markets and the methods by which investors access those markets. In this chapter we expand the discussion to discuss the strategic reasons for investing in commodity futures.

We begin by developing the economic case for commodity futures. We then review the existing literature on the diversification benefits of commodity futures. Last we examine several investable benchmarks that have been developed for the commodity futures markets.

Our discussion in this chapter focuses on the class of physical commodity futures. These commodity futures are sometimes referred to as "real assets"—assets that increase with inflation.[1] Real assets may also be defined by the tangible nature of their existence. A stock or a bond is represented by a piece of paper, but a real asset has a physical presence such as gold, oil, cattle, or wheat.[2]

ECONOMIC RATIONALE

We previously stated that commodities are an asset class distinct from stocks and bonds. In this section we clarify that distinction and demonstrate where and why commodity prices react differently than capital asset prices.

Commodities and the Business Cycle

In Chapter 10 we demonstrated that commodity prices are not as directly impacted by changes in discount rates as stocks and bonds. We also discussed how commodity prices are not determined by the discounted value of future cash flows. Instead, commodity prices are determined by the current supply and demand of the underlying commodity. Since commodity prices are driven by different economic fundamentals as stocks and bonds, they should be expected to have little correlation or even negative correlation with the prices of capital assets.

There are three arguments why commodity prices should, in fact, be negatively correlated with the prices of stocks and bonds. The first is the relationship

---

[1] See Kenneth Froot, "Hedging Portfolios with Real Assets," *The Journal of Portfolio Management* (Summer 1995), pp. 60–77.

[2] Under this definition, real estate also qualifies as a real asset because there is a tangible nature to the investment (i.e., a building, a shopping center, an apartment complex).

that commodity futures prices have with inflation. Inflation is well documented to have a detrimental impact on the values of stocks and bonds. However, inflation is expected to have a positive impact on commodity futures prices for two reasons.

First, physical commodity prices such as oil are an underlying source of inflation. As the cost of raw materials increases, so does the producers' price inflation and the consumer price inflation. In fact, commodity prices are a component of the producer price index and the consumer price index. Therefore, higher commodity prices mean higher inflation.

Also, higher inflation means higher short-term interest rates. This is also has a beneficial impact on commodity futures investments because of their collateral yield. As we discussed in the prior chapter, commodity futures contracts can be purchased with a down payment known as the initial margin. The initial margin can be contributed in the form of cash or in U.S. Treasury bills. This means that one component of return from an investment in commodity futures is the interest that is earned on the margin deposit that supports the futures contract.[3] Higher inflation therefore, means a higher interest rate on the margin on deposit, and a higher return from investing in commodity futures contracts.

Exhibit 1 documents the relationship between inflation, commodity futures, and stocks and bonds. This chart plots the correlation of monthly returns between stocks, bonds, and commodities with the rate of inflation. The time period is January 1990 through December 2000.[4]

Exhibit 1: Correlation with Inflation

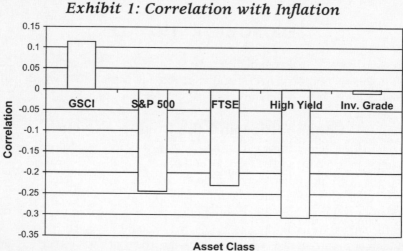

[3] If the futures margin is deposited in cash, then the futures broker may pay a higher interest rate on that deposit. Alternatively, if the futures margin is deposited in Treasury bills, as the T-bills mature, newer, higher yielding T-bills may be used to replace them.

[4] We use the Goldman Sachs Commodity Index as our proxy for commodity prices. There are, in fact, several commodity indices that we will discuss later in the chapter. Data for the GSCI was provided by Heather Shemilt at Goldman Sachs.

Exhibit 2: Correlation with the Change in Inflation

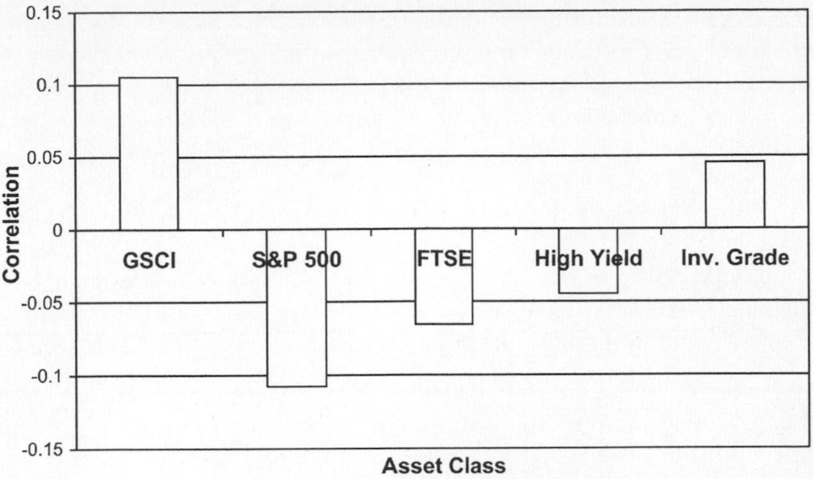

As can be seen, commodity futures prices are positively correlated with inflation. Conversely, capital assets such as stocks and bonds are negatively correlated with inflation. Therefore, throughout the course of the business cycle, as inflation increases, capital asset values decrease, but commodity futures values increase. The reverse is also true, as inflation decreases, capital asset prices increase, but commodity futures prices decrease.

Notice that the Financial Times Stock Index (FTSE) of the 100 largest stocks traded on the London Stock Exchange is also negatively correlated with the U.S. inflation rate. This is important to note because an investor seeking international diversification as a means to escape the ravages of domestic inflation did not find it in foreign stocks.

Even more important, commodity futures prices are positively correlated with *the change* in the inflation rate while capital assets are negatively correlated with changes in the rate of inflation.[5] This is important because changes in the rate of inflation tend to reflect inflation shocks (i.e., unanticipated changes that force investors to revise their expectations about future inflation). A positive change in the inflation rate means that investor's expectations regarding future inflation rates will increase. Stocks and bond prices react negatively to such revised expectations while commodity futures prices react positively.

Exhibit 2 demonstrates the reaction of capital assets and commodity assets to changes in the rate of inflation. All capital assets except investment grade bonds react negatively to changes in the inflation rate, while commodities react positively.

---

[5] See Philip Halpern and Randy Warsager, "The Performance of Energy and Non-Energy Based Commodity Investment Vehicles in Periods of Inflation," *The Journal of Alternative Assets* (Summer 1998), pp. 75–81.

Exhibit 3: The Business Cycle and Stock, Bond, and Commodity Prices

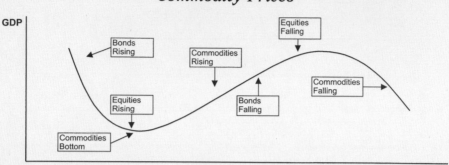

A second reason why commodity returns may be negatively correlated with the returns to stocks and bonds is that commodity futures prices are impacted by short-term expectations while stocks and bonds are affected by long-term expectations. For example, in a strong economy financial assets may decline over fears of increased inflation or sustainability of the economic growth. These are long-term concerns. Conversely, commodity prices will react favorably because they are influenced by the high demand for raw materials under the current market conditions. The result is that commodity futures prices and stock and bond prices can react very differently at different parts of the business cycle. Exhibit 3 diagrams this counter-cyclical price move.

This counter-cyclical movement between commodity futures and stocks and bonds is demonstrated by research conducted by Goldman Sachs & Co.[6] When the economy is below capacity (as measured by long-run GDP), equity returns have been at their highest, but commodity prices have been at their lowest. This occurs at the bottom of an economic cycle. As economic growth accelerates, stock prices begin to decline but commodity prices increase. When the economy heats up and exceeds long-run GDP, the return to commodity futures exceeds that for stocks. These results are displayed in Exhibit 4.

Exhibit 4 demonstrates that financial assets such as stocks and bonds are primarily anticipatory. Their value is derived from expectations regarding long-term earnings and coupon payments. Consequently, they perform best when the economy appears the worst but the prospects for improvement are the highest.

Real assets, on the other hand, show the opposite pattern. Commodity prices are determined not so much by the future prospects of the economy, but by the level of current economic activity. Consequently commodity prices are at their lowest when economic activity is at its lowest, and vice versa.

---

[6] See Goldman Sachs & Co., "The Strategic Case for Using Commodities in Portfolio Diversification," Goldman Sachs Research Series on Commodities as an Asset Class (July 1996).

Exhibit 4: Business Cycle and the Returns to Stocks and Commodities

Description of the Business Cycle	S&P 500 Returns	Commodity Returns
Low Output and Slow Growth	18.49%	–5.28%
Low Output and Fast Growth	12.08%	11.23%
High Output and Fast Growth	7.21%	29.35%
High Output and Slow Growth	–2.85%	27.53%

Commodities are represented by the Goldman Sachs Commodity Index
Source: Goldman Sachs & Co., "The Strategic Case for Using Commodities in Portfolio Diversification" (June 2001).

A third argument for the negative correlation between commodity prices and capital assets is based on economic production.[7] Consider the three primary inputs to economic production: capital, labor, and raw materials. The returns to these three factors should equal the price of production. In the short to intermediate term, the cost of labor should remain stable. Therefore, for any given price level of production, an increase in the return to capital must mean a reduction in the return to raw materials, and vice versa. The result is a negative correlation between commodity prices and the prices of capital assets.

In sum, commodity prices are expected to be at the very least uncorrelated with the returns to stocks and bonds. Additionally, there are three reasons to expect commodity prices to be negatively correlated with stocks and bonds. First, inflation has a positive effect on commodity prices but a negative impact on stocks and bonds. Second, commodity prices are impacted by a different set of expectations than that for stocks and bonds. Last, in the production process there is a tradeoff between the returns to capital and the returns to raw materials.

Event Risk

In Chapters 6 and 7 we demonstrated how financial assets and hedge fund strategies are exposed to significant event risk. For example, our analysis of the returns to hedge funds around the financial turmoil of August and September 1998 indicated that most hedge fund strategies experienced significant negative returns. Additionally, we demonstrated that most arbitrage strategies have exposure to event risk, which can result in significant negative returns.

Commodities, by contrast, tend to have *positive* exposure to event risk. The reason is that the surprises that occur in the commodities markets tend to be those that unexpectedly reduce the supply of the commodity to the market. Events such as OPEC agreements to reduce the supply of crude oil, a cold snap in winter, war, or political instability can drive up energy prices. Similarly, events such as droughts, floods, and crop freezes all reduce the supply of agricultural products. Last, strikes and labor unrest can drive up the prices of both precious and industrial metals.

[7] See Robert Greer, "Institutional Use of Physical Commodity Indices," in *Commodity Derivatives and Finance* (London: Euromoney Books, 1999).

Exhibit 5: Goldman Sachs Commodity Index

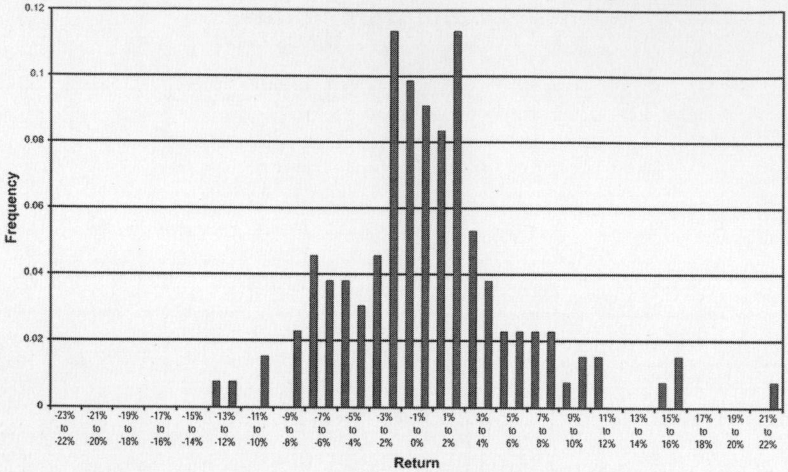

| E(Return) | 0.74% | Std Dev: | 5.47% | Sharpe: | 0.0531 |
| Skewness: | 0.819 | Kurtosis: | 2.313 | | |

These patterns of unexpected shocks to the commodity prices should provide a pattern of positively skewed returns. In Chapter 6 we demonstrated that many hedge fund strategies have positively skewed distributions — that is, more return observations to the right of the median (positive) than to the left of the median (negative). Positively skewed return distributions will have a beneficial impact to a diversified portfolio because they can provide an upward return bias to the portfolio.

This positive skew to commodity returns is verified when we consider the distribution of returns to commodity futures. Exhibit 5 demonstrates the frequency distribution for the Goldman Sachs Commodity Index, an investable index of commodity futures. We will discuss the GSCI in more detail later in this chapter. For now, the focus is on the pattern of returns associated with an investment in the GSCI.

Using monthly data from January 1990 through December 2000, we graph the frequency distribution of returns for the GSCI. This distribution is shifted to the right-hand side of the graph. This indicates a positive bias to commodity futures returns: large positive returns occur more frequently than large negative returns.

Furthermore, these patterns of commodity shocks are expected to be uncorrelated. For example, OPEC agreements to cut oil production should be uncorrelated with droughts in the agricultural regions around the world or with labor strikes affecting metals mining. The point is that the global supply and demand factors for each individual commodity market that determine the price of each commodity are very different. The primary factors that determine the supply and demand for, and the price of, oil are very different from those that affect the price of wheat, gold or aluminum. Consequently, we would expect the price patterns of commodities to be uncorrelated with each other. This has important implications for commodity indices.

Exhibit 6: Annual Returns in Years of Market Stress

Year	S&P 500	Commodities
1973	−14.69%	74.96%
1974	−26.47%	39.51%
1977	−7.16%	10.37%
1981	−4.92%	−23.01%
1987	5.25%	23.77%
Oct. 1987	−21.54%	1.05%
1990	−3.10%	29.08%
1998	26.66%	−35.75%
2000	−10.14%	49.74%

Commodities are represented by the Goldman Sachs Commodity Index

Equally important is that shocks to the commodities markets are expected to be at the least, uncorrelated with the financial markets, and more likely, to be negatively correlated with the financial markets. The reason follows from our discussion above — most shocks to the commodity markets tend to reduce the supply of raw materials to the market. The sudden decrease of raw materials should have a positive impact on commodity prices, but a negative impact on financial asset prices, whose expected returns will be reduced by the higher cost of production inputs.

Consider Exhibit 6. This exhibit demonstrates several years where there were significant shocks to the supply and demand of physical commodities. Again, we use the GSCI as a benchmark for commodity returns. In the early and mid 1970s there were a series of oil price shocks. This was a boon for commodity prices, but disaster for financial asset prices. In contrast, 1981 was a year of severe recession for the United States. Financial asset prices declined but so did commodities, as there was simply insufficient demand both for finished goods and raw materials to support either financial asset prices or commodity prices.

1990 was the year of the Iraqi invasion of Kuwait. This political instability had a negative impact on financial asset prices, but a positive impact on commodity prices. Last, in 1998, there was a glut of cheap crude oil and petroleum products on in the market. In late 1997, OPEC voted to increase production just as the southeast Asian economies were slipping into a steep recession. In addition under the UN "food for oil" program, new oil production came on line from Iraq. Further, an extremely mild winter (recall "El Nino") resulted in a build up of petroleum inventories around the world. The result, in 1998, was plenty of cheap raw materials, which in turn translated to strong stock market gains in the United States.

In conclusion, commodity price shocks tend to favor supply disruptions rather than sudden increases in supply. These disruptions provide positive returns for commodities at the same time that they provide negative returns for financial assets. Therefore, the event risk associated with commodities tends to favor investors in the commodity markets while detrimentally impacting investors in the financial markets. In the next section we discuss the empirical literature that supports the notion of commodities within a diversified portfolio.

THE EMPIRICAL EVIDENCE SUPPORTING COMMODITY FUTURES AS AN ASSET CLASS

While commodities within an investment portfolio are considered to be a new phenomenon, the fact is that organized commodity trading has been in existence far longer than stock and bond trading. The first commodity exchange was the Osaka rice exchange that began trading in Japan in the 1400s. By contrast, the New York Stock Exchange did not begin trading until the early 1800s. Nonetheless, commodity futures investing is relatively new compared to stock and bond investing.

In his seminal paper more than two decades ago, Greer introduced the idea of investing in commodity futures as a portfolio diversification tool.[8] In his article he proposed an unleveraged index of commodity futures prices be used as an inflation hedge for a stock portfolio. He demonstrated that a combination of a commodity futures index and large capitalized stocks provided a better risk and return profile than a portfolio constructed solely of stocks.

Five years later, Zvi Bodie examined how commodity futures contracts can supplement a portfolio of stocks and bonds to improve the risk and return trade-off in an inflationary environment.[9] Studying the period of 1953-1981, he found that the inclusion of commodity futures shifts the efficient frontier up and to the left. He concluded that a portfolio of stocks, bonds, Treasury bills, and commodity futures improved the risk and return than an investment portfolio constructed without commodity futures.

In more recent research, Ankrim and Hensel,[10] Lummer and Scott,[11] Kaplan and Lummer,[12] Gibson,[13] and Anson[14] all examine adding commodity futures to an investment portfolio through an investment in a passive commodity futures index. All five studies conclude that an investment in a passive commodities futures index provides a good diversifier for stocks and bonds as well as an effective hedge against inflation.

Satyanarayan and Varagnis extend the investment analysis of commodity futures to an international portfolio.[15] They find that commodity futures returns

[8] See Robert Greer, "Conservative Commodities: A Key Inflation Hedge," *The Journal of Portfolio Management* (Summer 1978).

[9] See Zvi Bodie, "Commodity Futures as a Hedge Against Inflation," *The Journal of Portfolio Management* (Spring 1983), pp. 12–17.

[10] Ernest Ankrim and Chris Hensel, "Commodities in Asset Allocation: A Real Asset Alternative to Real Estate?" *Financial Analysts Journal* (May/June 1993), pp. 20–29.

[11] Scott Lummer and Laurence Siegel, "GSCI Collateralized Futures: A Hedging and Diversification Tool for Institutional Investors," *Journal of Investing* (Summer 1993), pp. 75–82.

[12] Paul Kaplan and Scott Lummer, "GSCI Collateralized Futures as a Hedging and Diversification Tool for Institutional Investors: An Update," working paper, Ibbotson Associates (November 1997).

[13] Roger Gibson, "The Rewards of Multiple Asset Class Investing," *Journal of Financial Planning* (March 1999), pp. 50–59.

[14] Mark Anson, "Spot Returns, Roll Yield, and Diversification with Commodity Futures," *The Journal of Alternative Investments* (Winter 1998), pp. 16–32.

[15] See Sudhakar Satyanarayan and Panos Varangis, "Diversification Benefits of Commodity Assets in Global Portfolios," *The Journal of Investing* (Spring 1996), pp. 69–78.

are negatively correlated with the returns to all developed markets and with three of six emerging markets. One reason why all developed markets are negatively correlated with the returns to commodity futures is that developed markets are the primary consumers of commodity inputs. Conversely, emerging markets tend to be net suppliers of commodity inputs. Consequently, it is not surprising to find that some emerging markets are positively correlated with commodity futures prices.

Anson extends the analysis of commodity futures to utility theory. He finds that the marginal utility of commodity futures investing increases with an investor's level of risk aversion. That is, the more risk averse the investor, the greater the utility from investing in commodity futures.[16]

Froot compares three classes of real assets: real estate, commodity futures, and the stocks of companies that are commodity producers.[17] He finds that when commodity futures are the initial hedge in a portfolio, it renders the other real assets ineffective. Yet, when commodity futures are added to the portfolio as a secondary hedge after other real assets have already been added, commodity futures still remain a significant portfolio diversifier. However, he concludes that the same cannot be said for real estate. Once commodity futures have been added to an investment portfolio, real estate does little to reduce portfolio volatility. The same conclusion is reached for commodity-based equity. In other words, commodity futures provide a more effective hedge against unexpected inflation than do either real estate or the stock of commodity producing companies.

In conclusion, prior empirical studies have found commodity futures to have significant diversification potential for financial assets. All of the studies to date have found that the addition of commodity futures to a portfolio of stocks and bonds has the ability to reduce the risk of the portfolio for a given level of return. Further, each of these studies used an investable commodity futures index to reach their conclusions.

COMMODITY FUTURES INDICES

In this section we review several investable commodity futures indices, analyze their construction, and consider their application to a diversified portfolio.

Description of a Commodity Futures Index

The first commodity indices were designed to reflect price changes either in the cash/spot markets or in the futures markets. However, these indices did not reflect the total return that can be earned from commodity futures contracts. Therefore, they were not investable. An example of a price change index is the Commodity Research Bureau (CRB) Commodities Index.

---

[16] See Mark Anson, "Maximizing Utility with Commodity Futures," *The Journal of Portfolio Management* (Summer 1999), pp. 86–94.

[17] See Kenneth Froot, "Hedging Portfolios with Real Assets," *The Journal of Portfolio Management* (Summer 1995), pp. 60–77.

A commodity futures index should represent the total return that would be earned from holding only long positions in unleveraged physical commodity futures. Financial futures should not be included because, as we demonstrated in Chapter 10, financial futures contracts are economically linked to the underlying financial assets. Therefore, there is no diversification benefit from adding long positions in financial futures to a portfolio of financial assets.

In Chapter 10 we also described how a futures contract may be purchased by paying only a small portion of the total price of the underlying commodity called the initial margin. The initial margin typically represents 5% to 10% of the futures price. Therefore, futures contracts are purchased with leverage. For example, a 10% initial margin requirement translates into a leverage ratio of 10 to 1. This means that for every dollar invested in a commodity futures contract, the investor would receive $10 of commodity price exposure. The application of leverage can enhance an investor's return, but at the same time can also exacerbate an investor's losses. Therefore, the leverage associated with a futures contract can increase the volatility of the investment.

In contrast, commodity futures indices are constructed to be unleveraged. The face value of the futures contracts are fully supported (collateralized) either by cash or by Treasury bills. Futures contracts are purchased to provide economic exposure to commodities equal to the amount of cash dollars invested in the index. Therefore, every dollar of exposure to a commodity futures index represents one dollar of commodity price risk.

For example, the current initial margin for gold is $1,350. With gold selling at $250 and 100 ounces of gold being the size of the contract, one futures contract has economic exposure to gold of $25,000. A managed futures account would typically pay the initial margin of $1,350 and receive economic exposure to gold equivalent to $25,000. The percentage of equity capital committed to the futures contract is equal to $1,350/$25,000 = 5.4%. In contrast, a commodity futures index will fully collateralize the gold futures contract. This means $25,000 of U.S. Treasury bills will be held to fully support the face value of the gold futures contract. In fact, the face value of every futures contract included in a commodity index will be fully collateralized by an investment in U.S. Treasury bills.

In this way, an unleveraged commodity futures index represents the returns an investor could earn from continuously holding a passive long-only position in a basket of commodity futures contracts. The passive index must reflect all components of return from commodity futures contracts: price changes, collateral yield, and roll yield.

Finally, we note that a commodity futures index has several differences compared to a managed futures account. Managed futures accounts represent the returns that can be earned from the active investment style of a Commodity Trading Advisor (CTA) or a Commodity Pool Operator (CPO). In a managed futures account the CTA or CPO has discretion over the trading positions taken.

First, managed futures accounts are just that — actively managed accounts — while commodity futures indices are designed to provide passive exposure to the commodity futures markets. Second, CTAs and CPOs tend to invest across the spectrum of the futures markets, including financial futures as well as commodity futures in their investment portfolio. Third, CTAs and CPOs may invest both long and short in futures contracts. Commodity futures indices, in contrast, invest in long-only positions. Last, managed futures accounts tend to apply leverage in the purchase and sale of commodity futures contracts. We will have more to say about the managed futures industry in Chapter 13.

Sources of Index Return

The total return from an unleveraged commodity futures index comes from three primary sources: changes in spot prices of the underlying commodity, the interest earned from the Treasury bills used to collateralize the futures contracts, and the roll yield. Each component can be an important part of the return of a commodity index in any given year.

Spot Prices

As we indicated in Chapter 10, spot commodity prices are determined by the supply and demand characteristics of each commodity market. We demonstrated, for example, how the price of crude oil plummeted in 1998 due to over-production by OPEC members, extra production by Iraq, and the slow down in southeast Asia due to the Asian Contagion of late 1997. This supply imbalance drove crude oil prices down. However, in early 1999, OPEC members reached an agreement to cut production and restrict the supply of crude oil into the marketplace. This changed the supply and demand equilibrium from one of excess supply to one of excess demand, and crude oil prices rose significantly.

These price changes in the spot market are reflected directly in the commodity futures markets. Recall the following equation from Chapter 10:

$$F = Se^{(r + c - y)(T - t)} \tag{1}$$

where

> F is the futures price
> S is the current spot/cash price of the underlying commodity
> r is the risk-free rate of return
> c is the cost of storage
> y is the convenience yield
> $T - t$ is the time to maturity of the contract

Other factors remaining equal (storage cost, risk-free rate, and convenience yield), when the spot price of the underlying commodity increases in value, so will the futures price. The reverse is also true, as spot prices decline, so will the futures price. Therefore, changes in the current cash price of a commodity flow right through to the futures price.

This is important to understand, because as we discussed above, most of the shocks with respect to physical commodities tend to be events that reduce the current supply. That is, physical commodities have positive event risk. Supply and demand shocks to the physical commodity markets almost always result in positive price changes for both the spot market and the futures market.

Collateral Yield

As we discussed above, a commodity futures index is unleveraged. It is unleveraged because the economic exposure underlying the basket of futures contract is fully collateralized by the purchase of U.S. Treasury bills. Therefore, for every $1 invested in a commodity futures index the investor receives $1 dollar of diversified commodity exposure plus interest on $1 dollar invested in U.S. Treasury bills.

The interest earned on the Treasury bills used as collateral is called the *collateral yield*, and it can be a significant part of the total return to a commodity futures index. Further, changes in inflation rates will be reflected in the yield on Treasury bills. This is another way that a commodity futures index can hedge against inflation.

Roll Yield

Roll yield is the least obvious source of return for commodity futures. Roll yield is derived from the shape of the commodity futures term structure. Recall our discussion from Chapter 10 that commodity futures markets can either be in backwardation, where futures prices are below the expected spot price, or contango, where futures prices are above the current spot price for the underlying commodity.

When the futures markets are in backwardation, a positive return will be earned from a simple "buy and hold" strategy. The positive return is earned because as the futures contract gets closer to maturity, its price must converge to that of the spot price of the commodity. Since the spot price is greater than the futures price, this means that the futures price must increase in value. This convergence is known as "rolling up the yield curve," or simply, "roll yield." A demonstration should help.

Consider Exhibit 7. This exhibit demonstrates the term structure for crude oil futures contracts in June and July 2000. Notice that the futures prices decline the longer the maturity of the futures contract. Therefore, the term structure is downward sloping. This is a demonstration of backwardation — the futures prices are below the current spot price for crude oil.

Recall that a backwardated market indicates that producers of commodities are willing to hedge their commodity price risk by selling their future production at lower prices than the current spot price of the commodity. The farther out in time that they sell their future production, the greater the discount they must offer to investors to entice them to purchase the futures contracts. As a futures contract gets closer to maturity, less price risk remains, and an investor will harvest part of the price discount as profit by rolling up the futures yield curve. Rolling up the term structure results in profit harvesting.

Exhibit 7: Term Structure for Crude Oil Futures

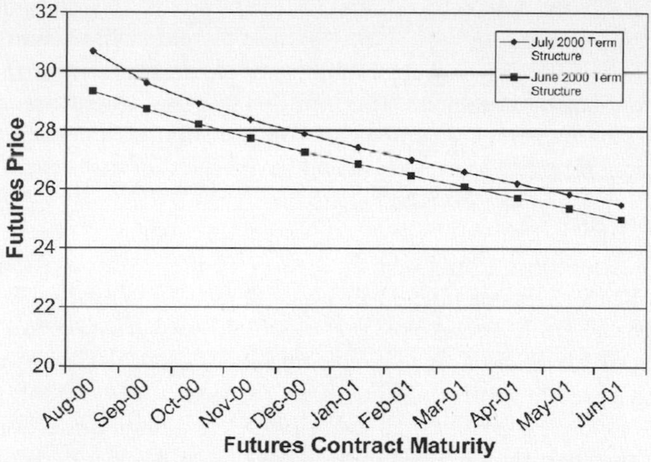

Exhibit 8: Calculation of the Roll Yield for Crude Oil Futures

Contract Maturity	Price as of July 2000	Less Price at June 2000	Less Change in Spot Price	Equals Roll Yield
Aug-00	$30.67	$29.31	$0.50	$0.86
Sep-00	$29.60	$28.71	$0.50	$0.39
Oct-00	$28.90	$28.20	$0.50	$0.20
Nov-00	$28.35	$27.72	$0.50	$0.13
Dec-00	$27.88	$27.26	$0.50	$0.12
1-Jan	$27.42	$26.85	$0.50	$0.07
1-Feb	$27.00	$26.47	$0.50	$0.03
1-Mar	$26.60	$26.10	$0.50	$0.00
1-Apr	$26.21	$25.73	$0.50	–$0.02
1-May	$25.84	$25.36	$0.50	–$0.02
1-Jun	$25.49	$24.99	$0.50	$0.00

In July 2000 the futures term structure is slightly above the June crude oil term structure that existed in June, reflecting an increase in crude oil spot prices of about $0.50. The increase in spot prices shifted the whole term structure upwards. In addition to the price appreciation, the owner of a long crude oil can earn the roll yield.

Exhibit 8 calculates the roll yield associated with each futures contract over the one month holding period of June to July 2000. As a futures contract approaches maturity, there is less price risk, and therefore less of a discount is required to entice buyers into the market. Therefore, part of the price discount can be harvested by rolling up the yield curve.

For example, suppose an investor purchased at the beginning of June 2000 the crude oil futures contract maturing in August 2000. On June 1, 2000, the August futures contract was priced at $29.31. One month later, on July 5, 2000, the August crude oil futures contract was priced at $30.67. Of the $1.36 increase in price for the August futures contract, 50 cents was due to an increase in spot prices. The remainder, 86 cents, was the roll yield earned from the buy-and-hold strategy.

As can be seen, the roll yield is greater the closer the futures contract is to maturity. This is because a greater amount of uncertainty is reduced the closer the futures contract is to maturity. The farther out on the term structure an investor goes, the less uncertainty can be resolved as a futures contract rolls up the curve. Consequently, as an investor moves farther out on the term structure, the roll yield declines, and can even be negative.

How large can this roll yield be? A study of crude oil futures prices found that a long position in the first nearby futures contract (the contract closest to maturity) earned an average annual roll yield of 9% over the period 1987–1995.[18] Additionally, the study found that the roll yield was greatest for commodity futures contracts that were closer to maturity.

Notice that the roll yield can also be negative. In a contango market, when futures prices are greater than spot prices, the futures prices will roll down the term structure resulting in lost value as the futures price converges to the spot price. Recall from Chapter 10, in a contango market, commodity consumers are the natural hedgers, and they purchase futures contracts. Investors who sell short the futures contracts to the commodity consumers will collect the futures premium as the futures contract rolls down the term structure.

Adding the Three Return Components

The total return of any commodity futures index is the combined return of the above three components: changes in spot prices, collateral yield, and roll yield. In Exhibit 9 we present the annual total return for the GSCI over the period 1970–2000 including the three sub-components of total return.

Exhibit 9 indicates that each component of return can add significant value to the total return associated with commodity futures. For instance, spot returns range from −30.5% to +48.7%. Similarly, roll yield ranges from −14.6% to +21.4%, and collateral yield ranges from +2.7% to +13.2%. Overall, the GSCI earned an average annual total return of 15.3%.[19]

One frequent question associated with commodity futures is how can there be a positive return if there is little or no inflation. The answer is that changes in inflation are primarily reflected in changes in the spot prices for commodities. This is but one component of the total return associated with an investment in commodity futures. With or without inflation, commodity producers still need to hedge their future production, and this creates a positive roll yield. Also, even if inflation is low, real interest rates may be high. Therefore, the yield on U.S. Treasury bills used as collateral can be significant. As a result, inflation is not a necessary condition for earning attractive returns from an investment in commodity futures.

---

[18] See Daniel Nash, "Relative Value Trading in Commodities," working paper (July 15, 1996).

[19] The author is indebted to Heather Shemilt and Frances Orabona of Goldman Sachs & Co. for providing the data for this analysis.

Exhibit 9: Spot Returns, Collateral Yield, and Roll Yield

Date	GSCI TR Annual Returns	GSCI Collateral Yield	GSCI Roll Yield	GSCI Spot Annual Returns
31-Dec-70	15.1%	7.3%	2.9%	4.9%
3-Jan-72	20.7%	5.3%	9.1%	6.3%
29-Dec-72	42.9%	5.7%	5.2%	31.9%
31-Dec-73	75.0%	12.2%	14.1%	48.7%
31-Dec-74	39.5%	10.8%	8.0%	20.7%
31-Dec-75	−17.2%	4.8%	8.5%	−30.5%
30-Dec-76	−11.9%	4.4%	−2.5%	−13.8%
30-Dec-77	10.4%	5.8%	3.8%	0.8%
29-Dec-78	31.6%	9.3%	1.1%	21.2%
31-Dec-79	33.8%	13.2%	−2.5%	23.2%
31-Dec-80	11.1%	12.5%	−14.4%	13.0%
31-Dec-81	−23.0%	10.4%	−8.5%	−25.0%
31-Dec-82	11.6%	11.6%	0.0%	−0.1%
30-Dec-83	16.3%	9.8%	−0.8%	7.3%
31-Dec-84	1.1%	9.5%	1.1%	−9.5%
31-Dec-85	10.0%	8.1%	1.6%	0.3%
31-Dec-86	2.0%	6.0%	14.8%	−18.8%
31-Dec-87	23.8%	7.1%	13.5%	3.2%
30-Dec-88	27.9%	8.4%	7.3%	12.2%
29-Dec-89	38.3%	11.0%	14.9%	12.4%
31-Dec-90	29.1%	9.6%	13.3%	6.1%
31-Dec-91	−6.1%	5.1%	8.4%	−19.6%
31-Dec-92	4.4%	3.6%	−1.5%	2.3%
31-Dec-93	−12.3%	2.7%	−5.3%	−9.6%
30-Dec-94	5.3%	4.5%	−9.7%	10.5%
29-Dec-95	20.3%	6.6%	1.2%	12.6%
31-Dec-96	33.9%	6.7%	21.4%	5.8%
31-Dec-97	−14.1%	4.3%	0.0%	−18.4%
31-Dec-98	−35.7%	3.1%	−14.6%	−24.3%
31-Dec-99	40.9%	6.5%	−11.9%	46.2%
29-Dec-00	49.7%	8.6%	14.2%	26.9%
Average	15.3%	7.6%	3.0%	4.7%

Source: Goldman Sachs provided GSCI index data; estimates of Collateral and Roll Yield were calculated by the author.

COMMODITY INDICES

It may surprise investors that there are several commodity futures indices in existence. These indices have all the benefits of a stock index: They are transparent, they are liquid, you can trade in the underlying component parts of the index, and they are investable. Even if an investor, such as a pension plan, cannot invest directly into commodity futures indices, it may still gain exposure through a commodity-linked note of the type described in Chapter 10.

An investment manager can use commodity futures indices in two ways. First, a commodity futures index can be used to implement a specific view on the expected returns from commodities as an asset class. This is a tactical bet by the investment manager that commodities will outperform stocks and bonds given the current position of the business cycle.

Alternatively, commodity futures indices can be used to provide passive portfolio diversification. Exhibit 3 demonstrated that commodity prices peak and bottom out at different parts of the business cycle than do financial assets. Within this context, commodities have a strategic purpose: to diversify the investment portfolio's risk and return, without any view as to the current state of the business cycle.

Unlike equity stock indices, where an investor can maintain her positions almost infinitely, commodity futures contracts specify a date for delivery. In order to maintain a continuous long-only position, expiring futures contracts must be sold and new futures contracts must be purchased. This provides the roll yield discussed above.

The Goldman Sachs Commodity Index

The GSCI is designed to be a benchmark for investment in the commodity markets and as a measure of commodity market performance over time. It is also designed to be a tradable index that is readily accessible to market participants. It is a long-only index of physical commodity futures. Not only is the GSCI comprised of physical commodity futures contracts, a futures contract trades on the index itself. In other words, investors can purchase a futures contract tied to the future expected spot value of the GSCI.

The GSCI was introduced in 1991. Although the GSCI was not published prior to that time, Goldman Sachs has calculated the historical value of the GSCI and related indices dating back to January 1970, based on historical prices of futures contracts and using the selection criteria and index construction established in 1991. The GSCI has been normalized to a value of 100 on December 31, 1969.

The GSCI is composed only of physical commodity futures. Financial futures contracts (on securities, currencies, or interest rates) are not included. The limitation to only physical commodity futures focuses the construction of the index on real assets that are the inputs to the global production process. Additionally, the GSCI is composed of the first nearby futures contract in each commodity (the futures contract that is closest to maturity).

The GSCI is a production-weighted index that is designed to reflect the relative significance of each of the constituent commodities to the world economy while preserving the tradability of the index by limiting eligible futures contracts to those with adequate liquidity. The GSCI is constructed using 5-year averages of a particular commodity's contribution to world production. This is done to mitigate the effect of any aberrant year with respect to the production of a commodity.

Exhibit 10: GSCI Commodity Group Weights as of July 2001

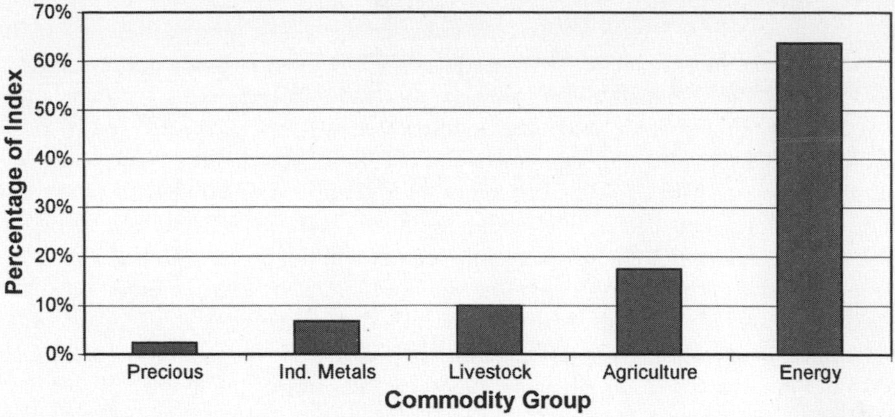

The GSCI is constructed with 26 physical commodities across five main groups of real assets: precious metals, industrial metals, livestock, agriculture, and energy. Exhibit 10 presents the weights of these five commodity groups in the GSCI as of July 2001. Energy is the largest component of the index. This reflects the importance of energy products in the global production process. Precious metals, on the other hand, represent the smallest component of the GSCI. While precious metals may be held as a store of value, they are a smaller input to global production.

The GSCI physical weights are set once a year (in January) and then the dollar percentage values are allowed to float for the remainder of the year. There is no limit to the weight any one commodity may become of the index and no minimum weight for any commodity. The GSCI is a (production) value weighted index. Value-weighted indices represent a momentum investment strategy because those commodity futures contracts that do well represent an increasing portion of the index.

Last, we consider the distribution of returns associated with the GSCI. In Exhibit 5 we plotted the monthly return distribution for the GSCI over the period 1990–2000. In that exhibit we reported a positive value for skew (0.82). This indicates that returns are biased to the upside.

The GSCI has a large positive value of kurtosis (2.313). From our discussion in Chapter 6, we know that this condition of leptokurtosis means that commodity returns experience large outlier returns more frequently than might be expected with a normal distribution. This indicates that commodity futures are exposed to event risk: the risk of sudden shocks to the global supply and demand for physical commodities. From our discussion of commodity event risk above, we expect that exposure to event risk to have a beneficial impact on commodity returns.

Dow Jones-AIG Commodity Index

The DJ-AIGCI is designed to provide both liquidity and diversification with respect to physical commodities.[20] It is a long-only index composed of futures contracts on 20 physical commodity products. These products include energy (crude oil, heating oil, unleaded gasoline, and natural gas), precious metals (gold and silver), industrial metals (copper, aluminum, zinc, and nickel), grains (wheat, corn, soybeans, and soybean oil), livestock (live cattle and lean hogs), and the "soft" commodities (cocoa, coffee, cotton, and sugar). The DJ-AIGCI is composed of commodities traded on U.S. commodity exchanges and also on the London Metals Exchange (LME). Contracts on the LME provide exposure to industrial metals such as aluminum, nickel, and zinc.

Unlike the GSCI, to determine the weightings of each commodity in the index, the DJ-AIGCI relies primarily on liquidity data. This index considers the relative amount of trading activity associated with a particular commodity to determine its weight in the index. Liquidity is an important indicator of the interest placed on a commodity by financial and physical market participants. The index also relies to a lesser extent on dollar-adjusted production data to determine index weights. Therefore, the index weights depend primarily on endogenous factors in the futures markets (liquidity), and secondarily, on exogenous factors to the futures markets (production).

The component weightings are also determined by several rules to ensure diversified commodity exposure. Disproportionate weighting to any particular commodity or sector could increase volatility and negate the concept of a broad-based commodity index. Therefore, the DJ-AIGCI index also applies two important diversification rules:

1. No related group of commodities (e.g., energy products, precious metals, livestock, or grains) may constitute more than 33% of the index weights.
2. No single commodity may constitute less than 2% of the index.

The DJ-AIGCI is re-weighted and re-balanced every January. Re-balancing and re-weighting is designed to reduce the exposure of the index to commodities that have appreciated in value and to increase the index's exposure to commodities that have underperformed. During the course of the year, commodity weights are free to increase or decrease as their values increase or decrease, subject to the two limits imposed above. This represents a momentum type of index.

Exhibit 11 presents the weights as of June 2001 associated with the DJ-AIGCI. Notice that the addition of natural gas at 6% plus petroleum products at 25% is close to the 33% limit for any commodity sector (in this case, energy).

Exhibit 12 presents a frequency distribution of the monthly returns to the DJ-AIGCI Index over the time period 1990–2000.[21] Similar to the GSCI, this dis-

---

[20] Information on the DJ-AIGCI can be found at the Dow Jones website, www.dj.com and using the dowjones weblinks to the DJ-AIGCI.

[21] The Dow Jones-AIGCI Index has been in operating existence only since 1998. Therefore, to calculate returns prior to 1998, Dow Jones and AIG had to calculate index returns back in time using the index construction rules currently in place.

tribution of returns demonstrates a positive skew indicating that more positive returns are experienced more frequently than negative returns. Additionally, the distribution of returns also demonstrates slight leptokurtosis, indicating a small exposure to outlier events.

Exhibit 11: Dow Jones-AIG Commodity Index Weights as of June 2001

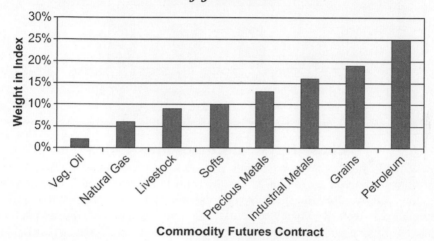

Exhibit 12: Distribution of Returns for the DJ-AIGCI

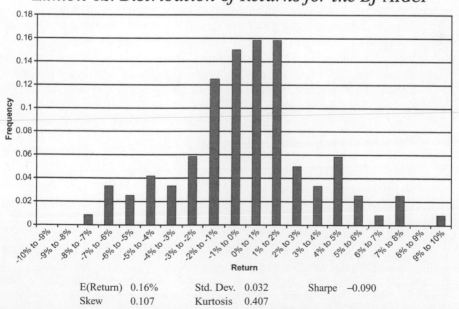

E(Return)	0.16%	Std. Dev.	0.032	Sharpe	−0.090
Skew	0.107	Kurtosis	0.407		

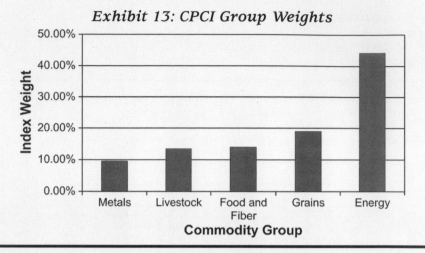

Exhibit 13: CPCI Group Weights

Chase Physical Commodity Index

The Chase Physical Commodity Index (CPCI) was created in 1993.[22] It is a total return commodity index that measures the reinvested daily returns of a portfolio of commodity futures and the daily interest associated with fully collateralized futures investments. The index contains 19 different commodity futures contracts representing five major commodity groups: grains (wheat, corn, soybeans, soybean meal, and soybean oil), metals (gold, silver, and copper), energy (crude oil, heating oil, unleaded gasoline, and natural gas), livestock (live cattle, feeder cattle, and lean hogs), and food and fiber (cocoa, coffee, sugar, and cotton).

The constituents of the CPCI are selected and weighted based on several criteria, including their value in world trade, availability of exchange-traded futures contracts listed on a U.S. commodity futures exchange, and sufficient trading volume and open interest in order to meet minimum liquidity standards.

The CPCI differs from the GSCI and the DJ-AIGCI in that once the weights are established, they remain constant throughout the year. This weighting scheme presents a contrarian view because the index rebalances by selling winners and buying losers. Even if there is no mean reversion for commodity prices, the fact that commodities in the index are less than perfectly correlated provides the opportunity to profit by selling expensive commodity futures contracts and purchasing cheap contracts.

Exhibit 13 presents the weights of the five major real asset groups in the CPCI as of June 2001. Similar to the GSCI and the DJ-AIGCI, energy is the largest group. However, the CPCI has a higher allocation to metals, feedstock, and food and fiber.

Exhibit 14 presents the frequency distribution for the CPCI. Similar to the GSCI, we find a positive skew to the distribution and fat tails. Therefore, this index is also exposed to event risk, and the event risk provides a positive bias to the return distribution.

---

[22] Information on the CPCI was provided by Robert Greer at JP Morgan Chase.

Exhibit 14: Distribution of Returns for the CPCI

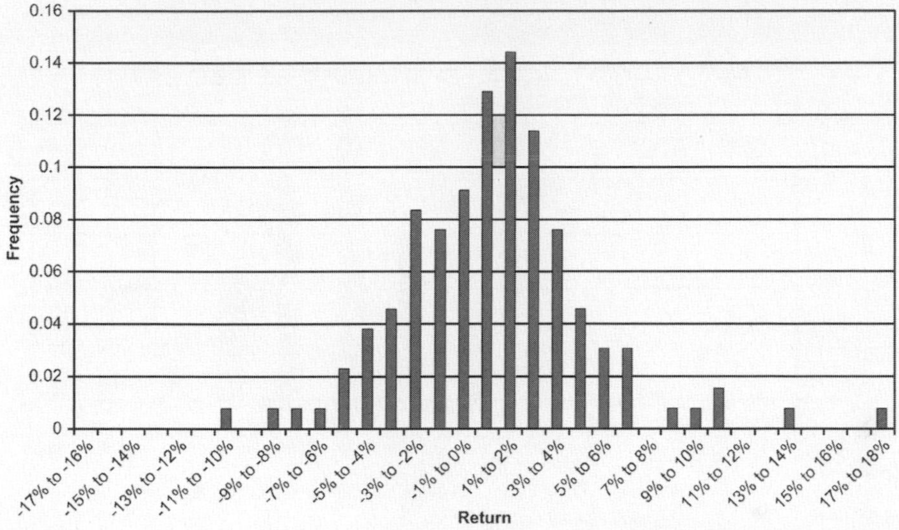

| E(Return) 0.83% | Std. Dev. 3.99% | Sharpe 0.0958 | Skew 0.6370 | Kurtosis 2.4463 |

MLM Index

Mount Lucas Management introduced the MLM Index (MLMI) in 1988.[23] It was the first passive index of returns to futures investing. The MLMI differs significantly from the previous futures indices in three ways.

First, the MLMI is designed to be a trend following index. The MLMI uses a 12-month look back window for calculating the moving average unit asset value for each futures market in which it invests. Once a month, on the day prior to the last trading day, the algorithm examines the current unit asset value in each futures market compared to the average value for the prior 12 months. If the current unit asset value is above the 12-month moving average, the MLMI purchases the futures contract. If the current unit asset value is below the 12-month moving average, the MLMI takes a short position in the futures contract.

This highlights the second difference associated with the MLMI. This index can be both long and short futures contracts whereas the GSCI, DJ-AIGCI, and the CPCI only take long positions in futures contracts.

The theory behind the MLMI is that the mismatch in commercial firms' futures positions is greatest, and investors can profit the most, when the underlying futures market is moving broadly from one price level to another, either up or down. The object of this index construction is to capture the potential profits represented by such broad market trends.

---

[23] Information regarding the MLMI was provide by Karin Deutsch and Raymond Ix at Mount Lucas Management.

Exhibit 15: Distribution of Returns for the MLMI

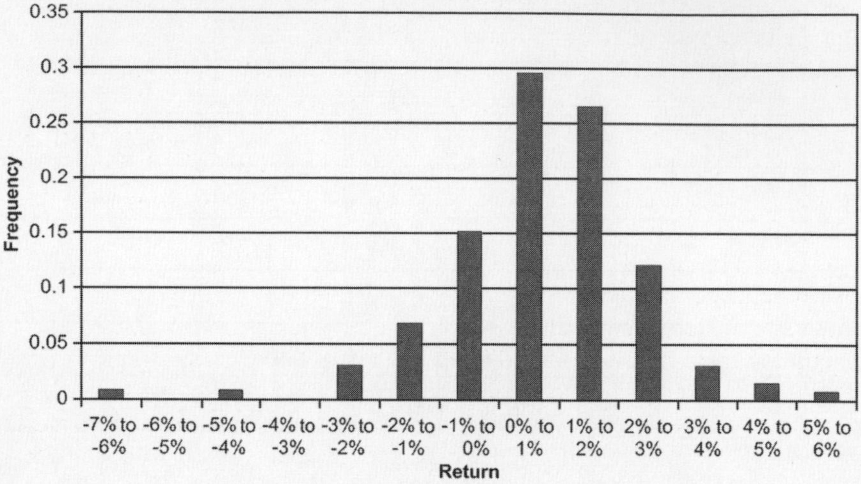

| E(Return) 0.73% | Std. Dev. 0.016 | Sharpe 0.173 | Skew −0.562 | Kurtosis 2.476 |

The last difference with respect to the MLMI is that it invests in both physical commodity, financial, and currency futures. There are 25 futures contracts in seven major categories: grains (corn, soybeans, soybean meal, soybean oil, and wheat), livestock (live cattle), energy (heating oil, crude oil, natural gas, and unleaded gasoline), metals (gold, silver, and copper), food and fiber (coffee, cotton, and sugar), financials (5-year Treasury notes, 10-year Treasury notes, and Treasury bonds), and currencies (Australian dollars, British pounds, Canadian dollars, German Marks, Swiss francs, and Japanese yen).[24]

The MLMI is equal-weighted. The purpose of its construction is to capture the pricing trend of each commodity without regard to its production value or trading volume in the market. Therefore, the price trend for each commodity in the index is given the same consideration. Given its trend following design, the MLMI re-balances every month based on the prior 12-month moving average.

In Exhibit 15, we present the probability distribution for the MLMI index. It has a negative value for skew, indicating a distribution of returns with a bias towards negative returns as well as a large value of kurtosis indicating exposure to outlier events.

Comparison of Commodity Futures Indices

It is worthwhile to summarize some of the differences between the commodity indices discussed above. The GSCI, for example, is economically weighted. The

---

[24] There is one additional difference with respect to the MLMI. Two versions of the index are calculated. One version is unleveraged, and one version is three times levered.

weights in the index are determined solely by exogenous economic data (e.g., production values for the global economy). The argument for constructing such an index is analogous to that for the capitalization weighted S&P 500; the most economically important commodities should influence a portfolio tracking an index.[25]

In contrast, the DJ-AIGCI is primarily activity weighted. Those commodities that are most actively traded determine its construction. This index relies upon endogenous variables (trading volume and liquidity) to determine its weights. This approach assures maximum liquidity for portfolios tracking the index.

Last, the CPCI is a value-weighted index. It maintains a constant relationship between the quantities of the various physical commodity futures. For example, no matter whether the price of crude oil goes up or down, the index will maintain the same ratio of crude oil contracts to gold contracts, wheat contracts, coffee contracts, etc. This constant re-balancing forces the index to sell those commodities that have appreciated in value and purchase those commodities that have declined in value. Selling high and buying low can be an additional source of return, particularly if commodity prices tend to revert to a long-term mean, or even if they exhibit less than perfect correlation.

In Exhibit 16 we present a comparison of the return and risk profile for the four commodity futures indices discussed above. In Exhibit 16, we use monthly return data to compare the expected return, the Sharpe ratio, the skew of the distribution of returns, and the level of kurtosis associated with each distribution. We also include data regarding the S&P 500 as a standard for comparison.

First, we note that the GSCI, the DJ-AIGCI, and the CPCI have a positive skew to the distribution. From our discussion of return distributions in Chapter 6, we can conclude that a positive skew indicates that the mean of the distribution is to the right of (greater than) the median of the distribution. This means that there are more frequent large return observations to the right of the distribution (positive returns) and there are more small and mid-range positive return observations to the left of the distribution. In other words, large positive outlying returns occur more frequently than large negative outlying returns, indicating a bias to the upside.

Exhibit 16: Expected Monthly Return, Sharpe Ratios, Skew, and Kurtosis

	S&P 500	GSCI	DJ-AIGCI	CPCI	MLMI
E(Return)	1.20%	0.74%	0.16%	0.83%	0.73%
Std. Dev.	3.92%	5.47%	3.18%	3.99%	1.61%
Sharpe	0.19	0.0531	−0.09	0.0958	0.173
Skew	−0.499	0.82	0.107	0.637	−0.562
Kurtosis	1.443	2.313	0.407	2.446	2.476

[25] See Greer, "Institutional use of Physical Commodity Indices."

This is good news for investors. Any return distribution that demonstrates a positive skew (i.e., more frequent large positive returns than large negative returns) is a potentially valuable portfolio addition.

The positive skew is largest for the GSCI and lowest for the DJ-AIGCI. One explanation could be the production weighting of the GSCI versus the liquidity weighting of the DJ-AIGCI. It could be that greater exposure to the most economically important commodity futures provides the greatest source of positive upside potential.

The MLMI is the only futures index that has a negative skew associated with it. This value indicates a negative bias to event risk. There is, however, a trade-off. The MLMI has much less dispersion in its returns than the other three indices. The standard deviation of the MLMI returns is 70% less than that for the GSCI, 60% less than that for the CPCI, and 50% less than that for the DJ-AIGCI. This should be expected given the construction of the MLMI. Its trend following strategy should reduce its exposure to extreme outlier events. In addition, the MLMI has the largest Sharpe ratio of the four commodity futures indices. Therefore, the MLMI may have negative exposure to event risk, but it does have the best reward-to-risk ratio.

The GSCI, CPCI, and the MLMI all have similar (in fact, almost identical) positive values of kurtosis, indicating "fat tails" in the distribution of returns. For the GSCI, this could be due to the momentum style of the GSCI. Commodity prices are allowed to run up or down in the GSCI, changing the weights of the index dramatically. For the MLMI, the large value of kurtosis could be due to sudden changes in commodity price trends. Given a sudden price spike or trough in commodity prices, it may take time for the MLMI to apply its 12-month moving average to adjust for the trend. This could lead to fat tails.

Finally, the large value of kurtosis for the CPCI is puzzling because the index continually re-balances itself. This re-balancing should reduce the exposure to any one commodity or group by selling off some of the winners and buying some of the underperformers. We would expect this to reduce the exposure of the index to large outlier returns. However, the reverse appears to be true.

Conversely, the DJ-AIGCI specifically limits the exposures of commodity sectors so that the index does not become "top heavy" with respect to any particular commodity or sector. This cap may reduce the exposure of outlier events within the DJ-AIGCI compared to the GSCI. This cap, in fact, acts like a short call option position that truncates the distribution of returns above the allowable percentage limit in the index. Truncating a return distribution will reduce an investor's exposure to large outlier returns. The result is a lower value of leptokurtosis.

Other Commodity Indices

We take time to note a few other commodity indices. First, there is the JP Morgan Commodity Index. This index is composed of energy, agricultural, and metal products. It has a smaller basket of commodities than the GSCI, CPCI or the DJ-AIGCI indices. With the merger of Chase and JP Morgan, this index is expected to be phased out in favor to the CPCI.

There is also the Bridge-CRB index. This is a "naive" commodity index because it equally weights each commodity within the index. For example, frozen concentrated orange juice is given the same weight as crude oil. There are 17 physical commodities, each with a weight of 5.88%. No consideration is given to production or liquidity in constructing the index.

Last, Forstmann Leff has designed the Investable Commodity Index. This is also an equally weighted index across 16 physical commodity futures. Equal weighting is maintained to provide an unbiased measure of performance.

CONCLUSION

This chapter was designed to introduce the reader to the economic rationale behind investing in commodity futures. Its second purpose was to introduce several commodity futures indices that can be used for performance benchmarking.

In this sense, commodity futures investing has developed further than the hedge fund industry because several well-defined and transparent benchmarks have been invented to track the performance of commodity futures investing. However, investment capital committed to commodity futures is considerably smaller than that invested with hedge funds. One estimate has only $8 billion invested in commodity futures products.[26]

One reason is the lack of understanding of the product. Therefore, this chapter was designed to provide an introduction to commodity futures investing. A second reason is the perceived view that commodity futures are extremely risky investments, best left for cowboy speculators and flamboyant floor traders. In the next chapter we will disarm this myth and consider whether commodity futures have a place within an investment portfolio.

---

[26] My thanks to Robert Greer of JP Morgan Chase for providing this estimate.

Chapter 12

Commodity Futures in a Portfolio Context

In the prior two chapters we first identified commodity futures as a distinct asset and we discussed the economics associated with the pricing of commodity futures. In addition, we indicated that commodity futures prices are influenced by factors different than those for financial assets. This led us to the conclusion that commodity futures have the potential to be excellent diversifying agents for a stock and bond portfolio.

In this chapter we consider commodity futures within a portfolio context. First, we compare the economic statistics of commodity futures to those for stocks and bonds. Next we build portfolios of commodity futures, stocks, and bonds and observe the risk and return of these portfolios compared to those constructed without commodity futures. Last, we examine commodity futures as a defensive investment. Our analysis concludes that commodity futures are indeed valuable diversification tools.

ECONOMIC SUMMARY OF COMMODITY FUTURES

In this section we briefly review the inflation protection offered by commodity futures. We also compare the risk and return profile of commodity futures compared to stocks and bonds over a long period of time.

Inflation Protection

Bonds are a contingent claim on the earning power of a corporation. They have a senior claim on revenue earned by a corporation. However, bonds perform poorly when the purchasing power of money declines in an inflationary environment.

Conversely, stocks, as the residual claim on the physical assets of a corporation provide better purchasing power protection. However, stocks also represent a claim on the future earning potential of the corporation. When this earning power is eroded due to inflationary concerns, stocks also decline in value.

Real assets such as commodity futures can hedge this decline in value due to inflation. In Chapter 11 we introduced four investable commodity futures indices — the GSCI, the DJ-AIGCI, the CPCI, and the MLMI.

Exhibit 1 presents the correlation of the four indices with domestic U.S. inflation over the time period 1990–2000. We also include the S&P 500 for domestic stocks, EAFE for international stocks, and the Lehman U.S. Treasury Bond Index for bonds. Exhibit 1 demonstrates that stocks and bonds are negatively correlated with the rate of inflation. Higher inflation means lower returns to stocks and bonds, and vice versa. Conversely, all of the commodity indices are positively correlated with inflation. Higher inflation means higher returns to commodity futures and vice versa. Therefore, commodity futures offer good inflation protection for financial assets.

An argument might be made that an investor could purchase Treasury Inflation Protected Securities (TIPS) as a hedge against inflation. It is true that the cash flows accruing to TIPS are adjusted to maintain their value in an inflationary environment. However, TIPS do not offer inflation protection for other assets in the portfolio.

TIPS are designed to have the coupon rate increase so that the price of a TIPS does not decline when inflation increases. This preserves or *maintains* the value of the TIPS investment. However, the preservation of TIPS value does not offer relief for other assets in the portfolio. In contrast, commodity futures increase in value when inflation goes up. This increase in value can be used to shelter some of the decline in value suffered by financial assets in the portfolio.

Note also, that the returns earned by international stocks experience the same level of negative correlation with the U.S. inflation rate. One reason is that price increases of raw materials affect foreign economies just as much as the U.S. economy. Consequently, an investor seeking a hedge against domestic inflation did not find it by diversifying into foreign stocks.

Average Return and Volatility

Commodity futures are often perceived to be extremely volatile, with large price swings up and down. We expect commodity futures to be riskier than U.S. Treasury bonds, but we also expect the return to be greater to compensate for the additional risk.

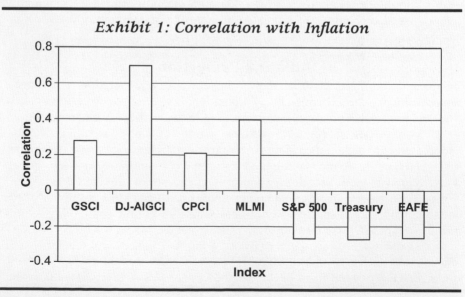

Exhibit 1: Correlation with Inflation

Exhibit 2: Average Returns for Stocks, Bonds, and Commodity Futures

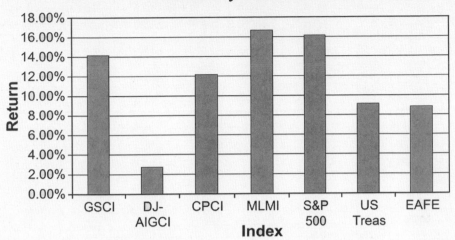

Note: DJ-AIGCI data are available only from 1991.

Exhibit 3: Volatility of Stocks, Bonds, and Commodity Futures

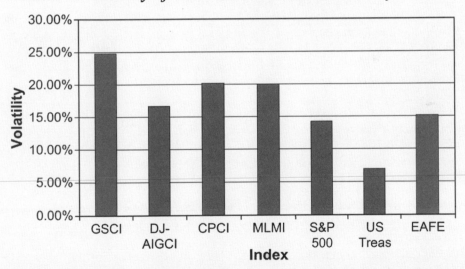

Note: DJ-AIGCI data are available only from 1991.

We might also expect commodity futures to have greater volatility than that for large capitalization stocks (because futures prices are subject to short term fluctuations), but not significantly greater. In turn, we expect to earn an average rate of return greater than stocks for this additional volatility. These expectations are summarized in Exhibits 2 and 3.

Exhibit 4: Correlation Matrix

	GSCI	DJ-AIGCI	CPCI	MLMI	S&P 500	US Treas	EAFE
GSCI	1.0000	0.9486	0.9190	0.3699	−0.3777	−0.2480	−0.2235
DJ-AIGCI	0.9486	1.0000	0.9589	−0.0439	−0.4343	−0.3424	−0.2797
CPCI	0.9190	0.9589	1.0000	0.3646	−0.2543	−0.2936	−0.1484
MLMI	0.3699	−0.0439	0.3646	1.0000	−0.5343	−0.0092	−0.3973
S&P 500	−0.3777	−0.4343	−0.2543	−0.5343	1.0000	0.3869	0.4513
US Treas	−0.2480	−0.3424	−0.2936	−0.0092	0.3869	1.0000	0.0803
EAFE	−0.2235	−0.2797	−0.1484	−0.3973	0.4513	0.0803	1.0000

Exhibit 2 indicates that commodity futures outperformed the returns to international stocks and bonds over the period 1973–2000 and were about the same as U.S. stocks.[1] This was a diverse period of time including oil price shocks, oil gluts, three recessions, droughts, floods, La Nina, and several periods of monetary tightening and easing. In sum, 1973–2000 is a sufficiently long time period to provide a reasonable estimate of the long-term returns to stocks, bonds, and commodity futures.

Exhibit 3 presents the standard deviation of returns (volatility) to these three asset classes over the same time period.[2] Not surprisingly, commodity futures exhibit higher volatility than bonds. However, the volatility is not excessive. The DJ-AIGCI and the MLMI have annual volatility less than 20%, and the GSCI has the highest standard deviation of returns at close to 25%.

Although commodity futures exhibit greater volatility than stocks or bonds, they should not be viewed as a risky investment. Exhibit 4 presents a correlation matrix of commodity futures with domestic stocks, international stocks, and U.S. Treasury bonds. Exhibit 4 demonstrates that each commodity futures index is negatively correlated with the returns to domestic stocks, U.S. Treasury bonds, and foreign stocks.

Therefore, an investment in commodity futures should not be analyzed in a vacuum. Instead, commodity futures are best considered within a portfolio context, where their diversification potential can be achieved. In the next section, we consider commodity futures as part of a diversified portfolio.

COMMODITY FUTURES AND THE EFFICIENT INVESTMENT FRONTIER

Having established commodity futures as a distinct new asset class in Chapters 10 and 11, we consider how this asset class performs when considered in a diversified portfolio of stocks and bonds. In this section, we construct efficient frontiers for stocks, bonds, and passive commodity futures.

---

[1] The data for the DJ-AIGCI are available only from 1991. Consequently, the returns presented to the DJ-AIGCI are not comparable to the other indices. We include the information for completeness.

[2] Once again, we note that data for the DJ-AIGCI prior to 1991 are not available, and therefore, the information for this index is not strictly comparable to the other indices. It is included for completeness.

Exhibit 5: Efficient Frontier for Stocks and Bonds

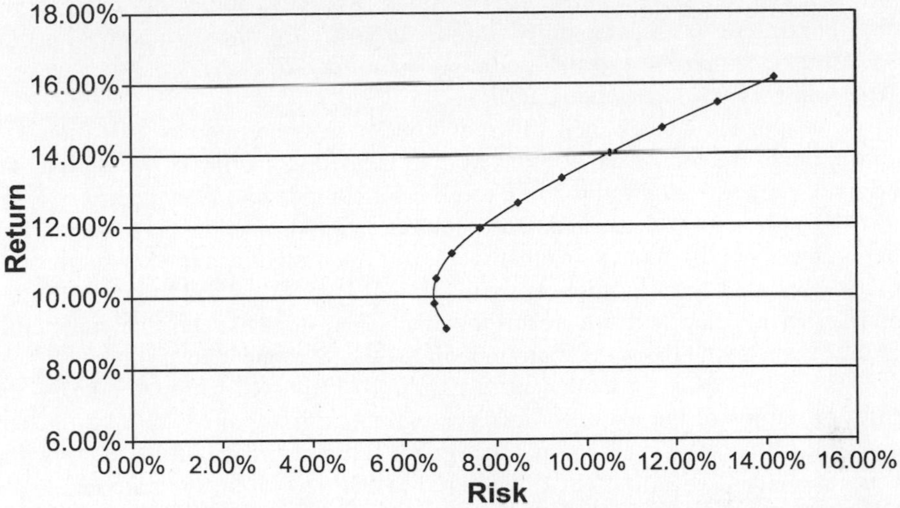

The efficient frontier is a graphical depiction of the trade off between risk and return. It provides a range of the risk and return that can be achieved in a balanced portfolio of investable assets. First, we graph the efficient frontier using domestic stocks and bonds to provide a benchmark of risk and return data points that can be achieved without commodity futures. We then add commodity futures to the investment portfolio and observe how the efficient frontier changes with the addition of this new asset class.

Exhibit 5 presents the initial frontier using stocks and bonds. At the highest return point on the frontier, the portfolio consists of 100% stocks. At the lowest return point, the portfolio consists completely of U.S. Treasury bonds. In between the portfolio mix of assets ranges from 90% stocks and 10% bonds to 10% stocks and 90% bonds.

The efficient frontier in Exhibit 5 indicates that higher return may be achieved only at the cost of assuming more risk. Along the efficient frontier, there is no other combination of stocks and bonds that will yield a higher return for a given level of risk, or a lower level of risk for a given level of return. This is why the frontier is efficient; it provides a graphical description of the best portfolios that may be achieved using stocks and bonds.

The efficient frontier changes when commodity futures are added to the mix. Exhibit 6 demonstrates the efficient frontier when commodity futures are added to the stock and bond portfolio. Initially, we use the GSCI to represent an asset allocation to commodity futures.

Again, the two endpoints of the graph are defined by 100% stocks at the highest return level and 100% bonds at the lowest return level. In between, the allocation to commodity futures remains constant at 10%, with a 5% less allocation to stocks and a 5% less allocation to bonds. For example, in Exhibit 5, we plot risk and return data points at 90% stocks and 10% bonds, 80% stocks and 20% bonds, etc. With commodity futures, in Exhibit 6, the data points become 85% stocks, 5% bonds, and 10% commodity futures, 75% stocks, 15% bonds, and 10% commodity futures, and so forth.

In Exhibit 6, the new efficient frontier including commodity futures is above and to the left of the original frontier plotted in Exhibit 5. We include the original frontier from Exhibit 5 in Exhibit 6 for comparison. The original efficient investment frontier without commodity futures clearly lies below the efficient frontier with commodity futures. In other words, the addition of commodity futures into the investment portfolio pushes the investment frontier up and to the left into a more efficient risk and return area of the graph. This demonstrates that commodity futures improve the risk and return tradeoff for the investment portfolio.

Reflect back for a moment to Exhibit 3. The GSCI had the highest volatility of returns of the major indices presented. At first glance, an investor may discount the value of investing in commodity futures because of the higher volatility associated with the GSCI compared to the S&P 500. Such a comparison ignores the negative correlation of the returns to the GSCI with the returns to stocks and bonds. The impact of this negative correlation can only be felt within a diversified portfolio. As a stand-alone investment, the diversification potential of commodity futures vis a vis stocks and bonds cannot be observed. It can only be appreciated within a portfolio context.

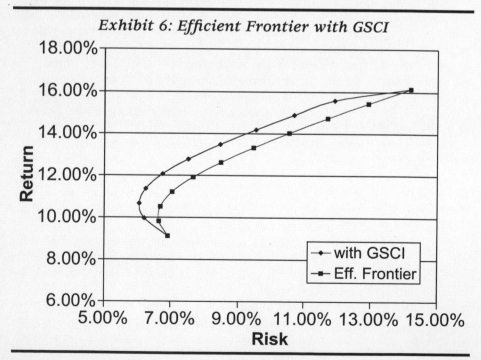

Exhibit 6: Efficient Frontier with GSCI

Exhibit 7: Efficient Frontier with DJ-AIGCI

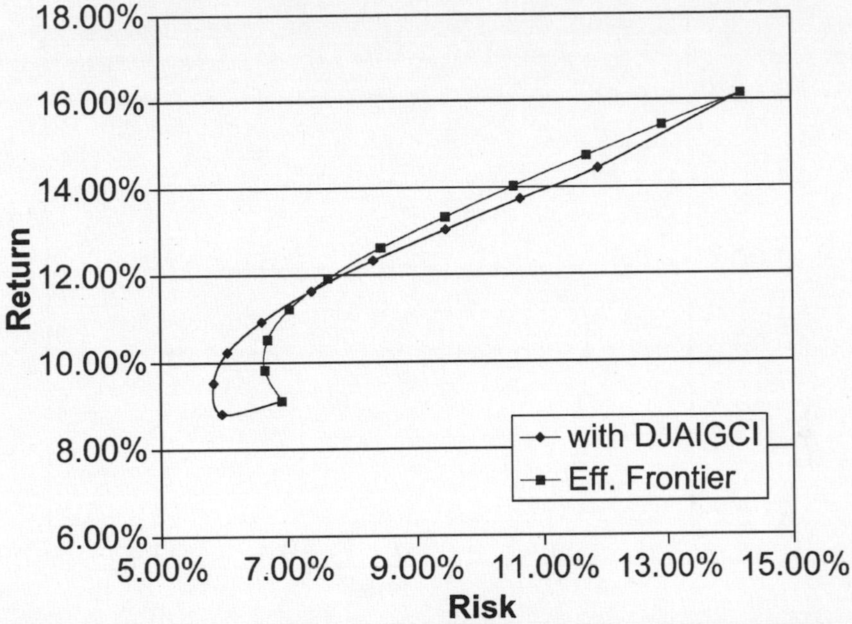

In Exhibit 7, we again present both the efficient frontier with the DJ-AIGCI and without commodity futures. In this case, the benefits of commodity futures investing are less apparent. At the higher range of risk and return, the two efficient frontiers are almost identical. However, at the lower end of the risk and return range, the frontier with the DJ-AIGCI is more efficient.

This highlights an important point. It is at the lower spectrum of risk and return where the more risk averse investors reside. These investors are only willing to incur a small amount of risk to achieve a modest return. Yet, it is within this range that the DJ-AIGCI index has its greatest impact. Therefore, its utility is greater the more risk averse the investor.

Maximizing utility with commodity futures is an important concept because greater the risk aversion of the investor, the greater the benefit of investing in commodity futures. This point may seem counter-intuitive because commodity futures are often perceived as risky investments. However, the returns to commodity futures tend to be negatively correlated with the returns to financial assets. Therefore, when considered within a portfolio context, commodity futures can provide positive utility to a risk averse investor. In fact, Anson demonstrates that the greater the risk aversion of the investor, the greater will be the marginal utility of investing in commodity futures.[3]

[3] See Mark Anson, "Maximizing Utility with Commodity Futures," *The Journal of Portfolio Management* (Summer 1999).

Exhibit 8: Efficient Frontier with CPCI

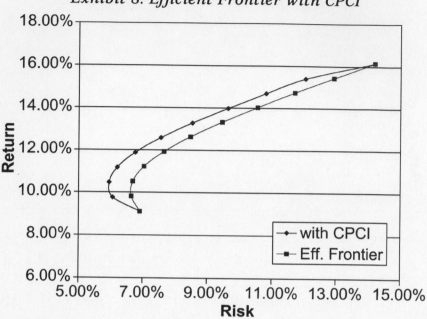

Exhibit 8 plots the efficient frontier with a 10% constant allocation to commodity futures represented by the CPCI. Similar to Exhibit 6, the efficient frontier including the CPCI lies completely above and to the left of the original efficient frontier with stocks and bonds. This means that at every data point on the original frontier, there is a more efficient portfolio that can be achieved if commodity futures are included in the portfolio. Simply put, a traditional stock and bond portfolio is inefficient compared to a similar portfolio that includes a 10% allocation to the CPCI commodity futures.

Last, Exhibit 9 presents the efficient frontier for a portfolio of stocks, bonds and 10% commodity futures as represented by the MLMI. Similar to Exhibits 6 and 8, the efficient frontier that includes an allocation to commodity futures completely dominates the efficient frontier obtained with stocks and bonds alone. Every data point that includes commodity futures provides a better risk and return tradeoff than a portfolio comprised only of stocks and bonds. Once again, the stock and bond portfolio is inferior to a portfolio containing stocks, bonds, and a 10% allocation to commodity futures.

It is important to note again that the GSCI, the DJ-AIGCI, the CPCI, and the MLMI are all *investable* commodity futures indices. They were all designed with the investor in mind, and an investor can allocate a portion of her portfolio assets to any of these four indices just as she might make an allocation to emerging market stocks, for instance. Therefore, each index is an appropriate proxy for investing in the commodity futures markets.

Exhibit 9: Efficient Frontier with MLMI

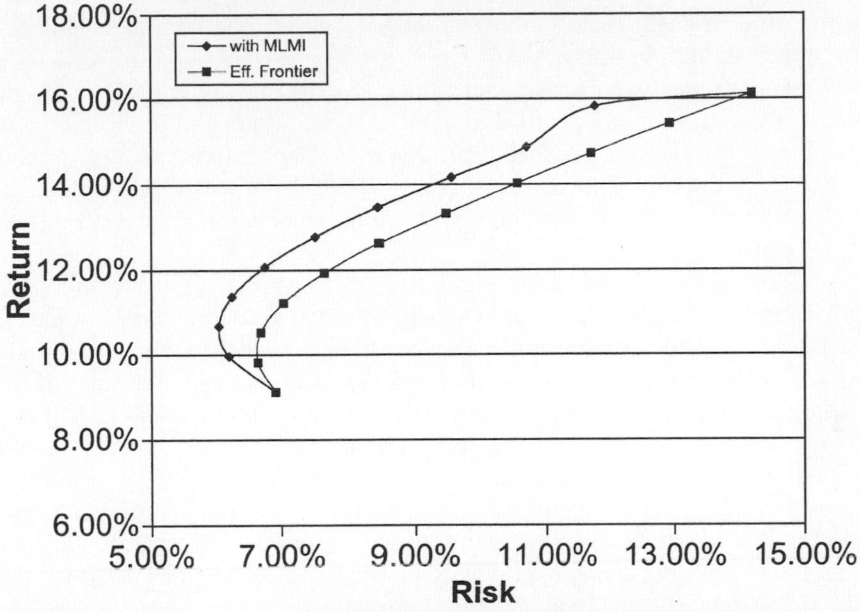

The above discussion was intended to demonstrate that commodity futures are best analyzed within a portfolio context. Only then can their full investment benefit be appreciated. The ability of commodity futures returns to move in the opposite direction of the returns to stocks and bonds provides a powerful tool for portfolio diversification. This is consistent with our discussion in Chapter 11 regarding how commodity futures react differently than stocks and bonds to different parts of the economic cycle. Exhibits 6 through 9 translate this business cycle concept into portfolio construction. In the next section, we consider another useful element of commodity futures investing: downside risk protection.

COMMODITY FUTURES AS A DEFENSIVE INVESTMENT

It is an unfortunate fact of life that when things hit the fan, they tend to do it all at the same time. For example, a number of studies have examined the correlation of the U.S. domestic and international equity markets during periods of market stress or decline. The conclusion is that the equity markets around the world tend to be more highly correlated during periods of economic stress.[4] This means that

---

[4] See Claude Erb, Campbell Harvey, and Tadas Viskanta, "Forecasting International Equity Correlations," *Financial Analysts Journal*, (November/December 1994); and Rex Sinquefield, "Where Are the Gains from International Diversification?" *Financial Analysts Journal* (January/February 1996).

international equity markets tend to decline at the same time as the U.S. stock market. Therefore, international equity diversification may not provide the requisite diversification when a U.S. domestic investor needs it most — during periods of economic turmoil or decline.

One reason why international equity investments might not provide suitable diversification for a U.S. stock portfolio is that almost all traditional assets react in similar fashion to macroeconomic events. A spike in oil prices, for example, will be felt across all economies, and inflation fears will be uniform around the globe. Further, international equity markets are becoming increasing linked for four reasons.

First, policy makers from major industrial nations regularly attend economic summits where they attempt to synchronize fiscal and monetary policy. The Maastricht Treaty and the birth of "Euroland" is an example. Second, corporations are expanding their operations and revenue streams beyond the site of their domestic incorporation. Third, the increased volume of international capital flows means that economic shocks will be felt globally as opposed to country specific. Last, nations such as Japan have undergone a "Big Bang" episode where domestic investors have greater access to international investments. This provides for an even greater flow of capital across international boundaries. As a result, the equity markets are becoming a single, global asset class and distinctions between international and domestic stocks are beginning to fade.

This is one reason why "skill-based" investing has become so popular with investors. Hedge funds and other "skill-based" strategies might be expected to provide greater diversification than international equity investing because the returns are dependent upon the special skill of the manager rather than any broad macroeconomic events or trends.

Yet, diversification need not rely on active "skill-based" strategies. Diversification benefits can be achieved from the passive addition of a new asset class such as commodity futures.

The greatest concern for any investor is downside risk. If equity and bond markets are becoming increasingly synchronized, international diversification may not offer the protection sought by investors. The ability to protect the value of an investment portfolio in hostile or turbulent markets is the key to the value of any macroeconomic diversification.

Within this framework, an asset class distinct from financial assets has the potential to diversify and protect an investment portfolio from hostile markets. Commodity futures make a good choice for downside risk protection.

To demonstrate this downside risk protection, we start with a standard portfolio of stocks and bonds. We begin with a portfolio that is 60% the S&P 500 and 40% U.S. Treasury bonds. In Exhibit 10 we provide a frequency distribution of the monthly returns to this portfolio over the time period 1990–2000. This exhibit shows the return pattern for monthly returns to a 60%/40% stock/bond portfolio over this time period.

Exhibit 10: Frequency Distribution, 60/40 Stocks/Bonds

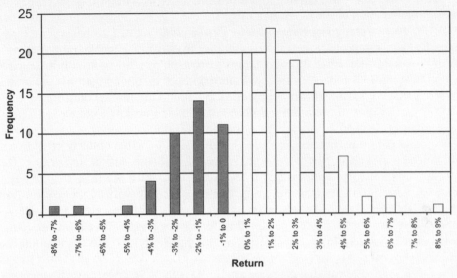

Our concern is the shaded part of the return distribution. This shows where the returns to the stock and bond portfolio were negative. That is, the shaded part of the distribution shows both the size and the frequency with which the combined portfolio of 60% S&P 500 plus 40% U.S. Treasury bonds earned a negative return in a particular month. It is this part of the return distribution that an investor attempts to avoid or limit.[5]

We find that the average monthly return to a 60/40 stock/bond portfolio in the shaded part of the distribution of Exhibit 10 is a negative 2.07%. In other words, when the standard stock/bond portfolio earned a negative return in any given month, on average the magnitude of that return was −2.07%.

These negative returns are exactly the returns that investors want to reduce through diversification. We consider how this shaded part of the curve changes when we add in commodity futures.

In Exhibit 11 we change the standard stock/bond investment portfolio by providing a 10% allocation to commodity futures. The resulting portfolio is 55% S&P 500 stocks, 35% U.S. Treasury bonds, and 10% GSCI. Exhibit 11 plots the frequency distribution for this portfolio.

Once again, we are concerned with the shaded part of the frequency distribution of returns for this stock/bond/commodities portfolio. Although the distribution looks similar, it has in fact changed significantly from Exhibit 10. The average monthly return to the 55/35/10 stock/bond/commodities portfolio in the

---

[5] See Steve Strongin and Melanie Petsch, "Managing Risk in Hostile Markets," Goldman Sachs Commodities Research, April 24, 1996.

shaded part of Exhibit 11 is −1.79%. In other words, when the stock/bond/commodities portfolio earned a negative return in any given month, on average the magnitude of the return was −1.79%.

This is an improvement in return over Exhibit 10 of 28 basis points per month. That is, the addition of the commodity futures to the stock and bond portfolio provided on average 28 basis points per month of protection in hostile markets. This is a 13% reduction in downside risk. Further, notice that this reduction in risk came with a conservative allocation to commodity futures of 10%.

In Exhibit 10, we observed 42 months out of a total of 132 that had a negative return for the 60/40 stock/bond portfolio. This a frequency of 31.2%, or about 3.8 months per year. Therefore, on average, an allocation to the GSCI is expected to provide approximately 1.06% (3.8 × 0.28%) of annual downside protection.

Exhibit 12 provides a frequency distribution for a portfolio that consists of 55% S&P 500, 35% U.S. Treasury bonds, and a 10% allocation to the DJ-AIGCI. Exhibit 12 provides a similar analysis to that of Exhibit 11. The average negative return in the shaded part of Exhibit 12 is −1.81%. This is an improvement over Exhibit 10 of 26 basis points per month, or about 0.99% (3.8 months × 0.26%) per year.

Exhibit 13 provides the same analysis for the CPCI. This exhibit shows a plot of the frequency distribution for a 55/35/10 stock/bond/CPCI portfolio. The average return in the shaded part of the distribution is −1.86%. Therefore, the CPCI provides 21 basis points of downside risk protection per month, or about 0.8% (3.8 months × 21 bp) of annual protection against hostile markets.

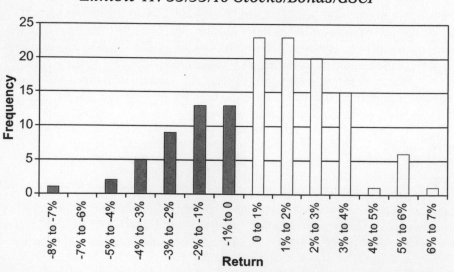

Exhibit 11: 55/35/10 Stocks/Bonds/GSCI

Exhibit 12: 55/35/10 Stocks/Bonds/DJ-AIGCI

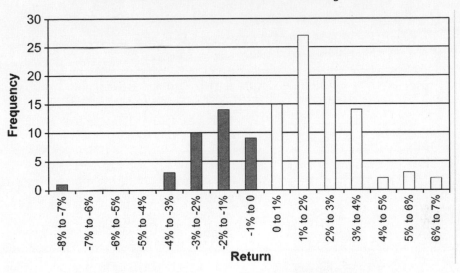

Exhibit 13: 55/35/10 Stocks/Bonds/CPCI

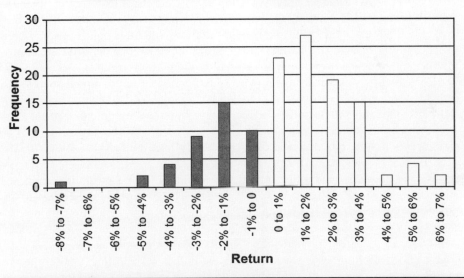

Exhibit 14 plots the frequency distribution for a portfolio consisting of 55% S&P 500, 35% U.S. Treasury bonds, and 10% MLMI. Once again the shaded part of the distribution of portfolio returns improves significantly. The average return in the downside part of the return distribution is −1.88%. Therefore, the MLMI provided 19 basis points of monthly downside protection, or about 0.72% (3.8 months × 0.19%) of annual protection against hostile markets.

Exhibit 14: 55/35/10 Stocks/Bonds/MLMI

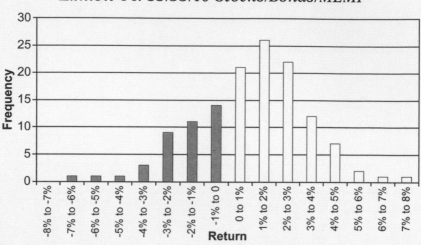

Let's look at the impact of Exhibits 11 through 14. These graphs demonstrate that a small allocation to commodity futures benchmarked to a passive futures index can provide average annual protection against downside exposure of 0.72% to 1.06%. To put this in context, compare these results to the world of active equity investing where an annual alpha, or excess return, of 100 basis points is considered excellent performance. Yet, a 10% passive allocation to commodity futures can provide return protection on par with excess return offered by active managers.

Finally, we consider the downside protection of international stocks. We indicated above that the equity markets are becoming less distinct and resembling more of a global asset class. This reduces the diversification potential of international stocks. To demonstrate this idea, we build a portfolio consisting of U.S. stocks, U.S. bonds and foreign stocks. The exact allocation is 55% S&P 500, 35% U.S. Treasury bonds, and 10% EAFE.[6]

Exhibit 15 provides the frequency distribution for this portfolio. Again, we concentrate on the shaded part of the distribution. The average monthly return to the downside portion of this distribution is −2.11%. That is, a 10% allocation to international stocks provided an *additional* exposure to downside risk of −4 basis points. Therefore, an allocation to international stocks did not diversify an investment portfolio comprised of domestic stocks and bonds. In fact, a 10% allocation to international stocks *increased* the exposure to downside risk. Therefore, international stocks did not protect the standard 60/40 stock/bond portfolio from hostile markets.

We also consider what might be sacrificed to achieve this downside protection. It is possible that in protecting against some downside exposure, an investor must accept a reduction in positive returns in the non-shaded (positive) part of the return distributions. We examine this possibility in Exhibit 16.

[6] EAFE is an international stock index developed and maintained by Morgan Stanley Capital International.

Exhibit 15: 55/35/10 U.S. Stocks/U.S. Bonds/EAFE

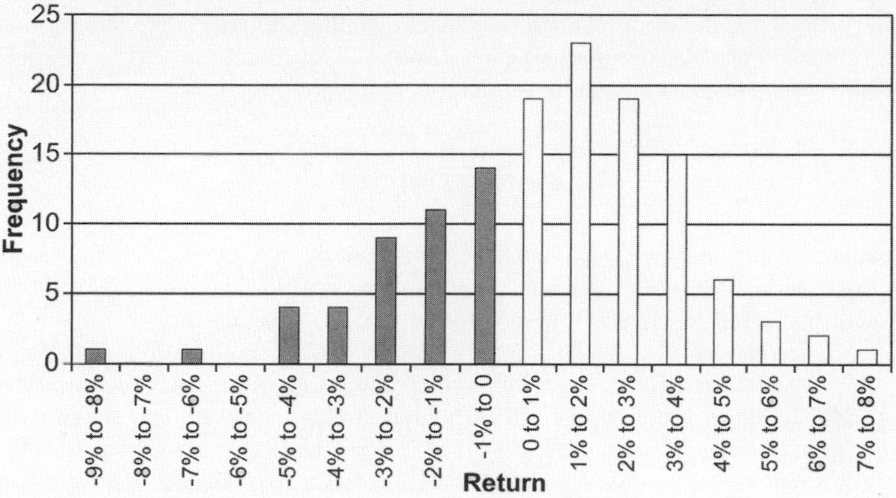

Exhibit 16: Downside Risk Protection
(Monthly Returns 1990-2000)

Portfolio Composition	Expected Return	Standard Deviation	Sharpe Ratio	Average Downside	Downside Protection
60/40 US Stocks/US Bonds	0.91%	2.60%	0.177	-2.07%	N/A
55/35/10 Stocks/Bonds/GSCI	0.90%	2.39%	0.187	-1.79%	0.28%
55/35/10 Stocks/Bonds/DJ-AIGCI	0.92%	2.30%	0.205	-1.81%	0.26%
55/35/10 Stocks/Bonds/CPCI	0.91%	2.38%	0.192	-1.86%	0.21%
55/35/10 Stocks/Bonds/MLMI	0.90%	2.33%	0.191	-1.88%	0.19%
55/35/10 Stocks/Bonds/EAFE	0.86%	2.66%	0.155	-2.11%	-0.04%

The expected monthly return to the standard 60/40 stock portfolio over this period was 0.91%. Compare this to the expected monthly return to a 55/35/10 stock/bond/commodity futures portfolio in Exhibit 16. The expected return for a portfolio with the GSCI is 0.90% per month, a reduction of 1 basis point per month or 12 basis points per year in expected return to achieve an expected 1.06% of average annual downside protection. This seems like a very reasonable tradeoff.

In fact, for the DJ-AIGCI, the expected monthly return actually improves to 0.92% per month, while it remains the same with the CPCI at 0.91%, and is 0.90% with the MLMI. In each case, considerable downside protection is achieved with only a minimal sacrifice of expected monthly return, if at all.

We note that the addition of international equities to the standard 60/40 stock and bond portfolio resulted in a decline of the expected monthly return down to 0.86%, a reduction in average monthly return of 5 basis points.

Finally, we compare the Sharpe ratios for the standard 60/40 stock/bond portfolio to those portfolios including commodity futures and international equity. In each case, the allocation to 10% commodity futures results in a significant improvement in the Sharpe ratio. However, an allocation to 10% international equities results in a significant decline in the Sharpe ratio.

CONCLUSION

Chapters 10 and 11 were concerned with the introduction to commodity futures as an asset class distinct from financial assets such as stocks and bonds. In this chapter we considered the diversification value of this new asset class.

The greatest value of commodity futures is achieved within a portfolio context. Analyzing commodity futures as a stand-alone investment ignores the fact that the returns to commodity futures tend to be negatively correlated with the returns to financial assets. We discussed in Chapter 11 that the returns to commodity futures tend to peak and trough at different parts of the economic cycle in contrast to stocks and bonds. This counter-cyclical effect provides the potential for portfolio diversification.

This diversification potential was revealed in two separate ways. First, we demonstrated how a 10% allocation of commodity futures provided an efficient investable frontier that dominated the efficient frontier that was achieved with stocks and bonds alone. Second, we demonstrated how a 10% allocation to commodity futures provided significant downside protection in hostile markets. In contrast, we found that international stocks provided no downside exposure and, in fact, increased the exposure to hostile markets for a standard 60/40 stock/bond portfolio.

Chapter 13

Managed Futures

Managed futures refers to the active trading of futures contracts and forward contracts on physical commodities, financial assets, and currencies. The purpose of the managed futures industry is to enable investors to profit from changes in futures prices. This is similar to the purpose of the commodity futures indices described in Chapters 10, 11, and 12. The difference with managed futures is the active component.

The managed futures industry is another skill-based style of investing. Investment managers attempt to use their special knowledge and insight in buying and selling futures and forward contracts to extract a positive return. These futures managers tend to argue that their superior skill is the key ingredient to derive profitable returns from the futures markets.

There are three ways to access the skill-based investing of the managed futures industry: public commodity pools, private commodity pools, and individual managed accounts. *Commodity pools* are investment funds that pool the money of several investors for the purpose of investing in the futures markets. They are similar in structure to hedge funds, and are considered a subset of the hedge fund marketplace.

Every commodity pool must be managed by a general partner. Typically, the general partner for the pool must register with the Commodity Futures Trading Commission and the National Futures Association as a Commodity Pool Operator (CPO). However, there are exceptions to the general rule, and these are discussed in detail in Chapter 8.

Public commodity pools are open to the general public for investment in much the same way a mutual fund sells its shares to the public. Public commodity pools must file a registration statement with the Securities and Exchange Commission before distributing shares in the pool to investors. An advantage of public commodity pools is the low minimum investment and the frequency of liquidity (the ability to cash out).

Private commodity pools are sold to high net worth investors and institutional investors to avoid the lengthy registration requirements of the SEC and sometimes to avoid the lengthy reporting requirements of the CFTC (see the discussion in Chapter 8). Otherwise, their investment objective is the same as a public commodity pool. An advantage of private commodity pools is usually lower brokerage commissions and greater flexibility to implement investment strategies and extract excess return from the futures markets.

Commodity pool operators (for either public or private pools) typically hire one or more Commodity Trading Advisors (CTAs) to manage the money deposited with the pool. CTAs are professional money managers in the futures markets.

Like CPOs, CTAs must register with the Commodity Futures Trading Commission (CFTC) and the National Futures Association (NFA) before managing money for a commodity pool. In some cases a managed futures investment manager is registered as both a CPO and a CTA. In this case, the general partner for a commodity pool may also act as its investment adviser.

Last, wealthy and institutional investors can place their money directly with a CTA in an *individually managed account*. These separate accounts have the advantage of narrowly defined and specific investment objectives as well as full transparency to the investor.

CTAs may invest in both exchange-traded futures contracts and forward contracts. A forward contract has the same economic structure as a futures contract with one difference; it is traded over the counter. Forward contracts are private agreements that do not trade on a futures exchange. Therefore, they can have terms that vary considerably from the standard terms of an exchange listed futures contracts. Forward contracts accomplish the same economic goal as a futures contract but with the flexibility of custom tailored terms.

In this chapter, we examine the managed futures industry. First, we provide a brief history of the managed futures industry. We then review the prior empirical research regarding the benefits to investing in managed futures. Next, we examine the return distribution of managed futures returns. Last, we conduct an analysis of downside risk protection for managed futures within a portfolio context.

HISTORY OF MANAGED FUTURES

Organized futures trading began in the United States in the 1800s with the founding of the Chicago Board of Trade (CBOT) in 1848. It was founded by 82 grain merchants and the first exchange floor was above a flour store. Originally, it was a cash market where grain traders came to buy and sell supplies of flour, timothy seed, and hay.

In 1851, the earliest futures contract in the United States was recorded for the forward delivery of 3,000 bushels of corn, and two years later, the CBOT established the first standard futures contract in corn. Since then, the heart and soul of the CBOT has been its futures contracts on agricultural crops grown primarily in the midwestern states: corn, wheat, and soybeans. Therefore, commodity futures exchanges were founded initially by grain producers and buyers to hedge the price risk associated with the harvest and sale of crops.

Other futures exchanges were established for similar reasons. The Chicago Mercantile Exchange (CME), for example, lists futures contracts on livestock. Chicago was once famous for its stockyards where cattle and hogs were herded to the market. Ranchers and buyers came to the CME to hedge the price risk associated with the purchase and sale of cattle and hogs.

Other exchanges are the New York Mercantile Exchange (NYMEX) where futures contracts on energy products are traded. The Commodity Exchange of New York (now the COMEX division of the NYMEX) lists futures contracts on precious and industrial metals. The New York Coffee, Sugar, and Cocoa Exchange lists futures contracts on (what else?) coffee, sugar, and cocoa. The New York Cotton Exchange lists contracts on cotton and frozen concentrated orange juice.[1] The Kansas City Board of Trade lists futures contracts on wheat and financial products such as the Value Line stock index.

Over the years, certain commodities have risen in prominence while others have faded. For instance, the heating oil futures contract was at one time listed as inactive on the NYMEX for lack of interest. For years, heating oil prices remained stable, and there was little interest or need to hedge the price risk of heating oil. Then along came the Arab Oil Embargo of 1973, and this contract quickly took on a life of its own as did other energy futures contracts.

Conversely, other futures contracts have faded away because of minimal input into the economic engine of the United States. For instance, rye futures traded on the CBOT from 1869 to 1970, and barley futures traded from 1885 to 1940. However, the limited importance of barley and rye in finished food products led to the eventual demise of these futures contracts.

As the wealth of America grew, a new type of futures contract has gained importance: financial futures. The futures markets changed dramatically in 1975 when the CBOT introduced the first financial futures contract on Government National Mortgage Association mortgage-backed certificates. This was followed two years later in 1977 with the introduction of a futures contract on the U.S. Treasury Bond. Today this is the most actively traded futures contract in the world.

The creation of a futures contract that was designed to hedge financial risk as opposed to commodity price risk opened up a whole new avenue of asset management for traders, analysts, and portfolio managers. Now, it is more likely that a financial investor will flock to the futures exchanges to hedge her investment portfolio than a grain purchaser will trade to hedge commodity price risk. Since 1975, more and more financial futures contracts have been listed on the futures exchanges. For instance, in 1997 stock index futures and options on the Dow Jones 30 Industrial Companies were first listed on the CBOT. The S&P 500 stock index futures and options (first listed in 1983) are the most heavily traded contracts on the CME. Additionally, currency futures were introduced on the CME in the 1970s (originally listed as part of the International Monetary Market).

With the advent of financial futures contracts more and more managed futures trading strategies were born. However, the history of managed futures products goes back more than 50 years.

---

[1] The New York Coffee, Sugar, and Cocoa Exchange and the New York Cotton Exchange have merged to form the New York Board of Trade, where each exchange exists as a separate subsidiary of the NYBOT.

The first public futures fund began trading in 1948 and was active until the 1960s. This fund was established before financial futures contracts were invented, and consequently, traded primarily in agricultural commodity futures contracts. The success of this fund spawned other managed futures vehicles, and a new industry was born.

The managed futures industry has grown from just $1 billion under management in 1985 to $35 billion of funds invested in managed futures products in 2000. The stock market's return to more rational pricing in 2000 helped fuel increased interest in managed futures products. Still, managed futures products are a fraction of the estimated size of the hedge fund marketplace of $400 to $500 billion. Yet, issues of capacity are virtually non-existent in the managed futures industry compared to the hedge fund marketplace where the best hedge funds are closed to new investors.

Similar to hedge funds, CTAs and CPOs charge both management fees and performance fees. The standard "1 and 20" (1% management fee and 20% incentive fee) are equally applicable to the managed futures industry although management fees can range from 0% to 3% and incentive fees from 10% to 35%.

Unfortunately, until the early 1970s, the managed futures industry was largely unregulated. Anyone could advise an investor as the merits of investing in commodity futures or form a fund for the purpose of investing in the futures markets. Recognizing the growth of this industry, and the lack of regulation associated with it, in 1974 Congress promulgated the Commodity Exchange Act (CEA) and created the Commodity Futures Trading Commission (CFTC).

Under the CEA, Congress first defined the terms Commodity Pool Operator and Commodity Trading Advisor. Additionally, Congress established standards for financial reporting, offering memorandum disclosure, and bookkeeping. Further, Congress required CTAs and CPOs to register with the CFTC. Last, upon the establishment of the National Futures Association (NFA) as the designated self-regulatory organization for the managed futures industry, Congress required CTAs and CPOs to undergo periodic educational training.

Today, there are four broad classes of managed futures trading; agricultural products, energy products, financial and metal products, and currency products. Before examining these categories we review the prior research on the managed futures industry.

PRIOR EMPIRICAL RESEARCH

There are two key questions with respect to managed futures: (1) Will an investment in managed futures improve the performance of an investment portfolio?; and (2) Can managed futures products produce consistent returns?

The case for managed futures products as a viable investment is mixed. Elton, Gruber, and Rentzler, in three separate studies examine the returns to public commodity pools.[2] In their first study, they conclude that publicly offered commodity funds are not attractive either as stand-alone investments or as additions to a portfolio containing stocks and/or bonds. In their second study, they find the historical return data reported in the prospectuses of publicly offered commodity pools are not indicative of the returns that these funds actually earn once they go public. In fact, they conclude that the performance discrepancies are so large that the prospectus numbers are seriously misleading. In their last study, they did not find any evidence that would support the addition of commodity pools to a portfolio of stocks and bonds and that commodity funds did not provide an attractive hedge against inflation. Last, they find that the distribution of returns to public commodity pools to be negatively skewed. Therefore, the opportunity for very large negative returns is greater than for large positive returns.

Irwin, Krukemeyer, and Zulauf,[3] Schneeweis, Savanyana, and McCarthy,[4] and Edwards and Park[5] also conclude that public commodity funds offer little value to investors as either stand-alone investments or as an addition to a stock and bond portfolio. However, Irwin and Brorsen find that public commodity funds provide an expanded efficient investment frontier.[6]

For private commodity pools, Edwards and Park[7] find that an equally weighted index of commodity pools have a sufficiently high Sharpe Ratio to justify them as either a stand-alone investment or as part of a diversified portfolio. Conversely, Schneeweis et al conclude that private commodity pools do not have value as stand-alone investments but they are worthwhile additions to a stock and bond portfolio.[8]

With respect to separate accounts managed by CTAs, McCarthy, Schneeweis, and Spurgin[9] find that an allocation to an equally weighted index of CTAs provides valuable diversification benefits to a portfolio of stocks and bonds. In a subsequent study, Schneeweis, Spurgin, and Potter find that a portfolio allocation

---

[2] See Edwin Elton, Martin Gruber, and Joel Rentzler, "Professionally Managed, Publicly Traded Commodity Funds," *Journal of Business*, vol. 60, no. 2 (1987), pp. 175–199; "New Public Offerings, Information, and Investor Rationality: The Case of Publicly Offered Commodity Funds," *Journal of Business*, vol. 62, no. 1 (1989), pp. 1–15; "The Performance of Publicly Offered Commodity Funds," *Financial Analysts Journal* (July-August 1990), pp. 23–30.

[3] See Scott Irwin, Terry Krukemyer, and Carl Zulauf, "Investment Performance of Public Commodity Pools: 1979–1990," *The Journal of Futures Markets*, vol. 13, no. 7 (1993), pp. 799–819.

[4] See Thomas Schneeweis, Uttama Savanayana, and David McCarthy, "Alternative Commodity Trading Vehicles: A Performance Analysis," *The Journal of Futures Markets*, vol. 11, no. 4 (1991), pp. 475–487.

[5] See Franklin Edwards and James Park, "Do Managed Futures Make Good Investments," *The Journal of Futures Markets*, vol. 16, no. 5 (1996), pp. 475–517.

[6] See Scott Irwin and B. Wade Brorsen, "Public Futures Funds," *The Journal of Futures Markets*, vol. 5, no. 3 (1985), pp. 463–485.

[7] See Edwards and Park, "Do Managed Futures Make Good Investments?"

[8] See Schneeweis, Savanayana, and McCarthy, "Alternative Commodity Trading Vehicles: A Performance Analysis."

[9] See David McCarthy, Thomas Schneeweis, and Richard Spurgin, "Investment Through CTAs: An Alternative Managed Futures Investment," *The Journal of Derivatives* (Summer 1996), pp. 36–47.

to a dollar weighted index of CTAs results in a higher portfolio Sharpe ratio.[10] Edwards and Park find that an index of equally weighted CTAs performs well as both a stand-alone investment and as an addition to a diversified portfolio.[11]

An important aspect of any investment is the predictability of returns over time. If returns are predictable, then an investor can select a commodity pool or a CTA with consistently superior performance. Considerable time and effort has been devoted to studying the managed futures industry to determine the predictability and consistency of returns. Unfortunately, the results are not encouraging.

For instance, Edwards and Ma find that once commodity funds go public through a registered public offering, their average returns are negative.[12] They conclude that prior pre-public trading performance for commodity pools is of little use to investors when selecting a public commodity fund as an investment. The lack of predictability in historical managed futures returns is supported by the research of McCarthy, Schneeweis, and Spurgin,[13] Irwin, Zulauf, and Ward,[14] and the three studies by Elton, Gruber, and Renzler.[15] In fact, Irwin *et al* conclude that a strategy of selecting CTAs based on historical good performance is not likely to improve upon a naive strategy of selecting CTAs at random.

In summary, the prior research regarding managed futures is unsettled. There is no evidence that public commodity pools provide any benefits either as a stand-alone investment or as part of a diversified portfolio. However, the evidence does indicate that private commodity pools and CTA managed accounts can be a valuable addition to a diversified portfolio. Nonetheless, the issue of performance persistence in the managed futures industry is unresolved. Currently, there is more evidence against performance persistence than there is to support this conclusion.

In the next section, we begin to analyze the performance in the managed futures industry by examining the return distributions for different CTA investment styles. We then consider the potential for downside risk protection from managed futures.

---

[10] See Thomas Schneeweis, Richard Spurgin, and Mark Potter, "Managed Futures and Hedge Fund Investment for Downside Equity Risk Management," in *The Handbook of Managed Futures: Performance, Evaluation and Analysis*, Carl C. Peters and Ben Warwick, editors, New York: McGraw Hill Companies, Inc., 1997.

[11] Edwards and Park, "Do Managed Futures Make Good Investments?"

[12] See Franklin Edwards and Cindy Ma, "Commodity Pool Performance: Is the Information Contained in Pool Prospectuses Useful?" *The Journal of Futures Markets*, vol. 8, no. 5 (1988), pp. 589–616.

[13] McCarthy, Schneeweis, and Spurgin, "Investment Through CTAs: An Alternative Managed Futures Investment."

[14] Scott Irwin, Carl Zulauf, and Barry Ward, "The Predictability of Managed Futures Returns," *The Journal of Derivatives* (Winter 1994), pp. 20–27.

[15] Elton, Gruber, and Rentzler, "Professionally Managed, Publicly Traded Commodity Funds," "New Public Offerings, Information, and Investor Rationality: The Case of Publicly Offered Commodity Funds," and "The Performance of Publicly Offered Commodity Funds."

RETURN DISTRIBUTIONS OF MANAGED FUTURES

Similar to our analysis for hedge funds and passive commodity futures, we examine the distribution of returns for managed futures. We use the Barclays Managed Futures Index to determine the pattern of returns associated with several styles of futures investing.

Managed futures products may be good investments if the pattern of their returns is positively skewed. One way to consider this concept is that it is similar to owning a Treasury bill plus a lottery ticket. The investor consistently receives low, but positive returns. However, every once and a while an extreme event occurs and the CTA is able to profit from the movement of futures prices. This would result in a positive skew.

In Chapter 11, we saw that this was the case for passive commodity futures. They earned consistent positive returns, and every once in a while there is a commodity price shock that tends to push prices upward. As a result, the distribution of returns for passive commodity futures tend to be positively skewed.

To analyze the distribution of returns associated with managed futures investing, we use the Barclays CTA managed futures indices that divide the CTA universe into four actively traded strategies: (1) CTAs that actively trade in the agricultural commodity futures; (2) CTAs that actively trade in currency futures; (3) CTAs that actively trade in financial and metal futures; and, (4) CTAs that actively trade in energy futures.

Managed futures traders have one goal in mind: to capitalize on price trends. Most CTAs are considered to be trend followers. Typically, they look at various moving averages of commodity prices and attempt to determine whether the price will continue to trend up or down, and then trade accordingly. Therefore, it is not the investment strategy that is the distinguishing factor in the managed futures industry, but rather, the markets in which CTAs and CPOs apply their trend following strategies.[16]

In this chapter we use the Mount Lucas Management Index (MLMI) as a benchmark by which to judge CTA performance. Recall from our discussion in Chapter 11 that the MLMI is a passive futures index. It applies a mechanical and transparent rule for capitalizing on price trends in the futures markets. It does not represent active trading. Instead, it applies a consistent rule for buying or selling futures contracts depending upon the current price trend in any particular commodity futures market. In addition, the MLMI invests across agricultural, currency, financial, energy, and metal futures contracts. Therefore, it provides a good benchmark by which to examine the four managed futures strategies.

Exhibits 15 and 16 in Chapter 11 demonstrate that the MLMI has a negative skew of −0.562. Therefore, a simple or naive trend following strategy will produce a distribution of returns that has more negative return observations below the

---

[16] In fact, one article has noted that the managed futures industry suffers because too many CTAs are following similar trend following strategies. See Daniel Collins, "A New Life for Managed Futures," *Futures* (April 1, 2001).

median than positive observations above the median. In reviewing the distribution of returns for manage futures strategies, we keep in mind that the returns are generated from active management. As we indicated in our discussion of hedge funds in Chapter 6, one demonstration of skill is the ability to shift a distribution of returns from a negative skew to a positive skew. Therefore, if CTAs do in fact have skill, we would expect to see distribution of returns with a positive skew.

Further, the passive MLMI strategy produces a distribution of returns with considerable leptokurtosis; the value of kurtosis for the MLMI is 2.476. This indicates that the tails of the distribution that have greater probability mass than a normal, bell-shaped distribution. This indicates that a passive trend following strategy has significant exposure to outlier events. Consequently, we would expect to observe similar leptokurtosis associated with managed futures.

Last, the average return for the MLMI strategy was 0.73% per month. If managed futures strategies can add value, we would expect them to outperform the average monthly return earned by the naive MLMI strategy.

Managed Futures in Agricultural Commodities

In our discussion of commodity futures in Chapter 10 we indicated that commodity prices are more likely to be susceptible to positive price surprises. The reason is that most of the news associated with agricultural products is usually negative. Droughts, floods, storms, and crop freezes are the main news stories. Therefore, new information to the agricultural market tends to result in positive price shocks instead of negative price shocks. (There is not much price reaction to the news that "the crop cycle is progressing normally.") We would expect the CTAs to capture the advantage of these price surprises and any trends that develop from them.

Exhibit 1 presents the return distribution for Barclays Agricultural CTA index. We use data over the period 1990–2000. From a quick review of this distribution, it closely resembles a bell curve type of distribution. However, in Exhibit 5, we show that this distribution in fact has a positive skew of 0.18. Therefore, compared to the negative skew observed for the passive MLMI, we can conclude that managed futures did add value compared to a passive strategy.

In addition, the value of kurtosis, while still positive at 0.69, is much smaller than that for the MLMI. In fact, the tails of the distribution for the Barclays Agricultural CTA index have probability mass close to that for a normal distribution. Therefore, CTAs were able to shift the distribution of commodity futures returns from a negative skew to a positive skew while reducing the exposure to tail risk.

Unfortunately, there is a tradeoff for this skill. The average return to the Barclays Agricultural CTA index of 0.58% per month is less than that for the MLMI index of 0.73%. Additionally, the Sharpe ratio for the managed futures strategy is lower than that for the MLMI. Consequently, the results for managed futures trading in the agriculture markets is mixed. On the one hand we observe a positive shift to the distribution of returns, but a reduction in the risk and return tradeoff as measured by the Sharpe ratio.

Exhibit 1: Barclay Agriculture CTA Returns

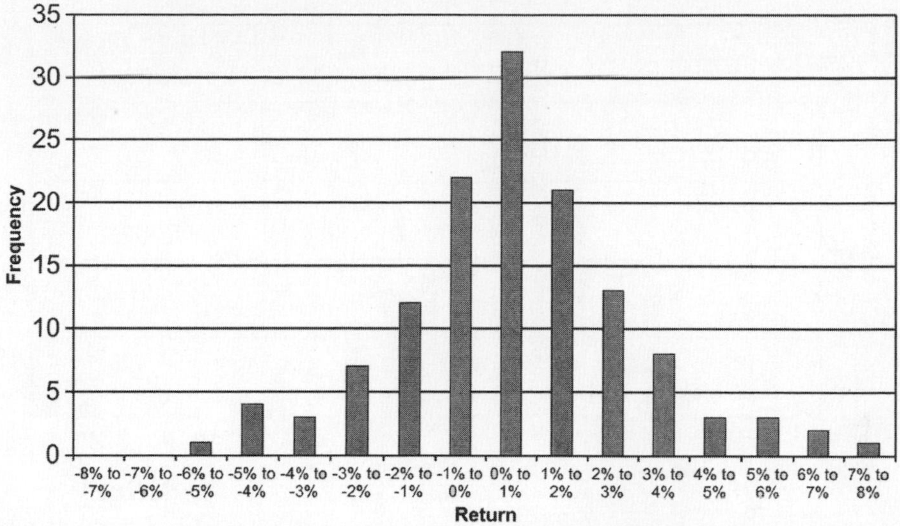

Managed Futures in Currency Markets

The currency markets are the most liquid and efficient markets in the world. The reason is simple, every other commodity, financial asset, household good, cheeseburger, etc. must be denominated in a currency. As the numeraire, currency is the commodity in which all other commodities and assets are denominated.

Daily trading volume in exchange listed and forward markets for currency contracts is in the hundreds of billions of dollars. Given the liquidity, depth, and efficiency of the currency markets, we would expect the ability of managed futures traders to derive value to be small.

Exhibit 2 provides the distribution of returns for actively managed currency futures. We can see from this graph and Exhibit 5, that CTAs produced a distribution of returns with a very large positive skew of 1.39. This is considerably greater than that for the MLMI, and presents a strong case for skill. In addition, the average monthly return for CTAs trading in currency futures is 0.8% per month, an improvement of the average monthly return for the MLMI.

Unfortunately, this strategy also provides a higher value of kurtosis, 3.15, indicating significant exposure to outlier events. This higher exposure to outlier events translates into a higher standard deviation of returns for managed currency futures, and a lower Sharpe ratio.

The evidence for skill-based investing in managed currency futures is mixed. On the one hand, CTAs demonstrated an ability to shift the distribution of returns compared to a naive trend following strategy from negative to positive. On the other hand, more risk was incurred through greater exposure to outlier events resulting in a lower Sharpe ratio than that for the MLMI.

Exhibit 2: Barclay Currency CTA Returns

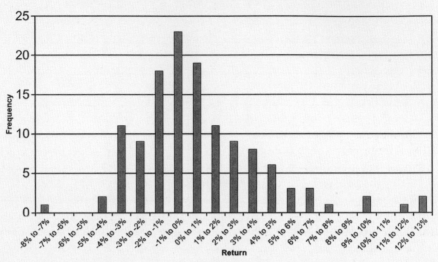

Managed Futures in the Financials and Metals Markets

As we discussed above, with the advent of the GNMA futures contract in the 1970s, financial futures contracts have enjoyed greater prominence than traditional physical commodity futures. However, considerable liquidity exists in the precious metals markets because gold, silver, and platinum are still purchased and sold primarily as a store of value rather than for any productive input into a manufacturing process. In this fashion, precious metal futures resemble financial assets.

In Chapter 6 we demonstrated how financial assets tend to have a negative skew of returns during the period 1990–2000 with a reasonably large value of leptokurtosis. Therefore, a demonstration of skill with respect to managed futures is again the ability to shift the distribution of returns to a positive skew.

Exhibit 3 and Exhibit 5 demonstrate this positive skew. Managed futures in financial and precious metal futures have a positive skew of 0.58 and a small positive kurtosis of 0.49. Therefore, CTAs were able to shift the distribution of returns to the upside while reducing exposure to outlier returns.

The average monthly return, however, is 0.63%, less than that for the MLMI. Additionally, the Sharpe ratio for this CTA strategy is less than that for the MLMI. Once again, we find mixed evidence that managed futures can add value beyond that presented in a mechanical trend following strategy.

Managed Futures in the Energy Markets

The energy markets are chock full of price shocks associated with news events. These news events tend to be positive for the price of energy related commodities and futures contracts thereon. The Arab Oil Embargo in 1973 and 1977, the Iraq/

Iran war of the early 1980s, the Iraqi invasion of Kuwait in 1990, as well as sudden cold snaps, broken pipelines, oil refinery fires and explosions, and oil tanker shipwrecks all tend to increase the price of oil and oil related products.

If there is skill in the managed futures industry with respect to energy futures contracts, we would expect to see a positively skewed distribution with a large expected return. In addition, we would expect to see a large value of kurtosis that reflects the exposure to these outlier events.

Exhibits 4 and 5 present the results for managed futures in the energy markets.[17] The results are consistent with our expectations for skew and kurtosis. CTAs did manage to produce a positively skewed distribution of returns. Additionally, a large value of leptokurtosis is observed, consistent with the energy price shocks that affect this market in particular.

Yet, the average return for managed futures in the energy markets is a −0.06% per month. Therefore, even though CTAs are able to shift the distribution of returns to a positive skew, the distribution is centered around a negative mean return. While a positive skew to a distribution is a favorable characteristic of any asset class, it has no utility to an investor if the asset class still loses money. Therefore, we must conclude that managed futures in the energy markets did little to add value for an investor.

Given the mixed and disappointing results observed in Exhibits 1 through 5, we explore another possible use for managed futures: downside risk protection. We examine this prospect in the next section.

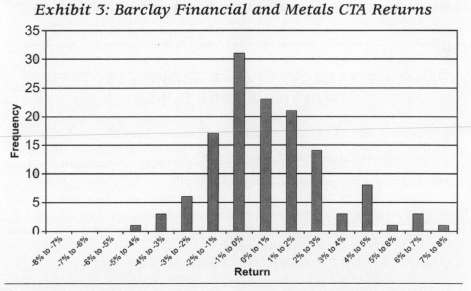

Exhibit 3: Barclay Financial and Metals CTA Returns

[17] Unfortunately, the Barclays Energy CTA index stopped at the end of 1998. This period captures the decline of the energy markets in 1998 due to the world oil glut, but does not include the rebound in energy prices throughout 1999 and 2000.

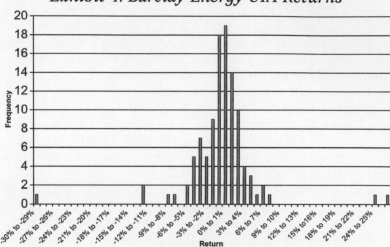

Exhibit 4: Barclay Energy CTA Returns

Exhibit 5: Return Distributions for Managed Futures

	MLMI	CTA Agriculture	CTA Currency	CTA Financial	CTA Energy
Expected Return	0.73%	0.58%	0.80%	0.63%	−0.06%
Standard Deviation	1.61%	2.33%	3.58%	2.21%	5.55%
Sharpe Ratio	0.173	0.055	0.098	0.081	−0.091
Skew	−0.562	0.182	1.394	0.587	0.309
Kurtosis	2.476	0.693	3.147	0.491	14.616

MANAGED FUTURES AS DOWNSIDE RISK PROTECTION FOR STOCKS AND BONDS

This section is similar to that presented in Chapter 12 for passive commodity futures. As we discussed in Chapter 12, the greatest concern for any investor is downside risk. If equity and bond markets are becoming increasingly synchronized, international diversification may not offer the protection sought by investors. The ability to protect the value of an investment portfolio in hostile or turbulent markets is the key to the value of any macroeconomic diversification.

Within this framework, an asset class distinct from financial assets has the potential to diversify and protect an investment portfolio from hostile markets. It is possible that "skill-based" strategies such as managed futures investing can provide the diversification that investors seek. Managed futures strategies might provide diversification for a stock and bond portfolio because the returns are dependent upon the special skill of the CTA rather than any macroeconomic policy decisions made by central bankers or government regimes.

Exhibit 6: 55/35/10 Stocks/Bonds/CTA Agriculture

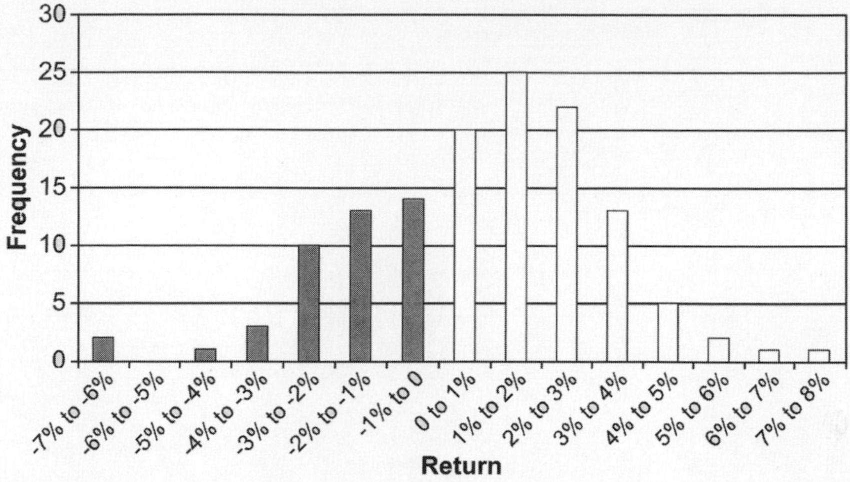

Recall that in Exhibit 10 in Chapter 12 we presented the return distribution for a portfolio that was 60% the S&P 500 and 40% U.S. Treasury bonds. Our concern is the shaded part of the return distribution. This shows where the returns to the stock and bond portfolio were negative. That is, the shaded part of the distribution shows both the size and the frequency with which the combined return of 60% S&P 500 plus 40% U.S. Treasury bonds earned a negative return in a particular month. The average monthly return in the shaded part of the distribution was −2.07%. It is this part of the return distribution that an investor attempts to avoid or limit.

We attempt to protect against the downside of this distribution by making a 10% allocation to managed futures to our initial stock and bond portfolio. Therefore, the new portfolio is a blend of 55% S&P 500, 35% U.S. Treasury bonds, and 10% managed futures. If managed futures can protect against downside risk, we can conclude that it is a valuable addition to a stock and bond portfolio.

Once again, we use the MLMI as a benchmark to determine if CTAs can improve the downside protection over a passive trend following strategy. Recall that in Chapter 12, we found that the MLMI provided 19 basis points of downside protection for stocks and bonds (see Exhibits 14 and 16 in Chapter 12). Therefore, to demonstrate special skill (and to earn their fees), CTAs in managed futures products must provide greater than 19 basis points of downside risk protection.

Exhibit 6 presents the return distribution for a 55/35/10 stock/bond/CTA agriculture portfolio. Exhibit 10 presents summary statistics for this portfolio. The average downside return in the shaded part of Exhibit 6 is −1.81%. This is an improvement of 26 basis points over the shaded downside area presented in Exhibit 10 in Chapter 12. We can conclude that CTAs managing futures in the agricultural sector did, in fact, exhibit skill by providing additional downside protection beyond that offered by the passive MLMI.

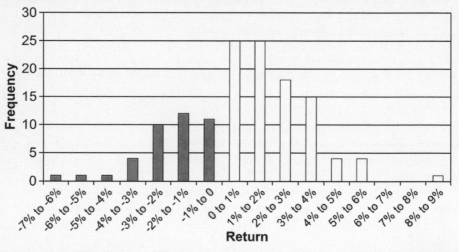

Exhibit 7: 55/35/10 Stocks/Bonds/CTA Currency

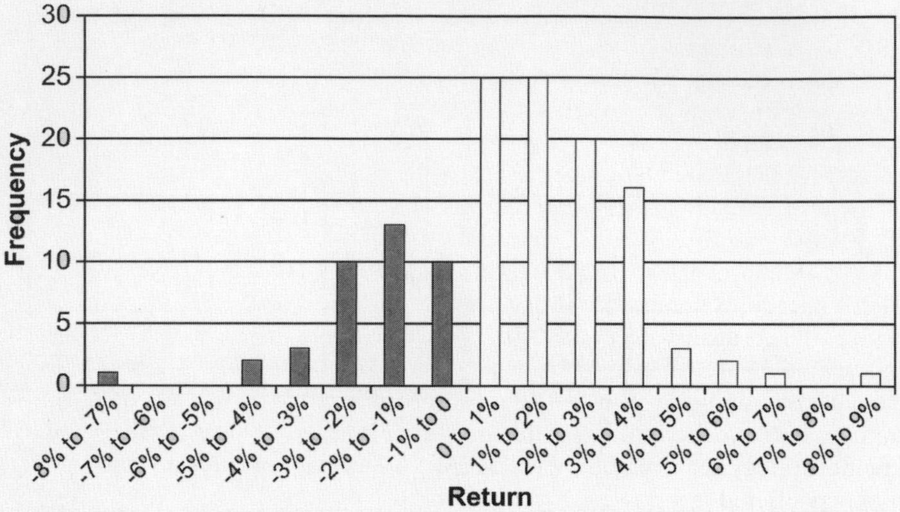

Exhibit 8: 55/35/10 Stocks/Bonds/CTA Financials and Metals

In Exhibit 10 we show that this downside protection came at the expense of 3 basis points per month of expected return. Given that, on average, the 60/40 stock/bond portfolio experiences 3.8 downside months per year (see Chapter 12), the annual expected trade off is (26 bp × 3.8) − (3 bp × 12) = 63 basis points.

Exhibit 7 presents the return distribution for a 55/35/10 stocks/bonds/CTA currency portfolio. This portfolio also provides downside protection to a stock and bond portfolio. The average monthly downside return is −1.96%. Therefore, currency managed futures provided 0.11% of average monthly downside risk protection. This is less than provided by the MLMI, and consequently, CTAs in this sector did not demonstrate additional skill with respect to downside protection.

In Exhibit 8 we present the portfolio return distribution with a 10% allocation to CTA managed futures in financial and metal futures contracts. The average monthly downside return of this portfolio is −1.95%, indicating an improvement of 0.12% per month over the standard stock and bond portfolio. However, again, this is less than the protection offered by the MLMI, and CTA skill is not apparent.

Last, Exhibit 9 presents the return distribution for a 55/35/10 stock/bond/ CTA energy portfolio. The average monthly downside return in this portfolio is − 1.86%, an improvement of 21 basis points over that for stocks and bonds alone. This outperforms the downside risk protection offered by the MLMI.

Once again, we cannot provide firm support for the managed futures industry. Although all managed futures strategies provided downside protection to a stock and bond portfolio, only two strategies (agriculture and energy futures trading) outperformed the downside protection provided by the passive trend following strategy represented by the MLMI. CTAs trading currency and financial products offered less downside protection than that provided by the MLMI. Perhaps currency and financial futures are sufficiently linked to financial assets that they offer less downside protection. In any event, our conclusion regarding the diversification potential of managed futures products is unsettled.

These results are summarized in Exhibit 10 where we present average downside return compared to the 60/40 stock/bond portfolio as well as the expected returns, standard deviations, and Sharpe ratios for the four portfolios containing managed futures products. We also present the same information for the 55/35/10 stock/bond/MLMI portfolio.

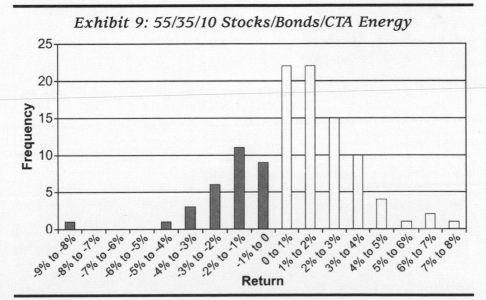

Exhibit 9: 55/35/10 Stocks/Bonds/CTA Energy

Exhibit 10: Downside Risk Protection
(Monthly Returns 1990-2000)

Portfolio Composition	Expected Return	Standard Deviation	Sharpe Ratio	Average Downside	Downside Protection
60/40 US Stocks/US Bonds	0.91%	2.60%	0.177	−2.07%	N/A
55/35/10 Stocks/Bonds/CTA Agriculture	0.88	2.37	0.182	−1.81	0.26%
55/35/10 Stocks/Bonds/CTA Currency	0.90	2.39	0.190	−1.96	0.11
55/35/10 Stocks/Bonds/CTA Financial & Metals	0.89	2.39	0.182	−1.95	0.12
55/35/10 Stocks/Bonds/CTA Energy	0.92	2.38	0.197	−1.86	0.21
55/35/10 Stocks/Bonds/MLMI	0.90	2.33	0.191	−1.88	0.19

In each case, a portfolio with a 10% allocation to managed futures provided a higher Sharpe ratio than that for the 60/40 stock/bond portfolio. This highlights the concept that managed futures products cannot be analyzed on a stand-alone basis. However, when considered within a portfolio context, some benefit from managed futures products can be achieved.

However, in only one case, managed energy futures products, did CTAs provide a Sharpe ratio greater than the passive strategy offered by the MLMI. Even CTA managed agriculture futures did not provide a higher Sharpe ratio than the MLMI. In fact, if we compare Exhibit 16 in Chapter 12 to Exhibit 10 in this chapter, it appears that almost all of the passive commodity futures indices outperformed the active CTA strategies in terms of both downside risk protection and Sharpe ratios.

The downside risk protection demonstrated by managed futures products is consistent with the research of Schneeweis, Spurgin, and Potter and Anson.[18] Specifically, they find that a combination of 50% S&P 500 stocks and 50% CTA managed futures outperforms a portfolio comprised of the S&P 500 plus protective put options. Unfortunately, our research indicates that only in limited circumstances do managed futures products offer financial benefits greater than that offered by a passive futures index.

CONCLUSION

In this chapter we examined the benefits of managed futures products. Prior empirical research has not resolved the issue of whether managed futures products can add value either as a stand-alone investment or as part of a diversified portfolio.

On a stand-alone basis, our review indicates that managed futures products fail to outperform a naive trend following index represented by the MLMI. The MLMI is a transparent commodity futures index that mechanically applies a

---

[18] See Thomas Schneeweis, Richard Spurgin, and Mark Potter, "Managed Futures and Hedge Fund Investment for Downside Equity Risk Protection," *Derivatives Quarterly* (Fall 1996), pp. 62–72. See also Mark Anson, "Managing Downside Risk in Return Distributions Using Hedge Funds, Managed Future and Commodity Futures," working paper (2001).

simple price trend following rule for buying or selling commodity futures. We did not find sufficient evidence to conclude that skill-based CTA trading can outperform this passive index of commodity futures.

On a portfolio basis, the results were more encouraging. We found that managed futures products did provide downside risk protection that, on average, ranged from 0.11% to 0.26% per downside month. Unfortunately, only in limited circumstances (energy futures products) did CTA managed products outperform passive commodity futures indices either on a Sharpe ratio basis or with respect to downside risk protection.

Section III

Private Equity

Chapter 14

Introduction to
Venture Capital

The private equity sector purchases the private stock or equity-linked securities of non-public companies that are expected to go public or provides the capital for public companies (or their divisions) that may wish to go private. The key component in either case is the private nature of the securities purchased. Private equity, by definition, is not publicly traded. Therefore, investments in private equity are illiquid. Investors in this marketplace must be prepared to invest for the long haul; investment horizons may be as extended as 5 to 10 years.

"Private equity" is a generic term that encompasses four distinct strategies in the market for private investing. First, there is venture capital, the financing of start-up companies. Second, there are leveraged buyouts (LBOs) where public companies repurchase all of their outstanding shares and turn themselves into private companies. Third, there is mezzanine financing, a hybrid of private debt and equity financing. Last, there is distressed debt investing. These are private equity investments in established (as opposed to start up) but troubled companies.

Private equity is as old as Columbus' journey to America. Queen Isabella of Spain sold her jewelry to finance Columbus' small fleet of ships in return for whatever spoils Columbus could find in the New World. The risks were great but the potential rewards were even greater. This in a nutshell summarizes the private equity market: a large risk of failure but the potential for outstanding gains.

In this chapter we focus on the best known of the private equity categories: venture capital. Venture capital is the supply of equity financing to start-up companies that do not have a sufficient track record to attract investment capital from traditional sources (e.g., the public markets or lending institutions). Entrepreneurs that develop business plans require investment capital to implement those plans. However, these start-up ventures often lack tangible assets that can be used as collateral for a loan. In addition, start-up companies are unlikely to produce positive earnings for several years. Negative cash flows are another reason why banks and other lending institutions as well as the public stock market are unwilling to provide capital to support the business plan.

It is in this uncertain space where nascent companies are born that venture capitalists operate. Venture capitalists finance these high-risk, illiquid, and unproven ideas by purchasing senior equity stakes while the firms are still privately held. The ultimate goal is to make a buck. Venture capitalists are willing to underwrite new ventures with untested products and bear the risk of no liquidity only if they can expect a reasonable return for their efforts. Often, venture capitalists set expected target rates of return of 33% or more to support the risks they bear. Successful start-up companies funded by venture capital money include Cisco Systems, Cray Research, Microsoft, and Genentech.

We begin with a brief history of venture capital. We then consider the role of a venture capitalist in a start-up company. Last, we review the current structure of the industry.

THE HISTORY OF VENTURE CAPITAL

The first modern venture capital firm was American Research and Development. It was formed in 1946 as a publicly traded closed-end fund. Its investment objective was to finance companies in growth industries, at that time broadcasting, aerospace, and pharmaceuticals.

Over the next 12 years, a small number of venture capital firms (less than 20) were established. Most were structured as closed-end funds like American Research and Development. In 1958 two new developments were introduced into the venture capital industry.

First, Congress created the Small Business Investment Companies (SBICs). SBICs are licensed and regulated by the Small Business Administration. These are government-backed but privately owned investment companies that provide both management assistance and venture financing for start-up companies. These companies include Citicorp Venture Capital and Clinton Capital. SIBCs have provided financing to successful household names such as Apple Computer, Federal Express, and Intel Corporation. Today, there are an estimated 300 SBICs in the United States, concentrated in states with high levels of entrepreneurial talent such as California, Massachusetts, New York, and Texas.[1]

The second development in 1958 was the formation of the first venture capital limited partnership, Draper, Gaither, and Anderson. Limited partnerships have become the standard tool for investing in venture capital by wealthy and institutional investors. Although imitators soon followed, limited partnerships accounted for a small number of the venture capital vehicles throughout the 1960s and 1970s. Furthermore, the annual flow of money into venture capital limited partnerships or closed end funds never exceeded a few hundred million dollars during this time period.[2]

A third important watershed in the development of the venture capital industry was a change in the "prudent person" standard in the rules governing the pension fund industry in the 1970s. Since 1974, corporate pension plans have

---

[1] See W. Keith Schilit, "Structure of the Venture Capital Industry," *The Journal of Private Equity* (Spring 1998).

[2] See Paul Gompers and Josh Lerner, "The Use of Covenants: An Empirical Analysis of Venture Partnership Agreements," *Journal of Law and Economics* (October 1996).

been governed by the Employee Retirement Income Security Act of 1974 (ERISA). ERISA was established to ensure proper investment guidelines for the mounting pension liabilities of corporate America.

Initially, ERISA guidelines prohibited pension funds from investing in venture capital funds because of their illiquid and high-risk status. In 1979, the Department of Labor (which oversees ERISA) issued a clarification of the prudent person rule to indicate that venture capital and other high-risk investments should not be considered on a stand-alone basis, but rather on a portfolio basis. In addition, the rule clarified that the prudent person test is based on an investment review process and not on the ultimate outcome of investment results. Therefore, as long as a pension fund investment fiduciary follows sufficient due diligence in considering the portfolio effects of investing in venture capital, the prudent person test is met. The change in the prudent person rule allowed pension funds for the first time to wholly endorse venture capital investing.

The 1980s saw yet another new development in the venture capital industry: The Gatekeeper. Although many pension funds and wealthy investors access the venture capital industry through investment funds or limited partnerships, few investors have devoted resources to evaluate and monitor these investments. Investors' lack of experience and expertise in venture capital led to the birth of investment advisers to fill this gap.

In the 1980s, investment advisers came to prominence to advise pension funds and wealthy investors on the benefits of venture capital investing. These gatekeepers got their name because venture capital funds and limited partnerships could no longer access pension fund investment staffs directly. Venture capitalists now had to go through the investment adviser to get a capital commitment from a pension fund. In turn, gatekeepers pooled the resources from their clients and became a dynamic force in the venture capital industry. By 1991, up to one-third of all pension fund commitments to venture capital and one-fifth of all venture money raised came through a gatekeeper.[3]

Venture capital financing increased steadily in the 1980s from about $1.5 billion in commitments in 1980 to over $5 billion in commitments in 1987. During this time, the number of active venture capital investment vehicles increased four-fold. However, the stock market crashes in 1987 and 1989 as well as the recession of 1990–1991 reduced the capital commitments to about $2.5 billion by 1991.

The 1990s saw the longest economic growth cycle ever experienced in the United States. Since the last U.S. recession ended in 1991, the economy has sustained strong growth with a minimum of inflation. This is the perfect environment for venture capital to blossom.

Exhibit 1 demonstrates the growth of investment capital committed to venture capital from 1990 through 2000. For the first half of the decade (1990–1995), the annual commitments to venture capital generally ranged from $5 billion to $7 billion. However, starting in 1996, the venture capital industry experi-

---

[3] Id.

enced exponential growth. The average annual growth rate of venture capital commitments between 1995 and 2000 was 82%. From 1990 through 1999, investing in venture capital increased nine-fold.

This growth was fueled by three factors: robust returns in the stock market in the United States, a strong initial public offering (IPO) market, and low inflation. These three factors allowed investors to simultaneously increase their risk tolerance and to extend their investment horizons. Increased risk tolerance allowed investors to bear the high risks of start-up companies. Extended investment horizons allowed investors to accept long lock-up periods associated with venture capital investing.

Exhibit 2 demonstrates the returns to venture capital compared to the S&P 500 over a 1-year, 3-year, 5-year, and 10-year investment horizon (1991–2000). We include the returns for late stage, early stage, and balanced venture capital funds. We can see that over each time horizon, the returns to venture capital dominate those of the S&P 500. This should be expected because investors should be compensated for the risk of start-up companies and the lack of liquidity of their holdings.

The 1-year, 3-year, and 5-year returns to venture capital appear excessive compared to the broader stock market. These returns were fueled by excessively optimistic expectations concerning the ability of new Internet companies to earn extraordinary profits as well as an extraordinarily robust U.S. economy.

Exhibit 1: Growth of Venture Capital Investing, 1990–2000

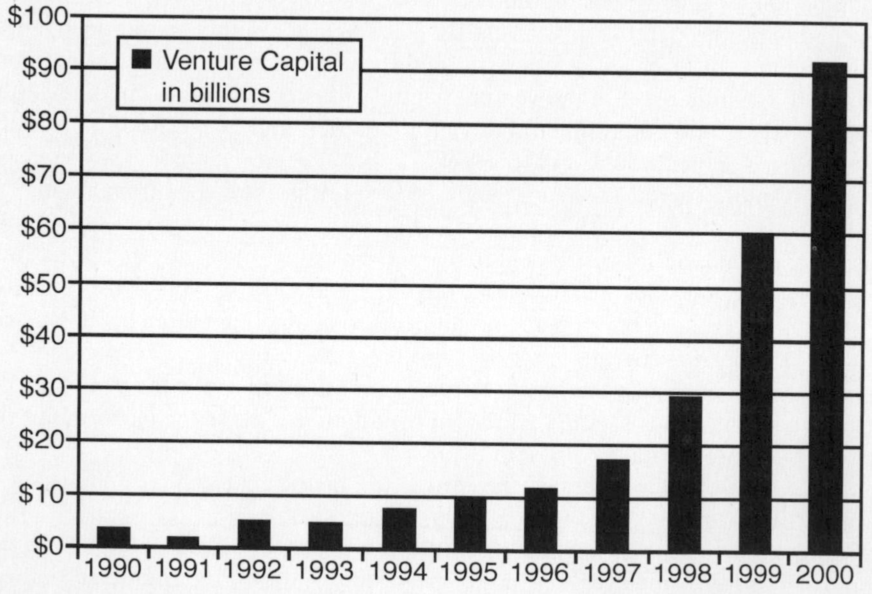

Source: Thomson Financial Venture Economics

Exhibit 2: Returns to Venture Capital

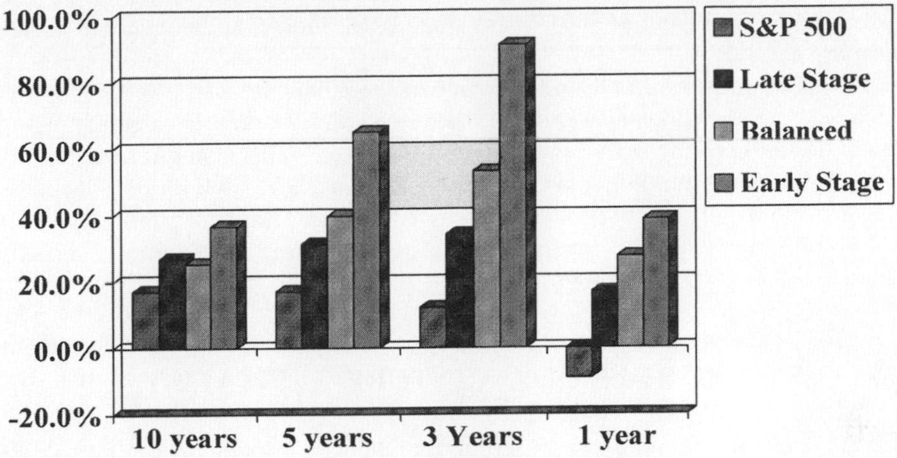

Source: Thomson Financial Venture Economics

A more realistic appraisal of venture capital returns is the 10-year horizon. Over a full economic cycle, venture capital returns should be expected to earn a premium over the public stock market of 5% to 7%.[4] Over the 10-year cycle, for example, balanced and late stage venture capital investments earned a premium over the S&P 500 of 8% and 10%, respectively. Exhibit 2 demonstrates this long-term premium.

The new millennium began with a bang, but by the end of its first full year of 2000, ended with a whimper. The Nasdaq stock market, the primary listing ground for private companies going public through IPOs, came crashing down to earth. Throughout the late 1990s, the valuations associated with companies listed on the Nasdaq became inflated compared to companies listed in the S&P 500 and the Dow Jones 30 Industrial Companies.

Exhibit 3 demonstrates the value of the Nasdaq composite index compared to the S&P 500 and the Dow Jones Industrials from the beginning of 1997 through the first quarter of 2001.[5] The thin line on top of the graph represents the value of the Nasdaq, while the dashed line in the middle is the S&P 500 and the thick line at the bottom represents the Dow Jones 30 Industrials. As can be seen, the Nasdaq tracked closely the valuations of the S&P 500 and the Dow Jones until the beginning of 1999. Then valuations began to diverge with the Nasdaq soaring in value compared to the S&P 500 and the Dow Jones. This created a valuation "bubble" fueled by the belief that technology stocks would take over the world.

---

[4] See Keith Ambachtsheer, "How Should Pension Funds Managed Risk," *Journal of Applied Corporate Finance* (Summer 1998), pp. 1–6.

[5] To compare the values of these stock indices, we measure the value of $1,000 invested in each index over the period January 1997 through March 2001.

However, the bubble in burst in 2000 when new technology companies failed to produce the earnings and revenue growth forecast by optimistic Wall Street analysts. By the beginning of 2001, these three stock indices had converged back to similar values.

Going forward in the new decade of the 2000s, rational pricing has come back to the stock market as well as the venture capital market. The decline in optimism has reduced the cash flows to venture capital funds. Commitments to venture capital funds in the first six months of 2001 were $21.4 billion, a decline of $27.7 billion from the first six months of 2000. Also, there were only 18 initial public offerings of U.S. companies in the first quarter of 2001 compared to 135 IPOs in the first quarter of 2000.

THE ROLE OF A VENTURE CAPITALIST

Venture capitalists have two roles within the industry. Raising money from investors is just the first part. The second is to invest that capital with start-up companies.

Venture capitalists are not passive investors. Once they invest in a company, they take an active role either in an advisory capacity or as a director on the board of the company. They monitor the progress of the company, implement incentive plans for the entrepreneurs and management, and establish financial goals for the company.

Besides providing management insight, venture capitalists usually have the right to hire and fire key mangers, including the original entrepreneur. They also provide access to consultants, accountants, lawyers, investment bankers, and most importantly, other business that might purchase the start-up company's product.

Exhibit 3: Nasdaq, S&P 500, and Dow Jones Industrials

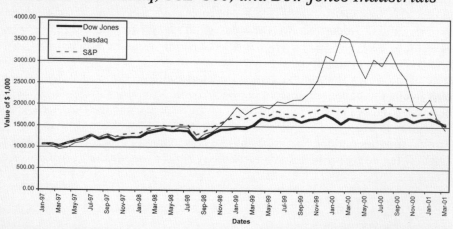

In seeking viable start-up companies to finance, venture capitalists focus on certain aspects of the entrepreneur's business opportunity. These are a business plan, intellectual property rights, prior history of the company, prior history of the management team, regulatory matters, and an exit plan.

Business Plans

The most important document upon which a venture capitalist will base her decision to invest in a start-up company is the business plan. The business plan must be comprehensive, coherent, and internally consistent. It must clearly state the business strategy, identify the niche that the new company will fill, and describe the resources needed to fill that niche.

The business plan also reflects the start-up management team's ability to develop and present an intelligent and strategic plan of action. Therefore, the business plan not only describes the business opportunity but also gives the venture capitalist an insight to the viability of the management team.

Last, the business plan must be realistic. One part of every business plan is the assumptions about revenue growth, cash burn rate, additional rounds of capital injection, and expected date of profitability and/or IPO status. The financial goals stated in the business plan must be achievable. Additionally, financial milestones identified in the business plan can become important conditions for the vesting of management equity, the release of deferred investment commitments, and the control of the board of directors.

Intellectual Property Rights

Most start-ups in the technology and other growth sectors base their business opportunity on the claim to proprietary technology. It is very important that a start-up's claim and rights to that intellectual property be absolute. Any intellectual property owned by the company must be clearly and unequivocally assigned to the company by third parties (usually the entrepreneur and management team). A structure where the entrepreneur still owns the intellectual property but licenses it to the start-up company are disfavored by venture capitalists because license agreements can expire or be terminated leaving the venture capitalist with a shell of a start-up company.

Generally, before a venture capitalist invests with a start-up company, it will conduct patent and trademark searches, seek the opinion of a patent counsel, and possibly ask third parties to confidentially evaluate the technology owned by the start-up company.

Additionally, the venture capitalist may ask key employees to sign non-competition agreements, where they agree not to start another company or join another company operating in the same sector as the start-up for a reasonable period of time. Key employees may also be asked to sign non-disclosure agreements because protecting a start-up company's proprietary technology is an essential element to success.

Prior Operating History

Venture capitalists are not always the first investors in a start-up company. In fact, they may be the third source of financing for a company. Many start-up companies begin by seeking capital from friends, family members, and business associates. Next they may seek a so called "angel investor": a wealthy private individual or an institution that invests capital with the company but does not take an active role in managing or directing the strategy of the company. Then come the venture capitalists.

As a result, a start-up company may already have a prior history before presenting its business plan to a venture capitalist. At this stage, venture capitalists ensure that the start-up company does not have any unusual history such as a prior bankruptcy or failure.

The venture capitalist will also closely review the equity stakes that have been previously provided to family, friends, business associates, and angel investors. These equity stakes should be clearly identified in the business plan and any unusual provisions must be discussed. Equity interests can include common stock, preferred stock, convertible securities, rights, warrants, and stock options. There must still be sufficient equity and upside potential for the venture capitalist to invest. Finally, all prior security issues must be properly documented and must comply with applicable securities laws.

The venture capitalist will also check the company's articles of incorporation to determine whether it is in good legal standing in the state of incorporation. Further, the venture capitalist will examine the company's bylaws, and the minutes of any shareholder and board of directors meetings. The minutes of the meetings can indicate whether the company has a clear sense of direction or whether it is mired in indecision.

The Start-up Management Team

The venture capitalist will closely review the resumes of every member of the management team. Academic backgrounds, professional work history and references will all be checked. Most important to the venture capitalist will be the professional background of the management team. In particular, a management team that has successfully brought a previous start-up company to the IPO stage will be viewed most favorably.

In general, a great management team with a good business plan will be viewed more favorably than a good management team with a great business plan. The best business plan in the world can still fail from inability to execute. Therefore, a management team that has demonstrated a previous ability to follow and execute a business plan will be given a greater chance of success than an unproven management team with a great business opportunity.

However, this is where a venture capitalist can add value. Recognizing a great business opportunity but a weak management team, the venture capitalist can bring his or her expertise to the start-up company as well as bring in other, more seasoned management professionals. While this often creates some friction with the original entrepreneur, the ultimate goal is to make money. Egos often succumb when there is money to be made.

Last, the management team will need a seasoned chief financial officer (CFO). This will be the person primarily responsible for bringing the start-up company public. The CFO will work with the investment bankers to establish the price of the company's stock at the initial public offering. Since the IPO is often the exit strategy for the venture capitalist as well as some of the founders and key employees, it is critical that the CFO have IPO experience.

Legal and Regulatory Issues

We have already touched on some of the legal issues regarding non-competition agreements, non-disclosure agreements, and proper filings for the issuance of equity and debt securities. In addition, the venture capitalist must also determine if patent protection is needed for the start-up's proprietary intellectual property, and if so, initiate the legal proceedings.

Also, in certain industries, federal regulatory approval is necessary before a product can be sold in the United States. Nowhere is this more important than the biotechnology and healthcare sectors. The business plan for the company must also address the time lag between product development and regulatory approval. Additionally, the venture capitalist must consider the time lag before operating profits will be achieved after regulatory approval of a new healthcare product.

Finally, there should be no litigation associated with the start-up company or its management team. Litigation takes time, money, and emotional wear and tear. It is can be a distraction for the company and its key employees. Outstanding or imminent litigation will raise the hurdle rate even higher before a venture capitalist will invest.

Exit Plan

Eventually, the venture capitalist must liquidate her investment in the start-up company to realize a gain for herself and her investors. When a venture capitalist reviews a business plan she will keep in mind the timing and probability of an exit strategy.

An exit strategy is another way the venture capitalist can add value beyond providing start-up financing. Venture capitalists often have many contacts with established operating companies. An established company may be willing to acquire the start-up company for its technology as part of a strategic expansion of its product line. Alternatively, venture capitalists maintain close ties with investment bankers. These bankers will be necessary if the start-up company decides to seek an IPO. In addition, a venture capitalist may ask other venture capitalists to invest in the start-up company. This helps to spread the risk as well as provide additional sources of contacts with operating companies and investment bankers.

Venture capitalists almost always invest in the convertible preferred stock of the start-up company. There may be several rounds (or series) of financing of preferred stock before a start-up company goes public. Convertible preferred shares are the accepted manner of investment because these shares carry a priority over common stock in terms of dividends, voting rights, and liquidation preferences. Furthermore, venture capitalists have the option to convert their shares to common stock to enjoy the benefits of an IPO.

Other investment structures used by venture capitalists include convertible notes or debentures that provide for the conversion of the principal amount of the note or bond into either common or preferred shares at the option of the venture capitalist. Convertible notes and debentures may also be converted upon the occurrence of an event such as a merger, acquisition, or IPO. Venture capitalists may also be granted warrants to purchase the common equity of the start-up company as well as stock rights in the event of an IPO.

Other exit strategies used by venture capitalists are redemption rights and put options. Usually, these strategies are used as part of a company reorganization. Redemption rights and put options are generally not favored because they do not provide as large a rate of return as an acquisition or IPO. These strategies are often used as a last resort when there are no other viable alternatives. Redemption rights and put options are usually negotiated at the time the venture capitalist makes an investment in the start-up company (often called the Registration Rights Agreement).

Usually, venture capitalists require no less than the minimum return provided for in the liquidation preference of a preferred stock investment. Alternatively, the redemption rights or put option might be established by a common stock equivalent value that is usually determined by an investment banking appraisal. Last redemption rights or put option values may be based on a multiple of sales or earnings. Some redemption rights take the highest of all three valuation methods: the liquidation preference, the appraisal value, or the earnings/sales multiple.

In sum, there are many issues a venture capitalist must sort through before funding a start-up company. These issues range from identifying the business opportunity to sorting through legal and regulatory issues. Along the way, the venture capital must assess the quality of the management team, prior capital infusions, status of proprietary technology, operating history (if any) of the company, and timing and likelihood of an exit strategy.

THE CURRENT STRUCTURE OF THE VENTURE CAPITAL INDUSTRY

The structure of the venture capital industry has changed dramatically over the past 20 years. We focus on three major changes: sources of venture capital financing, venture capital investment vehicles, and specialization within the industry.

Sources of Venture Capital Financing

The structure of the venture capital marketplace has changed considerably since 1985. What is most notable is the leading sources of venture capital financing. For example, over the period 1985–1990, the leading source of venture capital financing was pension funds. This came as a result of the revisions to the prudent person standard for pension fund investing in 1979. Over the 1985–1990 period, pension funds accounted for almost 60% of venture capital funding. Endowments and intermediaries, on the other hand, were a negligible source of venture capital funds. Also, in 1985–1990, government agencies accounted for about 11% of the total source of venture capital funds.[6]

By 1999, the landscape of venture capital financing had changed considerably. Pension funds accounted for only about 20% of the source of venture capital funds. Government agencies supplied almost no money to venture capital in 1999, squeezed out by private sources. The federal and state governments no longer need to support the venture capital industry. Virtually all money comes from institutional and other investors willing to take the risk of start-up companies in return for sizeable gains.

To replace the decline of pension funds and government agencies, three new sources of venture capital funds have grown over the last 15 years: endowments, intermediaries, and individuals. Endowments, with their perpetual investment horizons, are natural investors for private equity. Also, as the wealth of the United States has grown, wealthy individuals have allocated a greater share of their wealth to venture capital investments. Last, intermediaries such as hedge funds, cross over funds, and interval funds have entered the venture capital market. Together, endowments, intermediaries, and individuals accounted for almost one half of the source of venture capital funds in 1999. Exhibit 4 demonstrates the changing sources of venture capital financing in the United States.

Exhibit 5 demonstrates another trend in the venture capital industry, the surge of financing for Internet-related companies. Exhibit 5 is the complement to Exhibit 4, it presents the uses of venture capital financing in 1999. Companies whose business opportunity depended solely on an Internet application received more than twice as much venture capital financing as the next largest category, communications. In fact, the four categories that are technology related (computers, semiconductors, computer software, and Internet) accounted for 60% of the use of venture capital financing in 1999.

Venture Capital Investment Vehicles

As the interest for venture capital investments has increased, venture capitalists have responded with new vehicles for venture financing. These include limited partnerships, limited liability companies, corporate venture funds, and venture capital fund of funds.

---

[6] See Steven Lipin, "Venture Capitalists "R" Us," The *Wall Street Journal* (February 22, 2000), p. C1.

Exhibit 4: Sources of Venture Capital Funds

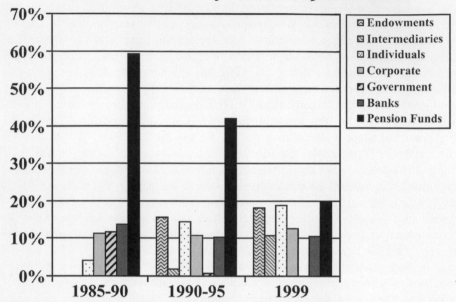

Source: Thomson Financial Venture Economics

Exhibit 5: Uses of Venture Capital 1990–2000, in Billions

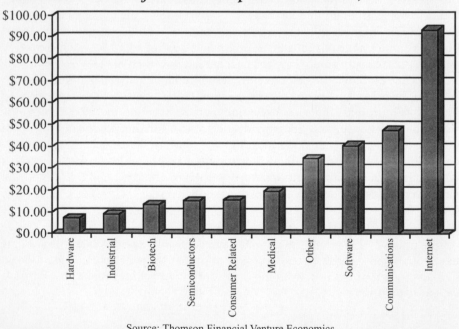

Source: Thomson Financial Venture Economics

Limited Partnerships

The predominant form of venture capital investing in the United States is the limited partnership. Recall our discussion with respect to the regulation of hedge funds in Chapter 8. In that chapter we indicated that hedge funds operated either as "3(c)(1)" or "3(c)(7)" funds to avoid registration as an investment company under the Investment Company Act of 1940. The same regulatory exemptions apply to venture capital funds.

As a limited partnership, all income and capital gains flow through the partnership to the limited partner investors. The partnership itself is not taxed. The appeal of the limited partnership vehicle has increased since 1996 with the "Check the Box" provision of the U.S. tax code.

Previously, limited partnerships had to meet several tests to determine if their predominant operating characteristics resembled more a partnership than a corporation. Such characteristics included, for instance, a limited term of existence. Failure to qualify as a limited partnership would mean double taxation for the investment fund; first at the fund level and second, at the investor level.

This changed with the U.S. Internal Revenue Services decision to let entities simply decide their own tax status by checking a box on their annual tax form as to whether they wished to be taxed as a corporation or as a partnership. "Checking the box" greatly encouraged investment funds to establish themselves as a limited partnership.

Limited partnerships are generally formed with an expected life of 7 to 10 years with an option to extend the limited partnership for another 1–5 years. The limited partnership is managed by a general partner who has day to day responsibility for managing the venture capital fund's investments as well as general liability for any lawsuits that may be brought against the fund. Limited partners, as their name implies, have only a limited (investor) role in the partnership. They do not partake in the management of the fund and they do not bear any liability beyond their committed capital.

All partners in the fund will commit to a specific investment amount at the formation of the limited partnership. However, the limited partners do not contribute money to the fund until it is called down or "taken down" by the general partner. Usually, the general partner will give one to two months notice of when it intends to make additional capital calls on the limited partners. Capital calls are made when the general partner has found a start-up company in which to invest. The general partner can make capital calls up to the amount of the limited partners' initial commitments.

An important element of limited partnership venture funds is that the general partner/venture capitalist has also committed investment capital to the fund. This assures the limited partners of an alignment of interests with the venture capitalist. Typically, limited partnership agreements specify a percentage or dollar amount of capital that the general partner must commit to the partnership.

Limited Liability Companies

A recent phenomenon in the venture capital industry is the limited liability company (LLC). Similar to a limited partnership, all items of net income or loss as well as capital gains are passed through to the shareholders in the LLC. Also, like a limited partnership, an LLC must adhere to the safe harbors of the Investment Company Act of 1940. In addition, LLCs usually have a life of 7 to 10 years with possible options to extend for another 1 to 5 years.

The managing director of an LLC acts like the general partner of a limited partnership. She has management responsibility for the LLC including the decision to invest in start-up companies the committed capital of the LLC's shareholders. The managing director of the LLC might itself be another LLC or a corporation. The same is true for limited partnerships; the general partner need not be an individual, it can be a legal entity like a corporation.

In sum, LLCs and limited partnerships accomplish the same goal — the pooling of investor capital into a central fund from which to make venture capital investments. The choice is dependent upon the type of investor sought. If the venture capitalist wishes to raise funds from a large number of passive and relatively uninformed investors, the limited partnership vehicle is the preferred venue. However, if the venture capitalist intends to raise capital from a small group of knowledgeable investors, the LLC is preferred.

The reason is twofold. First, LLCs usually have more specific shareholder rights and privileges. These privileges are best utilized with a small group of well-informed investors. Second, an LLC structure provides shareholders with control over the sale of additional shares in the LLC to new shareholders. This provides the shareholders with more power with respect to the twin issues of increasing the LLC's pool of committed capital and from whom that capital will be committed.

Corporate Venture Capital Funds

With the explosive growth of technology companies in the late 1990s, many of these companies found themselves with large cash balances. Microsoft, for example, had a cash and cash equivalent balance of almost $30 billion in 2000. Microsoft and other companies need to invest this cash to earn an appropriate rate of return for their investors.

A corporate venture capital fund is an ideal use for a portion of a company's cash. First, venture capital financing is consistent with Microsoft's own past; it was funded with venture capital 20 years ago. Second, Microsoft can provide its own technological expertise to help a start-up company. Last, the start-up company can provide new technology and cost savings to Microsoft. In a way, financing start-up companies allows Microsoft to "think outside of the box" without committing or diverting its own personnel to the task.

Corporate venture capital funds are formed only with the parent company's capital, outside investors are not allowed to join. In addition to Microsoft, other corporate venture funds include Xerox Venture Capital, Hewlett-Packard Co. Corporate Investments, Intel Capital, and Amoco Venture Capital. Investments in start-up companies is a way for large public companies to supplement their research and development budgets. In addition to access to new technology, corporate venture capital funds also gain the ability to generate new products, identify new or diminishing industries, acquire a stake in a future potential competitor, derive attractive returns for excess cash balances, and learn the dynamics of a new marketplace.

Perhaps the best reason for corporate venture capital funds is to gain a window on new technology. Consider the case of Supercomputer Systems of Wisconsin. Steve Chen, the former CEO of Cray Research left Cray to start his own super computer company. Cray Research is a super computer company that was itself a spin-off from Control Data Corp., which in turn was an outgrowth of Sperry Corporation. When Mr. Chen founded his new company, IBM was one of his first investors even though IBM had shifted its focus from large mainframe computers to laptop computers, personal computers, and service contracts.[7]

Another example is Intel Capital, Intel Corporation's venture capital subsidiary. The goal of Intel Capital is to develop a strategic investment program that focuses on making equity investments and acquisitions to grow the Internet economy, including the infrastructure, content, and services in support of Intel's main business which is providing computer chips to power personal and laptop computers. To further this goal, Intel Capital has provided venture capital financing to companies like Peregrine Semiconductor Corp., a start-up technology company that designs, manufactures and markets high-speed communications integrated circuits for the broadband fiber, wireless, and satellite communications markets.

In fact, in year 2000, Intel was the most active venture capital investor. Through affiliated funds, Intel made 210 investments compared to 145 investments made by Goldman Sachs (second most active investor) and 142 investments made by Chase Capital Partners (third most active investor).

There are, however, several potential pitfalls to a corporate venture capital program. These may include conflicting goals between the venture capital subsidiary and the corporate parent. In addition, the 5- to 10-year investment horizon for most venture capital investments may be a longer horizon than the parent company's short-term profit requirements. Further, a funded start-up company may be unwilling to be acquired by the parent company. Still, the benefits from corporate venture capital programs appear to outweigh these potential problems. As of 1998, there were almost 100 corporate venture capital subsidiaries in the United States.[8]

Another pitfall of corporate venture capital funds is the risk of loss. Just as every venture capitalist experiences losses in her portfolio of companies, so too will the corporate venture capitalist. This can translate into significant losses for the parent company.

Take the case of Dell Computers. Dell took a charge of $200 million in the second quarter of 2001 as a result of losses from Dell Ventures, the company's

---

[7] See Schilit, "Structure of the Venture Capital Industry."
[8] *Id.*

venture capital fund. Additionally, in June 2001, Dell reported that its investment portfolio has declined in value by more than $1 billion.[9]

Intel Corp. reported in year 2001 that its technology portfolio declined more than $7 billion in value. For example, in the second quarter of 2000, Intel reported a $2.1 billion gain from the sale of its venture capital investments. Gains from Intel's technology portfolio helped to keep its earnings growth intact. Conversely, in the second quarter of 2001, Intel reported only a $3 million gain from the sale of its investments from its venture capital subsidiary.[10]

Dell and Intel are not alone. Microsoft Corp.'s investment holdings appeared to decline by $3 billion from their peak value.[11] Microsoft, Dell, and Intel all invested in Internet start-ups because it was in their long-term business interests. For example, web sites offering video, music, and other entertainment programs generate a greater demand for high-speed Internet access. This in turn should increase the demand for more powerful computers and faster computer chips. Unfortunately, the decline in technology stocks demonstrated in Exhibit 3 eroded the value of these venture capital investments.

Perhaps the most extreme case of non-performing corporate venture capital investments is that of Comdisco Inc. Comdisco sought bankruptcy protection in July 2001 after making $3 billion in loans to start up companies that were unable to repay most of the money.[12] The company wrote off $100 million in loans made by its Comdisco Ventures unit, which leases computer equipment to start up companies. In addition, Comdisco also took a $206 million reserve against earnings from investments in those ventures.

Venture Capital Fund of Funds

A venture capital fund of funds is a venture pool of capital that, instead of investing directly in start-up companies, invests in other venture capital funds. The venture capital fund of funds is a relatively new phenomenon in the venture capital industry. The general partner of a fund of funds does not select start-up companies in which to invest. Instead, she selects the best venture capitalists with the expectation that they will find appropriate start-up companies to fund.

A venture capital fund of funds offers several advantages to investors. First, the investor receives broad exposure to a diverse range of venture capitalists, and in turn, a wide range of start-up investing. Second, the investor receives the expertise of the fund of funds manager in selecting the best venture capitalists

---

[9] See Joseph Menn, "Tech Giants Lose big on Start-up Ventures," *Los Angeles Times* (June 11, 2001).

[10] See Cesca Antonelli, "Chipmaker's Profit Plunges 94%; Intel Still Beats Analysts Forecasts," *Bloomberg News* (July 18, 2001); and Joseph, Menn, "Tech Giants Lose Big on Start-up Ventures."

[11] See Joseph Menn, "Tech Giants Lose Big on Start-up Ventures." Microsoft includes a "catch-all" investment category on its balance sheet titled: Equities and Other Investments. From September 2000 to March 2001, that figure declined from $20.5 billion to $17.5 billion.

[12] See Jeff St. Onge, "Comdisco Seeks Bankruptcy Protection from Creditors," *Bloomberg News* (July 16, 2001).

with whom to invest money. Last, a fund of funds may have better access to popular, well-funded venture capitalists whose funds may be closed to individual investors. In return for these benefits, investors pay a management fee (and, in some cases, an incentive fee) to the fund of funds manager. The management fee can range from 0.5% to 2% of the net assets managed.

Fund of fund investing also offers benefits to the venture capitalists. First, the venture capitalist receives one large investment (from the venture fund of funds) instead of several small investments. This makes fund raising and investor administration more efficient. Second, the venture capitalist interfaces with an experienced fund of funds manager instead of several (potentially inexperienced) investors.

Specialization within the Venture Capital Industry

Like any industry that grows and matures, expansion and maturity lead to specialization. The trend towards specialization in the venture capital industry exists on several levels, by industry, geography, stage of financing, and "special situations." Specialization is the natural by-product of two factors. First, the enormous amount of capital flowing into venture capital funds has encouraged venture capitalists to distinguish themselves from other funds by narrowing their investment focus. Second, the development of many new technologies over the past decade has encouraged venture capitalists to specialize in order to invest most profitably.

Specialization by Industry

Specialization by entrepreneurs is another reason why venture capitalists have tailored their investment domain. Just as entrepreneurs have become more focused in their start-up companies, venture capitalists have followed suit. The biotechnology industry is a good example.

The biotech industry was born on October 14, 1980, when the stock of Genentech, Inc. went public. On that day, the stock price went from $39 to $85 and a new industry was born. Today, Genentech is a Fortune 500 company with a market capitalization of $28 billion. Other successful biotech start-ups include Cetus Corp., Biogen, Inc., Amgen Corp., and Centacor, Inc.

The biotech paradigm has changed since the days of Genentech. Genentech was founded on the science of gene mapping and slicing to cure diseases. However, initially it did not have a specific product target. Instead, it was concerned with developing its gene mapping technology without a specific product to market.

Compare this situation to that of Applied Microbiology, Inc. of New York. It has focused on two products with the financial support of Merck and Pfizer, two large pharmaceuticals.[13] One of its products is an antibacterial agent to fight gum disease contained in a mouthwash to be marketed by Pfizer.

Specialized start-up biotech firms have led to specialized venture capital firms. For example, Domain Associates of Princeton, New Jersey focuses on funding

---

[13] See W. Keith Schilit, "The Nature of Venture Capital Investments," *The Journal of Private Equity* (Winter 1997), pp. 59–75.

new technology in molecular engineering. However, specialization is not unique to the biotech industry. Other examples include Communication Ventures of Menlo Park, California. This venture firm provides financing primarily for start-up companies in the telecommunications industry. Another example is American Health Capital Ventures of Brentwood, Tennessee that specializes in funding new healthcare companies.

Specialization by Geography

With the boom in technology companies in Silicon Valley, Los Angeles, and Seattle, it is not surprising to find that many California based venture capital firms concentrate their investments on the west coast of the United States. Not only are there plenty of investment opportunities in this region, it is also easier for the venture capital firms to monitor their investments locally. The same is true for other technology centers in New York, Boston, and Texas.

As another example, consider Marquette Ventures based in Chicago. This venture capital company invests primarily with start-up companies in the Midwest. Although it has provided venture capital financing to companies outside of this region, its predominate investment pattern is with companies located in the midwestern states.[14] Similarly, the Massey Birch venture capital firm of Nashville, Tennessee has provided venture financing to a number of companies in its hometown of Nashville as well as other companies throughout the southeastern states.

Regional specialization has the advantage of easier monitoring of invested capital. Also, larger venture capital firms may overlook viable start-up opportunities located in more remote sections of the United States. Regional venture capitalists step in to fill this niche.

The downside of regional specialization is twofold. First, regional concentration may not provide sufficient diversification to a venture capital portfolio. Second, a start-up company in a less-exposed geographic region may have greater difficulty in attracting additional rounds of venture capital financing. This may limit the start-up company's growth potential as well as exit opportunities for the regional venture capitalist.

Stage of Financing

Venture capitalists also distinguish themselves by the point at which they will invest in a start-up company. Some venture capitalists provide first stage, or "seed capital" while others wait to invest in companies that are further along in their development. For a first time entrepreneur, seed financing can be difficult to find. Without a prior track record, most venture capitalists are skeptical of new product ideas.

Seed financing is usually in the range of $500,000 to $3 million. Examples of seed financing companies are Technology Venture Investors of Menlo Park, California, Advanced Technology Ventures of Boston, and Onsent, located in Silicon Valley.[15] First stage venture capitalists tend to be smaller firms because

---

[14] *Id.*
[15] *Id.*

large venture capital firms cannot afford to spend the endless hours with an entrepreneur for a small investment, usually no greater than $1 to $2 million.

A new development to fill this niche is the venture capital "feeder fund."
These have been established where large venture capitalists provide capital to
seed venture capitalists in return for the opportunity to make a later stage investment in the start-up company if it is successful.

Most venture capital firms invest either in mid or late stage rounds of
equity. Later stage financing provides for a quicker return of capital as well as a
lower risk investment. Returns are expected to be lower than that for seed financing. In many cases the start-up company has a viable product by the time a second
or third round of venture financing is sought. Also, with the increase flow of
money into venture funds, venture capitalists have found that they have larger
pools of capital to deploy. Later stage financing provides the most efficacious
means to deploy large chunks of investor capital.

As an example of how different venture capital firms invest at different
points of a start up company life cycle consider the example of CacheFlow Inc.[16]
CacheFlow is a company that provides for local storage or "caching" of frequently used Internet data via a technology gadget added to customers' computer
networks. CacheFlow started operations with $1 million in seed capital raised
from a dozen angel investors in March 1996.

In October 1996, CacheFlow received its first venture capital infusion,
selling 3.2 million shares of Series A convertible preferred stock at 87.5 cents per
share to Benchmark Capital Partners for a 25% stake in the company. In December 1997, CacheFlow raised a middle round of venture capital financing from
U.S. Ventures. U.S. Ventures paid $6 million for Series B preferred convertible
preferred stock for 17% of the company. Finally, in March 1999, CacheFlow
received $8.7 million in late stage venture capital from Technology Crossover
Ventures. This venture capital group paid $4.575 a share for Series C convertible
preferred stock for 7% of the company.

CacheFlow went public in November 1999 at a price of $24 a share and
closed at $126.38 a share on its first day of trading. Its stock price reached a peak
value of $165 a share in December 1999. Based on the purchase prices for the differ-
ent series of convertible preferred stock, by the end of the first day of trading, Series
A holders had a return of over 14,000%, Series B stockholders had a gain of over
5,400%, and Series C stock holders had a gain of over 2,600%.

Unfortunately, since December 1999, CacheFlow's stock price has not
fared so well. CacheFlow's stock price declined by 51% in November 2000 when
its revenue growth failed to please analysts and investors. In addition, CacheFlow
announced in February 2001 that its third quarter revenues were only about $21
million, less than half of what analysts had projected. The company announced
that it was restructuring to reduce costs and aggressively managing its headcount.

---

[16] For a great case history on a start-up company, see Suzanne McGee, "Venture Capital "R" Us; Cache-
Flow: The Life Cycle of a Venture-Capital Deal," The *Wall Street Journal* (February 22, 2000), p. C1.

By August 2001, its stock price had declined to $2.59. Exhibit 6 demonstrates the rise and fall of the fortunes of CacheFlow Inc.

Special Situation Venture Capital

In any industry, there are always failures. Not every start-up company makes it to the IPO stage. However, this opens another specialized niche in the venture capital industry: the turnaround venture deal. Turnaround deals are as risky as seed financing because the start-up company may be facing pressure from creditors. The turnaround venture capitalist exists because mainstream venture capitalists may not be sufficiently well-versed in restructuring a turnaround situation.

Consider the following example.[17] A start-up company is owned 50% by early and mid-stage venture capitalists and 50% by the founder. Product delays and poor management have resulted in $10 million in corporate assets and $15 million in liabilities. The company has a negative net worth and is technically bankrupt.

The turnaround venture capitalist offers the founder/entrepreneur of the company $1 million for his 50% ownership plus a job as an executive of the company. The turnaround venture capitalist then offers the start-up company's creditors 50 cents for every one dollar of claims. The total of $8.5 million might come from a $1 million dollar contribution from the turnaround venture capitalist and $7.5 million in bank loans secured by the $10 million in assets. Therefore, for $1 million the turnaround venture capitalist receives 50% of the start-up company and restores it to a positive net worth.

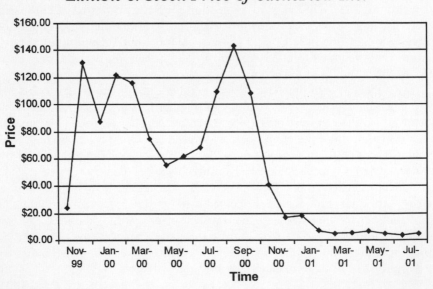

Exhibit 6: Stock Price of CacheFlow Inc.

---

[17] A similar example is in Schilit, "The Nature of Venture Capital Investments."

The founder of the company is happy because he receives $1 million for a bankrupt company plus he remains as an executive. The other venture capitalists are also happy because now they will be dealing with another venture specialist plus the company has been restored to financial health. With some additional hard work the company may proceed on to an IPO. The creditors, however, will not be as pleased, but may make the deal anyway because 50 cents on the dollar may be more than they could expect to receive through a formal liquidation procedure.

An example of such a turnaround specialist is Reprise Capital Corp. of Garden City, New Jersey. In 1997, this company raised $25 million for turn-around venture capital deals.

In summary, the growth of the venture capital industry has created the need for venture capital specialists. The range of new business opportunities is now so diverse that it is simply not possible for a single venture capital firm to stay on top of all opportunities in all industries. Therefore, by necessity, venture capitalists have narrowed their investment domain to concentrate on certain niches within the start-up universe. Specialization also leads to differentiation, which allows venture capitalists to distinguish themselves from other investment funds.

CONCLUSION

The venture capital industry has grown tremendously over the past 50 years, but the fundamental concept remains unchanged: investing private capital with promising but untested business opportunities in order to reap long-term returns that offer a significant premium above the general stock market.

The long bull market of the 1990s combined with the greatest period of economic expansion in U.S. history helped to fuel extraordinary growth in the venture capital industry. However, a slow down in the technology sector as well as the U.S. and global economies have cooled the return expectations of venture capitalists and investors alike. As a result, commitments to venture capital funds declined in year 2001 compared to year 2000. Looking forward, venture capital will remain a popular and rewarding alternative equity investment strategy. However, the stellar returns earned in 1999 should not be expected to repeat any time in the near future.

credit, specifically that card histories of successful buyout transactions di

Chapter 15

Introduction to Leveraged Buyouts

L everaged buyouts are a way to take a company with publicly traded stock private, or a way to put a company in the hands of the current management (sometimes referred to *management buyouts* or *MBOs*). LBOs use the assets or cash flows of the company to secure debt financing either in bonds issued by the corporation or bank loans, to purchase the outstanding equity of the company. In either case, control of the company is concentrated in the hands of the LBO firm and management, and there is no public stock outstanding.

LBOs represent a mechanism to take advantage of a window of opportunity to increase the value of a corporation. Leverage buyouts can be a way to unlock hidden value or exploit existing but underfunded opportunities.

We begin this chapter with a brief history of the LBO market. Next we provide a theoretical example of how LBOs work. We then discuss how LBOs add value, providing short case histories of successful buyout transactions. As successful as LBO transactions have been, there are risks and we examine these risks in light of the large leverage ratios used to fund buyouts. We also examine the fee structures of LBO funds and other methods by which LBO funds make money. Last, we consider some of the corporate governance advantages of LBOs.

THE HISTORY OF LBOs

Although LBOs began after the Second World War, it was not until the 1970s that the investment value of LBOs became apparent. In 1976 a new investment firm was created on Wall Street, Kohlberg Kravis Roberts & Co. (KKR).[1] The founders of KKR had previously worked at Bear Stearns and Company, and they helped to pioneer the LBO transaction as early as 1968. No firm has had a greater impact on the leveraged buyout market than KKR. Indeed, many of the transactions discussed in this chapter were originated by KKR.

KKR began with just $3 million of its own funds to invest, but soon raised enough capital from other investors to finance the buyout in 1977 of A.J. Industries, a small manufacturing conglomerate. The transaction was for $94 million and consisted of $62 million in bank debt and $32 million of KKR and inves-

---

[1] Their offices are actually in midtown Manhattan.

tor equity. At that time, there were no investors willing to provide subordinated debt to finance a LBO transaction.

This changed with KKR's buyout of Houdaille Industries in 1979. This transaction was financed with 86% debt in the form of senior and subordinated notes. The Houdaille deal demonstrated to the market that for leveraged buyouts there were many investors willing to purchase the debt of an LBO in addition to providing the equity.

The 1980s witnessed the rise of another key element of LBOs: the junk bond. Junk bonds are subordinated debt typically with little in the way of collateral protection. These bonds are just one step above equity, often have a low credit rating, and trade similar to equity. Junk financing is popular because the bond terms can be flexible like private bank financing, but at the same time, appeal to a broader investor base.

Michael Milken became famous for developing Drexel Burnham Lambert's junk bond business. By the mid 1980s, Michael Milken was one of the most powerful men on Wall Street (even though he operated out of the Beverly Hills, CA office of Drexel Burnham Lambert). The deals that Michael Milken and KKR put together demonstrated that a company's cash flows and strength of management team were more creditworthy assets than traditional forms of collateral such as property, plant, and equipment.[2]

Fed by junk bond financing, LBO deals reached a crescendo in 1989 when KKR bought the giant food conglomerate RJR Nabisco Inc. for $31 billion in a deal that was documented in the book and movie titled *Barbarians at the Gate*.

In the 1990s, LBO transactions hit two walls. First, there was the U.S. recession of 1990–1991 which, while brief, pushed out credit spreads to unfriendly levels. By the end of 1991, 26 of 83 large LBOs completed between 1985 and 1989 had defaulted on their debt financing. Second, in 1998, the default by the Russian government on its treasury bonds once again sent credit spreads spiraling upwards. While in the 1980s, debt accounted for as much as 95% of some LBO deals, by the end of the 1990s, high debt loads of over 75% became unattractive.

The new millennium started much more quietly in the LBO market than in years past. Compared to the $31 billion LBO of RJR Nabisco, in 2000, only five LBO deals over $1 billion were completed.[3] Yet, in 2000, LBO funds raised about $65 billion compared to $48 billion in 1999. Exhibit 1 presents the growth of the LBO market from 1990 through 2000.

The sheer number of LBO firms seeking investor capital have spurred this growth. While in the 1970s only two firms dominated the market, KKR and Forstmann Little & Co., there are now 850 LBO funds competing for money and companies. The growth of this market has led to lower returns for investors. Exhibit 2 presents the annual return to LBO investment firms from 1990 through 2000.

---

[2] Michael Milken was subsequently arrested, indicted, and convicted of securities fraud for the role he played in financing several corporate takeovers in the 1980s. The subsequent securities scandal resulted in the demise of Drexel Burnham Lambert.

[3] See Debra Sparks, "The Return of the LBO," *Business Week* (October 16, 2000).

Exhibit 1: LBO Fund Commitments, 1990–2000

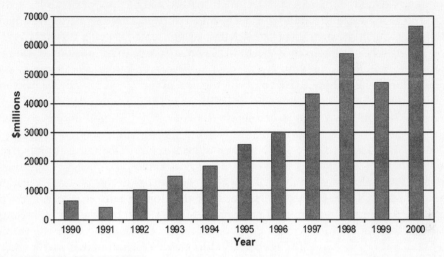

Total 1990–2000: $323.591 billion

Source: Thomson Financial Venture Economics

Exhibit 2: Annual Returns to LBO Funds, 1990–2000

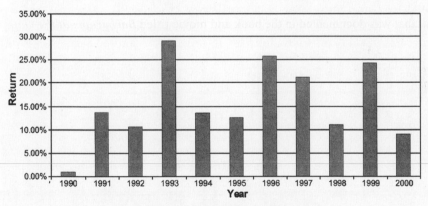

Source: Thomson Financial Venture Economics

As can be seen, the returns earned by LBO investment pools have declined over the 1990s as too much money chased too few deals. The biggest LBO deal in 2000 was Donaldson, Lufkin & Jeanrette Inc.'s $3.8 buyout of U.S. meat produce IBP Inc. (formerly known as Iowa Beef Processors). Unfortunately, this deal lost out to a higher bid from Tyson Foods.

Currently, the major challenge facing LBO firms is finding sufficient deals in which to invest their capital. The large pool of industrial conglomerates in the 1980s that were ripe to buyout, strip down, and then resell have disappeared. This was a ready-made pipeline for LBO transactions, but it has dried up as more and more companies specialize within one industry. With so much money pouring into the LBO market, LBO investment firms have been forced to consider alternative investment vehicles for their investor capital. We will discuss this topic further in Chapter 17.

Another by-product of the flow of capital into LBO funds is the decline in the leverage ratio. In 1989, the average equity contributed to the buyout was about 10% of the bid price. However, by the end of the 1990s buyout funds were putting more equity into their deals. In 1998, the average equity in an LBO deal was 32%, in 1999 it was 36%, and in 2000 it was 38%.[4] Exhibit 3 demonstrates the larger equity component of LBO deals in the 1990s. As the amount of leverage in each LBO deal declines, so does the potential return. Declining returns may stem the tide of investor capital flowing into LBO funds.

Perhaps the last frontier of LBO development is exchange-traded private equity. In March, 2001 a new online network run by former Bear, Stearns & Co. employees opened with the goal to become the NASDAQ of the private equity market. The New York Private Placement Exchange (NYPPE) is an electronic communications network (ECN) designed to serve as matchmaker and marketplace for buyers and sellers of all types of private equity including venture capital interests, interests in LBO funds, interests in hedge funds, and restricted securities of both public and private companies.

The NYPPE has applied to the Securities and Exchange Commission for trading exchange status. The ECN's goal is to create a secondary market for private deals much like the trading of public stock. The NYPPE has concentrated on two specialties: (1) providing liquidity to investors in limited partnerships of the type that are constructed for venture capital, LBO and hedge funds and (2) the offering of newly issued private placements of restricted securities.

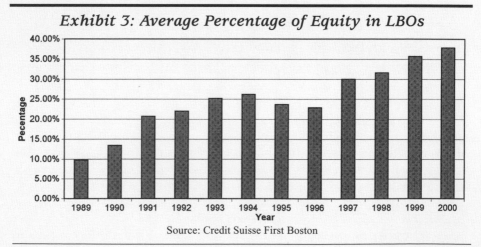

Exhibit 3: Average Percentage of Equity in LBOs

Source: Credit Suisse First Boston

---

[4] "Still Looking: Flush with Cash, Buyout Funds Hope for a Deal Rebound," *The Investment Dealers' Digest* (April 9, 2001).

A THEORETICAL EXAMPLE OF A LEVERAGED BUYOUT

In a perfect world, everyone makes money, and no one is unhappy. We will discuss some spectacular LBO failures below. In the meantime, we describe how a theoretical LBO should work.

Imagine a company that is capitalized with a market value of equity of $500 million and a face value of debt of $100 million. The company generates an EBITDA (earnings before interest and taxes plus depreciation and amortization) of $80 million. EBITDA represents the free cash flow from operations that is available for the owners and debtors of the company. This is a 13.3% return on capital for the company's shareholders and debtholders.

An LBO firm offers $700 million to purchase the equity of the company and to pay off the outstanding debt. The debt is paid off at face value of $100 million and $600 million is offered to the equity holders (a 20% premium over the market value) to entice them to tender their shares to the LBO offer.

The $700 million LBO is financed with $600 million in debt (with a 10% coupon rate) and $100 million in equity. The company must pay yearly debt service of $60 million to meet its interest payment obligations. After the LBO, the management of the company improves its operations, streamlines its expenses, and implements better asset utilization. The result is that the cash flow of the company improves from $80 million a year to $120 million a year.[5] By foregoing dividends and using the free cash flow to pay down the existing debt, the management of the company can own the company free and clear in about seven years.

This means that, after seven years, the LBO firm can claim the annual cash flow of $120 million completely for itself. Using a growth rate of 2% per year and a discount rate of 12%, this cash flow is worth:

$120 million/(0.12 − 0.02) = $1.2 billion

Therefore, the total return on the investment for the LBO transaction is:

$[$1.2 \text{ billion}/$100 \text{ million}]^{1/7} − 1 = 42.6\%$

The amount of 42.6% represents the annual compounded return for this investment.

As this example demonstrates, the returns to LBO transactions can be quite large, but the holding period may also be commensurately long. At the end of seven years, the management of the company can reap the $1.2 billion value through one of four methods:

1. The management can sell the company to a competitor or another company that wishes to expand into the industry.

---

[5] Studies of LBOs indicate that coporate cash flows increase 96% from the year before the buyout to three years after the buyout. See Michael Jensen, "The Modern Industrial Revolution, Exit, and the Failure of Internal Control Systems," *The New Corporate Finance*, 2nd Edition, Donald H. Chew, Jr. (ed.) (New York: Irwin/McGraw Hill, 1999).

2. Through an initial public offering. Consider the example of Gibson Greetings. This company was purchased from RCA for $81 million with all but $1 million financed by bank loans and real estate leasebacks. When Gibson Greetings went public, the 50% equity interest owned by the LBO firm was worth about $140 million, equal to a compound annual rate of return of over 200%.

3. Another LBO. The management of the company doubled its value from $600 million to $1.2 billion. They can now refinance the company in another LBO deal where debt is reintroduced into the company to compensate management for their equity stake. In fact, the existing management may even remain as the operators of the company with an existing stake in the second LBO transaction, providing them with the opportunity for a second go round of leveraged equity appreciation.

4. Straight refinancing. This is similar to number 3 above, where a company reintroduces debt into its balance sheet to pay out a large cash dividend to its equity owners.

Consider United Defense Industries Inc. This company is the main contractor on the U.S. Army's Bradley fighting vehicle and in the development of the Crusader field artillery system. The Carlyle Group, an LBO firm operating out of Washington D.C., purchased United Defense in 1997 from the FMC Corp and Harsco Corp. for $850 million with $173 million in equity and the rest in debt. By July 2001, United Defense had paid down its debt to $235 million. At that point, the Carlyle Group added more debt to United Defense's balance sheet by arranging for a loan of $850 million. Of the $850 million refinancing, The Carlyle Group used $400 million to pay a dividend to its investors which include pension funds, endowments, and wealthy individuals.

HOW LBOS CREATE VALUE

The theoretical example given above is a good starting point for describing an LBO transaction, but there is no standard format for a buyout, each company is different, and every LBO deal has different motivations. However, there are five general categories of LBOs that illuminate how these transactions can create value.

LBOs that Improve Operating Efficiency

A company may be bought out because it is shackled with a non-competitive operating structure. For large public companies with widespread equity ownership, the separation of ownership and management can create agency problems with ineffective control mechanisms. Management may have little incentive to create value because it has a small stake in the company, and monitoring of management's actions by a diverse shareholder base is likely to be just as minimal.

Under these circumstances, management is likely to be compensated based on revenue growth. This may result in excess expansion and operating inefficiencies resulting from too much growth. These examples often occur in mature industries with stable cash flows. Consider the following case history.

Safeway Corporation

In 1986, KKR took Safeway, a grocery/supermarket chain, private at a cost of $4.8 billion. The transaction was financed with 86% debt financing. At the time Safeway had an expensive cost structure that was not competitive with the rest of the supermarket food industry. Its employees earned wages that were 33% above the industry average. In sum, Safeway had stores that were losing money, inefficient inventory controls, and other poor operating procedures.

Drastic measures were implemented: renegotiations with unions, employee layoffs, and store closings. For example, Safeway sold its poorest performing division in Salt Lake City to Borman's Supermarkets for $75 million, and sold all 121 stores in its Dallas division to different grocery chains. Within two years, all divisions lacking wage parity with Safeway's competitors had been divested. This resulted in a reduction of over 1,000 stores and a 40% reduction in employees.

In addition, regional managers were compensated not by how much they generated in sales (the prior incentive scheme), but instead, on how well their operations earned a return on the market value of capital employed. As a result, managers worked harder to keep costs in line, closed under-performing stores, and expanded the business only when it appeared profitable.

The freedom to cut costs and the necessity to meet high debt service forced the management of Safeway to think of profits first, and expansion second. It worked, and KKR eventually took public again the company after it had improved its operations and profitability. The LBO investors earned an annualized return of almost 43%.

Safeway is an example where value creation came not from entrepreneurial input, but rather from greater operating efficiencies. The grocery chain industry is a mature industry. New innovations are rare; it is a high volume, low margin business. Margin expansion comes not from brilliant insights into new strategies, but rather, from increasing operating efficiencies. As a result, Safeway is best categorized as an efficiency buyout.[6] Efficiency buyouts often result in a reduction in firm assets and revenue, but eventually, an increase in firm profits.

Such a buyout introduces more concentrated ownership and a better incentive scheme to mitigate agency problems. Management is given a stake in the company with an incentive scheme tied not to increasing revenues, but to increasing operating margins and equity value. In addition a high leverage ratio is used to ensure that management has little discretion to pursue inefficient projects.

---

[6] See Robert Hoskisson, Mike Wright, and Lowel W. Busenitz, "Firm Rebirth: Buyouts as Facilitators of Strategic Growth and Entrepreneurship," *The Academy of Management Executive* (February 2001).

Last, the LBO firm replaces the diverse shareholder base and provides the active oversight that was lacking by the prior (widespread) equity owners.

Unlocking an Entrepreneurial Mindset

Another way an LBO can create value is by helping to free management to concentrate on innovations. Another frequent LBO strategy is the unwanted division. Often an operating division of a conglomerate is chained to its parent company and does not have sufficient freedom to implement its business plan. An LBO can free the operating division as a new company, able to control its own destiny.

Duracell Corporation

Duracell was a division of Kraft Foods, a consumer product, but different from the consumer foods primarily produced by Kraft. Duracell was too small and too different from its parent company to warrant much attention. The buyout of Duracell was led by its management in a MBO because they felt that they could increase the value of the company if they were freed from a bureaucratic parent company.

Duracell was taken private in 1988. The goal of management was not to sell assets and shrink the company (although it did consolidate its production by eliminating small plants). Instead, the company increased its budget for research and development, producing batteries that were not only longer lived, but also were more environmentally friendly. Additionally, management pursued an overseas expansion plan, to become a dominant supplier around the globe. Finally, management implemented an aggressive marketing and advertising campaign.

In short, once unshackled from a corporate parent, Duracell was free to pursue its expansion plans with the capital that it previously did not receive from its corporate parent. However, this capital was costly, and more than ever, the management of Duracell had to focus on cash flows and efficient use of existing assets — there was no corporate parent with deep pockets to bail it out.

In response to the pressure to manage its debt service and increase the value of equity, Duracell adopted the concept of economic value added (EVA). EVA is a method for evaluating projects and performance by including a charge against profits for the cost of capital that a company employs.[7] The capital charge under EVA measures the return that investors could expect to earn by investing their money in a portfolio of stocks with similar risk as the company.

The EVA approach to value creation has gained popular attention because it reflects economic reality rather than accounting conventions such as earnings per share or return on equity. Accounting-based measures can be distorted by non-cash charges, early revenue recognition, and other accounting con-

---

[7] The formula for EVA is: Net Operating Profits after Tax − (Cost of Capital) × (Total Capital Employed). See Al Ehrbar, *EVA: The Real Key to Creating Wealth* (New York: John Wiley & Sons, Inc., 1998). Many firms have adopted EVA as a way to measure their performance including Coca-Cola, Briggs & Stratton, and Boise Cascade. In addition, the California Public Employees' Retirement System (CalPERS) uses EVA in its annual review of corporate governance of corporations based in the United States.

ventions. This may lead to a temptation by management to manipulate accounting-based performance measures such as earnings per share. Conversely, EVA measures the opportunity cost of capital based on the risk undertaken to achieve a revenue stream. As a result, EVA redirects management's focus from accounting numbers to equity value creation.

Duracell was a success story. It managed to increase its cash flows from operations at an annual rate of 17% from 1989 through 1995. Eventually, KKR negotiated the sale of Duracell to the Gillette corporation, resulting in a compound annual return of 40%. Management's shares were valued in excess of $45 at the time compared to the price of $5 a share at the time of the buyout.[8]

Duracell is a prime example of an entrepreneurial LBO. Once freed from Kraft Foods, Duracell was able to implement new innovations such as mercury-free alkaline batteries. Not only was the production process cheaper, its new environmentally friendly batteries appealed to the public. Additionally, Duracell developed rechargeable nickel hydride batteries for use in laptop personal computers. Last, rather than build new production facilities as it had done previously, Duracell formed manufacturing joint ventures in Germany, Japan, India, and China. This helped Duracell to expand internationally while deploying its capital most efficiently under the principles of EVA.

It is important to note that in an entrepreneurial LBO, the leverage ratio cannot be as high as for an operating efficiency LBO. The reason is that there must be sufficient flexibility for the managers/entrepreneurs to pursue their new initiatives. Whereas in the Safeway example management's actions needed to be restricted, in the Duracell example management's actions needed to be indulged. A moderate amount of leverage is usually required (50% to 70%) which provides sufficient discipline, but still allows for innovative flexibility.

The Overstuffed Corporation

One of the mainstream targets of many LBO firms are conglomerates. Conglomerate corporations consist of many different operating divisions or subsidiaries, often in completely different industries. Wall Street analysts are often reluctant to follow or "cover" conglomerates because they do not fit neatly into any one industrial category. As a result, these companies can be misunderstood by the investing public, and therefore, undervalued. Consider the following case history.

Beatrice Foods
In yet another KKR deal, Beatrice Foods (a food processing conglomerate) was bought out in an LBO in 1986 for $6.2 billion. This was a 45% premium over the company's market value one month earlier.

---

[8] For more details on the Safeway and Duracell buyouts, see George Baker and George David Smith, "Leveraged Management Buyouts at KKR: Historical Perspectives on Patient Equity, Debt Discipline and LBO Governance," *Private Equity and Venture Capital: A Practical Guide for Investors and Practitioners*, Rick Lake and Ronald Lake (eds.) (London: Euromoney Books, 2000).

Over the next two years, the management of the company, with KKR's assistance, sold off $7 billion of assets, reaping an $800 million gain over the initial LBO price. This is a clear demonstration of how the market and Wall Street analysts can undervalue a company. The LBO transaction paid for itself in the asset sales alone. This is all the more impressive when we recall that when KKR purchased the company for $6.2 billion, this price was at a 45% premium to the company' current stock price. Beatrice Foods is an excellent example of an undervalued conglomerate.

As might be expected, sales for the streamlined company declined from $11.4 billion to $4.2 billion after the $7 billion of asset sales. Yet, profits increased from about $300 million to almost $1 billion. Finally, after the sale of assets, the total debt of Beatrice Foods rose only slightly from $300 million to $376 million. The annual compounded return on this transaction was in excess of 40%.

Beatrice Foods is similar in some respects to the Safeway example. In each case, entrepreneurial insight was not required. Instead, strong operating management was the key to a successful LBO. In Safeway's case, management's job was to eliminate inefficient and unprofitable divisions. Safeway sold off these divisions and made them someone else's problem.

Similarly, Beatrice Food's management also pared down its assets, not necessarily to improve operations, but instead, to give the company a better focus and identity. Beatrice was "overstuffed" in that it had too many products across too many markets, resulting in a lack of coverage by the investment community and a lack of understanding of its core value.

Last, what Safeway and Beatrice needed was strong monitoring by their shareholders. In their public form this was difficult to do for both companies because of their widespread shareholder base. However, in the LBO format, the equity of both companies was concentrated in the hands of the LBO fund. This resulted in close monitoring of their operations. What these companies needed was not more growth, but rather, a business plan that focussed on streamlining and improving core divisions.

Buy and Build Strategies

Another LBO value creation strategy involves combining several operating companies or divisions through additional buyouts. The LBO firm begins with one buyout and then acquires more companies and divisions that are strategically aligned with the initial LBO portfolio company. The strategy is that there will be synergies from combining several different companies into one. In some respects, this strategy is the reverse of that for conglomerates. Rather than strip a conglomerate down to its most profitable divisions, this strategy pursues a "buy and build" approach. This type of strategy is also known as a "leveraged build-up."

Berg Electronics
The buyout firms of Hicks, Muse, Tate & Furst and Mills & Partners jointly purchased Berg Electronics from the DuPont Corporation in 1993 for a purchase

price of $335 million. At that time, DuPont's evaluation of Berg indicated that it generated about $18 million in profit on revenue of $380 million. Berg manufactured computer connectors as well as socket and cable assembly products for the telecommunications industry.

Berg Electronics was used as a platform for further leveraged transactions in the same industry. Over the next five years, Berg Electronics made eight acquisitions under the direction of Hicks, Muse and Mills & Partners including the acquisition of AT&T's connector business and Ericsson AB's connector division. By 1997, Berg had sales of $785 million and profits of over $180 million and employed 7,800 workers in 22 countries.

In early 1998, the buyout firms distributed shares in Berg to their investment partners and retained 20% of the firm for themselves. In August 1998, Framatome Connectors International, based in France and the third largest maker of electrical connectors, purchased Berg Electronics for $35 a share, for a total of $1.85 million, a 41% gain in purchase price before including the effects of leverage. It is estimated that based on the initial equity contributed, the Berg Electronics transaction earned a return in excess of 1,000%.[9]

LBO Turnaround Strategies

With a slowdown in the United States as well as global economies throughout 2000, turnaround LBOs have become increasingly popular. Unlike traditional buyout firms that look for successful, mature companies with low debt to equity ratios and stable management, turnaround LBO funds look for underperforming companies with excessive leverage and poor management. The targets for turnaround LBO specialists come from two primary sources: (1) ailing companies on the brink of Chapter 11 bankruptcy and (2) underperforming companies in another LBO fund's portfolio.

One LBO firm that pursues such a strategy is Questor Management Co. This company was founded in 1995 and has specialized in turnaround and distressed investments of troubled companies in other LBO firm's portfolios.

Aegis Communications Group

Aegis Communications Group is a teleservices company that offers integrated marketing services including customer acquisition, customer care, high volume outbound database telemarketing, and marketing research. Aegis was the result of a buy and build strategy.

In December 1996, Thayer Capital Partners, through its buyout fund, Thayer Equity Investors III, purchased majority stakes in two teleservice companies, Edward Blank Associates and LEXI International Inc. In 1997, these two companies were combined with a third company in Thayer Capital's portfolio to build IQI, Inc. Thayer Capital then used IQI, Inc. as a merger partner with ATC Commu-

---

[9] See Hoskisson, Wright, and Busenitz, "Firm Rebirth: Buyouts as Facilitators of Strategic Growth and Entrepreneurship."

nications Group in July 1998 to form Aegis Communications Group. After the merger, Thayer Capital became Aegis Communications' largest shareholder.

Unfortunately, after the merger Aegis' share price dropped from $3 to $1 within a year. In August 1999, Thayer Capital brought in Questor to help revive the company. Aegis was suffering from high employee turnover, and an over leveraged balance sheet. Questor purchased $46.75 million in Series F senior voting convertible preferred stock in Aegis that was used to repay about $43 million in existing bank debt. As a result of its capital infusion, Questor was able to control approximately 47% of Aegis' voting stock.

Although Thayer Capital's equity was diluted by Questor's investment, initially, the company's fortunes were reversed, and its stock price increased from less than $1.00 to about $2.50 by the beginning of 2000. Questor's investment showed a gain of approximately 150% in less than one year. Unfortunately, since then, the stock price of Aegis has drifted back below $1.00.

LBO FUND STRUCTURES

In this section we discuss how LBO funds are structured as well as discuss their fees. While LBO funds are very similar to venture capital funds in design, they are much more creative in fee generation.

Fund Design

Almost all LBO funds are designed as limited partnerships. This is very similar to the way hedge funds and venture capital funds are established. In fact many LBO funds have the name "partners" in their title. Recent examples include TH Lee Group Arnault Partners, a European LBO fund formed in March 2001; Thomas H. Lee Equity Partners Fund V, a $6.1 billion LBO fund (the largest fund in 2000), and Thomas Weisel Capital Partners II, a new LBO fund seeking to raise $2.5 billion.

Every LBO fund is run by a general partner. The general partner is typically the LBO firm, and all investment discretion as well as day to day operations vest with the general partner. Limited partners, as their name applies, have a very limited role in the management of the LBO fund. For the most part, limited partners are passive investors who rely on the general partner to source, analyze, perform due diligence, and invest the committed capital of the fund.

Some LBO funds have advisory boards comprised of the general partner and a select group of limited partners. The duties of the advisory board are to advise the general partner on conflicts of issue that may arise as a result of acquiring a portfolio company or collecting fees, provide input as to when it might be judicious to seek independent valuations of the LBO fund's portfolio companies, and to discuss whether dividend payments for portfolio companies should be in cash or securities.

Similar to hedge funds and venture capital funds, LBO funds must be aware of the regulatory restrictions that apply to the offering of interests in their fund. To avoid being deemed an investment company, LBO funds take advantage of the 3(c)(1) and 3(c)(7) provisions of the Investment Company Act of 1940. These provisions were discussed at length in Chapter 8 with respect to hedge funds and are equally applicable to LBO funds.

Fees

If there was ever an investment structure that could have its cake and eat it too, it would be an LBO firm. LBO firms have any number of ways to make their money.

First, consider how LBO firms gather capital. KKR for instance, received in 2000 a $1 billion capital contribution from the State of Oregon pension fund for its newest LBO fund, the Millennium Fund. LBO firms charge a management fee for the capital committed to their investment funds. The management fee generally ranges from 1% to 3% depending on the strength of the LBO firm. On KKR's newest fund, for instance, the management fee offered to some investors is 1% per year. Given that KKR expects to raise between $5 billion and $6 billion, this would indicate an annual management fee in the range of $50 to $60 million a year.

In addition, LBO firms share in the profits of the investment pool. These incentive fees usually range from 20% to 30%. Incentive fees are profit sharing fees. For instance, an incentive fee of 20% means that the LBO firm keeps one dollar out of every five earned on LBO transactions.

LBO firms also may charge fees to the corporation that it is taken private of up to 1% of the total selling price for arranging and negotiating the transaction. As an example, KKR earned $75 million for arranging the buyout of RJR Nabisco, and $60 million for arranging the buyout of Safeway Stores.

Not only do LBO firms earn fees for arranging deals, they can earn break-up fees if a deal craters. Consider the Donaldson, Lufkin & Jenrette LBO of IBP Inc. This $3.8 billion buyout deal, first announced in October, 2000 was subsequently topped by a $4.1 billion takeover bid from Smithfield Foods Inc. in November, 2000. This bid was in turn topped by a $4.3 billion takeover bid from Tyson Foods Inc. in December 2000. Despite losing out on the buyout of IBP, as part of the LBO deal terms, DLJ was due a $66.5 million breakup fee from IBP because it was sold to another bidder.

In addition to earning fees for arranging the buyout of a company or for losing a buyout bid, LBO firms may also charge a divestiture fee for arranging the sale of a division of a private company after the buyout has been completed. Further, a LBO firm may charge director's fees to a buyout company if managing partners of the LBO firm sit on the company's board of directors after the buyout has occurred. In fact there are any number of ways for a LBO firm to make money on a buyout transaction.

In summary, LBO firms are "Masters of the Universe" when it comes to fee structures. It is no wonder that they have become such popular and profitable investment vehicles.

RISKS OF LBOs

LBOs have less risk than venture capital deals for several reasons. First, the target corporation is already a seasoned company with public equity outstanding. Indeed, many LBO targets are mature companies with undervalued assets.

Second, the management of the company has an established track record. Therefore, assessment of the key employees is easier than a new team in a venture capital deal.

Third, the LBO target usually has established products or services and a history of earning profits. However, management of the company may not have the freedom to fully pursue their initiatives. An LBO transaction can provide this freedom.

Last, the exit strategy of a new IPO in several years time is much more feasible than a venture capital deal because the company already had publicly traded stock outstanding. A prior history as a public company, demonstrable operating profits, and a proven management team make an IPO for a buyout firm much more feasible than an IPO for a start-up venture.

The obvious risk of LBO transactions is the extreme leverage used. This will leave the company with a high debt to equity ratio and a very large debt service. The high leverage can provide large gains for the equity owners, but it also leaves the margin for error very small. If the company cannot generate enough cash flow to service the coupon and interest payments demanded of its bondholders, it may end up in bankruptcy, with little left over for its equity investors. "Leveraged Fallouts" are an inevitable fact of life in the LBO marketplace.

Consider the example of Robert Campeau's buyout of the department store chain Allied Stores in December 1986. Campeau bid $3.6 billion for the stores, a 36% premium over the common share price at that time. With such a high offer, shareholders quickly tendered their shares and the company became private. The deal was highly leveraged. Of the $3.6 billion, $3.3 billion was financed by callable senior and subordinated notes.

Upon completion of the LBO, Campeau quickly sold a large portion of Allied Stores' assets for $2.2 billion and paid down the outstanding debt. As a result, sales of Allied Stores declined from $4.2 billion in 1986 to $3.3 billion in 1988. In addition to asset sales, employment declined significantly from 62,000 employees in 1986 to 27,000 in 1988. As a result, the Allied Stores, which lost $50 million in 1986, turned a profit in 1988.

Unfortunately, the debt to equity ratio of Allied Stores remained high, and the company could not generate sufficient cash flow to meet its debt service. The chain filed for bankruptcy in 1990.

Another example of a retailing LBO is the management buyout of Macy's Department Stores in 1986. Unlike the Allied Stores example, the management of Macy's attempted to keep the company intact rather than sell off chunks of assets. Macy's was purchased for $3.5 billion, about a 20% premium over the existing stock price at that time. Over the next two years, sales increased from $4.7 billion to $5.7 billion as Macy's management pursued a course of expansion rather than contraction. Unfortunately, the cost of expansion as well as the high debt service turned Macy's from a profitable company to a money losing venture. By 1988, Macy's debt service was $570 million.[10] That is, its interest payments (not the face value of debt) totaled almost $600 million. By the end of 1991, Macy's had over $5.4 billion dollars of debt on its balance sheet. The large debt ratio plus the recession of 1991 forced Macy's into Chapter 11 bankruptcy protection in January 1992.

Although high debt levels eventually forced Allied Stores and Macy's into bankruptcy, there are several advantages to using large leverage ratios. First, high levels of debt financing allows equity investors with only a small amount of capital to realize large gains as debt levels are paid down. Second, a high debt level means a small equity level and this allows the management of a buyout company to purchase a significant equity stake in the company. This "carrot" provides for a proper alignment of management's interests with that of the LBO investment firm. Last, high debt levels and debt service payments are a useful "stick" to keep management operating at peak levels of efficiency to ensure that the debt is paid down at timely intervals.

CORPORATE GOVERNANCE AND LBOs

One of the interesting by-products of an LBO transaction is the development of strong corporate governance principles. Corporate governance is the process by which the managers of a corporation align their interests with the equity owners of the business (the shareholders). Corporate governance plays a key part in a successful LBO transaction. We briefly describe the corporate governance issue and then consider how LBOs address this problem.

Agency Costs and Firm Management

The objectives of senior management may be very different from that of a corporation's equity owners. For instance, management may be concerned with keeping their jobs, and presiding over a large empire. Conversely, shareholders want value creation. As we previously noted, in a large company, equity ownership may be so widely dispersed that the owners of the company cannot make their objectives known to management, or even control management's natural tendencies. This raises the issue of agency costs.

In a corporation, senior management is the agent for the shareholders. Shareholders, as the owners of the company, delegate day-to-day decision-making authority to management with the expectation (or hope) that management of the

---

[10] See W. Keith Schilit, "The Nature of Venture Capital Investments," *The Journal of Private Equity* (Winter 1997), pp. 59–75.

company will act in the best interests of the shareholders.[11] The separation of ownership and control of the corporation results in agency costs.

Agency costs come in three forms. First, there is the cost to properly align management's goals with that of shareholders. Alignment usually is achieved in the form of incentives for management that may include stock options, bonuses, and other performance-based compensation. Second, there is the cost of monitoring management. This may include auditing financial statements, shareholder review of management perquisites, and independent reviews of management's compensation structure. Last, agency costs can include the erosion of shareholder value from management-led initiatives that are not in the best interests of value creation.

In a well-known study, Jensen and Meckling demonstrate that the agents of a company (management) will act in the best interests of the principals (shareholders) only if appropriate incentives are given to the agents and the agents are monitored. [12] This is where LBO firms come in.

LBO firms replace a diverse group of shareholders with a highly concentrated group of equity owners. The concentrated and private nature of the shareholders allows the management of the buyout firm to concentrate on maximizing cash flows, not earnings per share. Management no longer has to account to outside analysts or the media regarding its earnings growth.

With a majority of the remaining equity of the once public/now private company concentrated in the hands of the LBO firm, the interaction between equity owners and management becomes particularly important. After a company is taken private, LBO firms maintain an active role in guiding and monitoring the management of the company. In addition, the LBO firm most often will establish incentive goals for the management of the company such as when the management may collect a bonus and for how much.

After a transaction is complete, an LBO firm remains in continuous contact with the management of the buyout firm. As the majority equity owner, the LBO firm has the right to monitor the progress of management, ask questions, and demand accountability. Often an LBO firm will ask for detailed monthly reports from either the CEO or CFO of the company so that the LBO firm can monitor the progress management has made towards implementing their business plan. A constant dialogue between the management of a company and its equity investors is the essence of corporate governance.

Establishing a New Business Plan

For a successful LBO, it is imperative that the management of the company and the LBO firm agree on the business plan for the company going forward. This is very different from how a public corporation operates. Rarely does a public com-

---

[11] At CalPERS, we often refer to ourselves as "Shareowners" rather than "Shareholders."

[12] See Michael Jensen and William Meckling, "Theory of the Firm: Managerial Behavior, Agency Costs and Ownership Structure," *The Journal of Financial Economics* (October 1976), pp. 305–60.

pany submit its business plan to its shareholders for approval. The reason is two-fold. First, the shareholder base is so disperse that it is impractical to seek shareholder approval. Second, most shareholders are not sufficiently knowledge-able that they can fully assess the business plan.

The corporate governance paradigm changes with an LBO company. As the supermajority shareholder of the private company (up to 80% to 90% of the equity may be owned by the LBO firm, the remainder with management), the LBO firm is able to provide clear and complete direction to its agents (the man-agement of the company). Although the specific business plans vary from LBO company to company, there are three common goals.

First, the management of the company and the LBO firm must come up with a plan to unlock the intrinsic value of the company. This might mean shed-ding marginally profitable divisions or subsidiaries and concentrating on the com-pany's core strength. It might mean cutting back on expansion plans to focus on improving the profitability of existing operations. It might mean streamlining operations by reducing the existing workforce and cutting back on overhead. In sum, there must be some economic rationale why the LBO makes sense.

Second, a plan to meet the existing debt service and to pay down debt must be implemented. This is a key control over the management of the company. If the debt cannot be paid down, there will be no appreciation of the equity of the company, and bankruptcy may result. Management is forced to focus on maximiz-ing profits and utilizing assets most efficiently. It is not in management's best interests to be wasteful or to pursue empire-building if this means that their equity stake in the private company will depreciate.

Last, the management and the LBO firm must work together to develop the long-term value of the equity in the company. Since management of the com-pany also has an equity stake, its interests are perfectly aligned with that of the LBO firm. LBO transactions take time to come to fruition, the average length of investment is between 6 and 7 years. During this time, the value of the equity position must be increased and an exit strategy must be fulfilled. It is not enough to unlock the hidden value of a buyout company, both the management and the LBO firm must be able to cash in this value.

Ideally, LBO firms should not interfere with management's implementa-tion of the business plan, but rather, should act as a sounding board or consultant for management's ideas. LBO firms can bring their prior experience to the man-agement of a company as well as their access to investment bankers, lawyers, con-sultants, accountants, and other professionals.

Spillover of Corporate Governance to the Public Market

The principles of corporate governance that LBO firms apply to their private com-panies have three important benefits for the public market.

First, the strong governance principles that an LBO firm implements in its private firms should remain when those firms are taken public again. Proper management incentives and monitoring mechanisms have already been established. Even if the private company is sold to another corporation (possibly a public company), the robust corporate governance principles should have an impact on the acquiring company's bottom line.

Second, LBO transactions are a warning to management of public companies. If a company has a poor incentive scheme and minimal shareholder monitoring, it may be ripe for an LBO acquisition. Further, there is no guarantee that the existing management of a public company will remain after the LBO transaction. The LBO firm will have the final say as to who remains and who departs. This threat may provide an incentive for the management of public companies to adopt strong corporate governance principles that increase shareholder value.

Last, the incentive and monitoring schemes implemented by LBO firms for their portfolio companies provide guidance to management and shareholders alike. Management of public companies can view how new concepts such as EVA can increase shareholder value while providing for just performance compensation. Conversely, shareholders can observe the impact that the owners of a business can have on a company's performance if they can concentrate their power at a shareholder meeting. Shareholder power is a powerful tool, and LBOs have used this tool most effectively.

The Dismantling of Conglomerates

We indicated earlier that conglomerates are popular targets for LBO firms, although there are very few left. As business schools churned out tens of thousands of MBA graduates in the 1960s, 1970s, and 1980s, diversification became all of the rage. "Don't put your eggs all in one basket," a lesson learned in business school, became a motto for many companies as they bought unrelated businesses in an attempt to diversify their operating risks.

Examples (in the 1980s) include Mobil Corporation's purchase of the retail store chain Montgomery Ward and Exxon Corporation's establishment of a personal computer division, Exxon Information Systems. Homogeneous, single-industry firms were discouraged, diversification was the new game in town.

Unfortunately, diversification at the corporate level is unnecessary and redundant. Investors could just as easily purchase shares of Mobil and Montgomery Ward if they wished to diversify their portfolio with oil and retailing stocks, or Exxon Corporation and IBM if they wanted oil and personal computer exposure. In addition, corporations on a diversification binge had to pay large premiums to the market in expensive tender offers.

Ultimately, this led to depressed share prices of the conglomerate. The large premiums paid by the conglomerates represented corporate waste because there was no reason to pay a large premium for something shareholders could already do themselves, and at a cheaper price. As a result the share prices of conglomerates languished because there were no synergies to be gained by wanton diversification.

However, this is where LBOs added value. Not only did they buy out conglomerates by the bucket full, they paid top dollar, thereby returning to shareholders of the conglomerates some of the prior corporate waste from diversification. Further, they streamlined the conglomerate, spinning off unrelated divisions into pure plays. This added value for the LBO firm's investors as well as for the new shareholders of the pure-play spinoffs.

Last, more than any other factor, LBO firms stopped the unnecessary diversification of large corporations. The pickings were just too easy for LBO firms, and eventually, conglomerates faded away to a corporate form of the past.

MERCHANT BANKING

As a final discussion we take a moment to briefly describe merchant banking. Merchant banking is a first cousin of leveraged buyouts. Sometimes, it is difficult to distinguish between the two.

Merchant banking is the practice of buying non-financial companies by financial institutions. Most investment banking companies and large money-center banks have merchant banking units. These units buy and sell non-financial companies for the profits that they can generate for the shareholders of the merchant bank. In some cases the merchant banking units establish limited partnerships similar to LBO funds. At that point there is very little distinction between a merchant banking fund and the LBO funds discussed above.

Consider the example of DLJ's attempted purchase of IBP, Inc. In October 2000, DLJ announced a $3.8 billion buyout of IBP. The terms included $750 million in equity, $1.65 billion in debt borrowing, and the assumption of $1.4 billion of IBP liabilities.

DLJ Merchant Banking Partners III contributed 55% of the equity for the transaction. This merchant banking fund was created with capital contributed by DLJ and its employees. DLJ Merchant Banking Partners III operated as a private LBO fund because only DLJ and its employees could invest in the fund; outside investors were excluded.

Merchant banking started as a way for Wall Street investment banks and Midtown money center banks to take a piece of the action that they helped to fund. If a bank loaned money to an LBO group to purchase a company, the merchant banking unit of the bank would invest some equity capital and get an equity participation in the deal. Soon the merchant banking units of investment banks established their own buyout funds and created their own deals.

While merchant banking is designed to earn profits for the investment bank, it also allows the bank to leverage its relationship with the buyout company into other money-generating businesses such as underwriting, loan origination, merger advice, and balance sheet recapitalization. All of these ancillary business translate into fee generation for the investment bank.

For instance, as part of the IBP buyout, DLJ arranged the debt financing for IBP consisting of three separate tranches: a $500 million in 5.5-year revolving credit, a $500 million 5.5-year term loan, and a $650 million 7-year term loan. DLJ eventually lost its buyout bid for IBP to Tyson Foods Inc. (which bid $4.3 billion for IBP). However, had the buyout been completed, DLJ would have collected significant fees for arranging the $1.65 billion credit facility. Nonetheless, DLJ's merchant banking unit still earned a $66.5 million breakup fee.

The risk of merchant banking is that an investment bank will continue to throw good money after bad to a company owned by its merchant banking unit. An example is Goldman Sachs' purchase of AMF Bowling Inc. Goldman led a $1.37 billion leveraged buyout of the bowling company in 1996 along with buyout firms Kelso & Co. and the Blackstone Group.[13]

Goldman Sachs subsequently brought AMF Bowling public again in November 1997 in an IPO that raised about $263 million at a share price of $19.50. After the IPO, Goldman Sachs remained the majority shareholder with about 54% of the company. A year later, in December 1998, Goldman Sachs paid almost $48 million for $343 million face value of zero-coupon convertible debentures. At that time, AMF's share price had declined over 80% to the $4 to $5 range.[14]

From the time of its buyout, AMF went on a buying spree, increasing its bowling centers from about 300 to in 1996 to over 500 by 1998. Unfortunately, AMF expanded just at a time when customer demand for its bowling equipment, accessories, and bowling center packages declined. The leverage from the buyout and its acquisition binge quickly pushed AMF's total debt to over $1.2 billion. Eventually, AMF's debt burden combined with its operating losses became so large that AMF Bowling Worldwide, the main operating subsidiary of AMF Bowling Inc. filed for Chapter 11 bankruptcy in July 2001. It is estimated that the cost to Goldman through its equity and bond purchases was at least $400 million.[15]

CONCLUSION

Over the last 25 years, leveraged buyouts have become a mainstream investment product. Most institutional investors now commit some component of their portfolios to leveraged buyouts. Indeed, the primary investors in LBO funds are pension and endowment funds. The State of Oregon's $1 billion dollar commitment to KKR's newest buyout fund is a good indication of the institutional level of interest in buyouts.

Leveraged buyout funds rival venture capital funds in the amount of money committed for investment. From 1990–2000 the total amount of money

---

[13] See Gregg Wirth, "Bum Deals: As a Buyout Binge Looms, Will Wall Street Learn from its Merchant Banking Mistakes?" *Investors Dealers Digest* (February 12, 2001).

[14] In July 1999 AMF repurchased approximately 45% of its outstanding debentures.

[15] See Wirth, "Bum Deals."

committed to leverage buyouts was $323 billion compared to a total for venture capital funds of $272 billion.[16] The reasons are twofold. First, LBOs are less risky than venture capital investments because they target established companies with existing profits. Second, LBO firms have been able to generate positive returns comparable to venture capital.

However, LBO returns have eroded in recent years. This is a result of the tremendous inflows of capital into LBO funds which, in turn, means greater equity commitments to each deal and less leverage. While lower leverage reduces the risk of a buyout transaction, it also reduces the return.

Finally, the maturation of the industry has resulted in greater specialization. KKR continues to focus on undervalued divisions and conglomerates. Other firms, such as Clayton & Dublier, have turnaround management skills and invest in troubled companies that need workout solutions. Hicks, Muse, Tate & Furst collects and resells fast-growing businesses in an industry such as radio stations. Moving forward, it is expected that LBO firms will continue to carve out specialty niches where they can most easily and profitably exploit their particular strengths.

---

[16] As reported in *Venture Economics*. However, venture capital funds have accelerated the pace of their fund raising over the past two years.

Chapter 16

Debt as Private Equity

In this chapter we discuss two forms of private equity that appear as debt on an issuer's balance sheet. Mezzanine debt is closely linked to the leveraged buyout market, while distressed debt investors pursue companies whose fortunes have taken a turn for the worse. Like venture capital and LBOs, these strategies pursue long-only investing in the securities of target companies, and these strategies can result in a significant equity stake in a target company. In addition, like venture capital and LBOs, these two forms of private equity investing provide alternative investment strategies within the equity asset class.

Since mezzanine debt and distressed debt investors purchase the bonds of a target company, it may seem inappropriate to classify these strategies within the equity asset class. However, we will demonstrate in this chapter that these two strategies derive a considerable amount of return as equity components within a company's balance sheet.

For now, it is important to recognize that mezzanine debt and distressed debt investing can be distinguished from traditional long-only investing. The reason is that these two forms of private equity attempt to capture investment returns from economic sources that are mostly independent of the economy's long-term macroeconomic growth. For instance, the debt of a bankrupt company is more likely to rise and fall with the fortunes of the company and negotiations with other creditors than with the direction of the general stock market. While the direction of the stock market and the health of the overall economy may have some influence on a distressed company, it is more likely that the fortunes of the company will be determined by the hands of its creditors.

We divide this chapter into two sections: one for mezzanine debt, and one for distressed debt. Mezzanine debt follows naturally from our discussion of leveraged buyouts because it often forms part of the financing for a buyout transaction. Conversely, distressed debt may arise from an LBO deal that has gone sour. In each case, through a purchase of debt securities, an investor can achieve a significant equity participation in a target company.

MEZZANINE DEBT

Mezzanine debt is often hard to classify because the distinction between debt and equity can blur at this level of financing. Oftentimes, mezzanine debt represents a hybrid, a combination of debt of equity. Mezzanine financing gets its name because it is inserted into a company's capital structure between the "floor" of equity and the "ceiling" of senior, secured debt. It is from the in between nature of this type of debt that mezzanine derives its name.

Mezzanine financing is not used to provide cash for the day-to-day operations of a company. Instead, it is used during transitional periods in a company's life. Frequently, a company is in a situation where its senior creditors (banks) are unwilling to provide any additional capital and the company does not wish to issue additional stock. Mezzanine financing can fill this void.

Mezzanine debt has become increasingly popular for two reasons. First, the slow down in the U.S. economy means that banks and other senior debt lenders are less aggressive about providing capital. Second, there are fewer lending options in the bank market. As a result of many mergers and consolidations in the banking sector, the number of participants in syndicated bank loans has declined from 110 lenders in 1998 to 49 by April 2001.[1]

Still, mezzanine financing is a niche market, operating between "story credits" and the junk bond market. Story credits are private debt issues that have a good "story" to sell them. Generally, these are senior secured financings with good credit and an interesting story to tell. However, not all firms have good credit or interesting stories. Mezzanine debt may be their best source of financing.

Also, junk bond issues tend to be large, $300 million and up. Generally these are offered by large public companies. Conversely, mezzanine debt tends to be issued in smaller chunks, in the $25 million to $300 million range. Therefore, mezzanine debt provides a nice niche of financing for small to mid-cap companies.

Some investors, such as insurance companies, view mezzanine as a traditional form of debt. Insurance companies are concerned with the preservation of capital, the consistency of cash flows, and the ability to make timely interest payments. Other investors, such as mezzanine limited partnerships, LBO firms, and commercial banks, focus on the capital appreciation, or equity component of mezzanine debt. Often these firms demand an equity "kicker" be attached to the mezzanine debt. This kicker is usually in the form of equity warrants to purchase stock at a discounted strike price.

In this section we discuss how mezzanine financing is used to bride a gap in time, capital structure, or transaction structure. We also discuss the sources of mezzanine financing and the expected returns associated with these lenders. Next, we discuss the advantages of mezzanine financing both from a lender/investor perspective and from the borrower/issuing company perspective. Last, we review important provisions that are associated with inter-creditor agreements between the mezzanine lenders and the senior debtholders.

Mezzanine Financing to Bridge a Gap in Time

Mezzanine financing has three general purposes. First, it can be financing used to bridge a gap in time. This might be a round of financing to get a private company

---

[1] See "Still Looking: Flush with Cash, Buyout Firms Hope for a Deal Rebound," *The Investment Dealer's Digest* (April 9, 2001).

to the IPO stage. In this case, mezzanine financing can either be subordinated debt convertible into equity, or preferred shares, convertible into common equity upon the completion of a successful IPO.

Examples of this time-gap financing include Extricity, Inc. a platform provider for business-to-business relationship management. In May 2000, Extricity raised $50 million in mezzanine financing from a broad group of corporate and financial investors. Within a matter of days after its mezzanine round, Extricity also filed a registration statement for an IPO, but subsequently withdrew its registration statement as the market for IPOs cooled off. However, the mezzanine round of financing was sufficient to get Extricity through the next 10 months until March 2001, when the company was purchased for $168 million by Peregrine Systems Inc., a business-software maker.

Similarly, the Internet company iComs, Inc. raised $20 million in mezzanine financing while awaiting its IPO window of opportunity. The mezzanine debt was structured as subordinated convertible debt plus warrants. This financing was later supplemented by a sale of 14% of the company to Lycos, Inc. As of July 2001, iComs had yet to go public.

The above examples demonstrate a common use of mezzanine financing in an uncertain economy. The slow down in the US economy has led to a substantial decrease in IPOs. Initial public offerings declined 86% from the first quarter of 2000 to the first quarter of 2001. The delay in many IPOs drove private companies to seek a mezzanine round of financing, to bridge the time until the company can launch a successful IPO.

Mezzanine financing may also be used to fill a gap in time associated with project finance. Project finance focuses on the completion of a specific corporate project as opposed to general growth or production. For instance, a real estate developer needs to finance the construction of a new office building. Upon completion of the office building, the developer will be able to execute a first mortgage using the completed building as collateral for the loan. However, the bank is unwilling to bear the construction risk and will not provide the mortgage financing until the building is completed. In order to complete the construction process, the developer will seek mezzanine financing to bride the gap of time while the office building is under construction. Then the long-term financing will be received and the mezzanine debt retired.

An example is the $235 million high-yield issue for the construction of an 800 room Hilton Hotel Corporation hotel in Austin, Texas. The construction of this hotel had been delayed several times until financing was finalized in March 2001. U.S. Bancorp Piper Jaffray underwrote the financing for the project that consisted of $100 million in Series A senior debt and $135 million in Series B mezzanine debt. The senior bonds will mature in 2015, 2020, and 2030 and the mezzanine debt can be called sooner.

Another example of time-gap, or project, financing is that of RangeStar Wireless, a telecommunications company. In May 2000, this company announced the completion of a $25 million dollar round of mezzanine financing to complete the development of its Invisible Antenna project.

Mezzanine financing that is used to bridge a gap in time for project financing is usually deployed quickly. There may be less time in which to complete the deal, and due diligence may not be as rigorous. As a result, time-gap mezzanine financing bears more risk and will be priced accordingly, usually with a coupon rate of 12%–14% with equity kickers that bring the total return up to the 20% to 30% range.[2] Alternatively, mezzanine debt used to finance another round of private capital before an IPO may have more time to complete the due diligence process, but will still be priced expensively commensurate with the considerable risk of a private company.

Mezzanine Financing to Bridge a Gap in the Capital Structure

A second and more common use of mezzanine financing is to bridge a gap in the capital structure of a company. In this case, mezzanine financing is used not because of time constraints but rather because of financing constraints between senior debt and equity. Mezzanine financing provides the layer of capital beyond what secured lenders are willing to provide while minimizing the dilution of a company's outstanding equity.

Mezzanine debt is used to fill the gap between senior debt represented by bank loans, mortgages and senior bonds, and equity. Consequently, mezzanine debt is junior, or subordinated, to the debt of the bank loans, and is typically the last component of debt to be retired.

Under this definition, mezzanine financing is used to fund acquisitions, corporate re-capitalizations, or production growth. More generally, mezzanine financing is used whenever the equity component of a transaction is too low to attract senior lenders such as banks and insurance companies. Senior lenders may require a lower debt-to-equity ratio than the borrower is willing to provide. Most borrowers dislike reducing their equity share price through offerings that dilute equity ownership. Consider the following examples.

In 2000, the Indian Group Tata acquired the British organization Tetley Group. The financing package for the acquisition included £60 million of equity, £140 million of senior debt, a vendor loan of £20 million, and £50 million of mezzanine debt in the form of subordinated debt with warrants. Further, bank lenders were reluctant to loan funds until a mezzanine tranche of financing was in place.

To highlight the niche nature of mezzanine financing, consider the case of Superior Candy Co., a 45-year old candy company that wanted to acquire a competitor of similar size. The Great Candy Co. agreed to be acquired by Superior for $12 million. Unfortunately Superior Candy could only obtain $7.7 million

---

[2] See Bailey S. Barnard, "Mezzanine Financing Demystified," *Mergers & Acquisitions Insights* (April 2000).

from its senior lender. This transaction was too small to attract the attention of traditional Wall Street houses to finance an issue of junk bonds. Fortunately, Superior Candy completed the deal by obtaining the remaining capital from a mezzanine fund in return for issuing subordinated debt with warrants that gave the mezzanine investor less than 20% of the company.[3]

As a final example of how mezzanine financing can be used to plug a gap in a company's capital structure, consider the recapitalization of Elis Group. The company was originally bought out by the LBO firm BC Partners in 1997. In 2000, Goldman Sachs, BNP Paribas, and Credit Agricole Indosuez arranged the Eu1.13 billion re-financing of the buyout that was split into five tranches: a Eu400 million 7-year term loan at 200 basis points over Libor, a Eu50 million 7-year term loan at 250 basis points over Libor, a Eu400 million 8-year term loan at 250 basis points over Libor, a Eu50 million 7-year revolver, and a $130 million 10-year mezzanine tranche that was priced at 450 basis points over Libor. To demonstrate the flexibility of mezzanine financing, this layer of debt was priced in U.S. dollars to encourage U.S. mezzanine investors to participate.

To illustrate the equity-like nature of mezzanine financing, in a subsequent IPO of Elis Group stock, the mezzanine tranche was taken out before any of the senior Eu 1 billion senior debt. Simply stated, one form of equity (mezzanine) was replaced with another (common shares).

Mezzanine Financing to Bridge a Gap in an LBO

The third popular use of mezzanine debt is a tranche of financing in many LBO deals. For instance, LBO target companies may not have the ability to access the bond markets right away, particularly if the target company was an operating division of a larger entity. It may not have a separate financial history to satisfy SEC requirements for a public sale of its bonds. Consequently, a mezzanine tranche may be necessary to complete the financing of the buyout deal. Alternatively, a buyout candidate may not have enough physical assets to provide the necessary collateral in a buyout transaction. Last, bank lenders may be hesitant to lend if there is not sufficient equity committed to the transaction. Mezzanine debt is often the solution to solve these LBO financing problems.

In Europe, mezzanine debt is an especially popular form of LBO financing because of the disclosure requirements associated with a bond offering. Most buyout firms choose the mezzanine financing route to bypass the bond markets and keep the company private. However, this usually means paying coupon rates of 17% to 18% in Europe plus providing equity kickers in the form of warrants.[4]

Consider the buyout of U.K. food group Rank Hovis McDougall. In early 2001, Rank Hovis was bought out by Doughty Hanson in a £1.139 billion LBO. The buyout included a 10-year mezzanine tranche of £245 million. JP Morgan

---

[3] Lawrence M. Levine, "Filling a Financing Shortfall with Mezzanine Capital," *Mergers & Acquisitions* (November–December 1998).

[4] See Mairin Burns, "High Yield is Back in Europe but Mezz Debt Lives On," *Buyouts* (February 5, 2001).

Chase subsequently restructured the buyout financing to include £600 million of asset securitization, £300 million of senior debt, and £200 million of mezzanine financing.

LBO firms frequently run into trouble with bank lenders when they try to over leverage the target company. Most banks look at a lending limit of four times cash flow. Consider the Eu1.048 billion buyout in early 2001 of European company Lafarge Specialty Materials. The deal was originally proposed with a bank loan of Eu765 million. This amount of financing was right at the limit of four times EBITDA but the deal had only a 27% equity contribution, below the 30% that many banks require today. The amount of debt financing was thought to be too aggressive. To complete the deal, Salomon Smith Barney and the Royal Bank of Scotland underwrote a mezzanine tranche of Eu100 million.[5]

The use of mezzanine financing to complete an LBO deal is not limited to European transactions. It is also popular in the United States. Consider the $750 million of CB Richard Ellis Services Inc., the largest commercial property broker in the United States. In February 2001, the company agreed to be bought out by an investor group led by Blum Capital Partners. The purchase price was financed with a combination of about 63% debt and the remainder, equity. Blum Capital received a commitment from Credit Suisse First Boston and DLJ Investment Funding Inc. for debt financing that included a $400 million tranche of senior debt and a $75 million tranche of mezzanine debt.

The mezzanine tranche often reflects a layer of quasi-equity to banks in an LBO deal. Usually, the mezzanine tranche receives an equity kicker to solidify its status as "equity." Consider the leveraged buyout of Buffets Inc. by the private equity firm Caxton-Iseman Capital in July 2000. CSFB Mezzanine Club contributed $55 million in mezzanine debt in the form of senior subordinated notes plus warrants. Similarly, the buyout of Wilmar Industries, Inc. by Partheon Investors in June 2000 contained a $40 million mezzanine tranche in the form of subordinated notes plus warrants in addition to senior lending of $133 million. In each case, an equity kicker was added to the mezzanine tranche to reflect the equity-like nature of the financing.

Mezzanine Funds

Mezzanine funds must pay attention to the same securities laws as hedge funds, venture capital funds, and buyout funds. This means that mezzanine funds must ensure that they fall within either the 3(c)(1) or the 3(c)(7) exemptions of the Investment Company Act of 1940. These "safe harbor" provisions ensure that mezzanine funds do not have to adhere to the filing, disclosure, record keeping, and reporting requirements as do mutual funds.

There are two key distinctions between venture capital funds and mezzanine funds. The first is the return expectations. Mezzanine funds seek total rates

---

[5] Id.

of return in the 15% to low twenties range. Compare this to LBO funds that seek returns in the mid-to-high twenties and venture capital funds that seek returns in excess of 30%.

For example, senior bank debt in a private equity transaction is usually priced at 200 to 250 basis points over Libor, while mezzanine financing usually bears a coupon rate of 400 to 500 basis points over Libor. In addition, mezzanine financing will contain some form of equity appreciation such as warrants or the ability to convert into common stock that raises the total return towards 20%. Exhibit 1 demonstrates the year-by-year returns to mezzanine financing over the period 1990–2000.

Mezzanine financing is the most expensive form of debt because it is the last to be repaid. It ranks at the bottom of the creditor totem pole, just above equity. As a result, it is expected to earn a rate of return only slightly less than common equity. Exhibit 1 demonstrates that rates of return are quite favorable: generally in the 14%–15% range, but have been as high as 30% in any given year.

Second, mezzanine funds are staffed with different expertise than a venture capital fund. Most venture capital funds have staff with heavy technology related experience including former senior executives of software, semiconductor, and Internet companies. In contrast, mezzanine funds tend to have financial professionals, experienced in negotiating "equity kickers" to be added on to the mezzanine debt offering.

Exhibit 1: Returns to Mezzanine Debt

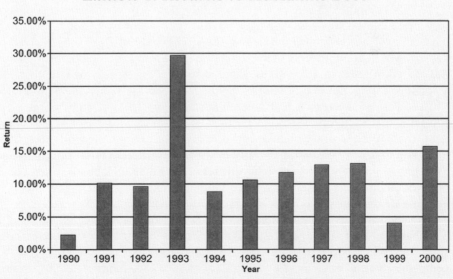

Source: Thomson Financial Venture Economics

Exhibit 2: Mezzanine Fund Commitments

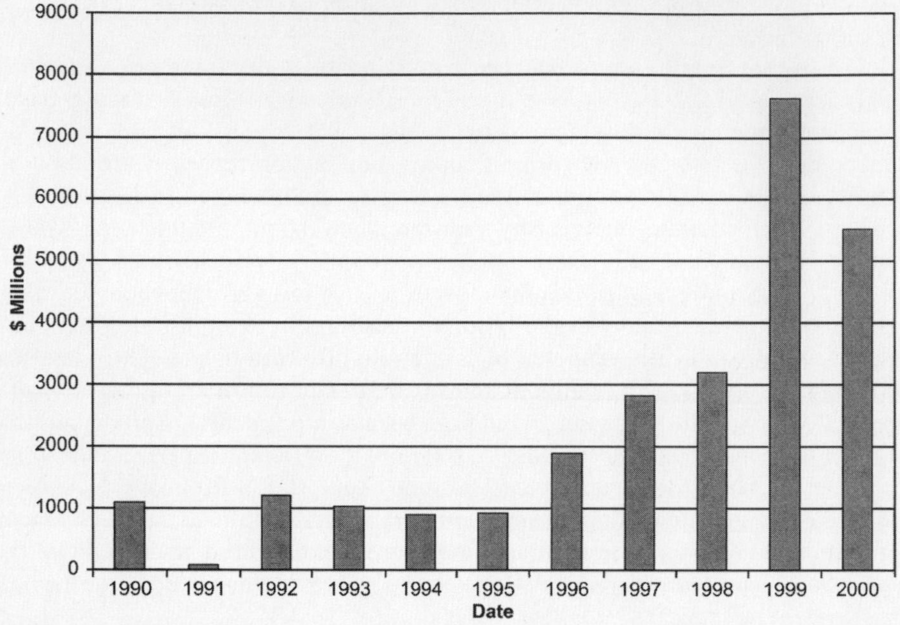

1990–2000 Total $26.2 billion

Source: Thomson Financial Venture Economics

Mezzanine funds have not attracted the flow of investor capital compared to venture capital funds or leveraged buyout funds. However, mezzanine funds have enjoyed steady growth throughout the 1990s. Exhibit 2 presents the year by year growth of commitments to mezzanine funds. From 1990–2000, the total capital raised in mezzanine funds is $26.2 billion. This is only one-tenth of the amount of capital raised by venture capital funds over the same time period.

Part of the reason that mezzanine financing has not attracted as much capital is that with a robust economy throughout most of the 1990s, mezzanine debt was not a necessary component of many transactions. Second, mezzanine financing tends to be small, generally in the $20 million to $300 million range. Last, mezzanine debt, while it yields greater returns than junk bonds, cannot compete with the returns earned by venture capitalists and leveraged buyout funds.

Mezzanine funds look for businesses that have a high potential for growth and earnings, but do not have a sufficient cash flow to receive full funding from banks or other senior creditors. Banks may be unwilling to lend because of a short operating history or a high debt to equity ratio. Mezzanine funds look for companies that, over the next 4 to 7 years, can repay the mezzanine debt through a debt refinancing, an initial public offering, or an acquisition.

Mezzanine funds are risk lenders. This means that in a liquidation of the company, mezzanine investors expect little or no recovery of their principal. Consequently, mezzanine investors must assess investment opportunities outside of conventional banking parameters. Existing collateral and short-term cash flow are less of a consideration. Instead, mezzanine investors carefully review the management team and its business plan to assess the likelihood that future growth will be achieved by the issuing company. In sum, similar to stockholders, mezzanine debt investors assume the risk of the company's success or failure.

Recent mezzanine funds that have raised capital from investors and are now closed to new investors include the $1 billion Goldman Sachs Mezzanine Fund II, a $1.6 billion dollar fund closed by Donaldson, Lufkin and Jenrette, CSFB's $550 million Mezzanine Club, Deutsche Bank's $1 billion DB Capital Mezzanine Partners, and the Merrill Lynch $1.1 billion ML Mezzanine Partners fund.

Investors in mezzanine funds are generally pension funds, endowments, and foundations. These investors do not have the internal infrastructure or expertise to invest directly in the mezzanine market. Therefore, they enter this alternative investment strategy as limited partners through a mezzanine fund.

Similar to hedge funds, venture capital funds and LBO funds, mezzanine funds are managed by a general partner who has full investment discretion. Many mezzanine funds are managed by merchant banks who have experience with gap financing or by mezzanine professionals who previously worked in the mezzanine departments of insurance companies and banks.

Other Mezzanine Lenders

Pension and endowment funds are not the only investors in mezzanine debt. The high coupon rates plus the chance for some upside potential also appeals to more conservative investors.

Insurance Companies

As previously noted, insurance companies are a major source of mezzanine financing. They are a natural provider of mezzanine debt because the duration of their liabilities (life insurance polices and annuities) are best matched with longer-term debt instruments.

These investors take more of a fixed income approach and place a high value on the scheduled repayment of principal. Insurance companies are more concerned with a higher coupon payment than with the total return represented by equity warrants. Therefore, insurance companies act more like traditional lenders than like equity investors. They provide mezzanine financing to higher quality credit names and emphasize the preservation versus appreciation of capital.

Traditional Senior Lenders

Interestingly, banks and other providers of senior secured debt often participate in mezzanine financing. This financing takes the form of "stretch" financing where a bank lends more money than it believes is prudent given existing assets. This excess advance of debt beyond the collateral value of a company's business assets is the "stretch" part of the financing, and is often called an "airball."[6]

Stretch financing may be provided, for instance, when an LBO firm agrees to put up more equity for a buyout deal. Generally, the amount looked for is 30% or more equity in the LBO. In addition, the senior lender may ask for an equity kicker such as warrants to compensate it for stretching its financing beyond the assets available.

Traditional Venture Capital Firms

As the economy has softened, venture capital firms have looked for ways to maintain their stellar returns. Additionally, the large flows of capital into venture funds have created the need for venture capital funds to expand their investment horizons. As a result, there has been a greater interest in mezzanine financing.

Consider the example of Metrika Inc, a privately owned developer and manufacturer of quantitative medical devices. In April 2001, this company raised $26 million in mezzanine financing to scale up production and market Metrika's quantitative testing device of hemoglobin A1c, a measure of long-term glucose control for people with diabetes. The financing was led by Oak Hill Capital Partners, L.P., a private equity partnership founded by Robert M. Bass and Sutter Hill Ventures. Oak Hill Capital invests across a wide variety of private equity transactions. However, Sutter Hill Ventures is one of Silicon Valley's original venture capital firms. Founded in 1962, Sutter Hill Ventures generally provides venture capital financing for technology and health care based start-up companies.

As the example above demonstrates, the lines between mezzanine financing and venture capital can become blurred. With respect to pre-IPO companies, it is difficult to distinguish where venture capital ends and mezzanine financing begins. The typical distinction is the debt form of mezzanine financing. As we demonstrated in Chapter 14, Venture capitalists have traditionally invested in the preferred equity of start-up companies.

Advantages of Mezzanine Debt to the Investor

Mezzanine debt is a hybrid. It has debt-like components but usually provides for some form of equity appreciation. This appeals to investors who are more conservative but like to have some spice in their portfolios.

High Equity-Like Returns

The high returns to mezzanine debt compared to senior debt appeals to traditional fixed income investors such as insurance companies. Mezzanine debt typically has a coupon rate that is 200 basis points over that of senior secured debt. Additionally, given an insurance company's long-term investment horizon, it may be less concerned with short-term earnings fluctuations.

---

[6] See Bailey Barnard, "Mezzanine Financing Demystified."

Further, mezzanine debt often has an equity kicker, typically in the form of warrants. These warrants may have a strike price as low as $0.01 per share. The amount of warrants included is inversely proportional to the coupon rate. The higher the coupon rate, the fewer the warrants that need to be issued.

Nonetheless, the investor receives both a high coupon payment plus participation in the upside of the company should it achieve its growth potential. The equity component can be significant, representing up to 5% to 20% of the outstanding equity of the company. For this reason, mezzanine debt is often viewed as an investment in the company as opposed to a lien on assets.

Priority of Payment
Although mezzanine debt is generally not secured by collateral, it still ranks higher than equity and other unsecured creditors. Therefore, mezzanine debt is senior to trade creditors.

Schedule of Repayment
Like senior secured debt, mezzanine debt usually has a repayment schedule. This schedule may not start for several years as senior debt is paid off, but it provides the certainty of when a return of capital is expected.

Board Representation
A subordinated lender generally expects to be considered an equity partner. In some cases, mezzanine lenders may request board observation rights. However, in other cases, the mezzanine lender may take a seat on the board of directors with full voting rights.

Restrictions on the Borrower
Although mezzanine debt is typically unsecured, it still may come with restrictions on the borrower. The mezzanine lender may have the right to approve or disapprove of additional debt, acquisitions made by the borrower, changes in the management team, and the payment of dividends.

Advantages to the Company/Borrower
Mezzanine debt is a tool for plugging holes in a company's business plan. It can be shaped and molded to meet the company's business needs. Its malleability appeals to corporate issuers.

Flexibility
There are no set terms to mezzanine financing. Subordinated debt comes in all shapes, maturities, and sizes. The structure of mezzanine debt can be as flexible as needed to accommodate the parties involved. For example the repayment of principal is usually deferred for several years and can be tailored to fit the borrowers cash flow projections.

Exhibit 3: Term Sheet for a Mezzanine Debt Transaction

Company	Company XYZ
Financing Amount	$50 million
Issue Date	7/1/01
Securities	Subordinated Series A notes, maturity 2009
Interest	12% coupon payable semiannually, first payment due 1/1/02
Conversion Terms	None
Warrants	50 warrants per $1,000 face value, exercise price $0.50, first exercisable 1/1/05
Principal Repayment	Semiannual with first payment 7/1/05. All remainder due at maturity.
Collateral Security	None
Board Representation	None
Registration	No SEC registration. The debentures and warrants will be sold under SEC regulation 144A. However, Company XYZ will register the warrants and the additional shares thereto should the company go public.

Semi-Equity

Mezzanine lenders focus on the total return of the investment over the life of the debt. Therefore, they are less concerned with collateral or short-term earnings fluctuations. In fact, subordinated unsecured debt resembles a senior class of equity, and most senior lenders consider a company to have strengthened its balance sheet by adding this layer of capital.

Lengthening of Maturity

The borrower can improve its cash flow by lengthening the maturity of the debt repayment associated with mezzanine financing. This is because the payback of the mezzanine debt is often delayed until the fifth or sixth year, with final payment in years 8 through 10.

No Collateral

The borrower does not have to pledge any collateral for mezzanine debt.

Less Equity Dilution

The borrower has not immediately diluted the equity of its outstanding shares. True, mezzanine debt almost always comes with some form of equity kicker that will eventually dilute the number of outstanding common shares. However, this "kicker" may not kick in for several years, affording the company a chance to implement its business plan and improve its share price before it is subject to dilution.

Cheaper than Common Equity

Even though senior lenders may consider mezzanine financing to be a form of equity, it does not carry all the risks of equity. Therefore, it does not need to yield the same total return as expected by shareholders.

Exhibit 3 shows a typical term sheet for a mezzanine debt offering.

Negotiations with Senior Creditors

The subordination of mezzanine debt is typically accomplished in an agreement with the company's existing creditors. The agreement is usually called an "inter-creditor agreement." The inter-creditor agreement may be negotiated separately between the senior creditors and the mezzanine investor, or it may be incorporated directly into the loan agreement between the mezzanine investor and the company. In either case, this agreement places certain restrictions on both the senior creditor and the mezzanine investor.

Subordination

The subordination may be either a blanket subordination or a springing subordination.[7] A *blanket subordination* prevents any payment of principal or interest to the mezzanine investor until the senior debt is fully repaid. A *springing subordination* occurs when the mezzanine investor receives payments while the senior debt is outstanding. However, if a default occurs or a covenant is violated, the subordination "springs" up to stop all payments to the mezzanine investor until the default is cured or fully repaid.

Acceleration

The violation of any covenant may result in the senior debt lender accelerating the senior loan. This means that the senior lender can declare the senior debt due and payable immediately. This typically forces a default and allows the senior lender to enforce the collateral security.

Drawdown

The order of drawdown is important to senior lenders. Because senior lenders often view mezzanine capital as a form of equity financing, they will require that mezzanine debt be fully drawn before lending the senior debt.

Restrictions to Amending Credit Facility Documents

Inter-creditor agreements usually restrict amendments to the credit facility so that the terms of the inter-creditor agreement cannot be circumvented by new agreements between the individual lenders and the borrower.

Assignment

Senior lenders typically restrict the rights of the mezzanine investor to assign its interests to a third party. Generally, senior lenders will allow an assignment providing the assignee signs a new inter-creditor agreement with the senior lender.

Insurance Proceeds

Mezzanine lenders typically want any insurance proceeds to be deployed to purchase new assets for the borrower and not to repay senior debt. The reason is the

---

[7] See Chapman Tripp and Sheffield Young, "Mezzanine Finance: One Person's Ceiling is Another Person's Floor," *Finance Law Focus* (November 1998).

equity-like nature of mezzanine financing. Mezzanine investors consider their debt to be a long-term investment in the company where a significant return component depends upon the operations of the company appreciating in value.

Takeout Provisions

A takeout provision allows the mezzanine investor to purchase the senior debt once it has been repaid to a certain level. This is one of the most important provisions in an inter-creditor agreement and goes to the heart of mezzanine investing. By taking out the senior debt, the mezzanine investor becomes the most senior level of financing in the company, and in fact, can take control of the company. At this point the mezzanine investor usually converts its debt into equity (either through convertible bonds or warrants) and becomes the largest shareholder of the company.

From the above discussion, it can be seen that inter-creditor agreements are a matter of give and take between senior secured lenders and mezzanine investors. Mezzanine investors are willing to grant senior lenders certain provisions that protect the capital at risk of the senior lenders. In return, mezzanine investors have the ability to buyout the senior debt and then assert their equity rights in the company. In the next section, we discuss another form of debt investment that can be transformed into a private equity stake in a company.

DISTRESSED DEBT

The slowdown in the U.S. economy in 2001 opened a door for a form of private equity investing that had been growing slowly but steadily throughout the 1990s: distressed debt investing. Distressed debt investing is the practice of purchasing the debt of troubled companies. These companies may have already defaulted on their debt or may be on the brink of default. Additionally, distressed debt may be that of a company seeking bankruptcy protection.

The key to distressed debt investing is to recognize that the term "distressed" has two meanings. First, it means that the issuer of the debt is troubled — its liabilities may exceed its assets — or it may be unable to meet its debt service and interest payments as they become due. Therefore, distressed debt investing almost always means that some workout, turnaround, or bankruptcy solution must be implemented for the bonds to appreciate in value.

Second, "distressed" refers to the price of the bonds. Distressed debt often trades for pennies on the dollar. This affords a savvy investor the opportunity to make a killing if she can identify a company with a viable business plan but a short-term cash flow problem.

In this section we begin with a short discussion on the growth of the distressed debt marketplace. We then describe the nature of investors that seek value in distressed debt. Next, we provide a brief overview of the bankruptcy process and how this can influence the value of distressed debt. Last, we provide examples of how investors used distressed debt to gain an equity stake in a company.

Exhibit 4: Face Value of Distressed Portfolios

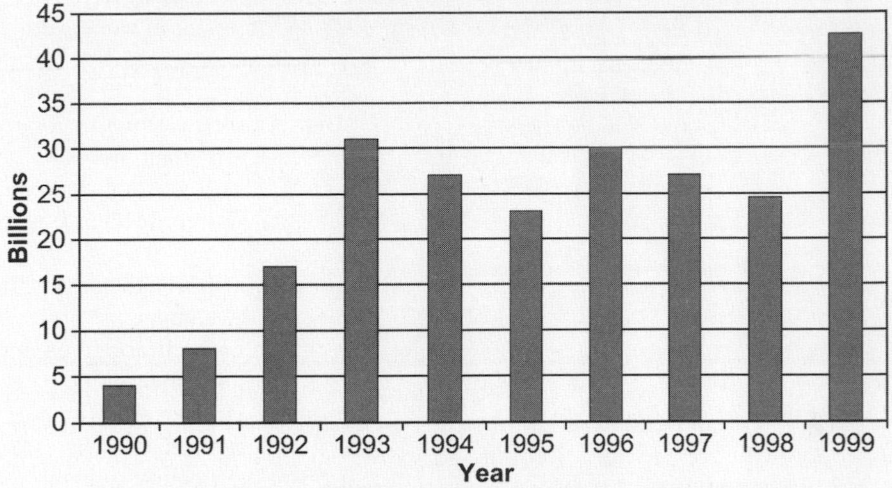

Source: Jesse Snyder, "Who's Fueling Debt Purchases?" *Collections and Credit Risk* (June 1999).

The Growth of the Distressed Debt Market

Exhibit 4 presents the face value of all distressed portfolios over the time period of 1990–1999. As can be seen, the distressed market has nearly doubled between 1998 and 1999. Several factors influenced this growth.

First, many more types of commercial loans are available for resale. In addition to the traditional industrial loans that are routinely bought and sold, there are many new types of charge off loan portfolios that include auto deficiencies; credit card paper; medical and healthcare receivables; personal loans; retail sales agreements; insurance premium deficiencies; and aviation, boat, and recreational vehicle loans.

Second, many more banks and other lenders are managing their assets from a global portfolio perspective as opposed to an account level basis. Proactive risk management techniques are being applied that prune or "groom" the portfolio to achieve a desired risk and return balance. The result is that banks are selling non-performing and sub-performing loans in the market at attractive discounts to get them off their books.

Exhibit 5 lists the top ten distressed debt sellers in 1998. Six of the top ten sellers were banks, with the other four being a finance company, a credit card company, a national retailer, and a charge off repackaging company.

Third, debt loads continue to grow. Commercial and industrial loans reached $943 billion in January 1999, a 10.57% increase from 1998.[8] Residential mortgage credit is expected to reach $4.6 trillion by the end of 2001. Last, consumer installment credit surpassed $1.3 trillion in January 1999.

---

[8] See Jesse Snyder, "Who's Fueling Debt Purchases?" *Collections & Credit Risk* (June 1999).

Exhibit 5: Sellers of Distressed Debt in 1998

Company	Amount
Citicorp Credit Services	$2,300,000,000
MBNA Corp.	$2,000,000,000
Household Finance	$1,000,000,000
Chase Manhattan Bank	$750,000,000
Sears Credit Group	$650,000,000
Charge-Off Clearinghouse	$550,000,000
Bank of America	$550,000,000
First U.S.A. Bank	$450,000,000
Providian National Bank	$430,000,000
Discover Card Operations	$370,000,000

Source: Jesse Snyder, "Who's Fueling Debt Purchases?" *Collections and Credit Risk* (June 1999).

Finally, the U.S. robust economy through most of the 1990s spawned thousand of new companies, not all of which were successful. This also added to the supply of distressed debt. Looking forward, the slowing U.S. economy in 2000–2001 has increased the supply of distressed debt securities, providing investors with ample opportunity to swoop in and scoop up deals. This slowdown is reflected in default rates and other statistics of distressed debt.

In May 2001, Moody's Investor Service estimated the high-yield default rate in the U.S. at 8.1%, and forecasted that the default rate for junk bonds would be 10% by the end of 2001.[9] This is equivalent to about $65 billion in distressed debt. This compares to a default rate of 13% at the peak of the last U.S. recession when $28 billion worth of bonds fell into distress. In the first six months of 2001, total bond defaults were $45.5 billion, according to Fitch, a bond rating service. In the month of April 2001 alone, issuers defaulted on payments on $11 billion in high-yield bonds, a record volume for a single month.[10]

Vulture Investors and Hedge Fund Managers

Distressed debt investors are often referred to as "vulture investors," or just "vultures" because they pick the bones of underperforming companies. They buy the debt of troubled companies including subordinated debt, junk bonds, bank loans, and obligations to suppliers. Their investment plan is to buy the distressed debt at a fraction of its face value and then seek improvement of the company.

Sometimes this debt is used as a way to gain an equity investment stake in the company as the vultures agree to forgive the debt they own in return for stock in the company. Other times, the vultures may help the troubled company to get on its feet, thus earning a significant return as the value of their distressed debt recovers in value. Still other times distressed debt buyers help impatient creditors to cut their losses and wipe a bad debt off their books. The vulture, in return, waits patiently for the company to correct itself and for the value of the distressed debt to recover.

---

[9] See Ian Springsteel, "Worse Than Imagined," *Investment Dealers Digest* (July 2, 2001).

[10] See Dane Hamilton, "One Firm's Poison is Another's Treat," *The National Post* (June 1, 2001).

Exhibit 6: Returns to Distressed Debt

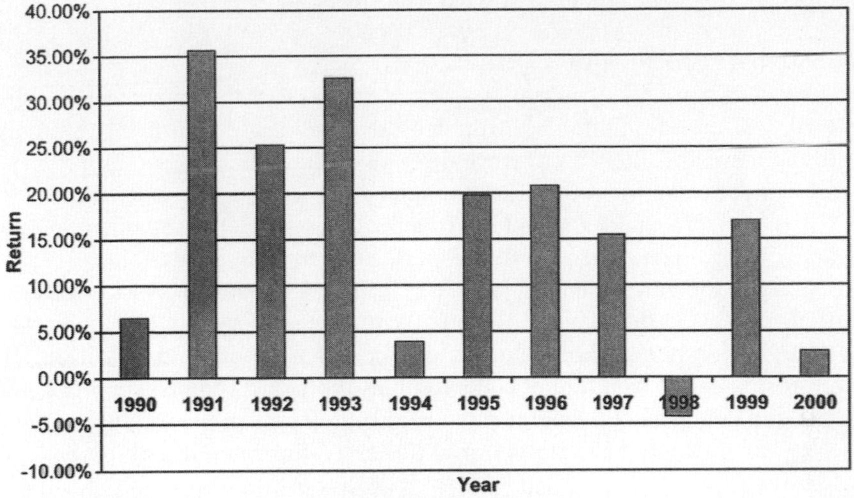

Source: Hedge Fund Research Inc.

There is no standard model for distressed debt investing, each distressed situation requires a unique approach and solution. As a result, distressed debt investing is mostly company selection. There is a low covariance with the general stock market.

The returns for distressed debt investing can be very rewarding. Distressed debt obligations generally trade at levels that yield a total return of 20% or higher. For example, by the beginning of 2001 an estimated 15% to 20% of all leveraged bank debt loans traded at 80 cents on the dollar or less.[11]

Exhibit 6 presents the year-by-year returns to distressed investing over the period 1990–2000. As can be seen, these returns can exceed 30% in any given year. The average annual compounded return over this time was 15%.

Finally, the growth of the distressed market has attracted another player to the game: the hedge fund manager. Exhibit 7 illustrates that the amount of money committed to hedge fund managers that operate in the distressed market grew steadily from 1990 until 1998. In that year, the twin catastrophes of the Russian bond default and the Long Term Capital Management bailout wreaked havoc in the distressed bond arena. As a result of the poor performance of distressed debt in 1998, capital commitments to distressed debt hedge fund managers declined in 1999 and 2000.

Distressed Debt and Bankruptcy

Distressed debt investing and the bankruptcy process are inextricably intertwined. Many distressed debt investors purchase the debt while the borrowing company is currently in the throes of bankruptcy. Other investors purchase the debt before a company enters into bankruptcy proceedings with the expectation of gaining con-

---

[11] See Riva D. Atlas, "Company in Trouble? They're Waiting," The *New York Times* (January 21, 2001).

trol of the company. In either case a brief summary of Chapter 11 Bankruptcy is appropriate to understanding distressed debt investing.

Overview of Chapter 11

Chapter 11 of the U.S. Bankruptcy Code recognizes the corporation as a going concern.[12] It therefore affords a troubled company protection from its creditors while the company attempts to work through its operational problems. Only the debtor company can file for protection under Chapter 11.

Generally, under a Chapter 11 bankruptcy, the debtor company proposes a plan of reorganization that describes how creditors and shareholders are to be treated under the new business plan. The claimants in each class of creditors are entitled to vote on the plan. If all impaired classes of security holders vote in favor of the plan, the bankruptcy court will conduct a confirmation hearing. If all requirements of the bankruptcy code are met, the plan is confirmed and a newly reorganized company will emerge from bankruptcy protection.

The process of Chapter 11 Bankruptcy is illustrated in Exhibit 8.

Classification of Claims Under the bankruptcy code, a reorganization plan may place a claim in a particular class only if such claim is substantially similar to the other claims in that class. For instance, all issues of subordinated debt by a company would constitute one class of creditors under a bankruptcy plan. Similarly, all secured bank loans (usually the most senior of creditor claims) are usually grouped together as one class of creditors. Finally, at the bottom of the pile is common equity, the last class of claimants in a bankruptcy.

Exhibit 7: Commitments to Distressed Debt Hedge Funds

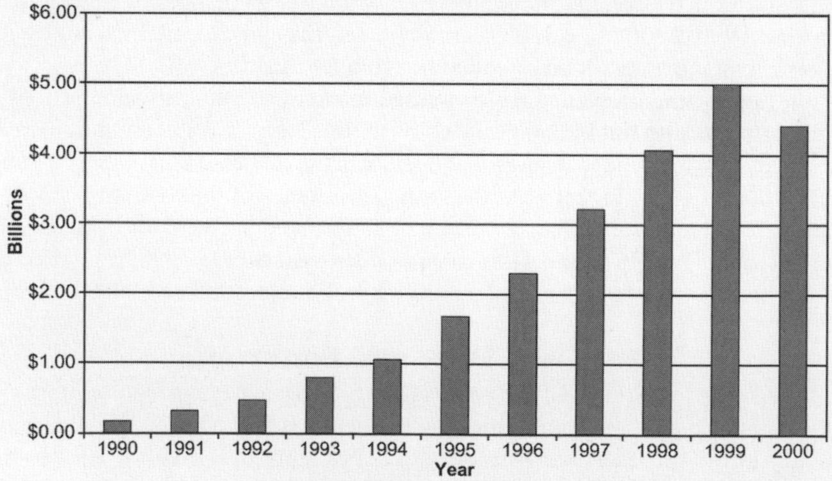

Source: Hedge Fund Research, Inc.

---

[12] See 11 U.S.C. sections 101 and sequence.

Exhibit 8: An Overview of the Chapter 11 Bankruptcy Process

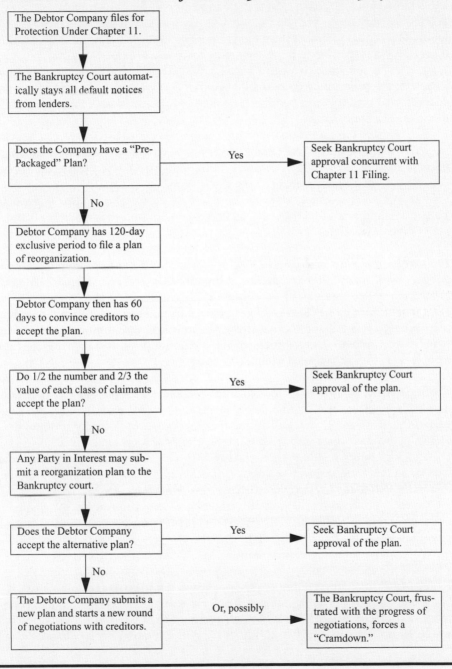

Plan of Reorganization The debtor has an exclusive right to file a plan of reorganization within 120 days of seeking Chapter 11 bankruptcy protection.[13] If the debtor company files a plan during this 120-day window, it has another 60 days to lobby its creditors to accept the plan. During this time (120 days plus 60 days) no other party in interest may file a competing reorganization plan.[14]

After the exclusive period ends, any claimant may file a reorganization plan with the bankruptcy court. At this point the gloves come off and senior and subordinated creditors can petition the bankruptcy court to have their reorganization plan accepted.

This is the interesting part of a bankruptcy process and it can become very acrimonious. In the Federated/Macy's case discussed below, the negotiations became so intense that the bankruptcy court appointed Cyrus Vance, the former U.S. Secretary of State, to mediate the discussions.

A plan is accepted when all classes of claimants vote in favor of the plan. This is an important point because any one class of creditors can block a debtor's plan of reorganization.

Prepackaged Bankruptcy Filing Sometimes a debtor company agrees in advance with its creditors on a plan of organization before it formerly files for protection under Chapter 11. Creditors usually agree to make concessions up front in return for equity in the reorganized company. The company then files with the bankruptcy court, submits its already negotiated plan of reorganization, and quickly emerges with a new structure. The discussion of Loews Cinemas below is an example of a prepackaged Chapter 11 filing.

Voting within a Class To constitute an acceptance of a plan of reorganization either (1) the class must be completely unimpaired by the plan (i.e., the class will be paid in full) or (2) one half in number and two-thirds in dollar amount of claims in the class must vote in favor of the reorganization plan.

All claims within a class must receive the same treatment. If the members of a class vote in favor of a reorganization less than unanimously, and any dissenting claimants in the class receive at least what they would have obtained in a Chapter 7 Liquidation plan, the dissenters are bound to receive the treatment under the reorganization plan. The reason is that the dissenters are no worse off than they would be under a liquidation of the company, and may be better off if the reorganized company is successful.

Blocking Position A single creditor can block a plan of reorganization if it holds one-third of the dollar amount of any class of claimants. Recall, that acceptance of a plan is usually predicated on a vote of each class of security holders, which requires support of two-thirds of the dollar amount of the claims in each

---

[13] See 11 U.S. C., section 1121(b).

[14] However, the bankruptcy court may increase or reduce this exclusive period "for cause."

class of creditors. Therefore, a single investor can obtain a blocking position by purchasing one-third of the debt in any class. A blocking position will force the debtor company to negotiate with the blocking creditor.

The Cramdown Under Section 1129(b) of the bankruptcy code, a reorganization plan may be confirmed over the objection of any impaired class that votes against it so long as the plan (1) does not unfairly discriminate against the member of that class, and (2) is fair and equitable with respect to the members of that class.[15] This provision of the bankruptcy court is called the *cramdown* because it empowers the bankruptcy court judge to confirm a plan of reorganization over the objections of an impaired class of security holders (the plan is "crammed down" the throat of the objecting claimants).

Cramdowns are usually an option of last resort if the debtor and creditors cannot come to agreement. Bankruptcy courts have considerable discretion to determine what constitutes "unfair discrimination" and "fair and equitable" treatment for members of a class. In practice cramdown reorganizations are rare. Eventually, the debtor and creditors come to some resolution.

Absolute Priority A plan of reorganization must follow the rule of priority with respect to its security holders. Senior secured debtholders, typically bank loans, must be satisfied first. The company's bondholders come next. These may be split between senior and subordinated bondholders. The company's shareholders get whatever remains. As the company pie is split up it is usually the case that senior secured debt is made whole and that subordinated debt receives some payment less than its face value with the remainder of its obligation is transformed into equity in the reorganized company. Last, the original equity holders often receive nothing. Their equity is replaced by that converted from the subordinated debt.

It may seem unfair that the original equity holders are wiped out, but this is the residual risk that is born by every shareholder in every company. As the U.S. Supreme Court has stated, "one of the painful facts of bankruptcy is that the interests of shareholders become subordinated to the interests of creditors."[16]

Also, throughout the bankruptcy process, the debtor company's outstanding debt may be freely bought and sold. This allows distressed debt investors the opportunity to purchase undervalued debt securities with the anticipation that the debtor company will implement a successful reorganization.

The ability in the bankruptcy process to wipe out the ownership of existing shareholders and to transform the debt of senior and subordinated creditors into the company's new equity class is a key factor in distressed debt investing. The examples below demonstrate how distressed debt investors may gain control of a company through Chapter 11 Bankruptcy proceedings.

---

[15] See 11 U.S.C., section 1129(b)(1).
[16] See Commodity Futures Trading Commission v. Weintraub, 471 U.S. 343, at 355 (1985).

Using Distressed Debt to Recycle Private Equity

LBO firms are a great source for distressed debt. "Leveraged fallouts" occur frequently, leaving large amounts of distressed debt in their wake. However, this provides an opportunity for distressed debt buyers to jump in, purchase cheaply non-performing bank loans and subordinated debt, eliminate the prior private equity investors, and assert their own private equity ownership.

Consider Regal Cinemas Inc., the largest U.S. theater chain. Regal was originally taken private in 1998 in a combined effort of Hicks, Muse, Tate & Furst and KKR. The two buyout firms each put up about $500 million in equity to purchase the firm for $1.5 billion. Over the next two years, Regal added $1.2 billion to its balance sheet in bank debt and subordinated notes.

Unfortunately, over capacity of movie theaters, a slowing U.S. economy, and fewer blockbuster movies resulted in a loss of $167 million for Regal in the first 9 months of 2000. In December 2000, bank lenders refused to let the company pay interest to its subordinated bondholders because it would violate loan covenants. Regal's debt officially became distressed.

In stepped distressed debt buyers Philip Anschutz and Oaktree Capital Management. Together, they purchased 65% of Regal's outstanding bank debt and 95% of its subordinated debt. In September 2001, Regal announced a prepackaged bankruptcy plan where holders of Regal's bank debt would receive all of the equity in the re-organized company. In effect, Anschutz and Oaktree Capital replaced the private equity ownership of KKR and Hicks, Muse in Regal Cinemas with their own private equity stake. In fact, in May 2001, KKR had already written off its $492 million investment in Regal Cinemas.

Distressed Buyouts

Even as leveraged buyout firms create distress situations, they also actively invest in this arena. After all, bankruptcy court and creditor workouts provide opportunities to purchase undervalued assets. Often, creditors are sufficiently worried about receiving any recovery that they bail out of their positions when possible, opening up the door for buyout firms to scoop up assets on the cheap. Consider the following example.

Vlasic Foods International Inc., the maker of Vlasic pickles[17] and Swanson and Hungry Man frozen dinners, filed for Chapter 11 bankruptcy in early 2001, listing $458 million in assets and $649 million in debts, including almost $200 million in outstanding junk bonds. Vlasic was originally purchased by Campbell Soups in 1978. Twenty years later, Campbell Soup spun out Vlasic to a group of senior managers. A group of 22 banks lent Vlasic $560 million to pay Campbell as part of the split off. Vlasic incurred additional debt over the next two years to finance its operations.

In June 2001, the U.S. Bankruptcy Court in Delaware agreed to a cash bid by Hicks, Muse, Tate & Furst of $370 million for the assets of Vlasic. Following the strict priority of bankruptcy proceedings, the $370 million was first used to pay secured creditors in full. The remainder, about $70 million, was used to

---

[17] Remember the TV commercials with the cartoon stork that talked like Groucho Marx?

pay unsecured creditors approximately 35–40 cents on the dollar. Existing equity shareholders received no payment; their value was wiped out by the bankruptcy.

Consider the advantages to Hicks, Muse of the Vlasic deal. First, the buy-out firm acquires for $370 million, assets that have a book value of $458 million. This does not take into account the productive ability of those assets to generate a market value in excess of their book value.

Second, Hicks, Muse acquired several well-known brand names. In fact, the A.J. Heinz & Co. had initially bid $195 million for Vlasic's pickle and barbecue sauce divisions while the company was in bankruptcy. It is possible that Hicks, Muse could negotiate a better deal with Heinz or another packaged food company for the sale of those assets.

Third, Hicks, Muse acquired the company free and clear of any outstanding debt. This was all wiped out through the bankruptcy proceedings. This allows for the opportunity to refinance the company with new debt while keeping the company out of bankruptcy proceedings.

Last, all shareholder equity was wiped out in the bankruptcy proceedings. Hicks, Muse is now the sole owner of Vlasic Foods. Going forward, Hicks, Muse will probably apply its same business plan that it uses for many buyouts: streamline operations, sell unrelated business units to generate cash, provide stronger management, and promote Vlasic's well-known brand names.

Compare this example of Hicks, Muse to the one previous with respect to Regal Cinemas. LBO firms can be both suppliers and acquirers of distressed assets. It might be fair to say that "what goes around, comes around." Better yet, private equity firms specialize in seeking undervalued companies. However, not every private equity deal succeeds, and these underperforming companies, through distressed debt, can become another source of private equity investing.

Converting Distressed Debt to Private Equity in a Pre-Packaged Bankruptcy

In February 2001, Loews Cineplex Entertainment Corp., the largest publicly traded U.S. movie theater chain, and one of the largest movie theater chains in the world, filed for Chapter 11 Bankruptcy. At the same time, it signed a letter of intent with Oaktree Capital Management, LLC and the Onex Corporation to sell Loews Cineplex and its subsidiaries to the investor group. This was a "pre-packaged" bankruptcy where the debtor agrees in advance to a plan of reorganization before formerly filing for Chapter 11 Bankruptcy.

The letter agreement proposed that Onex and Oaktree convert their distressed debt holdings of about $250 million of senior secured bank debt and $180 million of unsecured company bonds into 88% of the equity of the reorganized company. Unsecured creditors, including subordinated debtholders, would receive the other 12% of equity.[18] All existing equity interests would be wiped out by the

---

[18] Oaktree Capital also owned about 60% of Loews' senior subordinated notes.

reorganization. Last, the remaining holders of bank debt would receive new term loans as part of the bankruptcy process equal in recovery to about 98% of the face amount of current debt.

In this prepackaged example, Onex and Oaktree became the majority equity owners of Loews by purchasing its bank and subordinated debt. Furthermore, their bank debt was converted to a private equity stake because all public shares of Loews were wiped out through the bankruptcy proceedings. Loews two largest shareholders, Sony Corporation (40% equity ownership) and Vivendi Universal SA (26%) lost their complete equity stake in Loews. In effect, the bankruptcy proceeding transformed Loews from a public company to a private one.

Using Distressed Debt for a Takeover

As a good example of how a corporation can use distressed debt to take control of another company, consider the merger of Federated Department Stores and R.H. Macy & Co. Federated was able to gain control of Macy's with an initial investment in distressed debt of only $109 million.

Federated itself was a victim of the leveraged fallouts of the late 1980s and early 1990s. Federated was taken private in an LBO by Robert Campeau in 1988, the same gentleman that took Allied Department Stores private in 1986. Campeau's vision was to create a huge retailing empire anchored by two separate retailing chains: Allied and Federated. Unfortunately, the high debt burden of both buyouts forced both companies into Chapter 11 bankruptcy in January 1990.

Federated Department Stores emerged from bankruptcy in February 1992 after creditors agreed to swap $4.8 billion in claims for equity in the reorganized company. This helped to reduce Federated's debt from $8.3 billion to $3.5 billion, and reduced its interest payments from $606 million to $259 million. The connection to Robert Campeau was severed. In an ironic twist of fate, Federated emerged from bankruptcy just nine days after Macy's filed for Chapter 11 bankruptcy protection. Macy's was another victim of a leveraged fallout.

Soon after the Macy's bankruptcy filing, Federated made overtures to acquire its long-time rival. This was another twist of fate because Macy's had bid against Robert Campeau in 1988 for control of Federated. Macy's rebuffed Federated's inquiries because it believe that the company could be better served if it remained independent.[19]

With Macy's mired in negotiations with its senior creditors regarding a plan of reorganization and a takeover out of the question (there was no equity to takeover), Federated decided to become one of Macy's creditors. In January 1994, Federated purchased one half of Macy's most senior secured debt from Macy's largest creditor: the Prudential Insurance Co. of America. Prudential held a senior loan of $832.5 million that was secured by 70 of Macy's best stores. With accrued interest, the total of the distressed debt was $1 billion, representing one-sixth of Macy's total debt.[20]

---

[19] See Richard Siklos, "Macy's Holiday Revival," *The Financial Post* (December 24, 1994).
[20] See "Federated Buys Large Share of Macy Debt," *Facts on File World News Digest* (January 6, 1994).

Federated paid $109.3 million for one half of this loan with a promissory note to pay the remainder in three years. In addition, Federated received an option from Prudential to purchase the remaining half of Prudential's senior loan within three years. Overnight, Federated became Macy's largest and most senior creditor.

Given its new standing as a senior secured creditor, Federated received standing from the bankruptcy court to (1) challenge Macy's plan of reorganization (Federated now had a blocking position within the senior secured class of creditors); (2) propose a competing plan to the bankruptcy court; and (3) obtain non-public financial information regarding Macy's business prospects.

Federated proposed converting its bank debt into equity and assuming Macy's existing liabilities. Macy's continued to resist. Specifically, Macy director Laurence A. Tisch teamed up with counsel for bondholders holding $1.2 billion in subordinated debt and demanded a reorganization plan valued at least $4 billion.[21] Meanwhile Federated received support from Fidelity Management & Research Co. which signed a "lock-up letter" stating that it would only support a plan that gave the banks full recovery in return for the banks support of Federated's plan.[22] The lock-up letter worked and Federated was able to merge the two companies in December 1994 when it agreed to convert its senior loan to equity and to assume $4.1 billion in outstanding Macy's debts.[23]

Distressed Debt as an Undervalued Security

Distressed debt is not always an entrée into private equity; it can simply be an investment in an undervalued security. In this instance, distressed debt investors are less concerned with an equity stake in the troubled company. Instead, they expect to benefit if the company can implement a successful turnaround strategy.

Consider the bankruptcy of Montgomery Ward & Co. in July 1997. Montgomery Ward was the first mail-order merchant in 1872 (Sears was second) and became a successful and savvy mass merchandiser throughout most of the 1900s.[24] However, it failed to ride the wave of the post-World War II economic boom and was eventually eclipsed by other large retailers such as Sears and J.C. Penney's.

As a result, Montgomery Ward went through several owners in the 1970s and 1980s including Marcor Inc., Mobil Oil Corporation, and a senior management buyout. Despite its varied ownership, Montgomery Ward could not turn

---

[21] See Karen Donovan, "Macy Merger Squeezes out Weil Gotshal; Bankruptcy Judge Approves Federated's Takeover Plan," *The National Law Journal* (December 19, 1994).

[22] Id.

[23] There was significant legal maneuvering before the deal was completed including the appointment of Cyrus R. Vance, the former U.S. Secretary of State to mediate the discussions between Macy's, Federated, and other outstanding creditors.

[24] In fact, it was a Montgomery Ward copywriter who invented the character and illustrated poem "Rudolph the Red-Nosed Reindeer," for Santa Claus to give to children in Montgomery Ward department stores. Rudolph was an instant hit and helped to draw large crowds to Montgomery Ward stores.

itself around. Its lack of brand-name goods, dingy stores, and out of date image kept customers away and led to its July 1997 Chapter 11 bankruptcy filing.[25]

The Ward's bankruptcy provided an opportunity for distressed investors, vendors, and bank lenders alike. By October 1997, Ward's unsecured debt was trading around 35 cents on the dollar. At that price, distress debt investors such as the Third Avenue Value Fund, bought $17 million of Ward's debt from its vendors.[26] In addition, secured lender New York Life accepted an unsolicited bid from Merrill Lynch & Co. for its entire senior Montgomery Ward debt of $40 million. Nationwide Insurance Cos. also sold $31.5 million of its secured debt.

From a distressed investor's point of view the Montgomery Ward's bankruptcy provided a good opportunity because GE Capital Inc. already owned more than 50% of Ward's. Additionally, it was one of its largest creditors having provided $1 billion in financing for the retailer's previous reorganization plan. It seemed reasonable to believe that GE Capital would provide additional relief to get the company out of bankruptcy. In fact, GE Capital did step up to the plate and paid $650 million for the remainder of the company (plus its Signature Group direct marketing arm) as well as wiping clean the $1 billion in debt. Montgomery Ward emerged from bankruptcy in August 1999.

However, GE Capital did not step up as much as some distressed debt investors had hoped. Secured creditors were paid in full, but unsecured creditors received only 26 to 28 cents on the dollar. Those distressed debt investors who purchased senior claims at a discount profited nicely. However, those who purchased vendor claims (unsecured debt) lost money.

As an unfortunate postscript, Montgomery Ward still could not make a go of it and filed for bankruptcy again in December 2000. This time there was no reorganization. The company went out of business.

Distressed Debt Arbitrage

If there is any way to skin an arbitrage, hedge fund managers will think of it. While this is not a private equity form of investing, it is a form of equity arbitrage best suited for hedge fund managers.

The arbitrage is constructed as follows. A hedge fund manager purchases distressed debt which she believes is undervalued. At the same time, she shorts the company's underlying stock. The idea is that if the bonds are going to decline in value, the company's stock price will decline even more dramatically because equity holders have only a residual claim behind debtholders.

Conversely, if the company's prospects improve, both the distressed debt and equity will appreciate significantly. The difference then will be between the coupon payment on the debt versus dividends paid on the stock. Since a company

---

[25] See Jef Feeley, "Wards Emerges From Bankruptcy Court to Clouded Future," *Bloomberg News* (August 2, 1999).

[26] See Rekha Balu, "Debt Traders Capitalize on Vendor Uncertainty; Buying, Selling Ward's Stakes could Affect Proceedings," *Crain's Chicago Business* (October 6, 1997).

coming out of a workout or turnaround situation almost always conserves its cash and does not pay cash stock dividends, the hedge fund manager should earn large interest payments on the debt compared to the equity.

Risks of Distressed Debt Investing

There are two main risks associated with distressed debt investing. First, business risk still applies. Just because distressed debt investors can purchase the debt of a company on the cheap does not mean it cannot go lower. This is the greatest risk to distressed debt investing, a troubled company may be worthless and unable to pay off its creditors. While creditors often convert their debt into equity, the company may not be viable as a going concern. If the company cannot develop a successful plan of reorganization, it will only continue its spiral downwards.

It may seem strange, but creditworthiness doesn't apply. The reason is that the debt is already distressed because the company may already be in default and its debt thoroughly discounted. Consequently, failure to pay interest and debt service has already occurred.

Instead, vulture investors consider the business risks of the company. They are concerned not with the short-term payment of interest and debt service, but rather, the ability of the company to execute a viable business plan. From this perspective, it can be said that distressed debt investors are truly equity investors. They view the purchase of distressed debt as an investment in the company as opposed to a lending facility.

Consider the case of Iridium LLC, a satellite-telephone system with $1.5 billion in high-yield debt. Motorola Inc. started Iridium in 1997, and owned 18% of the company. Iridium launched a network of 66 satellites to build a global telephone network. After Iridium went public in 1997, its market capitalization reached almost $11 billion.

However, Iridium's business plan eventually fell apart as it failed to attract enough customers to make the business viable. Iridium's phones were too bulky, about the size of a brick, much larger than the small, pocket-sized cellular phones to which consumers had become accustomed. In addition, service was unreliable, the satellite phones worked poorly in buildings and cars. Instead of the 600,000 subscribers that Iridium had projected, it could only muster 20,000.

As a consequence, Iridium could not meet the interest payments on $800 million of senior bank debt. Still, in May 1999, distressed debt investors jumped to buy Iridium's 14% subordinated notes for 26 cents on the dollar when it appeared that Iridium would be able to restructure its senior bank loans. However, the restructuring failed, and with over $3 billion in debt Iridium filed for Chapter 11 bankruptcy in August 1999.

At the time of its bankruptcy, Iridium's subordinated notes were trading at 14.5 cents on the dollar. Unfortunately, Iridium's financial woes continued as the company sank further and further into losses and debt. By March 2000, Iridium's subordinated bonds were trading at 2 to 3 cents on the dollar. Iridium was finally put out of its misery in November 2000 when the bankruptcy court liquidated the company for a paltry $25 million. Its bonds were worthless.

The second main risk is the lack of liquidity. The distressed debt arena is a fragmented market, dominated by a few players. Trading out of a distressed debt position may mean selling at a significant discount to the book value of the debt. For example, at the time of the Loews bankruptcy filing, its senior subordinated notes were trading at an offer of 15, but with a bid of 10, a gap of 5 cents or $50 dollars for every $1000 face value bond.

In addition, purchasers of distressed debt must have long-term investment horizons. Workout and turnaround situations do not happen overnight. It may be several years before a troubled company can correct its course and appreciate in value.

CONCLUSION

In this chapter we identified two forms of debt investing that are really variations on private equity investing. Mezzanine financing is the epoxy of the financing world. It fits in where traditional debt and equity cannot. Like epoxy, mezzanine financing is thoroughly flexible. Its shape and size is dependent upon the specifics of the financing needed. In addition, mezzanine can strengthen a debtor company's balance sheet, providing the "glue" between debt and equity.

Borrowers like mezzanine capital because it provides an inexpensive way to raise money without immediately diluting the outstanding equity of the company. Investors, on the other hand, like the high yields offered by mezzanine debt plus the ability to share in some of the appreciated value of the debtor company.

Distressed debt rarely occurs because of some spectacular event that renders a company's products worthless overnight. Usually, a company's financial condition deteriorates over a period of time due to inefficient or tired management. The management of a company that was once established in the marketplace may become tired or rigid, unable or unwilling to cope with new market dynamics. As a result the company fails to execute its business plan or worse yet, tries to implement an obsolete business plan.

This is where private equity managers earn their bread and butter. Revitalizing a company and implementing new business plans are their specialty. The adept distressed investor is able to spot these tired companies, identify their weaknesses, and bring a fresh approach to the table. By purchasing the debt of the company, the distressed debt investor creates a seat for herself at the table with the ability to turn the company around.

Chapter 17

The Economics of Private Equity

The prior three chapters have been descriptive in nature. In Chapter 14 we provided a narrative overview of the venture capital market. Similar descriptions were provided for leveraged buyouts, mezzanine debt, and distressed debt investing. In this chapter we consider the risks and returns associated with private equity investing.

Consistent with our prior analysis of hedge funds and commodities, we begin with an examination of how these classes of private equity have performed relative to the broader stock market. We also review the distribution of returns associated with the different classes of private equity. Last, we consider private equity within a portfolio context.

THE PERFORMANCE OF PRIVATE EQUITY

In this section we compare the performance of each class of private equity to that of the S&P 500. Our purpose is simply to determine which form of investing fared better over the period 1990–2000: private equity or a passive equity index investment.

Venture Capital

Recall from our discussion in Chapter 14 that venture capitalists seek to earn a long-term rate of return in excess of 5% to 7% above that of the general stock market. This risk premium provides compensation for three main risks. First, there is the business risk of a start-up company. Although many start-ups successfully make it to the IPO stage, many more fail to succeed. A venture capitalist must earn a sufficient return to compensate her for bearing the risk of corporate failure. Although public companies can also fail (see our distressed examples in Chapter 16), venture capital is unique in that the investor takes on the business risk before a company has the ability to fully implement its business plan.

Second, there is the lack of liquidity. There is no public market for trading venture capital interests. What secondary trading exists is limited to other private equity investors.

This is a fragmented market with inefficiencies. The tailored nature of a venture capitalists portfolio will not suit all buyers all of the time. Further, another

333

venture capital firm may not have the time or ability to perform as thorough a due diligence as the initial investing firm. The common solution is to discount heavily another venture capitalists' portfolio in a secondary transaction.

Third, there is the lack of diversification associated with a venture capital portfolio. The capital asset pricing model (CAPM) teaches us that the only risk that investors should be compensated for is the risk of the general stock market, or systematic risk. Unsystematic, or company specific risk can be diversified away. However, the CAPM is predicated upon security interests being freely transferable. This is not possible in the venture capital marketplace. The lack of liquidity prohibits transferability. Consequently, company specific risk must be rewarded.

Also, the CAPM requires diversification. Yet, as we discussed in Chapter 14, venture capital firms are becoming more specialized. This specialization developed as a result of the intensive knowledge base needed to invest in the technology, telecom, and biotech industries. Unfortunately, specialization leads to concentrated portfolios, the very anathema of the CAPM.

Specialization might be the most important development in the venture capital world. Not only does specialization help private equity managers invest more efficiently, it allows them to earn a higher return over the market. Another way to state this observation is that specialization may lead to a higher long-term risk premium over a market benchmark to reflect the increased risk associated with concentrated portfolios.

In light of these risks, we examine the returns to venture capital compared to the S&P 500 stock index, our proxy for the market return. In Exhibit 1, we graph the value of $1,000 invested at the beginning of 1990 through the end of year 2000. This 11-year period should be sufficient to reveal any long term risk premium earned by venture capitalists.[1]

Not surprising, venture capital returns exceed those for the general stock market. For most of the 1990s, venture capital earned a steady excess return over the S&P 500. However, beginning in 1998, venture capital returns skyrocket compared to the S&P 500.

Clearly, this was an unusual time, when many technology stocks traded beyond any bounds of rationality. During this time, many newly minted Wall Street analysts outdid themselves with outrageous forecasts of performance and almost criminally deficient stock price projections. We demonstrated in Chapter 14 how this technology bubble burst with the NASDAQ composite first soaring above the S&P 500 and the Dow Jones Industrial, and then crashing back down to earth.

With the year 2000 and most of year 2001 under our belts, it is clear that many start-up companies were simply overvalued. Nonetheless, going forward, higher risk premiums for venture capital remain warranted for two reasons. First, there is continued trend towards specialization within the industry. As stated pre-

---

[1] For venture capital, LBOs and mezzanine debt, we use data from the Venture Economics database. This information presents the average returns from reporting investment firms. For distressed debt, we use data from Hedge Fund Research, Inc.

viously, this should allow venture capitalists to derive greater returns to compensate them for greater concentration in their portfolios.

Second, the slowdown in the U.S. economy has dried up alternative sources of capital for pre-IPO companies. This means venture capitalists will be called upon to provide greater commitments to start-up companies, and these commitments should be made at attractive prices.

As a last point, it should be noted that venture capital returns are dependent upon a healthy public stock market. A strong public securities market supports the IPO market — the major exit strategy of most venture capitalists.

Leveraged Buyouts

Like venture capital firms, leverage buyout firms also concentrate on company selection as opposed to market risk. However, leveraged buyout funds have less risk than venture capital funds for two reasons.

First, leverage buyouts take private public companies that are considerably beyond their IPO stage (or they buy out established operating divisions of public companies). The business risk associated with start-up companies does not exist. Typically, buyouts target successful but undervalued companies. These companies generally have long-term operating histories, generate a positive cash flow, and have established brand names and identities with consumers.

Exhibit 1: Value of an Investment in Venture Capital

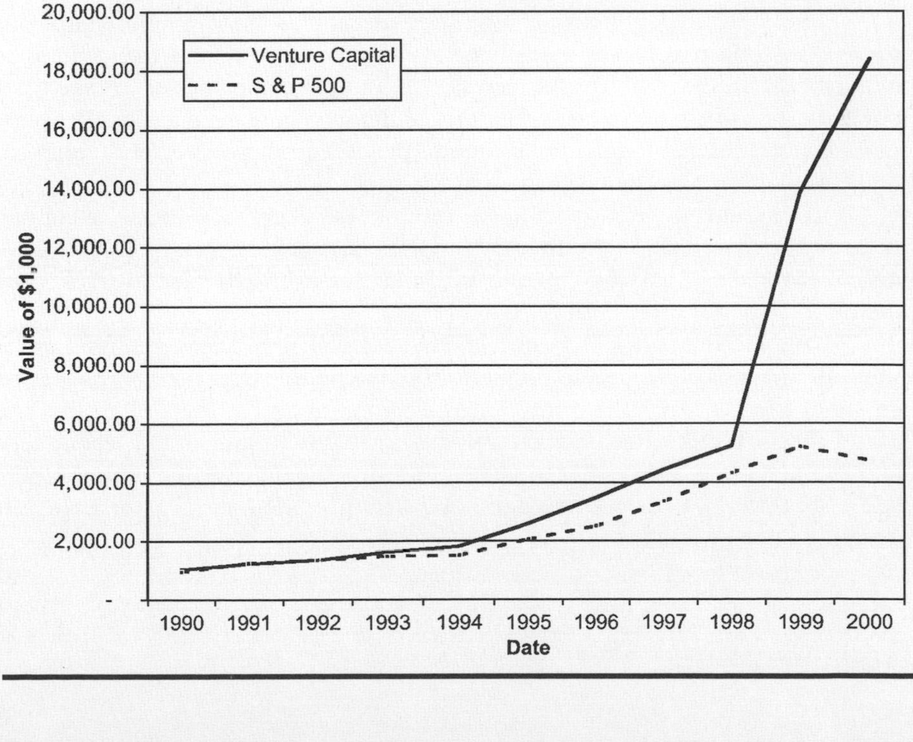

Exhibit 2: Value of an Investment in LBOs

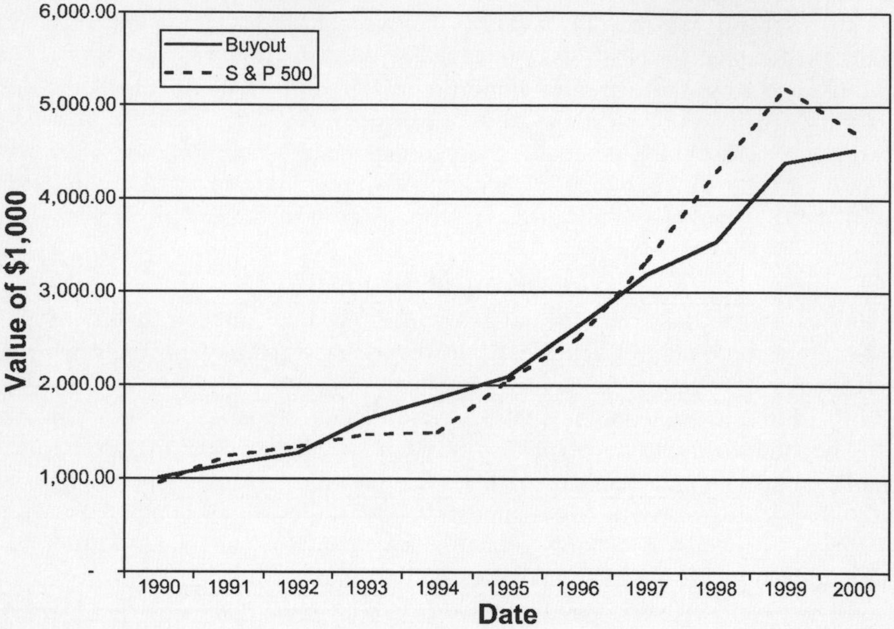

Second, LBO firms tend to be less specialized than venture capitalists. While LBO firms may concentrate in one sector from time to time, they tend to be more eclectic in their choices for targets. LBO target companies can range from movie theaters to grocery stores.[2] Therefore, although they maintain smaller portfolios than traditional long-only managers, they tend to have greater diversification than their venture capital counterparts.

Consequently, we expect to see returns less than that for venture capital, but possibly, more than that earned by the broader stock market. In Exhibit 2 we present the value of a $1,000 investment in an average LBO fund as tracked by Venture Economics versus that for the S&P 500.

We see that LBO firms in fact earn a lower return than venture capital firms. However, with respect to the S&P 500, the returns over the 11-year period are about even. While LBO firms earned a premium to the S&P 500 in the first half of the 1990s, the stock market outperformed LBO funds in the second half until the decline in the market in year 2000. In the end, over the period 1990–2000, the S&P 500 and the average LBO firm provided an investor with just about the same total return.

---

[2] For instance, at the time that KKR was writing down its investment in Regal Cinemas, it was racking up large gains from its investment in Randall's Food Markets, Inc.

Exhibit 3: Value of an Investment in Mezzanine Debt

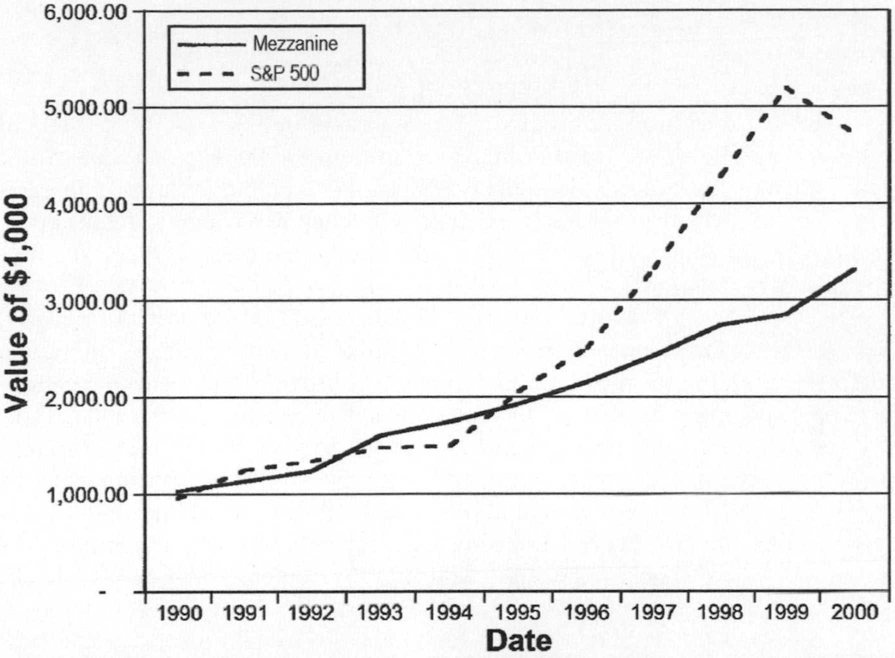

Mezzanine Debt

Recall our discussion of mezzanine debt in Chapter 16. Mezzanine financing is a hybrid. It has debt-like components such as coupon payments and debt service schedules, but at the same time, it also provides for equity appreciation, usually in the form of warrants or some conversion factor. Consequently, we expect it to perform less than the equity investments of venture capital or LBO firms. In addition, given its debt component, we expect it to perform less than the S&P 500.

Exhibit 3 confirms our expectations. Mezzanine debt performed about the same as the S&P 500 during the first half of the 1990s. During this time, the large coupon payments on mezzanine debt plus some equity appreciation provided returns that were similar to the S&P 500. However, in the last part of the 1990s when equity returns surged, mezzanine debt could not keep pace. The debt component of this gap financing weighed it down, preventing it from sharing fully in the stock market's appreciation during this extraordinary time.

Mezzanine debt's under performance compared to the S&P 500 should not be viewed negatively because mezzanine financing is designed to under perform the stock market. This may seem like an odd statement, but it's true. Because of its debt component, an investor has some downside protection. If the company's fortunes decline and the stock price with it, the investor will at least have the principal repayment and large coupon payments to reward her. Consequently, mezzanine debt is similar to a put option plus equity. The investor has some protection on the downside, but in return must sacrifice some appreciation on the upside.

Distressed Debt

Distressed debt investors are usually equity investors in debt's clothing. Most of the time, the vultures are looking to swoop in, purchase cheap debt securities, convert them to stock, turn around the company, and reap the rewards of appreciation. Consequently, they are less concerned with coupon payments, debt service, or repayment schedules. They are in it for the equity that can be squeezed out of distressed debt situations.

The risks they bear are large; as we discussed in the previous chapter, "distressed" means companies in trouble. Similar to venture capital, there is a large business risk associated with distressed debt investing. The management of the troubled company must arrest the company's decline and turn it around. Typically, management can stop a company's decline by seeking Chapter 11 Bankruptcy protection. However, the harder part is coming up with a plan of reorganization that will reward senior and unsecured creditors. If successful, distressed debt investors can reap a bonanza. Consequently, distressed debt investors are exposed to event risk, either the event that the company will declare bankruptcy or that the company will not be able to emerge from bankruptcy protection.

Like LBO and venture capital funds, distressed debt investors also tend to run concentrated portfolios of companies. However, distressed debt investors tend to invest across industries as opposed to concentrating in a single industry. This may lead to better diversification than venture capital funds.

Within the risk spectrum, distressed debt investors fall in between venture capitalists and LBO firms. Like LBO firms, distressed debt investors purchase securities of companies that have an established operating history. In most cases these companies are way past their IPO stage. However, unlike LBO firms that target successful but stagnant companies, distressed investing targets troubled companies. These companies have progressed past stagnation, and may already be in bankruptcy proceedings.

Like venture capital firms, distressed debt investors assume considerable business risk. However, distressed debt investing is less risky than venture capital because the company already has a proven product and operating history. The company's current problems might be due to poor execution of an existing business plan, an obsolete business plan, or simply poor cash management. These problems can be fixed whereas a start-up company with a product that doesn't sell cannot.

Exhibit 4 presents the value of distressed debt investing compared to the S&P 500. As can be seen, distressed debt investors were consistently rewarded for accepting the extra business risk of investing in troubled companies. Additionally, distressed debt investors earned returns that were greater than that for LBO firms, but less than that for venture capital firms.

Exhibit 4: Value of an Investment in Distressed Debt

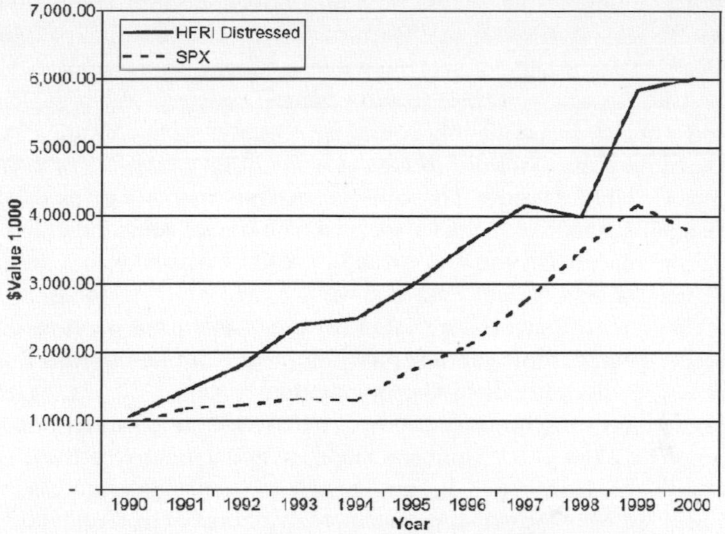

We also note that distressed debt investors performed poorly in 1998 when the Russian bond default and Long Term Capital Management sent shock waves through the credit markets. This forced investors to flee to safety in U.S. Treasury securities and AAA rated bonds. The heightened scrutiny of credit risk adversely impacted the returns to distressed debt.

PRIVATE EQUITY RETURN DISTRIBUTIONS

In this section we perform the analysis that was previously deployed for hedge funds, commodities, and managed futures. Through the process of graphing the returns to private equity we try to understand the nature of the risks associated with this form of investing.

In Chapter 6 we introduced the concepts of skewness and kurtosis. These are statistical measures that help to describe the distribution of returns earned from an investment in an asset class.

Recall that skewness and kurtosis are defined by the third and fourth moments of the distribution, respectively. A normal (bell-shaped) distribution has no skewness because it is a symmetrical distribution. The values of kurtosis in the following exhibits are measured relative to a normal, bell-shaped distribution. A positive value for kurtosis indicates a distribution with "fatter" than normal tails, (a condition called leptokurtosis) while a negative value indicates a distribution with "thinner" than normal tails (platykurtosis).

Normal distributions can be defined by the first two moments of the distribution — the mean and the variance. Therefore, for a normal distribution, a Sharpe ratio is an appropriate measure for risk and return. However, if higher moments of the distribution are present, a Sharpe ratio may not capture the complete risk and return tradeoff.[3] This is why we plot the distribution to observe if it exhibits non-normal properties that might not be captured by a Sharpe ratio analysis.

We take the data contained in the Venture Economics database, and recalibrate them to plot a frequency distribution of the returns associated with venture capital, LBOs, and mezzanine debt. For distressed debt investing, we use the return information in the HFRI database. The following exhibits provide a graphical depiction of the range and likelihood of returns associated with private equity investing. We calculate the mean, standard deviation, skew, and kurtosis associated with each strategy.

As benchmarks for our analysis, we use the returns to the S&P 500 and high-yield bonds. Recall our discussion in Chapter 6 that private equity portfolios are exposed to considerable market risk. Therefore, we use the S&P 500 as a benchmark for venture capital, LBOs, and mezzanine debt.

Exhibit 5 presents the distribution of quarterly returns associated with the S&P 500 over the period 1980–2000. This distribution exhibits a negative skew of −0.41 and a positive value of kurtosis of 1.25. These results are almost the same as those presented in Chapter 6 when we presented the monthly returns of the S&P 500.[4]

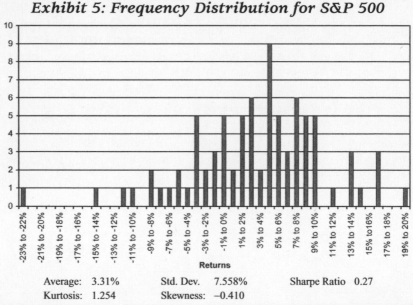

Exhibit 5: Frequency Distribution for S&P 500

Average:	3.31%	Std. Dev.	7.558%	Sharpe Ratio 0.27
Kurtosis:	1.254	Skewness:	−0.410	

---

[3] For a detailed examination of symmetric performance measures and asymmetric return distributions, see Mark Anson, "Symmetric Performance Measures and Asymmetric Trading Strategies: A Cautionary Example," *Journal of Alternative Investments* (2001).

[4] In Chapter 6 we used the monthly returns of the S&P 500 to be consistent with the monthly reporting format of most hedge funds. In this chapter we use the quarterly returns of the S&P 500 to be consistent with the quarterly reporting format of most private equity firms.

In Chapter 6 we used high-yield bonds to analyze hedge funds that had exposure to credit risk, and we found that the return distribution for high-yield debt is distinctly non-normal. We demonstrated that high yield debt had a negative skew value of −0.434, as well as a large positive value of kurtosis of 4.233. We continue to use Exhibit 4 from Chapter 6 as our benchmark for credit risk.[5]

The distribution of returns to high-yield bonds demonstrated a significant downside tail. This "fat" tail reflects the event risk of downgrades, defaults, and bankruptcies. As we explained in Chapter 6, credit risk is simply another way to describe event risk.

A negative skew indicates that the mean of the distribution is to the left of (less than) the median of the distribution. This means that there are more frequent large return observations to the left of the distribution (negative returns) and there are more small and mid-range positive return observations to the right of the distribution. In other words, large negative outlying returns occur more frequently than large positive outlying returns, indicating a bias to the downside.

A positive skew indicates the reverse of a negative skew. It indicates that the mean of the distribution is to the right of the median and that there are more frequent large positive returns than there are large negative returns. A positive skew demonstrates a bias to the upside.

Venture Capital

Exhibit 6 presents the frequency distribution for the quarterly returns to venture capital over the time period 1980–2000. It is clear that venture capital investments generate a return pattern with large positive values for both skewness and kurtosis. The implication is that there are more large positive returns than negative returns associated with venture capital investing (the large positive skew). In addition, the large positive value of kurtosis (leptokurtosis) indicates that there are many more large outliers associated with venture capital returns than associated with a normal distribution.

The large value of positive kurtosis (27.16) for venture capital is partly influenced by the recent history of the venture capital market. Returns of almost 100% in 1999 were true outliers, unlikely to repeat any time in the near or distant future. These large positive returns helped to generate the large tails associated with the venture capital distribution.

The second reason for the large outlier returns is the very nature of venture capital investing. When a company does well it can be a "20 bagger" or better, generating tremendous returns for its venture capital investors.[6] Unfortunately, many start-up companies go bust and the venture capitalist loses her investment.

---

[5] The returns for distressed debt investing are reported on a monthly basis. Therefore, the high-yield returns presented Exhibit 4 from Chapter 6 are appropriate to use as a benchmark for distressed debt because they are also reported on a monthly basis. We do this to ensure that we are comparing "apples to apples."

[6] The terminology "20 bagger" comes from Peter Lynch, the former manager of the Fidelity Magellan Fund. He often referred to a stock in baseball terms. Therefore, a "two-bagger" was a stock that doubled your money, a three-bagger tripled your money, and so on. A 20-bagger indicates a company that appreciates in value twenty-fold compared to the cost of the venture capital investment.

Exhibit 6: Frequency Distribution for Venture Capital

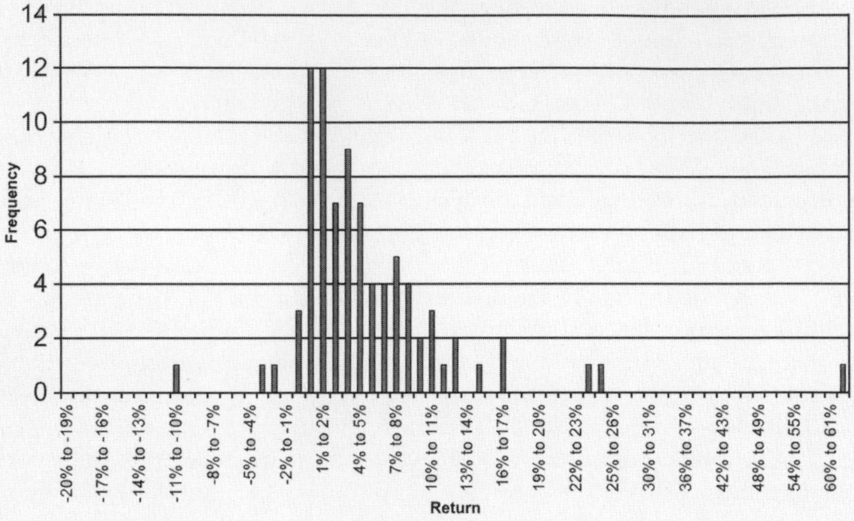

Average:	5.37%	Std. Dev.	8.31%	Sharpe Ratio 0.49
Kurtosis:	27.16	Skewness:	4.28	

This return pattern is ideal for posting a large positive skew with a large positive value of kurtosis. If a company goes bust, the most a venture capitalist can lose is the money she invested. However, if the company is successful, the gains can be extraordinary.

Venture capital returns have a positive skew of 4.28 compared to a negative skew for the S&P 500 of −0.41 over the same time period. This demonstrates that the concentrated company selection of venture capitalists was able to avoid the negatively skewed pattern of the broader stock market returns. This is a demonstration of company selection skill. In sum, a large positive skew combined with a large value of kurtosis translated into large positive returns for venture capital investors.

Leveraged Buyouts

Exhibit 7 presents the frequency distribution for LBOs. Similar to venture capital returns, the returns to LBOs demonstrate both positive skew (1.55) and kurtosis (3.38), though less so than venture capital. The return distribution associated with LBOs is exposed to large outlier returns, but far less than venture capital. This is consistent with our discussion above.

LBO firms have far less business risk than venture capital firms. LBO firms target successful but undervalued companies. These firms have operating management in place, an established product and brand name, an operating history, and stable balance sheets. LBO firms then implement a better business plan that generates a larger cash flow, and add leverage to boost the returns to equity.

Exhibit 7: Frequency Distribution for LBOs

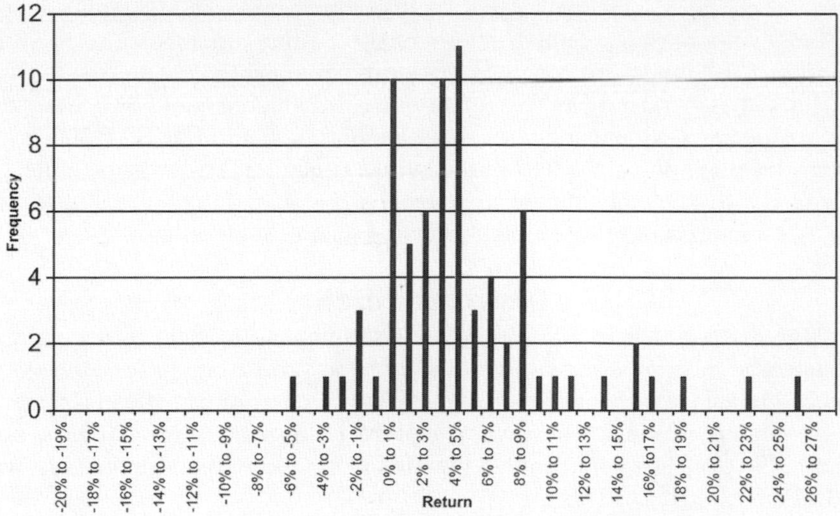

Average:	4.85%	Std. Dev.	5.59%	Sharpe Ratio 0.64
Kurtosis:	3.38	Skewness:	1.55	

When LBOs work well, they can generate returns in the 40% range. However, when they work poorly, they may end up in Chapter 11 Bankruptcy protection. Even then, an LBO investment is not a total loss because the reorganization plan might allow the company to emerge from bankruptcy with the LBO equity still intact.

Similar to venture capital, the ability to generate returns that are positively skewed with a positive value of kurtosis means more large positive returns than large negative returns. This is a favorable return pattern for investors, and demonstrates skill on the part of LBO firms. We also note that LBO firms generated returns that had less volatility than the S&P 500 and a higher Sharpe ratio.

Mezzanine Debt

Given its status as a hybrid, part debt and part equity, we would expect to see lower returns than for venture capital and LBOs, but also lower volatility of returns. Both cases are observed — mezzanine debt earns less than venture capital and LBOs, but there is also less risk.

With respect to skew and kurtosis, we observe a positive skew and a positive value of kurtosis. Recall from Chapter 6 that the distribution of returns associated with high-yield debt demonstrated a negative skew of −0.434 and a positive kurtosis of 4.233. The distribution of returns for junk financing had more large negative returns than large positive returns. This was reflective of the credit/event risk associated with high-yield bonds.

Conversely, with respect to mezzanine debt, in Exhibit 8 we observe a positive skew of 1.25 associated with its return distribution consistent with private equity investing. The negative skew generally associated with credit risky securities (debt) has been overcome by the equity component of the mezzanine debt. In addition, mezzanine debt demonstrates a positive value of kurtosis (3.35) similar to that for LBO funds. We conclude that mezzanine debt is exposed to outlying events about as frequently as that for LBO funds, which is more frequently than what is expected from either a normal distribution or that for the S&P 500.

Investors do get the best of the hybrid structure: the downside protection associated with a debt investment while receiving a distribution of returns that has more in common with private equity investing than debt investing.

Distressed Debt

Although distressed debt is a way to convert outstanding debt into equity, the investor must bear the event risk that the company will cease to function. As we discussed in the prior chapter, distressed companies may already be in Chapter 11 Bankruptcy proceedings. However, Chapter 11 Bankruptcy protection is not a panacea, the company could end up liquidating similar to the Montgomery Ward and Iridium examples in Chapter 16.

Consequently, credit risk still exists. From Chapter 6 we know that event risk translates into a negative skew value with a large value of kurtosis. Consistent with this type of risk, Exhibit 9 demonstrates a negative skew value of −0.73 and a large positive value of kurtosis of 5.63. These values are very similar to those found for high-yield bonds indicating an event risk profile similar to credit risky bonds.

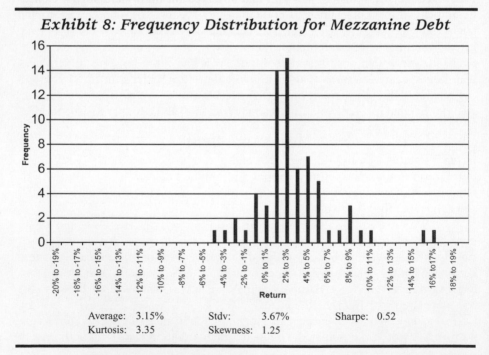

Exhibit 8: Frequency Distribution for Mezzanine Debt

Average: 3.15%		Stdv: 3.67%	Sharpe: 0.52
Kurtosis: 3.35		Skewness: 1.25	

Exhibit 9: Frequency Distribution for Distressed Debt

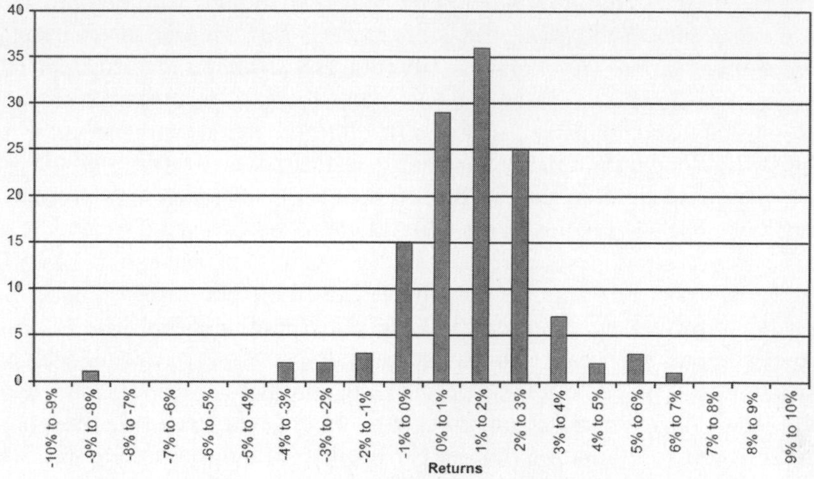

| Average: | 1.210% | Stdv: | 1.902% | Sharpe Ratio | 0.40 |
| Skewness: | -0.733 | Kurtosis: | 5.626 | | |

Our conclusion is that distressed debt investing, while producing very favorable returns over the period 1990–2000, still exposed investors to considerable event risk. This risk was on par with that observed for high-yield bonds. Consequently, investors in distressed debt should expect to bear the event risk associated with troubled companies — that is, that the company will cease its operations.

PRIVATE EQUITY WITHIN A DIVERSIFIED PORTFOLIO

The popularity of private equity investments has led to many studies on the value of investing in these vehicles.[7] However, the amount of assets committed to private equity investments will depend on the value of portfolio diversification to the investor. In other words, the utility of investing in private equity will be different depending upon an investor's level of risk aversion. In this section, we examine the utility of investing in private equity funds within a diversified portfolio context.

Prior research has demonstrated that private equity has good diversification properties. Gompers and Lerner examine the correlation of the returns to private

---

[7] See, Alon Brav and Paul Gompers. "Myth or Reality? The Long-Run Underperformance of Initial Public Offerings: Evidence from Venture and Non-Venture Capital-Backed Companies," *Journal of Finance* (December 1997), pp. 1791–1821; Paul Gompers and Josh Lerner, "Money Chasing Deals? The Impact of Fund Inflows on the Valuation of Private Equity Investments," *Journal of Financial Economics* (2000), pp. 281–325; Paul Gompers and Josh Lerner, "The Challenge of Performance Assessment," in *Private Equity and Venture Capital*, Rick Lake and Ronald Lake (eds.) (London: Euromoney Books, 2000); and Paul Gompers, "Grandstanding in the Venture Capital Industry," *The Journal of Financial Economics* (1996), pp. 131–156.

equity with that of several asset classes.[8] Using information reported by Warburg, Pincus, they find that the correlation of private equity returns with that of corporate and Treasury bonds to be 10% and 7%, respectively. With the S&P 500 and small cap stocks, the correlation with private equity returns was 60% and 68%, respectively. However, when Gompers and Lerner adjust the Warburg, Pincus private equity returns with estimated marks to market, they find that the correlations with corporate bonds, Treasury bonds, large cap stocks, and small cap stocks, increases to 19%, 14%, 74%, and 78%, respectively. Nonetheless, the less than perfect correlation of private equity with major asset classes indicates it has useful properties of diversification.

There are, however, concerns about the returns to private equity. First, Gompers and Lerner conclude that inflows to private equity funds have a substantial impact on the pricing of private equity investments.[9] The implication is that there is too much money chasing too few deals, and that the positive valuations associated with private equity investments may be due to new capital inflows instead of real economic value.

Second, Gompers demonstrates that young venture capital firms bring private companies to the public market earlier than older venture capital firms in order to establish a positive reputation.[10] He concludes that this type of signaling causes real wealth losses in the form of underpriced IPOs and lower-valued equity stakes, and that this loss is borne by the limited partners in the venture fund.

Despite these potential caveats, empirical research indicates that private equity has favorable risk and return characteristics. We examine these properties within a portfolio framework.

Building a Diversified Portfolio with Private Equity

To determine whether private equity investments add value to a diversified portfolio, we maximize portfolio value over five asset classes: large-capitalization stocks, small-capitalization stocks, investment-grade bonds, cash, and private equity. For large-cap stocks we use the S&P 500 total return index, for small-cap stocks we use the NASDAQ total return index, for long-term bonds we use the Salomon Smith Barney Broad Investment Grade (BIG) Bond Index, and for cash we use the 3-month U.S. Treasury bill rate.

We use the term "private equity" generally to describe the four forms of private investing we have previously discussed: venture capital, leveraged buyouts, mezzanine financing, and distressed debt investing. We obtain information on the historical returns for these four sources of private equity from Venture Economics and Hedge Fund Research Inc.[11]

---

[8] See Gompers and Lerner, "The Challenge of Performance Assessment."

[9] See Gompers and Lerner, "Money Chasing Deals?"

[10] See Gompers, "Grandstanding in the Venture Capital Industry."

[11] Venture Economics is a Thomson Financial company. It offers information on the private equity industry, including conferences, market statistics, journals, and databases. It has been in business since 1961. Hedge Fund Research Inc. is a database that contains information on many different types of investment styles for hedge funds. Unfortunately, it is not possible to measure the diversification potential of every individual private equity fund on a stock and bond portfolio. Therefore, we use an index of returns for each of the four private equity categories to determine the impact on expected utility

Exhibit 10: Correlation Matrix

	3Mo T-Bill	SBBIG	Nasdaq	S&P 500	Venture Capital	Buyouts	Mezzanine	Distressed
3Mo T-Bill	1.000	0.232	−0.148	−0.052	−0.094	−0.282	−0.243	−0.163
SBBIG	0.232	1.000	−0.026	0.158	−0.228	−0.180	−0.003	−0.098
Nasdaq	−0.148	−0.026	1.000	0.841	0.681	0.408	−0.090	0.504
S&P 500	−0.052	0.158	0.841	1.000	0.427	0.352	0.047	0.499
Venture Capital	−0.094	−0.228	0.681	0.427	1.000	0.384	−0.129	0.243
Buyouts	−0.282	−0.180	0.408	0.352	0.384	1.000	0.114	0.380
Mezzanine	−0.243	−0.003	−0.090	0.047	−0.129	0.114	1.000	0.106
Distressed	−0.163	−0.098	0.504	0.499	0.243	0.380	0.106	1.000

There are several caveats associated with an index of private equity returns. First, private equity managers tend to use conservative assumptions in the computation of their returns. As a result, private equity values tend to lag the rest of the financial markets because fund managers usually wait until there is a realizable event associated with a private equity investment that provides a measure of market value. This event could be an initial public offering, a second round of financing, or a third-party follow-on investment.[12]

Second, private equity managers tend to report the net asset value of their funds on a quarterly basis. Monthly return data are rare. Quarterly reporting can mask month-to-month fluctuations in value.

Last, there is usually some source of bias associated with a database. In Chapter 7 we described the data biases associated with hedge fund data. The same biases apply with respect to private equity databases.

In Exhibits 5 through 9, the Sharpe ratios for the four categories of private equity are higher than those for the S&P 500. On a stand-alone basis, it would appear that private equity funds are a superior investment choice. However, private equity should not be considered in isolation because this ignores its diversification potential with respect to other asset classes.

The diversification potential of private equity is demonstrated in Exhibit 10, which presents a correlation matrix of the quarterly returns of the four classes of private equity compared to the traditional stock and bond asset classes.[13] For instance, the returns to all four classes of private equity are negatively correlated with investment-grade bonds and U.S. Treasury bills, and have low correlation with the returns to large-cap and small-cap stocks. In conclusion, the less than perfect correlation (and, in some cases, negative correlation) of private equity returns with the returns to stocks, bonds, and cash indicate excellent diversification potential.

---

[12] We also note that private equity indices are not fully investable due to issues of capacity, minimum net worth requirements imposed by the private equity managers, and regulatory restrictions as to the number of investors that may invest in a private investment vehicle.

[13] In Exhibit 10 we use quarterly data from 1990–2000 to ensure consistency of the data, and we convert the monthly returns for distressed debt into quarterly returns to be comparable with those for the other classes of private equity.

A Model for Maximizing Portfolio Value

When presented with various outcomes of portfolio return and volatility, an investor will choose the portfolio that provides the best balance of risk and return. This balance will depend upon each investor's level of risk aversion. The issue we examine is whether the addition of private equity to a portfolio of stocks and bonds will increase an investor's expected utility beyond that obtained with only stocks and bonds.

Several prior empirical studies describe an investor's utility function as:[14]

$$E(U_i) = E(R_p) - A_i \sigma^2(R_p)$$

where

$E(U_i)$ is the expected utility of the i-th investor

$E(R_p) = \Sigma_i w_i E(R_i)$ is the expected return of the portfolio

$\sigma^2(R_p) = \Sigma_i \Sigma_j w_i w_j \sigma_i \sigma_j \rho_{ij}$ is the variance of the portfolio returns

A_i is a measure of relative risk aversion for the i-th investor

w_i and w_j are the portfolio weights of the i-th and j-th asset classes

σ_i and σ_j are the volatilities of the i-th and j-th asset classes

ρ_{ij} is the correlation coefficient between the i-th and j-th asset classes

The expected utility in the equation may be viewed as the expected return on the investor's portfolio minus a risk penalty. The risk penalty is equal to the risk of the portfolio multiplied by the investor's level of risk aversion. This is another way to say that the equation is just a risk-adjusted expected rate of return for the portfolio, where the risk adjustment depends on the level of the investor's risk aversion.[15]

Whether we call the equation the expected utility or the risk-adjusted return, solving this function requires quadratic programming. This is because solving for $E(U)$ involves both squared terms (the individual asset variances) as well as multiplicative terms (the covariances of the various asset classes). The important point to realize is that quadratic solutions recognize that the risk of the portfolio depends upon the interactions among the asset classes.

---

[14] See Philippe Jorion, "Risk Management Lessons Learned from Long Term Capital Management," Working paper, 2000; William Sharpe, "Asset Allocation," in *Managing Investment Portfolios: A Dynamic Process*, John Maginn and Donald Tuttle (eds.) (New York: Warren, Gorham and Lamber, 1990); and Richard Grinold and Ronald Kahn, *Active Portfolio Management* (New York: McGraw Hill, 2000).

[15] It should be noted that the equation is based on the mean and variance and does not include the higher moments such as skew and kurtosis. Three comments are necessary. First, incorporating higher moments into a utility function can lead to the counter economic results of increasing marginal utility and increasing absolute risk aversion. Increasing marginal utility would mean that the more an investor invests in private equity, the greater the utility. There would be no point of saturation. Second, the impact of skew or kurtosis for an asset class should have a lesser impact within a diversified portfolio. Last, an advantage of defining expected utility in the text as a risk-adjusted return is that the absolute risk aversion of the investor decreases with the expected return. For a more detailed discussion on these issues, see Mark Anson, "Maximizing Expected Utility with Private Equity," *The Journal of Investing* (2001).

There are two problems with determining the utility of private equity investing. First, utility functions are hard to define in terms of all of the factors that affect investors' behavior. Second, even if a utility function could be specified for each investor, these functions would be as varied and as different as the investors they attempt to describe. Consequently, there is no single answer to the utility of private equity investing.

Instead of trying to describe the unique benefits of private equity for every investor, we develop a simple scale to measure risk aversion. We set A_i equal to 0 for a risk neutral investor, 1 for a low risk aversion investor, 2 for a moderate risk aversion investor, and 3 for a high risk aversion investor. At $A_i = 0$, the investor is neutral to risk, and expected return is all that matters. Conversely, as A_i increases from 0 to 3, portfolio volatility becomes a greater concern in the investor's utility function, and the investor will seek greater diversification to manage her risk.

Analyzing Private Equity within a Portfolio Context

A constrained optimization program is run to solve the equation at each level of risk aversion.[16] In Exhibit 11 we present the base case of maximizing utility without using any class of private equity. We can see that a risk neutral investor allocates her entire portfolio to small-cap stocks. This is because the risk-neutral investor is not encumbered by concerns over risk; maximizing return is all that matters. An investor who is unconcerned with risk will not have her behavior affected by the volatilities or correlations of the various asset classes. This type of investor invests in the asset class that yields the highest expected returns: small-capitalization stocks.

However, as the investor's level of risk aversion increases, we see that she diversifies her portfolio between small-cap stocks and the less volatile investment-grade bonds. The reason is that these asset classes have less than perfect correlation with each other. By diversifying across a number of asset classes, the investor can reduce the volatility of her investment portfolio. This volatility dampening effect has greater utility as the level of risk aversion increases.

At $A_i = 3$, the high risk averse investor shifts almost three-fourths of her portfolio away from small-cap stocks and into investment-grade bonds. No allocation is made to cash at any level of risk aversion. This is due to the relatively low returns earned by this asset class over the time period studied.

The results for each category of private equity are presented in Exhibits 12 through 15. These exhibits demonstrate that, as an investor's risk aversion increases, so does her allocation to private equity.

---

[16] To solve the utility maximization equation, we program an optimization as follows:

Maximize $E(U) = \Sigma_i w_i E(R_i) - A_i \Sigma_i \Sigma_j w_i w_j \sigma_i \sigma_j \rho_{ij}$

subject to the constraints $\Sigma w_i = 1$, and $0 \le w_i \le 1$, where $A_i = 0, 1, 2, 3$ for different levels of relative risk aversion.

Exhibit 11: Maximizing Utility without Private Equity

Risk Neutral Investor ($A = 0$)

Tbill	SBBIG	NASDAQ	S&P 500
0.000	0.000	1.000	0.000

Expected Utility	Expected Return	Standard Deviation	Sharpe Ratio
0.048	0.048	0.135	0.261

Low Risk Aversion ($A_i = 1$)

Tbill	SBBIG	NASDAQ	S&P 500
0.000	0.231	0.769	0.000

Expected Utility	Expected Return	Standard Deviation	Sharpe Ratio
0.031	0.041	0.104	0.277

Moderate Risk Aversion ($A_i = 2$)

Tbill	SBBIG	NASDAQ	S&P 500
0.000	0.601	0.399	0.000

Expected Utility	Expected Return	Standard Deviation	Sharpe Ratio
0.025	0.031	0.055	0.334

High Risk Aversion ($A_i = 3$)

Tbill	SBBIG	NASDAQ	S&P 500
0.000	0.724	0.276	0.000

Expected Utility	Expected Return	Standard Deviation	Sharpe Ratio
0.023	0.028	0.040	0.373

In Exhibit 12, we see that a risk neutral investor will allocate all of her portfolio to venture capital. The reason is the superior returns earned by venture capital over this time period (it even outperforms small-cap stocks). The superior returns of venture capital are enough to outweigh its risk except for the high risk averse investor. We can see that such an investor diversifies her portfolio between venture capital and investment-grade bonds.

In Exhibit 13, with respect to LBOs, the low risk, moderate risk, and high risk aversion investor allocates approximately 64%, 84%, and 90%, respectively, of her portfolio to leveraged buyout investments. The allocation to LBOs is made to balance the risk of small-cap stocks. Small-cap stocks outperformed LBO firms over this time period, but they were also riskier. Therefore, as an investor's level of risk aversion increases, she makes a larger and larger allocation to LBO firms to balance the risk of small-cap stocks in her portfolio.

Exhibit 12: Maximizing Utility with Venture Capital

Risk Neutral Investor ($A = 0$)

Tbill	SBBIG	NASDAQ	S&P 500	Venture
0.000	0.000	0.000	0.000	1.000

Expected Utility	Expected Return	Standard Deviation	Sharpe Ratio
0.071	0.071	0.107	0.545

Low Risk Aversion ($A_i = 1$)

Tbill	SBBIG	NASDAQ	S&P 500	Venture
0.000	0.000	0.000	0.000	1.000

Expected Utility	Expected Return	Standard Deviation	Sharpe Ratio
0.060	0.071	0.107	0.545

Moderate Risk Aversion ($A_i = 2$)

Tbill	SBBIG	NASDAQ	S&P 500	Venture
0.000	0.000	0.000	0.000	1.000

Expected Utility	Expected Return	Standard Deviation	Sharpe Ratio
0.048	0.071	0.107	0.545

High Risk Aversion ($A_i = 3$)

Tbill	SBBIG	NASDAQ	S&P 500	Venture
0.000	0.269	0.000	0.000	0.731

Expected Utility	Expected Return	Standard Deviation	Sharpe Ratio
0.039	0.057	0.077	0.578

Exhibit 13: Maximizing Utility with Leveraged Buyouts

Risk Neutral Investor ($A = 0$)

Tbill	SBBIG	NASDAQ	S&P 500	LBO
0.000	0.000	1.000	0.000	0.000

Expected Utility	Expected Return	Standard Deviation	Sharpe Ratio
0.048	0.048	0.135	0.261

Low Risk Aversion ($A_i = 1$)

Tbill	SBBIG	NASDAQ	S&P 500	LBO
0.000	0.000	0.354	0.000	0.646

Expected Utility	Expected Return	Standard Deviation	Sharpe Ratio
0.036	0.040	0.064	0.431

Moderate Risk Aversion ($A_i = 2$)

Tbill	SBBIG	NASDAQ	S&P 500	LBO
0.000	0.000	0.159	0.000	0.841

Expected Utility	Expected Return	Standard Deviation	Sharpe Ratio
0.033	0.038	0.048	0.523

High Risk Aversion ($A_i = 3$)

Tbill	SBBIG	NASDAQ	S&P 500	LBO
0.000	0.000	0.094	0.000	0.906

Expected Utility	Expected Return	Standard Deviation	Sharpe Ratio
0.031	0.037	0.045	0.547

Exhibit 14: Maximizing Utility with Mezzanine Debt

Risk Neutral Investor ($A = 0$)

Tbill	SBBIG	NASDAQ	S&P 500	Mezzanine
0.000	0.000	1.000	0.000	0.000

Expected Utility	Expected Return	Standard Deviation	Sharpe Ratio
0.048	0.048	0.135	0.261

Low Risk Aversion ($A_i = 1$)

Tbill	SBBIG	NASDAQ	S&P 500	Mezzanine
0.000	0.000	0.569	0.000	0.431

Expected Utility	Expected Return	Standard Deviation	Sharpe Ratio
0.033	0.039	0.077	0.347

Moderate Risk Aversion ($A_i = 2$)

Tbill	SBBIG	NASDAQ	S&P 500	Mezzanine
0.000	0.000	0.320	0.000	0.680

Expected Utility	Expected Return	Standard Deviation	Sharpe Ratio
0.030	0.034	0.047	0.464

High Risk Aversion ($A_i = 3$)

Tbill	SBBIG	NASDAQ	S&P 500	Mezzanine
0.000	0.000	0.237	0.000	0.763

Expected Utility	Expected Return	Standard Deviation	Sharpe Ratio
0.028	0.033	0.039	0.518

Similar results are presented in Exhibits 14 and 15 for mezzanine debt and distressed debt. A risk neutral investor will select small-cap stocks over either of these forms of debt due to the greater return earned by small-cap stocks. However, as the level of risk aversion increases, an investor will allocate a larger part of her portfolio to either mezzanine debt or distressed debt to balance the risks associated with small cap stocks. The allocation to mezzanine debt and distressed debt increases as an investor's level of risk aversion increases.

The important point of this analysis is that the Sharpe ratios and utility values for each category of private equity in Exhibits 12 through 15 dominate those in Exhibit 11 (which contains no component of private equity). Simply stated, the investor achieves a higher expected utility and a higher Sharpe ratio at each level of risk aversion, and with each component of private equity than she does without a component of private equity in her portfolio. [17]

---

[17] As a final point, the marginal utility of private equity is positive at each level of risk aversion where the marginal utility is determined by $\partial E(U)/\partial w_{pe} = E(R_{pe}) - 2A_i\sigma_{pe}\Sigma_j w_j\sigma_j\rho_{pej}$. See Anson, "Maximizing Utility with Private Equity."

Exhibit 15: Maximizing Utility with Distressed Debt

Risk Neutral Investor ($A = 0$)

Tbill	SBBIG	NASDAQ	S&P 500	Distressed
0.000	0.000	1.000	0.000	0.000

Expected Utility	Expected Return	Standard Deviation	Sharpe Ratio
0.048	0.048	0.135	0.261

Low Risk Aversion ($A_i = 1$)

Tbill	SBBIG	NASDAQ	S&P 500	Distressed
0.000	0.000	0.282	0.000	0.718

Expected Utility	Expected Return	Standard Deviation	Sharpe Ratio
0.037	0.041	0.061	0.461

Moderate Risk Aversion ($A_i = 2$)

Tbill	SBBIG	NASDAQ	S&P 500	Distressed
0.000	0.000	0.104	0.000	0.896

Expected Utility	Expected Return	Standard Deviation	Sharpe Ratio
0.034	0.039	0.049	0.541

High Risk Aversion ($A_i = 3$)

Tbill	SBBIG	NASDAQ	S&P 500	Distressed
0.000	0.000	0.045	0.000	0.955

Expected Utility	Expected Return	Standard Deviation	Sharpe Ratio
0.032	0.038	0.046	0.559

In summary, the four categories of private equity investing demonstrated positive portfolio benefits. In fact, private equity replaced investment-grade bonds (from Exhibit 11) as an effective portfolio diversifying agent. Each component of private equity improved the risk to reward performance of the investment portfolio.

CONCLUSION

This chapter was concerned with the economics of private equity. Initially, we observed that the more risky categories of private equity, venture capital, and distressed debt earned risk premiums in excess of that of the S&P 500 while LBOs and mezzanine debt did not. However, all four categories of private equity earned higher Sharpe ratios than the S&P 500 indicating a superior risk and return profile than the broader stock market.

We also found that the return distributions for venture capital, LBOs, and mezzanine debt compared favorably to the S&P 500. Specifically, these three classes of private equity demonstrated skill by avoiding the negative skew associated with the returns to the broad stock market. Distressed debt, however, was found to have a similar return distribution to that of high-yield bonds. This is consistent with the event risk to which distressed debt investors are exposed.

Last, in our examination of private equity in a portfolio context, we found that private equity was an effective diversifying agent. Specifically, we found that each class of private equity was adept at diversifying the risks associated with publicly traded stocks. The conclusion is that private equity is a valuable addition to a diversified stock portfolio.

Chapter 18

Alternative Investment Strategies in Private Equity

Private equity is the largest of the alternative investment strategies. In the year 2000, a total of $165 billion was invested in venture capital, LBOs, mezzanine debt, and distressed debt, combined. The popularity of these investment strategies has encouraged private equity managers to expand the applications of their investment insights. In this chapter we consider four new venues of private equity investing.

The four new ventures for private equity investors include crossover funds, PIPE transactions, interval funds, and private equity in private equity. Crossover funds are a hybrid structure with a private equity component. PIPE transactions are private investments in public companies. Interval funds provide a retail outlet for private equity. Last, private investments in private equity firms are possible.

CROSSOVER FUNDS

Crossover funds contain both private and public securities in their portfolio. This is not a new phenomenon with private equity managers. What is new is that private equity managers may employ a long/short strategy with respect to that portion of their portfolio that is committed to publicly traded securities. Long/short investing has traditionally been the venue of hedge fund managers. Consequently, private equity managers may have found a new product niche within the alternative asset universe.

A Graphical Illustration of Crossover Funds

Private equity investments typically have the greatest duration of any long-only investment class. Duration is a way to measure the rate of change in the value of an asset compared to the change in value of a benchmark such as the S&P 500. This is simply another way to say that private equity investments have the greatest exposure to market risk compared to other long-only investments such as a passive equity index investment program.

In Chapter 4 we presented a graphical way to compare long-only investments to hedge funds. Long only managers typically invest in either the equity or bond market, but do not leverage their investment bets. Therefore, their investment programs have considerable market risk exposure, but very little leverage or credit risk exposure.

At one end of the scale are money market cash managers who take almost no credit or market risk to avoid "breaking the buck." At the other end of the scale are private equity managers. They take no credit risk, but have the greatest exposure to market risk. In between, we find growth managers, equity index managers, value managers, and fixed income managers. Exhibit 1 summarizes this exposure to market risk.

Private equity investments have the greatest exposure to market risk for several reasons. First is the relative lack of liquidity for private equity investments. Private equity pools typically have lock-up periods of several years. The lock-up period forces private equity investors to maintain a long-term exposure to the equity market.

Second, private equity investments are often concentrated in new and emerging industry sectors or companies. It may be years before these new and emerging sectors and companies achieve their full potential and value. Additionally, these new sectors or companies can exhibit considerable volatility, and this volatility can be exacerbated by a sector's or company's covariance with the general stock market.

Finally, private equity investments are often made in companies that have no publicly traded securities. It may be years before an initial public offering occurs that allows a private equity investor the opportunity to cash out of her investment.

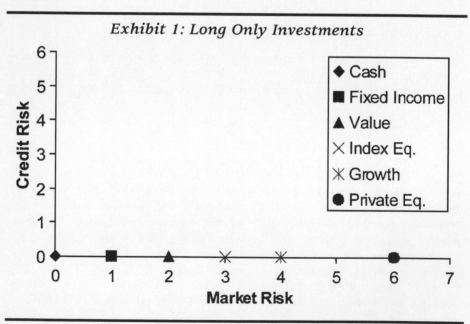

Exhibit 1: Long Only Investments

Exhibit 2: Long Only Plus Crossover Funds

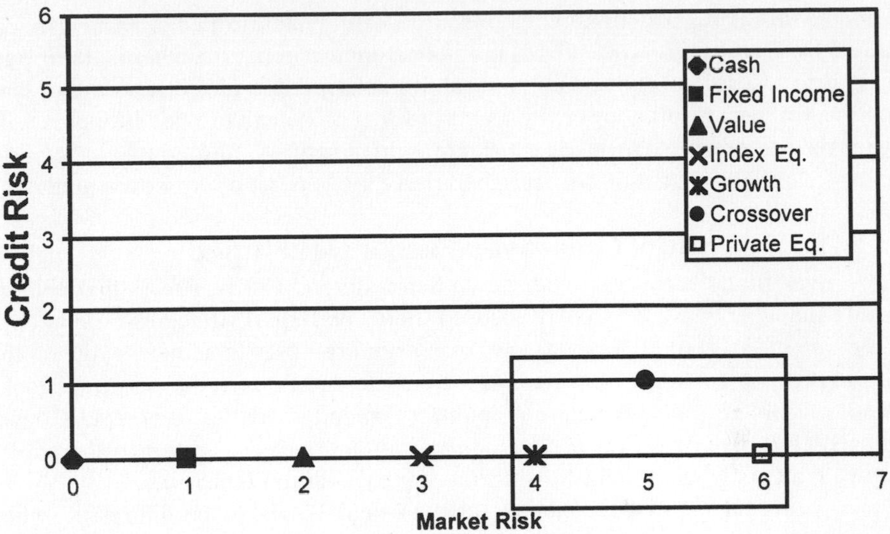

The graphical analysis changes considerably for hedge fund managers. In Chapter 6 we established three general classes of hedge funds: those hedge funds that are exposed to credit risk (e.g. relative value arbitrage, fixed income arbitrage, etc.), those hedge funds that are exposed to market risk (equity long/short and global macro funds), and those funds that have minimal exposure to either market or credit risk (market neutral and market timing funds). Into this mix we add crossover funds.[1]

These are funds that combine components of private equity and public market securities. These funds are true hybrids — they combine parts of private equity management with hedge fund investment strategies. They have considerable market exposure because of the nature of their investment strategy, equity long short plus private equity. Additionally, this type of fund also applies leverage either directly through borrowing cash, or implicitly through borrowing securities to short. Therefore, crossover funds have some exposure to credit risk.

We call this type of fund a crossover fund because when we overlay this strategy on to Exhibit 1 we get the illustration demonstrated in Exhibit 2. In this figure, we can see that crossover funds fill the gap between private equity and public equity. In other words, along the axis of market exposure, there is a leap from growth investing in public securities to lock-up investing in private equity funds.

Crossover funds help to bridge this gap by filling the hole between public equity and private equity. We demonstrate this bridge by the rectangle in Exhibit

---

[1] To see a graphical depiction of hedge funds and crossover funds, see Mark Anson, "Cross Over Funds: A New Venue for Private Equity," *The Journal of Private Equity* (2001).

2. Within this rectangle it is clear that crossover funds fall in between public and private equity investing.

In this regard, crossover funds are not intended to hedge an investment portfolio. Instead, crossover funds are opportunistic in nature. That is, their purpose is to expand the investment opportunity set available to investors rather than to hedge it. As a result, they create a new product niche and provide investors with two sources of outperformance: private equity returns, and equity long/short returns. In the next section we describe briefly the genesis of crossover funds.

How Crossover Funds Developed

Crossover funds are a relatively new phenomenon. The reason is that private equity managers have previously focused their investment strategies on the long-only side of the market. Yet, there are many opportunities to achieve value on the short side of the market. However, in the private equity universe, shorting stocks is not possible because there are no publicly traded securities to borrow. Consequently, it is necessary for private equity managers to cross over to the public equity markets where establishing a short equity position is feasible.

In Chapter 4 we establish three critical issues to be addressed when selecting a hedge fund manager. One key issue is: What makes the hedge fund manager so smart? A hedge fund manager must prove either that she is smarter than other investors or, if she is not smarter, that she is better informed. The same issue applies to crossover funds. Crossover managers typically fall into the second category; they are better informed than other investors.

Hedge fund managers that are smarter typically have better computer algorithms that allow them to extract more information from the same data used by other investors. Their competitive advantage comes not from collecting data, but from filtering it. Conversely, crossover managers derive their competitive edge from the collection of data.

In Chapter 14 we indicated that private equity investing has become more specialized. This is very different from the original beginnings of the market where private equity firms tended to be generalists. Now, however, private equity managers tend to focus on one industry such as telecommunications, and often, within that industry, on one sector, such as cellular communications. The nature of this specialization leads to large proprietary databases.

In short, private equity managers are better informed within their industry and sector domain. In general, private equity managers spend years gathering data, analyzing companies, and understanding the macroeconomic and regulatory environment in which a sector operates. Consequently, they become experts in that sector or segment of the economy. This expertise allows them to identify good companies and bad companies. However, in the private equity universe, they can only maximize their competitive information with respect to good companies. It is not possible to short bad companies because there is no publicly traded stock. Bad companies simply don't enter into their portfolio, and consequently, are not part of their investment strategy.

However, private equity managers can take their proprietary databases and sector expertise and cross over to the public securities markets to take advantage of both good and bad companies. Only in the public securities market can they maximize the full value of their proprietary knowledge through both long and short equity positions.

Consider the following language from the offering document of a private equity manager who crossed over to the public securities side of the equity market:

> The General Partner will utilize its industry expertise, contacts,
> and databases developed over the past 11 years to identify _____
> company investment ideas outside of traditional sources...

This crossover manager knows the exact nature of its competitive advantage. The manager has a superior information set that it has developed over the past 11 years, and it takes advantage of this information set by crossing over to the public markets side of the equity market.

Examples of Crossover Funds

As indicated, crossover funds generally germinate from the private equity side of the investment spectrum. Some funds state that they will pursue an equity long/short strategy but will also consider a limited amount of private equity investment. Other funds specifically label themselves as crossover funds and use this label in describing their investment strategy. In either case, crossover funds tend to specialize in a particular sector of the economy.

Consider the following language from a healthcare crossover fund:

> The adviser believes that an investment strategy that focuses on
> public market investing, but also combines a limited amount of
> private investing and a sophisticated approach to trading that
> includes short selling, will be the most effective way to exploit
> these dynamics. The _____ Fund will seek to achieve this by
> leveraging the public market expertise of portfolio manager
> _____ alongside the venture capital expertise of _____ in
> private healthcare investing.

Although it does not label itself as a crossover fund, this fund follows the basic paradigm: an equity long/short program combined with private equity investing. This fund was an outgrowth from a private equity investment firm.

However, consider the following language from the disclosure document of a long/short technology fund:

> The [Manager] intends to pursue a "crossover" strategy which
> includes investing in both public and late stage private companies
> ("Late Stage Investments"). Late Stage Investments are securities

transactions of privately held (non-publicly traded) companies that are expected to become public or be acquired within twelve months of investment. The [Manager] anticipates that Late Stage Investments will comprise up to 25% of [the Fund's] assets at the time of such investment.

This fund manager knows exactly where it fits along the equity investment opportunity set. This fund was also developed by a private equity investment firm. Note further that this manager limits the amount of the portfolio that will be committed to private equity investments. This is typical. Often, the amount committed to private equity investments in a crossover fund is stated explicitly in the offering memorandum for the fund. However, If the amount of private equity investing is not specified in the offering memorandum, it will be negotiated with the limited partners and specified in the limited partnership agreement.

Issues with Crossover Funds

Crossover funds are true hybrids: They are a combination of hedge fund and private equity fund. As a result there may be a conflict with respect to the terms and conditions under which these funds operate. We highlight some of the main issues below.

Fees

Fortunately (and not surprisingly), fees are one area where hedge funds and private equity funds agree. Both types of funds charge management fees and profit sharing fees. In the hedge fund marketplace, the industry standard for fees is "1 and 20." That is, hedge funds generally charge a 1% management fee and a 20% profit sharing fee. However, hedge fund fees can range from 0 to 3% for management fees, and from 15% to 30% for incentive fees. Nonetheless, the clear majority of hedge funds charge "1 and 20." The private equity marketplace charges fees similar to hedge funds. Generally, they charge a management fee of 1% to 2% with a 20% "carry" or profit sharing fee.

Lock-Up Period

Although more hedge funds are beginning to require a lock-up period, most hedge funds generally do not have this constraint. Liquidity is usually provided on a quarterly or semi-annual basis. Some hedge funds even allow their investors to cash out of the fund on a monthly basis. The reason is that hedge funds tend to buy and sell publicly traded securities. This public nature of their security holdings allows the hedge funds to provide periodic liquidity to their investors.

This is in contrast to private equity funds where the lock-up period can be for several years. Typically the lock-up period is in the 7- to 10-year range, and can be even longer. The reason for the lock-up is the private nature of the equity investments. Private equity funds tend to invest in non-public entities in the case of venture capital funds, for example. Alternatively, private equity funds may take companies private in a leverage buyout. Additionally, other strategies such as mezzanine financing typically invest in privately issued securities through an unregistered (with the SEC) offering. It may be years before a private company issues securities either publicly or privately where a new valuation can be computed and an exit opportunity becomes available.

Because of the hybrid nature of a crossover fund, the lock-up period will need to be balanced against the portion of the portfolio dedicated to private equity. Further, those investors who have traditionally invested with hedge funds may not appreciate the need for a lock-up period with respect to the private equity component of the portfolio. In general, if the private equity portion of the fund is limited to no more than 25%, a lock-up period of 1 to 2 years should be reasonable. There should be sufficient liquidity in the public securities portion of the crossover fund to provide for the liquidity needs of the fund's investors.

Fee Recapture

Hedge funds typically apply "high water marks" with respect to incentive fees. This is another way of saying that a hedge fund manager may not receive an incentive fee until the value of the limited partnership units exceeds its previous high net asset value. The volatile nature of hedge fund management may result in a hedge fund suffering a loss of value. Under a high water mark provision, the hedge fund manager may not receive any additional incentive fees until she has recouped the previously lost value. In other words, once a hedge fund manager achieves a net asset value, this net asset value leaves a "high water mark," and the hedge fund manager may not charge an incentive fee until she exceeds the previous highest net asset value.[2]

Private equity funds, in contrast, do not contain a high water mark provision. Instead, they typically employ a "clawback" provision. A clawback provision requires the private equity manager to return previously collected incentive fees if there is an insufficient return to the investors in the fund. Clawback provisions may be associated with a minimum return that the private equity manager promises to her investors. This means that the limited partners in a private equity fund have the right to "clawback" a part of the general partner's incentive fee if she fails to perform under the terms of the private equity fund agreement.

Crossover funds tend to have a high water mark instead of a clawback provision. This reflects the fact that the predominant component of the fund is usually its public securities investment strategy. However, it is not unusual to have both a clawback provision and a high water mark. Generally, both provisions are found in a crossover fund where the private equity component is large, in the 40% plus range.

Advisory Committee

Hedge funds often have advisory committees consisting of limited partners invested in the fund. Advisory committees have no management duties (to protect

---

[2] In fact, it can be argued that hedge fund managers have a "free option" with respect to incentive fees. See Mark Anson, "Hedge Fund Incentive Fees and the Free Option," *The Journal of Alternative Investments* (Fall 2001).

the limited liability status of the limited partner investors). Instead, they act in an advisory capacity to the hedge fund manager with respect to matters of valuation of investments, potential conflicts of interest, and the expansion of the fund for new limited partner investors.

Private equity funds, in contrast, rarely have advisory committees. Limited partners generally take a less active role in the affairs of the private equity fund.

Depending on the size of the public market investments compared to the private equity investments, an advisory committee may be appropriate. In fact such a committee would be useful not only for the reasons enumerated above, but also to ensure that the general partner stays within the allowable percentage allocation to private equity investments.

Rollover of Investments

Rollover provisions are common in private equity funds but not in hedge funds. If a private equity investment comes to fruition during the lock-up period — for example, a private equity company has an initial public offering or the company is acquired — then the private equity manager has the right to rollover the cash proceeds into additional private equity investments.

Rollover provisions are not used in the hedge fund marketplace because of the public nature of the securities that are purchased. Rollover provisions are not necessary because the hedge fund manager is freely able to buy and sell securities to effect its strategy. Any proceeds received from the sale of one security are used to purchase another security. For this reason, hedge funds generally do not need lock-up periods. Investors can liquidate their investment and walk away when ready.

Again, the necessity of a rollover provision in a crossover fund will depend upon the size of the private equity component. Crossover funds with a private equity component equal to 40% or more may need such a provision to provide the crossover manager the ability to maximize the value of the private equity component of the fund.

Summary of Crossover Funds

Private equity managers have entered a domain traditionally populated by hedge fund managers: long/short equity investing. Previously, a long and short equity investment strategy was performed only by hedge fund managers. However, private equity managers are beginning to apply their sector expertise beyond the non-public equity market. These funds typically contain both a private equity component as well as a long/short strategy in public securities.

Private equity managers tend to specialize within one industry or sector. They have spent many years developing proprietary databases to analyze companies within their chosen sector. This industry expertise provides them with a competitive advantage in evaluating good and bad companies. However, it is not feasible to short securities in the private equity market. Consequently, the value of a private equity manager's database can only be maximized in the public equity arena.

PIPES

Hedge funds, mutual funds, venture capitalists, and leveraged buyout firms are all pursuing a new form of equity investment called a PIPE. PIPE stands for "Private Investment in a Public Entity." In a PIPE investment, an investor or group of investors bargains directly with a public company to acquire a private equity position. These are private placements of the company's stock that are purchased by investors outside of the normal public arena.

The PIPEs market began because many small, newer companies have found it difficult to raise funds through a traditional stock offering. This is even more important given the compressed time frame for companies operating in the technology sector.

In this section we examine the growth and structure of the PIPEs market. We also consider the benefits and risks of PIPE transactions both from an investor and issuer perspective. Last we show how leveraged buyout funds have embraced this type of financing.

How PIPEs Work

In a typical situation, a start-up company will take its stock public, for example, at $20 dollars a share, only to see its share price slip back to $5. The start-up company may be unable to find additional public market financing on attractive terms. This is where a PIPE transaction is most applicable.

PIPEs are a form of private placement. Public companies agree to sell unregistered securities, usually at a discount to institutional investors. Since the securities sold are not registered with the Securities and Exchange Commission (SEC), the investors cannot resell them into the market until a registration statement has been filed and declared effective by the SEC. Typically, a condition of the PIPE transaction is that the issuer subsequently file a registration statement with the Securities and Exchange Commission.[3]

PIPE transactions may be a private sale of common stock, convertible notes, or convertible preferred stock. Consider the following three examples.

On May 21, 2001, Restoration Hardware Inc. (ticker RSTO) raised $24.5 million by selling unregistered common stock to a group of select investment firms including Capital Research and Management Company, Fidelity Management and Research Company, and Baron Asset Management. The private stock was priced at $5.43 per share, which was 25% below the closing price of $7.25 on May 21. Also, Restoration Hardware committed to file a registration statement with the SEC in one to two months. In the meantime, the investors could not sell their shares because they were not registered.

---

[3] Usually this is in the form of an S-3 registration statement. This is a "short form" registration statement that requires the least amount of information and is the least costly, but will nonetheless serve the purpose of registering the PIPE securities for public resale. See Mark Anson, "Playing the PIPES: The Benefits and Risks of Private Investments in Public Entities," *The Journal of Private Equity* (2001).

As an example of a PIPE sale of convertible debt, consider the case of Internet Pictures Corporation (ticker IPIX), a Tennessee-based company that provides Internet-based imaging used in e-commerce, communications, and entertainment. iPIX allows Internet users to receive a 360 degree view of a building site, a home, or a device listed on a web page.

iPIX had previously received $200 million of venture and public financing. Unfortunately, the company reported a loss of $17.1 million for the first quarter of 2001, and its share price declined from a post IPO high of $45.00 to $0.40 in April 2001.

In May 2001, iPIX entered into a PIPE transaction with Paradigm Capital Partners and the Memphis Angels, two investment groups best known for early stage venture financing. The two groups provided iPIX with $10 million in exchange for convertible notes that could be exercised for up to 60 million of common stock at a price of $0.25 (for 52 million shares) and $0.50 (for the remaining 8 million shares). This financing was part of a two-tranche plan with an additional $20 million of convertible preferred stock to be issued later with a conversion price of $0.25 for common shares.

Last, as an example of preferred shares issues through a PIPE, consider Net2000 Communications (ticker NTKK), a provider of broadband telecommunications services with operations in over 20 markets. On March 29, 2001 Net2000 entered into an agreement to issue 65,000 of shares of series D convertible pay-in-kind preferred stock for $65 million. The private stock was issued to Boston Ventures, BancBoston Capital, The Carlyle Group, PNC Equity Management, and Nortel Networks. The preferred stock was convertible into 22 million shares of Net2000 common stock based on a conversion price of $2.955. On March 29, 2001, this represented a slight discount from the closing price of $3.00.

PIPE transactions are often presented to institutional investors in a term sheet format. Exhibit 3 presents a term sheet that reflects the deal points of the iPIX PIPE financing.

As the three examples above demonstrate, the most attractive feature of a PIPE transaction from an investor's point of view is the ability to buy the equity of a company at a discounted price. The less liquid the PIPE, the steeper the discount. The investor must bear the liquidity risk until the PIPE securities are either registered or converted.

However, not all PIPE transactions are priced at a discount. Consider Breakaway Solutions Inc. (ticker: BWAY), a Boston-based provider of consulting services for small companies. Breakaway is the only publicly traded company that focuses exclusively on companies that have market capitalizations below $500 million even though this segment of the market accounts for 53% of industry-wide expenditures on consulting services. As a result, Breakaway does not face a competitive bid on 60% of its contracts, and it is one of the fastest growing companies in the e-services industry.

In May 2000, Breakaway's dominant position in the e-services industry made it an attractive investment even though the company had just gone public a scant 8 months prior. Nonetheless, Putnam Investments approached Breakaway for a PIPE transaction. Putnam paid $26 a share for 1.5 million of private stock in Breakaway, well above the closing price of $22.50 at the time the deal was announced.[4]

Why Companies are Willing to Issue PIPEs

PIPEs are often offered at steep discounts to existing market prices for a company's stock. Yet companies are willing to distribute their stock at below market prices for several reasons.

First, new public companies generally have only a small percentage of outstanding public stock (the "float"). Insiders, venture capitalists, and other angel investors may still own a large portion of convertible preferred shares or restricted stock that has yet to be publicly registered. Consequently, the outstanding float may be in the range of 5% to 30%.

With such a small percentage of stock outstanding, issuing new public shares will only further dilute the public stock price of the company. Of the 1,262 companies that went public between 1998 and 2000, 152 of them (12%) are trading below $1.[5] Under these circumstances, a private placement of public equity can ensure that the additional stock stays out of the public market until the company has a better chance to implement its business strategy.

Exhibit 3: Term Sheet for the iPIX PIPE Transaction

Company	Internet Pictures Corporation
Financing Amount	$10 million Tranche A $20 million Tranche B
Securities	Tranche A: Convertible notes plus warrants Maturity = August 14, 2002 Tranche B: Series B Convertible Preferred Stock
Interest	Tranche A: 8% per year in cash or preferred stock at Investor's option. Payable at maturity of the note. Tranche B: 8% per year of the Original Issue Price ($20).
Conversion Terms	Tranche A: Convertible into common at $0.25 (for 52 million shares) and $0.50 (for 8 million shares). Tranche B: Convertible into common at $0.25 per share.
Floor	None
Floating or Adjustable Conversion	None
Warrants	Tranche A: 250,000 warrants to purchase Series B Preferred Stock at prices of $20 and $40 per share.
Registration	The company will file a registration statement with the SEC within 20 days of the closing of each tranche.

---

[4] See Stephen Lacey, "Breakaway Solutions Pipes to $39 Million," *IPO Reporter* (June 5, 2000). Unfortunately, by the end of the year, Breakaway's stock price had declined to less than $1.00.

[5] See Britt Tunick, "Equity Credit Lines Offer Cash for Companies in Need," *BuyOuts* (May 7, 2001).

Second, Wall Street analysts can be without mercy when a new technology company fails to achieve its sales or profit targets. When this happens, the public stock of a new company can be hammered. PIPEs can provide a form of financing that will not react violently to performance numbers that do not live up to the ambitious forecasts of Wall Street analysts.

Third, the new company decides to whom it will sell its shares. This is in contrast to a public offering, where the company cannot control to whom its shares are distributed.

Fourth, public offerings of stocks are expensive. They require expensive banking fees, and doing a road show for investors. It has been documented that the average cost for an IPO is 11% of the proceeds, while the average cost for a secondary offering is 7.1% of the total proceeds.[6]

Additionally, private placements can occur much more quickly than a public offering. A private placement usually takes a few weeks to complete while a public offering may take several months. The difference in this timing can be crucial for a company that is burning through cash quickly or needs the money in the near term for an acquisition or other time-intensive project.

Finally, the market for initial and secondary public offerings has cooled quite a bit from early 2000. For example, in the first quarter of 2000 there were 185 IPOs of new stock, while in the first quarter of 2001 there were only 17 IPOs. Consequently, the market for public offerings has dried up considerably.

For these reasons, it is to the advantage of a new company to find a long-term equity partner, an investor who is willing to hold on to the company's stock as the company asserts itself in the marketplace. This investor/partner may be willing to purchase the stock of the company in a private transaction. The trade off for the company is that it must sell its stock at a discount to the market price.

The Size of the PIPEs Market

It is not surprising that with a slowing economy, PIPE transactions have declined in 2001. In the first quarter of 2001, $2.5 billion was invested in 184 PIPE transactions with public companies. This amount was a sharp decline from $8.4 billion invested with 385 PIPE transactions in the first quarter of 2000. Still, the number of PIPE transactions in the first quarter of 2001 exceeded those of IPOs (17) and secondary offering of public stock (65).[7]

PIPEs fall into two broad categories, traditional PIPEs and structured PIPEs. Traditional PIPEs are straightforward private purchases of commons equity and preferred stock with a fixed conversion into common shares. Structured PIPEs include the more exotic investments such as floating convertibles, reset convertibles, common stock with resets, and convertible preferred stock with resets.

[6] See Michael McDonough, "Death in One Act: The Case for Company Registration," *Pepperdine Law Review*, vol. 24 (1997), pp. 563–647.
[7] "PIPE Market Outpaces IPO and Secondary Markets in First Quarter; PIPEs Continue as the Primary Source of Equity Financing for Public Companies," *Business Wire* (April 4, 2001).

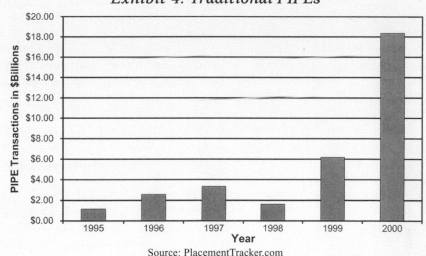

Exhibit 4: Traditional PIPEs

Source: PlacementTracker.com

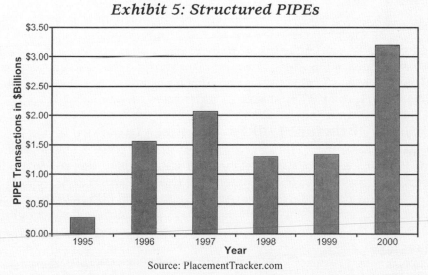

Exhibit 5: Structured PIPEs

Source: PlacementTracker.com

Exhibit 4 presents the growth in traditional PIPE transactions since 1995. As can be seen, the market for PIPEs has grown significantly over this 6-year period. Not surprisingly, the issuance of traditional PIPEs peaked in 2000. As noted above, the pace of PIPE transactions in the first quarter of 2001 has declined significantly from the first quarter of 2000.

Exhibit 5 presents the growth in structured PIPE transactions. Similar to traditional PIPEs, structured PIPE transactions peaked in 2000, but have declined in 2001.

Equity Lines of Credit

A variation on a PIPE transaction is an Equity Line of Credit (ELC). With an ELC, a company receives an established line of financing that it repays by issuing stock.

Consider the recent example of Igen International (ticker IGEN), a biotechnology company. Igen was short on cash, and was involved in an expensive lawsuit with another pharmaceutical company. Furthermore, with a depressed market for biotechnology stocks, a secondary public offering was not a favorable option.

Instead, Igen turned to a New York investment fund called Acqua Wellington, established in 1999 by a group of former bankers to offer equity lines of credit to new companies in return for discounted shares of a company's stock. Acqua Wellington has invested about $1.6 billion in 32 companies with plans to invest an additional $1.3 billion.[8]

Acqua agreed to purchase up to $60 million of Igen's stock in a private investment. In February 2001, Igen drew $9.5 million on this ELC in exchange for issuing 789,075 shares of its common stock, priced at about $12.04 per share. Compared to an average price of $14.27 in February 2001 for Igen's stock, this was a 15.6% discount. In addition, Igen has the option of drawing on another $50.5 million from Acqua Wellington over a 28-month period in exchange for further common shares.

ELCs are popular for several reasons. First, the issuing company holds the option on when to tap into the line of credit to issue more shares. Second, like a traditional PIPE, an equity line of credit does not dilute the share price of the company's outstanding stock. Last, repayment of the line of credit does not deplete the company's cash reserves because it is repaid with new shares. In return for the ELC, the company must issue its shares below the current market price.

Structured PIPEs: The Risks Involved

Despite the popularity of PIPEs, they have been severely criticized by the media.[9] Many PIPE transactions are structured with a "floating" conversion rate so that the amount of common shares that an investor will receive increases as the stock price of the company declines. As a result, critics contend that PIPE transactions can become "death spirals" since a company's stock price often drops after a PIPE financing. As the stock price drops, the company must commit to issue more and more equity to keep up with the floating conversion rate. This can result in massive dilution, driving a company's stock price down even further into a "death spiral."

These structured PIPE transactions are often referred to as "toxic" PIPEs because they are potentially poisonous to a company's financial health. Unscrupulous investors can take advantage of a company through a structured PIPE deal. A toxic PIPE works as follows:

---

[8] See Tunick, "Equity Credit Lines Offer Cash for Companies in Need."
[9] See Andrew Pollack, "A Lifeline, with Conditions," The *New York Times* (May 10, 2001); Steve Bergsman, "Toxic Cash-Burn Solutions," *CFO* (December 2000); and, Cynthia L. Webb, "Help Comes with a High Price: Distressed Firms Agree to Extraordinary Terms, Even at the Risk of Depressing Stock Prices," The *Washington Post* (April 16, 2001).

1. A young company goes public before it has a chance to fully establish its business strategy.
2. The company quickly burns through its IPO cash and needs more capital to survive.
3. With no profitability in sight, the public markets are closed to the new company.
4. Private equity investors agree to provide more cash in return for private securities that can be converted to common stock at a floating conversion rate, and at a steep discount to the company's current stock price.
5. The private equity investors short the stock of the company, driving its price downward.
6. The downward pressure on the company's outstanding stock triggers larger and larger conversion ratios resulting in greater and greater dilution of the company's stock.
7. The company must convert the private investors' private securities into common stock at a high conversion ratio and at a discount to the current market price. This dilution drives the company's public stock price down even further.
8. The private investors cover their shorts with the newly issued common stock and reap a bonanza. Alternatively, the private investors hold on to their stock, having converted enough so that they have gained control of the company.

Sound improbable? At least one company has sued its investors claiming that they hatched just such a scheme. Log On America Inc., a provider of high-speed Internet access, accused three firms of manipulating its stock price through short sales in an attempt to seize control of the company.

In a lawsuit filed in the U.S. District Court in New York City in August 2000, Log On alleged that three investment firms drove down its stock price so that they could convert preferred shares they held into more common shares. The lawsuit contended that the firms planned to acquire enough shares to take control of the company.[10]

In February 2000, Log On issued $15 million of convertible preferred shares to Promethean Asset Management LLC of New York, Citadel Limited Partnership of Chicago, and Marshall Capital Management Inc., a unit of Credit Suisse First Boston. The securities were structured so that they were convertible into more shares of common stock if the price of Log On's common stock declined. According to the lawsuit, the decline in Log On's stock was sufficient to result in the conversion of the preferred stock into 8 million shares of common stock, equal to roughly 50% of the company's equity. The lawsuit is still outstanding.[11]

---

[10] See Webb, "Help Comes with a High Price."

[11] At least one regulatory entity is reviewing the toxic effects of structural PIPES. For more details, see Mark Anson, "Playing the PIPES: The Benefits and Risks of Private Investments in Public Entities."

Not all structured PIPE deals result in the death of the company. As an example of a PIPE workout, consider the example of MicroStrategy, Inc. In June 2000, its secondary stock offering had fallen apart, and it was looking for another avenue of financing. A $125 million PIPE transaction was put together by Promethean Asset Management LLC, Citadel Investment Group LLC, and Angelo, Gordon & Co.[12]

The three investment groups purchased Series A preferred stock in MicroStrategy that was convertible into common shares. The conversion price of the common stock was based on the weighted average of shares over a 17-day trading period following the close of the deal in June 2000, about $33 a share. However, on the one-year anniversary of the PIPE transaction, the conversion rate could be reset based on the average price of the stock during a 10-day period in June 2001.

The more MicroStrategy's stock price fell, the more stock the three investment groups would receive. By April 3, 2001, MicroStrategy's stock price was trading at $1.75 a share and the conversion rate threatened to severely dilute existing shareholder's stake in the company. In order to avoid this dilution meltdown, MicroStrategy and the three investors restructured the PIPE deal to provide the company with a combination of common stock, cash, and a fixed-conversion rate senior security.

Summary of PIPEs

PIPEs have become an extremely popular form of equity financing for new and existing companies. However, while the benefits are many for the company, the risks can be extreme. Despite the publicity of toxic PIPEs, the great majority of PIPE transactions are not structured. They are straightforward private investments in a fixed amount of public equity. Furthermore, the publicity of toxic PIPEs and death spirals has resulted in three safeguards in the PIPE industry.

First, many PIPEs are now issued with a fixed conversion ratio, instead of a floating ratio. Second, for those PIPE transactions that contain a floating conversion ratio, a floor provision is usually included. This provision restricts the investor from converting into common shares below a certain price or above a certain conversion ratio. Last, more PIPE transactions are restricting investors from shorting the issuing company's public stock. The inability to short prevents investors from placing downward pressure on the company's outstanding stock price and initiating a death spiral.

PIPEs are an alternative investment strategy for private equity investors, hedge funds, and even traditional money management shops. With private equity deals becoming harder to find, the search for new sources of alternative returns has increased. Also, hedge funds have entered the game in search of new sources of return. Exhibit 6a provides a table of the top ten investors (as of June 29, 2001) in traditional PIPE transactions. As can be seen traditional money managers, hedge funds, and even pension funds invest in these securities. Exhibit 6b indicates the top ten investors in structured PIPEs. Here we see private equity investors as well as hedge fund managers as the primary purchasers. It is expected that

---

[12] See Webb, "Help Comes with a High Price."

this trend will continue as buyout firms, venture capital firms, hedge funds, and traditional investors seek new ways to put their investors' capital to work.

INTERVAL FUNDS

Interval funds are a retail entrée into the world of private equity. Previously, private equity investing was reserved for institutional investors and high net worth individuals. Interval funds operate somewhere between closed-end mutual funds and open-end mutual funds.

Interval funds resemble open-end mutual funds in that shares in the interval fund are offered continuously. Interval funds may also add on distribution fees, similar to marketing and distribution fees that open-end mutual funds are allowed to charge under Rule 12b-1 of the Investment Company Act of 1940. In addition, interval funds may also offer different classes of shares just like an open-end mutual fund.

Yet, like closed end mutual funds, they do not provide daily liquidity to investors. Closed-end mutual funds offer their shares to the public only once, at an initial public offering. There are no redemption rights in a closed-end fund. After the IPO, the fund is closed to new investors and investors may only buy and sell their shares in the fund via trading on a stock exchange.

Exhibit 6a: Top 10 Traditional PIPE Investors

Investment Manager	$ Invested In PIPEs
Janus Capital Corporation	$1,581,560,000
Putnam Investment Management	$484,372,868
Microsoft Corp.	$360,555,200
GE Capital Corporation	$360,500,025
Franklin Templeton Group	$283,936,749
Pequot Capital Management	$251,005,717
Soros Fund Management	$246,606,996
State of Wisconsin Investment Board	$217,632,998
E.M Warburg, Pincus & Co.	$205,295,924

Source: PlacementTracker.com

Exhibit 6b: Top 10 Structured PIPE Investors

Investment Manager	$ Invested in PIPEs
Rose Glen Capital Management	$654,293,575
Citadel Investment Group	$525,113,025
Angelo, Gordon & Co., L.P.	$394,122,161
Palladin Group	$342,963,366
Elliott Management Corporation	$298,346,291
Genesee Investments	$289,404,565
Promethean Asset Management	$257,858,657
Rhino Advisors	$247,011,706
Heights Capital Management	$222,636,002
Castle Creek Partners	$205,336,233

Source: PlacementTracker.com

They key distinction between interval funds, closed-end funds, and open-end funds is the timing of redemption rights. Interval funds may offer their shareholders redemption rights only at specified intervals (hence their name). Therefore, unlike an open-end mutual fund, redemption rights in an interval fund are not continuous. Further, unlike closed-end mutual funds, interval funds offer their shareholders periodic redemption rights.

In this section, we provide a brief history of the regulatory development of the interval fund. We then review the growth of the interval fund marketplace. Last, we consider their application to private equity and provide some examples of recent interval funds.

Open-End and Closed-End Mutual Funds

The retail mutual fund industry is regulated by the Securities and Exchange Commission (SEC) under the Investment Company Act of 1940 (the Company Act). Under the Company Act, mutual funds are referred to as "investment companies" and are classified into two broad groups: open-end companies and closed-end companies. Both types of companies offer their shares to retail investors through a public offering that must be registered with the SEC. However, there are numerous differences.

An open-end investment company generally bears more management and administrative burdens than a closed-end fund because it offers its shares on a continuous basis.[13] Under Section 5(a)(1) of the Company Act, an open-end mutual fund is one that is offering for sale or has outstanding any "redeemable security" of which it is the issuer.

A redeemable security means any security (other than short-term paper) under the terms of which the holder is entitled to receive approximately his proportionate share of the issuer's current net assets or the cash equivalent of his share of the net assets. This means that an open-end mutual fund must offer its shareholders daily liquidity equal to the cash value of each share's net asset value. Consequently, the fund's manager must adjust her investment strategy to cope with unexpected cash inflows and outflows. Usually, open-end mutual funds maintain a certain amount of cash to fund redemptions. Last, an open-end mutual fund cannot invest more than 15% of its total assets in illiquid investments (i.e., assets that are not readily marketable within seven days).

Under Section 5(a)(2) of the Company Act, a closed-end mutual fund is any investment company other than an open-end mutual fund. A closed-end fund generally makes only one offering of its shares. Since it does not need to worry about cash inflows or outflows, it can remain fully invested, holding cash balances only when it cannot find sufficient investment opportunities. A close-end fund can

---

[13] Because an open-end mutual fund offers its shares on a continuous basis, it must file annually an amendment to its original registration statement (called a "post-effective amendment") to keep its initial registration statement current. Closed-end mutual funds need only file an initial registration statement, no post-effective amendments are required. See Mark Anson, "Interval Funds: Retail Investing Comes to Private Equity," *The Journal of Investing* (2001).

also invest in less liquid assets without the 15% limitation that is imposed on open-end funds. However, there is a drawback for investors. After the initial public offering, the shares of closed-end funds often trade at a discount from their net asset value.[14] This discount may reflect the close-end fund's investment is less liquid securities, or the inability to tender shares back to the mutual fund issuer.

Interval funds were created in 1992 when the SEC decided to provide some relief from the discounts suffered by many closed-end mutual funds. The SEC implemented Rule 23c-3 to permit closed-end funds to have a policy of making periodic redemptions. The rule is intended to facilitate investment in less liquid securities, and to minimize market discounting of closed-end company shares. Interval funds, therefore, are classified as closed-end funds under the Company Act.

Exhibit 7 demonstrates the differences between closed-end mutual funds, open-end mutual funds, and interval funds.

Exhibit 7: Closed-End, Open-End, and Interval Mutual Funds

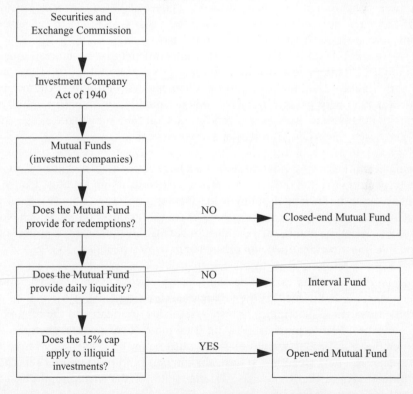

---

[14] If a closed-end company's shares trade in the secondary markets at a discount to net asset value, the mutual fund may be restricted in offering additional shares through a second public offering. This is because Section 23(b) of the Company Act prohibits closed-end companies from selling shares at a discount to net asset value.

Requirements of Rule 23c-3

Rule 23c-3 is known as a "safe harbor" under the securities laws. This means that if a regulated entity fulfills the requirements of the rule it will be exempted from certain provisions of the securities laws. The key exemption under Rule 23c-3 is that if a mutual fund follows all of the requirements of the rule, it shall not be deemed by the SEC to be a mutual fund that issues "redeemable securities." This is important because it means that the fund will be classified as a closed-end fund and therefore, will not be subject to the 15% limitation on investments in illiquid securities. However, there are several requirements to the rule.

1. *Redemption Policy.* An interval fund may only redeem its outstanding shares at intervals specified by Rule 23c-3. Redemptions are considered "Repurchase Offers" by the interval fund and may not be less than 5% of the outstanding shares nor more than 25% of the outstanding shares at any interval date. If the interval fund's shareholders tender more than the repurchase offer amount, the fund may repurchase an additional amount of stock not to exceed 2% of the stock outstanding. If there are more shares tendered than the fund is prepared to redeem, the fund must repurchase its shares on a pro rata basis.

Under Rule 23c-3, the redemption intervals may be no more frequently than quarterly. This is very different from an open-end mutual fund that must offer daily liquidity, and a closed-end fund that offers no liquidity. Alternatively, an interval fund may offer redemptions semi-annually, or annually. Finally, in addition to the interval repurchase offers, an interval fund may make a discretionary repurchase offer without limitation every two years.

2. *Fundamental Policy.* An interval fund must have a "fundamental policy" of providing redemption rights only at intervals specified in its prospectus. Under the Company Act, a fundamental policy is an operating policy of a mutual fund that may only be changed upon a majority vote of the shares outstanding, which would normally occur at the annual shareholders' meeting. All fundamental policies of a mutual fund must be identified and explained in its prospectus.

3. *Redemption Price.* Shares must be repurchased for cash at the net asset value of the interval fund determined on the "Repurchase Pricing Date" which is the date that the interval fund determines the net asset value applicable to the repurchase of its securities. The Repurchase Pricing Date must occur no later than the 14th day after the deadline by which investors must submit a repurchase request (a "Repurchase Request Deadline"). Last, the interval fund must pay its shareholders within 7 days of the Repurchase Pricing Date for the shares repurchased (a "Repurchase Payment Deadline").

4. *Fees.* Share repurchases are costly. There are transaction costs, bookkeeping costs, and administrative costs. Consequently, under Rule 23c-3, the interval fund

may deduct from the repurchase proceeds a repurchase fee not to exceed 2% of the proceeds for expenses directly related to the repurchase.

5. *Notification*. An interval fund must provide notice to its shareholders of its intention to repurchase shares. The notice must be made no less than 21 days and no more than 42 days before each Repurchase Request Deadline. The notification must indicate the number of shares that the interval fund is offering to repurchase as well as any fees that will be charged by the interval fund. In addition, the interval fund must file three copies of a "Notification of Repurchase Offer" (Form N-23c-3) with the SEC three business days after sending notification of the repurchase to its shareholders.

6. *Cancellation of the Repurchase*. A periodic repurchase offer may only be suspended by a vote of a majority of the interval fund's directors.

In summary, there are several regulatory hoops that an interval fund must jump through to abide by the requirements of Rule 23c-3. However, these hoops are not overly burdensome, and reasonable to apply. As a result, interval funds have grown significantly.

The Growth of Interval Funds

Since their introduction in 1992 with the promulgation of Rule 23c-3, interval funds have grown increasingly popular. They have grown from one fund in 1992 to 33 funds by the end of 1999. In 1999, 16 new interval funds were introduced. Assets under management have grown from $4 billion in 1992 to $28 billion in 1999.[15]

The popularity of interval funds stems from several factors. First, from an investor viewpoint, retail investors ("moms and pops") can invest in interval funds with the assurance of periodic liquidity. In addition, retail investors can obtain exposure to private equity investing that has been the traditional purview of institutional investors.

Second, from an interval fund's point of view, this investment format is preferred because the fund is not limited by the 15% cap on illiquid investments that is applied to open-end mutual funds. Therefore, they are ideal investment vehicles for the long-term investment horizon associated with private equity. In addition, an interval fund can continuously offer new shares to the investing public. Consequently, it has the ability to raise additional capital if new investment opportunities present themselves. Furthermore, an interval fund can charge 12b-1 fees (distribution fees) to its shareholders. In contrast, closed-end funds cannot charge distribution fees. Last, they do not need to offer daily liquidity like open-end mutual fund companies.

Third, as a registered investment company with the SEC, an interval fund is not subject to the 100 investor limitation that applies to a private equity invest-

---

[15] See Lori Pizani, "Interval Funds Gain Wider Acceptance," *Mutual Fund Market News* (January 24, 2000).

ment partnership that relies on Section 3(c)(1) of the Company Act. Interests in a Section 3(c)(1) fund must be sold in a private offering to no more than 100 beneficial owners. Additionally, registration with the SEC also avoids the requirements applicable to an investment partnership that relies on Section 3(c)(7) of the Company Act. Interests in a Section 3(c)(7) fund may only be sold to "qualified investors" — generally, institutional investors and entities that have investments of not less than $25 million and individual investors having investments of not less than $5 million.

Finally, interval funds typically charge management fees that are large for mutual funds, in the 2% to 3% range compared to the 50 basis point to 1% management fee charged by most retail mutual funds. Also, an interval fund may charge a performance fee similar to that of a private equity limited partnership fund. However, performance fees apply only if the fund sells its shares to "qualified clients" — those investors with a net worth exceeding $1.5 million or with assets currently with the fund manager of at least $750,000.

Examples of Private Equity Interval Funds

Initially, many interval funds were used for less liquid investments such as bank loans and other less marketable debt obligations. However, with the surge in private equity investing in the latter part of the 1990s, it was not long before the advantages of interval funds became apparent to private equity. In fact, many recent interval funds have been introduced for private equity investing. Consider the following examples.

Orbitex Life Sciences and Biotechnology Fund

This fund was launched on October 2, 2000 to invest in biotechnology companies. The fund intends to invest up to 25% to 30% of its assets in privately held, pre-IPO companies. This is consistent with the fact that about two-thirds of the biotechnology companies are privately held. In addition, the fund has the authority to sell short the stock of underperforming biotechnology companies.

The fund requires a $25,000 minimum investment and carries a 4% sales load. The fund charges a management fee of 2.75% and is offered at $26 a share. Redemptions will be made quarterly, and the fund will only purchase 5% of its outstanding shares in any given quarter.

Munder Capital @Vantage Fund

This fund closed its initial offering of shares on October 12, 2000. At that time, it had raised $200 million. The fund invests in internet and technology companies, and it may invest up to 40% of its assets in private or pre-IPO companies.

The fund requires a $10,000 minimum investment and charges a 4% sales charge. In addition, the fund charges a 3% annual management fee. Its redemption policy is 5% of the shares outstanding once every calendar quarter.

Exhibit 8: Recent Interval Funds

Fund	Investment Focus	Minimum Investment	Fees	Liquidity
Orbitex Life Sciences & Biotech	Biotechnology and Genomics, 30% in private equity	$25,000	4% sales charge and 2.75% annual fee	Up to 5% of outstanding shares once a quarter
Munder @Vantage	Internet and technology, 40% in private equity	$10,000	4% sales charge and 3% annual fee	Up to 5% of outstanding shares once a quarter
Seligman New Technologies	Technology, 35% to 100% in private equity	$10,000	3% sales charge and 3% annual expense ratio	Up to 5% of outstanding shares once a quarter

Seligman New Technologies Fund

This was one of the first interval funds formed to invest in private equity. This fund closed its initial public offering in 1999 after raising $580 million. The fund invests primarily in U.S. based technology companies. Seligman promoted the fund with the concept that 35% of its assets would be invested in the private equity of technology companies with the other 65% of its assets in the public equity of technology companies. However, the fund has the flexibility to increase the private equity component to as much as 100% of net assets.

The minimum investment was $10,000 with a 3% sales charge. In addition, the fund has an annual expense ratio of 3%. Its redemption policy is 5% of the outstanding shares on a quarterly basis.

Exhibit 8 summarizes the terms of these private equity interval funds.

Summary of Interval Funds

Interval funds provide a format for bringing private equity investing to the retail market. Previously, the private equity market was the domain of institutional investors and high net worth investors. In addition, investment advisers that had previously managed open-end mutual funds that invested only in public equity securities may now enter the venture capital investment arena.

Interval funds, however, will not replace traditional venture capitalists. The reason is that interval funds rarely invest in the early rounds of venture capital for start-up companies. Instead, they invest primarily in late stage private equity offerings, often the last stage of private equity before an IPO. This is usually the third or fourth round of venture capital financing. Occasionally, interval funds will also provide mezzanine financing.

As a last example, consider the Seligman New Technologies Fund. It has participated in several late stage tranches of venture capital. These private equity offerings include the $63 million offering of Series C preferred stock in Global Commerce Systems, Inc., the $22 million offering of Series C preferred stock of Technies.com, the $62.4 million offering of Series C preferred stock of OurHouse.com, and the $56.5 million of mezzanine financing for NeuVis.

Late stage investing also allows mutual fund companies to get in the door of hot technology companies before they go public. Often the stock of a new technology company skyrockets after its IPO making the company too expensive for mutual fund managers to purchase.

Finally, interval funds provide a valuable service in the life cycle of start-up companies because they funnel a new source of financing to the venture capital market: retail investors. Although retail investors may commit smaller increments of capital, collectively they constitute quite a force; the retail mutual fund market in the United States has over $5 trillion in assets.

PRIVATE EQUITY INVESTMENTS IN PRIVATE EQUITY

We conclude this chapter with a brief discussion of the most recent phenomenon in the private equity world: private equity investments in private equity investment firms.

For years, endowments, foundations, pension funds, and high net worth individuals have been placing their money in the trust of private equity managers. These managers then invest their clients' monies in venture capital deals, leveraged buyouts, mezzanine financing, and distressed debt. In return, the private equity managers receive both a management fee and a share of any profits.

The revenue stream derived from private equity management and incentive fees can be quite lucrative. An investment in this revenue stream can be just as profitable as the underlying investments made by the private equity investment manager.

An Example of Private Equity Investing in Private Equity Firms

In February 2001, the California Public Employees' Retirement System (CalPERS), the largest U.S. public pension fund, agreed to purchase an equity stake in the Carlyle Group Inc., one of the largest private equity investment firms in the world. The Carlyle Group is associated with many former politicians. For example, former Defense Secretary Frank Carlucci is its chairman and former Secretary of State James Baker is an adviser. Its managing partner, David Rubinstein, was a former aide in the Carter Administration.

The Carlyle Group's first fund, formed in 1990, has returned about 31% annually. In December 2000, the firm raised it largest buyout fund, totaling $3.8 billion to focus on buyouts in telecommunications and other federally regulated industries.

CalPERS paid $175 million for a 5% equity stake in the Carlyle Group. In addition, CalPERS agreed to invest up to $850 million in various Carlyle funds. The Carlyle Group decided to sell an equity stake to recapitalize the company after rapid growth and to provide capital after the firm repurchased a 10% equity stake owned by the Mellon family.

For CalPERS, not only does it get professional private equity investment management, it also gets a piece of the action. In addition, as a result of its private equity stake, it may consider this investment as a way to get a rebate on the fees it pays to The Carlyle Group.

Like all private equity investments, the best exit strategy is a public offering. An IPO for Carlyle might be possible in the future. In the meantime, the CalPERS' equity stake will appreciate as the value of the company's revenue stream grows.

CONCLUSION

The successful investing of private equity firms throughout most of the 1990s has attracted significant investor capital into the private equity markets. This flow of capital has three implications.

First, private equity managers will need to be creative to sustain the returns that they were able to generate in the recent past. This has led venture capital firms and LBO firms to consider alternative transactions such as crossover funds and PIPEs. The increased demand for private equity investments has led to the creation of new private equity products.

Second, the fees earned by private equity investors has attracted new investors into the market. Retail investment manager shops (mutual fund companies) have introduced interval funds to capture some of the return potential that has long been the domain of private equity firms. In addition, institutional investors have begun to consider equity stakes in private equity investment firms to capture some of the fee generation enjoyed by private equity firms.

Last, the dynamics of the private equity markets are changing rapidly. This change is necessary to keep up with the large flow of capital into the private equity markets.

Chapter 19

Performance Measurement for Private Equity

C hapters 14, 15, and 16 demonstrated that the past decade has resulted in tremendous growth for private equity investing. The commitment to private equity has grown in importance for both retail and institutional investors. However, very little has been produced regarding the pricing and benchmarking of private equity returns.

The private equity market is an example of a market where information is difficult to acquire. In the public equity markets, researchers often assume that the markets are efficient; that is, that there are no asymmetries of information among market participants. This assumption does not hold in the private equity market.

The problem becomes particularly acute in performance measurement. The benchmark chosen to measure the performance of a private equity manager is a key factor in assessment and allocation of capital to that manager. Additionally performance assessment is important for determining bonuses at endowments, pension funds, and foundations that are measured by the performance of their private equity portfolios.

In this chapter we present a method for measuring private equity performance relative to market indices. We begin by describing the problem of measuring private equity performance. We then examine the returns to private equity compared to several stock and bond indices to find an appropriate benchmark. This allows us to measure the excess risk-adjusted return earned by private equity managers. Last, we examine whether private equity portfolios are susceptible to stale or managed pricing, and attempt to determine which is the culprit.

THE PROBLEM

Part of the problem of performance measurement in the private equity arena is the structure of the marketplace. There are four main participants: issuers, intermediaries, investors, and information processors. The issuers generally share the trait of being locked out of the public markets. Private equity is generally one of the most expensive forms of capital financing (indeed see our discussion of PIPES in Chapter 18). Issuers of private equity are usually new and emerging firms that cannot raise money in the public markets.

The private nature of the securities offered requires intensive research to determine if they are priced fairly. There is no "semi-strong" form of market efficiency where security prices reflect all available public information.[1] Further, these instruments are closely held, so liquidity may not exist. For example, consider the case of CacheFlow Inc, a start up internet company that was mentioned in Chapter 14. Each series of preferred stock offered by this company was purchased by only one or two investors. There was virtually no market for Cache-Flow's securities outside of the venture capitalists that purchased the securities in the first place.

Consequently, private equity securities are thinly traded, if at all. Without a market for trading these securities, their value is often set by appraisal instead of an objective market price. The labor-intensive nature of valuing these securities makes the private equity arena a particularly inefficient market for pricing.

The pricing of private equity securities is further confounded by the intermediaries in this market. Approximately 80% of the capital committed to private equity is managed by intermediaries, limited partnerships that collect pools of investment capital. Each limited partnership is managed by a general partner, the private equity specialist.

The third group in the private equity arena is the investors, typically institutions and high net worth individuals. These investors commit their capital to an intermediary because they often lack the staff or expertise to make private equity investments directly. Typically, the general partner of the intermediary has broad discretion to invest the money as it sees fit.

The general partner of a private equity limited partnership has broad discretion not only to make investments, but also to determine their "fair value." Without publicly traded prices to determine fair value, most intermediaries have considerable flexibility to mark the value of the partnership's investment portfolio. Further, the general partner's incentive or profit sharing fees is dependent upon how the value of the partnership's portfolio changes. This has led one researcher to claim that many limited partnerships pursue "marketing supportive accounting," where the general partner is slow to mark down its portfolio positions to a reasonable estimate of fair value.[2]

Further, many general partners of private equity limited partnerships are reluctant to market their portfolio positions up or down until there is an objective market event that allows for re-pricing. This could be an additional round of private equity financing, an IPO, or a secondary trade of some of the securities in the

---

[1] The theory of efficient capital markets states that there are three forms of efficiency: weak, semi-strong, and strong. Weak market efficiency states that security prices reflect all past information. Semi-strong market efficiency states that security prices reflect all past and current publicly available information. Strong market efficiency states that security prices reflect all information, both private and public. It is generally believed that the public equity markets are semi-strong efficient; that is, the prices of publicly traded securities reflect all past and current public information regarding the underlying issuer.

[2] See Andrew Weisman, "The Dangers of Historical Hedge Fund Data," Nikko Securities International working paper, 2000.

over-the-counter market. However, an additional transaction may not happen for another 6 months or even for another year.

Companies that receive investment capital from private equity partnerships often remain privately held for many years after the investment has been made. These companies have no observable market price to present an objective value. Marking to market portfolio investments may not be possible. Consequently, many private equity firms maintain a conservative estimate of the value of their investments by keeping them at book value. Yet, this may not reflect the either the growth or decline of value of the private equity portfolio.

In sum, private equity limited partnerships hold various combinations of illiquid exchange-traded securities as well as privately issued, over-the-counter securities. The illiquid nature of these securities can lead to non-synchronous price changes given the movement of the overall stock market. For example, even publicly-traded securities in the small capitalization range of the stock market do not trade on a continuous basis.

The Capital Asset Pricing Model teaches us that the price of a security can be related to the amount of exposure it has to market risk. Market risk is the only risk that should be compensated because firm-specific risk can be diversified away through a portfolio approach to investing. However, the CAPM assumes that all securities are freely transferable, and this is not the case with private equity securities.

In the vernacular of investment management, private equity valuations suffer from "stale pricing." Stale pricing is the condition that the book value of private equity investments may not be "fresh" in the sense that it reflects current market value. Under the CAPM, fresh prices may be obtained monthly, weekly, and even daily, by observing how security prices react to concurrent movements in the broader stock market.

However, stale pricing will not necessarily react concurrently with a broad market index. Private equity prices may lag that of a readily observable benchmark. If this is the case, stale pricing can reduce estimates of volatility and correlation to broad-based securities indices.

Alternatively, it might be the case that private equity valuations suffer not from stale pricing, but from "managed pricing." Private equity managers have considerable discretion to mark the value of their portfolios. Consequently, they might "manage" their portfolio valuations, by pricing when it is convenient and profitable to do so. Managed pricing may also lead to a lag time between observable public market valuations and those in a private equity portfolio.

Last, we note in brief, that the proliferation of the fourth category of participants in the private equity market, information processors, has grown in an attempt to address these problems. Information processors come in the form of agents, consultants, gatekeepers, and advisers. They exist to reduce the problems of information asymmetry that are common to the private equity marketplace. Part of their respective jobs is to try to filter through the performance results of the limited partnership private equity funds to determine how stale the pricing might be.

There are two other potential problems with pricing private equity portfolios. First, one researcher has indicated that the flow of funds into venture capital limited partnerships may create an environment where too much money is chasing too few deals resulting in inflated private equity valuations.[3] However, this problem is not peculiar to the private equity market; it exists in the public equity markets, too. For instance, see Exhibit 3 in Chapter 14 which demonstrates the "too much money" phenomenon with respect to the prices of publicly traded securities in the NASDAQ market.

Second, private equity limited partnerships that are in the process of fund raising tend to be aggressive in the pricing of their portfolios. These funds may neglect to mark down portfolio values that are underwater and may value still private companies above cost.[4] This problem is peculiar to the private equity industry, and it may contribute to the managed pricing problem. In our next section we discuss some possible solutions to these problems.

PRIOR EFFORTS TO MEASURE
PRIVATE EQUITY PERFORMANCE

Some progress has been made to resolve the problems identified above. Industry groups have been formed to address the problem of stale or managed pricing. In addition, there have been efforts to mark-to-market private equity portfolios. Both of these methods have merit.

For example, the Institutional Limited Partners Association, the not-for-profit industry group that represents the interests of institutional investors in private equity partnerships, has attempted to establish reporting standards.[5] In addition, the British Venture Capital Association has introduced a set of valuation standards that its members must follow.[6] Nonetheless, these attempts to establish standard valuation practices still provide considerable flexibility to the private equity fund managers. For example, there is no clear distinction between early and late stage financing or the private equity firms that pursue these strategies. In sum, considerable discretion remains with the general partners of private equity funds to determine the valuations of their portfolios.

Further, the established guidelines generally emphasize the principle of *conservatism*. That is, private equity portfolios should not be marked to market

---

[3] See Paul Gompers and Josh Lerner, "Money Chasing Deals? The Impact of Fund Inflows on the Valuation of Private Equity Investments," *The Journal of Financial Economics* (2000).

[4] See Paul Gompers, "Grandstanding in the Venture Capital Industry," *The Journal of Financial Economics* (1996).

[5] See Institutional Limited Partners Association, "Proposal for a Standard Industry-Wide System for Measuring Interim Performance of Venture Capital Partnerships" (May 1990).

[6] See British Venture Capital Association, "Guidelines for the Valuation and Disclosure of Venture Capital Portfolios" (1993).

until an observable event (such as a new round of financing) that provides an objective valuation point. While these procedures might make the returns across different private equity funds more comparable, they make it more difficult to compare the returns to private equity to other asset classes. This means that private equity funds can demonstrate that they have outperformed their peers in the private equity marketplace, but they may not be able to demonstrate that they have outperformed the broader equity or (in the case of mezzanine or distressed debt) bond markets.

Another tenet of the principle of conservatism is to mark portfolio values down quickly and up slowly. That is, losses should be recognized as soon as they can be reasonably estimated. Conversely, gains should be recognized less quickly, only when they are assured.

Another solution to the problem of stale or managed prices is to mark to market each investment in a private equity portfolio on a periodic basis. This proposal does not wait until there is an observable and objective event such as an IPO. Instead, it reevaluates all holdings in the portfolio on a periodic basis (typically, quarterly) in an attempt to determine fair value.

This proposed solution is very time intensive, but it can produce reasonable results. Gompers and Lerner apply this approach to examine the returns from a single private equity group, the E.M. Warburg, Pincus & Co. private equity portfolio.[7] First, they use a single period CAPM regression model where the returns to the Warburg Pincus portfolio are measured against the returns to the public stock market. A single period model simply means that the current returns to the Warburg Pincus portfolio were regressed against the current returns to the publicly traded stock market.

In a CAPM regression model, the idea is to determine what amount of variation in the dependent variable (the Warburg Pincus private equity portfolio) that is determined by the variation in the independent variable (the stock market return). The important measure of performance is the constant term, or intercept, in the regression equation. This term represents the excess return earned by the private equity portfolio over and above that of the general stock market return. In other words, when the effects of the stock market have been controlled for, the residual return represented by the intercept determines whether the market-adjusted return earned by private equity is superior to or inferior to the performance of the broad stock market.

In their first regression, Gompers and Lerner find that the intercept is equal to 2.68% per quarter. This indicates that private equity can earn an excess return of 2.68% per quarter on a risk-adjusted basis.[8] They also find an R^2 of 0.28.

---

[7] See Paul Gompers and Josh Lerner, "The Challenge of Performance Assessment," *The Journal of Private Equity* (1997).

[8] However, it does not appear that Gompers and Lerner subtracted the cash rate of return from the excess return. If not, a Treasury bill return should be subtracted from the excess return to determine the true size of the private equity manager's alpha. Also, Gompers and Lerner do not distinguish between different types of private equity such as venture capital, leveraged buyouts, etc.

In their second regression, they use the same single period CAPM model, but they mark to market the private equity portfolio of Warburg Pincus. Mark to market is accomplished by taking every company in the Warburg Pincus portfolio and assigning it to a three-digit Securities Industry Classification. For each industry, Gompers and Lerner calculated an equal-weighted industry index from the public market values of firms in the same industry. They then adjust the portfolio investments by the change of value of the matched industry public market index.

They find the explanatory power of the single period CAPM regression increases when private equity investments are marked to market. The R^2 of the new equation increased to 0.492. Also, the intercept term declined to 1.97%. That is, once the private equity portfolio is marked to market, the excess return earned on the risk-adjusted portfolio is 1.97% per quarter, or about 8% per year.

A FRAMEWORK FOR MEASURING PRIVATE EQUITY PERFORMANCE

In this section we propose two methods by which to measure private equity performance. First, we describe how to adjust private equity investments for their exposure to market risk. We then consider several different benchmarks for each class of private equity.

Adjusting Private Equity Returns for Market Exposure

In Chapter 6, and again in Chapter 18 we demonstrated that private equity investments have the greatest exposure to market risk. Exhibit 1 in Chapter 18 demonstrates that private equity investments extend the furthest along the scale of market risk exposure. The reasons are now obvious: long holding periods, new companies subject to the whims of the economy, the lack of a well-developed secondary trading market, and nascent business plans that take time to come to fruition.

Given the large exposure to market risk that private equity investments provide, it is reasonable to ask if private equity funds are adding any value beyond the returns they receive from their market exposure. Essentially, private equity managers provide a package of returns that contains two essential ingredients: (1) the return earned for exposure to market risk; and (2) the private equity manager's active skill.[9]

The problem most investors face is separating the return due to market exposure from that earned from the private equity manager's skill. The solution most often pursued is to regress the historical returns from private equity investments on the concurrent returns of a broad based market index such as the Nasdaq or the Russell 1000. A broad market index is used as a proxy for market risk. In

---

[9] A similar claim can be made for those hedge funds that are exposed to market exposure such as those demonstrated in Exhibit 2 in Chapter 6.

this regression analysis, the return to the private equity investment is the dependent variable, and the return to the market index is the independent variable. The regression equation typically takes the form of:

$$R_{i,t}(\text{PE}) = \alpha + \beta R_{m,t} + \varepsilon_{i,t} \tag{1}$$

where

> $R_{i,t}(\text{PE})$ is the return to private equity investments at time t
> $R_{m,t}$ is the return on a broad-based market index at time t
> β is a measure of the systematic exposure of private equity returns to the broad-based market index
> $\varepsilon_{i,t}$ is a residual term which measures the variation of private equity returns that are not explained by movements in the broad-based market index or the private equity manager's skill
> α is the return due to the private equity manager's skill

This is a simple one-factor (the broad market return) regression model.[10] Equation (1) can be turned around to produce:

$$R_{i,t}(\text{PE}) - \beta R_{m,t} = \alpha + \varepsilon_{i,t} \tag{2}$$

Equation (2) is the risk-adjusted formula for private equity returns. It says that if we subtract the amount of exposure to the broad-based market index from the returns to private equity, what should be left is the excess return earned by the private equity manager. Equation (2) disentangles market returns from private equity returns to determine a measure of manager skill.

Equation (2) can be further refined by subtracting the return earned from investing in U.S. Treasury bills from the left hand side of the equation. If a private equity manager cannot find any viable investments, she should at least earn a rate of return equal to U.S. Treasury bills because this is the safest short-term investment available. Therefore, a private equity manager must earn a risk-adjusted return in excess of Treasury bills to demonstrate active skill, or alpha. Equation (2) can be expressed as:

$$[R_{i,t}(\text{PE}) - \text{Tbill}] - \beta[R_{m,t} - \text{Tbill}] = \alpha + \varepsilon_{i,t} \tag{3}$$

where

> $[R_{i,t}(\text{PE}) - \text{Tbill}]$ represents the net of fees return earned by private equity in excess of a cash rate of return;

---

[10] This is similar to the model used by Gompers and Lerner. They also use the three-factor Fama-French model which includes a factor for market risk, size, and book value. They find similar results to the one factor model. That is, the explanatory power of the three-factor regression equation increases if private equity investments are marked to market. See Gompers and Lerner, "The Challenge of Performance Assessment."

$[R_{m,t} -$ Tbill] represents the return on the market index in excess of the cash rate of return; and

α is the risk-adjusted excess return earned by the private equity manager.

Equation (3) can be used as a performance measure for private equity. First, the term β (beta) is a measure of the systematic risk of the private equity portfolio in relation to the market index. It is a measure of risk in relation to the broader stock or bond market. A value of beta greater than one indicates a portfolio that has greater variability than the overall stock or bond market. Conversely, a beta value less than one indicates a portfolio that has less variability than the overall stock or bond market.

The term α (alpha) is the intercept of the equation and it measures the return earned by the private equity portfolio after taking into account the effects of the broad stock or bond market and the current cash rate of return. The intercept represents the excess risk-adjusted return earned by the private equity manager over and above that for the market return and a cash return. It measures the return received due to the private equity manager's skill.

Private Equity Benchmarks

One of the problems with measuring private equity performance is determining the appropriate benchmark to use. For instance, in Chapter 14, we described how the returns to venture capital are closely linked to the over-the-counter stock market. Therefore, a natural starting point for venture capital would be to select the Nasdaq as an appropriate benchmark. We also include the Russell 1000 and Russell 2000 as potential benchmarks.

Last, we include the Post Venture Capital Index (PVCI) This index was developed by Thomson Financial *Venture Economics* and Warburg Pincus Counselors to provide a comprehensive post-venture capital public market index. The index contains public companies that were backed by venture capital before their IPO. The index composition increases as companies go public and decreases as companies drop out due to merger, acquisition or de-listing. Companies remain in the index for 10 years after their IPO and then are dropped. Venture-backed companies include traditional start-up and early stage venture-backed companies as well as later stage venture and private equity backed public companies.

In Chapter 15 we demonstrated how leveraged buyouts often take private established companies that suffer from some form of inefficiency. The nature of these mature companies would suggest that a stock market index with larger capitalized stocks might be a more appropriate benchmark for LBOs. The Russell 1000 or Russell 2000 might be good suggestions. In addition we include the Nasdaq and PVCI indices.

For mezzanine debt, the choice is less clear. This is because mezzanine is a hybrid product with components of debt and equity. Therefore, we use both debt and equity indices to determine which has the greatest explanatory power for the class of private equity.

Exhibit 1: Single Period Regression Analysis for Venture Capital

Market Index	Alpha	T statistic	Beta	T Statistic	R-square
Nasdaq	2.57%	3.25	0.39	6.29	33%
Russell 1000	2.93%	3.27	0.395	3.53	13%
Russell 2000	3.11%	3.49	0.28	3.44	13%
PVCI	3.35%	3.09	0.31	4.87	29%

Last, there is distressed debt. Once again, distressed debt can have a hybrid nature. It is the debt of a troubled company. Therefore, it could be treated as a high-yield bond investment. Alternatively, distressed debt is often converted to equity as part of the workout solution for the troubled company. Therefore, it may fluctuate in value similar to the equity stock market. Consequently, we also include both debt and equity benchmarks for distressed debt.

ANALYSIS OF PRIVATE EQUITY BENCHMARKS

To find an appropriate benchmark for each category of private equity, we examine a simple one period, one factor, regression model. We then expand these regressions to determine if there is managed or stale pricing associated with private equity investments.

For venture capital, LBOs, and mezzanine debt, we use data from *Venture Economics*. This database represents the returns earned from private equity limited partnerships that voluntarily report their returns to *Venture Economics*. For distressed debt we use data from Hedge Fund Research Inc. (HFRI). Similarly, the data from HFRI contains return information voluntarily reported by fund managers. The voluntary nature of this reporting is an important point that we will touch on in our conclusion to this chapter.

Simple One Period/One Factor Regression Results

In this section we use Equation (3) as our regression model to determine the amount of excess return associated with private equity. Exhibit 1 presents the regression results for venture capital. We regress the quarterly returns to venture capital as the dependent variable against the returns for the Nasdaq, Russell 1000, Russell 2000, and the PVCI. The returns are quarterly over the period 1980-2000.

In all cases the intercept, or alpha coefficient, and the beta coefficient are statistically significant at the 1% level. In other words, we can state that, with 99% confidence, the alpha and beta coefficients in each regression equation are significant in explaining the variability of the returns to venture capital.

For instance, with respect to venture capital returns regressed on the Nasdaq, the beta coefficient equals 0.39 and the alpha (or intercept) coefficient equals 2.57. The beta is a measure of the covariance of the returns to venture capital with those of the Nasdaq. A beta less than one indicates that the returns to venture capital are less volatile compared to the returns to the Nasdaq stock market. A beta greater than one indicates that the returns to venture capital are more volatile than the Nasdaq stock market. For all four regression equations, the beta values ranged from 0.28 with respect to the Russell 2000 to 0.40 for the Russell 1000. In each case, the returns to venture capital demonstrate less variability than the broader stock market.

The intercept value of 2.57 with respect to the Nasdaq regression indicates that, on average, the returns to venture capital generated a risk-adjusted return in excess of a cash rate of return of 2.57% per quarter or about 10% per year. The ability to generate risk-adjusted returns that are 10% greater than a cash rate of return is a clear demonstration of manager skill. The risk-adjusted return for the other three market indices is even greater: 2.93% pre quarter with respect to the Russell 1000; 3.11% per quarter for the Russell 2000; and 3.35% for the PVCI. Compared to each measure of market return, venture capital demonstrated sizeable risk-adjusted excess returns for investors.

Also, we note that the simple one period regression model of Equation (3) generated reasonable R-square measures. R-square measures the amount of variability in the dependent variable (venture capital returns) that is explained by the independent variable (the market indices). For example, R-square measures were 33% for the Nasdaq index and 29% for the PVCI.

The statistically significant results presented in Exhibit 1 demonstrate that a considerable portion of the returns to venture capital is dependent upon the performance of the broad stock market. This makes sense. A strong stock market provides for a healthy IPO market which, in turn, translates into good venture capital performance.

Exhibit 2 presents the results for the one period regression equations for LBOs, over the period 1980–2000. Again we use quarterly return data. The beta coefficients for each index are low, ranging from 0.018 for the PVCI to 0.079 for the Russell 1000. These low coefficients indicate the returns to the four market indices have a small economic impact in explaining the variability of the returns to leveraged buyout funds. This is reinforced by the low R-square measures presented in Exhibit 2. The largest is 1.6% indicating that only a very small portion of the variability in the returns to LBOs is explained by the movement of the public stock market.

The low explanatory power of the market indices demonstrates the company-specific investment style of LBO funds. LBO funds are less dependent upon the returns to the broad stock market. Their returns are based more on the unique characteristics of individual companies. Therefore, LBO funds are exposed more to company specific risk than systematic market risk.

Exhibit 2: Single Period Regression Analysis for LBOs

Market Index	Alpha	T statistic	Beta	T statistic	R-square
Nasdaq	3.13%	4.46	0.058	1.06	1.60%
Russell 1000	3.13%	4.41	0.079	0.86	1.00%
Russell 2000	3.23%	4.63	0.03	0.43	0.30%
PVCI	3.52%	4.45	0.018	0.38	0.30%

Exhibit 3: Single Period Regression Analysis for Mezzanine Debt

Market Index	Alpha	T statistic	Beta	T statistic	R-square
Nasdaq	1.66%	3.77	−0.025	−0.74	1.00%
Russell 1000	1.61%	3.61	−0.008	−0.15	0.03%
Russell 2000	1.60%	3.67	−0.004	−0.09	0.01%
High Yield Bonds	1.48%	2.89	0.019	0.42	0.30%

Despite the low beta values, in each case the value of the intercept is statistically significant at the 1% level (in fact the t-statistics for the alpha coefficient are almost identical in the four equations). The risk-adjusted returns in excess of cash range from 3.13% per quarter (for both the Nasdaq and the Russell 1000) to 3.52% for the PVCI. This indicates an annual risk-adjusted return in excess of a cash rate of about 12% to 14% per year.

Exhibit 3 presents the regression results for mezzanine debt. Reflecting mezzanine debt's dual nature as debt and equity, we regress the returns to mezzanine debt on both public equity and debt returns. Similar to LBOs the results are disappointing.

We find that the beta coefficient for mezzanine debt with respect to each equity index is negative and insignificant. This indicates that the returns to mezzanine debt move in the opposite direction of the stock market, although the effect is sufficiently small as to be insignificant. We also include the returns to high yield bonds to recognize the debt-like component of mezzanine debt. Here the beta is positive, but also insignificant. Further, the R-square measure is low, less than 1% in each regression. We conclude that mezzanine debt is not influenced by movements in either the public equity market or by the high-yield bond market.

However, the risk-adjusted excess return is statistically significant in each equation. The alpha coefficient ranged from 1.48% to 1.66% per quarter indicating an annual excess return of about 6% to 6.6% per year. This is what we would expect. Consistent with our discussions in Chapter 17, we would expect mezzanine debt to earn a lower excess return compared to venture capital or LBOs to reflect its lower risk.

The low R-squares associated with the regression equations for mezzanine debt indicate that it is a good portfolio diversification tool. The reason is that the returns to mezzanine debt are not influenced by general movements in either the stock or bond market.

Recall from our discussion in Chapter 16 that mezzanine debt is a form of "gap financing." It is used to plug a gap in time, capital structure, or LBO financing. Gaps in business plans occur regardless of the movements of the stock or bond markets. Consequently, there is no reason to expect mezzanine debt to be correlated with broad market indices. Its uncorrelated status makes it an ideal portfolio diversifier.

Exhibit 4: Single Period Regression Analysis for Distressed Debt

Market Index	Alpha	T statistic	Beta	T statistic	R-square
Nasdaq	1.82%	2.96	0.17	3.87	26%
Russell 1000	1.77%	2.86	0.33	3.90	26%
Russell 2000	1.90%	3.85	0.33	6.64	51%
High Yield	1.46%	2.01	0.16	2.80	16%

Last, in Exhibit 4, we present the regression results for distressed debt. Here, the results are more encouraging. In each case, the beta is statistically significant, for both equity and debt indices. The beta ranges from 0.33 for the Russell 2000 to 0.12 for the PVCI. It is also significant for high-yield bonds at 0.16. Distressed debt demonstrates a hybrid nature between debt and equity more so than mezzanine debt.

Further the R-square reaches a high of 51% based on the Russell 2000. The greater variability explained by the Russell 2000 might reflect the fact that distressed debt companies tend to be established companies that have run into financial trouble. These are companies significantly past their IPO stage. Therefore, indices such as the PVCI or the Nasdaq may have less explanatory power compared to a larger capitalized index such as the Russell 2000.

Last the quarterly alpha coefficient ranged from 1.46% with respect to the high yield index to 1.94% for the PVCI. This indicates that the average annual risk-adjusted return in excess of a cash return is about 6% to 8% per year. This is somewhat consistent with our discussion in Chapter 17 regarding the risks assumed by distressed debt investors.

In Chapter 17 we indicated that distressed debt investors are dealing with companies that have a great risk of survival. However, distressed debt investing is not as risky as venture capital because the target company usually has a long operating history with identifiable products. Therefore, the investment risk is less than venture capital. Consistent with this analysis, we find distressed debt managers produce an excess return slightly less than that for venture capital.

A Multi-Period Analysis of Private Equity Returns

We discussed above that the returns to private equity investing may suffer from stale or managed pricing. This means that examining private equity returns based on contemporaneous market returns may not fully reveal the extent to which private equity returns depend upon the returns to the broad stock or bond market. Therefore, the simple one period regression models we performed above may not provide accurate estimates of the systematic risk of private equity returns (as measured by β) or the risk-adjusted excess return as measured by α, the regression intercept.

In fact, the estimates of beta may be biased downwards while the estimates of alpha may be biased upwards because private equity pricing may not occur contemporaneously with changes in the public securities markets. This problem also occurs with respect to small, public firms where the trading of their securities is limited. The lack of liquidity associated with small firms can lead to stale or lagged prices.

To solve the problem of stale or managed pricing, Equation (1) can be expanded to include multi-period pricing effects:[11]

$$R_{i,t}(PE) - \alpha + \beta_0 R_{m,t} + \beta_1 R_{m,t-1} + \beta_2 R_{m,t-2} + \beta_3 R_{m,t-3} + \ldots + c_{i,t} \qquad (4)$$

Equation (4) is an equation where the returns to private equity in period t are regressed against the contemporaneous returns to the market as well as the lagged returns to the market from prior periods $t - 1$, $t - 2$, $t - 3$, and so forth. Equation (4) is a "multi-period" extension of regression Equation (1).

If the returns to private equity are due to either stale or managed pricing, we should see a significant influence from prior market returns. That is, stale or managed pricing may result in a delay between the time that changes in the value of the public securities market are observed and the time when these changes in value are reflected in the returns to private equity portfolios. By including prior market returns in our regression equation, we can observe the non-synchronous or delayed market effects on private equity returns.

In Equation (4), the summed beta of $\beta_0 + \beta_1 + \beta_2 + \beta_3 + \ldots$, provides a more accurate measure of how the returns to private equity co-vary with the public securities market. In other words, by summing the regression coefficients for both contemporaneous and lagged market effects we should be able to obtain a better measure of the systematic risk associated with private equity. In addition, by taking into account both contemporaneous and lagged stock/bond market effects, we should also obtain a better estimate of alpha, the measure of the private equity manager's skill.

With respect to Equation (4), we can perform the same transformations to achieve the same risk-adjusted return (in excess of a cash rate) demonstrated in Equation (3). Equation (5) presents this transformation.

$$[R_{i,t}(PE) - Tbill] - \beta_0[R_{m,t} - Tbill] - \beta_1[R_{m,t-1} - Tbill] \\ - \beta_2[R_{m,t-2} - Tbill] - \beta_3[R_{m,t-3} - Tbill] = \alpha + \varepsilon_{i,t} \qquad (5)$$

We regress the returns to private equity on the contemporaneous market return as well as the market return for the prior three quarters. In this way, we can observe the full impact of the public securities markets on the returns to private equity.[12] We note that the Treasury bill returns in equation (5) must also be lagged to coincide with the lagged stock or bond market returns.

---

[11] This method has been applied successfully to hedge funds. See Clifford Asness, Robert Krail, and John Liew, "Do Hedge Funds Hedge?" *The Journal of Portfolio Management* (Fall 2001).

[12] We also went further than one year in our lagged variables but found no measurable increase in explanatory power.

Exhibit 5 presents the results for venture capital. Once again, we regress the current returns to venture capital against the current return to the public stock market as well as the return to the public stock market for the prior three quarters. With respect to the Nasdaq stock market, the results are illuminating. Each beta coefficient is significant at the 1% level. This means that the returns to the Nasdaq stock market for both the current quarter as well as the prior three quarters are all statistically significant in explaining the current returns to venture capital. This is a strong demonstration of stale or managed pricing. Similar results are demonstrated for venture capital returns and the PVCI, and to a lesser extent, with respect to the Russell 1000 and Russell 2000 indices.

Further, the R-square measure increases in each regression equation in Exhibit 5. For example, the R-square measures for both the Nasdaq and the PVCI are now at 50%, a considerable improvement over the results in Exhibit 1.

The summed betas in Exhibit 5 demonstrate a much higher covariance with the market returns than that presented in Exhibit 1. For example, the summed betas in Exhibit 5 with respect to the Nasdaq equal 0.92 compared to 0.39 for the single period model displayed in Exhibit 1. Simply put, when we allow for stale or managed pricing, we find that the returns to private equity have a much greater exposure to the returns to the public securities markets. Similar results are found for each of the lagged stock market indices presented in Exhibit 5.

Last, we find that alpha (the intercept term) declines significantly when we account for lagged market returns. For example, the alpha term in Exhibit 5 with respect to the Nasdaq stock market is 1.15% per quarter (4.6% per year) compared to 2.57% (10.28% per year) presented in Exhibit 1. Therefore, this measure of the private equity manager's skill declines by more than one half when we account for lagged market returns. This indicates that a considerable amount of manager skill observed from quarter to quarter can be explained by prior market returns.

Exhibit 6 presents the results for LBO returns. We find that there is also a lagged effect for LBO returns. The market return observed three quarters prior is significant in explaining the returns to LBO portfolios in the current quarter. Specifically, we find the coefficient β_3 to be significant in the regression equation with respect to Nasdaq (at the 10% level), the Russell 1000 (at the 5% level) and the Russell 2000 (at the 1%). This demonstrates a consistent lagged effect to determining the returns earned from leveraged buyouts.

The summed beta is also greater. For example the summed beta for LBO returns regressed the Russell 2000 is 0.44 in Exhibit 6 compared to 0.03 in Exhibit 1 with respect to the Russell 2000. Last, the excess return earned by LBO funds declines in Exhibit 6 when lagged market returns are included.

The alpha term in Exhibit 6 with respect to the Russell 2000 is 2.81% per quarter compared to 3.23% displayed in Exhibit 2. Therefore, lagged market returns have some impact in explaining manager alpha in LBO funds but not nearly the same impact as for venture capital. We conclude the excess return generated by LBO fund managers is reasonably robust to contemporaneous and lagged market returns. In other words, LBO fund managers add significant, genuine excess return through their skill.

Exhibit 5: Multi-Period Regression Analysis for Venture Capital

Market Index	Alpha	T statistic	Beta(0)	T statistic	Beta(1)	T statistic	Beta(2)	T statistic	Beta (3)	T statistic	R-square
Nasdaq	1.15%	1.47	0.42	7.34	0.16	2.62	0.20	3.40	0.14	2.41	50%
Russell 1000	2.28%	2.36	0.42	3.72	0.08	0.71	0.21	1.83	0.12	1.07	19%
Russell 2000	2.75%	2.94	0.32	3.76	0.08	0.92	0.16	1.97	0.03	0.34	18%
PVCI	0.51%	0.43	0.36	6.19	0.23	3.57	0.23	3.70	0.15	2.27	50%

Exhibit 6: Multi-Period Regression Analysis for Leveraged Buyouts

Market Index	Alpha	T statistic	Beta(0)	T statistic	Beta 1	T statistic	Beta(2)	T statistic	Beta (3)	T statistic	R-square
Nasdaq	2.60%	3.26	0.060	1.06	0.03	1.33	0.006	0.92	0.11	1.80	8%
Russell 1000	2.57%	3.14	0.100	1.09	0.07	0.75	0.027	0.28	0.20	2.15	8%
Russell 2000	2.81%	3.93	0.078	1.11	0.10	1.39	0.061	0.84	0.20	2.90	13%
PVCI	2.69%	3.08	0.031	0.7	0.07	1.38	−0.018	−0.37	0.03	0.61	6%

Exhibit 7 presents the lagged regression results for mezzanine debt. We continue to find very weak results. Lagged market returns have almost no impact on the returns to mezzanine debt. We find only weak significance for β_3 with respect to the Nasdaq (at the 13% level of significance) and the Russell 2000 (at the 14% level of significance). Additionally, the sum of the lagged beta is only 0.074 with respect to the Nasdaq and 0.20 for the Russell 2000. We conclude that contemporaneous and lagged market variables have very little explanatory power with respect to mezzanine debt returns.

R-square measures remain low; no greater than 5%. Mezzanine debt does appear to be an uncorrelated asset class with respect to both debt and equity. This is consistent with our results in Chapter 17 where we found mezzanine debt to be an excellent portfolio diversification agent. In addition, this is consistent with our discussion of mezzanine debt in Chapter 16 where we indicated that the tailored nature of mezzanine debt indicates that it may be more dependent upon the fortunes of the individual firm as opposed to those of the general stock market.

Last, we find very little diminution of the alpha terms in Exhibit 7 compared to Exhibit 3. This demonstrates that a consistent, robust excess return is earned from mezzanine debt investments.

Exhibit 8 presents the results for lagged market returns and distressed debt. We find that the lagged values of the Russell 2000 have significant explanatory power for the returns to distressed debt. The first two betas, β_0 and β_1, are both significant at the 1% level, and the contemporaneous and lagged market returns explain 72% (the R-square measure) of the returns to distressed debt. Further, the summed beta in Exhibit 8 with respect to the Russell 2000 is equal to about 0.67, demonstrating considerable covariance with the stock market return, much larger than the 0.33 value observed in the single beta regression in Exhibit 4.

Last, the alpha coefficient declines significantly. In Exhibit 8, using the Russell 2000 as the market index, the quarterly alpha value is 0.9%. This indicates that distressed debt managers provided a risk-adjusted excess return of 3.6% per year, much less than the 7.6% annual excess return indicated in Exhibit 4. This indicates that lagged market returns are a significant factor in determining the returns to distressed debt.

Exhibit 9 summarizes our results. We compare the single period beta coefficient for each component of private equity and each market index to that for the summed beta in the lagged regressions. It is apparent that when prior market returns are included in the regression equation, the impact of the market returns is much greater in explaining the variability of returns to private equity.

Furthermore, as the explanatory power of the lagged market returns increases, the alpha, or excess return declines. In every category of private equity and for every market index, the excess return in the multiperiod regression is less than that observed in the single period regressions. Consequently, part of a manager's excess return that is reported in the current quarter of performance might be a reflection of prior market returns earned in previous quarters.

Exhibit 7: Multi-Period Regression Analysis for Mezzanine Debt

Market Index	Alpha	T statistic	Beta(0)	T statistic	Beta(1)	T statistic	Beta(2)	T statistic	Beta (3)	T statistic	R-square
Nasdaq	1.25%	2.37	-0.016	-0.46	0.025	0.65	0.005	0.140	0.060	1.54	4%
Russell 2000	1.21%	2.56	0.032	0.70	0.056	1.19	0.051	1.084	0.068	1.49	5%
High Yield	1.19%	1.98	0.038	0.67	-0.054	-0.77	0.080	1.160	-0.015	-0.26	3%
PVCI	1.34%	2.47	-0.007	-0.24	-0.017	-0.54	-0.003	-0.100	0.026	0.03	3%

Exhibit 8: Multi-Period Regression Analysis for Distressed Debt

Market Index	Alpha	T statistic	Beta (0)	T statistic	Beta (1)	T statistic	Beta (2)	T statistic	Beta (3)	T statistic	R-square
Nasdaq	1.77%	2.08	0.163	3.30	0.077	1.47	-0.009	-0.170	-0.048	-0.87	30%
Russell 1000	1.18%	1.50	0.404	4.48	0.262	3.02	-0.003	-0.030	-0.124	-1.46	43%
Russell 2000	1.04%	2.21	0.429	8.95	0.220	4.95	0.064	1.440	-0.039	-0.91	72%
High Yield	1.40%	1.68	0.130	1.79	0.034	0.36	0.010	0.095	-0.012	0.08	16%

Exhibit 9: Exposure to Market Risk — Single Period Beta versus Multi-Period Beta

Private Equity Category	Market Index	Multi-Period Beta B(0)+B(1)+B(2)+B(3)	Single Period Beta Beta(0)	Difference	Multi-Period Alpha	Single Period Alpha	Difference
Venture Capital	Nasdaq	0.916	0.390	0.526	1.15%	2.57%	-1.42%
	Russell 1000	0.832	0.395	0.437	2.28%	2.93%	-0.65%
	Russell 2000	0.595	0.285	0.310	2.75%	3.11%	-0.36%
	PVCI	0.983	0.312	0.671	0.51%	3.35%	-2.84%
Leveraged Buyouts	Nasdaq	0.258	0.058	0.200	2.60%	3.13%	-0.53%
	Russell 1000	0.404	0.079	0.325	2.58%	3.13%	-0.55%
	Russell 2000	0.440	0.029	0.411	2.81%	3.23%	-0.42%
	PVCI	0.111	0.018	0.093	2.69%	3.53%	-0.84%
Mezzanine Debt	Nasdaq	0.074	-0.026	0.100	1.25%	1.66%	-0.41%
	Russell 1000	0.224	-0.008	0.232	1.03%	1.61%	-0.58%
	Russell 2000	0.207	-0.004	0.211	1.21%	1.60%	-0.39%
	High Yield	0.049	0.019	0.030	1.19%	1.48%	-0.29%
Distressed Debt	Nasdaq	0.184	0.172	0.012	1.77%	1.82%	-0.05%
	Russell 1000	0.539	0.328	0.211	1.18%	1.77%	-0.59%
	Russell 2000	0.674	0.334	0.340	1.04%	1.90%	-0.86%
	High Yield	0.170	0.161	0.009	1.40%	1.46%	-0.06%

STALE VERSUS MANAGED PRICING

Summarizing our results so far, we have found that lagged market returns have a significant impact in explaining the returns reported by venture capital funds, distressed debt funds and LBO funds. Mezzanine debt indicated only a small lagged effect with respect to stock market returns. These results indicate that private equity portfolios reflect changes in the prices of marketable securities over a period of time up to one year. In other words, there is non-synchronous (lagged) pricing between private equity portfolios and stock and bond market returns.

We now come to the crux of our final issue: Are these non-synchronous private equity returns due to stale pricing or managed pricing? The non-contemporaneous impact of market returns on private equity portfolios could be due to the structure of the private equity market. That is, illiquid securities which are marked to market only when there are observable, but infrequent events (such as an IPO, new round of financing, etc.). This would result in stale prices where private equity portfolios are "refreshed" with a time delay compared to the public securities markets.

Alternatively, the lagged impact of market returns on private equity portfolios could be due to private equity managers who actively manage the pricing of their portfolios. It is possible that private equity fund managers mark the value of their portfolios up or down when it is favorable to do so.

Based on the nature of profit-sharing fees earned by private equity fund managers they might be reluctant to mark down their portfolios and quick to mark up their investment portfolios. In other words, if managed pricing is the source of these lagged effects, then private equity managers may be more aggressive in marking up their portfolios when the public securities market is performing well, but less aggressive in marking down their portfolios when the public securities market is performing poorly. It is in their economic interest to pursue this form of managed pricing.

Under these circumstances, when the public stock and bond markets are performing well, we would expect private equity managers to be quick to mark *up* the value of their portfolios. Lagged market returns would then have a smaller impact (and the lagged betas would be smaller in value). However, when the public stock and bond markets are performing poorly, we would expect private equity managers to smooth out the downside impact on their portfolios. In other words, private equity managers may be slower to mark *down* their portfolios. Lagged market returns would then have a larger impact in explaining the returns to private equity (and the lagged beta coefficients would be larger).

The above theory assumes that private equity managers are unscrupulous and actively manage their portfolio values to enhance their profit sharing fees instead of benefiting their investors.[13] There is a converse to this hypothesis.

---

[13] There is some evidence to support the selfish behavior of venture capital firms. See Gompers, "Grandstanding in the Venture Capital Industry."

Alternatively, investors might effectively monitor private equity managers through annual audits and advisory committees. Under these circumstances, private equity managers may not be able to manage the pricing of their investment portfolios to their advantage.

If private equity managers are monitored effectively by investors, then it is more likely that they will be quick to mark down the value of their portfolios in down markets and slow to mark up the value of their portfolios in up markets. This is the essence of conservatism discussed earlier in this chapter. This will lead to the lagged market returns having a greater impact in up markets than in down markets.

Another consideration is the risk to reputation. Private equity manages who have a positive track record with investors will be less likely to pursue managed pricing to their benefit because it may harm their reputation with investors. To protect their reputation, these scrupulous managers would then be quick to mark down their portfolio values (small lagged effect) and slow to mark up their portfolios (large lagged effect).

To summarize, if private equity manages manage the pricing of their portfolios to their advantage, we would expect the lagged betas to have a greater impact in down markets. Conversely, if private equity managers are properly monitored, or do not wish to risk the damage to their reputation, then we would expect the lagged betas to have a greater impact in up markets.

Finally, if managed pricing is not prevalent, then the performance of the lagged betas should be symmetrical. That is, there should be minimal difference in the lagged beta coefficients between up and down markets. In this case the culprit for the significance of lagged market returns would be stale pricing.

To address the issue of managed pricing, we run the multi-period regressions of Equation (5) with dummy variables.[14] A dummy variable is a way to split the world into two distinct states. In state one, the stock or bond market performs well. In state two, the stock or bond market performs poorly. Dummy variables are often referred to as binary variables because they describe only two states of the world (up/down, bad/good, perform well/perform poorly, etc.). Dummy variables are often multiplied against the independent variables in the regression equation to capture this binary view of the world. Our new equation looks like this:

$$R_{i,t}(\text{PE}) - \text{Tbill} = \alpha + \beta_0[R_{m,t} - \text{Tbill}] + D \times [\beta_1(R_{m,t-1} - \text{Tbill})]$$
$$+ D \times [\beta_2(R_{m,t-2} - \text{Tbill})] + D \times [\beta_3(R_{m,t-3} - \text{Tbill})] + \varepsilon_{i,t} \qquad (6)$$

To conduct this analysis, we run Equation (6) twice. In the first analysis, we set the dummy variable (D) equal to 1 when the stock markets perform well, and 0 when the market performs poorly. We then calculate the size of the lagged betas. In the second analysis, we set the dummy variable equal to 1 when the stock markets perform poorly and 0 when the markets perform well. Again we

---

[14] For an application of this technique to hedge funds, see Asness, Krail, and Liew, "Do Hedge Funds Hedge?"

calculate the sum of the lagged betas. By performing this procedure we can observe the values for the lagged betas in up markets versus those in down markets. If the non-synchronous pricing in private equity portfolios is due to managed pricing, we would expect to see asymmetry in the values of the lagged betas between up and down markets.

To simplify this analysis, we consider only those regression equations from Exhibits 4 through 8 that demonstrated the greatest lagged effect. For venture capital returns, the R-square measure was highest for the Nasdaq (the PVCI was just about equal in explanatory power). For LBOs, mezzanine debt, and distressed debt, the lagged effect was greatest using the Russell 2000 stock index.

Our results are presented in Exhibit 10. For each category of private equity, we divide this Exhibit into two states of the world: up markets and down markets. We present each beta coefficient associated with lagged market returns as well its t-statistic. We also present the R-square measure for both up market and down market regression equations.

For venture capital, Exhibit 10 demonstrates an asymmetry in lagged pricing. Specifically, all of the beta coefficients (lagged and contemporaneous) in up markets are large and are all significant at either the 1% or 2.5% level. In addition, the R-square measure remains large at 51%.

Conversely, with respect to down markets only the first beta coefficient (β_0) is significant at the 1% level. None of the lagged beta coefficients are significant at either the 1% or 5% level. Further, the R-square measure is low, at 18%.

The above results build a prima facie case for managed pricing. The size and significance of the lagged beta coefficients in up markets and the lack of significance of any lagged beta coefficient in down markets indicates that venture capital managers apply the rule of conservatism. They are slow to incorporate positive stock market returns into their portfolios, preferring to wait until they are assured of earning these returns. Conversely, when the stock market performs poorly, venture capital managers are quick to incorporate these negative returns into their private equity portfolios.[15]

The results for LBOs are similar. Recall from Exhibit 6 that β_3 was the one variable that was significant in the lagged regression equation. In Exhibit 10 we find asymmetric pricing with respect to β_3. In up markets, the t-statistic for β_3 is significant at the 1% level while the t-statistic for β_3 is insignificant in the down market regression equation. In addition, the R-square measure is larger in the up markets regression equation compared the results in down markets. This is another indication of managed pricing applying the rule of conservatism, although not as strongly as that for venture capital.

---

[15] It is interesting to note that the excess return earned by venture capitalists in up markets is a negative 4.45%, while it is a positive 7.23% in down markets. This could mean that in strong stock markets, the venture capitalist does not add much excess value because a surging stock market ensures excellent returns to venture capital. Conversely, in down markets, it appears that venture capitalist provide considerable excess return.

Exhibit 10: Managed Pricing in Private Equity Returns

Category	Alpha	T statistic	B(0)	T statistic	B(1)	T statistic	B(2)	T Statistic	B(3)	T statistic	R-square
Venture Capital											
Up Markets	-4.45%	-3.53	0.66	7.77	0.23	2.69	0.26	3.06	0.19	2.26	51%
Down Markets	7.23%	5.45	0.41	3.14	0.24	1.58	0.28	1.83	0.16	1.09	18%
Leveraged Buyouts											
Up Markets	0.31%	0.21	0.12	1.02	0.11	0.95	0.08	0.72	0.36	3.21	15%
Down Markets	4.49%	3.99	0.06	0.52	0.10	0.84	0.03	0.26	0.15	1.27	4%
Mezzanine Debt											
Up Markets	0.80%	0.81	-0.01	-0.07	0.06	0.82	0.02	0.24	0.08	1.05	3%
Down Markets	2.32%	3.43	0.06	0.81	0.05	0.64	0.08	1.12	0.07	0.96	4%
Distressed Debt											
Up Markets	-0.78%	-0.59	0.43	4.32	0.24	2.34	0.06	0.61	-0.03	-0.31	37%
Down Markets	4.26%	7.34	0.84	8.76	0.26	3.66	-0.15	-2.07	-0.21	2.96	72%

Mezzanine debt continues to be the enigma that it was in our prior regression equations. No beta coefficient, either contemporaneous or lagged, is statistically significant in either up or down markets. The lagged effects are symmetric in that there is no impact in explaining the variability of returns to mezzanine debt in either up or down markets. There is no evidence of managed pricing let alone lagged pricing with respect to mezzanine debt.

Last, distressed debt displays opposite pricing effects from venture capital and LBOs. The significance of the lagged betas is greater in down markets compared to up markets and the R-square measure is greater for down markets (72%) than for up markets (37%). This indicates that managed pricing is practiced more extensively in down markets than in up markets contrary to the rule of conservatism.[16]

CONCLUSION

In reviewing appropriate benchmarks for private equity we found that the Nasdaq is a suitable performance measure for venture capital, particularly when lagged market returns are included in measuring venture capital returns. The PVCI also proved to be a reliable performance measure for both contemporaneous and lagged returns.

For leveraged buyouts, the Russell 2000 proved to be a useful benchmark when allowing for lagged market returns. However, none of the four benchmarks examined provided useful information with respect to contemporaneous market returns.

Mezzanine debt remains a mystery. Despite its hybrid nature between debt and equity, none of the equity or bond indices were useful in explaining the returns to mezzanine debt. Contemporaneous and lagged market variables had almost no impact in explaining the variability of mezzanine debt returns. Consequently, we did not find a suitable benchmark for mezzanine debt.

Last, distressed debt demonstrated both equity and high yield properties as the Russell 2000 stock index and the High Yield Bond Index were significant in explaining the returns to distressed debt. In particular, including contemporaneous and lagged market returns for the Russell 2000 explained 70% of the variability in the returns to distressed debt.

Finally, there is considerable evidence of managed pricing in private equity portfolios. We observed asymmetric pricing with respect to lagged market variables. For venture capital and LBO funds, we found that when the stock and bond markets increase, private equity managers were slower to mark up their

---

[16] What is surprising is the negative sign with respect to beta coefficients β_2 and β_3. These coefficients are statistically significant at the 5% and 1% level, respectively. This indicates that distressed debt managers extensively use lagged market returns in pricing their portfolios in down markets, but price their portfolios contrary to what was observed in the stock market two and three quarters previously.

portfolios (leading to greater significance in lagged market returns in explaining the returns to private equity portfolios). Conversely, when stock and bond markets performed poorly, we found that private equity managers were quick to mark down the value of their portfolios. This is contrary to private equity managers' incentive schemes, but consistent with proper monitoring by investors and the risk to reputation that might be suffered by improper pricing.

The risk to reputation should be discussed a bit further. The data used in this analysis came from *Venture Economics* which collects data from several hundred private equity fund managers. These managers report their data voluntarily to *Venture Economics*. Therefore, there might be a form of self-selection bias associated with this data. In other words, it might be the case that only those private equity managers with sterling reputations and conservative pricing report their results to *Venture Economics*. While this is admirable on their part, there may many other private equity manager who do not report their return data to *Venture Economics* who do manage their portfolio values to their advantage.

To be blunt, human nature being what it is, it does not take much imagination to consider that some managers might mark to market their portfolios more quickly in up markets to capture larger incentive fees (and slower in down markets to forestall the loss of incentive fees).[17] It is in their economic interest to do so.

Yet, it appears that private equity investors manage to monitor private equity managers effectively such that human nature does not affect the valuation of the underlying private equity portfolios. Most private equity fund managers agree to an annual outside audit by an auditing firm chosen by the investors in the fund. Additionally, most private equity fund managers conduct quarterly portfolio reviews with their investors. As a result, it is difficult for private equity managers to manage the pricing of their investment portfolios to their advantage. Inevitably, they would be caught either by their investors or by the outside auditors.

As a result, we find conservative pricing demonstrated by venture capital and LBO fund managers. However, this does not mean that private equity investors can relax. They must maintain their vigilance with respect to the pricing of private equity portfolios lest human nature have its way.

For example, we found contrary results with respect to distressed debt. Our lagged regressions showed greater explanatory power in down markets than up markets, indicating greater managed pricing in down markets than up markets. The data for distressed debt returns came from HFRI, which is a database of primarily hedge fund managers. This may indicate that investors need to be more vigilant in monitoring the pricing activities of hedge fund managers than those of

---

[17] In fact, Gompers has documented the human nature aspect of nascent venture capital managers bringing start-up companies to the public markets earlier that might otherwise be prudent in order to establish a reputation in the private equity marketplace. See Gompers, "Grandstanding in the Venture Capital Industry." Therefore, there may be a difference between new private equity managers who wish to establish a reputation and established private equity managers who wish to protect their reputation. The former may be more aggressive in pricing their portfolios while our results indicate that the latter tend to be more conservative in pricing their portfolios.

private equity managers. Although our results for distressed debt are inconsistent with the results observed for other categories of private equity, they are consistent with results observed by Asness, Krail, and Liew in a study of hedge funds.[18]

Finally, we noted earlier that the data used for the analysis in this chapter was voluntarily reported by private equity managers. This may indicate a form of self-selection bias. Possibly, those managers who voluntarily report their return information to databases have a reputation to protect. As a result, the return information reported to the private equity databases may come only from those scrupulous managers who do not manage the pricing of the private equity investment portfolios to their advantage. In other words, this universe of data may unintentionally exclude return information from private equity managers who do not apply the same scruples to portfolio pricing as those managers who voluntarily report their return information.

---

[18] See Asness, Krail, and Liew, "Do Hedge Funds Hedge?" They find that hedge fund managers manage the pricing of their portfolios to their advantage.

Section IV

Credit Derivatives

Chapter 20

Introduction to Credit Derivatives

Credit derivatives are financial instruments that are designed to transfer the credit exposure of an underlying asset or issuer between two or more parties. They are individually negotiated financial contracts which may take the form of options, swaps, forwards or credit linked notes where the payoffs are linked to, or derived from, the credit characteristics of the referenced asset or issuer. With credit derivatives, a financial manager can either acquire or hedge credit risk.

Many asset managers have portfolios which are very sensitive to changes in the spread between riskless and risky assets and credit derivatives are an efficient way to hedge this exposure. Conversely, other asset managers may use credit derivatives to target specific exposures as a way to enhance portfolio returns. In each case, the ability to transfer credit risk and return provides a new tool for portfolio managers to improve performance.

Credit derivatives, therefore, appeal to financial managers who invest in high-yield bonds, bank loans, or other credit dependent assets. The possibility of default is a significant risk for asset managers, and one that can be effectively hedged by shifting the credit exposure.

In their simplest form, credit derivatives may be nothing more than the purchase of credit protection. The ability to isolate credit risk and manage it independently of underlying bond positions is the key benefit of credit derivatives. Prior to the introduction of credit derivatives, the only way to manage credit exposure was to buy and sell the underlying assets. Because of transaction costs and tax issues, this was an inefficient way to hedge or gain exposure.

Credit derivatives, therefore, represent a natural extension of the financial markets to unbundle the risk and return buckets associated with a particular financial asset, such as credit risk. They offer an important method for investment managers to hedge their exposure to credit risk because they permit the transfer of the exposure from one party to another. Credit derivatives allow for an efficient exchange of credit exposure in return for credit protection.

Before we can discuss credit derivatives we must first review the underlying risk which these new financial instruments transfer and hedge. We begin this chapter with a discussion of credit risk. We then review the credit risks inherent in three important financial markets: high-yield bonds, leveraged bank loans, and sovereign debt. Each of these markets is especially attuned to the nature and amount of credit risk undertaken with each investment. Finally, we provide several examples of how credit derivatives may be used in these markets.

CREDIT RISK

A fixed income debt instrument represents a basket of risks. There is the risk from changes in interest rates (duration and convexity risk), the risk that the issuer will refinance the debt issue (call risk), and the risk of defaults, downgrades, and widening credit spreads (credit risk). The total return from a fixed income investment such as a corporate bond is the compensation for assuming all of these risks. Depending upon the rating on the underlying debt instrument, the return from credit risk can be a significant part of a bond's total return.

There are three important types of credit risk: default risk, downgrade risk, and credit spread risk. *Default risk* is the risk that the issuer of a bond or the debtor on a loan will not repay the outstanding debt in full. Default risk can be complete in that no amount of the bond or loan will be repaid, or it can be partial in that some portion of the original debt will be recovered. *Downgrade risk* is the risk that a national rating agency will lower its credit rating for an issuer based on perceived earnings capacity. *Credit spread risk* is the risk that the spread over a reference riskless rate will increase for an outstanding debt obligation. Credit spread risk and downgrade risk differ in that the latter pertains to a specific, formal credit review by an independent agency while the former is the financial markets' reaction to perceived credit deterioration.

Credit risk is influenced by both macroeconomic events and company specific events. For instance, credit risk typically increases during recessions or slowdowns in the economy. In an economic contraction, revenues and earnings decline across a broad swath of industries, reducing the interest coverage with respect to loans and outstanding bonds for many companies caught in the slowdown. Additionally, credit risk can be affected by liquidity crisis when investors seek the haven of liquid U.S. government securities.

Company specific events are unrelated to the business cycle and impact a single company at a time. These events could be due to a deteriorating client base, an obsolete business plan, non-competitive products, outstanding litigation, or for any other reason that shrinks the revenues and earnings of a particular company.

There are two common methods of measuring credit risk. The first is a company's credit rating. Nationally Recognized Statistical Rating Organizations (NRSROs) categorize corporations according to their credit risk. These firms include Standard & Poor's, Moody's Investors Services, and Fitch. Credit ratings are assigned on the basis of a variety of factors including a company's financial statements and an assessment of management.

Second, credit risk can be measured by the credit risk premium. This is the difference between the yield on a credit risky asset and that of a comparable default-free U.S. Treasury security. The premium is the compensation that investors must be paid to hold the credit risky asset. As a company's credit quality deteriorates, a larger credit risk premium will be demanded to compensate investors for the risk of default.

In fact, the non-U.S. Treasury fixed income market is often referred to as the "spread product" market. This is because all other fixed income products, such as bank loans, high-yield bonds, investment-grade corporate bonds, or emerging market debt, trade at a credit spread relative to U.S. Treasury securities. Hence the term "spread products."

The Effect of Credit Risk

Several parties are affected by credit risk. First, bond issuers and corporate borrowers are affected because their ability and expense of borrowing money, either from the capital markets or from banks, depends upon their credit rating. A higher credit rating means not only cheaper financing, it also means a broader pool of capital from which to borrow. Many pension funds, endowments, mutual funds, and high net worth investors have limits on the amount of high-yield investments they may make. Therefore a smaller pool of investors exist to purchase high-yield debt, and this increases the cost to borrowers.

Investors are also affected by credit risk. The credit rating at the time of purchase of a bond or making of a commercial loan determines the coupon that either the investor or the bank will receive. However, should the credit rating deteriorate after the investment is made, the value of the underlying bond or loan will also deteriorate.

Most commercial loans pay floating rates, depending upon the movement of an underlying risk-free rate (a comparable U.S. Treasury rate). Therefore, banks are less exposed to interest rate risk. However, the credit risk premium is usually set at the time the loan is made. If the credit premium subsequently increases, the bank will not be fully compensated for the credit risk it bears.

Traditional Methods of Managing Credit Risk

Credit risk has been traditionally managed by underwriting standards, diversification, and asset sales.[1] Consider a bank that is analyzing a corporate client for a bank loan. The bank will first consider the company's financial position, its revenue growth, earnings potential, interest coverage, and operating leverage. Next the bank will consider the corporation's balance sheet, its ratio of debt to equity and short-term liabilities to long-term liabilities. Then the bank will review the industry in which the company operates. It will consider competitive pressures, consolidation, new products, and growth prospects. The bank will then set a limit on the amount it will loan and will consider the loan amount against the bank's total limit for the industry in which the company operates.

Diversification is the second traditional method of managing credit risk. Banks build loan portfolios consisting of commercial loans across several different industries. This reduces the likelihood that all of the loans will suffer defaults at the same time. It is simply an application of "don't put all of your loans in one basket."

[1] See Robert Neal, "Credit Derivatives: New Financial Instruments for Controlling Credit Risk," *Economic Review* (Federal Reserve Bank of Kansas City), Second Quarter 1996.

Exhibit 1: High-Yield Bond Market

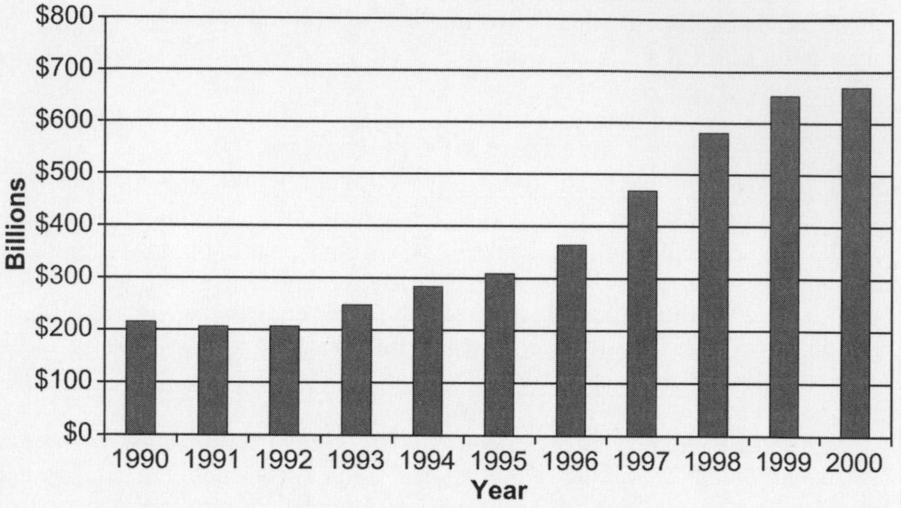

Source: Credit Suisse First Boston

Last, banks have sold their loan portfolios to reduce their exposure to certain industries or clients. While effective, this method can be difficult to implement. The reason is that banks build custom loan portfolios that match the particular balance sheet composite for the bank as well as its target audience of commercial borrowers. A loan portfolio for one bank will not perfectly suit another bank. Therefore, the sale of a loan portfolio usually entails a considerable discount.

However, this issue has largely been eliminated over the past decade with the increase in collateralized debt obligations. These are notes that are securitized by a pool of bank loans. The loans are packaged together, and new securities are issued to outside investors. We will discuss these securities at length in Chapter 21.

HIGH-YIELD BONDS

The high-yield bond market has become a large economic force in the capital markets. The term "high yield" generally means those bonds that have a large credit risk premium compared to a comparable risk-free bond. High-yield bonds are generally considered to be those bonds that lack an investment grade credit rating. This includes are securities that are rated less than BBB by Standard & Poor's and less than Baa by Moody's Investor Services. Despite the demise of Drexel Burnham Lambert, the junk bond market grew dramatically throughout the 1990s. Exhibit 1 demonstrates the growth of this market over the time period 1990–2000.

Exhibit 2: Salomon Smith Barney High-Yield Index

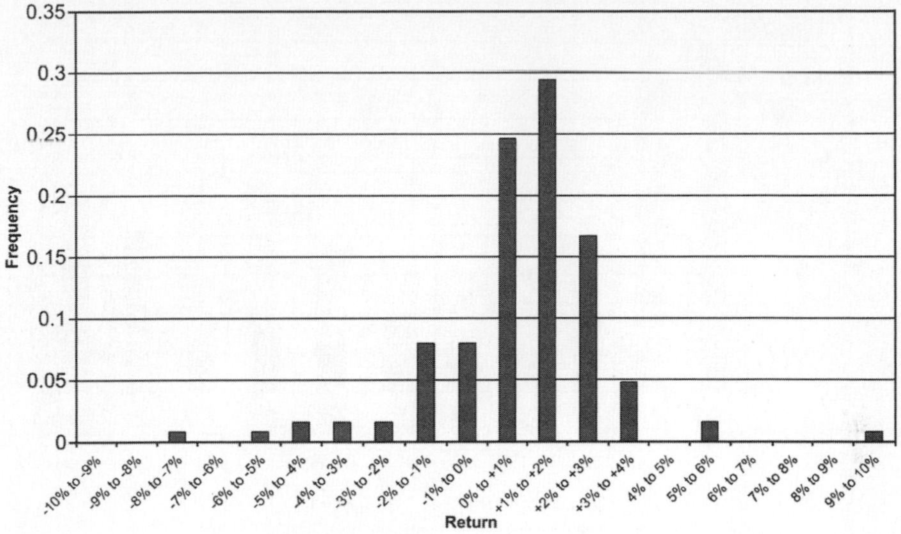

| Kurtosis | 4.233 | E(Return) | 0.78% | Sharpe | 0.157 |
| Skewness | -0.434 | Std. Dev. | 2.13% | Risk Free | 0.005 |

High-Yield Credit Risk

The high-yield bond market is subject to considerable credit risk. Consider Exhibit 2. This is the return distribution for high-yield bonds. As we have previously discussed in other chapters, credit risky assets have a negative skew and a large value of leptokurtosis. These two statistics indicate that high yield bonds are subject to considerable downside exposure. This risk is translated in the form of defaults, downgrades, or increased credit spreads.

For example, Exhibit 3 lists the default rates for high-yield bonds over the period 1990–2000. A bond is usually considered defaulted when it misses a coupon or principal repayment, or the issuer of the bond files for Chapter 11 bankruptcy protection. Not surprising, high-yield bond defaults were greatest during the last recession of 1990–1991, peaking at a rate close to 9%. This is a demonstration of the macroeconomic business cycle impact on the high-yield market.[2]

In 2000, a total of 115 issuers defaulted on 176 bond issues. This produced a record default volume of $27.9 billion. The highest industry default rate was transportation at 18.1% followed by building and materials at 16.2%, food, beverage and tobacco at 15.6%, and insurance companies at 15%.[3]

---

[2] See Mariarosa Verde, Robert Grossman, and Paul Manusco, "High Yield Defaults Soar in 2000," *Fitch Loan Products Special Report* (February 12, 2001).
[3] Id.

Exhibit 3: High-Yield Default Rates

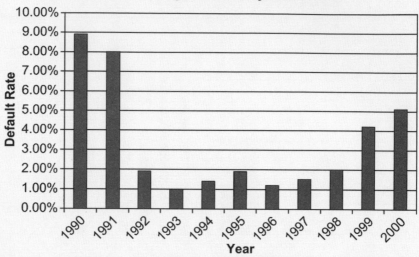

Source: Credit Suisse First Boston

Exhibit 4: Ratio of Downgrades to Upgrades for Corporate Bonds

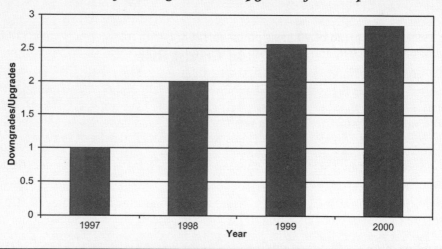

In addition to defaults, high-yield bonds are also subject to downgrades. Year 2000 was also notable for the number of downgrades issued by rating agencies. For example, Standard & Poor's had 983 global corporate rating actions in 2000. Of this amount, 727 were rating downgrades and 256 were upgrades for a ratio of downgrades to upgrades of 2.84 to 1.[4] This is a trend that has been building since the "Asian Contagion" of 1997 began a credit crisis. (See Exhibit 4.)

---

[4] See "Ratings Roundup: Downgrades Dominated in 2000," Standard & Poor's (March 1, 2001).

Exhibit 5: Credit Spread for BBB Rated Bonds over Treasury Bonds

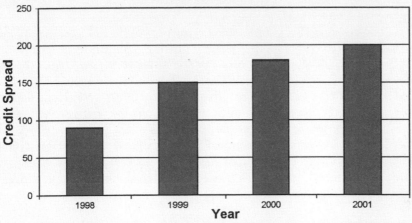

Finally, there is also credit spread risk. For instance, in June 2001, bonds rated BBB– (lowest level of investment grade) by Standard & Poor's were trading at an average credit spread over U.S. Treasuries of 200 basis points. Compare this to a credit spread of 180 basis points in 2000, a credit spread of 150 basis points in 1999, and a spread of 90 basis points in 1998. For an investor holding a $1,000 bond between 1998 and 2001 with a duration of 5, this was an average loss of about $55 in value. (See Exhibit 5.)

Credit risk is not all one sided, improved credit quality will lead to higher bond prices. For example, in 2000, $261 billion of corporate bonds were upgraded. In addition to credit upgrades, there are other events that have a positive impact on high-yield bonds. Mergers and acquisitions generally lead to either a credit upgrade as a weaker company is acquired by a stronger company, or the bonds are redeemed as part of a change of control provision in the bond indenture. For example, in 2000, Standard & Poor's found that mergers and acquisitions had a positive effect on credit ratings with the ratio of upgrades to downgrades as a result of M&A activity equal to 1.17 to 1.[5] Last, as the leveraged loan market has grown, companies have found it advantageous to redeem outstanding high-yield bonds and replace them with cheaper bank loans. Bond redemptions also provide a positive credit event for high-yield bondholders.

LEVERAGED BANK LOANS

The leveraged loan market is typically defined as bank loans that are made to companies that have a credit rating below investment grade, or loans that are

[5] Id.

priced at LIBOR + 150 basis points or more. Similar to high-yield bonds, bank loans are subject to the risk that the borrower will pay down the loan faster than expected or refinance the loan (call risk) as well as the risk of default, downgrade, and increased credit spread.

The corporate bank loan market typically consists of syndicated loans to large and mid-sized corporations. They are floating-rate instruments, often priced in relation to LIBOR. Corporate loans may be either *revolving credits* (known as *revolvers*) that are legally committed lines of credit, or term loans that are fully funded commitments with fixed amortization schedules. Term loans tend to be concentrated in the lower credit rated corporations because revolvers usually serve as backstops for commercial paper programs of fiscally sound companies.

Term bank loans are re-priced periodically. Because of their floating interest rate nature, they have reduced market risk resulting from fluctuating interest rates. Consequently, credit risk takes on greater importance in determining a commercial loan's total return.

The Growth of the Leveraged Loan Market

The leveraged loan market rivals that of the high-yield bond market. Exhibit 6 shows that in year 2000 the size of the leveraged loan market has exceeded that of the high-yield bond market.

This growth has been fueled by several factors. First, over the past several years, the bank loan market and the high-yield bond market have begun to converge. This is due partly to the relaxing of commercial banking regulations which has allowed many banks to increase their product offerings, including high-yield bonds. Contemporaneously, investment banks and brokerage firms have established loan trading and syndication desks to compete with those of commercial banks.

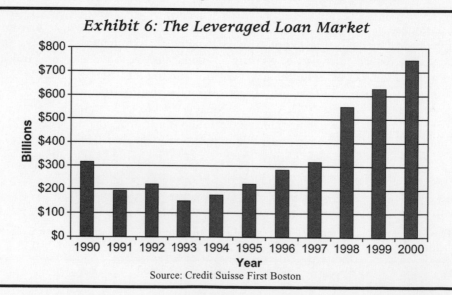

Exhibit 6: The Leveraged Loan Market

Source: Credit Suisse First Boston

Exhibit 7: Institutional Investors in the Loan Market

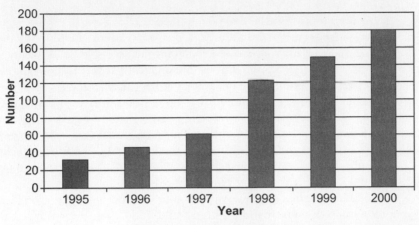

Source: Credit Suisse First Boston

In addition to banks and brokerage firms, insurance companies have become increasingly involved in the bank loan business as demonstrated by the Citicorp/Travelers Insurance merger. As regulatory barriers continue to fall, it is expected that there will be fewer distinctions between commercial banks, brokerage firms, and insurance companies. Integration of these three branches of financial service firms should lead to greater expansion of the leveraged loan market.

A third reason is the acceptance of bank loans as a form of investment by institutional investors. Pension funds, endowment funds, mutual funds, and high net worth individuals have all entered the market for bank loan investing. Exhibit 7 demonstrates the growth of institutional investors in the bank loan market from 1995 to 2000. It is estimated that institutional investors now account for more than 25% of the leveraged loan market.[6] Institutional investors seek bank loans because they meet their need for higher spreads and match up well against their liabilities.

The entrance of institutional investors has led to a change in the structure of many syndicated loans. Where the tenor of a bank loan was previously in the 2- to 4-year range, longer-term loans are being arranged to meet the longer investment horizons of institutional investors. Often a syndicated loan will be offered with different tranches constructed not by differences in credit ratings but by differences in maturity. For example, Allied Waste's loan facility established in 2000 had three tranches. Tranche A was a $2.25 billion term loan that had a maturity of 2005, Tranche B was for $1 billion with a maturity of 2006, and Tranche C was for $1.25 billion with a maturity of 2007. The tranches of these "alphabet" loans will have different pricing despite having the same credit quality. The different pricing reflects the different maturities of the tranches. The A tranche is usually

---

[6] See "Changes in the Global Loan Market are Reflected in the Dynamic Growth of Syndicated Loan Ratings," Moody's Investors Services (September 2000).

priced in the range of Libor + 150 to 250, with subsequent tranches priced at Libor + 250 and up.

These investors are further enticed to the bank loan market by the securitization of bank loans through collateralized loan obligations. These obligations are in a format that investors already understand: the asset-backed security. We will discuss collateralized loan obligations in more detail in the next chapter.

Last, a new and more efficient capital market has emerged for bank loans. Many commercial banks have realized that their strength is best displayed in reviewing the creditworthiness of borrowers and originating new loans, but not necessarily holding those loans on their balance sheet. Consistent with the development of the collateralized loan obligation market, banks can now repackage these loans and sell them to other investors. In this way banks can better manage their risk capital and generate higher returns on equity.

All of this integration may result in more risk. For example, hybrid debt instruments with both bank loan and high-yield bond characteristics are now available in the capital markets. These hybrid commercial loans typically have a higher prepayment penalty than standard commercial loans, but only a second lien (or no lien) on assets instead of the traditional first claim. Additionally, several commercial loan tranches may now be offered as part of a financing package where the first tranche of the bank loan is fully collateralized and has a regular amortization schedule, but the last tranche has no security interest and only a final bullet payment at maturity. These new commercial loans have the structure of high-yield bonds, but have the floating-rate requirement of a bank loan. Consequently, the very structure of these hybrid bank loans make them more susceptible to credit risk.

Attracting Investors in the Bank Loan Market

In addition to some of the factors mentioned above, there are two reasons why investors are attracted to the bank loan market. First, bank loans generally have a more senior position within the capital structure of a borrowing corporation. This higher priority of claim on assets affords investors greater protection than high-yield bonds.

A recent study by Fitch found that over the period 1997–2000, bank loans had significantly greater recovery rates than high-yield bonds. Bank loans recovered on average 73% of par value while senior unsecured bonds recovered only 35% of par value and subordinated bonds recovered only 17% of par value.[7] These recovery rates are consistent with a study by Moody's Investor services that found that senior secured bank loans recovered 70.26% of their par value while senior unsecured bonds recovered 55.15% and junior subordinated debt recovered 20.39%.[8]

A second reason for bank loan popularity is that they are less volatile investments. The reason is that bank loans typically have floating coupon rates

---

[7] See Steven O'Shea, Sharon Bonelli, and Robert Grossman, "Bank Loan and Bond Recovery Study: 1997–2000," Fitch (March 19, 2001).

[8] See "Bank Loan Loss Given Default," Moody's Investors Service (November 2000).

instead of fixed coupon rates associated with high-yield bonds. This lower volatility can lead to higher Sharpe ratios. Exhibit 8 presents the average annual return, standard deviation and Sharpe ratios for U.S. Treasury bonds, AAA-rated bonds, high-yield debt, and leveraged loans over the period 1992-2000. [9]

Exhibit 8 demonstrates that leveraged loans have very favorable Sharpe ratios compared to other sectors of the fixed-income market. For example, the Sharpe ratio for leveraged loans is almost three times greater than that for high-yield bonds even though high-yield bonds have a larger average annual return. However, high-yield bonds are much riskier as revealed by the higher standard deviation of high-yield bond returns compared to leveraged loans.

EMERGING MARKET DEBT

Credit risk is not unique to the domestic U.S. financial markets. When investing in the sovereign debt of a foreign country, an investor must consider two crucial risks. One is political risk — the risk that even though the central government of the foreign country has the financial ability to pay its debts as they come due, for political reasons (e.g., revolution, new government regime, trade sanctions), the sovereign entity decides to forfeit (default) payment. The second type of risk is credit risk — the same old inability to pay one's debts as they become due.

A sovereign government relies on two forms of cash flows to finance its government programs and to pay its debts: taxes and revenues from state-owned enterprises. Taxes can come from personal income taxes, corporate taxes, import duties, and other excise taxes. State-owned enterprises can be oil companies, telephone companies, national airlines and railroads, and other manufacturing enterprises.

In times of economic turmoil such as a recession, cash flows from state owned enterprises decline along with the general malaise of the economy. Additionally, tax revenues decline as corporations earn less money, as unemployment rises, and as personal incomes decline. Lastly, with a declining foreign currency value, imports decline, reducing revenue from import taxes.

Exhibit 8: Expected Returns, Standard Deviations, and Sharpe Ratios

	Expected Return	Standard Deviation	Sharpe Ratio
U.S. Intermediate Treasury	6.84%	7.12%	0.203
AAA Rated Corporate Bonds	7.72%	7.94%	0.292
High-Yield Bonds	8.45%	9.45%	0.322
Leveraged Loans	7.61%	2.43%	0.908

[9] The source data for this table comes from DeRosa-Farag, "State of the Credit Markets," Credit Suisse First Boston (April 2001).

Exhibit 9: JP Morgan EMBI Index

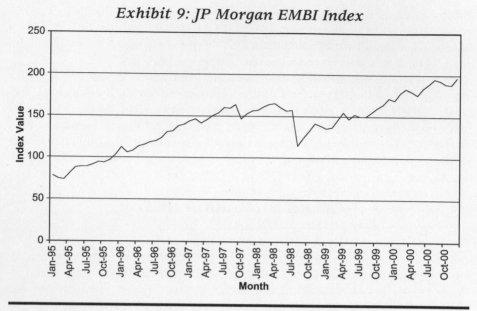

The extreme vicissitudes of the sovereign debt market are no more apparent than in the emerging market arena. Here, the "Asian Tigers" — Hong Kong, Taiwan, Korea, and Singapore — enjoyed a real average growth rate over the 1986–1998 period of about 8% per year. During this period, investors could have earned an average of almost 14% by investing in the public (or quasi-public) debt of these countries.

However, the fortunes of the emerging markets countries can deteriorate rapidly. Exhibit 9 presents the daily price chart for J.P. Morgan's Emerging Bond Index (EMBI) for the year 1995–2000. EMBI is a weighted average of the returns to sovereign bonds for 27 emerging market countries from Latin America, Eastern Europe, and Asia.

As Exhibit 9 demonstrates, the performance of the EMBI index was generally positive for most of this time period. However, there were two periods of notable decline. The first was in October 1997, when the "Asian Contagion" hurt the emerging markets. In this month, the index declined by 10.5%. Second, in August 1998, the Russian government defaulted on its bonds, sending the index down by 27.4%.

For example, consider the Russian government 10% bond due in 2007. In July 1997 when this bond was issued, its credit spread over a comparable U.S. Treasury bond was 3.50%. However, by the time the Russian government defaulted on its bonds, the credit spread had increased to 53% (5,300 basis points) over comparable U.S. Treasury securities. This spread widening led to billions of dollars of losses as Russian bonds traded for just pennies on the dollar.[10]

Once again, we note that credit risk is not all one sided. Even though there was a rapid decline in the credit quality of emerging market sovereign debt

---

[10] See "Financial Firms Lose $8 Billion so Far," The *Wall Street Journal* (September 3, 1998), p. A2.

in 1997, such a steep retreat presented opportunities for credit quality improvement. From its low point in August 1998 to the end of 2000, the index posted a gain of 72%, for an average annual return of 27.2%.

Risk Profile of Emerging Market Debt

The discussion above demonstrated that emerging market debt is subject to considerable event risk. Sudden drops of the JP Morgan's EMBI index indicate the extent to which credit events can hit quickly and harshly in emerging market debt. A default in one emerging market country can lead to widening credit spreads across all emerging markets. In addition, as the Russian bond example demonstrates, emerging market debt is subject to considerable default risk.

To analyze this risk, we graph the frequency distribution of the returns for the JP Morgan EMBI index over the time period 1990–2000. The results of this distribution are presented in Exhibit 10. We can see that emerging market debt has a large negative skew value indicating a bias towards negative returns. In addition, the returns to emerging market bonds have a large positive value of kurtosis. The combination of negative skew and large kurtosis means that this distribution of returns has considerable exposure to downside risk. This is similar to our discussion with respect to high-yield bonds. The two classes of fixed income investments demonstrate exposure to event risk, the risk of financial events that deteriorate the creditworthiness of an issuer.

Exhibit 10: Frequency Distribution for JP Morgan Emerging Composite

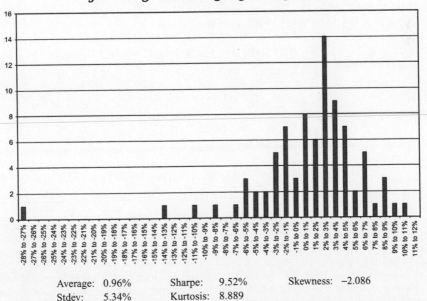

Average: 0.96%	Sharpe: 9.52%	Skewness: −2.086
Stdev: 5.34%	Kurtosis: 8.889	

CREDIT OPTIONS

In the prior sections of this chapter we provided a demonstration of credit risk and it importance in determining asset value. In this section we review one of the basic credit derivative structures: credit options. These instruments may be used for transferring or accumulating credit exposure.

Credit Put Option

In its simplest form, a credit option can be a binary option. With a binary credit option, the option seller will pay out a sum if and when a default event occurs with respect to a referenced credit (e.g., the underlying issuer is unable to pay its obligations as they become due). Therefore, a binary option represents two states of the world: default or no default; it is the clearest example of credit protection. At maturity of the option, if the referenced credit has defaulted the option holder receives a payout. If there is no default at maturity of the option, the option buyer receives nothing and forgoes the option premium. A binary credit option could also be triggered by a ratings downgrade.

A European binary credit option pays out a sum only at maturity if the referenced credit is in default. An American binary option can be exercised at any time during its life. Consequently, if an American binary credit option is in the money (a default event has occurred), it will be exercised immediately because delaying exercise will reduce the present value of the fixed payment.

Consider an American credit put option that pays the holder of the option the difference between the strike price and market value of the bond if a high-yield bond is in default.[11] If the bond is not in default, the pay off to the put option is zero. This option may be described as:

$$P[B(t)] = \begin{cases} X - B(t) \text{ if the bond is in default} \\ 0 \text{ otherwise} \end{cases}$$

where

X = the strike price of the put option
$B(t)$ = the market value of the bond at default[12]

Exhibit 11 presents a binary credit option where the payout is dependent upon whether the referenced credit is in default. This protects the investor only

---

[11] Typically, the market price of the bond is fixed at some period of time after the default such as one month from the default date. Also, the condition of default must be specified. This could be a failure to make a timely payment of interest or principal or it may be triggered by a Chapter 11 bankruptcy filing.

[12] Mathematical formulae have been developed to determine the value of credit options. These equations can be quite complicated. Generally, they fall into two types of pricing methodologies: structural versus term structure. For more information regarding credit option pricing formulae, see Mark Anson, *Credit Derivatives*, (New Hope, PA: Frank J. Fabozzi Associates, 1999).

after default has occurred. The bond may have declined in price before the issuing company declares a default.

Instead of waiting for an actual default to occur, the strike price of the option can be set to a minimum net worth of the underlying issuer below which default is probable. For instance, if the firm value of the referenced credit (assets − liabilities) falls to $100 million, then the binary credit option will be in the money.

Alternatively, a binary credit put options may be based on credit ratings as the threshold or trigger. For instance, in January 1998 bondholders forced the International Finance Corporation of Thailand (IFCT) to redeem $500 million in bonds several years before their maturity. The bond issue contained a provision that allowed investors to put the bonds back to the issuer at face value should the sovereign credit rating of Thailand fall below investment grade.

This binary credit put option may be expressed as:

$$P[V(t); \$500 \text{ million}] = \begin{cases} \$500 \text{ million} - V(t); \text{ if credit rating is below} \\ \qquad\qquad\qquad\qquad \text{investment grade} \\ \$0; \text{ if credit rating is above investment grade} \end{cases}$$

Exhibit 12 demonstrates the payout to the credit put option on the IFCT bonds.

Credit Call Options

In addition to the binary put option described above, the IFCT bonds also provided that investors would receive an additional 50 basis points of coupon income should the credit rating of Thailand decline by two notches. Further, investors would receive 25 basis points of coupon income for every subsequent decline in credit rating thereafter. These call options were in effect until a below investment grade credit rating was reached. Then the bonds were putable as described above.

Exhibit 11: Payout Function for a Binary Credit Put Option

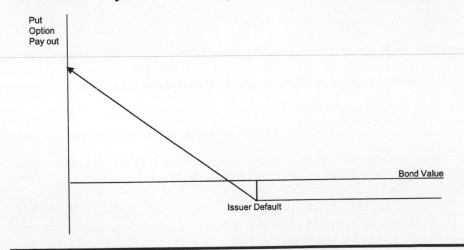

Exhibit 12: Binary Credit Put Option on IFCT Bonds

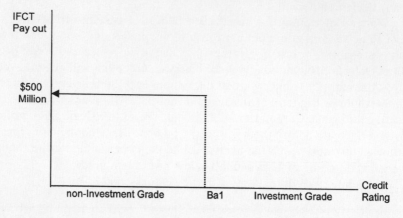

Exhibit 13: Binary Credit Call Options on IFCT Bonds

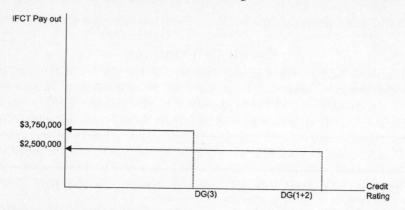

DG(1+2) indicates the first two credit downgrades
DG(3) indicates the third downgrade

The ability to earn additional yield as the credit rating of Thailand declined is the same as a series of binary call options. These options may be expressed as:

$$C[CR(t); ICR] = \begin{cases} \$2{,}500{,}000; \text{ if } CR(t) \text{ is two grades below } ICR \\ \$0; \text{ if } CR(t) \text{ is not two grades below } ICR \end{cases}$$

where $CR(t)$ is the current credit rating for Thailand at time t, ICR is the initial credit rating of Thailand at the issuance of the bonds, and $\$2{,}500{,}000 = 0.005 \times \$500{,}000{,}000$.

The payout function for these binary credit call options are displayed in Exhibit 13. The bonds suffered three credit downgrades before they hit the non-investment grade level and became putable.

Exhibit 14: Credit Call Option Written on a Credit Spread

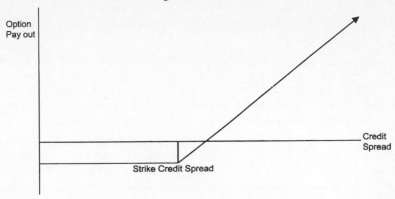

The reader may question why the IFCT would issue bonds with attached binary credit options. The reason is one of cost. Options are not free. By attaching credit options to its bonds, the IFCT was in fact selling these options to its investors in return for paying a lower coupon rate. Through the "sale" of these credit options, the IFCT was able to initially lower its funding costs by 100 basis points. Unfortunately, the credit rating of Thailand deteriorated, resulting, ultimately, in a greater expense to IFCT.

Finally, credit options can be written on the level of a credit spread for a credit risky asset above that for a risk free asset. If the credit spread widens, the referenced asset will decline in value, but the option will increase in value. This type of credit option is structured so that the option is in the money when the credit spread exceeds a specified spread level. The payoff is determined by taking the difference in credit spreads multiplied by a specified dollar amount and a risk factor that is determined by measures of duration and convexity.[13]

Exhibit 14 demonstrates a credit call option written on a credit spread. The option payout function starts below zero because the option is costly. However, once the credit spread of the underlying issuer or bond reaches the strike credit spread, the option payout fund turns positive and increases in value as the credit spread of the risky asset increases.

CREDIT SWAPS

There are two basic kinds of credit swaps: credit default swaps and total return swaps. Credit default swaps are used to shift credit exposure to a credit protection seller.

---

[13] For more details on this type of option, see Mark Anson, "Credit Derivatives in Portfolio Management," in Frank J. Fabozzi (ed.), *Professional Perspectives on Fixed Income Portfolio Management, Volume I* (New Hope, PA: Frank J. Fabozzi Associates, 2000).

Total return credit swaps are a way to increase an investor's exposure to credit risk and the returns commensurate with that risk. Credit swaps are an important component of the collateralized debt obligations that we will discuss in the next chapter.

Credit Default Swap

A credit default swap is similar to the binary put options discussed above in that its primary purpose is to hedge the credit exposure to a referenced asset or issuer. In this sense, credit default swaps operate in a similar fashion to a standby letter of credit. A credit default swap is the simplest form of credit insurance.

There are two types of credit default swaps. The first type is a bilateral contract where the credit protection buyer pays a periodic premium on a predetermined amount (the notional amount) in exchange for a contingent payment from the credit protection seller to reimburse the buyer for any losses suffered from a specified credit event. Credit events may be defined as a failure to pay, bankruptcy, repudiation, restructuring, acceleration, or a credit event upon a merger. The premium, notional amount, tenor (maturity of the swap), periodicity of payments, referenced asset, and credit events are negotiated between the credit protection buyer and the credit protection seller in an International Swaps and Derivatives Association swap agreement.

The credit default swap may be negotiated with respect to any credit risky asset such as a portfolio of bank loans, a basket of high-yield bonds, or a collection of emerging market bond issues. The credit protection buyer continues to receive the total return on the underlying assets. However, if the total return is negative due to a credit event, the buyer has the contractual right to seek reimbursement from the credit protection seller. Exhibit 15 demonstrates a simple credit default swap.

A variation on the credit default swap is for the owner of the credit risky asset to pass on the total return of the asset to the credit protection seller in return for a certain payment. The credit protection buyer gives up the uncertain returns of the credit risky asset in return for certain payments from the credit protection seller. The credit protection seller now receives both the upside and the downside of the return associated with the credit risky asset. Exhibit 16 demonstrates this swap.

Exhibit 15: Credit Default Swap with Transfer of Default Risk

Exhibit 16: Credit Default Swap with Transfer of Total Return

Exhibit 17: Total Return Credit Swap

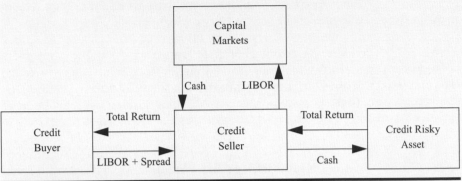

Large banks are the natural dealers for credit default swaps because it is consistent with their letter of credit business. Banks may sell credit default swaps as a natural extension of their credit lending business. Alternatively, a bank may use a credit default swap to hedge the credit exposure that exists on its balance sheet.

Credit default swaps are very flexible. For instance, a credit default swap may state in the contract the exact amount of insurance payment in the event of a credit event. Alternatively, a credit default swap may be structured so that the amount of the swap payment by the credit protection seller is determined after the credit event. Usually, this is determined by the market value of the referenced asset after the credit event has occurred.

Total Return Credit Swap

A total return credit swap is different from a credit default swap in that the latter is used to hedge a credit exposure while the former is used to increase or gain credit exposure. A total return swap transfers all of the economic exposure of a referenced asset or a referenced basket of assets to the credit swap buyer. A total return credit swap includes all cash flows from the referenced asset as well as any capital appreciation or depreciation of those assets.

If the total return payer owns the underlying referenced assets, it has transferred its economic exposure to the total return receiver in return for a payment usually tied to LIBOR. Effectively, the total return payer has a neutral position with respect to the underlying credit risky asset that will earn LIBOR plus a spread. However, the total return payer has only transferred the economic exposure of the referenced assets to the total return buyer, it has not transferred the physical ownership of the assets. The total return payer must continue to finance the underlying assets at its marginal cost of borrowing or the opportunity cost of investing elsewhere the capital tied up by the referenced assets.

Exhibit 17 displays a total return credit swap. Assume the credit seller borrows money from the capital markets at LIBOR. It uses the borrowed cash to purchase the credit risky asset, and receives the total return from the asset. The credit seller then enters into a swap agreement with the credit buyer where the buyer will receive the total return from the credit risky asset in return for paying to the credit seller LIBOR + spread.

From the credit seller's perspective, all cash flows net out to the spread over LIBOR. Therefore, the credit seller's profit is equal to the spread times the dollar value of the credit swap. From the credit buyer's perspective, it receives the total return on a credit risky asset without having to use its own capital to purchase the asset. These types of swaps are often known as "renting a balance sheet" because the referenced asset remains on the seller's balance sheet at the seller's cost of funds.[14]

Risks of Credit Swaps

While credit derivatives offer investors alternative strategies to access credit risky assets, they come with specialized risks. These risks apply equally to credit options as well as credit swaps.

First, there is operational risk. Operational risk is the risk that traders or portfolio managers could imprudently use credit swaps. Since these are off-balance sheet contractual agreements, excessive credit exposures can be achieved without appearing on an investor's balance sheet. Without proper accounting systems and other back-office operations, an investor may not be fully cognizant of the total credit risk exposure.

Second, there is counterparty risk. This is the risk that the counterparty to a swap agreement will default on its obligations. It is ironic that a credit protection buyer, for example, can introduce a new form of credit risk into her portfolio (counterparty credit risk) from the purchase of a credit default swap. For a credit protection buyer to suffer a loss two things must happen: (1) there must be a credit event on the underlying credit risky asset and (2) the credit protection seller must default on its obligations to the credit protection buyer.

Another source of risk is liquidity risk. Currently, there are no exchange-traded credit derivatives. Instead, they are traded over the counter as customized contractual agreements between two parties. The very nature of this customization makes credit derivatives illiquid. Credit derivatives will not suit all parties in the financial markets, and a party to a custom tailored credit derivative contract may not be able to obtain the "fair value" of the contract if he tries to sell his position.

Last, there is pricing risk. As the derivative markets have matured, the mathematical models used to price derivative contracts have become increasingly complex. These models are dependent upon assumptions regarding underlying economic parameters. Consequently, the pricing of credit derivatives is sensitive to the assumptions of the models.

---

[14] Another form of credit derivative is a credit forward contract. These contracts act like one-period total return credit swaps. For more detail, see Mark Anson, *Credit Derivatives*.

CONCLUSION

This chapter was designed to be a brief introduction to credit risk and new derivative products that may be used to access credit risky assets. Credit derivatives provide new tools for banks, insurance companies, and institutional investors to buy, sell, diversify, and trade units of credit risk. In addition, credit derivatives allow investors to achieve favorable yields to match their outstanding liabilities.

In our next chapter we introduce the collateralized debt obligation market. This market would not be as successful and large without the initial development of the credit derivative market. Wall Street and investors have embraced these alternative strategies to access credit return.

Chapter 21

Collateralized Debt Obligations

Collateralized debt obligations (CDOs) are a form of asset-backed security (ABS) where a pool of fixed income instruments are repackaged into highly rated securities. These structures were born in the late 1980s as banks began to repackage leveraged loans that were not easily transferable into securities that could be bought and sold. These securities were called collateralized loan obligations (CLOs), and they were backed by a portfolio of secured or unsecured bank loans made to a variety of commercial borrowers.

In the early 1990s a new variation of this structure was created, collateralized bond obligations (CBOs). A CBO is a security that is backed by a portfolio of senior or subordinated bonds issued by a variety of corporate or sovereign issuers. CBOs are just another form of a debt instrument that is backed not by the credit of a single issuer, but instead, is supported by the credit of many different issuers.

From these two streams of asset-backed securities, CDOs were born. A CDO is simply a security that is backed by a portfolio of bonds and loans together. In fact, the term "CDO" is often used broadly to refer to any CLO or CBO structure. In its simplest form, a CDO is a trust or special purpose vehicle that purchases loans and bonds from banks, insurance companies and other sellers, and then issues new securities to investors where the new securities are collateralized by the bonds and loans contained in the trust.

In this chapter we provide an introduction to the CDO marketplace. We describe the various uses for CDOs as well as the risks and benefits. We also provide some examples of recent CDO structures. Last, we consider how CDO structures may be combined with other forms of alternative investment strategies such as private equity and hedge funds.

GENERAL STRUCTURE OF CDOS

As just explained, the term CDOs can be used to broadly refer to any collateralized bond obligation or collateralized loan obligation. These two categories describe a large portion of the CDO marketplace. However, there are also investment vehicles that combine both bonds and loans into a single asset-backed pool. These structures are best referred to as collateralized debt obligations because the underlying pool of collateral contains both bonds and loans. Therefore, the term

CDO may also refer to a hybrid asset-backed structure where the supporting collateral is a combination of debt instruments including bank loans, high-yield corporate bonds, emerging market sovereign debt, and even other CDO securities.

Size of the Market for CBOs and CLOs

The growth in CBOs and CLOs has been significant in the 1990s as insurance companies, mutual funds, investment banks, and European banks have all jumped into the marketplace. Exhibit 1 (a) presents the growth of the CBO market from 1995–2000. The market has grown from $2 billion in new CBOs in 1995 to over $40 billion in new CBOs sold in 2000. Exhibit 1(b) demonstrates the historical growth of the CBO market. The total outstanding amount of CBO securities reached almost $155 billion by year 2000.

Exhibit 1: Market Value of CBOs
a. Market Value of New CBOs

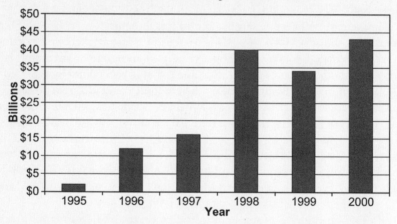

b. Market Value of all Outstanding CBOs

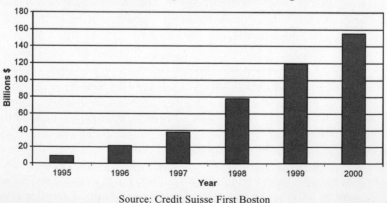

Source: Credit Suisse First Boston

Exhibit 2: Market Value of CLOs
a. Market Value of New CLOs

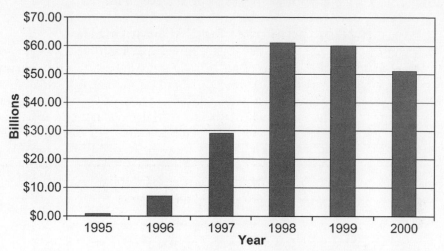

b. Market Value of All Outstanding CLOs

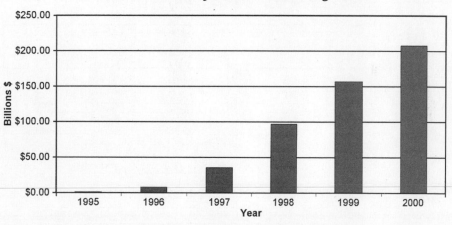

Source: Credit Suisse First Boston

The market for CLOs has seen similar growth. Exhibit 2(a) presents the growth in new CLOs over the same time period. Not surprisingly, this market peaked in 1998 at about $61 billion in new issues. The liquidity crisis of 1998 spilled over to 1999 resulting in a slight decline in new CLO structures. Year 2000 witnessed a slowdown in the U.S. stock market and economy. Consequently, new CLO issuance declined to about $51 billion. Despite the slowdown in the U.S. economy in 2000, the overall CLO market grew tremendously. Exhibit 2(b) shows that the total outstanding CLO securities exceeded $200 billion by year 2000.

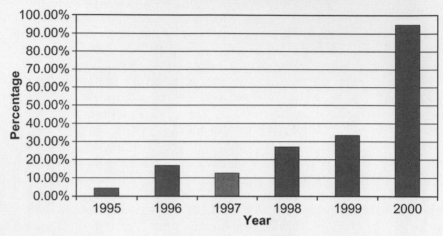

Exhibit 3: CBOs as a Percentage of New High-Yield Bond Issuance

Source: Credit Suisse First Boston

Exhibit 4: CLOs as a Percentage of New Leveraged Loan Volume

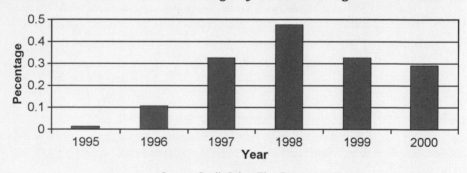

Source: Credit Suisse First Boston

It is also interesting to consider what percentage of the market share CBOs constitute of the new high-yield bond issuance. Exhibit 3 shows that CBOs have become a greater percentage of new high-yield issues. For instance, in 2000, almost all new high-yield issues were repackaged through a CBO structure.

CLO structures have declined, however, relative to the highly leveraged loan market. Consistent with the results in Exhibit 2, Exhibit 4 demonstrates that CLO structures peaked in 1998 as a percentage of the new highly leveraged loan volume.

Overview of the CDO Marketplace

The asset-backed nature of CDO securities may be used to effect two main types of transactions: *balance sheet CDOs* and *arbitrage CDOs*. Banks and insurance companies are the primary sources of balance sheet CDOs. They use these structures to manage their commercial loan investments listed on their balance sheet. Therefore, balance sheet CDOs tend to be in the form of collateralized loan obligation structures.

The goal of a balance sheet CDO is typically to reduce regulatory capital requirements. By selling a portion of their loan portfolios, banks and insurance companies can free up regulatory capital required to support those loans.

Although CLO structures were invented in the late 1980s, it was not until the ROSE Funding No. 1 CLO in November 1996 that the value of CLOs to manage balance sheet risk became apparent. In that transaction National Westminister Bank sold $5 billion of high quality commercial bank loans to the ROSE CLO. This sale represented 15% to 20% of Nat West's total loan book (about 2,000 corporate loans). The transaction not only provided new funding to Nat West, it also released up to $400 million of regulatory capital.[1]

Since the Nat West transaction, banks have realized that they can use the asset-backed securities market to manage their balance sheets. The dramatic increase in technology and financial engineering in the 1990s allows banks to manage their credit risks more finely. In today's financial markets, many banks have concluded that their expertise lies in analyzing credit risk and originating loans to match that risk, but not necessarily in holding the loans on their balance sheet.[2]

In contrast to banks, money managers are the main suppliers of arbitrage CDOs. Arbitrage CDOs are most often in the form of a CBO structure because the money managers tend to have more experience managing high-yield bonds than leveraged loans. However, arbitrage CDOs can contain bonds, mortgages, commercial loans, and even investments in other CDO structures. The ultimate goal is to make a profit instead of managing balance sheet risk.

Further, within these two broad categories are several sub-categories that further segment the CDO marketplace. For instance, balance sheet CDOs can be either cash funded or can be synthetically constructed through the use of credit derivatives. Similarly, arbitrage CDOs can be funded with cash or through the use of credit derivatives.

Exhibit 5 presents an overview of the different segments of the CDO market. We present examples of each segment in our discussions below.

Special Purpose Vehicles

At the center of every CDO structure is a special purpose vehicle (SPV). This is a term to describe a legal entity that is established to accomplish a specific transaction such as a CDO structure. SPVs are usually set up as either a Delaware or Massachusetts business trust or as a special purpose corporation (SPC), usually Delaware based.

---

[1] See Charles Smithson and Gregory Hayt, "Tools for Reshaping Credit Portfolios: Managing Credit Risk," *The RMA Journal* (May 2001).

[2] See Kenneth E. Kohler, "Collateralized Loan Obligations: A Powerful New Portfolio Management Tool for Banks," *Securitization Conduit* (Summer 1998).

Exhibit 5: Overview of Collateralized Debt Obligations

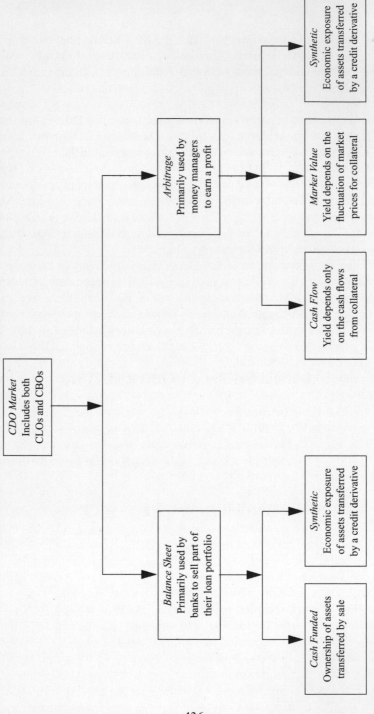

In the case of a balance sheet CDO, the SPV will be established as a CLO trust. The selling bank will be the sponsor for the trust, meaning that it will bear the administrative and legal costs of establishing the trust. In the case of an arbitrage CDO, the SPV is usually a CBO trust and the sponsoring entity is typically a money manager.

SPVs are often referred to as "bankruptcy remote." This means that if the sponsoring bank or money manager goes bankrupt, the CDO trust will not be affected. The trust assets remain secure from any financial difficulties suffered by the sponsoring entity.

The SPV owns the collateral placed in the trust, and issues notes and equity against the collateral it owns. These collateralized debt obligations may be issued in different classes of securities or "tranches." Each tranche of a CDO structure may have its own credit rating. The most subordinated tranche of the CDO is usually called the equity tranche.

These securities are issued privately to institutional investors and high net worth individuals. The collateral held by the SPV produces cash flows that are used to pay interest and dividends on the notes and equity issued by the SPV. The majority of principal on the securities issued by the SPV is paid at the end of the life of the SPV, usually from final principal pay-offs or the sale of the SPV assets.

BALANCE SHEET CDO STRUCTURES

Balance sheet CDO structures are typically constructed as collateralized loan obligations. Following Exhibit 5, we consider two examples of balance sheet CDO structures: cash funded and synthetic. We diagram how these structures work and discuss the benefits to a bank or other lending institution from sponsoring a CLO structure.

Cash Funded Balance Sheet CDO

In a balance sheet CDO, the seller of the assets is usually a bank that seeks to remove a portion of its loan portfolio from its balance sheet. The bank constructs a CLO special purpose vehicle to dispose of its balance sheet assets into the CLO structure. Exhibit 6 demonstrates this type of CLO structure.

Notice that there are several players in a CLO structure. First, the bank receives funding from the capital markets. Then the bank loans money to a commercial borrower. In return for lending cash, the bank receives a secured loan obligation from the borrower. The bank then pools several of these loans (it can be as many as several hundred) and sells the pool of loans to the CLO trust in return for cash. The CLO trust in turn issues securities to outside investors in the form of debt securities. These debt securities represent a claim on the pool of commercial loans contained in the CLO trust. The CLO trust uses the cash received from the sale of the CLO securities to pay the bank for the purchase of the commercial loans.

Exhibit 6: Structure of a Balance Sheet CLO

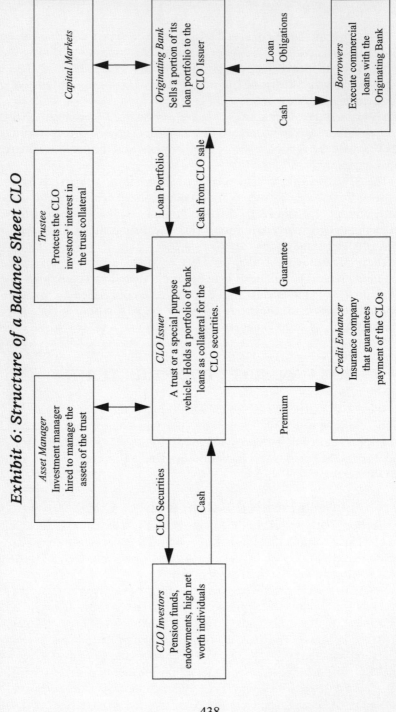

Capital Markets

Originating Bank
Sells a portion of its loan portfolio to the CLO Issuer

Borrowers
Execute commercial loans with the Originating Bank

Loan Obligations

Cash

Trustee
Protects the CLO investors' interest in the trust collateral

Loan Portfolio

Cash from CLO sale

CLO Issuer
A trust or a special purpose vehicle. Holds a portfolio of bank loans as collateral for the CLO securities.

Guarantee

Credit Enhancer
Insurance company that guarantees payment of the CLOs

Premium

Asset Manager
Investment manager hired to manage the assets of the trust

CLO Securities

Cash

CLO Investors
Pension funds, endowments, high net worth individuals

438

CLO trusts usually have a professional asset manager to manage the assets contained in the trust. This can be the selling bank where the bank is hired under a separate agreement to manage the portfolio of loans that it sold to the CLO trust. Also, the CLO trust will have a trustee whose job it is to protect the security interests of the CLO investors in the trust's assets. Usually, this is not the bank or an affiliate because of conflict of interest provisions. Last, the CLO trust may purchase a credit enhancement from an outside insurance provider. The credit enhancement guarantees from a third party timely payment of interest and principal on the CLO securities up to a specified amount, and ensures that they will receive an investment-grade credit rating.

Many bank CLOs are self-liquidating. All interest and principal payments from the commercial loans are passed through to the CLO investors. Other balance sheet CLOs provide for the reinvestment of loan payments into additional commercial loans to be purchased by the CLO trust. After the initial reinvestment period, the CLO trust enters into an amortization period when the loan proceeds are used to pay down the principal of the outstanding CLO tranches.

Synthetic Balance Sheet CDO

Synthetic balance sheet CDOs differ from the cash funded variety in several important ways. First, cash funded CDOs are constructed with an actual sale and transfer of the loans or assets to the CDO trust. Ownership of the assets is transferred from the bank's balance sheet to that of the CDO trust. In a synthetic CDO, however, the sponsoring bank or other institution transfers the total return profile of a designated basket of loans or other assets via a credit derivative transaction, usually a credit default swap or a credit return swap. Therefore, the bank transfers its risk profile associated with its assets, but not the legal ownership of assets.

Second, in a cash flow CDO, the proceeds received from the sale of the CDO securities are used to purchase the collateral for the CDO trust. The cash flows from the collateral held by the CDO trust are then used to pay the returns on the CDO securities. Conversely, the cash proceeds from a synthetic balance sheet CDO are usually invested in U.S. Treasury securities. The interest received from these securities is used to fund the swap payments to the bank.

Third, a synthetic balance sheet CDO can use leverage. The use of leverage can boost the returns received by the CDO investors, thereby increasing the attractiveness of the CDO securities.

Last, a synthetic balance sheet CDO is less burdensome in transferring assets. Certain commercial loans may require borrower notification and consent before being transferred to the CDO trust. This can take time and increases the administration costs.

Exhibit 7 demonstrates a synthetic balance sheet CDO. Assume that a bank establishes a SPV in the form of a trust for a balance sheet CLO. The bank wishes to reduce its exposure to a basket of loans on its balance sheet.[3]

---

[3] We omitted the asset manager and trustee from this exhibit to make the diagram less cluttered. These two entities are still used, but are not crucial to our example.

Exhibit 7: Synthetic Balance Sheet CLO

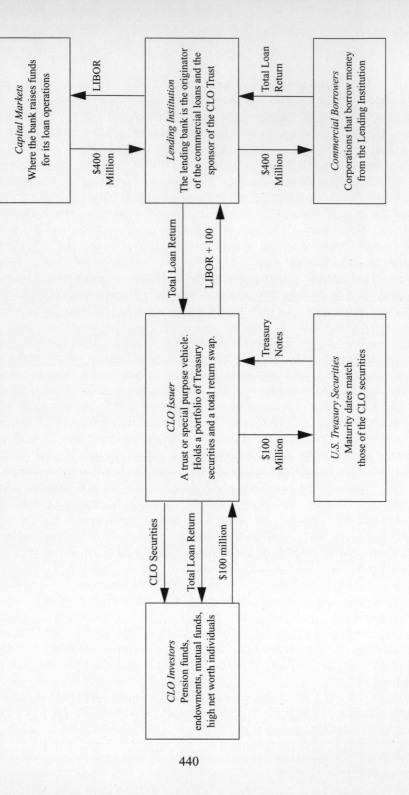

The CLO trust issues medium term notes to investors that the trust records on its balance sheet as a liability and the investors record on their balance sheets as a privately issued 144A security.[4] The proceeds from the sale of the CLO securities are used to purchase U.S. Treasury securities with the same maturity as the CLO securities. The CLO securities receive an investment-grade credit rating because they are backed by default-free U.S. Treasury securities.

Next the SPV enters into a total return swap with the bank where the SPV will pay to the bank LIBOR + 100 basis points in return for receiving the total return on the referenced basket of bank loans. The total return from the bank loans includes both interest payments plus any appreciation or depreciation of the loan value. The SPV in turn passes through to the CLO security holders the total return from the loan portfolio.

Notice that the CLO security holders are insulated from the derivative transaction with the bank. The CLO trust acts as a middleman or buffer between the CLO security holders and the bank so that the CLO investors do not have to enter a swap directly with the bank. This could be problematic for certain pension funds or endowment funds that do not have the authority to negotiate swap agreements.

Assume that the CLO trust sells $100 million of securities to institutional and high net worth investors and that the trust securities mature in four years. The CLO trust uses the $100 million to purchase U.S. Treasury notes that mature in four years and accrue interest at 6% annually. In addition, the CLO trust enters into a 4-year total return swap with the bank where the CLO trust will pay to the bank LIBOR + 100 basis points annually, and the bank will pay the CLO trust the total return on its loan portfolio. The notional value of the swap transaction is $400 million. The average annual interest rate earned on the bank loans is LIBOR + 250 basis points.

In Exhibit 7, the notional value of the total return swap does not equal the face value of CLO trust securities sold. This is a demonstration of the leverage that can be applied in a synthetic balance sheet CLO compared to the cash funded CLO discussed earlier. Under the swap agreement, the CLO trust agrees to pay the bank LIBOR + 100 on a notional value of $400 million, while receiving from the bank the total return on a $400 million basket of loans. The total return on the loan basket equals the average interest payment of LIBOR + 250, plus any price appreciation or depreciation associated with the bank loans.

Take a moment to review all of the cash flows for the bank displayed in Exhibit 7. All of the cash flows net out to a single fee of 100 basis points for the bank. The bank receives $400 million from the capital markets and uses this cash to build a commercial loan portfolio. The bank pays for its funding at straight LIBOR. From the commercial loans, the bank receives LIBOR + 250 in interest payments plus any appreciation or depreciation in the value of the loans (together the interest payments plus any change in loan value equals the Total Loan Return).

---

[4] These private securities are typically offered in the form of SEC Rule 144A. Under this rule, the securities do not need to be registered with the SEC via a registration statement, but may be sold only to Qualified Institutional Buyers.

The bank passes on the interest payments and any appreciation or depreciation to the CLO trust under the terms of the total return swap agreement. The CLO trust agrees to pay the bank LIBOR + 100 which covers the banks funding costs at LIBOR plus adds 100 basis points.

Exhibit 8 demonstrates that all of these inflows and outflows cancel out leaving the bank with 100 basis points times the notional value of the swap, or an annual cash flow of $4 million.

The CLO investors receive the return on all of the CLO trust's assets and contractual agreements. This includes the net income on the swap agreement of 150 basis points plus any increase or decrease in the value of the basket of bank loans plus the interest earned on the U.S. Treasury securities. If there is no change in the value of the loans, then at maturity of the CLO securities, investors will receive the 4-year Treasury rate plus 150 basis points on a notional value of $400 million.

This highlights the use of leverage in the synthetic balance sheet CLO. Investors in the CLO trust committed only $100 million of capital but received 150 basis points of income on $400 million of bank loan exposure. This is equivalent to earning 600 basis points on $100 million. Plus the investors in the CLO trust receive the return earned on the 4-year U.S. Treasury notes. Therefore, investors in the CLO trust receive a rate of return that is 600 basis points greater than a comparable Treasury note. The ability to add 600 basis points of credit spread return on an investment grade security far exceeds the return that an investor could earn if it purchased the loans outright from the bank.

If this sounds like a great deal for the investors, it is even a better deal for the bank. Not only does the bank reduce its risk exposure to a basket of bank loans, it also frees up regulatory capital associated with these risky assets because it has transferred the risk (but not the assets) to the CLO trust. On top of this risk reduction, the bank receives a swap fee of $4 million per year. In other words, through a synthetic balance sheet CLO, the bank is paid to reduce its risks. The bank gets its cake and eats it too.

Exhibit 8: Net Gain or Loss for the Synthetic Balance Sheet CLO

	Cash Inflow	Cash Outflow	Net Gain/Loss
Raise $400 million from Capital Markets	$400,000,000		
Loan $400 million to commercial borrowers		$400,000,000	
Net Gain or Loss			$0
Receive interest on bank loans	LIBOR + 250		
Pay bank loan interest to the CLO Trust		LIBOR + 250	
Net Gain or Loss			0
Receive loan appreciation or depreciation	Change in Loan		
Pay loan appreciation/depreciation to the CLO Trust		Change in Loan	
Net Gain or Loss			0
Receive swap payments from the CLO Trust	LIBOR + 100		
Pay interest on borrowings from Capital Markets		LIBOR	
Net Gain or Loss			100 basis points

The $100 million of U.S. Treasury securities serves as collateral for the CLO trust's side of the total return swap with the sponsoring bank. If the basket of referenced loans declines in value, the Treasury securities will pay for this decline. For this reason, the CLO trust's position is often referred to as the "first loss position." This means that the first $100 million of loss on the basket of bank loans will be absorbed by the CLO trust. The remaining $300 million "second loss position" is retained by the bank because it still owns the basket of loans. Therefore, the bank can receive regulatory capital relief only for the first loss position of $100 million.

In practice, the CLO trust is constructed so that if the first loss position is fully drawn upon, the trust will liquidate. The trust will pay out any remaining accrued interest to the holders of the trust certificates and then close its operations. The CLO securities will be rendered worthless.

Benefits to Banks from CLOs

Although there is a growing demand from investors for CLO structures, banks are equally motivated to build CLO trust structures. Risk reduction as indicated above is just one of several benefits to banks from CLOs.

Reducing Risk-Based/Regulatory Capital

Reducing risk-based/regulatory capital is the single most important motivation for a bank to form a CLO trust. Under the 1988 Basle Accord adopted by the G-10 group of industrialized nations, banks in these nations are required to maintain risk-based capital equal to 8% of the outstanding balance of commercial loans.[5] The 8% regulatory capital charge required for commercial loans is the highest percentage of capital required to be held against any asset type.

Using a CLO trust to securitize and sell a portfolio of commercial loans can free up regulatory capital that must be committed to support the loan portfolio. Consider a bank with a $500 million loan portfolio that it wishes to sell. It must hold risk-based capital equal to 8% × $500 million = $40 million to support these loans. The bank sponsors a CLO trust where the trust purchases the $500 million loan portfolio from the bank and finds outside investors to purchase all of the CLO securities. The bank no longer has any exposure to the basket of commercial loans and now has freed $40 million of regulatory capital that it can use in other parts of its balance sheet.

Unfortunately, sometimes the equity tranche of the CLO trust is unappealing to outside investors and cannot be sold. Under this circumstance, the sponsoring bank may have to retain an equity or "first loss" position in the CLO trust. If this is the case, the regulatory capital standards require the bank to maintain risk-based capital equal to its "first loss" position. For example, if the sponsoring bank had to retain a $10 million equity piece in the CLO trust to attract

---

[5] For a more detailed discussion on the Basle Accord and it impact on regulatory capital, see Mark Anson, *Credit Derivatives* (New Hope, PA: Frank J. Fabozzi Associates, 1999).

other investors, it must take a one-for-one regulatory capital charge for this first loss position. This means that only $40 million − $10 million = $30 million of regulatory capital will be freed by the CLO trust.

Increasing Loan Capacity

In our regulatory capital example above, not only does the bank free up $40 million of regulatory capital, it also receives cash proceeds from the sale of its loans to the CLO trust. The funds generated by the loan securitization can be used to originate additional commercial loans at either better rates or better credit quality or it can be used to purchase different assets for the bank's balance sheet. Either way, the bank has generated a large cash inflow that it can use to strengthen its balance sheet.

Improving ROE and ROA Measures

With its cash in hand, the bank can reduce its overall balance sheet by paying down its liabilities. In fact, if the bank can reduce its overall capital base and at the same time increase the proportion of higher yielding assets, it will increase its return on equity (ROE) and return on assets (ROA).

Continuing with our example from above. Assume that the bank's cost of funds is LIBOR and that the $500 million portfolio of loans earns on average LIBOR + 100 basis points. Therefore, the bank earns $5 million per year on this loan portfolio. The required regulatory capital is $40 million for a ROE of $5 million ÷ $40 million = 12.5%.

The bank uses the $500 million received from the sale to the CLO trust to loan out in the residential mortgage market. The bank receives loan income of LIBOR + 0.75% on the residential mortgages. However, the regulatory capital required to support residential mortgages is one half of that for commercial loans, or $20 million. The bank's return on equity is now: $3.75 million ÷ $20 million = 18.75%.

Reducing Credit Concentrations

The selling bank may be at the limit of its credit exposure to one industry or group of borrowers. It may find this industry profitable in terms of commercial loans, but cannot increase its exposure. By selling part of its loan portfolio, it has produced more "dry powder" to lend to that borrower or industry.

Preserving Customer Relations

A bank is often in the uncomfortable position of accepting more exposure to a bank client that it wishes. In order to maintain its relationship with its borrowers, the bank can reduce its exposure to the client by selling a portion of the bank's loan portfolio pertaining to the client to the CLO trust. In a CLO, the portfolio manager for the trust is often the bank so that the borrowing client need not even know that its loan has been sold to the CLO trust.

Exhibit 9: Growth of Institutional Investors in the Bank Loan Market

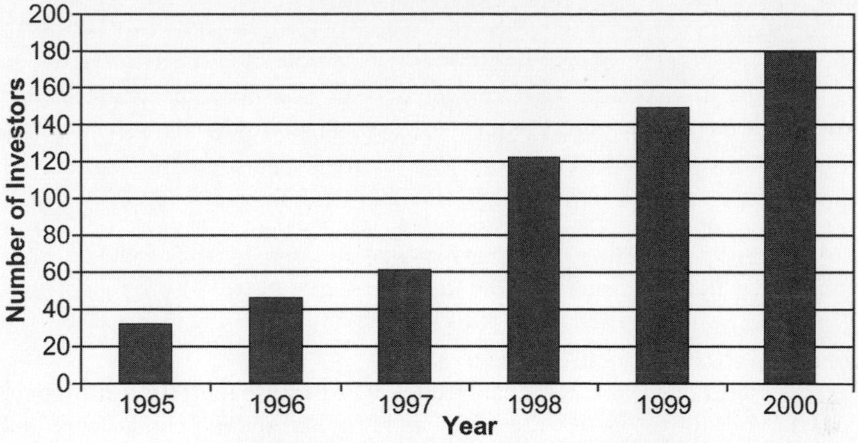

Source: Standard & Poor's Portfolio Management Data

Competitive Positioning

As Exhibit 2 demonstrates, the market for CLO trusts has grown significantly during the period 1995–2000. There is a large investor base of pension funds, endowments, mutual funds, insurance companies, and high net worth individuals that seek to invest in bank loans.[6] The number of institutional loan investors has grown significantly from 1995 through the year 2000. Exhibit 9 shows the growth of investor interest in this market.

CLO trusts are the natural format for achieving this exposure. Furthermore, large banks desiring to position themselves in this increasingly competitive marketplace may wish to establish a program of CLO trusts in order to attract and maintain qualified investors for the CLO securities.

Credit Enhancements

Most CLO structures contain some form of credit enhancement to ensure that the CLO securities sold to investors will receive an investment grade rating. These enhancements can be internal or external. Generally, credit enhancements are made at the expense of lower coupon rates paid on the CLO securities. While we discuss credit enhancements with respect to CLO trusts, these provisions are equally applicable to CBO trusts.

Subordination

Subordination is the most common form of credit enhancement in a CDO transaction and it flows from the structure of the CLO trust. This in an internal credit enhancement.

[6] See Smithson and Hayt, "Tools for Reshaping Credit Portfolios; Managing Credit Risk."

For instance, CLO trusts typically issue several class or tranches of securities. The lower level, or subordinated tranches, provide credit support for the higher rated tranches. As we discussed previously, the equity tranche in a CLO trust provides the "first loss" position with respect to a basket of loans. This tranche provides credit enhancement for every class of CLO securities above it.[7]

Junior tranches of a CDO are rated lower than the senior tranches but in return receive a higher interest rate commensurate with their subordinated status and therefore greater credit risk. The payment structure of a CDO can vary, but it is usually is one of three forms: sequential pay, fast pay/slow pay, or pro rata.

In a sequential-pay CDO, the senior tranches must be paid in full before any principal is paid to the junior tranches. In a fast pay/slow pay CDO, the senior tranches are paid down faster than the junior tranches. Last, in a pro rata payment, the senior and junior tranches are paid down at the same rate. Most CDO structures go with a sequential-pay format.

This payment structure is often referred to as the "waterfall." As interest and principal payments are received from the underlying collateral, they flow down the waterfall, first to the senior tranches of the CLO trust and then to the lower rated tranches. Subordinated tranches must wait for sufficient interest and principal payments to flow down the tranche structure before they can receive a payment.

Over Collateralization

Over collateralization results from the senior/junior nature of tranches in a CDO. For example, consider a CDO trust with a market value of collateral trust assets of $100. The CDO trust issues two tranches. Tranche A is the senior tranche and consists of $80 million of securities. Tranche B consists of $20 million of subordinated securities and is paid after the senior tranche is paid in full. The level of over collateralization for the senior tranche is $100/$80 = 125%. The funds used to purchase the excess collateral come from the subordinated tranche; tranche B provides the over collateralization to tranche A. Over collateralization is an internal credit enhancement.

Spread Enhancement

Another internal enhancement can be excess spread of the loans contained in the CLO trust compared to the interest promised on the CLO securities. The excess spread may arise because the assets of the CLO trust are of lower credit quality than the CLO securities, and therefore yield a higher interest rate than that paid on the CLO securities. A higher yield on the trust assets may also result from a different term structure. This excess spread may be used to cover any losses asso-

---

[7] Most CLO structures are "de-linked." That is, there is no link with the selling bank, the CLO trust holds ownership over the loan assets. In this case the credit rating of the bank does not affect the CLO trust. In some cases, however, the CLO trust remains linked with the selling bank. In this case, the bank sells the risk to the CLO trust via a credit-linked note or a credit swap so that the CLO trust must depend upon the creditworthiness of the selling bank to collect on the trust's assets.

ciated with the CLO trust loan portfolio. If there are no losses on the loan portfolio, the excess spread accrues to the equity tranche of the CLO trust.

Cash Collateral or Reserve Account

Excess cash is held in highly rated instruments such as U.S. Treasury securities or high-grade commercial paper that provide security to the debt holder of the CLO trust. Cash reserves are often used in the initial phase of a cash flow transaction. During this phase, cash proceeds received by the trust from the sale of its securities are used to purchase the underlying collateral and the reserve account. Cash reserves are not the most efficient form of credit support because they generally earn a lower rate of return than that required to fund the CLO securities. Therefore, there is a clear tradeoff: a higher cash reserve account means greater credit support but at the expense of lower interest payments on the CLO securities.

External Credit Enhancement

An external credit enhancement is provided by an outside third party in the form of insurance against defaults in the loan portfolio. This insurance may be a straightforward insurance contract, the sale of a put option, or the negotiation of a credit default swap to protect the downside from any loan losses. The effect is to transfer the credit risks associated with the CLO trust collateral from the holders of the CLO trust securities to the insurance company.

ARBITRAGE CDOS

An arbitrage CDO seeks to make a profit. The profit is earned by selling CLO/CBO securities to outside investors at a price that is higher than that paid for the assets placed into the CLO/CBO structure. Most often an arbitrage CDO consists of bonds purchased on the open market. These bonds are then placed into the CDO trust and the manager of the trust sells new securities (the CBOs) to new investors. An arbitrage profit is earned if the CDO trust can sell its securities at a lower yield than that paid for the bond collateral contained in the trust.

Exhibit 10 presents the structure for a CBO trust. Many of the same players that were introduced in Exhibit 6 are used in the formation of a CBO trust. The difference is that the seller of the assets to the trust is usually not a bank, but an investment management firm interested in making money through the CBO structure. In Exhibit 10, the seller of the bonds will earn a profit from the CBO trust if the "Cash from CBO Sale" exceeds the cash paid for the original bonds.

Cash Flow Arbitrage CDO

In a cash flow arbitrage CDO, the repayment of the CDO securities are dependent upon cash flows from the underlying pool of bonds and loans. These structures typically invest in high-yield bonds with average ratings of B to BB.

Exhibit 10: Structure of an Arbitrage CDO/CBO

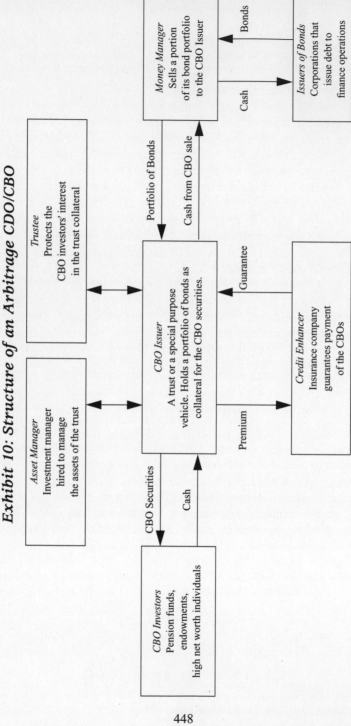

In a cash flow CBO, the trust holds the bonds and receives the debt service (principal and interest payments). The CBO trust securities are sold to match the payment schedules of the bonds held as collateral by the trust. As the collateral pays down, the CBO trust pays down its securities.

In some cases, the cash flow arbitrage CDO is static. This means that the collateral held by the CBO trust does not change, it remains static throughout the life of the trust. Other CBO trusts are actively managed. The money manager who sponsors the fund may buy and sell high-yield bonds or other assets for the trust over its term.

Cash flow arbitrage CBO trusts are dependent upon default and recovery rates. For example, assume that a CBO trust has two tranches or classes of securities. Tranche A is the senior class and represents $100 million in CBO securities. Class B is the subordinated, or equity class, and is $50 million of securities. Underlying the CBO trust is $150 million of high-yield bonds that pay income to the trust of LIBOR + 4%.

The senior tranche is promised payments of principal plus LIBOR + 1%, the subordinate tranche receives whatever is left after the senior tranche is fully paid. For simplicity, we assume that the CBO trust is organized for one year with a bullet payment at the end of one year and that LIBOR is equal to 5%.

We demonstrate several scenarios: no default of high-yield bonds, a 1% default rate, 2% default rate, and so on up to a 5% default rate. The historical recovery rate for defaulted high-yield debt is about 40%. Therefore if 5% of the bonds default, the CBO trust would expect to recover $5\% \times 40\% = 2\%$, resulting in a net loss of 3%.[8]

Under the no default scenario, at maturity of the CBO trust, the subordinated equity tranche of the CBO trust will receive:

$150 million $\times$ (1+[LIBOR + 4%]) − $100 million $\times$ (1+[LIBOR + 1%])
= $57.5 million

On an original investment of $50 million, this is a return of 15%.

Under the next scenario, 1%, or $1.5 million of the high-yield bonds held by the CBO trust, default. With a recovery rate of 40%, this is a net loss of $0.9 million that must be absorbed by equity tranche. Under this loss scenario, the equity tranche will receive:

$148.5 million $\times$ (1 + [LIBOR + 4%]) + $0.6 million
− $100 million $\times$ (1 + [LIBOR + 1%]) = $56.465 million

On an original investment of $50 million, this is a return of 12.93%

These scenarios can be used to generate a yield table of the equity tranche for this CBO structure. Exhibit 11 provides a graph of the default rate and

---

[8] We also assume that recovery on any defaulted bond is made by the maturity of the CBO trust. In practice, recovery can take several years, stretching out the payments to the equity tranche of the CBO. Last, we assume that all accrued income is lost on defaulted debt, and that any recovery pertains only to the face value of the debt.

the resulting yield to maturity for the equity tranche. As can be seen, the return to the equity tranche declines quickly as the default rate rises. At a default rate of 5%, the return to the equity tranche is less than 5%.

The important point to this example is that the return on investment for both tranches depends only on the cash flows received by the CBO trust. The critical factors associated with these cash flows are the default rate for the high-yield bonds held by the CBO trust and the recovery rate on those bonds once they default.

At no time does the market value of the high-yield bonds affect the return to the CBO investors. Although the prices of the high-yield bonds may fluctuate up and down, this does not affect the returns to the CBO security holders as long as the underlying collateral pays its coupons and principal at maturity.

Market Value Arbitrage CDO

With these CDO structures, the return earned by investors is linked to the market value of the underlying collateral contained in the CDO trust. These structures are used when the maturity of the collateral assets purchased by the trust does not match precisely the maturity of the CDO securities. In fact, this is usually the case.

Consider the example of a CBO trust that buys high-yield bonds. It is unlikely that the trust will be able to sell securities that perfectly mimic the maturity of the high-yield bonds held as collateral. Therefore, the cash flows associated with a market value arbitrage CDO come from not only the interest payments received on the collateral bonds, but also from the sale of these bonds to make the principal payments on the CBO securities. Therefore, the yield on the CBO securities is dependent upon the market value of the high-yield bonds at the time of resale.

Exhibit 11: Projected Return for Equity in a Cash Flow Arbitrage CBO

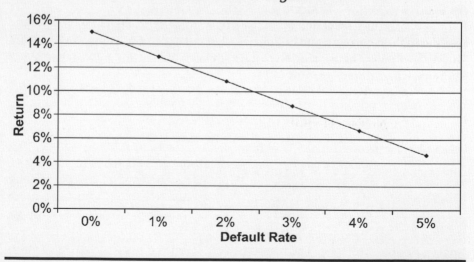

Exhibit 12: Expected Return for the Equity Tranche of a Market Value CBO

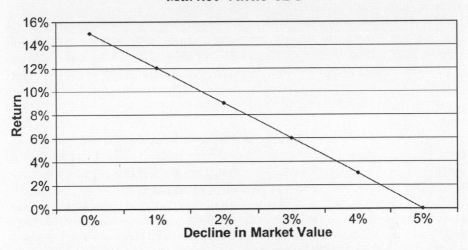

Given the dependency on market prices, market value arbitrage CDOs use the total rate of return as a measure of performance. The total rate of return takes into account the interest received from the high-yield bonds as well as their appreciation or depreciation in value.

Let's use the same example as above for the cash flow CBO structure. There are two tranches, a $100 million tranche paying LIBOR + 1% and an equity tranche. The CBO trust lasts for one year, and at the end of one year, both tranches of securities receive a bullet payment. The difference is that at the end of one year, the CBO trust must sell its underlying high-yield bond portfolio to fund the redemption of the CBO trust securities.

Under this scenario, we assume not that there are defaults, but instead that the high-yield bond portfolio has suffered a decline in value of 0% to 5%. Under the 0% decline in value scenario, the return to the equity tranche in a market value CBO will be the same as under the cash flow example, 15%.

Under a decline of value of 1%, the return to the equity tranche will equal:

$150 million × (1 +[LIBOR + 4%]) − $100 million
   × (1+[LIBOR+1%]) − $1.5 million = $56 million

This equals a total return of $56 million ÷ $50 million = 12%.

In Exhibit 12 we provide a graph similar to Exhibit 11 that plots the return to the equity tranche versus the decline in value of the high yield bond portfolio. As we can see, a decline in market value results in a more precipitous decline (compared to a cash flow arbitrage CBO) in the return to the equity tranche of this CBO trust. The reason is that there is no opportunity for the trust collateral to recover the lost value. The high-yield bonds must be sold to fund the redemptions of the CBO securities. This decline in value is locked in at the time of the liquidation of the trust.

Practically, a market value CBO trust will also experience defaults just like cash flow CBO trusts. When this occurs, the market value trust must take into account defaults and recovery rates as well as changes in market value. In fact it is likely that as default rates increase, the market value of the bond portfolio will decrease. These complementary effects can erode the return to the equity tranche even faster than indicated in Exhibits 11 and 12.

Synthetic Arbitrage CDOs

Synthetic arbitrage CDOs simulate the risk transference similar to a cash sale of assets without any change in the legal ownership of the assets. The risk is transferred by a credit default swap or a total return credit swap.

Synthetic arbitrage CDOs are used by asset management companies, insurance companies, and other investment shops with the intent of exploiting a mismatch between the yield of underlying securities and the lower cost of servicing the CDO securities. These structures are less administratively burdensome when compared to cash funded structures particularly when attempting to transfer only a portion of a credit risk.

Synthetic CDO trusts can also be used to provide economic exposure to high-yield assets that may be relatively scarce and difficult to acquire in the cash market. Last, synthetic CDO trusts can employ leverage. In Exhibit 7 we demonstrated a synthetic balance sheet CLO where the leverage ratio was 4 to 1.

The mechanics of a synthetic arbitrage CDO are similar to those demonstrated in Exhibit 7. The CDO trust enters into a swap agreement on a reference portfolio of fixed income securities. The portfolio may be fully funded or only partially funded at the time of the swap agreement (there is often a "ramping up" period when credit risky assets are selected for the reference portfolio). Under the swap agreement, the CDO trust will pay LIBOR plus a spread to the sponsoring money manager, and in return, receive the total return on the reference portfolio. The total return includes interest received from the securities in the reference portfolio as well as any price appreciation or depreciation. The reference portfolio is funded on the balance sheet of the sponsoring institution.

One key difference of a synthetic arbitrage CDO compared to a cash flow CDO is that the swap payments are made periodically, usually on a quarterly basis. Therefore, the underlying collateral must be marked to market each quarter to determine the total return on the credit swap. This exposes the CDO securities holder to market risk similar to a market value arbitrage CLO trust discussed above.

Profiting from an Arbitrage CDO Trust

We have mentioned several times that the motivation for an arbitrage CDO trust is to earn a profit. We provide an example of how this is done.

Exhibit 13: An Arbitrage CBO Trust

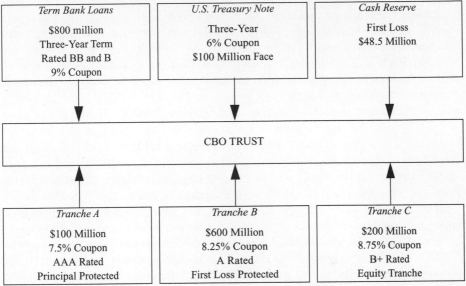

Term Bank Loans	U.S. Treasury Note	Cash Reserve
$800 million	Three-Year	First Loss
Three-Year Term	6% Coupon	$48.5 Million
Rated BB and B	$100 Million Face	
9% Coupon		

CBO TRUST

Tranche A	Tranche B	Tranche C
$100 Million	$600 Million	$200 Million
7.5% Coupon	8.25% Coupon	8.75% Coupon
AAA Rated	A Rated	B+ Rated
Principal Protected	First Loss Protected	Equity Tranche

Assume a money manager establishes an arbitrage CBO to invest in high-yield bonds. The trust will have a life of three years and raises $900 million by selling three tranches of securities. The security tranches issued by the trust are divided by credit rating. In tranche A, debt with the highest priority is issued against the highest credit quality bonds in the trust collateral. This senior debt tends to have a lower return and volatility than that of the composite bond portfolio return and volatility.

The second or mezzanine tranche is securitized with the average credit quality bond in the pool. Here, the credit rating of tranche B may not be any greater than that of the average high-yield bond owned by the CBO trust, but this tranche still has the advantage of a diversified pool of bonds and the seniority to the last CBO tranche. The final tranche is subordinated to the two other CLO tranches and is securitized with the lowest credit quality bonds in the trust portfolio. For this tranche, the risk is the highest, but the bonds securing it are also the highest yielding.

Exhibit 13 provides a more detailed example of this arbitrage CBO trust. Consider a money manager that has a portfolio of high-yield bonds with credit ratings of the underlying issuers equal to B and BB. The bonds pay an average coupon of 9%, have a face value of $800 million, and a current market value of $750 million. The money manager sells these bonds to the trust for a fee of 20 basis points ($1,500,000). In addition, the money manager charges an annual management fee of 50 basis points for managing the face value of the Trust's assets: 50 bp × $900 million = $4,500,000.

Additionally, the CBO trust buys a $100 million 3-year U.S. Treasury note at an annual coupon of 6%. The Treasury note will be used to provide credit protection to Tranche A and allow for a AAA credit rating. Last, the CBO trust establishes a $48.5 million cash reserve account. The cash reserve comes from the difference in cash inflows from the sale of trust securities ($900 million), less the cash outflow to pay for the trust's assets ($750 for the high-yield bonds and $100 million for the Treasury note), less the transaction fee ($1,500,000). The cash reserve earns annual interest of 5%.

Tranche A has a $100 million face value, a coupon of 7.5% and is rated AAA. This tranche gets the highest credit rating possible because it is principal protected. The 3-year Treasury note will mature to a value of $100 million at the same time that the Tranche A securities become due and payable, and the proceeds from the Treasury note will be used to pay the Tranche A investors. However, the Tranche A investors receive a higher coupon than U.S Treasuries because they have a claim on a portion of the pass-through return earned from the high-yield bond portfolio.

The second tranche has a face value of $600 million, a stated coupon of 8.25%, and is rated single A. This tranche has a higher rating than the underlying bonds because it has first loss protection through the cash reserve. However, the first loss protection only covers $48.5 million worth of defaulted bonds. Therefore, this tranche does not have the same principal protection as Tranche A, and consequently receives a lower credit rating.

Tranche C is the equity tranche. It does not get paid until Tranches A and B receive their payments. Consequently, this tranche bears all of the residual risk of the CBO trust just as stockholders bear all of the residual risk in a corporation. This tranche has a face value of $200 million, a stated coupon of 8.75%, and is rated B+, the average credit rating of the high-yield bonds.

Where does the trust get the money to pay for the money manager's annual fee of $4.5 million? It receives the money from the spread. Note that the stated coupon on each tranche is less than the average interest coupon on the high-yield bonds. The difference between the interest income earned on the high-yield bonds and that paid to the CBO security holders is spread income to the CBO trust. The trust uses this spread income to pay the management fee. Any residual income left over accrues to the Tranche C security holders — the equity investors in the CLO trust.

It is often the case that the equity investor in the CBO tranche will be the money manager itself. The manager purchases the equity tranche for two reasons. The first is to reap the excess spread income received from the CBO trust. The second is to attract other investors who may not wish to bear the subordinated risk of the equity tranche.

The spread income that can be earned in a CBO trust is demonstrated in Exhibit 14. Together, the Treasury note, the cash reserve, and the high-yield bonds generate $80.425 million in annual income. The three CBO tranches and annual management fee, however, only require $79 million of annual cash payments. The difference of $1.425 million is the spread earned by selling CBO securities at a lower yield than earned by the high-yield bond portfolios.

In summary, there are three ways to make a profit from an arbitrage CDO. First, the money manager can earn a transaction fee for selling its high-yield portfolio to the CBO trust. Second, the money manager, as an equity investor in the CBO trust, can earn the spread or arbitrage income from the CBO trust. Last, the CBO sponsor usually is also the manager of the CBO trust and can earn management fees for its money management expertise.

EXAMPLES OF CDO STRUCTURES

As the discussion above indicated, CDOs can come in all shapes and sizes. Frequently, these investment vehicles have several classes of securities outstanding. We provide some examples below.

G-Force CDO

Exhibit 15 shows a structure for a CDO where the underlying collateral is subordinated commercial mortgage-backed securities (CMBS). This structure, G-Force, was offered by the General Motors Acceptance Corporation. These CMBS, from 21 different deals, were poured into the G-Force CDO Trust.[9] The Trust issued several different classes of notes and equity. Each class of security was privately placed pursuant to Rule 144A of the Securities Act of 1933.

Exhibit 14: CBO Trust Annual Cash Flows

Inflows	
Income from high-yield bonds, 9% on $800 million	$72,000,000
Income from Treasury note, 6% on $100 million	6,000,000
Income from Cash Reserve, 5% on $48.5 million	2,425,000
Total	$80,425,000
Outflows	
Coupon on Tranche A, 7.5% on $100 million	$7,500,000
Coupon on Tranche B, 8.25% on $600 million	49,500,000
Coupon on Tranche C, 8.75% on $200 million	17,500,000
Annual management fee	4,500,000
Total	$79,000,000
Net annual trust income	$1,425,000

[9] See David Graubard, "CDO Roundup: GMAC is Testing the Waters with CMBS-Backed Deal," *Asset Securitization Report* (February 19, 2001).

Exhibit 15: G-Force CDO Notes

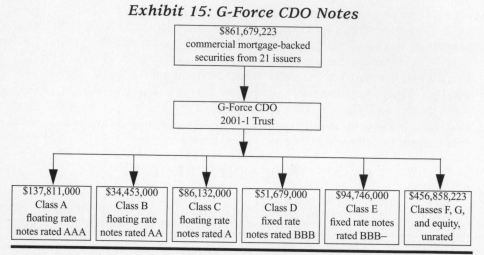

This is a balance sheet CDO. The G-Force CDO purchased the CMBS from the G2 Opportunity Fund, L.P. of which GMAC Commercial Mortgage Corp. was a founder. The G2 Opportunity Fund used the G-Force CDO to remove the risk of commercial mortgages from its balance sheet.

Several points should be noted about this structure. First, the most senior tranche of this CDO Trust receives the highest credit rating available, AAA. Therefore, even though the trust may contain less than investment grade securities, it still can issue tranches that have a high-investment grade rating.

The reason is simple. Class A notes are the first to receive coupon payments and to be redeemed. Even though the CDO trust contains subordinated CMBS that are less than AAA, there are enough mortgages to ensure the payment of the Class A obligations.

By purchasing CMBS from 21 different deals, G-Force was assured of a diversified portfolio of commercial mortgages. If there are defaults, it is most unlikely that all of these mortgages will default at the same time. Therefore, the diversity of the mortgage pool that supports the CDO trust ensures that Class A note holders will be paid in a timely fashion.

Second, as the G-Force CDO trust moves down the classes of notes, the ability to make full and timely payments becomes riskier. While Class A note holders have the greatest assurance of full and timely payments, this assurance began to erode as an investor purchases securities farther down into the classes. Therefore, Class B note holders received only a AA rating, Class C note holders received an A rating, and so forth.

The ratings continue to deteriorate until an investor reaches Classes F and G. These classes have no rating because they have the greatest risk: Classes F and G must wait until each tranche before them has been fully paid. Classes F and G are like subordinated debt; these notes generally have a low credit rating and are the last of the outstanding debt to be redeemed. Only equity ranks lower than Classes F and G.

Exhibit 16: HarbourView CDO III

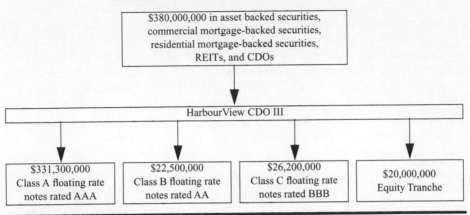

Finally, note the amount of residual commercial mortgages that supported Classes F and G and the equity tranche. There is a total $861 million of commercial mortgages used as collateral in the CDO trust to support investment-grade rated notes of only $404 million. The remaining $457 million of commercial mortgages is used for the subordinated debt and equity tranches. In other words, the CDO trust could lose $457 million of commercial mortgages before the investment grade classes would be affected. This is another way of stating that the coverage ratio for the investment-grade tranches is 53% of the CDO trust. Tranches F and G as well as the equity tranche were designated as subordinate to support the investment-grade ratings of Tranches A through E.

HarbourView CDO III

Not all CDOs have such a large subordinated coverage ratio as the G-Force CDO. Also, CDO trusts do not have to be as specialized as the G-Force CDO. Consider the CDO structure for the HarbourView CDO III trust shown in Exhibit 16.

There are two key differences in this trust compared to that of the G-Force CDO product. First, the collateral underlying the trust is much more diversified. The HarbourView CDO trust has an investment portfolio consisting of asset-backed securities, commercial mortgage-backed securities, residential mortgage-backed securities, real estate investment trusts, and even other collateralized debt obligations.[10] This is in contrast to the G-Force CDO that invested exclusively in commercial mortgages.

Second, a greater proportion of the overall CDO is investment grade. Class A notes are rated AAA and constitute over 80% of the issued securities by the CDO trust. This reflects a very high credit quality of investments by the HarbourView CDO compared to that of the G-Force CDO. In fact, the only tranche that is not rated investment grade is the equity tranche. The coverage ratio of the subordinated secu-

---

[10] See "HarbourView CDO III Rated AAA/AA/BBB by Fitch," *Business Wire* (April 25, 2001).

rities to the investment grade tranches is only 5% compared with 53% for the G-Force CDO. This is another reason why the G-Force CDO was a balance sheet CDO, it removed lower rated mortgages from its balance sheet into that of the CDO trust.

This is an example of an arbitrage CDO. HarbourView is a wholly-owned subsidiary of OppenheimerFunds Inc., a mutual fund manager based in New York City. OppenheimerFunds has a well-known high-yield department that manages high-yield mutual funds for retail investors. The HarbourView CDO is a way for OppenheimerFunds and HarbourView to earn additional management fee income for their expertise in the high-yield market. It is also a way for OppenheimerFunds to diversify its revenue base between retail investors and institutional investors.

NEW DEVELOPMENTS IN CDOS

In our discussion of distressed debt investing in Chapter 16, we noted how default rates have increased in the United States during the time period 2000-2001. In fact, one rating service, Fitch, has determined the high-yield bond default amount to be $45.5 billion in the first six months of 2001. This increase in default rates has led to an increased interest in distressed debt-backed CDOs.

As second new development has been the extension of CDOs to hedge funds. This comes as a result of the tremendous amount of capital pouring into the hedge fund market. Last, CDOs have been applied to private equity investments. These three new developments demonstrate how barriers are being broken between different segments of the alternative investment market.

Distressed Debt CDOs

A recent development in the CDO market is a distressed debt CDO. As its name implies, the primary collateral component is distressed debt. Distressed debt included both securities for which the issuer is in default of the bond payments, and non-defaulted securities that trade in distressed ranges in anticipation of a future default by the issuing entity. Distressed debt securities are generally defined as those loans or subordinated debt that trade at a coupon rate 10% or greater compared to a U.S. Treasury rate. In Chapter 20 we referred to the group of credit risky assets as "spread products." Distressed debt may be referred to as "big spread products."

Distressed debt CDOs usually have a combination of defaulted securities, distressed, but unimpaired securities, and non-distressed securities. The CDO manager will use historical default rates and estimated recovery amounts as well as the timing of default and recovery for distressed assets and non-distressed assets. In addition, for securities already in default, the CDO manager may use simulation models to determine how historical recovery patterns may change in times of additional market stress or lack of liquidity.

The appeal of the CDO structure is the ability to provide a series of tranches of collateralized securities that can have an investment-grade credit rating even though the underlying collateral in the CDO is almost exclusively distressed debt.

Investors are then able to sample the distressed debt market more effectively by choosing a distressed debt CDO tranche that matches their level of risk aversion. The CDO securities can receive a higher investment rating than the underlying distressed collateral through one or several of the credit enhancements described above.

Suppliers of Distressed Debt

To date, the main suppliers of assets for distressed debt CDOs have been banks. Banks use these CDOs to manage the credit exposure on their balance sheets. Assets for a CDO are purchased at market value. When a bank sells a distressed loan or bond to a distressed debt CDO it will usually receive a loss because it issued the loan or purchased the bond at par value. It was after the issuance of the loan or bond purchase that the asset became distressed resulting in a decline in market value.

Still banks are willing to provide the collateral to distressed debt CDOs for several reasons. First, it stops the deterioration of value on the bank's balance sheet. Any further decline in value of the distressed loan will be at the expense of the CDO and the holders of the CDO's equity tranches.

Second, by removing distressed loans from its balance sheet, the bank reduces its non-performing asset ratio. This allows it to obtain regulatory capital relief from its relevant banking authority, and this regulatory capital can be used for other bank business.[11]

Consider the Patriarch Partners distressed loan CDO. In January 2001, Patriarch purchased a portfolio of $1.35 billion of troubled loans from FleetBoston Financial Corp representing about 10% of FleetBoston's troubled loan portfolio. The purchase price was $1 billion, a 26% discount from the face value of the loans. The trust collateral consisted of 188 commercial loans from 91 borrowers.[12]

To finance the purchase of the loans, Patriarch Partners sold $925 million in AAA rated bonds and $75 million of A rated bonds. To receive an investment-grade credit rating for its CDO bonds, Patriarch had to establish a credit enhancement. It established a large reserve account of about $275 million. Patriarch was able to establish this reserve account because of the $1 billion it paid to FleetBoston, $725 was in cash and $275 million was in the form of a zero-coupon note. Therefore, Patriarch had $275 million from the sale of the trust securities that it could allocate to the reserve account. This CDO structure is presented in Exhibit 17.

From Patriarch's perspective, if it can successfully collect on all of the troubled loans, it stands to collect considerable income from the excess spread between the loan collateral and the interest paid on the trust securities. For instance, the AAA rate CDO tranche was priced at an interest rate of about LIBOR + 50 basis points, considerably less than that received from the commercial loans.

---

[11] The amount of regulatory capital that banks are required to maintain is determined by the Basle Committee on Banking Regulations and Supervisory Practices, which established global regulatory capital standards for industrialized nations. See Anson, *Credit Derivatives*.

[12] See Mark Pittman, "Patriarch Purchase of Fleet Loans a Bet on Collecting on Bad Debts," *Bloomberg News* (January 11, 2001).

Exhibit 17: Patriarch CLO Trust of Distressed Bank Loans

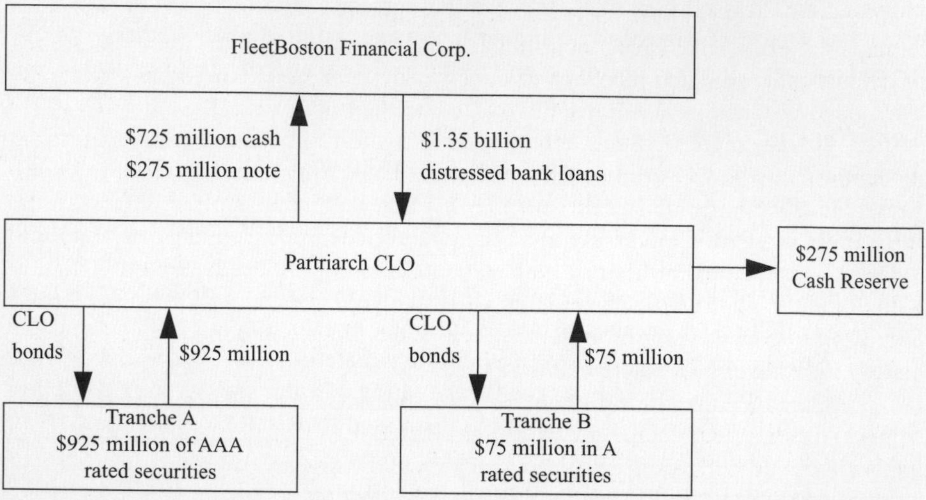

```
┌─────────────────────────────────────────────────────────────────┐
│                    FleetBoston Financial Corp.                    │
└─────────────────────────────────────────────────────────────────┘
        ▲                            │
   $725 million cash            $1.35 billion
   $275 million note            distressed bank loans
        │                            ▼
┌─────────────────────────────────────────────────────┐     ┌──────────────┐
│                  Partriarch CLO                      │ ──▶ │ $275 million │
└─────────────────────────────────────────────────────┘     │ Cash Reserve │
  CLO          ▲              CLO           ▲                └──────────────┘
  bonds   $925 million        bonds    $75 million
    │         │                 │          │
    ▼         │                 ▼          │
┌──────────────────────┐   ┌──────────────────────┐
│     Tranche A        │   │     Tranche B        │
│  $925 million of AAA │   │  $75 million in A    │
│   rated securities   │   │   rated securities   │
└──────────────────────┘   └──────────────────────┘
```

From FleetBoston's perspective, it could sell the loans without taking a complete write-off. In addition, FleetBoston was able to reduce its loan-loss reserves by $75 million by removing the troubled loans from its balance sheet. FleetBoston can also profit because the value of the $275 million zero-coupon bonds are tied to the amount collected from the troubled loans.[13]

Defaulted Securities

For defaulted securities, the timing and amount of recovery is the most important determinant for building credit tranches from the CDO trust. Recovery usually depends upon the stage of the distressed cycle that the issuer has entered.

If the issuer has just defaulted on the security, or has just sought the protection of Chapter 11 bankruptcy proceedings, the existing market price for the debt may be a poor indication of the ultimate recovery that will be achieved.[14] To get a better determination on the defaulted debt's true value, the CDO manager must review fair value opinions, the company's business plan included with the plan of reorganization filed with the bankruptcy court, competing plans offered by other creditors, and third-party appraisal reports.

Conversely, the later in the stage of bankruptcy that an issuer has progressed, the more dependable will be the market price of the outstanding defaulted securities. For example, if each creditor class has approved a company's plan of reorganization, and all that is waiting is the bankruptcy court's final approval, the market price of defaulted debt should be a reasonable estimate of its fair value.

---

[13] Id.

[14] See "Framework for Rating Distressed Debt CDOs," *Fitch Structured Finance, Loan Products Special Report* (July 27, 2001).

Distressed Assets

Distressed assets are those securities that are not yet impaired, but trade with the anticipation of default. These securities need to be analyzed by default rates, timing of default, and estimated recovery value. Consideration here is not given to the life cycle of bankruptcy proceedings, but instead, to the life cycle of the company.

For example a young company with a short operating history may have its debt rated CCC by various rating agencies. This rating is reflective of the company's nascent earnings stream and the fact that its business plan may yet to be fully implemented. Conversely, an older, established company with a long and deteriorating operating history may have outstanding debt also rated CCC but with a much higher yield. The reason is that the younger company, while short on operating history is long on potential, while the older company with the longer history may have an obsolete business plan.

Consider the timing of default for these two companies. For the older company, default may come much sooner than that for the new company because its fortunes are declining. In addition, the new company may be able to attract more rounds of financing based on the potential of its business plan while investors may have lost patience with the older company and additional financing may not be forthcoming.

While the default rate may be higher for the older company, estimates of recovery value may also be higher for the older company than the newer company. This is because the older company has had time to acquire physical assets which serve as collateral for its debt, while the newer company may have yet to generate much in the way of physical assets on its balance sheet. Therefore, while the probability and timing of default for the older company may be greater, so too is its recovery value.

A final consideration is the industry in which both the old and new companies operate. If it is an industry that has a long-term default rate that exceeds the long term average default rate for high-yield debt, then the CDO assumptions must be adjusted accordingly, and the equity tranche may need to assume a larger slice of the total CDO trust.

Non-Distressed Assets

Non-distressed assets are usually a minority of the distressed debt CDO. These assets may be investment grade, but more likely, have credit ratings below BBB (the bottom tier of investment grade debt). This can include loans or notes with credit ratings from BBB– to CCC+.

Non-distressed assets are usually analyzed with respect to "yield to worst" and portfolio concentrations. Yield to worst means the yield that would be earned on the security in the worst case scenario, usually a default or the declaration of bankruptcy. This yield takes into account the existing cash flows, the expected time to bankruptcy, and an estimate of recovery value. CDO trusts with a higher yield to worst than that of the average for similarly rated assets would be expected to experience default rates in excess of that for the rated category. Higher expected default rates means a larger equity tranche to absorb these losses.

In addition, CDO trusts with a greater concentration in a particular industry or with respect to a particular issuer may also require higher equity participation. The reason is that a credit event with respect to that concentrated industry or issuer could result is a disproportionate amount of defaults.

Hedge Fund CDOs

In March 2001, Ferrell Capital Management began marketing CDO securities that were backed by investments in hedge funds. The Ferrell CDO is backed primarily by the AIG International Relative Value Fund, which is the underlying asset via a $200 million investment. The hedge fund invests in commodity arbitrage, currency arbitrage, and merger arbitrage in both the United States and Europe.

It is expected that hedge fund managers will follow the lead of the Ferrell CDO and issue CDOs directly themselves, eliminating third-party issuers. For hedge fund managers, the CDO technology provides new ways to earn arbitrage spreads, particularly for those hedge fund managers that invest in distressed debt and fixed income arbitrage. These hedge fund managers already have the skill set for credit risk analysis, the ideal background for arbitrage CBOs or CLOs.

In fact, Standard & Poor's is examining a number of proposals for hedge fund of funds securitizations, and hopes to publish rating criteria within a year. To rate these transactions, S&P will use a similar approach to rating traditional CDOs.[15] S&P will review the hedge fund of fund's investment strategies, underlying asset characteristics, risk measurement, management processes, and level of liquidity. S&P will also assess the level and quality of management of the hedge fund of funds as well as the correlation of returns among different fund of funds and the overall leverage applied in each product. Additionally, S&P will review the underlying hedge funds themselves, taking into account return history, volatility of returns, redemption provisions, and risk controls.

Private Equity CDO

Another intersection in the alternative investment marketplace is that of CDOs and private equity. In July 2001, JP Morgan Partners and Prime Edge sponsored a new CDO trust that raised €150 million (about $128 million) by selling CDO securities that are collateralized by investments in private equity funds.[16] Furthermore, Standard & Poor's issued an investment-grade credit rating for the CDO securities in what was the first stand-alone credit rating for a private equity vehicle.

The €150 million was invested in a diversified pool of 35 pre-approved European private equity fund managers. The CDO trust issued three tranches of

[15] See "Standard & Poor's Vast Hedge Fund of Funds Securitization Potential," *PR Newswire* (October 1, 2001).

[16] See Dan Primack, "Prime Edge and JP Morgan Partners Put Private Equity into Debt," *Private Equity Week* (June 11, 2001).

securities. Tranche A carried a AA rating (with an insurance guarantee from Allianz Risk Transfer) and had a term of 12 years and raised €72 million. Tranche B was rated BBB, also had a term of 12 years, and raised €33 million. The equity or subordinated tranche of €45 million was unrated.

RISKS OF CDOS

There are considerable risks associated with CDO trusts. We provide a short discussion below, but the list is by no means comprehensive. For instance, if hedge funds begin to offer CDOs all the economic risks of the CDO must be considered as well as the risks peculiar to hedge fund management.

Default Risk

Default risk is the single greatest risk associated with an investment in a CDO structure. The lower down the totem pole of tranches the investor acquires, the greater the risk.

A recent example of the risks associated with CDOs is provided by the American Express Company.[17] As a result of its investments in CDOs, it was forced to take a more than $1 billion pretax charge for losses associated with these investments.

The investments were made by the company's money management unit, American Express Financial Advisors. In the late 1990s, AEFA decided to increase the high-yield bond portion of its portfolio to 12% of a pool of assets AEFA managed for the parent company, and to include in its high-yield bond portfolio CDO investments. AEFA purchased CDO securities in about 60 different trusts, and in some cases, bought the lower rated or equity tranches of the CDO.[18]

Unfortunately, with high-yield default rates increasing significantly from prior years, the riskier tranches of CDO structures began to default, resulting in large losses. American Express initially reported a loss from these investments of $182 million in April 2001. In July, the company announced an additional $826 million charge from its investments in CDOs. Of this amount, $403 million was due to problems related to the investment-grade tranches of CDOs it owned, and the remainder from losses and planned sales of high-yield bonds and lower-grade CDO tranches.[19]

The experience of American Express also illustrates another risk with CDO investing. Investors all too often rely on the reports generated by the CDO manager to determine the value of the collateral in the CDO.

To its credit, once the problem came to light, American Express performed its own analysis of the credit risk associated with the CDO collateral. In its analysis, American Express used an estimate that default rates would continue in the 8% to 9% range and stay constant for the next 18 months. This assumption

---

[17] See Paul Beckett, Mitchell Pacelle and Tom Lauricella, "How American Express Got in Over its Head with Risky Securities," *The Wall Street Journal* (July 27, 2001), p. A1.
[18] Id.
[19] Id.

led to the significant charges associated with its CDO portfolio. These estimates were more conservative than the more optimistic estimates generated by the CDO managers. Also, American Express analyzed the credit risk associated with about 8,500 bonds underlying the CDO trusts in which it had invested.[20]

The lesson is that in times of stress, CDO managers may be slower or reluctant to write down or write off the investments contained in the CDO trust. The investor may need to perform its own analysis to determine the extent of the damage.

Downgrade Risk

Downgrade risk refers to a reduction in credit rating of the CDO trust securities themselves (and not the underlying collateral). Prior to 2001 no AAA rate CDO tranche had ever been downgraded. However, with the general slowdown of the U.S. economy and the increase in default rates, downgrades were inevitable. In July 2001, Standard & Poor's downgraded, six AAA rated CDO tranches because of losses associated with the underlying trust collateral. While a downgrade will not hurt an investor if she holds her CDO trust security to maturity and receives full payments, it might harm her in the interim if she decides to sell her securities.

Differences in Periodicity

It may be that the frequency with which payments are received on the underlying collateral does not coincide with the frequency with which payments must be made on the CDO securities. This risk can be compounded when payments on different assets are received with different frequencies.

For instance, consider a CDO collateralized by both high-yield bonds and commercial loans. High-yield bonds pay interest semi-annually while commercial loans typically pay interest quarterly. If the trust's assets (the underlying bond and loan collateral) pay interest more frequently than the trust securities, then the transaction may be subject to negative carry (the trust has to hold the interest payments received from the collateral securities in low interest bearing accounts and wait for the payment date on its securities). Alternatively, if the trust assets pay interest less frequently than the securities issued by the trust, the trust may be faced an interest deficiency (the trust must find some way to fund the interest payments due on its securities).

This problem is often solved through the use of a swap agreement with an outside party, where the trust swaps the payments on the underlying collateral in return for interest payments that are synchronized with that of the trust securities.

Difference in Payment Dates

A risk due to the difference in payment dates arises from a mismatch between the dates on which payments are received on the underlying trust collateral, and the dates on which the trust securities must be paid. For example, consider a CBO

---

[20] Id.

trust whose underlying collateral consists entirely of high-yield bonds that pay semi-annual interest each July and January. Unfortunately, the CDO trust securities pay semi-annual interest in March and October. Similar to the problem of periodicity, this mismatch can be cured in a swap with an outside counterparty.

Basis Risk

Basis risk occurs when the index used for the determination of interest earned on the CDO trust collateral is different from the index used to calculate the interest to be paid on the CDO trust securities. For instance, the interest paid on most bank loans is calculated on a LIBOR plus a spread, but other assets may be based on a certificate of deposit rate in the United States. The combination of these assets in a single CDO trust will result in different bases used to determine the interest payments on the CDO trust securities. One way to counter this problem is to issue one or more tranches with a fixed interest rate. This way the underlying index will not affect the required payment to the CDO securities. However, this may lead to spread compression risk.

Spread Compression

Spread compression risk arises when credit spreads decline or compress over time, reducing interest rate receipts from the underlying collateral. Arbitrage CDOs based on high-yield bonds and commercial loans are susceptible to this risk.

For example, suppose a CDO trust is based on a portfolio of leveraged loans earning LIBOR + 200. The trust issues securities that, in the aggregate, pay an average of LIBOR + 100. Over the life of the trust, some of the commercial loans mature and must be replaced with new collateral for the CDO trust. However, in the interim, credit spreads have declined so that the same credit quality loan is now priced at LIBOR + 100. The CDO trust has now lost its arbitrage, and further, there is no excess spread to cushion any defaults that may occur with the new loans.

Yield Curve Risk

CDO trust portfolios with assets across a spectrum of maturity ranges will be impacted by changes in the yield curve represented by shifts in the curve, its shape, and its steepness.

For example, falling interest rates may result in a reduction of the positive spread between the CDO trust assets and its securities. This will have the similar impact as the spread compression described above if the trust securities have a fixed coupon rate instead of a floating coupon rate. In addition, high yielding collateral may be called away in the case of high-yield bonds, or prepaid in the case of commercial loans and replaced with lower yielding collateral. This will erode the arbitrage of the CDO trust.

The slope of the yield curve will also impact the profitability of an arbitrage CDO. For example, throughout most of the 1990s, the US yield curve was upward sloping. Consequently, there has been a negative carry between holding cash reserve accounts and the higher interest that must be paid on long term CDO trust securities.

CONCLUSION

This chapter was designed to introduce the reader to the basics of the collateralized debt obligation market. This is a huge market, with issuance now over $100 billion per year, and with new entrants every day.

The CDO market has also witnessed the intersection of other alternative investment strategies, including private equity, hedge funds, and distressed debt. Although commercial loans and high-yield bonds are the most popular form of assets for a CDO, just about any type of underlying asset can be used to collateralize a CDO trust. For instance, commodity-linked notes would be appropriate for a CBO trust structure. In addition, the first CDO trust backed by municipal bonds is expected to be introduced by the end of 2001.

In sum, the expanse of the CDO marketplace is limited only by the imagination of money managers, banks, and investment bankers to bundle new assets into trust structures. The limiting factor is getting the rating agencies to review and issue an investment-grade credit rating for the tranches of the CDO trust securities. To that end, the rating agencies must be able to develop a coherent method for analyzing the underlying collateral. Without investment-grade credit ratings, CDOs will not be able to sell their securities.

Section V

Corporate Governance

Chapter 22

Corporate Governance as an Alternative Investment Strategy

In Chapter 15 we discussed how leveraged buyouts have a positive impact on the corporate governance of target companies. Most public companies have widespread equity ownership. Shareholders tend to be scattered about the investor universe. As a result, monitoring the management of the company may not be easy. A single shareholder may be able to raise only a small voice. The advantage rests with management not with shareholders.

This advantage shifts with a leveraged buyout. LBOs introduce a more concentrated ownership structure. In effect, the leveraged buyout firm replaces the diverse shareholder base and provides a measure of active oversight that was lacking with a fragmented equity ownership structure. Leveraged buyout firms pursue an active corporate governance program where the managers of the company are held accountable for their actions by the equity owners.

It is clear from the returns earned by LBO firms, that solid corporate governance initiatives can add value and enhance the wealth of shareholders. However, corporate governance need not be limited to leveraged buyout firms. Any shareholder can be an active owner. In fact, corporate governance is often referred to as "Shareholder Activism." We use both terms interchangeably in this chapter.

It may seem odd to discuss corporate governance in the context of alternative assets. Yet, shareholder activism is certainly not a mainstream investment strategy. In fact, there are three reasons why corporate governance should be classified as an alternative equity investment strategy.

First, this strategy actively engages the executive management of public companies with the purpose of strengthening the companies' internal controls and financial performance. In this respect, corporate governance programs are very similar to private equity investment portfolios. Second, corporate governance programs target the internal controls of public companies independent of the current state of the equity market. Therefore, shareholder activism can provide a positive return stream that has less than perfect correlation with equity market returns. Last, corporate governance programs tend to have small, concentrated investment portfolios, similar to private equity and hedge funds. Therefore, corporate governance fulfills the characteristics of an alternative investment strategy, the same as private equity or hedge fund portfolios.

We begin this chapter by discussing the nature of agency problems and the lack of corporate control. Next, we discuss equity index investing and the role it plays in corporate governance. We then provide a brief introduction to corporate governance programs. We also review prior empirical studies regarding the benefits of shareholder activism. Last, we provide some empirical results from the California Public Employees' Retirement System's (CalPERS) corporate governance program.

AGENCY PROBLEMS AND THE LACK OF CORPORATE CONTROL

Shareholders are the ultimate decision-makers for any public company. After all, they own the company and can choose to do with it what they will. However, it is not practical for shareholders to make every day to day decision concerning the operations of the company. Consequently, shareholders delegate this authority to the managers of the company. The managers as agents are supposed to act in the best interests of their principals—the shareholders. However, problems may arise when the agents do not act in the best interest of their principals.

Agency Theory and Problems

In their seminal paper, Jensen and Meckling postulated agency problems in the management of public corporations.[1] An agency problem can arise when managers of public companies pursue their own economic self-interest instead of maximizing shareholder wealth. For instance, managers may work less vigorously on behalf of the shareholders, pursuing instead luxurious offices, corporate power, higher salaries and bonuses, and other perquisites of their employment. In essence, managers are human beings and are prone to pursue their own agendas instead of those for shareholders.

This problem is particularly acute in large public companies where the shareholders are widely dispersed. In this circumstance, there may not be sufficient incentives for individual owners to expend their financial or reputational resources to monitor the behavior of managers.

There are three solutions to the agency problem. The first is to ensure that managers have as significant ownership stake in the company as the shareholders. The goal of increasing shareholder wealth is then perfectly consistent with increasing the agent's wealth.

If the managers of the company do not have a significant ownership stake in the company, then compensation schemes must be adjusted to align the agents' self-interest with that of the shareholders. Specifically, compensating managers based on objective performance that increases shareholder wealth such as share price performance will provide consistency of shareholder and manager goals.

---

[1] See Michael Jensen and William Meckling, "Theory of the Firm: Managerial Behavior, Agency Costs and Ownership Structure," *Journal of Financial Economics* (October 1976), pp. 305–360.

Last, a corporate monitoring system can alleviate the agency problem as well as the need for large equity stakes by managers or incentive schemes that align economic interests. Corporate internal controls can provide effective monitoring of management's performance and behavior which ensure that shareholders' best interests are fulfilled.

The twin problems of human behavior and the inability to monitor effectively can lead to a breakdown in corporate internal control systems. We next consider how some of these controls breakdown and how they may be corrected.

Failure of Internal Corporate Control Systems

In the early 1990s there was a change in many boardrooms across corporate America. Many CEOs were removed by their board of directors. These companies included American Express, General Motors, Chrysler, IBM, Kodak and Westinghouse. These highly publicized departures were examples where internal corporate controls worked, even if they were a bit late. Unfortunately, all too often, the board of directors takes vital action only after the company is in a severe financial mess. Then the bankruptcy court or a takeover by another company is the frequent solution.

Corporate control systems are the responsibility of a company's board of directors. Directors are elected by the shareholders and have the final responsibility for the activities of the firm. It is the board's job to hire and fire the CEO, to establish appropriate compensation schemes, and to ensure appropriate controls are in place so that shareholders' interests are best served. The board of directors has access to confidential corporate information and the power to provide effective oversight of the company's managers.

There are several control points that can lead to a more efficient allocation of a corporation's resources and ensure shareholder wealth maximization. Unfortunately, all too frequently these control points fail to function properly.

Board Agenda

Although the CEO of every corporation must answer to the board of directors, it is most often the case that the agenda for every board meeting is set by the CEO rather than the directors themselves. This is often out of necessity because the CEO is the person most knowledgeable about the company's business affairs. However, this allows the CEO to control the amount of information as well as the content that is fed to the board of directors. Directors can operate effectively only when they have complete information.

Further, some directors may not have sufficient financial or industry expertise to interpret the information provided by the CEO. Even if the information provided by the CEO is concise, pertinent, and well-organized, the director may have only limited time to digest the information and make an intelligent decision. Unfortunately, some board agenda items may be too complicated to arrive at the right decision within the limited time frame of a one-day board meeting.

Board Composition

Another unfortunate fact of corporate America is that the CEO has considerable input into who will sit on his or her board of directors. Cronyism is not out of the question. Board members who have a current or prior affiliation with the CEO are often selected, raising questions of objectivity.

Furthermore, few boards of directors use recruiting agencies to find appropriate candidates for board vacancies. Frequently, board vacancies are filled by word of mouth, personal networks, or informal referrals, instead of a rigorous and objective search. A good solution is for the company to establish and update annually the criteria for selecting candidates for nomination to the board of directors.

Even then there may be a lack of cohesiveness among board members. A board of directors is a group of individuals working towards a common goal. Yet, most board members have businesses and professions to run outside of the corporate boardroom. They are busy people that have only a limited time to interact. Under these circumstances it is not unusual that directors might be inhibited from speaking their minds and providing useful insight.

Last, all too frequently, many board members are also managers (insiders) of the corporation. Insiders acting as board members present a conflict of interest because one of the functions of the board is to review the performance and compensation of the corporation's managers. Ideally, a board of directors should have only one insider sit on the board: the CEO.

Equity Alignment

Jensen and Meckling indicate that one of the best ways to resolve the agency problems is to have managers own a significant stake in the company. Further, this ownership stake must be sufficiently large to have an impact on the manager's wealth.[2]

Yet, many CEOs and directors have small equity stakes in the companies they manager and direct. In a study of the equity holdings of CEOs of the 1,000 largest corporations in the United States, the median holding was 0.2% of the company's outstanding equity.[3]

Another issue is the amount of equity held by directors. Frequently, these holdings are small or non-existent. Equity ownership of the underlying company is rarely a condition of board membership. This problem can be solved by compensating directors, in part, in the form of stock and stock options. While a few companies have adopted this compensation scheme, equity participation by board members continues to be small.

Board Size

The saying "Nothing gets done by committee" can apply to a board of directors as well. The larger the board size, the less likely it is to take concerted action. With

---

[2] Id.

[3] See Michael Jensen, "The Modern Industrial Revolution, Exit, and the Failure of Internal Control Systems," in Donald H. Chew, Jr. (ed.), *The New Corporate Finance*, 2d ed., (New York: Irwin/McGraw-Hill, 1999).

a large board of directors, a consensus must be reached. Not only does this take time, but it can also result in mild rather than decisive action.

While there is no ideal board size, smaller is better, generally less than 10 board members is preferred. Larger boards are easier for the CEO to control because it is often the case that when searching for a consensus, a large board will look to the CEO for guidance. This defeats the independent oversight by the board of directors.

Large corporate boards can be made effective through the use of committees. In particular, a corporate board of directors should have an audit committee, a nominating committee, and a compensation committee. Each of these committees should consist only of independent directors (it would not make sense to have a compensation committee populated by corporate insiders).

Joint CEO/Chairman Role

Perhaps the single largest breakdown with respect to internal corporate control mechanisms is the combination of the CEO's title with that of the Chairman of the Board. In both roles the joint CEO/Chairman has total control of the corporation. Not only does the joint CEO/Chairman have control over the corporation's day to day operations, but also over the board of directors that oversees managers for the corporation.

There is simply too great a conflict of interest with respect to the joint CEO/Chairman because it is too easy for him or her to act in his/her self-interest instead of those of the company's shareholders. Without the leadership of an independent director it is difficult for the board of directors to perform its critical oversight function.

In summary, corporate governance often does not work in the United States as it should. Agency problems, human nature, large and unwieldy boards of directors, and CEO power and control contribute to this breakdown. The failure of corporations to act in the best interests of shareholders can lead to a diminution of shareholder value. This provides an opportunity for shareholder activism to enhance returns. In short, corporate governance is an alternative investment strategy for equity portfolios.

EQUITY INDEX INVESTING

Equity index investing is a proxy for investing in an asset class. It is an efficient way to gain economic exposure to the publicly traded equity markets. The chosen index is assumed to represent the risk and return properties of an asset class to which the investor wishes to obtain exposure.

In the United States, the public equity market is so large that a number of different indices have been constructed to capture different parts of the stock market. For example, the S&P 500 is designed to track the largest capitalized stocks in the United States. Conversely, the Russell 1000 and 2000 are designed to track large, mid, and small cap stocks. Last, the Wilshire 5000 is designed to capture the full public equity market in the United States. The size and growth of equity index investing has distinct implications for corporate governance programs.

Exhibit 1: Ten Largest Index Asset Managers

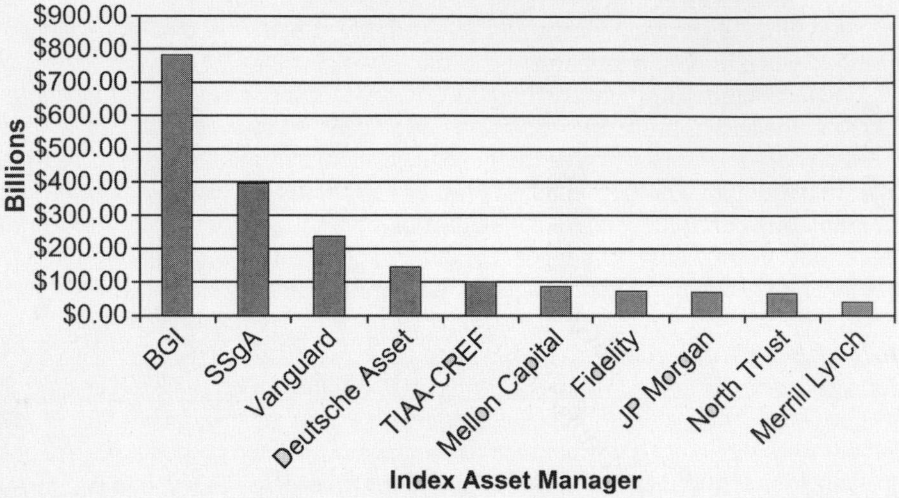

Source: *Pensions & Investments*, September 17, 2001.

A large equity index will represent the actively traded securities within a public stock market. The index represents the total of all active management decisions regarding those public companies because an investor is buying into the ideas of all active management in that asset class.[4] While the decisions of active equity managers cannot be observed, the impact those decisions have on equity prices can be observed. As a result, index investing means tracking not only the actions of the best investment managers in the equity marketplace, it also means tracking the mediocre and just plain bad equity managers. Similarly, equity index investing means tracking not only the good performing companies, but also, the mediocre.

Index investing is often referred to as "passive" investing. However, an investor does not need to be a passive index investor. It is possible to enjoy the benefits of efficient equity asset class exposure while attempting to improve the overall risk and return profile of the asset class. This is the goal of shareholder activism.

The Size of the Equity Index Market

Equity index investing is a popular strategy with both institutional and retail investors. The size of this market is huge. Exhibit 1 presents the amount of index assets managed by the ten largest providers of index management. The total is almost $2 trillion dollars. The industry total for all index providers approaches $2.5 trillion dollars. In the United States, about 18% of tax-exempt institutional equity assets are indexed, and foreign equities represent about 25% of the equity index assets.[5]

---

[4] See Keith P. Ambachtsheer and D. Don Ezra, *Pension Fund Excellence* (New York: John Wiley & Sons, 1998).

[5] *Id.*

Exhibit 2: U.S. Institutional Tax-Exempt Index Funds

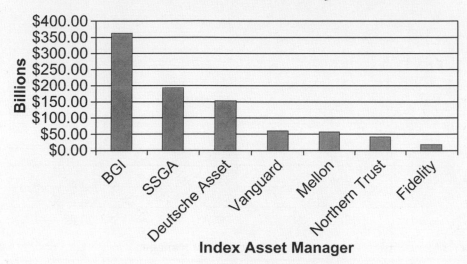

Source: *Pensions & Investments*, September 17, 2001.

Exhibit 3: Growth of Index Investing

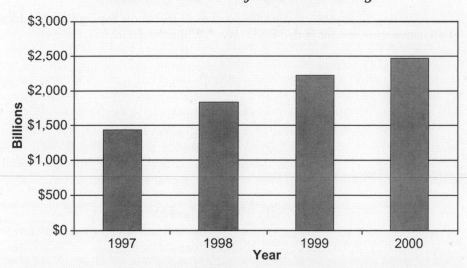

Source: *Pensions & Investments*, September 17, 2001.

Exhibit 2 presents the size of the market for U.S. institutional tax-exempt investors. The total size of this market is over $1 trillion. Last, Exhibit 3 demonstrates the growth in index investing. From 1997 to 2000, this market grew at a compound annual growth rate of 14.5%.

Exhibit 4: Instutional Equity Ownership in the United States

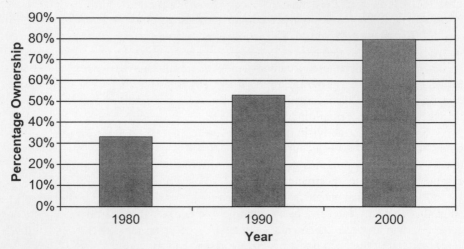

The sheer size of the equity index market makes it fertile ground for corporate governance programs. This is especially true among institutional investors who have sufficient resources to apply a corporate governance program. Institutional investors have a distinct advantage due to their size. Institutional ownership (pension funds, endowments, money management firms, and family offices) of the U.S. equity market has more than doubled over the past 20 years. Exhibit 4 demonstrates the growth of institutional ownership.

The size of the institutional market means that large institutions trade primarily among themselves in an effort to manage risk and enhance returns. Concerted action on the part of institutional investors can have an impact on the performance of public companies. Therefore, corporate governance can have an impact not only on targeted companies, but also the broader stock market. The lessons made public and learned by one corporation can influence the performance of other public corporations.

An Example

Consider the following example. An institutional investor holds 1% of XYZ company stock in its passive index fund worth $100 million. The management of the company has pursued "empire-building" strategies that are costly but do nothing to increase shareholder wealth. As a result, the company has declined in value by 5% each year for the last three years. Yet, the management of the company seems content to build their empire despite the lost value to shareholders.

Unfortunately, the institutional investor cannot sell the stock because it must pursue a buy and hold strategy in its index fund. Passive index investing imposes a significant constraint on an investor: the inability to sell an underperforming stock. Index investors achieve a breadth of equity exposure cheaply and efficiently. However, they must accept the poor financial performance of those underachieving companies that are contained in their chosen index.

If the management of XYZ company continues to pursue its strategy, the institutional investor can expect to lose next year another 5% or $5 million from its investment. Under these circumstances, the institutional investor would be better off if it pursued a program of corporate governance with XYZ company. In fact, the institutional investor has an incentive to spend up to $5 million to stop management's empire building strategy.

Shareholder activism need not be limited to a single company. A reasonable strategy to pursue is a course of action aimed at improving the overall performance of public companies contained in the investor's index fund. This is the essence of corporate governance.

Not only can an active shareholder bring about a change in a specific company, that company can serve as an example to other public corporations. By effecting changes in the behavior and management of corporate agents, active shareholders can improve the financial performance. Moreover, more companies may alter their behavior and management practices to avoid conflict and public scrutiny from other investors. Publicity can be a useful and an effective tool for shareholder activism. Consequently, a broad based and highly public corporate governance program can result in widespread benefits for a large index fund investment.

These "spillover" effects can boost the performance of the overall equity asset class in addition to specific stocks. Spillover effects, however, are difficult to measure. Nonetheless there is anecdotal evidence that these benefits do exist. For example, the Business Roundtable (an association of CEOs of public companies) released a Statement of Corporate Governance in 1997 that lists their recommendations on best practices regarding corporate governance. Several of the recommended practices were key issues among shareholder proposals throughout the 1990s.[6]

Pension funds and other institutional index investors have a fiduciary duty of care to manage their plan assets prudently. While there is no distinct fiduciary duty to monitor investments, this duty is often subsumed as part of the concept of a prudent investor. The duty to monitor investments is particularly important with respect to indexed investments.

A BRIEF REVIEW OF CORPORATE GOVERNANCE PROGRAMS

Corporate governance programs are another way of describing shareholder activism. Over the past decade, institutional investors have begun to flex their muscles with respect to underperforming corporations. Specifically, these investors have engaged

---

[6] See Diane Del Guercio and Jennifer Hawkins, "The Motivation and Impact of Pension Fund Activism," *The Journal of Financial Economics* (June 1999).

the management of poor performing companies in proxy proposals, direct discussions with executive management, and direct negotiations on corporate goals and vision. The goal of shareholder activism is perfectly selfish: to enhance shareholder wealth.

Informed shareholders no longer rely on the discipline of the financial markets to correct corporate performance. In the 1980s, many academics and economists argued that poor performing companies would be subject to takeovers and acquisitions. This corrective action of the financial markets was expected to provide the proper incentives to managers to take corrective action before they lost their jobs through a merger.

However, the era of highly leveraged buyouts and takeovers came to an end with the takeover of RJR Nabisco. This buyout marked both the peak and the end of the junk bond financing of the 1980s. Afterward, the burden of corporate control fell to the shareholders of public companies.

A Definition of Corporate Governance

In a nutshell, corporate governance may be described as the prudent and active use of shareholder rights to increase shareholder wealth. Shareholders must act like owners and continue to exercise their ownership rights in a public company. Over 60 years ago, Graham and Dodd first commented:[7]

> The choice of a common stock is a single act, its ownership is a
> continuing process. Certainly, there is just as much reason to exer-
> cise care and judgment in being a shareholder as in becoming one.

Corporate governance is then shareholder activities intended to monitor and influence corporate management.

All companies experience inevitable periods of stock price appreciation and depreciation as profitability increases and wanes. These periods will occur whether or not a corporation practices good principles of governance. However, accountable governance may mean the difference between prolonged periods of underperformance and responding quickly to a new course of corporate action.

SEC Rule 14a-8

Rule 14a-8 under the Securities and Exchange Commission Act of 1934 is the Shareholder Proposal Rule. Under this rule, shareholders may submit proposals to a public company for inclusion in that company's proxy materials. Shareholder proposals are brief statements requesting certain action by the management of a public company. In effect, the shareholder/principal formally requests that the agents/managers follow a course of action for the shareholder's/principal's benefit.

These proposals are included on the company's proxy statement at the expense of the company (the company has to print and distribute the proxy state-

---

[7] Benjamin Graham and David Dodd, *Security Analysis*, 1st ed. (New York: McGraw Hill, 1934).

ments) along with management's response to the proposal and management's voting recommendation. Once added to the company's proxy statement, the shareholder proposal must be presented at the annual shareholders' meeting of the public company. In between the proxy mailing date and the annual meeting, managers and dissident shareholders may contact other shareholders to gather support for their proposals. The proposal is voted on by shareholders at the annual meeting for the company, along with other issues such as the election of directors. In sum, the proxy process provides active shareholders with a convenient format for presenting their ideas regarding the company's corporate governance.

Even if a shareholder proposal passes by the requisite majority, the management of the company does not have to implement the requested action. A passed shareholder proposal is not binding on the corporation unless the corporation's bylaws make such proposals binding on the management of the company. Nonetheless, the passing of a shareholder proposal is a strong indication to management of the course of action it should pursue to please the owners of the company (if they value their jobs).

Del Guercio and Hawkins examine shareholder proposals submitted by large institutional investors over the period 1987–1993.[8] They find that the most prevalent proposals request confidential voting by shareholders, rescinding of poison pills and other anti-takeover provisions, and independence of the board of directors. These proposals are designed to strengthen the corporate controls and financial performance.

The proxy process was made easier for active investors in 1992 when the SEC passed new rules that allowed shareholders to communicate more directly with one another. Prior to 1992, the only way for shareholders to communicate with each other without running afoul of the SEC rules regarding shareholder groups was through the proxy process. However, in 1992, the SEC relaxed the restrictions in its proxy rules with respect to disclosure of communications among shareholders.

The new rules significantly lowered the costs of corporate governance programs. Institutional investors could now pursue less formal governance programs that direct proxy proposals. Private communications with management as well as other shareholders became more common. However, the threat of a shareholder proposal in a public proxy statement remains a serious threat.

Prior Research on Corporate Governance Programs

Although corporate governance investment programs are a relatively new phenomenon, considerable research has examined their financial impact. The ultimate goal of corporate governance is to increase shareholder wealth. However, prior studies are divided as to whether corporate governance programs add value.

For example, Wahal finds an insignificant stock price reaction over a seven-day event period around the proxy mailing dates for a sample of 211 share-

---

[8] See Del Guercio and Hawkins, "The Motivation and Impact of Pension Fund Activism."

holder proposals.[9] However, in a subsample of CalPERS-targeted companies, significant positive stock returns were observed, indicating that CalPERS is a positive influence on firm performance.

Del Guercio and Hawkins also find no significant stock price effect from shareholder proposals at the proxy date or in the three years following the targeting of companies.[10] However, they do find that shareholder proposals are followed by significant additional corporate governance activity and broad corporate change such as asset sales and restructuring. Further, they find that firms targeted by CalPERS or subject to a proposal on anti-takeover issues are significantly more likely to receive a takeover bid.

Karpoff, Malatesta, and Walking find no significant stock price reaction to shareholder proxy proposals and no operating performance improvement over one to three years following the shareholder proposal.[11] Gillan and Starks find that shareholder proposals sponsored by institutional investors receive considerable support from other investors, and have a small but measurable negative impact on stock prices.[12] Forjan finds that there is a negative stock price reaction when shareholder proposals are submitted to management.[13] However, in a subsample of shareholder proposals that succeed, the stock price reaction is positive.

Smith finds that CalPERS has been successful in changing the corporate governance structure in almost 75% of the cases studied.[14] For those shareholder proposals submitted by CalPERS that are successful, he finds a significant positive stock price reaction. For those proposals that are unsuccessful, the share price reaction is negative. Smith concludes that CalPERS is successful in monitoring managers and increasing shareholder wealth.

Similarly, Nesbitt studies the wealth effects associated with CalPERS corporate governance program.[15] He finds, over the period 1987–1992, that companies that are contacted by CalPERS by letter experience positive long-term performance in excess of the S&P 500. Specifically, Nesbitt finds significant stock price performance in excess of the S&P 500 for a sample of companies contacted by CalPERS.

In summary, the empirical evidence regarding the economic impact of shareholder proposals is unsettled. Some studies show no increase in shareholder wealth from the submission of shareholder proposals, some studies show a nega-

---

[9] S. Wahal, "Pension Fund Activism and Firm Performance," *The Journal of Financial and Quantitative Analysis* (1996).

[10] See Del Guercio and Hawkins, "The Motivation and Impact of Pension Fund Activism."

[11] See Johathan Karpoff, Paul Malatesta, and Ralph Walking, "Corporate Governance and Shareholder Initiatives: Empirical Evidence," *The Journal of Financial Economics* (November 1996).

[12] See Stuart Gillan and Laura Starks, "Corporate Governance Proposals and Shareholder Activism: The Role of Institutional Investors," *The Journal of Financial Economics* (2000).

[13] James Forjan, "The Wealth Effects of Shareholder Sponsored Proposals," *Review of Financial Economics* (January 1999).

[14] Michael Smith, "Shareholder Activism by Institutional Investors: Evidence from CalPERS," *The Journal of Finance* (1996).

[15] Stephen Nesbitt, "Long-Term Rewards from Shareholder Activism: A Study of the "CalPERS" Effect," *The Journal of Applied Corporate Finance* (Winter 1994).

tive impact on shareholder wealth, and some studies show a positive impact on shareholder wealth. In the next section we consider a different form of shareholder activism, and its impact on shareholder wealth.

EXAMINING THE BENEFITS OF A CORPORATE GOVERNANCE PROGRAM

The empirical studies cited above provide mixed evidence concerning the value added from corporate governance programs. However, most of these studies examine only brief time periods associated with corporate governance programs. Further, shareholder proposals are only one tactic that may be used in corporate governance programs.

In this section we analyze the value added with respect to the CalPERS' corporate governance program over the time period 1992–2001, a period of sufficient time and macroeconomic diversity to provide a realistic look at the constructive nature of a corporate governance program. In addition, rather than examining shareholder proposals we consider the economic impact of the publication of CalPERS' Focus List of public companies.

CalPERS' Focus List

Since 1992, CalPERS has focussed its attention on companies considered by several measures to be "poor" financial performers. By centering its attention and resources in this way, CalPERS believes that it can demonstrate to those who might question the value of corporate governance, specific and tangible economic results.[16]

The CalPERS' Focus List was first born in 1992 when CalPERS publicly identified 10 large public corporations in a published list. CalPERS announced that these companies were poor performers, and therefore, should bear the public scrutiny associated with their under performance. Further, CalPERS stated that it would continue to monitor closely the performance of these companies and would consider shareholder proposals and other actions necessary to improve the financial performance of companies placed on the Focus List.

In fact, CalPERS takes an active role with those companies placed on its Focus List. This activity begins several months before the Focus List is released. CalPERS begins the process in the spring of every year by screening a universe of approximately 1,500 public companies across all industries and levels of market capitalization. Over the course of 2 to 3 months CalPERS reduces this universe to a list of 20 to 25 companies that it believes demonstrate poor financial performance as well as poor corporate governance principles. These companies become candidates for CalPERS' Focus List.

---

[16] See The California Public Employees' Retirement System, "Corporate Governance Core Principles and Guidelines," April 13, 1998.

CalPERS contacts potential corporate candidates in late summer or early autumn of each year. Over the course of the next four to six months, CalPERS meets directly with the executive management and directors of candidate companies to discuss its concerns and to provide management with an opportunity to make a case for exclusion from the Focus List.

Sometimes, potential candidates react immediately to CalPERS initial contact by initiating share buybacks, or by implementing new internal controls in the hopes that a positive short-term boost to their share price might persuade CalPERS to exclude them from the Focus List. These changes are made in response to the concerns expressed by CalPERS as a large institutional investor, and also, to forestall inclusion on the Focus List.

The final Focus List is usually published in February or March of the year following initial contact. Some potential candidates are excluded because they agree to make changes to their control procedures, or have already implemented them. The remaining candidates that do make the Focus List are included because of lack of progress or responsiveness to CalPERS' shareholder concerns. Focus List graduates are based on three criteria: return on capital, corporate governance principles, and stock price performance.

Return on capital is measured using the principles of Economic Value Added (EVA). We discussed EVA briefly in Chapter 15 with respect to the case history for the Duracell Corporation. Briefly, EVA is a method for evaluating projects and performance by including a charge against profits for the cost of capital that a company employs.[17] Capital charges under EVA measure the return that investors could expect to earn by investing their money in a portfolio of stocks with similar risk as the company.

The EVA approach to value creation reflects economic reality because EVA measures the opportunity cost of capital based on the risk undertaken to achieve a revenue stream. This is in contrast to accounting ratios such as earnings per share or return on equity that can be distorted by non-cash charges, early revenue recognition, and capitalized expenses. These accounting conventions are applied at the discretion of management and may lead to a temptation by management to manipulate accounting-based performance measures such as earnings per share. The beauty of EVA is that it redirects management's focus from accounting numbers to equity value creation.

Stock price performance is relatively straightforward. CalPERS' measures a company's stock price performance relative to its peers for a 5-year period. Those companies that have large underperformance are eligible for the Focus List.

Last, CalPERS' considers a company's corporate governance principles. Issues such as staggered/classified boards of directors, lack of independent directors, a combined CEO/Chairman of the Board, and poison pills are just some of the key issues that makes a company eligible for the list.

In sum, eligible candidates for CalPERS' Focus List must demonstrate poor financial performance and poor corporate governance principles. As mentioned

---

[17] The formula for EVA is: Net Operating Profits after Tax − (Cost of Capital) × (Total Capital Employed).

above, sooner or later all companies experience a period of underperformance. However, it is those companies that have poor corporate governance principles that are more likely to experience a prolonged (even fatal) period of underperformance.

A Test of CalPERS' Focus List

CalPERS' has published its Focus List each year since 1992. Although the list originally included 12 companies, in recent years, the list has not been fixed at any specific number to allow the CalPERS' investment staff the flexibility to include only the most egregious candidates.

We examine the stock price reaction of all companies included on the Focus List over the 10-year period 1992–2001. The sample size of companies is 97. The study period is rich in economic detail including two periods of Federal Reserve tightening of interest rates (1992–1993, and 1999–2000) as well as three periods of Federal Reserve easing (1994, 1997–1998, and 2001). In addition there was the "Tequila Crisis" of 1994–1995, the Asian Contagion of 1997–1998, and the bursting of the technology bubble in 2000–2001.

The key purpose is to determine whether the Focus List is an effective way to increase shareholder wealth. If corporate underperformance is the result of lack of effort or poor decision making that can be corrected through public scrutiny or improved corporate controls, then inclusion on the Focus List might be expected to reinvigorate the company to improve its effort and financial performance. At the very least, inclusion on the Focus List should arrest the declining fortunes of those companies that are targeted. Examining a company's stock price performance before inclusion on the Focus List, at the time of announcement of the Focus List, and after inclusion on the Focus List might provide some evidence of the economic value of corporate governance programs.[18]

We examine three periods of performance associated with companies that appear on CalPERS' focus list. The first period is the six months leading up to the date of publication of CalPERS' annual list. As noted above, one of the criteria for Focus List inclusion is poor stock price performance. Consequently, we might expect to see negative stock price performance leading up to the announcement date. Conversely, there might be a concerted effort by companies to improve their stock price performance in an attempt to avoid inclusion in the Focus List. This could lead to positive stock price performance leading up to the publication of the Focus List.

There are also competing economic effects at the time of publication by CalPERS of its Focus List. On the one hand, there might be a negative stock price impact as investors react unfavorably to the identification of CalPERS' target firms. Yet, many investors may view inclusion on CalPERS' Focus List a positive development because of CalPERS' underlying commitment to work with those companies to improve their corporate controls and stock price performance.

---

[18] This type of analysis is known as an "event study." For details on event studies, see Mark Anson, "Financial Market Dislocations and Hedge Fund Returns," working paper, 2001.

Exhibit 5: Shareholder Wealth and CalPERS' Focus List

Time Period	Excess Return	T statistic
T-180 to T-91	1.27%	0.317
T-90 to T-1	5.32%	1.33
T(0) to T+4	1.11%	1.41
T+5 to T+94	12.70%	3.17
T+95 to T+184	5.70%	1.65

Finally, we examine the performance of companies after the publication date of the Focus List. Here, the results should be unequivocal. If there is value to CalPERS' corporate governance program, we should see a positive stock price performance after the publication date of the Focus List.

The economic results of CalPERS' Focus List program are contained in Exhibit 5. In this exhibit, we examine five periods of stock price performance. The first period is 180 to 90 (trading) days before release of the Focus List. This is approximately a 4-month period prior to release of the Focus List. The second period is from 90 days before release of the Focus List up to the Focus List publication date. The third period is the publication day of the Focus List plus four trading days after the announcement of the list. Last, we also measure the stock price performance for two 90-day periods after the publication of the Focus List.

In Exhibit 5, we observe significant, positive, excess stock price performance after the release of the Focus List. We also observe positive excess returns before the release of the Focus List and at the time the list is published, but these returns are statistically insignificant. In summary, soon after the Focus List is received, the corporations contained in the list experience significant positive price effects to their share prices. Further, this positive price impact does not erode in subsequent periods. In summary, significant, lasting economic value is added through the CalPERS' Focus List.

The results of this analysis differ from that of Caton, Goh, and Donaldson.[19] They study the financial performance of companies contained in the Focus List released by the Council of Institutional Investors and find significant negative excess returns associated with the release date of the list.[20] One difference may the purpose of the Council's Focus List versus that of CalPERS'. The Focus List produced by the Council serves mostly as identification. It is intended to focus scrutiny on companies with poor corporate governance, but the Council normally does not pursue any further action. Conversely, CalPERS' goal is not only to

---

[19] See Gary L. Caton, Jeremy Goh, and Jeffrey Donaldson, "The Effectiveness of Institutional Activism," *Financial Analysts Journal* (July/August 2001). Also, the methodology used in this chapter was different than Caton *et al*. We formed portfolio of companies to account for the clustering of event dates while Caton *et al* test individual companies. Testing individual companies assumes that there is no correlation among the excess returns. The lack of correlation may be violated when companies share the same event date (such as the release of a list of companies at the same time).

[20] The Council of Institutional Investors is an industry association or more than 120 large U.S. pension funds, both public and private.

identify those corporations that have poor performance and governance, but also to work with those companies to improve their governance procedures and financial performance. As a result, investors may react more favorably to companies contained on CalPERS' Focus List compared to that of the Council's.

Relation to the Overall Stock Market

As a last piece of the corporate governance puzzle, we examine the stock returns of those companies with respect the S&P 500. This should provide insight as to whether a corporate governance program is largely correlated with the broader stock market, or whether a corporate governance program has a low correlation with the broad stock market. It is the last condition, low correlation with the S&P 500, that is often cited as a determining characteristic of an alternative investment strategy.

The CalPERS Focus List has been released every year since 1992. This list generally includes 10 to 12 companies each year. To determine the correlation of the Focus List companies with the S&P 500, we form 10 portfolios, one portfolio for each year from 1992–2001. In each portfolio are the companies contained in CalPERS' Focus List for that year. The returns to these portfolios are regressed against the returns to the S&P 500 to measure their correlation with the stock index. The results are presented in Exhibit 6.

The correlation of the Focus List Portfolio returns with the S&P 500 are generally low. The average correlation across the ten portfolios is 0.558. This low correlation is comparable to those for hedge fund of fund strategies with the S&P 500 presented in Chapter 3, and those of private equity portfolios presented in Chapter 17. In summary, CalPERS' Focus List portfolios produced returns with low correlation to the market returns similar to other categories of alternative assets.

Exhibit 6: Average Correlation with the S&P 500 = 0.558

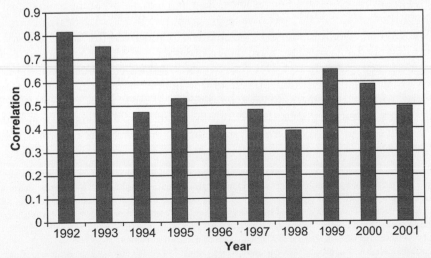

CONCLUSION

CalPERS corporate governance program provides significant, positive economic value added while producing portfolios of companies that have a low correlation with the broad stock market. Despite the economic benefits that can be derived from corporate governance, these programs are not implemented by institutional investors to the same extent as other alternative investment strategies. The reasons are several.

First, there is the risk of legal liabilities for investors that pursue confrontational discussions with corporate executives. Shareholder proposals may lead to costly and time consuming proxy battles should a corporate target decide to fight back against the principles of corporate governance.

Second, there is the "free rider" problem. When a large institutional investor pursues a successful plan of corporate governance, all shareholders benefit. Those shareholders who contribute nothing to the corporate governance initiative receive just as much benefit as the institutional investor who actively pursued the governance plan of action. Therefore, an investor who decides to implement a corporate governance program must realize in advance that many will benefit from its actions while it will bear all of the costs.[21]

Third, many institutional investors do not have either the staff or the expertise to pursue corporate governance initiatives. Institutions such as CalPERS and TIAA-CREF are rare in that they have dedicated corporate governance units within their investment departments.

Last, many institutions have a passive investment approach through index funds. These investors may not believe that lost value in an index fund is a sufficient economic incentive to risk their reputation as well as their financial resources on such public and active investment strategies.

Yet, the cost of corporate governance programs is small relative to the size of an investor's assets. For instance, Romano indicates that the annual cost to CalPERS of its corporate governance program is 0.002% (0.2 basis points) of CalPERS' domestic investments.[22] Del Guercio and Hawkins find that pension funds that pursue a corporate governance program spend less than one-half of a basis point per year.[23] In fact, Del Guercio and Hawkins conclude that if the California State Teachers Retirement System (the fund with the smallest investments in target companies in their study) were to improve stock prices only 0.5% at its target firms, it could increase its portfolio by $2 million. The implication is that there is an even greater incentive at larger institutional investors to initiate a corporate governance program.

---

[21] CalPERS acknowledges the free rider issue. However, CalPERS realizes that it is a leader in investment management, and it is willing to assume a leadership role in corporate governance. Given the size of CalPERS' portfolio, it might be said that corporate governance is not only CalPERS' duty, but also its destiny.

[22] See Roberta Romano, "Less is More: Making Institutional Investor Activism a Valuable Mechanism of Corporate Governance," *Yale Journal of Regulation*, Summer 2001.

[23] See Del Guercio and Hawkins, "The Motivation and Impact of Pension Fund Activism."

Furthermore, an institutional investor need not apply corporate governance alone. There are many other investors that share the same goal. For instance, the Council of Institutional Investors was founded in 1987 to address the similar concerns for large investors. One objective of the Council is to establish goals and guidelines for the effective governance of publicly traded corporations. To this end, the Council believes that all publicly traded companies and their shareholders and other constituencies benefit from written, disclosed governance procedures and policies.[24]

In conclusion, corporate governance is an alternative investment strategy for institutional investors. Further, this strategy is particularly useful for equity index investors. Index investors must accept the good companies with the mediocre. However, corporate governance can improve the efficiency of the total asset class, providing wealth benefits to index investors. Finally, the data presented in this chapter with respect to the CalPERS' governance program demonstrate that this alternative strategy can enhance investment returns.

---

[24] More information on the Council of Institutional Investors may be found at www.cii.org.

Index